The Works Of Francis Beaumont And John Fletcher: The Maids Tragedy. Philaster. A King, And No King. The Scornful Lady. The Custom Of The Country

Francis Beaumont, John Fletcher, Alfred Rayney Waller, Arnold Glover

CAMBRIDGE ENGLISH CLASSICS

The Works of Francis Beaumont and John Fletcher

In ten volumes

Vol. I

FRANCIS BEAUMONT

Born 1584
Died 1616

JOHN FLETCHER

Born 1579
Died 1625

BEAUMONT AND FLETCHER

THE MAIDS TRAGEDY
PHILASTER
A KING, AND NO KING
THE SCORNFUL LADY
THE CUSTOM OF THE COUNTRY

THE TEXT EDITED BY
ARNOLD GLOVER, M.A.
OF TRINITY COLLEGE AND THE INNER TEMPLE

CAMBRIDGE:
at the University Press
1905

CAMBRIDGE UNIVERSITY PRESS WAREHOUSE,
C. F. CLAY, MANAGER.
London: FETTER LANE, E.C.
Glasgow: 50, WELLINGTON STREET.

Leipzig: F. A. BROCKHAUS.
New York: THE MACMILLAN COMPANY.
Bombay and Calcutta: MACMILLAN AND CO., LTD.

NOTE.

THE first collected edition of the plays of Beaumont and Fletcher was published in 1647 in folio (12½ ins. x 8⅛ ins. is the measurement of the copy used for the purpose of collation). The title-page runs thus :—

Comedies | and | Tragedies |
written by { Francis Beaumont And John Fletcher } Gentlemen. |
Never printed before, | And now published by the Authours | Originall Copies. | *Si quid habent veri Vatum præsagia, vivam.* | *London,* | Printed for *Humphrey Robinson,* at the three *Pidgeons,* and for | *Humphrey Moseley* at the *Princes Armes in* St *Pauls.*

This collection, which is referred to as the First Folio throughout the present edition, contained all the authors' previously unpublished plays (34) except *The Wild-Goose Chase,* which, at the date of the Folio, was supposed to be lost. The dedicatory epistles, commendatory poems and Catalogue of Plays, prefixed to the First Folio, are reprinted in the preliminary pages at the end of this Note (pp. ix—lvii).

NOTE

The second collected edition appeared in 1679 in folio (14⅜ ins. × 8¼ ins.); a reprint of the title-page is given on p. lix of the present volume. This collection, referred to henceforth as the Second Folio, contained (i) all the plays included in the First Folio, (ii) *The Wild-Goose Chase*, which had been published in folio in 1652, (iii) all the other then known plays of the authors which had been published previously to 1679.

William Marshall's portrait of John Fletcher faces the title-page of both folios with the following inscription engraved underneath :—

Felicis ævi ac Præsulis *Natus; comes* Beaumontis; *sic, quippe Parnassus*, biceps; FLETCHERUS *unam in Pyramida furcas agens. Struxit chorum plus simplicem Vates Duplex; Plus duplicem solus: nec ullum transtulit; Nec transferendus: Dramatum æterni sales*, Anglo *Theatro, Orbe, Sibi, superstites.*

FLETCHERE, facies absq; vultu pingitur; Quantus! vel umbram *circuit nemo tuam.*

J. Berkenhead.

Later collected editions of the works were published in 1711 (7 vols.); 1750, edited by Lewis Theobald, Thomas Seward and J. Sympson (10 vols.); 1778, edited by George Colman (10 vols.); 1812, edited by Henry Weber (14 vols.); 1843, edited by Alexander Dyce (11 vols.). It is unnecessary to refer in detail to these later editions which, very widely as they differ among themselves, agree in presenting an eclectic text, a text formed partly by a collation of the various old editions and partly by the adoption of conjectural emendations. During the progress of work upon the present issue another edition has been announced, under the general editorship of Mr A. H. Bullen, and the first volume was published last year. It follows the lines of its predecessors in presenting a modernised text, giving 'a fuller record than had been given by Dyce of *variæ lectiones*,' and pleading, in its prospectus, that, 'for the use of scholars, there should be editions of all our old authors in old spelling.'

The objects of the present edition, in accordance with the scheme of the series of ENGLISH CLASSICS of which it is a part, are to provide (i) a text in which there shall be no deviation from that adopted as its basis, in the matter of spelling, punctuation, the use of capitals and italics, save as recorded, and to give (ii) an apparatus of variant readings as an Appendix, comprising the texts of all the early issues, that is to say, of all editions prior to and including the Second Folio. Within these limits, and apart from mere variations in spelling and punctuation, every variation, whether deemed important or not, is recorded in the Appendixes to these volumes.

Of the 52 Plays in the Second Folio only 5 were published before the death of Beaumont and 9 before the death of Fletcher. The text has, therefore, given rise to a fruitful crop of conjectural emendations, but it has not been deemed a part of the editor's duty to garner them. Leaving these on one side, and desirous mainly of collecting every alternative reading in all the Quartos and in the two Folios, the text used in the preparation of the present edition, chosen after careful consideration, is that of the Second Folio, obvious printers' errors being corrected, recorded in the Appendix, and indicated in the text by the insertion of square brackets. This text is the latest with any pretence to authority, it includes all the plays, and it forms a convenient limit, beyond which no notice has been taken of alternative readings, and to which the variants, chronologically arranged from the earliest to the latest Quartos, can easily be referred. Some of the early Quartos no doubt offer better texts of some of the plays, especially in the matter of verse and prose arrangement, and had it been intended to print one text, and one text only, unaccompanied by a full apparatus of variorum readings, something might be said in favour of a choice among the Quartos and Folios, selecting here and there, in the case of each play, the particular text that seemed the best. But such choice could only be an extension of the eclectic method that has been rejected in dealing with alternative readings, it seemed to be equally unscientific, and, in view of the material in the Appendixes, needless.

In common with all the Quartos and the First Folio the Second Folio has failings, which will be noted in due course, but these have been exaggerated, and against them may be set the advantages detailed in the address of 'The Booksellers to the Reader,' reprinted on p. lx.

It has been thought that it would be useful to students to give lists of the different arrangements of prose and verse that obtain in the different quartos, and these will be found in the Appendix after the variants of each play.

The remaining volumes of this edition will follow as soon as can be arranged.

* * *

NOTE

The Syndics of the University Press have asked me to complete the work begun by Arnold Glover. It was a work greatly to his mind: he spent much labour upon it, being always keenly interested in critical, textual and bibliographical work in English literature; he welcomed a return to his earlier studies among the Elizabethans after five years given to the works of one of their most discerning critics; but he did not live to see the publication of the first volume of his new work. When he died in the January of this year, the text of volumes one and two had been passed for press, the material accumulated for the Appendixes to those volumes and the draft of the above 'Note' partly written. With the assistance of Mrs Arnold Glover, who had helped him in the laborious work of collation, I have checked and arranged this editorial material for press. I hope I have not let any error escape me which he would have detected.

A. R. WALLER.

CAMBRIDGE,
2 *August*, 1905.

CONTENTS.

TO

THE RIGHT HONOURABLE

PHILIP

Earle of Pembroke and Mountgomery:

Baron Herbert of Cardiffe and Sherland,

Lord Parr and Ross of Kendall; Lord Fitz-Hugh,

Marmyon, and Saint Quintin; Knight of the most noble Order of the Garter; and one of His Majesties most Honourable Privie Councell: And our Singular Good Lord.

MY LORD, *There is none among all the* Names *of* Honour, *that hath more encouraged the* Legitimate Muses *of this latter Age, then that which is owing to your* Familie; *whose* Coronet *shines bright with the native luster of its owne* Jewels, *which with the accesse of some Beames of* Sydney, *twisted with their* Flame *presents a* Constellation, *from whose* Influence *all good may be still expected upon Witt and Learning.*

At this Truth *we rejoyce, but yet aloofe, and in our owne valley, for we dare not approach with any capacity in our selves to apply your Smile, since wee have only preserved as* Trustees *to the* Ashes *of the Authors, what wee exhibit to your* Honour, *it being no more our owne, then those* Imperiall Crownes *and* Garlands *were the Souldiers, who were honourably designed for their Conveyance before the* Triumpher *to the* Capitol.

But directed by the example of some, who once steered in our qualitie, and so fortunately aspired to choose your Honour, *joyned with your (now glorified)* Brother, Patrons *to the flowing compositions of the then expired sweet* Swan *of* AVON SHAKESPEARE; *and since, more particularly bound to your* Lordships *most constant and diffusive* Goodnesse, *from which, wee did for many calme yeares derive a subsistence to our selves, and Protection to the Scene (now withered, and condemn'd, as we feare, to a long Winter and sterilitie) we have presumed to offer to your* Selfe, *what before was never printed of these* Authours.

Had they beene lesse then all the Treasure *we had contracted in the whole Age of* Poesie *(some few Poems of their owne excepted, which already published, command their entertainement, with all lovers of* Art *and* Language) *or were they not the most justly admir'd, and belov'd Pieces of* Witt *and the* World, *wee should have taught our selves a lesse Ambition.*

Be pleased to accept this humble tender of our duties, and till we faile in our obedience to all your Commands, vouchsafe, we may be knowne by the Cognizance *and* Character *of*

MY LORD,

Your Honours most bounden

John Lowin	*Joseph Taylor*
Richard Robinson	*Robert Benfeild*
Eylærd Swanston	*Thomas Pollard*
Hugh Clearke	*William Allen*
Stephen Hammerton	*Theophilus Byrd.*

TO THE READER.

POETRY *is the Child of* Nature, *which regulated and made beautifull by* Art, *presenteth the most Harmonious of all other compositions; among which (if we rightly consider) the* Dramaticall *is the most absolute, in regard of those transcendent* Abilities, *which should waite upon the* Composer; *who must have more then the instruction of Libraries (which of it selfe is but a cold contemplative knowledge) there being required in him a* Soule miraculously *knowing, and conversing with all mankind, inabling him to expresse not onely the Phlegme and folly* of thick-skin'd men, *but the strength and maturity* of the wise, *the Aire and insinuations of the* Court, *the discipline and Resolution of the Soldier, the Vertues and passions of every noble condition, nay the councells and characters of the greatest Princes.*

This you will say is a vast comprehension, and hath not hapned in many Ages. Be it then remembred to the Glory of our owne, *that all these are Demonstrative and met in* BEAUMONT & FLETCHER, *whom but to mention is to throw a cloude upon all former names and benight Posterity; This Book being, without flattery, the greatest* Monument *of the* Scene *that Time and Humanity have produced, and must Live, not only the* Crowne *and sole* Reputation *of our owne, but the stayne of all other* Nations *and* Languages, *for it may be boldly averred, not one indiscretion hath branded this Paper in all the Lines, this being the Authentick witt that made Blackfriers an Academy, where the three howers spectacle while* Beaumont *and* Fletcher *were presented, were usually of more advantage to the hopefull young Heire, then a costly, dangerous, forraigne Travell, with the assistance of a governing Mounsieur, or Signior to boot; And it cannot be denied but that the young spirits of the Time, whose Birth & Quality made them impatient of the sowrer wayes of education, have from the attentive hearing these pieces, got ground in point of wit and carriage of the most severely employed Students, while these Recreations were digested into Rules, and the very Pleasure did edifie. How many passable discoursing dining witts stand yet in good credit upon the bare stock of two or three of these single Scenes.*

And now Reader in this Tragicall Age *where the* Theater *hath been so much out-acted, congratulate thy owne happinesse, that in this silence of the Stage, thou hast a liberty to reade these inimitable Playes, to dwell and converse in these immortall Groves, which were only shewd our Fathers in a conjuring glasse, as suddenly removed as represented, the Landscrap is now brought home by this optick, and the Presse thought too pregnant before, shall be now look'd upon as greatest Benefactor to Englishmen, that must* acknowledge *all the felicity of* witt *and* words *to this Derivation.*

TO THE READER

You may here find passions raised to that excellent pitch and by such insinuating degrees that you shall not chuse but consent, & go along with them, finding your self at last grown insensibly the very same person you read, and then stand admiring the subtile Trackes of your engagement. Fall on a Scene of love and you will never believe the writers could have the least roome left in their soules for another passion, peruse a Scene of manly Rage, and you would sweare they cannot be exprest by the same hands, but both are so excellently wrought, you must confesse none, but the same hands, could worke them.

Would thy Melancholy have a cure? thou shalt laugh at Democritus *himselfe, and but reading one piece of this* Comick *variety, finde thy exalted fancie in Elizium; And when thou art sick of this cure, (for the excesse of delight may too much dilate thy* soule) *thou shalt meete almost in every leafe a soft purling passion or* spring *of sorrow so powerfully wrought high by the teares of innocence, and* wronged Lovers, *it shall perswade thy eyes to weepe into the streame, and yet smile when they contribute to their owne ruines.*

Infinitely more might be said of these rare Copies, but let the ingenuous Reader peruse them & he will finde them so able to speake their own worth, that they need not come into the world with a trumpet, since any one of these incomparable pieces well understood will prove a Preface *to the rest, and if the Reader can tast the best wit ever trod our English Stage, he will be forced himselfe to become* a breathing Panegerick *to them all.*

Not to detaine or prepare thee longer, be as capritious and sick-brain'd, as ignorance & malice can make thee, here thou art rectified, or be as healthfull as the inward calme of an honest Heart, Learning, *and* Temper *can state thy disposition, yet this booke may be thy fortunate* concernement *and Companion.*

It is not so remote in Time, but very many Gentlemen may remember these Authors & some familiar in their conversation deliver them upon every pleasant occasion so fluent, to talke a Comedy. He must be a bold man that dares undertake to write their Lives. What I have to say is, we have the precious Remaines, *and as the wisest contemporaries acknowledge they Lived a* Miracle, *I am very confident this volume cannot die without one.*

What more specially concerne these Authors and their workes is told thee by another hand in the following Epistle of the Stationer to the Readers.

Farwell, Reade, and feare not thine owne understanding, this Booke will create a cleare one in thee, and when thou hast considered thy purchase, thou wilt call the price of it a Charity to thy selfe, and at the same time forgive thy friend, and these Authors humble admirer,

JA. SHIRLEY.

The Stationer to the Readers.

Gentlemen, BEfore you engage farther, be pleased to take notice of these Particulars. You have here a *New Booke*; I can speake it clearely; for of all this large Volume of *Comedies* and *Tragedies*, not one, till now, was ever printed before. A *Collection of Playes* is commonly but a *new Impression*, the scattered pieces which were printed single, being then onely Republished together: 'Tis otherwise here.

Next, as it is all New, so here is not any thing *Spurious* or *impos'd*; I had the Originalls from such as received them from the *Authours* themselves; by Those, and none other, I publish this Edition.

And as here's nothing but what is genuine and Theirs, so you will finde here are no *Omissions*; you have not onely All I could get, but All that you must ever expect. For (besides those which were formerly printed) there is not any Piece written by these *Authours*, either Joyntly or Severally, but what are now publish'd to the World in this *Volume*. One only Play I must except (for I meane to deale openly) 'tis a *COMEDY* called the *Wilde-goose Chase*, which hath beene long lost, and I feare irrecoverable; for a *Person of Quality* borrowed it from the *Actours* many yeares since, and (by the negligence of a Servant) it was never return'd; therefore now I put up this *Si quis*, that whosoever hereafter happily meetes with it, shall be thankfully satisfied if he please to send it home.

Some *Playes* (you know) written by these *Authors* were heretofore Printed: I thought not convenient to mixe them with this *Volume*, which of it selfe is entirely New. And indeed it would have rendred the Booke so Voluminous, that *Ladies* and *Gentlewomen* would have found it scarce manageable, who in Workes of this nature must first be remembred. Besides, I considered those former Pieces had been so long printed and re-printed, that many Gentlemen were already furnished; and I would have none say, they pay twice for the same Booke.

One thing I must answer before it bee objected; 'tis this: When these *Comedies* and *Tragedies* were presented on the Stage, the *Actours* omitted some *Scenes* and Passages (with the *Authour's* consent) as occasion led them; and when private friends desir'd a Copy, they then (and justly too) transcribed what they *Acted*. But now you have both All that was *Acted*, and all that was not; even the perfect full Originalls without the least mutilation; So that were the *Authours* living, (and sure they can never dye) they themselves would challenge neither more nor lesse then what is here published; this Volume being now so compleate and finish'd, that the Reader must expect no future Alterations.

For *literall Errours* committed by the Printer, 'tis the fashion to aske pardon, and as much in fashion to take no notice of him that asks it; but in this also I have done my endeavour. 'Twere vaine to mention the *Chargeablenesse* of this Work; for those who own'd the *Manuscripts*, too well knew their value to make a cheap estimate of any of these Pieces, and though another joyn'd with me in the *Purchase* and Printing, yet the *Care* & *Pains* was wholly mine, which I found to be more then you'l easily imagine, unlesse you knew into how many hands the Originalls were dispersed. They are all now happily met in this Book, having escaped these *Publike Troubles*, free and unmangled. Heretofore when Gentlemen desired but a Copy of any of these *Playes*, the meanest piece here (if any may be called Meane where every one is Best) cost them more then foure times the price you pay for the whole *Volume*.

I should scarce have adventured in these slippery times on such a work as this, if knowing persons had not generally assured mee that these *Authors* were the most unquestionable *Wits* this Kingdome hath afforded. Mr. *Beaumont* was ever acknowledged a man of a most strong and searching braine; and (his yeares considered) the most *Judicious Wit* these later Ages have produced; he dyed young, for (which was an invaluable losse to this Nation) he left the world when hee was not full thirty yeares old. Mr. *Fletcher* survived, and lived till almost fifty; whereof the World now enjoyes the benefit. It was once in my thoughts to have Printed Mr. *Fletcher's* workes by themselves, because single & alone he would make a *Just Volume*: But since never parted while they lived, I conceived it not equitable to seperate their ashes.

It becomes not me to say (though it be a knowne Truth) that these *Authors* had not only High unexpressible gifts of *Nature*, but also excellent *acquired Parts*, being furnished with Arts and Sciences by that liberall education they had at the *University*, which sure is the best place to make a great Wit understand it selfe; this their workes will soone make evident. I was very ambitious to have got Mr. *Beaumonts* picture; but could not possibly, though I spared no enquirie in those *Noble Families* whence he was descended, as also among those Gentlemen that were his acquaintance when he was of the *Inner Temple*: the best Pictures and those most like him you'l finde in this *Volume*. This figure of Mr. *Fletcher* was cut by severall Originall Pieces, which his friends lent me, but withall they tell me, that his unimitable Soule did shine through his countenance in such *Ayre* and *Spirit*, that the Painters confessed, it was not easie to expresse him: As much as could be, you have here, and the *Graver* hath done his part. What ever I have seene of Mr. *Fletchers* owne hand, is free from interlining; and his friends affirme he never writ any one thing twice: it seemes he had that rare felicity to prepare and perfect all first in his owne braine; to shape and attire his *Notions*, to adde or loppe off, before he committed one word to writing, and never touched pen till all was to stand as firme and immutable as if ingraven in Brasse or Marble. But I keepe you too long from those *friends* of his whom 'tis fitter for you to read; only accept of the honest endeavours of

One that is a Servant to you all

HUMPHREY MOSELEY.

At the Princes Armes *in*
St Pauls *Church-yard.*
Feb. 14th 1646.

To the Stationer.

TEll the sad World that now the lab'ring Presse
H'as brought forth safe a Child of happinesse,
The Frontis-piece will satisfie the wise
And good so well, they will not grudge the price.
'Tis not all Kingdomes joyn'd in one could buy
(If priz'd aright) so true a Library
Of man: where we the characters may finde
Of ev'ry Nobler and each baser minde.
Desert has here reward in one good line
For all it lost, for all it might repine:
Vile and ignobler things are open laid,
The truth of their false colours are displayed:
You'l say the Poet's both best Judge and Priest,
No guilty soule abides so sharp a test
As their smooth Pen; for what these rare men writ
Commands the World, both Honesty and Wit.

GRANDISON.

IN MEMORY OF
Mr. JOHN FLETCHER.

MEe thought our Fletcher *weary of this croud,*
Wherein so few have witt, yet all are loud,
Unto Elyzium fled, where he alone
Might his own witt admire and ours bemoane;
But soone upon those Flowry Bankes, a throng
Worthy of those even numbers which he sung,
Appear'd, and though those Ancient Laureates strive
When dead themselves, whose raptures should survive,
For his Temples all their owne bayes allowes,
Not sham'd to see him crown'd with naked browes;
Homer *his beautifull* Achilles *nam'd,*
Urging his braine with Joves *might well be fam'd,*
Since it brought forth one full of beauties charmes,
As was his Pallas, and as bold in Armes;
King and *But when he the brave* Arbases *saw, one*
no King. *That saved his peoples dangers by his own,*
And saw Tigranes *by his hand undon*
Without the helpe of any Mirmydon,

He then confess'd when next hee'd Hector *slay,*
That he must borrow him from Fletchers *Play;*
This might have beene the shame, for which he bid
His Iliades *in a Nut-shell should be hid:*
Virgill *of his* Æneas *next begun,*
Whose God-like forme and tongue so soone had wonne;
That Queene of Carthage *and of beauty too,*
Two powers the whole world else were slaves unto,
Urging that Prince for to repaire his faulte
On earth, boldly in hell his Mistresse sought;
The Maides Tragedy. *But when he* Amintor *saw revenge that wrong,*
For which the sad Aspasia *sigh'd so long,*
Upon himselfe, to shades hasting away,
Not for to make a visit but to stay;
He then did modestly confesse how farr
Fletcher *out-did him in a Charactar.*
Now lastly for a refuge, Virgill *shewes*
The lines where Corydon Alexis *woes;*
But those in opposition quickly met
The faithfull Shepherdesse. *The smooth tongu'd* Perigot *and* Amoret*:*
A paire whom doubtlesse had the others seene,
They from their owne loves had Apostates *beene;*
Thus Fletcher *did the fam'd laureat exceed,*
Both when his Trumpet sounded and his reed;
Now if the Ancients yeeld that heretofore,
None worthyer then those ere Laurell wore;
The least our age can say now thou art gon,
Is that there never will be such a one:
And since t' expresse thy worth, our rimes too narrow be,
To help it wee'l be ample in our prophesie.

H. HOWARD.

On Mr John Fletcher, and his Workes, never before published.

TO flatter living fooles is easie slight:
But hard, to do the living-dead men right.
To praise a Landed Lord, is gainfull art:
But thanklesse to pay Tribute to desert.
This should have been my taske: I had intent
To bring my rubbish to thy monument,
To stop some crannies there, but that I found
No need of least repaire; all firme and sound.
Thy well-built fame doth still it selfe advance
Above the Worlds mad zeale and ignorance,

Though thou dyedst not possest of that same pelfe
(Which Nobler soules call durt,) the City wealth:
Yet thou hast left unto the times so great
A Legacy, a Treasure so compleat,
That 'twill be hard I feare to prove thy Will:
Men will be wrangling, and in doubting still
How so vast summes of wit were left behind,
And yet nor debts nor sharers they can finde.
'Twas the kind providence of fate, to lock
Some of this Treasure up; and keep a stock
For a reserve untill these sullen daies:
When scorn, and want, and danger, are the Baies
That Crown the head of merit. But now he
Who in thy Will hath part, is rich and free.
But there's a Caveat enter'd by command,
None should pretend, but those can understand.

HENRY MODY, Baronet.

ON

Mr. Fletchers Works.

THough Poets have a licence which they use
As th' ancient priviledge of their free Muse;
Yet whether this be leave enough for me
To write, great Bard, an Eulogie for thee:
Or whether to commend thy Worke, will stand
Both with the Lawes of Verse and of the Land,
Were to put doubts might raise a discontent
Between the Muses and the ——
I'le none of that. There's desperate wits that be
(As their immortall Lawrell) Thunder-free;
Whose personall vertues, 'bove the Lawes of Fate,
Supply the roome of personall estate:
And thus enfranchis'd, safely may rehearse,
Rapt in a lofty straine, [their] own neck-verse.
For he that gives the Bayes to thee, must then
First take it from the Militarie Men;
He must untriumph conquests, bid 'em stand,
Question the strength of their victorious band.
He must act new things, or go neer the sin,
Reader, as neer as you and I have been:
He must be that, which He that tryes will swear
I[t] is not good being so another Yeare.
And now that thy great name I've brought to [this],
To do it honour is to do amisse,
What's to be done to those, that shall refuse
To celebrate, great Soule, thy noble Muse?

Shall the poore State of all those wandring things,
Thy Stage once rais'd to Emperors and Kings?
Shall rigid forfeitures (that reach our Heires)
Of things that only fill with cares and feares?
Shall the privation of a friendlesse life,
Made up of contradictions and strife?
Shall He be entitie, would antedate
His own poore name, and thine annihilate?
Shall these be judgements great enough for one
That dares not write thee an Encomion?
Then where am I? but now I've thought upon't,
I'le prayse thee more then all have ventur'd on't.
I'le take thy noble Work (and like the trade
Where for a heap of Salt pure Gold is layd)
I'le lay thy Volume, that Huge Tome of wit,
About in Ladies Closets, where they sit
Enthron'd in their own wills; and if she bee
A Laick sister, shee'l straight flie to thee:
But if a holy Habit shee have on,
Or be some Novice, shee'l scarce looke upon
Thy Lines at first; but watch Her then a while,
And you shall see Her steale a gentle smile
Upon thy Title, put thee neerer yet,
Breath on thy Lines a whisper, and then set
Her voyce up to the measures; then begin
To blesse the houre, and happy state shee's in.
Now shee layes by her Characters, and lookes
With a stern eye on all her pretty Bookes.
Shee's now thy Voteresse, and the just Crowne
She brings thee with it, is worth half the Towne.
I'le send thee to the Army, they that fight
Will read thy tragedies with some delight,
Be all thy Reformadoes, fancy scars,
And pay too, in thy speculative wars.
I'le send thy Comick scenes to some of those
That for a great while have plaid fast and loose;
New universalists, by changing shapes,
Have made with wit and fortune faire escapes.
Then shall the Countrie that poor Tennis-ball
Of angry fate, receive thy Pastorall,
And from it learn those melancholy straines
Fed the afflicted soules of Primitive swaines.
Thus the whole World to reverence will flock
Thy Tragick Buskin and thy Comick Stock:
And winged fame unto posterity
Transmit but onely two, this Age, and Thee.

THOMAS PEYTON.
Agricola Anglo-Cantianus.

VERSES

ON THE
Deceased Authour, Mr John Fletcher, his Plays; and especially, *The Mad Lover.*

Whilst his well organ'd body doth retreat,
To its first matter, and the formall heat
Triumphant sits in judgement to approve
Pieces above our Candour and our love:
Such as dare boldly venter to appeare
Unto the curious eye, and Criticke eare:
Lo the Mad Lover *in these various times*
Is press'd to life, t' accuse us of our crimes.
While Fletcher *liv'd, who equall to him writ*
Such lasting Monuments of naturall wit?
Others might draw their lines with sweat, like those
That (with much paines) a Garrison inclose;
Whilst his sweet fluent veine did gently runne
As uncontrold, and smoothly as the Sun.
After his death our Theatres did make
Him in his own unequald Language speake:
And now when all the Muses out of their
Approved modesty silent appeare,
This Play of Fletchers *braves the envious light*
As wonder of our eares once, now our sight.
Three and fourfold blest Poet, who the Lives
Of Poets, and of Theaters survives!
A Groome, or Ostler of some wit may bring
His Pegasus to the Castalian spring;
Boast he a race o're the Pharsalian plaine,
Or happy Tempe *valley dares maintaine:*
Brag at one leape upon the double Cliffe
(Were it as high as monstrous Tennariffe)
Of farre-renown'd Parnassus he will get,
And there (t' amaze the World) confirme his seate:
When our admired Fletcher *vaunts not ought,*
And slighted everything he writ as naught:
While all our English wondring world (in's cause)
Made this great City eccho with applause.
Read him therefore all that can read, and those
That cannot learne, if y' are not Learnings foes,
And wilfully resolved to refuse
The gentle Raptures of this happy Muse.
From thy great constellation (noble Soule)
Looke on this Kingdome, suffer not the whole
Spirit of Poesie retire to Heaven,
But make us entertaine what thou hast given.

Earthquakes and Thunder Diapasons make
The Seas vast roare, and irresistlesse shake
Of horrid winds, a sympathy compose;
So in these things there's musicke in the close:
And though they seem great Discords in our eares,
They are not so to them above the Spheares.
Granting these Musicke, how much sweeter's that
Mnemosyne's *daughter's voyces doe create?*
Since Heaven, and Earth, and Seas, and Ayre consent
To make an Harmony (the Instrument,
Their own agreeing selves) shall we refuse
The Musicke which the Deities doe use?
Troys *ravisht* Ganymed *doth sing to* Jove,
And Phœbus *selfe playes on his Lyre above.*
The Cretan Gods, or glorious men, who will
Imitate right, must wonder at thy skill,
Best Poet of thy times, or he will prove
As mad as thy brave Memnon *was with love.*

ASTON COKAINE, Baronet.

Upon the Works of BEAUMONT, and FLETCHER.

HOw Angels *(cloyster'd in our humane Cells)*
Maintaine their parley, Beaumont-Fletcher *tels;*
Whose strange unimitable Intercourse
Transcends all Rules, and flyes beyond the force
Of the most forward soules; all must submit
Untill they reach these Mysteries *of Wit.*
The Intellectuall Language *here's exprest,*
Admir'd in better times, and dares the Test
Of Ours; for from Wit, Sweetnesse, Mirth, *and* Sence,
This Volume springs a new true Quintessence.

JO. PETTUS, Knight.

On the Works of the most excellent Dramatick Poet, Mr. *John F[l]etcher*, never before Printed.

HAile Fletcher, *welcome to the worlds great Stage;*
For our two houres, we have thee here an age
In thy whole Works, and may th' Impression *call*
The Pretor *that presents thy Playes to all:*

Both to the People, and the Lords *that sway*
That Herd, *and Ladies whom those Lords obey.*
And what's the Loadstone can such guests invite
But moves on two Poles, Profit *and* Delight,
Which will be soon, as on the Rack, confest
When every one is tickled with a jest:
And that pure Fletcher, *able to subdue*
A Melancholy *more then* Burton *knew.*
And though upon the by, to his designes
The Native *may learne English from his lines,*
And th' Alien *if he can but construe it,*
May here be made free Denison *of wit.*
But his maine end does drooping Vertue *raise,*
And crownes her beauty with eternall Bayes;
In Scænes where she inflames the frozen soule,
While Vice (*her paint washt off*) *appeares so foule;*
She must this Blessed Isle *and Europe leave,*
And some new Quadrant *of the* Globe *deceive:*
Or hide her Blushes on the Affrike *shore*
Like Marius, *but ne're rise to* triumph *more;*
That honour *is resign'd to* Fletchers *fame;*
Adde to his Trophies, that a Poets name
(*Late growne as odious to our* Moderne states
As that of King *to* Rome) *he vindicates*
From black aspertions, cast upon't by those
Which only are inspir'd to lye in prose.

And, By the Court of Muses be't decreed,
What graces spring from Poesy's richer seed,
When we name Fletcher *shall be so proclaim'd,*
As all that's Royall *is when* Cæsar's *nam'd.*

ROBERT STAPYLTON Knight.

To the memory of my most honoured kinsman, Mr. *Francis Beaumont.*

I'*Le not pronounce how strong and cleane thou writes,*
Nor by what new hard Rules thou took'st thy Flights,
Nor how much Greek *and* Latin *some refine*
Before they can make up six words of thine,
But this I'le say, thou strik'st our sense so deep,
At once thou mak'st us Blush, Rejoyce, and Weep.
Great Father Johnson *bow'd himselfe when hee*
(*Thou writ'st so nobly*) *vow'd* he envy'd thee.
Were thy Mardonius *arm'd, there would be more*
Strife for his Sword then all Achilles *wore,*

Such wise just Rage, had Hee been lately try'd
My life on't Hee had been o'th' Better side,
And where hee found false odds (through Gold or Sloath)
There brave Mardonius *would have beat them Both.*
Behold, here's FLETCHER *too! the World ne're knew*
Two Potent Witts co-operate till You;
For still your fancies are so wov'n and knit,
'Twas FRANCIS FLETCHER, *or* JOHN BEAUMONT *writ.*
Yet neither borrow'd, nor were so put to't
To call poore Godds and Goddesses to do't;
Nor made Nine Girles your Muses *(you suppose*
Women ne're write, save Love-Letters in prose)
But are your owne Inspirers, and have made
Such pow'rfull Sceanes, as when they please, invade.
Your Plot, Sence, Language, All's so pure and fit,
Hee's Bold, not Valiant, dare dispute your Wit.

GEORGE LISLE Knight.

On Mr. *JOHN FLETCHER'S* Workes.

SO shall we joy, when all whom Beasts and Wormes
Had turn'd to their owne substances and formes,
Whom Earth to Earth, or fire hath chang'd to fire,
Wee shall behold more then at first intire
As now we doe, to see all thine, thine owne
In this thy Muses Resurrection,
Whose scatter'd parts, from thy owne Race, more wounds
Hath suffer'd, then Acteon *from his hounds;*
Which first their Braines, and then their Bellies fed,
And from their excrements new Poets bred.
But now thy Muse inraged from her urne
Like Ghosts of Murdred bodyes doth returne
To accuse the Murderers, to right the Stage,
And undeceive the long abused Age,
Which casts thy praise on them, to whom thy Wit
Gives not more Gold then they give drosse to it:
Who not content like fellons to purloyne,
Adde Treason to it, and debase thy Coyne.
But whither am I strayd? I need not raise
Trophies to thee from other Mens dispraise;
Nor is thy fame on lesser Ruines built,
Nor needs thy juster title the foule guilt
Of Easterne Kings, who to secure their Raigne,
Must have their Brothers, Sonnes, and Kindred slaine.
Then was wits Empire at the fatall height,
When labouring and sinking with its weight,

From thence a thousand lesser Poets sprong
Like petty Princes from the fall of Rome.
When JOHNSON, SHAKESPEARE, *and thy selfe did sit,*
And sway'd in the Triumvirate of wit—
Yet what from JOHNSONS *oyle and sweat did flow,*
Or what more easie nature did bestow
On SHAKESPEARES *gentler Muse, in thee full growne*
Their Graces both appeare, yet so, that none
Can say here Nature ends, and Art begins
But mixt like th'Elements, and borne like twins,
So interweav'd, so like, so much the same,
None this meere Nature, that meere Art can name:
'Twas this the Ancients meant, Nature and Skill
Are the two topps of their Pernassus *Hill.*

J. DENHAM.

Upon Mr. *John Fletcher's* Playes.

FLETCHER, *to thee, wee doe not only owe*
All these good Playes, but those of others too:
Thy wit repeated, does support the Stage,
Credits the last and entertaines this age.
No Worthies form'd by any Muse but thine
Could purchase Robes to make themselves so fine:
What brave Commander is not proud to see
Thy brave Melantius *in his Gallantry,*
Our greatest Ladyes love to see their scorne
Out done by Thine, in what themselves have worne:
Th'impatient Widow ere the yeare be done
Sees thy Aspasia *weeping in her Gowne:*
I never yet the Tragick straine assay'd
Deterr'd by that inimitable Maid:
And when I venture at the Comick stile
Thy Scornfull Lady *seemes to mock my toile:*
Thus has thy Muse, at once, improv'd and marr'd
Our Sport in Playes, by rendring it too hard.
So when a sort of lusty Shepheards throw
The barre by turns, and none the rest outgoe
So farre, but that the best are measuring casts,
Their emulation and their pastime lasts;
But if some Brawny yeoman, of the guard
Step in and tosse the Axeltree a yard
Or more beyond the farthest Marke, the rest
Despairing stand, their sport is at the best.

EDW. WALLER.

To *FLETCHER* Reviv'd.

How have I been Religious? what strange Good
Ha's scap't me that I never understood?
Have I Hell guarded Hæresie *o'rethrowne?*
Heald wounded States? made Kings and Kingdomes one?
That Fate *should be so mercifull to me,*
To let me live t'have said I have read thee.
Faire Star ascend! the Joy! the Life! the Light
Of this tempestuous Age, this darke worlds sight!
Oh from thy Crowne of Glory dart one flame
May strike a sacred Reverence, whilest thy Name
(Like holy Flamens *to their God of Day)*
We bowing, sing; and whilst we praise, we pray.
Bright Spirit! whose Æternall motion
Of Wit, like Time, *still in it selfe did runne;*
Binding all others in it and did give
Commission, how far this, or that shall live:
Like Destinie *of Poems, who, as she*
Signes death to all, her selfe can never dye.
And now thy purple-robed Tragoedie,
In her imbroider'd Buskins, calls mine eye,
Valentinian *Where brave* Aëtius *we see betray'd,*
T'obey his Death, whom thousand lives obey'd;
Whilst that the Mighty Foole *his Scepter breakes,*
And through his Gen'rals *wounds his owne doome speaks,*
Weaving thus richly Valentinian
The costliest Monarch with the cheapest man.
Souldiers may here to their old glories adde,
The Mad Lover. The Lover *love, and be with reason* mad:
Not as of old, Alcides *furious,*
Who wilder then his Bull did teare the house,
(Hurling his Language with the Canvas stone)
'Twas thought the Monster roar'd the sob'rer Tone.
Tragi-comedies. *But ah, when thou thy sorrow didst inspire*
With Passions, blacke as is her darke attire,
Arcas. *Virgins as* Sufferers *have wept to see*
Bellario. *So white a Soule, so red a Crueltie;*
That thou hast griev'd, and with unthought redresse,
Dri'd their wet eyes who now thy mercy blesse;
Comedies. *Yet loth to lose thy watry jewell, when*
The Spanish Curate. *Joy wip't it off, Laughter straight sprung't agen.*
Now ruddy-cheeked Mirth *with Rosie wings,*
The Humorous Lieutenant. *Fanns ev'ry brow with gladnesse, whilest she sings*
Delight to all, and the whole Theatre
A Festivall in Heaven doth appeare:

VERSES

The Tamer Tam'd. The little French Lawyer. The custom of the Countrey.

Nothing but Pleasure, Love, and (like the Morne)
Each face a generall smiling doth adorne.
  Heare ye foule Speakers, that pronounce the Aire
Of Stewes and Shores, I will informe you where
And how to cloathe aright your wanton wit,
Without her nasty Bawd attending it.
View here a loose thought said with such a grace,
Minerva might have spoke in Venus face;
So well disguis'd, that t'was conceiv'd by none
But Cupid had Diana's linnen on;
And all his naked parts so vail'd, th' expresse
The Shape with clowding the uncomlinesse;
That if this Reformation which we
Receiv'd, had not been buried with thee,
The Stage (as this work) might have liv'd and lov'd;
Her Lines; the austere Skarlet had approv'd,
And th' Actors wisely been from that offence
As cleare, as they are now from Audience.
  Thus with thy Genius did the Scæne expire,
Wanting thy Active and inliv'ning fire,
That now (to spread a darknesse over all,)
Nothing remaines but Poesie to fall.
And though from these thy Embers we receive
Some warmth, so much as may be said, we live,
That we dare praise thee, blushlesse, in the head
Of the best piece Hermes to Love e're read,
That We rejoyce and glory in thy Wit,
And feast each other with remembring it,
That we dare speak thy thought, thy Acts recite:
Yet all men henceforth be afraid to write.

RICH. LOVELACE.

On Master *JOHN FLETCHERS* Dramaticall Poems.

GReat tutelary Spirit of the Stage!
FLETCHER! I can fix nothing but my rage
Before thy Workes, 'gainst their officious crime
Who print thee now , in the worst scæne of Time.
For me, uninterrupted hadst thou slept
Among the holly shades and close hadst kept
The mistery of thy lines, till men might bee
Taught how to reade, and then, how to reade thee.
But now thou art expos'd to th' common fate,
Revive then (mighty Soule!) and vindicate
From th' Ages rude affronts thy injured fame,
Instruct the Envious, with how chast a flame

Thou warmst the Lover; how severely just
Thou wert to punish, if he burnt to lust.
With what a blush thou didst the Maid adorne,
But tempted, with how innocent a scorne.
How Epidemick errors by thy Play
Were laught out of esteeme, so purg'd away.
How to each sence thou so didst vertue fit,
That all grew vertuous to be thought t' have wit.
But this was much too narrow for thy art,
Thou didst frame governments, give Kings their part,
Teach them how neere to God, while just they be;
But how dissolv'd, stretcht forth to Tyrannie.
How Kingdomes, in their channell, safely run,
But rudely overflowing are undone.
Though vulgar spirits Poets scorne or hate:
Man may beget, A Poet can create.

WILL. HABINGTON.

Upon Master *FLETCHERS* Dramaticall Workes.

W*Hat? now the Stage is down, darst thou appeare*
Bold FLETC[H]ER *in this tottring Hemispheare?*
Yes; Poets are like Palmes which, the more weight
You cast upon them, grow more strong & streight,
'Tis not *love*'s Thunderbolt, nor *Mars* his Speare,
Or *Neptune's* angry Trident, Poets fear.
Had now grim BEN *bin breathing, with what rage,*
And high-swolne fury had Hee lash'd this age,
SHAKESPEARE *with* CHAPMAN *had grown madd, and torn*
Their gentle Sock, *and lofty* Buskins *worne,*
To make their Muse welter up to the chin
In blood; *of* faigned *Scænes no need had bin,*
England *like* Lucians *Eagle with an Arrow*
Of her owne Plumes piercing her heart quite thorow,
Had bin a Theater and subject fit
To exercise in real *truth's their wit:*
Yet none like high-wing'd FLETCHER *had bin found*
This Eagles *tragick-destiny to sound,*
Rare FLETCHER's quill *had soar'd up to the sky,*
And drawn down Gods to see the tragedy:
Live famous Dramatist, let every spring
Make thy Bay flourish, and fresh Bourgeons *bring:*
And since we cannot have Thee trod o'th' stage,
Wee will applaud Thee in this silent Page.

JA. HOWELL. *P.C.C.*

VERSES

On the Edition.

FLETCHER (*whose Fame no Age can ever wast;*
Envy of Ours, and glory of the last)
Is now alive againe; and with his Name
His sacred Ashes wak'd into a Flame;
Such as before did by a secret charme
The wildest Heart subdue, the coldest warme,
And lend the Lady's eyes a power more bright,
Dispensing thus to either, Heat and Light.
He to a Sympathie those soules betrai'd
Whom Love or Beauty never could perswade;
And in each mov'd spectatour could beget
A reall passion by a Counterfeit:
When first Bellario *bled, what Lady there*
Did not for every drop let fall a teare?
And when Aspasia *wept, not any eye*
But seem'd to weare the same sad livery;
By him inspir'd the feign'd Lucina *drew*
More streams of melting sorrow then the true;
But then the Scornfull Lady *did beguile*
Their easie griefs, and teach them all to smile.
Thus he Affections could, or raise or lay;
Love, Griefe and Mirth thus did his Charmes obey:
He Nature taught her passions to out-doe,
How to refine the old, and create new;
Which such a happy likenesse seem'd to beare,
As if that Nature Art, Art Nature were.
Yet All had Nothing bin, obscurely kept
In the same Urne wherein his Dust hath slept,
Nor had he ris' the Delphick wreath to claime,
Had not the dying sceane expir'd his Name;
Dispaire our joy hath doubled, he is come,
Thrice welcome by this Post-liminium.
His losse preserv'd him; They that silenc'd Wit,
Are now the Authours to Eternize it;
Thus Poets are in spight of Fate reviv'd,
And Playes by Intermission longer liv'd.

THO. STANLEY.

On the Edition of Mr *Francis Beaumonts*, and Mr *John Fletchers* PLAYES never printed before.

I Am *amaz'd*; and this same *Extacye*
Is both my *Glory* and *Apology*.
Sober Joyes are dull Passions; they must beare
Proportion to the *Subject*: if *so*; where
Beaumont and *Fletcher* shall vouchsafe to be
That Subject; *That Joy* must be *Extacye*.
Fury is the *Complexion* of *great Wits*;
The *Fooles Distemper*: Hee, thats *mad* by *fits*,
Is *wise so* too. It is the *Poets Muse*;
The *Prophets God*: the *Fooles*, and *my excuse*.
For (in *Me*) nothing *lesse* then *Fletchers Name*
Could have *begot*, or *justify'd* this *flame*.
Beaumont
Fletcher } *Return'd?* methinks it should not be.
No, not in's *Works: Playes* are as *dead* as *He*.
The *Palate* of *this age gusts* nothing *High*;
That has not *Custard* in't or *Bawdery*.
Folly and *Madnesse* fill the *Stage*: The *Scæne*
Is *Athens*; *where*, the *Guilty*, and the *Meane*,
The *Foole 'scapes* well enough'; *Learned* and *Great*,
Suffer an *Ostracisme*; stand *Exulate*.

Mankinde is *fall'n againe*, *shrunke* a *degree*,
A *step* below his very *Apostacye*.
Nature her *Selfe* is out of *Tune*; and *Sicke*
Of *Tumult* and *Disorder*, *Lunatique*.
Yet *what World* would not cheerfully *endure*
The *Torture*, or *Disease*, t' *enjoy* the *Cure?*

This Booke's the *Balsame*, and the *Hellebore*,
Must *preserve bleeding Nature*, and *restore*
Our *Crazy Stupor* to a *just quick Sence*
Both of *Ingratitude*, and *Providence*.
That teaches us (at *Once*) to *feele*, and *know*,
Two deep Points: what we *want*, and what we *owe*.
Yet *Great Goods have their Ills*: Should we *transmit*
To *Future Times*, the *Pow'r* of *Love* and *Wit*,
In *this Example:* would they not *combine*
To make *Our Imperfections Their Designe?*
They'd *study* our *Corruptions*; and take more
Care to be *Ill*, then to be *Good*, *before*.

For *nothing but so great Infirmity,*
Could make Them worthy of such Remedy.

Have you not seene the Suns almighty Ray
Rescue th' *affrighted World*, and *redeeme Day*
From *blacke despaire:* how his *victorious Beame*
Scatters the *Storme*, and *drownes* the *petty flame*
Of *Lightning*, in the *glory* of his *eye*:
How *full* of *pow'r*, how *full* of *Majesty?*
When to *us Mortals*, *nothing* else was *knowne*,
But the *sad doubt*, whether to *burne*, or *drowne.*

Choler, and *Phlegme*, *Heat*, and *dull Ignorance*,
Have cast *the people* into *such* a *Trance*,
That *feares* and *danger* seeme *Great equally*,
And no *dispute* left now, but *how* to *dye.*
Just in *this nicke*, *Fletcher sets the world cleare*
Of all disorder and reformes us here.

The *formall Youth*, that knew *no* other *Grace*,
Or *Value*, but his *Title*, and his *Lace*,
Glasses himselfe: and in *this faithfull Mirrour*,
Views, *disaproves*, *reformes*, *repents* his *Errour.*

The *Credulous*, *bright Girle*, that *beleeves all*
Language, (in *Othes*) if *Good*, *Canonicall*,
Is *fortifi'd*, and *taught*, *here*, to *beware*
Of *ev'ry* specious *bayte*, of *ev'ry snare*
Save *one:* and *that* same *Caution* takes her *more*,
Then *all* the *flattery* she *felt before.*
She finds her *Boxes*, and her *Thoughts betray'd*
By the *Corruption* of the *Chambermaide:*
Then throwes her *Washes* and *dissemblings* By;
And *Vowes* nothing but *Ingenuity.*

The *severe States-man quits* his *sullen forme*
Of *Gravity* and *bus'nesse*; The *Luke-warme*
Religious his *Neutrality*; The *hot*
Braine-sicke Illuminate his *zeale*; *The Sot*
Stupidity; The *Souldier* his *Arreares*;
The *Court* its *Confidence*; The *Plebs* their *feares*;
Gallants their *Apishnesse* and *Perjurie*,
Women their *Pleasure* and *Inconstancie*;
Poets their *Wine*; the *Usurer* his *Pelfe*;
The *World* its *Vanity*; and *I* my *Selfe.*

Roger L'Estrange.

On the Dramatick Poems of Mr John Fletcher.

Wonder! who's here? Fletcher, *long buried*
Reviv'd? Tis he! hee's risen from the Dead.
His winding sheet put off, walks above ground,
Shakes off his Fetters, and is better bound.
And may he not, if rightly understood,
Prove Playes are lawfull? he hath made them Good.
Is any Lover Mad? *see here* Loves Cure;
Unmarried? to a Wife *he may be sure*
A rare one, For a Moneth; *if she displease,*
The Spanish Curate *gives a Writ of ease.*
Enquire The Custome of the Country, *then*
Shall the French Lawyer *set you free againe.*
If the two Faire Maids *take it wondrous ill,*
(*One of* the Inne, *the other of* the Mill,)
That th' Lovers Progresse *stopt, and they defam'd;*
Here's that makes Women Pleas'd, *and* Tamer tamd.
But who then playes the Coxcombe, *or will trie*
His Wit at severall Weapons, *or else die?*
Nice Valour *and he doubts not to engage*
The Noble Gentl'man, *in* Loves Pilgrimage,
To take revenge on the False One, *and run*
The Honest mans Fortune, *to be undone*
Like Knight of Malta, *or else* Captaine *be*
Or th' Humerous Lieutenant: *goe to Sea*
(A Voyage *for to starve*) *hee's very loath,*
Till we are all at peace, to sweare an Oath,
That then the Loyall Subject *may have leave*
To lye from Beggers Bush, *and undeceive*
The Creditor, discharge his debts; Why so,
Since we can't pay to Fletcher *what we owe.*
Oh could his Prophetesse *but tell one* Chance,
When that the Pilgrimes *shall returne from France.*
And once more make this Kingdome, as of late,
The Island Princesse, *and we celebrate*
A Double Marriage; *every one to bring*
To Fletchers *memory his offering.*
That thus at last unsequesters the Stage,
Brings backe the Silver, and the Golden Age.

Robert Gardiner.

VERSES

To the *Manes* of the celebrated Poets and Fellow-writers, *Francis Beaumont* and *John Fletcher*, upon the Printing of their excellent Dramatick Poems.

Disdaine not Gentle Shades, the lowly praise
Which here I tender your immortall Bayes.
Call it not folly, but my zeale, that I
Strive to eternize you that cannot dye.
And though no Language rightly can commend
What you have writ, save what your selves have penn'd;
Yet let me wonder at those curious straines
(The rich Conceptions of your twin-like Braines)
Which drew the Gods attention; who admir'd
To see our English Stage by you inspir'd.
Whose chiming Muses never fail'd to sing
A Soule-affecting Musicke; ravishing
Both Eare and Intellect, while you do each
Contend with other who shall highest reach
In rare Invention; Conflicts that beget
New strange delight, to see two Fancies met,
That could receive no foile: two wits in growth
So just, as had one Soule informed both.
Thence (Learned Fletcher) *sung the muse alone,*
As both had done before, thy Beaumont *gone.*
In whom, as thou, had he outliv'd, so he
(Snatch'd first away) survived still in thee.
What though distempers of the present Age
Have banish'd your smooth numbers from the Stage?
You shall be gainers by't; it shall confer
To th' making the vast world your Theater.
The Presse shall give to ev'ry man his part,
And we will all be Actors; learne by heart
Those Tragick Scenes and Comicke Straines you writ,
Un-imitable both for Art and Wit;
And at each Exit, *as your Fancies rise,*
Our hands shall clap deserved Plaudities.

John Web.

To the desert of the Author in his most Ingenious Pieces.

Thou art above their Censure, whose darke Spirits
Respects but shades of things, and seeming merits;
That have no soule, nor reason to their will,
But rime as ragged, as a Ganders Quill:
Where Pride blowes up the Error, and transfers
Their zeale in Tempests, that so wid'ly errs.

Like heat and Ayre comprest, their blind desires
Mixe with their ends, as raging winds with fires.
Whose Ignorance and Passions, weare an eye
Squint to all parts of true Humanity.
All is Apocripha *suits not their vaine:*
For wit, oh fye! and Learning too; prophane!
But Fletcher *hath done Miracles by wit,*
And one Line of his may convert them yet.
Tempt them into the State of knowledge, and
Happinesse to read and understand.
The way is strow'd with Lawrell, *and ev'ry Muse*
Brings Incense to our Fletcher: *whose Scenes infuse*
Such noble kindlings from her pregnant fire,
As charmes her Criticke Poets in desire,
And who doth read him, that parts lesse indu'd,
Then with some heat of wit or Gratitude.
Some crowd to touch the Relique of his Bayes,
Some to cry up their owne wit in his praise,
And thinke they engage it by Comparatives,
When from himselfe, himselfe he best derives.
Let Shakespeare, Chapman, *and applauded* Ben,
Weare the Eternall merit of their Pen,
Here I am love-sicke: and were I to chuse,
A Mistris corrivall 'tis Fletcher's *Muse.*

George Buck.

On Mr BEAUMONT.

(Written thirty years since, presently after his death.)

BEaumont *lyes here; and where now shall we have*
A Muse like his to sigh upon his grave?
Ah! none to weepe this with a worthy teare,
But he that cannot, Beaumont, *that lies here.*
Who now shall pay thy Tombe with such a Verse
As thou that Ladies didst, faire Rutlands *Herse?*
A Monument that will then lasting be,
When all her Marble is more dust than she.
In thee all's lost: a sudden dearth and want
Hath seiz'd on Wit, good Epitaphs are scant;
We dare not write thy Elegie, whilst each feares
He nere shall match that coppy of thy teares.
Scarce in an Age a Poet, and yet he
Scarce lives the third part of his age to see,
But quickly taken off and only known,
Is in a minute shut as soone as showne.

Why should weake Nature tire her selfe in vaine
In such a peice, to dash it straight againe?
Why should she take such worke beyond her skill,
Which when she cannot perfect, she must kill?
Alas, what is't to temper slime or mire?
But Nature's puzled when she workes in fire:
Great Braines (like brightest glasse) crack straight, while those
Of Stone or Wood hold out, and feare not blowes.
And wee their Ancient hoary heads can see
Whose Wit was never their mortality:
Beaumont *dies young, so* Sidney *did before,*
There was not Poetry he could live to more,
He could not grow up higher, I scarce know
If th' art it selfe unto that pitch could grow,
Were't not in thee that hadst arriv'd the hight
Of all that wit could reach, or Nature might.
O when I read those excellent things of thine,
Such Strength, such sweetnesse coucht in every line,
Such life of Fancy, such high choise of braine,
Nought of the Vulgar wit or borrowed straine,
Such Passion, such expressions meet my eye,
Such Wit untainted with obscenity,
And these so unaffectedly exprest,
All in a language purely flowing drest,
And all so borne within thy selfe, thine owne,
So new, so fresh, so nothing trod upon.
I grieve not now that old Menanders *veine*
Is ruin'd to survive in thee againe;
Such in his time was he of the same peece,
The smooth, even naturall Wit, and Love of Greece.
Those few sententious fragments shew more worth,
Then all the Poets Athens *ere brought forth;*
And I am sorry we have lost those houres
On them, whose quicknesse comes far short of ours,
And dwell not more on thee, whose every Page
May be a patterne for their Scene and Stage.
I will not yeeld thy Workes so meane a Prayse;
More pure, more chaste, more sainted then are Playes,
Nor with that dull supinenesse to be read,
To passe a fire, or laugh an houre in bed,
How doe the Muses suffer every where,
Taken in such mouthes censure, in such eares,
That twixt a whiffe, a Line or two rehearse,
And with their Rheume together spaule a Verse?
This all a Poems leisure after Play,
Drinke or Tabacco, it may keep the Day.
Whilst even their very idlenesse they thinke
Is lost in these, that lose their time in drinke.

Pity then dull we, we that better know,
Will a more serious houre on thee bestow,
Why should not Beaumont *in the Morning please,*
As well as Plautus, Aristophanes?
Who if my Pen may as my thoughts be free,
Were scurrill Wits and Buffons both to Thee;
Yet these our Learned of severest brow
Will deigne to looke on, and to note them too,
That will defie our owne, tis English stuffe,
And th' Author is not rotten long enough.
Alas what flegme are they, compared to thee,
In thy Philaster, *and* Maids-Tragedy?
Where's such an humour as thy Bessus? *pray*
Let them put all their Thrasoes *in one Play,*
He shall out-bid them; their conceit was poore,
All in a Circle of a Bawd or Whore;
A cozning dance, take the foole away,
And not a good jest extant in a Play.
Yet these are Wits, because they'r old, and now
Being Greeke and Latine, they are Learning too:
But those their owne Times were content t' allow
A thirsty fame, and thine is lowest now.
But thou shalt live, and when thy Name is growne
Six Ages older, shall be better knowne,
When th' art of Chaucers *standing in the Tombe,*
Thou shalt not share, but take up all his roome.

Joh. Earle.

UPON Mr FLETCHERS Incomparable Playes.

T*He Poet lives; wonder not how or why*
Fletcher *revives, but that he er'e could dye:*
Safe Mirth, *full* Language, *flow in ev'ry Page,*
At once he doth both heighten *and* aswage;
All Innocence and Wit, pleasant and cleare,
Nor Church *nor* Lawes *were ever Libel'd here;*
But faire deductions drawn from his great Braine,
Enough to conquer all that's False *or* Vaine;
He scatters Wit, and Sence so freely flings
That very Citizens *speake handsome things,*
Teaching their Wives *such unaffected grace,*
Their Looks *are now as handsome as their* Face.
Nor is this violent, he steals upon
The yeilding Soule untill the Phrensie's *gone;*

His very Launcings *do the Patient* please,
As when good Musicke *cures a* Mad Disease.
Small Poets rifle Him, yet thinke it faire,
Because they rob a man that well can spare;
They feed upon him, owe him every bit,
Th'are all but Sub-excisemen *of his Wit.*

J. M.

On the Workes of *Beaumont* and *Fletcher*, now at length printed.

GReat paire of Authors, whom one equall Starre
Begot so like in Genius, *that you are*
In Fame, as well as Writings, both so knit,
That no man knowes where to divide your wit,
Much lesse your praise; you, who had equall fire,
And did each other mutually inspire;
Whether one did contrive, the other write,
Or one fram'd the plot, the other did indite;
Whether one found the matter, th'other dresse,
Or the one disposed what th'other did expresse;
Where e're your parts betweene your selves lay, we,
In all things which you did but one thred see,
So evenly drawne out, so gently spunne,
That Art with Nature nere did smoother run.
Where shall I fixe my praise then? or what part
Of all your numerous Labours hath desert
More to be fam'd then other? shall I say,
I've met a lover so drawne in your Play,
So passionately written, so inflam'd,
So jealously inraged, then gently tam'd,
That I in reading have the Person seene,
And your Pen hath part Stage and Actor been?
Or shall I say, that I can scarce forbeare
To clap, when I a Captain do meet there,
So lively in his owne vaine humour drest,
So braggingly, and like himself exprest,
That moderne Cowards, when they saw him plaid,
Saw, blusht, departed guilty, and betraid?
You wrote all parts right; whatsoe're the Stage
Had from you, was seene there as in the age,
And had their equall life: Vices which were
Manners abroad, did grow corrected there:

They who possest a Box, and halfe Crowne spent
To learne Obscenenes, returned innocent,
And thankt you for this coznage, whose chaste Scene
Taught Loves so noble, so reform'd, so cleane,
That they who brought foule fires, and thither came
To bargaine, went thence with a holy flame.
Be't to your praise too, that your Stock and Veyne
Held both to Tragick and to Comick straine;
Where e're you listed to be high and grave,
No Buskin shew'd more solem[n]e, no quill gave
Such feeling objects to draw teares from eyes,
Spectators sate part in your Tragedies.
And where you listed to be low, and free,
Mirth turn'd the whole house into Comedy;
So piercing (where you pleas'd) hitting a fault,
That humours from your pen issued all salt.
Nor were you thus in Works and Poems knit,
As to be but two halfes, and make one wit;
But as some things we see, have double cause,
And yet the effect it selfe from both whole drawes;
So though you were thus twisted and combind
As two bodies, to have but one faire minde
Yet if we praise you rightly, we must say
Both joyn'd, and both did wholly make the Play,
For that you could write singly, we may guesse
By the divided peeces which the Presse
Hath severally sent forth; nor were gone so
(Like some our Moderne Authors) made to go
On meerely by the helpe of th'other, who
To purchase fame do come forth one of two;
Nor wrote you so, that ones part was to lick
The other into shape, nor did one stick
The others cold inventions with such wit,
As served like spice, to make them quick and fit;
Nor out of mutuall want, or emptinesse,
Did you conspire to go still twins to th' Presse:
But what thus joyned you wrote, might have come forth
As good from each, and stored with the same worth
That thus united them, you did joyne sense,
In you 'twas League, in others impotence;
And the Presse which both thus amongst us sends,
Sends us one Poet in a paire of friends.

Jasper Maine.

VERSES

Upon the report of the printing of the Dramaticall Poems of Master *John Fletcher*, collected before, and now set forth in one Volume.

Though when all Fletcher *writ, and the entire*
Man was indulged unto that sacred fire,
His thoughts, and his thoughts dresse, appeared both such,
That 'twas his happy fault to do too much;
Who therefore wisely did submit each birth
To knowing Beaumont *e're it did come forth,*
Working againe untill he said 'twas fit,
And made him the sobriety of his wit;
Though thus he call'd his Judge into his fame,
And for that aid allow'd him halfe the name,
'Tis knowne, that sometimes he did stand alone,
That both the Spunge and Pencill were his owne;
That himselfe judged himselfe, could singly do,
And was at last Beaumont *and* Fletcher *too;*
Else we had lost his Shepherdesse, *a piece*
Even and smooth, spun from a finer fleece,
Where softnesse raignes, where passions passions greet,
Gentle and high, as floods of Balsam meet.
Where dress'd in white expressions, sit bright Loves,
Drawne, like their fairest Queen, by milkie Doves;
A piece, which Johnson *in a rapture bid*
Come up a glorifi'd Worke, and so it did.
Else had his Muse set with his friend; the Stage
Had miss'd those Poems, which yet take the Age;
The world had lost those rich exemplars, where
Art, Language, Wit, sit ruling in one Spheare,
Where the fresh matters soare above old Theames,
As Prophets Raptures do above our Dreames;
Where in a worthy scorne he dares refuse
All other Gods, and makes the thing his Muse;
Where he calls passions up, and layes them so,
As spirits, aw'd by him to come and go;
Where the free Author did what e're he would,
And nothing will'd, but what a Poet should.
No vast uncivill bulke swells any Scene,
The strength's ingenious, a[n]d the vigour cleane;
None can prevent the Fancy, and see through
At the first opening; all stand wondring how
The thing will be untill it is; which thence
With fresh delight still cheats, still takes the sence;
The whole designe, the shadowes, the lights such
That none can say he shewes or hides too much:

Businesse growes up, ripened by just encrease,
And by as just degrees againe doth cease,
The beats and minutes of affaires are watcht,
And the nice points of time are met, and snatcht:
Nought later then it should, nought comes before,
Chymists, and Calculators doe erre more:
Sex, age, degree, affections, country, place,
The inward substance, and the outward face;
All kept precisely, all exactly fit,
What he would write, he was before he writ.
'Twixt Johnsons *grave, and* Shakespeares *lighter sound*
His muse so steer'd that something still was found,
Nor this, nor that, nor both, but so his owne,
That 'twas his marke, and he was by it knowne.
Hence did he take true judgements, hence did strike,
All pallates some way, though not all alike:
The god of numbers might his numbers crowne,
And listning to them wish they were his owne.
Thus welcome forth, what ease, or wine, or wit
Durst yet produce, that is, what Fletcher *writ.*

Another.

FLetcher, *though some call it thy fault, that wit*
So overflow'd thy scenes, that ere 'twas fit
To come upon the Stage, Beaumont *was faine*
To bid thee be more dull, that's write againe,
And bate some of thy fire, which from thee came
In a cleare, bright, full, but too large a flame;
And after all (finding thy Genius such)
That blunted, and allayed, 'twas yet too much;
Added his sober spunge, and did contract
Thy plenty to lesse wit to make't exact:
Yet we through his corrections could see
Much treasure in thy superfluity,
Which was so fil'd away, as when we doe
Cut Jewels, that that's lost is jewell too:
Or as men use to wash Gold, which we know
By losing makes the streame thence wealthy grow.
They who doe on thy workes severely sit,
And call thy store the over-births of wit,
Say thy miscarriages were rare, and when
Thou wert superfluous, that thy fruitfull Pen
Had no fault but abundance, which did lay
Out in one Scene what might well serve a Play;
And hence doe grant, that what they call excesse
Was to be reckon'd as thy happinesse,
From whom wit issued in a full spring-tide;
Much did inrich the Stage, much flow'd beside.

For that thou couldst thine owne free fancy binde
In stricter numbers, and run so confin'd
As to observe the rules of Art, which sway
In the contrivance of a true borne Play:
These workes proclaime which thou didst write retired
From Beaumont, *by none but thy selfe inspired;*
Where we see 'twas not chance that made them hit,
Nor were thy Playes the Lotteries of wit,
But like to Durers *Pencill, which first knew*
The lawes of faces, and then faces drew:
Thou knowst the aire, the colour, and the place,
The simetry, which gives a Poem grace:
Parts are so fitted unto parts, as doe
Shew thou hadst wit, and Mathematicks too:
Knewst where by line to spare, where to dispence,
And didst beget just Comedies from thence:
Things unto which thou didst such life bequeath,
That they (their owne Black-Friers) unacted breath.
Johnson *hath writ things lasting, and divine,*
Yet his Love-Scenes, Fletcher, *compar'd to thine,*
Are cold and frosty, and exprest love so,
As heat with Ice, or warme fires mixt with Snow;
Thou, as if struck with the same generous darts,
Which burne, and raigne in noble Lovers hearts,
Hast cloath'd affections in such native tires,
And so describ'd them in their owne true fires;
Such moving sighes, suc[h] undissembled teares,
Such charmes of language, such hopes mixt with feares,
Such grants after denialls, such pursuits
After despaire, such amorous recruits,
That some who sate spectators have confest
Themselves transform'd to what they saw exprest,
And felt such shafts steale through their captiv'd sence,
As made them rise Parts, and goe Lovers thence.
Nor was thy stile wholly compos'd of Groves,
Or the soft straines of Shepheards and their Loves;
When thou wouldst Comick be, each smiling birth
In that kinde, came into the world all mirth,
All point, all edge, all sharpnesse; we did sit
Sometimes five Acts out in pure sprightfull wit,
Which flowed in such true salt, that we did doubt
In which Scene we laught most two shillings out.
Shakespeare *to thee was dull, whose best jest lyes*
I'th Ladies questions, and the Fooles replyes;
Old fashion'd wit, which walkt from town to town
In turn'd Hose, which our fathers call'd the Clown;
Whose wit our nice times would obsceannesse call,
And which made Bawdry passe for Comicall:

Nature was all his Art, thy veine was free
As his, but without his scurility;
From whom mirth came unforc'd, no jest perplext,
But without labour cleane, chast, and unvext.
Thou wert not like some, our small Poets who
Could not be Poets, were not we Poets too;
Whose wit is pilfring, and whose veine and wealth
In Poetry lyes meerely in their stealth;
Nor didst thou feele their drought, their pangs, their qualmes,
Their rack in writing, who doe write for almes,
Whose wretched Genius, and dependent fires,
But to their Benefactors dole aspires.
Nor hadst thou the sly trick, thy selfe to praise
Under thy friends names, or to purchase Bayes
Didst write stale commendations to thy Booke,
Which we for Beaumonts *or* Ben. Johnsons *tooke:*
That debt thou left'st to us, which none but he
Can truly pay, Fletcher, *who writes like thee.*

William Cartwright.

On Mr Francis Beaumont
(then newly dead.)

HE that hath such acutenesse, and such witt,
As would aske ten good heads to husband it;
He that can write so well that no man dare
Refuse it for the best, let him beware:
BEAUMONT *is dead, by whose sole death appeares,*
Witt's a Disease consumes men in few yeares.

RICH. CORBET. D. D.

To Mr Francis Beaumont
(then living.)

HOw I doe love thee BEAUMONT, *and thy* Muse,
That unto me do'st such religion use!
How I doe feare my selfe, that am not worth
The least indulgent thought thy pen drops forth!
At once thou mak'st me happie, and unmak'st;
And giving largely to me, more thou tak'st.
What fate is mine, that so it selfe bereaves?
What art is thine, that so thy friend deceives?
When even there where most thou praisest me,
For writing better, I must envy thee.

BEN: JOHNSON.

VERSES

Upon Master FLETCHERS Incomparable Playes.

APollo sings, his harpe resounds; give roome,
For now behold the golden Pompe is come,
Thy Pompe of Playes which thousands come to see,
With admiration both of them and thee,
O Volume worthy leafe, by leafe and cover
To be with juice of Cedar washt all over;
Here's words with lines, and lines with Scenes consent,
To raise an Act to full astonishment;
Here melting numbers, words of power to move
Young men to swoone, and Maides to dye for love.
Love lyes a bleeding here, Evadne *there*
Swells with brave rage, yet comely every where,
Here's a mad lover, *there that high designe*
Of King and no King *(and the rare Plot thine)*
So that when 'ere wee circumvolve our Eyes,
Such rich, such fresh, such sweet varietyes,
Ravish our spirits, that entranc't we see
None writes lov's passion in the world, like Thee.

ROB. HERRICK.

On the happy Collection of Master *FLETCHER'S* Works, never before PRINTED.

FLETCHER *arise, Usurpers share thy Bayes,*
They Canton *thy vast Wit to build small* Playes:
He comes! his Volume *breaks through clowds and dust,*
Downe, little Witts, Ye must refund, Ye must.
Nor comes he private, here's great BEAUMONT *too,*
How could one single World encompasse Two?
For these Co-heirs had equall power to teach
All that all Witts both can and cannot reach.
Shakespear *was early up, and went so drest*
As for those dawning *houres he knew was best;*
But when the Sun shone forth, You Two *thought fit*
To weare just Robes, and leave off Trunk-hose-Wit.
Now, now 'twas Perfect; None must looke for New,
Manners and Scenes may alter, but not You;
For Yours are not meere Humours, *gilded straines;*
The Fashion lost, Your massy Sense *remaines.*
Some thinke Your Witts of two Complexions fram'd,
That One the Sock, *th'Other the* Buskin *claim'd;*

That should the Stage embattaile *all it's Force,*
FLETCHER *would lead the Foot,* BEAUMONT *the Horse.*
But, you were Both for Both; not Semi-witts,
Each Piece is wholly Two, yet never splits:
Y'are not Two Faculties (*and one* Soule *still*)
He th' Understanding, *Thou the quick free* Will;
But, as two Voyces *in one Song embrace,*
(FLETCHER'S *keen* Trebble, *and deep* BEAUMONTS Base)
Two, full, Congeniall Soules; still Both prevail'd;
His Muse and Thine were Quarter'd *not* Impal'd:
Both brought Your Ingots, Both toil'd at the Mint,
Beat, melted, sifted, till no drosse stuck in't,
Then in each Others scales weigh'd every graine,
Then smooth'd and burnish'd, then weigh'd all againe,
Stampt Both your Names upon't by one bold Hit,
Then, then 'twas Coyne, as well as Bullion-Wit.

Thus Twinns: But as when Fate one Eye deprives,
That other strives to double which survives:
So BEAUMONT *dy'd: yet left in Legacy*
His Rules and Standard-wit (FLETCHER) *to Thee.*
Still the same Planet, though not fill'd so soon,
A Two-born'd Crescent *then, now one* Full-moon.
Joynt Love *before, now* Honour *doth provoke;*
*So th' old Twin-*Giants *forcing a huge Oake*
One slipp'd his footing, th' Other sees him fall,
Grasp'd the whole Tree and single held up all.
Imperiall FLETCHER! *here begins thy Raigne,*
Scenes flow like Sun-beams from thy glorious Brain;
Thy swift dispatching Soule no more doth stay
Then He that built two Citties in one day;
Ever brim full, and sometimes running o're
To feede poore languid Witts that waite at doore,
Who creep and creep, yet ne're above-ground stood,
(*For Creatures have most Feet which have least Blood*)
But thou art still that Bird of Paradise
Which hath no feet *and ever nobly* flies:
Rich, lusty Sence, such as the Poet *ought,*
For Poems *if not Excellent, are Naught;*
Low wit in Scenes? in state a Peasant goes;
If meane and flat, let it foot Yeoman Prose,
That such may spell as are not Readers grown,
To whom He that writes Wit, shews he hath none.
Brave Shakespeare *flow'd, yet had his Ebbings too,*
Often above Himselfe, sometimes below;
Thou Alwayes Best; if ought seem'd to decline,
'Twas the unjudging Rout's mistake, not Thine:
Thus thy faire SHEPHEARDESSE, *which the bold Heape*
(*False to Themselves and Thee*) *did prize so cheap,*

Was found (*when understood*) *fit to be Crown'd,*
At worst 'twas worth two hundred thousand pound.
Some blast thy Works *lest we should track their Walke*
Where they steale all those few good things they talke;
Wit-Burglary must chide those it feeds on,
For Plunder'd folkes ought to be rail'd upon;
But (*as stoln goods goe off at halfe their worth*)
Thy strong Sence pall's *when they purloine it forth.*
When did'st Thou *borrow? where's the man e're read*
Ought begg'd by Thee *from those Alive or Dead?*
Or from dry Goddesses, *as some who when*
They stuffe their page with Godds, write worse then Men.
Thou was't thine owne *Muse, and hadst such vast odds*
Thou out-writ'st him whose verse made *all those* Godds:
Surpassing those our Dwarfish Age up reares,
As much as Greeks *or* Latines *thee in yeares:*
Thy Ocean Fancy knew nor Bankes nor Damms,
*We ebbe downe dry to pebble-*Anagrams;
Dead and insipid, all despairing sit
Lost to behold this great Relapse *of Wit:*
What strength remaines, is like that (*wilde and fierce*)
Till Johnson *made good Poets and right Verse.*
Such boyst'rous Trifles Thy Muse would not brooke,
Save when she'd show how scurvily they looke;
No savage Metaphors (*things rudely Great*)
Thou dost display, *not* butcher *a Conceit*;
Thy Nerves have Beauty, *which Invades and Charms*;
Lookes like a Princesse harness'd in bright Armes.
Nor art Thou Loud and Cloudy; *those that do*
Thunder so much, do't without Lightning too;
Tearing themselves, and almost split their braine
To render harsh what thou speak'st free and cleane;
Such gloomy Sense may pass for High *and* Proud,
But true-born Wit still flies above *the* Cloud;
Thou knewst 'twas Impotence *what they call* Height;
Who blusters strong i'th Darke, but creeps *it'h Light.*
And as thy thoughts were cleare, *so,* Innocent;
Thy Phancy gave no unswept Language vent;
Slaunderst not Lawes, *prophan'st no* holy Page,
(*As if thy Fathers* Crosier *aw'd the Stage*;)
High Crimes were still arraign'd, though they made shift
To prosper out foure Acts, *were plagu'd i'th* Fift:
All's safe, and wise; *no stiffe-affected Scene,*
Nor swoln, *nor* flat, *a True Full Naturall veyne*;
Thy Sence (*like well-drest Ladies*) *cloath'd as skinn'd,*
Not all unlac'd, nor City-startcht and pinn'd.
Thou hadst no Sloath, no Rage, no sullen Fit,
But Strength *and* Mirth, FLETCHER'S *a* Sanguin *Wit.*

Thus, two great Consul-*Poets all things swayd,*
Till all was English *Borne or* English *Made:*
Miter *and* Coyfe *here into One Piece spun,*
BEAUMONT *a* Judge's, *This a* Prelat's *sonne.*
What Strange Production is at last displaid,
(Got by Two Fathers, without Female aide)
Behold, two Masculines *espous'd each other,*
Wit *and the World were born without a* Mother.

J. BERKENHEAD.

To the memorie of Master *FLETCHER.*

THere's nothing gain'd by being witty: Fame
Gathers but winde to blather up a name.
Orpheus *must leave his lyre, or if it be*
In heav'n, 'tis there a signe, no harmony;
And stones, that follow'd him, may now become
Now stones againe, and serve him for his Tomb.
The Theban Linus, *that was ably skil'd*
In Muse and Musicke, was by Phœbus *kill'd,*
Though Phœbus *did beget him: sure his Art*
Had merited his balsame, not his dart.
But here Apollo's *jealousie is seene,*
The god of Physicks troubled with the spleene;
Like timerous Kings he puts a period
To high grown parts lest he should be no God.
Hence those great Master-wits of Greece that gave
Life to the world, could not avoid a grave.
Hence the inspired Prophets of old Rome
Too great for earth fled to Elizium.
But the same Ostracisme benighted one,
To whom all these were but illusion;
It tooke our FLETCHER *hence,* Fletcher, *whose wit*
Was not an accident to th' soule, but It;
Onely diffus'd. (Thus wee the same Sun call,
Moving it'h Sphære, and shining on a wall.)
Wit, so high plac'd at first, it could not climbe,
Wit, that ne're grew, but only show'd by time.
No fier-worke of sacke, no seldome show'n
Poeticke rage, but still in motion:
And with far more then Sphæricke excellence
It mov'd, for 'twas its owne Intelligence.
And yet so obvious to sense, so plaine,
You'd scarcely thinke't ally'd unto the braine:

So sweete, it gain'd more ground upon the Stage
Then Johnson *with his selfe-admiring rage*
Ere lost: and then so naturally it fell,
That fooles would think, that they could doe as well.
This is our losse: yet spight of Phœbus, *we*
Will keepe our FLETCHER, *for his wit is He.*

EDW. POWELL.

Upon the ever to be admired Mr. JOHN FLETCHER and His PLAYES.

W*Hat's all this preparation for? or why*
Such suddain Triumphs? FLETCHER *the people cry!*
Just so, when Kings approach, our Conduits run
Claret, as here the spouts flow Helicon;
See, every sprightfull Muse *dress'd trim and gay*
Strews hearbs and scatters roses in his way.
Thus th'outward yard set round with bayes *w'have seene,*
Which from the garden hath transplanted been:
Thus, at the Prætor's feast, with needlesse costs
Some must b'employd in painting of the posts:
And some as dishes made for sight, not taste,
Stand here as things for shew to FLETCHERS *feast.*
Oh what an honour! what a Grace 'thad beene
T'have had his Cooke in Rollo *serv'd them in!*
FLETCHER *the King of Poets! such was he,*
That earn'd all tribute, claim'd all soveraignty;
And may he that denye's it, learn to blush
At's loyall Subject, *starve at's* Beggars bush:
And if not drawn by example, shame, nor Grace,
Turne o're to's Coxcomb, *and the Wild-goose Chase.*
Monarch of Wit! great Magazine of wealth!
From whose rich Banke, *by a Promethean-stealth,*
Our lesser flames doe blaze! His the true fire,
When they like Glo-worms, being touch'd, expire.
'Twas first beleev'd, because he alwayes was,
The Ipse dixit, *and* Pythagoras
To our Disciple-wits; His soule might run
(By the same-dream't-of Transmigration)
Into their rude and indigested braine,
And so informe their Chaos-lump againe;
For many specious brats of this last age
Spoke FLETCHER *perfectly in every Page.*
This rowz'd his Rage to be abused thus:
Made's Lover mad, Lieutenant humerous.

Thus Ends of Gold and Silver-men *are made*
(As th'use to say) Goldsmiths of his owne trade;
Thus Rag-men *from the dung-hill often hop,*
And publish forth by chance a Brokers shop:
But by his owne light, now, we have descri'd
The drosse, from that hath beene so purely tri'd.
Proteus *of witt! who reads him doth not see*
The manners of each sex of each degree!
His full stor'd fancy doth all humours fill
*From th'*Queen *of* Corinth *to* the maid o'th mill;
His Curate, Lawyer, Captain, Prophetesse
Shew he was all and every one of these;
Hee taught (so subtly were their fancies seiz'd)
To Rule a Wife, and yet the Women pleas'd.
Parnassus *is thine owne, Claime't as merit,*
Law makes the Elder Brother to inherit.

G. Hills.

IN HONOUR OF M[r]

John Fletcher.

SO FLETCHER *now presents to fame*
His alone selfe and unpropt name,
As Rivers Rivers entertaine,
But still fall single into th'maine,
So doth the Moone in Consort shine
Yet flowes alone into its mine,
And though her light be joyntly throwne,
When she makes silver tis her owne:
Perhaps his quill flew stronger, when
Twas weaved with his Beaumont's *pen;*
And might with deeper wonder hit,
It could not shew more his, more wit;
So Hercules came by sexe and Love,
When Pallas sprang from single Jove;
He tooke his BEAUMONT *for Embrace,*
Not to grow by him, and increase,
Nor for support did with him twine,
He was his friends friend, not his vine.
His witt with witt he did not twist
To be Assisted, but t' Assist.
And who could succour him, whose quill
Did both Run sense and sense Distill?
Had Time and Art in't, and the while
Slid even as theirs wh'are only style,

Whether his chance did cast it so
Or that it did like Rivers flow
Because it must, or whether twere
A smoothnesse from his file and care,
Not the most strict enquiring nayle
Cou'd e're finde where his piece did faile
Of entyre onenesse; so the frame,
Was Composition, yet the same.
  How does he breede his Brother? and
Make wealth and estate understand?
Sutes Land to wit, makes Lucke match merit,
And makes an Eldest fitly inherit:
How was he Ben, *when* Ben *did write*
Toth' stage, not to his judge endite?
How did he doe what Johnson *did,*
And Earne what Johnson *wou'd have s'ed?*

Jos. Howe of Trin. Coll. Oxon.

Master *John Fletcher* his dramaticall Workes now at last printed.

I *Could prayse* Heywood *now: or tell how long,*
Falstaffe *from cracking Nuts hath kept the throng:*
But for a Fletcher, *I must take an Age,*
And scarce invent the Title for one Page.
Gods must create new Sphæres, that should expresse
The sev'rall Accents, Fletcher, *of thy Dresse:*
The Penne of Fates should only write thy Praise:
And all Elizium *for thee turne to Bayes.*
Thou feltst no pangs of Poetry, such as they,
Who the Heav'ns quarter still before a Play,
And search the Ephemerides *to finde,*
When the Aspect for Poets will be kinde.
Thy Poems (sacred Spring) did from thee flow,
With as much pleasure, as we reade them now.
Nor neede we only take them up by fits,
When love or Physicke hath diseas'd our Wits;
Or constr'e English to untye a knot,
Hid in a line, farre subtler then the Plot.
With Thee the Page may close his Ladies eyes,
And yet with thee the serious Student Rise:
The Eye at sev'rall angles darting rayes,
Makes, and then sees, new Colours; so thy Playes
To ev'ry understanding still appeare,
As if thou only meant'st to take that Eare;

The Phrase so terse and free of a just Poise,
Where ev'ry word ha's weight and yet no Noise,
The matter too so nobly fit, no lesse
Then such as onely could deserve thy Dresse:
Witnesse thy Comedies, Pieces of such worth,
All Ages shall still like, but ne're bring forth.
Other in season last scarce so long time,
As cost the Poet but to make the Rime:
Where, if a Lord a new way do's but spit,
Or change his shrugge this antiquates the Wit.
That thou didst live before, nothing would tell
Posterity, could they but write so well.
Thy Cath'lick Fancy will acceptance finde,
Not whilst an humour's living, but Man-kinde.
Thou, like thy Writings, Innocent and Cleane,
Ne're practis'd a new Vice, to make one Sceane,
None of thy Inke had gall, and Ladies can,
Securely beare thee sport without a Fanne.
But when Thy Tragicke Muse would please to rise
In Majestie, and call Tribute from our Eyes;
Like Scenes, we shifted Passions, and that so,
Who only came to see, turn'd Actors too.
How didst thou sway the Theatre! make us feele
The Players wounds were true, and their swords, steele!
Nay, stranger yet, how often did I know
When the Spectators ran to save the blow?
Frozen with griefe we could not stir away
Untill the Epilogue told us 'twas a Play.
What shall I doe? all Commendations end,
In saying only thou wert BEAUMONTS *Friend?*
Give me thy spirit quickely, for I swell,
And like a raveing Prophetesse cannot tell
How to receive thy Genius *in my breast:*
Oh! I must sleepe, and then I'le sing the rest.

T. Palmer of Ch. Ch. Oxon.

Upon the unparalelld Playes written by those Renowned Twinnes of Poetry BEAUMONT & FLETCHER.

W*Hat's here? another Library of prayse,*
Met in a Troupe t'advance contemned Playes,
And bring exploded Witt *againe in fashion?*
I can't but wonder at this Reformation,

VERSES

My skipping soule surfets with so much good,
To see my hopes into fruition *budd.*
A happy Chimistry! *blest viper,* joy!
That through thy mothers bowels gnawst thy way!
Witts flock in sholes, and clubb to re-erect
In spight of Ignorance *the Arcbitect*
Of Occidentall Poesye; *and turne*
Godds, to recall witts *ashes from their urne.*
Like huge Collosses *they've together mett*
Their shoulders, to support a world of Witt.
The tale of Atlas (*though of truth it misse*)
We plainely read Mythologiz'd *in this*;
Orpheus *and* Amphion *whose undying stories*
Made Athens *famous, are but* Allegories.
Tis Poetry has pow'r to civilize
Men, worse then stones, more blockish then the Trees.
I cannot chuse but thinke (*now things so fall*)
That witt is past its Climactericall;
And though the Muses *have beene dead and gone*
I know they'll finde a Resurrection.
Tis vaine to prayse; they're to themselves a glory,
And silence is our sweetest Oratory.
For he that names but FLETCHER *must needs be*
Found guilty of a loud hyperbole.
His fancy so transcendently aspires,
He showes himselfe a witt, who but admires.
Here are no volumes stuft with cheverle sence,
The very Anagrams *of Eloquence,*
Nor long-long-winded sentences that be,
Being rightly spelld, but Witts Stenographie.
Nor words, as voyd of Reason, as of Rithme,
Only cæsura'd to spin out the time.
But heer's a Magazine *of purest sence*
Cloath'd in the newest Garbe of Eloquence.
Scænes that are quick and sprightly, in whose veines
Bubbles the quintessence of sweet-high straines.
Lines like their Authours, *and each word of it*
Does say twas writ b' a Gemini *of Witt.*
How happie is our age! how blest our men!
When such rare soules live themselves o're agen.
We erre, that thinke a Poet dyes; for this,
Shewes that tis but a Metempsychosis.
BEAUMONT *and* FLETCHER *here at last we see*
Above the reach of dull mortalitie,
Or pow'r of fate: & thus the proverbe hitts
(*That's so much crost*) *These men live by their witts.*

ALEX. BROME.

COMMENDATORY

On the Death and workes of Mr John Fletcher.

MY name, so far from great, that tis not knowne,
Can lend no praise but what thou'dst blush to own;
And no rude hand, or feeble wit should dare
To vex thy Shrine with an unlearned teare.
I'de have a State of Wit convok'd, which hath
A power to take up on common Faith;
That when the stocke of the whole Kingdome's spent
In but preparative to thy Monument,
The prudent Councell may invent fresh wayes
To get new contribution to thy prayse,
And reare it high, and equall to thy Wit
Which must give life and Monument to it.
So when late ESSEX *dy'd, the Publicke face*
Wore sorrow in't, and to add mournefull Grace
To the sad pomp of his lamented fall,
The Common wealth serv'd at his Funerall
And by a Solemne Order built his Hearse.
But not like thine, built by thy selfe, in Verse,
Where thy advanced Image safely stands
Above the reach of Sacrilegious hands.
Base hands how impotently you disclose
Your rage 'gainst Camdens *learned ashes, whose*
Defaced Statua and Martyrd booke,
Like an Antiquitie and Fragment looke.
Nonnulla desunt's *legibly appeare,*
So truly now Camdens Remaines *lye there.*
Vaine Malice! how he mocks thy rage, while breath
Of fame shall speake his great Elizabeth!
'Gainst time and thee he well provided hath,
Brittannia *is the Tombe and Epitaph.*
Thus Princes honours; but Witt only gives
A name which to succeeding ages lives.
Singly we now consult our selves and fame,
Ambitious to twist ours with thy great name.
Hence we thus bold to praise. For as a Vine
With subtle wreath, and close embrace doth twine
A friendly Elme, by whose tall trunke it shoots
And gathers growth and moysture from its roots;
About its armes the thankfull clusters cling
Like Bracelets, and with purple ammelling
The blew-cheek'd grape stuck in its vernant haire
Hangs like rich jewells in a beauteous eare.
So grow our Prayses by thy Witt; we doe
Borrow support and strength and lend but show.

And but thy Male wit like the youthfull Sun
Strongly begets upon our passion.
Making our sorrow teeme with Elegie,
Thou yet unwep'd, and yet unprais'd might'st be.
But th' are imperfect births; and such are all
Produc'd by causes not univocall,
The scapes of Nature, Passives being unfit,
And hence our verse speakes only Mother wit.
Oh for a fit o'th Father! for a Spirit
That might but parcell of thy worth inherit;
For but a sparke of that diviner fire
Which thy full breast did animate and inspire;
That Soules could be divided, thou traduce
But a small particle of thine to us!
Of thine; which we admir'd when thou didst sit
But as a joynt-Commissioner in Wit;
When it had plummets hung on to suppresse
It's too luxuriant growing mightinesse:
Till as that tree which scornes to bee kept downe,
Thou grewst to govern the whole Stage alone.
In which orbe thy throng'd light did make the star,
Thou wert th' Intelligence did move that Sphære.
Thy Fury was compos'd; Rapture no fit
That hung on thee; nor thou far gone in witt
As men in a disease; thy Phansie cleare,
Muse chast, as those frames whence they tooke their fire;
No spurious composures amongst thine
Got in adultery 'twixt Witt and Wine.
And as th' Hermeticall Physitians draw
From things that curse of the first-broken Law,
That Ens Venenum, *which extracted thence*
Leaves nought but primitive Good and Innocence:
So was thy Spirit calcin'd; no Mixtures there
But perfect, such as next to Simples are.
Not like those Meteor-wits which wildly flye
In storme and thunder through th' amazed skie;
Speaking but th'Ills and Villanies in a State,
Which fooles admire, and wise men tremble at,
Full of portent and prodigie, whose Gall
Oft scapes the Vice, and on the man doth fall.
Nature us'd all her skill, when thee she meant
A Wit at once both Great and Innocent.
Yet thou hadst Tooth; but 'twas thy judgement, not
For mending one word, a whole sheet to blot.
Thou couldst anatomize with ready art
And skilfull hand crimes lockt close up i'th heart.
Thou couldst unfold darke Plots, and shew that path
By which Ambition climb'd to Greatnesse hath.

Thou couldst the rises, turnes, and falls of States,
How neare they were their Periods and Dates;
Couldst mad the Subject into popular rage,
And the grown seas of that great storme asswage,
Dethrone usurping Tyrants, and place there
The lawfull Prince and true Inheriter;
Knewst all darke turnings in the Labyrinth
Of policie, which who but knowes he sinn'th,
Save thee, who un-infected didst walke in't
As the great Genius of Government.
And when thou laidst thy tragicke buskin by
To Court the Stage with gentle Comedie,
How new, how proper th' humours, how express'd
In rich variety, how neatly dress'd
In language, how rare Plots, what strength of Wit
Shin'd in the face and every limb of it!
The Stage grew narrow while thou grewst to be
In thy whole life an Exc'llent Comedie.
To these a Virgin-modesty which first met
Applause with blush and feare, as if he yet
Had not deserv'd; till bold with constant praise
His browes admitted the unsought for Bayes.
Nor would he ravish fame; but left men free
To their owne Vote and Ingenuity.
When His faire Shepherdesse *on the guilty Stage,*
Was martir'd betweene Ignorance and Rage;
At which the impatient Vertues of those few
Could judge, grew high, cri'd Murther: though he knew
The innocence and beauty of his Childe,
Hee only, as if unconcerned, smil'd.
Princes have gather'd since each scattered grace,
Each line and beauty of that injur'd face;
And on th'united parts breath'd such a fire
As spight of Malice she shall ne're expire.
Attending, not affecting, thus the crowne
Till every hand did help to set it on,
Hee came to be sole Monarch, and did raign
In Wits great Empire, abs'lute Soveraign.

JOHN HARRIS.

On Mr. JOHN FLETC[H]ER's ever to be admired Dramaticall Works.

I'Ve thought upon't; and thus I may gaine bayes,
I will commend thee Fletcher, *and thy Playes.*
But none but Witts can do't, how then can I
Come in amongst them, that cou'd ne're come nigh?
There is no other way, I'le throng to sit
And passe it'h Croud amongst them for a Wit.

Apollo *knows me not, nor I the Nine,*
All my pretence to verse is Love and Wine.
By your leave Gentlemen. You Wits o'th' age,
You that both furnisht have, and judg'd the Stage.
You who the Poet and the Actors fright,
Least that your Censure thin the second night:
Pray tell me, gallant Wits, could Criticks think
There ere was solæcisme in FLETCHERS *Inke?*
Or Lapse of Plot, or fancy in his pen?
A happinesse not still alow'd to Ben!
After of Time and Wit h'ad been at cost
He of his owne New-Inne was but an Hoste.
Inspir'd, FLETCHER! *here's no vaine-glorious words:*
How ev'n thy lines, how smooth thy sense accords.
Thy Language so insinuates, each one
Of thy spectators has thy passion.
Men seeing, valiant; Ladies amorous prove:
Thus owe to thee their valour and their Love:
Scenes! chaste yet satisfying! Ladies can't say
Though Stephen *miscarri'd that so did the play:*
Judgement could ne're to this opinion leane
That Lowen, Tailor, *ere could grace thy Scene:*
'Tis richly good unacted, and to me
Thy very Farse appears a Comedy.
Thy drollery is designe, each looser part
Stuffs not thy Playes, but makes 'em up an Art
The Stage has seldome seen; how often vice
Is smartly scourg'd to checke us? to intice,
How well encourag'd vertue is? how guarded,
And, that which makes us love her, how rewarded?
Some, I dare say, that did with loose thoughts sit,
Reclaim'd by thee, came converts from the pit.
And many a she that to be tane up came,
Tooke up themselves, and after left the game.

HENRY HARINGTON.

the memory of the deceased but ever-living *Authour* in these his *Poems*, Mr. JOHN FLETCHER.

O*N the large train of* Fletchers *friends let me*
(Retaining still my wonted modesty,)
Become a Waiter in my ragged verse,
As Follower to the Muses *Followers.*
Many here are of Noble ranke and worth,
That have, by strength of Art, set Fletcher *forth*
In true and lively colours, as they saw him,
And had the best abilities to draw him;

Many more are abroad, that write, and looke
To have their lines set before Fletchers *Booke;*
Some, that have known him too; some more, some lesse;
Some onely but by Heare-say, some by Guesse,
And some, for fashion-sake, would take the hint
To try how well their Wits would shew in Print.
You, that are here before me Gentlemen,
And Princes of Parnassus *by the Penne*
And your just Judgements of his worth, that have
Preserv'd this Authours *mem'ry from the Grave,*
And made it glorious; let me, at your gate,
Porter it here, 'gainst those that come too late,
And are unfit to enter. Something I
Will deserve here: For where you versifie
In flowing numbers, lawfull Weight, and Time,
I'll write, though not rich Verses, honest Rime.
I am admitted. Now, have at the Rowt
Of those that would crowd in, but must keepe out.
Beare back, my Masters; Pray keepe backe; Forbeare:
You cannot, at this time, have entrance here.
You, that are worthy, may, by intercession,
Finde entertainment at the next Impression.
But let none then attempt it, that not know
The reverence due, which to this shrine they owe:
All such must be excluded; and the sort,
That onely upon trust, or by report
Have taken Fletcher *up, and thinke it trim*
To have their Verses planted before Him:
Let them read first his Works, and learne to know him,
And offer, then, the Sacrifice they owe him.
But farre from hence be such, as would proclaim
Their knowledge of this Authour, *not his Fame;*
And such, as would pretend, of all the rest,
To be the best Wits *that have known him best.*
Depart hence all such Writers, and, before
Inferiour ones, thrust in, by many a score,
As formerly, before Tom Coryate,
Whose Worke before his Praysers had the Fate
To perish: For the Witty Coppies tooke
Of his Encomiums *made themselves a* Booke.
Here's no such subject for you to out-doe,
Out-shine, out-live (though well you may doe too
In other Spheres:) For Fletchers *flourishing Bayes*
Must never fade while Phœbus *weares his Rayes.*
Therefore forbeare to presse upon him thus.
Why, what are you (cry some) that prate to us?
Doe not we know you for a flashy Meteor?
And stil'd (at best) the Muses *Serving-creature?*

Doe you comptroll? Y'have had your Jere: Sirs, no;
But, in an humble manner, let you know
Old Serving-creatures oftentimes are fit
T' informe young Masters, as in Land, in Wit,
What they inherit; and how well their Dads
Left one, and wish'd the other to their Lads.
And from departed Poets I can guesse
Who has a greater share of Wit, who lesse.
'Way Foole, another says. I, let him raile,
And 'bout his own eares flourish his Wit-flayle,
Till with his Swingle he his Noddle breake;
While this of Fletcher *and his* Works *I speake:*
His Works (*says* Momus) *nay, his* Plays *you'd say:*
Thou hast said right, for that to him was Play
Which was to others braines a toyle: with ease
He playd on Waves which were Their troubled Seas.
His nimble Births have longer liv'd then theirs
That have, with strongest Labour, divers yeeres
Been sending forth [*t*]*he issues of their Braines*
Upon the Stage; *and shall to th'* Stationers *gaines*
Life after life take, till some After-age
Shall put down Printing, *as this doth the* Stage;
Which nothing now presents unto the Eye,
But in Dumb-shews *her own sad* Tragedy.
'Would there had been no sadder Works abroad,
Since her decay, acted in Fields of Blood.
But to the Man againe, of whom we write,
The Writer *that made Writing his Delight,*
Rather then Worke. He *did not pumpe, nor drudge,*
To beget Wit, *or manage it; nor trudge*
To Wit-conventions with Note-booke, to gleane
Or steale some Jests to foist into a Scene:
He scorn'd those shifts. You that have known him, know
The common talke that from his Lips did flow,
And run at waste, did savour more of Wit,
Then any of his time, or since have writ,
(*But few excepted*) *in the Stages way:*
His Scenes *were* Acts, *and every* Act *a* Play.
I knew him in his strength; even then, when He
That was the Master of his Art and Me
Most knowing Johnson (*proud to call him* Sonne)
In friendly Envy swore, He had out-done
His very Selfe. *I knew him till he dyed;*
And, at his dissolution, what a Tide
Of sorrow overwhelm'd the Stage; *which gave*
Volleys of sighes to send him to his grave.
And grew distracted in most violent Fits
(*For* She *had lost the best part of her* Wits.)

In the first yeere, our famous Fletcher *fell,*
Of good King Charles *who grac'd these* Poems *well,*
Being then in life of Action: But they dyed
Since the Kings absence; or were layd aside,
As is their Poët. *Now at the Report*
Of the Kings *second comming to his Court,*
The Bookes *creepe from the* Presse *to Life, not* Action,
Crying unto the World, that no protraction
May hinder Sacred Majesty *to give*
Fletcher, *in them, leave on the* Stage *to live.*
Others may more in lofty Verses move:
I onely, thus, expresse my Truth and Love.
RIC. BROME.

Upon the Printing of Mr. JOHN FLETCHERS workes.

WHat meanes this numerous Guard? or do we come
To file our Names or Verse upon the Tombe
Of Fletcher, *and by boldly making knowne*
His Wit, betray the Nothing of our Owne?
For if we grant him dead, it is as true
Against our selves, No Wit, no Poet now;
Or if he be returnd from his coole shade,
To us, this Booke his Resurrection's made,
We bleed our selves to death, and but contrive
By our owne Epitaphs to shew him alive.
But let him live and let me prophesie,
As I goe Swan-like out, Our Peace is nigh;
A Balme unto the wounded Age I sing,
And nothing now is wanting but the King.
JA. SHIRLEY.

THE STATIONER.

AS after th' *Epilogue* there comes some one
To tell *Spectators* what shall next be shown;
So here, am I; but though I've toyld and vext,
'Cannot devise what to present 'ye next;
For, since ye saw no *Playes* this Cloudy weather,
Here we have brought Ye our whole Stock together.
'Tis new and all these *Gentlemen* attest
Under their hands 'tis Right, and of the Best;
Thirty foure Witnesses (without my taske)
Y'have just so many *Playes* (besides a *Maske*)
All good (I'me told) as have been *Read* or *Playd*,
If this Booke faile, tis time to quit the Trade.
H. MOSELEY.

POST[S]CRIPT.

WE forgot to tell the *Reader*, that some *Prologues* and *Epilogues* (here inserted) were not written by the *Authours* of this *Volume*; but made by others on the *Revivall* of severall *Playes*. After the *Comedies* and *Tragedies* were wrought off, we were forced (for expedition) to send the *Gentlemens* Verses to severall Printers, which was the occasion of their different Character; but the *Worke* it selfe is one continued Letter, which (though very legible) is none of the biggest, because (as much as possible) we would lessen the Bulke of the Volume.

A CATALOGUE

of all the Comedies and Tragedies

Contained in this Booke.

FIFTY
COMEDIES
AND
TRAGEDIES.

Written by {FRANCIS BEAUMONT AND JOHN FLETCHER,} Gentlemen.

All in one Volume.

Published by the Authors Original Copies, the Songs to each Play being added.

Si quid habent veri Vatum præsagia, vivam.

LONDON,
Printed by *J. Macock*, for *John Martyn*, *Henry Herringman*, *Richard Marriot*, MDCLXXIX.

FIFTY
COMEDIES
AND
TRAGEDIES.

Written by { FRANCIS BEAUMONT And JOHN FLETCHER, } Gentlemen.

All in one Volume.

Published by the Authors Original Copies, the Songs to each Play being added.

Si quid habent veri Vatum præsagia, vivam.

LONDON,
Printed by *J. Macock*, for *John Martyn*, *Henry Herringman*, *Richard Marriot*, MDCLXXIX.

THE
BOOK-SELLERS
TO THE
READER.

Courteous Reader, *THE First Edition of these Plays in this Volume having found that Acceptance as to give us Encouragement to make a Second Impression, we were very desirous they might come forth as Correct as might be. And we were very opportunely informed of a Copy which an ingenious and worthy Gentleman had taken the pains (or rather the pleasure) to read over; wherein he had all along Corrected several faults (some very gross) which had crept in by the frequent imprinting of them. His Corrections were the more to be valued, because he had an intimacy with both our Authors, and had been a Spectator of most of them when they were Acted in their life-time. This therefore we resolved to purchase at any Rate; and accordingly with no small cost obtain'd it. From the same hand also we received several Prologues and Epilogues, with the Songs appertaining to each Play, which were not in the former Edition, but are now inserted in their proper places. Besides, in this Edition you have the addition of no fewer than Seventeen Plays more than were in the former, which we have taken the pains and care to Collect, and Print out of 4to in this Volume, which for distinction sake are markt with a Star in the Catalogue of them facing the first Page of the Book. And whereas in several of the Plays there were wanting the Names of the Persons represented therein, in this Edition you have them all prefixed, with their Qualities; which will be a great ease to the Reader. Thus every way perfect and compleat have you, all both Tragedies and Comedies that were ever writ by our Authors, a Pair of the greatest Wits and most ingenious Poets of their Age; from whose worth we should but detract by our most studied Commendations.*

If our care and endeavours to do our Authors right (in an incorrupt and genuine Edition of their Works) and thereby to gratifie and oblige the Reader, be but requited with a suitable entertainment, we shall be encourag'd to bring Ben. Johnson'*s two Volumes into one, and publish them in this form; and also to reprint Old* Shakespear*: both which are designed by*

Yours,

Ready to serve you,

John Martyn.
Henry Herringman.
Richard Mariot.

[The Second Folio contained, between 'The Booksellers to the Reader' and 'A Catalogue,' eleven only of the Commendatory verses prefixed to the First Folio. These were those signed by Edw. Waller (see p. xxiii), J. Denham (p. xxii), Ben. Johnson (p. xl), Rich. Corbet (p. xl), Joh. Earle (p. xxxii), William Cartwright's first lines (p. xxxvii, to 'Fletcher *writ*' on p. xxxviii), Francis Palmer (p. xlvii, '*I Could prayse* Heywood,' etc.), Jasper Maine (p. xxxv), J. Berkenhead (p. xli), Roger L'Estrange (p. xxviii), Tho. Stanley (p. xxvii).]

A

CATALOGUE

Of all the

COMEDIES and TRAGEDIES

Contained in this BOOK, in the same Order as Printed.

THE
MAIDS TRAGEDY.

Persons Represented in the Play.

King.
Lysippus, *brother to the King.*
Amintor, *a Noble Gentleman.*
Evadne, *Wife to* Amintor.
Melantius } *Brothers to* Evadne.
Diphilus }
Aspatia, *troth-plight wife to* Amintor.
Calianax, *an old humorous Lord, and Father to* Aspatia.

Cleon } *Gentlemen.*
Strato }
Diagoras, *a Servant.*
Antiphila } *waiting Gentlewomen to* Aspatia.
Olympias }
Dula, *a Lady.*
Night }
Cynthia }
Neptune } *Maskers.*
Eolus }

Actus primus. Scena prima.

Enter *Cleon, Strato, Lysippus, Diphilus.*

C*Leon.* The rest are making ready Sir.

Strat. So let them, there's time enough.

Diph. You are the brother to the King, my Lord, we'l take your word.

Lys. Strato, thou hast some skill in Poetry, What thinkst thou of a Mask? will it be well?

Strat. As well as Mask can be.

Lys. As Mask can be?

Strat. Yes, they must commend their King, and speak in praise of the Assembly, bless the Bride and Bridegroom, in person of some God; th'are tyed to rules of flattery.

Cle. See, good my Lord, who is return'd!

Lys. Noble *Melantius*! [*Enter Melantius.* The Land by me welcomes thy vertues home to *Rhodes*, thou that with blood abroad buyest us our peace; the breath of Kings is like the breath of Gods; My brother wisht thee here, and thou art here; he will be too kind, and weary thee with often welcomes; but the time doth give thee a welcome above this or all the worlds.

Mel. My Lord, my thanks; but these scratcht limbs of mine have spoke my love and truth unto my friends, more than my tongue ere could: my mind's the same it ever was to you; where I find worth, I love the keeper, till he let it go,
And then I follow it.

Diph. Hail worthy brother!
He that rejoyces not at your return
In safety, is mine enemy for ever.

Mel. I thank thee *Diphilus*: but thou art faulty;
I sent for thee to exercise thine armes
With me at *Patria*: thou cam'st not *Diphilus*: 'Twas ill.

Diph. My noble brother, my excuse
Is my King's strict command, which you my Lord
Can witness with me.

Lys. 'Tis true *Melantius*,
He might not come till the solemnity
Of this great match were past.

Diph. Have you heard of it?

Mel. Yes, I have given cause to those that
Envy my deeds abroad, to call me gamesome;
I have no other business here at *Rhodes*.

Lys. We have a Mask to night,
And you must tread a Soldiers measure.

Mel. These soft and silken wars are not for me;
The Musick must be shrill, and all confus'd,
That stirs my blood, and then I dance with armes:
But is *Amintor* Wed?

Diph. This day.

Mel. All joyes upon him, for he is my friend:
Wonder not that I call a man so young my friend,
His worth is great; valiant he is, and temperate,
And one that never thinks his life his own,
If his friend need it: when he was a boy,
As oft as I return'd (as without boast)
I brought home conquest, he would gaze upon me,
And view me round, to find in what one limb
The vertue lay to do those things he heard:

Then would he wish to see my Sword, and feel
The quickness of the edge, and in his hand
Weigh it; he oft would make me smile at this;
His youth did promise much, and his ripe years
Will see it all perform'd. [*Enter Aspatia, passing by.*

Melan. Hail Maid and Wife!
Thou fair *Aspatia*, may the holy knot
That thou hast tyed to day, last till the hand
Of age undo't; may'st thou bring a race
Unto *Amintor* that may fill the world
Successively with Souldiers.

Asp. My hard fortunes
Deserve not scorn; for I was never proud
When they were good. [*Exit Aspatia.*

Mel. How's this?

Lys. You are mistaken, for she is not married.

Mel. You said *Amintor* was.

Diph. 'Tis true; but

Mel. Pardon me, I did receive
Letters at *Patria*, from my *Amintor*,
That he should marry her.

Diph. And so it stood,
In all opinion long; but your arrival
Made me imagine you had heard the change.

Mel. Who hath he taken then?

Lys. A Lady Sir,
That bears the light above her, and strikes dead
With flashes of her eye; the fair *Evadne* your vertuous Sister.

Mel. Peace of heart betwixt them: but this is strange.

Lys. The King my brother did it
To honour you; and these solemnities
Are at his charge.

Mel. 'Tis Royal, like himself;
But I am sad, my speech bears so unfortunate a sound
To beautiful *Aspatia*; there is rage
Hid in her fathers breast; *Calianax*
Bent long against me, and he should not think,
If I could call it back, that I would take
So base revenges, as to scorn the state (the King?
Of his neglected daughter: holds he still his greatness with

Lys. Yes; but this Lady
Walks discontented, with her watry eyes
Bent on the earth: the unfrequented woods
Are her delight; and when she sees a bank
Stuck full of flowers, she with a sigh will tell
Her servants what a pretty place it were
To bury lovers in, and make her maids
Pluck'em, and strow her over like a Corse.
She carries with her an infectious grief
That strikes all her beholders, she will sing
The mournful'st things that ever ear hath heard,
And sigh, and sing again, and when the rest
Of our young Ladies in their wanton blood,
Tell mirthful tales in course that fill the room
With laughter, she will with so sad a look
Bring forth a story of the silent death
Of some forsaken Virgin, which her grief
Will put in such a phrase, that ere she end,
She'l send them weeping one by one away.
Mel. She has a brother under my command
Like her, a face as womanish as hers,
But with a spirit that hath much out-grown
The number of his years. [*Enter Amintor.*
Cle. My Lord the Bridegroom!
Mel. I might run fiercely, not more hastily
Upon my foe: I love thee well *Amintor*,
My mouth is much too narrow for my heart;
I joy to look upon those eyes of thine;
Thou art my friend, but my disorder'd speech cuts off my love.
Amin. Thou art *Melantius*;
All love is spoke in that, a sacrifice
To thank the gods, *Melantius* is return'd
In safety; victory sits on his sword
As she was wont; may she build there and dwell,
And may thy Armour be as it hath been,
Only thy valour and thy innocence.
What endless treasures would our enemies give,
That I might hold thee still thus!
Mel. I am but poor in words, but credit me young man,
Thy Mother could no more but weep, for joy to see thee

After long absence; all the wounds I have,
Fetch not so much away, nor all the cryes
Of Widowed Mothers: but this is peace;
And what was War?

Amin. Pardon thou holy God
Of Marriage bed, and frown not, I am forc't
In answer of such noble tears as those,
To weep upon my Wedding day.

Mel. I fear thou art grown too sick; for I hear
A Lady mourns for thee, men say to death,
Forsaken of thee, on what terms I know not.

Amin. She had my promise, but the King forbad it,
And made me make this worthy change, thy Sister
Accompanied with graces above her,
With whom I long to lose my lusty youth,
And grow old in her arms.

Mel. Be prosperous.

Enter Messenger.

Messen. My Lord, the Maskers rage for you.

Lys. We are gone. *Cleon, Strato, Diphilus.*

Amin. Wee'l all attend you, we shall trouble you
With our solemnities.

Mel. Not so *Amintor.*
But if you laugh at my rude carriage
In peace, I'le do as much for you in War
When you come thither: yet I have a Mistress
To bring to your delights; rough though I am,
I have a Mistress, and she has a heart,
She saies, but trust me, it is stone, no better,
There is no place that I can challenge in't.
But you stand still, and here my way lies. [*Exit.*

Enter Calianax with Diagoras.

Cal. Diagoras, look to the doors better for shame, you let in all the world, and anon the King will rail at me; why very well said, by *Jove* the King will have the show i'th' Court.

Diag. Why do you swear so my Lord?
You know he'l have it here.

Cal. By this light if he be wise he will not.

Diag. And if he will not be wise, you are forsworn.

Cal. One may wear his heart out with swearing, and get thanks on no side, I'le be gone, look to't who will.

Diag. My Lord, I will never keep them out.
Pray stay, your looks will terrifie them.

Cal. My looks terrifie them, you Coxcombly Ass you! I'le be judg'd by all the company whether thou hast not a worse face than I—

Diag. I mean, because they know you and your Office.

Cal. Office! I would I could put it off, I am sure I sweat quite through my Office, I might have made room at my Daughters Wedding, they had near kill'd her among them. And now I must do service for him that hath forsaken her; serve that will. [*Exit Calianax.*

Diag. He's so humourous since his daughter was forsaken: hark, hark, there, there, so, so, codes, codes.
What now? [*Within. knock within.*

Mel. Open the door.

Diag. Who's there?

Mel. *Melantius.*

Diag. I hope your Lordship brings no troop with you, for if you do, I must return them. [*Enter Melantius.*

Mel. None but this Lady Sir. [*And a Lady.*

Diag. The Ladies are all plac'd above, save those that come in the Kings Troop, the best of *Rhodes* sit there, and there's room.

Mel. I thank you Sir: when I have seen you plac'd Madam, I must attend the King; but the Mask done, I'le wait on you again.

Diag. Stand back there, room for my Lord *Melantius*, pray bear back, this is no place for such youths and their Truls, let the doors shut agen; I, do your heads itch? I'le scratch them for you: so now thrust and hang: again, who is't now? I cannot blame my Lord *Calianax* for going away; would he were here, he would run raging among them, and break a dozen wiser heads than his own in the twinkling of an eye: what's the news now? [*Within.*
I pray can you help me to the speech of the Master Cook?

Diag. If I open the door I'le cook some of your Calvesheads. Peace Rogues.—again,—who is't?

Mel. *Melantius within, Enter Calianax to Melantius.*

Cal. Let him not in.

Diag. O my Lord I must; make room there for my Lord; is your Lady plac't?

Mel. Yes Sir, I thank you my Lord *Calianax*: well met,
Your causless hate to me I hope is buried.

Cal. Yes, I do service for your Sister here,
That brings my own poor Child to timeless death;
She loves your friend *Amintor*, such another false-hearted
Lord as you.

Mel. You do me wrong,
A most unmanly one, and I am slow
In taking vengeance, but be well advis'd.

Cal. It may be so: who placed the Lady there so near the presence of the King?

Mel. I did.

Cal. My Lord she must not sit there.

Mel. Why?

Cal. The place is kept for women of more worth.

Mel. More worth than she? it mis-becomes your Age
And place to be thus womanish; forbear;
What you have spoke, I am content to think
The Palsey shook your tongue to.

Cal. Why 'tis well if I stand here to place mens wenches.

Mel. I shall forget this place, thy Age, my safety, and through all, cut that poor sickly week thou hast to live, away from thee.

Cal. Nay, I know you can fight for your Whore.

Mel. Bate the King, and be he flesh and blood,
He lyes that saies it, thy mother at fifteen
Was black and sinful to her.

Diag. Good my Lord!

Mel. Some god pluck threescore years from that fond man,
That I may kill him, and not stain mine honour;
It is the curse of Souldiers, that in peace
They shall be brain'd by such ignoble men,
As (if the Land were troubled) would with tears
And knees beg succour from 'em: would that blood
(That sea of blood) that I have lost in fight,
Were running in thy veins, that it might make thee
Apt to say less, or able to maintain,

Shouldst thou say more,—This *Rhodes* I see is nought
But a place priviledg'd to do men wrong.

Cal. I, you may say your pleasure. [*Enter Amintor.*

Amint. What vilde injury
Has stirr'd my worthy friend, who is as slow
To fight with words, as he is quick of hand?

Mel. That heap of age which I should reverence
If it were temperate: but testy years
Are most contemptible.

Amint. Good Sir forbear.

Cal. There is just such another as your self.

Amint. He will wrong you, or me, or any man,
And talk as if he had no life to lose
Since this our match: the King is coming in,
I would not for more wealth than I enjoy,
He should perceive you raging, he did hear
You were at difference now, which hastned him.

Cal. Make room there.

Hoboyes play within.

Enter King, Evadne, Aspatia, Lords and Ladies.

King. *Melantius*, thou art welcome, and my love
Is with thee still; but this is not a place
To brabble in; *Calianax*, joyn hands.

Cal. He shall not have my hand.

King. This is no time
To force you to't, I do love you both:
Calianax, you look well to your Office;
And you *Melantius* are welcome home; begin the Mask.

Mel. Sister, I joy to see you, and your choice,
You lookt with my eyes when you took that man;
Be happy in him. [*Recorders.*

Evad. O my dearest brother!
Your presence is more joyful than this day can be unto me.

The Mask.

Night rises in mists.

Nigh. Our raign is come; for in the raging Sea
The Sun is drown'd, and with him fell the day:

Bright *Cinthia* hear my voice, I am the Night
For whom thou bear'st about thy borrowed light;
Appear, no longer thy pale visage shrowd,
But strike thy silver horn through a cloud,
And send a beam upon my swarthy face,
By which I may discover all the place
And persons, and how many longing eyes
Are come to wait on our solemnities. [*Enter Cinthia.*
How dull and black am I! I could not find
This beauty without thee, I am so blind;
Methinks they shew like to those Eastern streaks
That warn us hence before the morning breaks;
Back my pale servant, for these eyes know how
To shoot far more and quicker rayes than thou.

Cinth. Great Queen, they be a Troop for whom alone
One of my clearest moons I have put on;
A Troop that looks as if thy self and I
Had pluckt our rains in, and our whips laid by
To gaze upon these Mortals, that appear
Brighter than we.

Night. Then let us keep 'em here,
And never more our Chariots drive away,
But hold our places, and out-shine the day.

Cinth. Great Queen of shadows, you are pleas'd to speak
Of more than may be done; we may not break
The gods decrees, but when our time is come,
Must drive away and give the day our room.
Yet whil'st our raign lasts, let us stretch our power
To give our servants one contented hour,
With such unwonted solemn grace and state,
As may for ever after force them hate
Our brothers glorious beams, and wish the night
Crown'd with a thousand stars, and our cold light:
For almost all the world their service bend
To *Phœbus*, and in vain my light I lend,
Gaz'd on unto my setting from my rise
Almost of none, but of unquiet eyes.

Nigh. Then shine at full, fair Queen, and by thy power
Produce a birth to crown this happy hour;
Of Nymphs and Shepherds let their songs discover,

Easie and sweet, who is a happy Lover;
Or if thou woot, then call thine own *Endymion*
From the sweet flowry bed he lies upon,
On *Latmus* top, thy pale beams drawn away,
And of this long night let him make a day. (mine,
Cinth. Thou dream'st dark Queen, that fair boy was not
Nor went I down to kiss him; ease and wine
Have bred these bold tales; Poets when they rage,
Turn gods to men, and make an hour an age;
But I will give a greater state and glory,
And raise to time a noble memory
Of what these Lovers are; rise, rise, I say,
Thou power of deeps, thy surges laid away,
Neptune great King of waters, and by me
Be proud to be commanded. [*Neptune rises.*
Nep. *Cinthia*, see,
Thy word hath fetcht me hither, let me know why I ascend.
Cinth. Doth this majestick show
Give thee no knowledge yet?
Nep. Yes, now I see.
Something intended (*Cinthia*) worthy thee;
Go on, I'le be a helper.
Cinth. Hie thee then,
And charge the wind flie from his Rockie Den.
Let loose thy subjects, only *Boreas*
Too foul for our intention as he was;
Still keep him fast chain'd; we must have none here
But vernal blasts, and gentle winds appear,
Such as blow flowers, and through the glad Boughs sing
Many soft welcomes to the lusty spring.
These are our musick: next, thy watry race
Bring on in couples; we are pleas'd to grace
This noble night, each in their richest things
Your own deeps or the broken vessel brings;
Be prodigal, and I shall be as kind,
And shine at full upon you.
Nep. Ho the wind
Commanding *Eolus*! [*Enter Eolus out of a Rock.*
Eol. Great *Neptune*!
Nep. He.

Eol. What is thy will?
Nep. We do command thee free
Favonius and thy milder winds to wait
Upon our *Cinthia*, but tye *Boreas* straight;
He's too rebellious.
Eol. I shall do it.
Nep. Do, great master of the flood, and all below,
Thy full command has taken.
Eol. Ho! the main;
Neptune.
Nep. Here.
Eol. *Boreas* has broke his chain,
And struggling with the rest, has got away.
Nep. Let him alone, I'le take him up at sea;
He will not long be thence; go once again
And call out of the bottoms of the Main,
Blew *Proteus*, and the rest; charge them put on
Their greatest pearls, and the most sparkling stone
The bearing Rock breeds, till this night is done
By me a solemn honour to the Moon;
Flie like a full sail.
Eol. I am gone.
Cin. Dark night,
Strike a full silence, do a thorow right
To this great *Chorus*, that our Musick may
Touch high as heaven, and make the East break day
At mid-[n]ight. [*Musick.*

SONG.

Cinthia *to thy power, and them*
we obey.
Joy to this great company,
and no day
Come to steal this night away,
Till the rites of love are ended,
And the lusty Bridegroom say,
Welcome light of all befriended.
Pace out you watry powers below,
let your feet
Like the Gallies when they row,
even beat.

Let your unknown measures set
To the still winds, tell to all
That Gods are come immortal great,
To honour this great Nuptial.

The Measure. Second Song.

Hold back thy hours dark night, till we have done,
The day will come too soon;
Young Maids will curse thee if thou steal'st away,
And leav'st their blushes open to the day.
Stay, stay, and hide
the blushes of the Bride.
Stay gentle night, and with thy darkness cover
The kisses of her Lover.
Stay, and confound her tears, and her shrill cryings,
Her weak denials, vows, and often dyings;
Stay and hide all,
but help not though she call.

Nep. Great Queen of us and Heaven,
Hear what I bring to make this hour a full one,
If not her measure.
Cinth. Speak Seas King.
Nep. Thy tunes my *Amphitrite* joyes to have,
When they will dance upon the rising wave,
And court me as the sails, my *Trytons* play
Musick to lead a storm, I'le lead the way.

Song. Measure.

To bed, to bed; come Hymen, *lead the Bride,*
And lay her by her Husbands side:
Bring in the Virgins every one
That grieve to lie alone:
That they may kiss while they may say, a maid,
To morrow 'twill be other, kist and said:
Hesperus *be long a shining,*
Whil'st these Lovers are a twining.

Eol. Ho! *Neptune!*
Nept. *Eolus!*
Eol. The Seas go hie,

Boreas hath rais'd a storm; go and applie
Thy trident, else I prophesie, ere day
Many a tall ship will be cast away:
Descend with all the Gods, and all their power to strike a cal[m].
Cin. A thanks to every one, and to gratulate
So great a service done at my desire,
Ye shall have many floods fuller and higher
Than you have wisht for; no Ebb shall dare
To let the day see where your dwellings are:
Now back unto your Government in haste,
Lest your proud charge should swell above the waste,
And win upon the Island.
Nep. We obey. [*Neptune descends, and the Sea-gods.*
Cinth. Hold up thy head dead night; seest thou not day?
The East begins to lighten, I must down
And give my brother place.
Nigh. Oh! I could frown
To see the day, the day that flings his light
Upon my Kingdoms, and contemns old Night;
Let him go on and flame, I hope to see
Another wild-fire in his Axletree;
And all false drencht; but I forgot, speak Queen.
The day grows on I must no more be seen.
Cin. Heave up thy drowsie head agen, and see
A greater light, a greater Majestie,
Between our sect and us; whip up thy team;
The day breaks here, and you some flashing stream
Shot from the South; say, which way wilt thou go?
Nigh. I'le vanish into mists. [*Exeunt.*
Cin. I into day. [*Finis Mask.*
King. Take lights there Ladies, get the Bride to bed;
We will not see you laid, good night *Amintor*,
We'l ease you of that tedious ceremony;
Were it [my] case, I should think time run slow.
If thou beest noble, youth, get me a boy,
That may defend my Kingdom from my foes.
Amin. All happiness to you.
King. Good night *Melantius.* [*Exeunt.*

Actus Secundus.

Enter Evadne, Aspatia, Dula, *and other Ladies.*

DUL. Madam, shall we undress you for this fight?
The Wars are nak'd that you must make to night.

Evad. You are very merry *Dula.*

Dul. I should be far merrier Madam, if it were with me as it is with you.

Eva. Why how now wench?

Dul. Come Ladies will you help?

Eva. I am soon undone.

Dul. And as soon done:
Good store of Cloaths will trouble you at both.

Evad. Art thou drunk *Dula*?

Dul. Why here's none but we.

Evad. Thou think'st belike, there is no modesty
When we are alone.

Dul. I by my troth you hit my thoughts aright.

Evad. You prick me Lady.

Dul. 'Tis against my will,
Anon you must endure more, and lie still.
You're best to practise.

Evad. Sure this wench is mad.

Dul. No faith, this is a trick that I have had
Since I was fourteen.

Evad. 'Tis high time to leave it.

Dul. Nay, now I'le keep it till the trick leave me;
A dozen wanton words put in your head,
Will make you lively in your Husbands bed.

Evad. Nay faith, then take it.

Dul. Take it Madam, where?
We all I hope will take it that are here.

Evad. Nay then I'le give you o're.

Dul. So will I make
The ablest man in *Rhodes*, or his heart to ake.

Evad. Wilt take my place to night?

Dul. I'le hold your Cards against any two I know.

Evad. What wilt thou do?

Dul. Madam, we'l do't, and make'm leave play too.

Evad. *Aspatia*, take her part.

Dul. I will refuse it.
She will pluck down a side, she does not use it.
Evad. Why, do.
Dul. You will find the play
Quickly, because your head lies well that way.
Evad. I thank thee *Dula*, would thou could'st instill
Some of thy mirth into *Aspatia*:
Nothing but sad thoughts in her breast do dwell,
Methinks a mean betwixt you would do well.
Dul. She is in love, hang me if I were so,
But I could run my Country, I love too
To do those things that people in love do.
Asp. It were a timeless smile should prove my cheek,
It were a fitter hour for me to laugh,
When at the Altar the Religious Priest
Were pacifying the offended powers
With sacrifice, than now, this should have been
My night, and all your hands have been imployed
In giving me a spotless offering
To young *Amintors* bed, as we are now
For you: pardon *Evadne*, would my worth
Were great as yours, or that the King, or he,
Or both thought so, perhaps he found me worthless,
But till he did so, in these ears of mine,
(These credulous ears) he pour'd the sweetest words
That Art or Love could frame; if he were false,
Pardon it heaven, and if I did want
Vertue, you safely may forgive that too,
For I have left none that I had from you.
Evad. Nay, leave this sad talk Madam.
Asp. Would I could, then should I leave the cause.
Evad. See if you have not spoil'd all *Dulas* mirth.
Asp. Thou think'st thy heart hard, but if thou beest caught, remember me; thou shalt perceive a fire shot suddenly into thee.
Dul. That's not so good, let'm shoot any thing but fire, I fear'm not.
Asp. Well wench, thou mayst be taken.
Evad. Ladies good night, I'le do the rest my self.
Dul. Nay, let your Lord do some.

Asp. Lay a Garland on my Hearse of the dismal Yew.
Evad. That's one of your sad songs Madam.
Asp. Believe me, 'tis a very pretty one.
Evad. How is it Madam?

SONG.

Asp. *Lay a Garland on my Hearse of the dismal yew;*
Maidens, Willow branches bear; say I died true:
My Love was false, but I was firm from my hour of birth;
Upon my buried body lay lightly gentle earth.

Evad. Fie on't Madam, the words are so strange, they are able to make one Dream of Hobgoblins; *I could never have the power*, Sing that *Dula.*

Dula. *I could never have the power*
To love one above an hour,
But my heart would prompt mine eye
On some other man to flie;
Venus, *fix mine eyes fast,*
Or if not, give me all that I shall see at last.

Evad. So, leave me now.
Dula. Nay, we must see you laid.
Asp. Madam good night, may all the marriage joys
That longing Maids imagine in their beds,
Prove so unto you; may no discontent
Grow 'twixt your Love and you; but if there do,
Enquire of me, and I will guide your moan,
Teach you an artificial way to grieve,
To keep your sorrow waking; love your Lord
No worse than I; but if you love so well,
Alas, you may displease him, so did I.
This is the last time you shall look on me:
Ladies farewel; as soon as I am dead,
Come all and watch one night about my Hearse;
Bring each a mournful story and a tear
To offer at it when I go to earth:
With flattering Ivie clasp my Coffin round,
Write on my brow my fortune, let my Bier
Be born by Virgins that shall sing by course
The truth of maids and perjuries of men.

Evad. Alas, I pity thee. [*Exit Evadne.*
Omnes. Madam, goodnight.
1 *Lady.* Come, we'l let in the Bridegroom.
Dul. Where's my Lord?
1 *Lady.* Here take this light. [*Enter Amintor.*
Dul. You'l find her in the dark.
1 *Lady.* Your Lady's scarce a bed yet, you must help her.
Asp. Go and be happy in your Ladies love;
May all the wrongs that you have done to me,
Be utterly forgotten in my death.
I'le trouble you no more, yet I will take
A parting kiss, and will not be denied.
You'l come my Lord, and see the Virgins weep
When I am laid in earth, though you your self
Can know no pity: thus I wind my self
Into this willow Garland, and am prouder
That I was once your Love (though now refus'd)
Than to have had another true to me.
So with my prayers I leave you, and must try
Some yet unpractis'd way to grieve and die.
Dul. Come Ladies, will you go? [*Exit Aspatia.*
Om. Goodnight my Lord.
Amin. Much happiness unto you all. [*Exeunt Ladies.*
I did that Lady wrong; methinks I feel
Her grief shoot suddenly through all my veins;
Mine eyes run; this is strange at such a time.
It was the King first mov'd me to't, but he
Has not my will in keeping—why do I
Perplex my self thus? something whispers me,
Go not to bed; my guilt is not so great
As mine own conscience (too sensible)
Would make me think; I only brake a promise,
And 'twas the King that forc't me: timorous flesh,
Why shak'st thou so? away my idle fears. [*Enter Evadne.*
Yonder she is, the lustre of whose eye
Can blot away the sad remembrance
Of all these things: Oh my *Evadne*, spare
That tender body, let it not take cold,
The vapours of the night will not fall here.
To bed my Love; *Hymen* will punish us

For being slack performers of his rites.
Cam'st thou to call me?

Evad. No.

Amin. Come, come my Love,
And let us lose our selves to one another.
Why art thou up so long?

Evad. I am not well.

Amint. To bed then let me wind thee in these arms,
Till I have banisht sickness.

Evad. Good my Lord, I cannot sleep.

Amin. *Evadne*, we'l watch, I mean no sleeping.

Evad. I'le not go to bed.

Amin. I prethee do.

Evad. I will not for the world.

Amin. Why my dear Love?

Evad. Why? I have sworn I will not.

Amin. Sworn!

Evad. I.

Amint. How? Sworn *Evadne*?

Evad. Yes, Sworn *Amintor*, and will swear again
If you will wish to hear me.

Amin. To whom have you Sworn this?

Evad. If I should name him, the matter were not great.

Amin. Come, this is but the coyness of a Bride.

Evad. The coyness of a Bride?

Amin. How prettily that frown becomes thee!

Evad. Do you like it so?

Amin. Thou canst not dress thy face in such a look
But I shall like it.

Evad. What look likes you best?

Amin. Why do you ask?

Evad. That I may shew you one less pleasing to you.

Amin. How's that?

Evad. That I may shew you one less pleasing to you.

Amint. I prethee put thy jests in milder looks.
It shews as thou wert angry.

Evad. So perhaps I am indeed.

Amint. Why, who has done thee wrong?
Name me the man, and by thy self I swear,
Thy yet unconquer'd self, I will revenge thee.

Evad. Now I shall try thy truth; if thou dost love me,
Thou weigh'st not any thing compar'd with me;
Life, Honour, joyes Eternal, all Delights
This world can yield, or hopeful people feign,
Or in the life to come, are light as Air
To a true Lover when his Lady frowns,
And bids him do this: wilt thou kill this man?
Swear my *Amintor*, and I'le kiss the sin off from thy lips.
Amin. I will not swear sweet Love,
Till I do know the cause.
Evad. I would thou wouldst;
Why, it is thou that wrongest me, I hate thee,
Thou shouldst have kill'd thy self.
Amint. If I should know that, I should quickly kill
The man you hated.
Evad. Know it then, and do't.
Amint. Oh no, what look soe're thou shalt put on,
To try my faith, I shall not think thee false;
I cannot find one blemish in thy face,
Where falshood should abide: leave and to bed;
If you have sworn to any of the Virgins
That were your old companions, to preserve
Your Maidenhead a night, it may be done without this means.
Evad. A Maidenhead *Amintor* at my years?
Amint. Sure she raves, this cannot be
Thy natural temper; shall I call thy maids?
Either thy healthful sleep hath left thee long,
Or else some Fever rages in thy blood.
Evad. Neither *Amintor*; think you I am mad,
Because I speak the truth?
Amint. Will you not lie with me to night?
Evad. To night? you talk as if I would hereafter.
Amint. Hereafter? yes, I do. (patience mark
Evad. You are deceiv'd, put off amazement, and with
What I shall utter, for the Oracle
Knows nothing truer, 'tis not for a night
Or two that I forbear thy bed, but for ever.
Amint. I dream,—awake *Amintor*!
Evad. You hear right,
I sooner will find out the beds of Snakes,

And with my youthful blood warm their cold flesh,
Letting them curle themselves about my Limbs,
Than sleep one night with thee; this is not feign'd,
Nor sounds it like the coyness of a Bride.

Amin. Is flesh so earthly to endure all this?
Are these the joyes of Marriage? *Hymen* keep
This story (that will make succeeding youth
Neglect thy Ceremonies) from all ears.
Let it not rise up for thy shame and mine
To after ages; we will scorn thy Laws,
If thou no better bless them; touch the heart
Of her that thou hast sent me, or the world
Shall know there's not an Altar that will smoak
In praise of thee; we will adopt us Sons;
Then vertue shall inherit, and not blood:
If we do lust, we'l take the next we meet,
Serving our selves as other Creatures do,
And never take note of the Female more,
Nor of her issue. I do rage in vain,
She can but jest; Oh! pardon me my Love;
So dear the thoughts are that I hold of thee,
That I must break forth; satisfie my fear:
It is a pain beyond the hand of death,
To be in doubt; confirm it with an Oath, if this be true.

Evad. Do you invent the form:
Let there be in it all the binding words
Devils and Conjurers can put together,
And I will take it; I have sworn before,
And here by all things holy do again,
Never to be acquainted with thy bed.
Is your doubt over now?

Amint. I know too much, would I had doubted still;
Was ever such a marriage night as this!
You powers above, if you did ever mean
Man should be us'd thus, you have thought a way
How he may bear himself, and save his honour:
Instruct me in it; for to my dull eyes
There is no mean, no moderate course to run,
I must live scorn'd, or be a murderer:
Is there a third? why is this night so calm?

Why does not Heaven speak in Thunder to us,
And drown her voice?
Evad. This rage will do no good.
Amint. *Evadne*, hear me, thou hast ta'ne an Oath,
But such a rash one, that to keep it, were
Worse than to swear it; call it back to thee;
Such vows as those never ascend the Heaven;
A tear or two will wash it quite away:
Have mercy on my youth, my hopeful youth,
If thou be pitiful, for (without boast)
This Land was proud of me: what Lady was there
That men call'd fair and vertuous in this Isle,
That would have shun'd my love? It is in thee
To make me hold this worth—Oh! we vain men
That trust out all our reputation,
To rest upon the weak and yielding hand
Of feeble Women! but thou art not stone;
Thy flesh is soft, and in thine eyes doth dwell
The spirit of Love, thy heart cannot be hard.
Come lead me from the bottom of despair,
To all the joyes thou hast; I know thou wilt;
And make me careful, lest the sudden change
O're-come my spirits. (inviron me.
Evad. When I call back this Oath, the pains of hell
Amin. I sleep, and am too temperate; come to bed, or by
Those hairs, which if thou hast a soul like to thy locks,
Were threads for Kings to wear about their arms.
Evad. Why so perhaps they are.
Amint. I'le drag thee to my bed, and make thy tongue
Undo this wicked Oath, or on thy flesh
I'le print a thousand wounds to let out life.
Evad. I fear thee not, do what thou dar'st to me;
Every ill-sounding word, or threatning look
Thou shew'st to me, will be reveng'd at full.
Amint. It will not sure *Evadne*.
Evad. Do not you hazard that.
Amint. Ha'ye your Champions?
Evad. Alas *Amintor*, thinkst thou I forbear
To sleep with thee, because I have put on
A maidens strictness? look upon these cheeks,

And thou shalt find the hot and rising blood
Unapt for such a vow; no, in this heart
There dwels as much desire, and as much will
To put that wisht act in practice, as ever yet
Was known to woman, and they have been shown
Both; but it was the folly of thy youth,
To think this beauty (to what Land soe're
It shall be call'd) shall stoop to any second.
I do enjoy the best, and in that height
Have sworn to stand or die: you guess the man.

Amint. No, let me know the man that wrongs me so,
That I may cut his body into motes,
And scatter it before the Northern wind.

Evad. You dare not strike him.

Amint. Do not wrong me so;
Yes, if his body were a poysonous plant,
That it were death to touch, I have a soul
Will throw me on him.

Evad. Why 'tis the King.

Amint. The King!

Evad. What will you do now?

Amint. 'Tis not the King.

Evad. What, did he make this match for dull *Amintor*?

Amint. Oh! thou hast nam'd a word that wipes away
All thoughts revengeful: in that sacred name,
The King, there lies a terror: what frail man
Dares lift his hand against it? let the Gods
Speak to him when they please;
Till when let us suffer and wait.

Evad. Why should you fill your self so full of heat,
And haste so to my bed? I am no Virgin.

Amint. What Devil put it in thy fancy then
To marry me?

Evad. Alas, I must have one
To Father Children, and to bear the name
Of Husband to me, that my sin may be more honourable.

Amint. What a strange thing am I!

Evad. A miserable one; one that my self am sorry for.

Amint. Why shew it then in this,
If thou hast pity, though thy love be none,

Kill me, and all true Lovers that shall live
In after ages crost in their desires,
Shall bless thy memory, and call thee good,
Because such mercy in thy heart was found,
To rid a lingring Wretch.

Evad. I must have one
To fill thy room again, if thou wert dead,
Else by this night I would: I pity thee.

Amint. These strange and sudden injuries have faln
So thick upon me, that I lose all sense
Of what they are: methinks I am not wrong'd,
Nor is it ought, if from the censuring World
I can but hide it—Reputation,
Thou art a word, no more; but thou hast shown
An impudence so high, that to the World
I fear thou wilt betray or shame thy self.

Evad. To cover shame I took thee, never fear
That I would blaze my self.

Amint. Nor let the King
Know I conceive he wrongs me, then mine honour
Will thrust me into action, that my flesh
Could bear with patience; and it is some ease
To me in these extreams, that I knew this
Before I toucht thee; else had all the sins
Of mankind stood betwixt me and the King,
I had gone through 'em to his heart and thine.
I have lost one desire, 'tis not his crown
Shall buy me to thy bed: now I resolve
He has dishonour'd thee; give me thy hand,
Be careful of thy credit, and sin close,
'Tis all I wish; upon thy Chamber-floore
I'le rest to night, that morning visiters
May think we did as married people use.
And prethee smile upon me when they come,
And seem to toy, as if thou hadst been pleas'd
With what we did.

Evad. Fear not, I will do this.

Amint. Come let us practise, and as wantonly
As ever loving Bride and Bridegroom met,
Lets laugh and enter here.

Evad. I am content.

Amint. Down all the swellings of my troubled heart.
When we walk thus intwin'd, let all eyes see
If ever Lovers better did agree. [*Exit.*

Enter Aspatia, Antiphila *and* Olympias.

Asp. Away, you are not sad, force it no further;
Good Gods, how well you look! such a full colour
Young bashful Brides put on: sure you are new married.

Ant. Yes Madam, to your grief.

Asp. Alas! poor Wenches.
Go learn to love first, learn to lose your selves,
Learn to be flattered, and believe, and bless
The double tongue that did it;
Make a Faith out of the miracles of Ancient Lovers.
Did you ne're love yet Wenches? speak *Olympias*,
Such as speak truth and dy'd in't,
And like me believe all faithful, and be miserable;
Thou hast an easie temper, fit for stamp.

Olymp. Never.

Asp. Nor you *Antiphila*?

Ant. Nor I.

Asp. Then my good Girles, be more than Women, wise. At least be more than I was; and be sure you credit any thing the light gives light to, before a man; rather believe the Sea weeps for the ruin'd Merchant when he roars; rather the wind courts but the pregnant sails when the strong cordage cracks; rather the Sun comes but to kiss the Fruit in wealthy Autumn, when all falls blasted; if you needs must love (forc'd by ill fate) take to your maiden bosoms two dead cold aspicks, and of them make Lovers, they cannot flatter nor forswear; one kiss makes a long peace for all; but man, Oh that beast man!
Come lets be sad my Girles;
That down cast of thine eye, *Olympias*,
Shews a fine sorrow; mark *Antiphila*,
Just such another was the Nymph *Oenone*,
When *Paris* brought home *Helen*: now a tear,
And then thou art a piece expressing fully
The *Carthage* Queen, when from a cold Sea Rock,
Full with her sorrow, she tyed fast her eyes

To the fair *Trojan* ships, and having lost them,
Just as thine eyes do, down stole a tear, *Antiphila*;
What would this Wench do, if she were *Aspatia*?
Here she would stand, till some more pitying God
Turn'd her to Marble: 'tis enough my Wench;
Shew me the piece of Needle-work you wrought.
Ant. Of *Ariadne*, Madam?
Asp. Yes that piece.
This should be *Theseus*, h'as a cousening face,
You meant him for a man.
Ant. He was so Madam.
Asp. Why then 'tis well enough, never look back,
You have a full wind, and a false heart *Theseus*;
Does not the story say, his Keel was split,
Or his Masts spent, or some kind rock or other
Met with his Vessel?
Ant. Not as I remember.
Asp. It should ha' been so; could the Gods know this,
And not of all their number raise a storm?
But they are all as ill. This false smile was well exprest;
Just such another caught me; you shall not go so *Antiphila*,
In this place work a quick-sand,
And over it a shallow smiling Water.
And his ship ploughing it, and then a fear.
Do that fear to the life Wench.
Ant. 'Twill wrong the story.
Asp. 'Twill make the story wrong'd by wanton Poets
Live long and be believ'd; but where's the Lady?
Ant. There Madam.
Asp. Fie, you have mist it here *Antiphila*,
You are much mistaken Wench;
These colours are not dull and pale enough,
To shew a soul so full of misery
As this sad Ladies was; do it by me,
Do it again by me the lost *Aspatia*,
And you shall find all true but the wild Island;
I stand upon the Sea breach now, and think
Mine arms thus, and mine hair blown with the wind,
Wild as that desart, and let all about me
Tell that I am forsaken, do my face

(If thou hadst ever feeling of a sorrow)
Thus, thus, *Antiphila* strive to make me look
Like sorrows monument; and the trees about me,
Let them be dry and leaveless; let the Rocks
Groan with continual surges, and behind me
Make all a desolation; look, look Wenches,
A miserable life of this poor Picture.

Olym. Dear Madam!

Asp. I have done, sit down, and let us
Upon that point fix all our eyes, that point there;
Make a dull silence till you feel a sudden sadness
Give us new souls. [*Enter Calianax.*

Cal. The King may do this, and he may not do it;
My child is wrong'd, disgrac'd: well, how now Huswives?
What at your ease? is this a time to sit still? up you young
Lazie Whores, up or I'le sweng you.

Olym. Nay, good my Lord.

Cal. You'l lie down shortly, get you in and work;
What are you grown so resty? you want ears,
We shall have some of the Court boys do that Office.

Ant. My Lord we do no more than we are charg'd:
It is the Ladies pleasure we be thus in grief;
She is forsaken.

Cal. There's a Rogue too,
A young dissembling slave; well, get you in,
I'le have a bout with that boy; 'tis high time
Now to be valiant; I confess my youth
Was never prone that way: what, made an Ass?
A Court stale? well I will be valiant,
And beat some dozen of these Whelps; I will; and there's
Another of 'em, a trim cheating souldier,
I'le maul that Rascal, h'as out-brav'd me twice;
But now I thank the Gods I am valiant;
Go, get you in, I'le take a course with all.

[*Exeunt Omnes.*

Actus Tertius.

Enter Cleon, Strato, Diphilus.

CLE. Your sister is not up yet.

Diph. Oh, Brides must take their mornings rest, The night is troublesome.

Stra. But not tedious.

Diph. What odds, he has not my Sisters maiden-head to night?

Stra.. No, it's odds against any Bridegroom living, he ne're gets it while he lives.

Diph. Y'are merry with my Sister, you'l please to allow me the same freedom with your Mother.

Stra. She's at your service.

Diph. Then she's merry enough of her self, she needs no tickling; knock at the door.

Stra. We shall interrupt them.

Diph. No matter, they have the year before them. Good morrow Sister; spare your self to day, the night will come again. [*Enter Amintor.*

Amint. Who's there, my Brother? I am no readier yet, your Sister is but now up.

Diph. You look as you had lost your eyes to night; I think you ha' not slept.

Amint. I faith I have not.

Diph. You have done better then.

Amint. We ventured for a Boy; when he is Twelve,
He shall command against the foes of *Rhodes*.

Stra. You cannot, you want sleep. [*Aside.*

Amint. 'Tis true; but she
As if she had drunk *Lethe*, or had made
Even with Heaven, did fetch so still a sleep,
So sweet and sound.

Diph. What's that?

Amint. Your Sister frets this morning, and does turn her eyes upon me, as people on their headsman; she does chafe, and kiss, and chafe again, and clap my cheeks; she's in another world.

Diph. Then I had lost; I was about to lay, you had not got her Maiden-head to night.

Amint. Ha! he does not mock me; y'ad lost indeed;
I do not use to bungle.
Cleo. You do deserve her.
Amint. I laid my lips to hers, and [t]hat wild breath
That was rude and rough to me, last night [*Aside.*
Was sweet as *April*; I'le be guilty too,
If these be the effects. [*Enter Melantius.*
Mel. Good day *Amintor*, for to me the name
Of Brother is too distant; we are friends,
And that is nearer.
Amint. Dear *Melantius*!
Let me behold thee; is it possible?
Mel. What sudden gaze is this?
Amint. 'Tis wonderous strange.
Mel. Why does thine eye desire so strict a view
Of that it knows so well?
There's nothing here that is not thine.
Amint. I wonder much *Melantius*,
To see those noble looks that make me think
How vertuous thou art; and on the sudden
'Tis strange to me, thou shouldst have worth and honour,
Or not be base, and false, and treacherous,
And every ill. But—
Mel. Stay, stay my Friend, (me.
I fear this sound will not become our loves; no more, embrace
Amint. Oh mistake me not;
I know thee to be full of all those deeds
That we frail men call good: but by the course
Of nature thou shouldst be as quickly chang'd
As are the winds, dissembling as the Sea,
That now wears brows as smooth as Virgins be,
Tempting the Merchant to invade his face,
And in an hour calls his billows up,
And shoots 'em at the Sun, destroying all
He carries on him. O how near am I [*Aside.*
To utter my sick thoughts!
Mel. But why, my Friend, should I be so by Nature?
Amin. I have wed thy Sister, who hath vertuous thoughts
Enough for one whole family, and it is strange
That you should feel no want.

Mel. Believe me, this complement's too cunning for me.

Diph. What should I be then by the course of nature, They having both robb'd me of so much vertue?

Strat. O call the Bride, my Lord *Amintor*, that we may see her blush, and turn her eyes down; it is the prettiest sport.

Amin. *Evadne!*

Evad. My Lord! [*Within.*

Amint. Come forth my Love,
Your Brothers do attend to wish you joy.

Evad. I am not ready yet.

Amint. Enough, enough.

Evad. They'l mock me.

Amint. Faith thou shalt come in. [*Enter Evadne.*

Mel. Good morrow Sister; he that understands
Whom you have wed, need not to wish you joy.
You have enough, take heed you be not proud.

Diph. O Sister, what have you done!

Evad. I done! why, what have I done?

Strat. My Lord *Amintor* swears you are no Maid now.

Evad. Push!

Strat. I faith he does.

Evad. I knew I should be mockt.

Diph. With a truth.

Evad. If 'twere to do again, in faith I would not marry.

Amint. Not I by Heaven. [*Aside.*

Diph. Sister, *Dula* swears she heard you cry two rooms off.

Evad. Fie how you talk!

Diph. Let's see you walk.

Evad. By my troth y'are spoil'd.

Mel. *Amintor!*

Amint. Ha!

Mel. Thou art sad.

Amint. Who I? I thank you for that, shall *Diphilus*, thou and I sing a catch?

Mel. How!

Amint. Prethee let's.

Mel. Nay, that's too much the other way.

Amint. I am so lightned with my happiness: how dost thou Love? kiss me.

Evad. I cannot love you, you tell tales of me.

Amint. Nothing but what becomes us: Gentlemen,
Would you had all such Wives, and all the world,
That I might be no wonder; y'are all sad;
What, do you envie me? I walk methinks
On water, and ne're sink, I am so light.
Mel. 'Tis well you are so.
Amint. Well? how can I be other, when she looks thus?
Is there no musick there? let's dance.
Mel. Why? this is strange, *Amintor*!
Amint. I do not know my self;
Yet I could wish my joy were less.
Diph. I'le marry (too,) if it will make one thus.
Evad. *Amintor*, hark. [*Aside.*
Amint. What says my Love? I must obey.
Evad. You do it scurvily, 'twill be perceiv'd.
Cle. My Lord the King is here. [*Enter King and Lysi.*
Amint. Where?
Stra. And his Brother.
King. Good morrow all.
Amintor, joy on, joy fall thick upon thee!
And Madam, you are alter'd since I saw you,
I must salute you; you are now anothers;
How lik't you your nights rest?
Evad. Ill Sir.
Amint. I! 'deed she took but little.
Lys. You'l let her take more, and thank her too shortly.
King. *Amintor*, wert thou truly honest
Till thou wert Married?
Amint. Yes Sir.
King. Tell me then, how shews the sport unto thee?
Amint. Why well.
King. What did you do?
Amint. No more nor less than other couples use;
You know what 'tis; it has but a course name.
King. But prethee, I should think by her black eye,
And her red cheek, she should be quick and stirring
In this same business, ha?
Amint. I cannot tell, I ne're try'd other Sir, but I perceive
She is as quick as you delivered.
King. Well, you'l trust me then *Amintor*,

To choose a Wife for you agen?
Amint. No never Sir.
King. Why? like you this so ill?
Amint. So well I like her.
For this I bow my knee in thanks to you,
And unto Heaven will pay my grateful tribute
Hourly, and to hope we shall draw out
A long contented life together here,
And die both full of gray hairs in one day;
For which the thanks is yours; but if the powers
That rule us, please to call her first away,
Without pride spoke, this World holds not a Wife
Worthy to take her room.
King. I do not like this; all forbear the room
But you *Amintor* and your Lady. I have some speech with
You, that may concern your after living well.
Amint. He will not tell me that he lies with her: if he (do,
Something Heavenly stay my heart, for I shall be apt
To thrust this arm of mine to acts unlawful.
King. You will suffer me to talk with her *Amintor*,
And not have a jealous pang!
Amint. Sir, I dare trust my Wife
With whom she dares to talk, and not be jealous.
King. How do you like *Amintor*?
Evad. As I did Sir.
King. How's that!
Evad. As one that to fulfil your will and pleasure,
I have given leave to call me Wife and Love.
King. I see there is no lasting Faith in Sin;
They that break word with Heaven, will break again
With all the World, and so dost thou with me.
Evad. How Sir?
King. This subtile Womans ignorance
Will not excuse you; thou hast taken Oaths
So great, methought they did not well become
A Womans mouth, that thou wouldst ne're enjoy
A man but me.
Evad. I never did swear so; you do me wrong.
King. Day and night have heard it.
Evad. I swore indeed that I would never love

A man of lower place; but if your fortune
Should throw you from this height, I bade you trust
I would forsake you, and would bend to him
That won your Throne; I love with my ambition,
Not with mine eyes; but if I ever yet
Toucht any other, Leprosie light here
Upon my face, which for your Royalty I would not stain.

King. Why thou dissemblest, and it is in me to punish thee.

Evad. Why, it is in me then not to love you, which will
More afflict your body, than your punishment can mine.

King. But thou hast let *Amintor* lie with thee.

Evad. I ha'not.

King. Impudence! he saies himself so.

Evad. He lyes.

King. He does not.

Evad. By this light he does, strangely and basely, and
I'le prove it so; I did not shun him for a night,
But told him I would never close with him.

King. Speak lower, 'tis false.

Evad. I'm no man to answer with a blow;
Or if I were, you are the King; but urge me not, 'tis most true.

King. Do not I know the uncontrouled thoughts
That youth brings with him, when his bloud is high
With expectation and desires of that
He long hath waited for? is not his spirit,
Though he be temperate, of a valiant strain,
As this our age hath known? what could he do,
If such a sudden speech had met his blood,
But ruine thee for ever? if he had not kill'd thee,
He could not bear it thus; he is as we,
Or any other wrong'd man.

Evad. It is dissembling.

King. Take him; farewel; henceforth I am thy foe;
And what disgraces I can blot thee, look for.

Evad. Stay Sir; *Amintor*, you shall hear, *Amintor.*

Amint. What my Love?

Evad. *Amintor*, thou hast an ingenious look,
And shouldst be vertuous; it amazeth me,
That thou canst make such base malicious lyes.

Amint. What my dear Wife?

Evad. Dear Wife! I do despise thee;
Why, nothing can be baser, than to sow
Dissention amongst Lovers.
Amint. Lovers! who?
Evad. The King and me.
Amint. O Heaven!
Evad. Who should live long, and love without distaste,
Were it not for such pickthanks as thy self!
Did you lie with me? swear now, and be punisht in hell
For this.
Amint. The faithless Sin I made
To fair *Aspatia*, is not yet reveng'd,
It follows me; I will not lose a word
To this wild Woman; but to you my King,
The anguish of my soul thrusts out this truth,
Y'are a Tyrant; and not so much to wrong
An honest man thus, as to take a pride
In talking with him of it.
Evad. Now Sir, see how loud this fellow lyed.
Amint. You that can know to wrong, should know how
Men must right themselves: what punishment is due
From me to him that shall abuse my bed!
It is not death; nor can that satisfie,
Unless I send your lives through all the Land,
To shew how nobly I have freed my self.
King. Draw not thy Sword, thou knowest I cannot fear
A subjects hand; but thou shalt feel the weight of this
If thou dost rage.
Amint. The weight of that?
If you have any worth, for Heavens sake think
I fear not Swords; for as you are meer man,
I dare as easily kill you for this deed,
As you dare think to do it; but there is
Divinity about you, that strikes dead
My rising passions, as you are my King,
I fall before you, and present my Sword
To cut mine own flesh, if it be your will.
Alas! I am nothing but a multitude
Of walking griefs; yet should I murther you,
I might before the world take the excuse

Of madness: for compare my injuries,
And they will well appear too sad a weight
For reason to endure; but fall I first
Amongst my sorrows, ere my treacherous hand
Touch holy things: but why? I know not what
I have to say; why did you choose out me
To make thus wretched? there were thousand fools
Easie to work on, and of state enough within the Island.

Evad. I would not have a fool, it were no credit for me.

Amint. Worse and worse!
Thou that dar'st talk unto thy Husband thus,
Profess thy self a Whore; and more than so,
Resolve to be so still; it is my fate
To bear and bow beneath a thousand griefs,
To keep that little credit with the World.
But there were wise ones too, you might have ta'ne another.

King. No; for I believe thee honest, as thou wert valiant.

Amint. All the happiness
Bestow'd upon me, turns into disgrace;
Gods take your honesty again, for I
Am loaden with it; good my Lord the King, be private in it.

King. Thou may'st live *Amintor*,
Free as thy King, if thou wilt wink at this,
And be a means that we may meet in secret.

Amint. A Baud! hold my breast, a bitter curse
Seize me, if I forget not all respects
That are Religious, on another word
Sounded like that, and through a Sea of sins
Will wade to my revenge, though I should call
Pains here, and after life upon my soul.

King. Well I am resolute you lay not with her,
And so leave you. [*Exit King.*

Evad. You must be prating, and see what follows.

Amint. Prethee vex me not.
Leave me, I am afraid some sudden start
Will pull a murther on me.

Evad. I am gone; I love my life well. [*Exit Evadne.*

Amint. I hate mine as much.
This 'tis to break a troth; I should be glad
If all this tide of grief would make me mad. [*Exit.*

Enter Melantius.

Mel. I'le know the cause of all *Amintors* griefs,
Or friendship shall be idle. [*Enter Calianax.*

Cal. O *Melantius*, my Daughter will die. (room.

Mel. Trust me, I am sorry; would thou hadst ta'ne her

Cal. Thou art a slave, a cut-throat slave, a bloody treacherous slave.

Melan. Take heed old man, thou wilt be heard to rave,
And lose thine Offices.

Cal. I am valiant grown
At all these years, and thou art but a slave.

Mel. Leave, some company will come, and I respect
Thy years, not thee so much, that I could wish
To laugh at thee alone.

Cal. I'le spoil your mirth, I mean to fight with thee;
There lie my Cloak, this was my Fathers Sword,
And he durst fight; are you prepar'd?

Mel. Why? wilt thou doat thy self out of thy life?
Hence get thee to bed, have careful looking to, and eat warm things, and trouble not me: my head is full of thoughts more weighty than thy life or death can be.

Cal. You have a name in War, when you stand safe
Amongst a multitude; but I will try
What you dare do unto a weak old man
In single fight; you'l ground I fear: Come draw.

Mel. I will not draw, unless thou pul'st thy death
Upon thee with a stroke; there's no one blow
That thou canst give, hath strength enough to kill me.
Tempt me not so far then; the power of earth
Shall not redeem thee.

Cal. I must let him alone,
He's stout and able; and to say the truth,
However I may set a face, and talk,
I am not valiant: when I was a youth,
I kept my credit with a testie trick I had,
Amongst cowards, but durst never fight. (stay.

Mel. I will not promise to preserve your life if you do

Cal. I would give half my Land that I durst fight with that proud man a little: if I had men to hold, I would beat him, till he ask me mercy.

Mel. Sir, will you be gone?

Cal. I dare not stay, but I will go home, and beat my servants all over for this. [*Exit Calianax.*

Mel. This old fellow haunts me,
But the distracted carriage of mine *Amintor*
Takes deeply on me, I will find the cause;
I fear his Conscience cries, he wrong'd *Aspatia.*

Enter Amintor.

Amint. Mens eyes are not so subtil to perceive
My inward misery; I bear my grief
Hid from the World; how art thou wretched then?
For ought I know, all Husbands are like me;
And every one I talk with of his Wife,
Is but a well dissembler of his woes
As I am; would I knew it, for the rareness afflicts me now.

Mel. *Amintor*, We have not enjoy'd our friendship of late, for we were wont to charge our souls in talk.

Amint. *Melantius*, I can tell thee a good jest of *Strato* and a Lady the last day.

Mel. How wast?

Amint. Why such an odd one.

Mel. I have long'd to speak with you, not of an idle jest that's forc'd, but of matter you are bound to utter to me.

Amint. What is that my friend?

Mel. I have observ'd, your words fall from your tongue
Wildly; and all your carriage,
Like one that strove to shew his merry mood,
When he were ill dispos'd: you were not wont
To put such scorn into your speech, or wear
Upon your face ridiculous jollity:
Some sadness sits here, which your cunning would
Cover o're with smiles, and 'twill not be. What is it?

Amint. A sadness here! what cause
Can fate provide for me, to make me so?
Am I not lov'd through all this Isle? the King
Rains greatness on me: have I not received
A Lady to my bed, that in her eye
Keeps mounting fire, and on her tender cheeks

Inevitable colour, in her heart
A prison for all vertue? are not you,
Which is above all joyes, my constant friend?
What sadness can I have? no, I am light,
And feel the courses of my blood more warm
And stirring than they were; faith marry too,
And you will feel so unexprest a joy
In chast embraces, that you will indeed appear another.

Mel. You may shape, *Amintor*,
Causes to cozen the whole world withal,
And your self too; but 'tis not like a friend,
To hide your soul from me; 'tis not your nature
To be thus idle; I have seen you stand
As you were blasted; midst of all your mirth,
Call thrice aloud, and then start, feigning joy
So coldly: World! what do I here? a friend
Is nothing, Heaven! I would ha' told that man
My secret sins; I'le search an unknown Land,
And there plant friendship, all is withered here;
Come with a complement, I would have fought,
Or told my friend he ly'd, ere sooth'd him so;
Out of my bosom.

Amint. But there is nothing.

Mel. Worse and worse; farewel;
From this time have acquaintance, but no friend.

Amint. *Melantius*, stay, you shall know what that is.

Mel. See how you play'd with friendship; be advis'd
How you give cause unto your self to say, You ha'lost a friend.

Amint. Forgive what I have done;
For I am so ore-gone with injuries
Unheard of, that I lose consideration
Of what I ought to do—oh—oh.

Mel. Do not weep; what is't?
May I once but know the man
Hath turn'd my friend thus?

Amint. I had spoke at first, but that.

Mel. But what?

Amint. I held it most unfit
For you to know; faith do not know it yet.

Mel. Thou seest my love, that will keep company

With thee in tears; hide nothing then from me;
For when I know the cause of thy distemper,
With mine own armour I'le adorn my self,
My resolution, and cut through thy foes,
Unto thy quiet, till I place thy heart
As peaceable as spotless innocence. What is it?

Amint. Why, 'tis this—it is too big
To get out, let my tears make way a while.

Mel. Punish me strangely heaven, if he escape
Of life or fame, that brought this youth to this.

Amint. Your Sister.

Mel. Well said.

Amint. You'l wish't unknown, when you have heard it.

Mel. No.

Amint. Is much to blame,
And to the King has given her honour up,
And lives in Whoredom with him.

Mel. How, this!
Thou art run mad with injury indeed,
Thou couldst not utter this else; speak again,
For I forgive it freely; tell thy griefs.

Amint. She's wanton; I am loth to say a Whore,
Though it be true.

Mel. Speak yet again, before mine anger grow
Up beyond throwing down; what are thy griefs?

Amint. By all our friendship, these.

Mel. What? am I tame?
After mine actions, shall the name of friend
Blot all our family, and strike the brand
Of Whore upon my Sister unreveng'd?
My shaking flesh be thou a Witness for me,
With what unwillingness I go to scourge
This Rayler, whom my folly hath call'd Friend;
I will not take thee basely; thy sword
Hangs near thy hand, draw it, that I may whip
Thy rashness to repentance; draw thy sword.

Amint. Not on thee, did thine anger swell as high
As the wild surges; thou shouldst do me ease
Here, and Eternally, if thy noble hand
Would cut me from my sorrows.

Mel. This is base and fearful! they that use to utter lyes,
Provide not blows, but words to qualifie
The men they wrong'd; thou hast a guilty cause.
Amint. Thou pleasest me; for so much more like this,
Will raise my anger up above my griefs,
Which is a passion easier to be born,
And I shall then be happy.
Mel. Take then more to raise thine anger. 'Tis meer
Cowardize makes thee not draw; and I will leave thee dead
However; but if thou art so much prest
With guilt and fear, as not to dare to fight,
I'le make thy memory loath'd, and fix a scandal
Upon thy name for ever.
Amint. Then I draw,
As justly as our Magistrates their Swords,
To cut offenders off; I knew before
'Twould grate your ears; but it was base in you
To urge a weighty secret from your friend,
And then rage at it; I shall be at ease
If I be kill'd; and if you fall by me,
I shall not long out-live you.
Mel. Stay a while.
The name of friend is more than family,
Or all the world besides; I was a fool.
Thou searching humane nature, that didst wake
To do me wrong, thou art inquisitive,
And thrusts me upon questions that will take
My sleep away; would I had died ere known
This sad dishonour; pardon me my friend;
If thou wilt strike, here is a faithful heart,
Pierce it, for I will never heave my hand
To thine; behold the power thou hast in me!
I do believe my Sister is a Whore,
A Leprous one, put up thy sword young man.
Amint. How should I bear it then, she being so?
I fear my friend that you will lose me shortly;
And I shall do a foul action my self
Through these disgraces.
Mel. Better half the Land
Were buried quick together; no, *Amintor*,

Thou shalt have ease: O this Adulterous King
That drew her to't! where got he the spirit
To wrong me so?

Amint. What is it then to me,
If it be wrong to you!

Mel. Why, not so much: the credit of our house
Is thrown away;
But from his Iron Den I'le waken death,
And hurle him on this King; my honesty
Shall steel my sword, and on its horrid point
I'le wear my cause, that shall amaze the eyes
Of this proud man, and be too glittering
For him to look on.

Amint. I have quite undone my fame.

Mel. Dry up thy watry eyes,
And cast a manly look upon my face;
For nothing is so wild as I thy friend
Till I have freed thee; still this swelling breast;
I go thus from thee, and will never cease
My vengeance, till I find my heart at peace.

Amint. It must not be so; stay, mine eyes would tell
How loth I am to this; but love and tears
Leave me a while, for I have hazarded
All this world calls happy; thou hast wrought
A secret from me under name of Friend,
Which Art could ne're have found, nor torture wrung
From out my bosom; give it me agen,
For I will find it, wheresoe're it lies
Hid in the mortal'st part; invent a way to give it back.

Mel. Why, would you have it back?
I will to death pursue him with revenge.

Amint. Therefore I call it back from thee; for I know
Thy blood so high, that thou wilt stir in this, and shame me
To posterity: take to thy Weapon.

Mel. Hear thy friend, that bears more years than thou.

Amint. I will not hear: but draw, or I—

Mel. *Amintor.*

Amint. Draw then, for I am full as resolute
As fame and honour can inforce me be;
I cannot linger, draw.

Mel. I do—but is not
My share of credit equal with thine if I do stir?
Amint. No; for it will be cal'd
Honour in thee to spill thy Sisters blood,
If she her birth abuse, and on the King
A brave revenge: but on me that have walkt
With patience in it, it will fix the name
Of fearful Cuckold—O that word! be quick.
Mel. Then joyn with me.
Amint. I dare not do a sin, or else I would: be speedy.
Mel. Then dare not fight with me, for that's a sin.
His grief distracts him; call thy thoughts agen,
And to thy self pronounce the name of friend,
And see what that will work; I will not fight.
Amint. You must.
Mel. I will be kill'd first, though my passions
Offred the like to you; 'tis not this earth
Shall buy my reason to it; think a while,
For you are (I must weep when I speak that)
Almost besides your self.
Amint. Oh my soft temper!
So many sweet words from thy Sisters mouth,
I am afraid would make me take her
To embrace, and pardon her. I am mad indeed,
And know not what I do; yet have a care
Of me in what thou doest. (to save
Mel. Why thinks my friend I will forget his honour, or
The bravery of our house, will lose his fame,
And fear to touch the Throne of Majesty?
Amint. A curse will follow that, but rather live
And suffer with me.
Mel. I will do what worth shall bid me, and no more.
Amint. Faith I am sick, and desperately I hope,
Yet leaning thus, I feel a kind of ease.
Mel. Come take agen your mirth about you.
Amint. I shall never do't.
Mel. I warrant you, look up, wee'l walk together,
Put thine arm here, all shall be well agen.
Amint. Thy Love, O wretched, I thy Love, *Melantius*; why, I have nothing else.

Mel. Be merry then. [*Exeunt. Enter Melantius agen.*
Mel. This worthy young man may do violence
Upon himself, but I have cherisht him
To my best power, and sent him smiling from me
To counterfeit again; Sword hold thine edge,
My heart will never fail me: *Diphilus*,
Thou com'st as sent. [*Enter Diphilus.*
Diph. Yonder has been such laughing.
Mel. Betwixt whom?
Diph. Why, our Sister and the King,
I thought their spleens would break,
They laught us all out of the room.
Mel. They must weep, *Diphilus.*
Diph. Must they?
Mel. They must: thou art my Brother, and if I did believe
Thou hadst a base thought, I would rip it out,
Lie where it durst. (find it.
Diph. You should not, I would first mangle my self and
Mel. That was spoke according to our strain; come
Joyn thy hands to mine,
And swear a firmness to what project I shall lay before thee.
Diph. You do wrong us both;
People hereafter shall not say there past
A bond more than our loves, to tie our lives
And deaths together.
Mel. It is as nobly said as I would wish;
Anon I'le tell you wonders; we are wrong'd.
Diph. But I will tell you now, wee'l right our selves.
Mel. Stay not, prepare the armour in my house;
And what friends you can draw unto our side,
Not knowing of the cause, make ready too;
Haste *Diphilus*, the time requires it, haste. [*Exit Diphilus.*
I hope my cause is just, I know my blood
Tells me it is, and I will credit it:
To take revenge, and lose my self withal,
Were idle; and to scape impossible,
Without I had the fort, which misery
Remaining in the hands of my old enemy
Calianax, but I must have it, see [*Enter Calianax.*
Where he comes shaking by me: good my Lord,

Forget your spleen to me, I never wrong'd you,
But would have peace with every man.

Cal. 'Tis well;
If I durst fight, your tongue would lie at quiet.

Mel. Y'are touchie without all cause.

Cal. Do, mock me.

Mel. By mine honour I speak truth.

Cal. Honour? where is't?

Mel. See what starts you make into your hatred to my love and freedom to you;————————
I come with resolution to obtain a suit of you.

Cal. A suit of me! 'tis very like it should be granted, Sir.

Mel. Nay, go not hence;
'Tis this; you have the keeping of the Fort,
And I would wish you by the love you ought
To bear unto me, to deliver it into my hands.

Cal. I am in hope that thou art mad, to talk to me thus.

Mel. But there is a reason to move you to it. I would kill the King that wrong'd you and your daughter.

Cal. Out Traytor!

Mel. Nay but stay; I cannot scape, the deed once done,
Without I have this fort.

Cal. And should I help thee? now thy treacherous mind betrays it self.

Mel. Come, delay me not;
Give me a sudden answer, or already
Thy last is spoke; refuse not offered love,
When it comes clad in secrets.

Cal. If I say I will not, he will kill me, I do see't writ
In his looks; and should I say I will, he'l run and tell the
King: I do not shun your friendship dear *Melantius*,
But this cause is weighty, give me but an hour to think.

Mel. Take it—I know this goes unto the King,
But I am arm'd. [*Ex. Melant.*

Cal. Me thinks I feel my self
But twenty now agen; this fighting fool
Wants Policy; I shall revenge my Girl,
And make her red again; I pray, my legs
Will last that pace that I will carry them,
I shall want breath before I find the King.

Actus Quartus.

Enter Melantius, Evadne, *and a* Lady.

MEL. Save you.

Evad. Save you sweet Brother.

Mel. In my blunt eye methinks you look *Evadne.*

Evad. Come, you would make me blush.

Mel. I would *Evadne,* I shall displease my ends else.

Evad. You shall if you command me; I am bashful;
Come Sir, how do I look?

Mel. I would not have your women hear me
Break into commendation of you, 'tis not seemly.

Evad. Go wait me in the Gallery—now speak.

Mel. I'le lock the door first. [*Exeunt Ladies.*

Evad. Why?

Mel. I will not have your guilded things that dance in visitation with their Millan skins choke up my business.

Evad. You are strangely dispos'd Sir.

Mel. Good Madam, not to make you merry.

Evad. No, if you praise me, 'twill make me sad.

Mel. Such a sad commendation I have for you.

Evad. Brother, the Court hath made you witty,
And learn to riddle.

Mel. I praise the Court for't; has it learned you nothing?

Evad. Me?

Mel. I *Evadne,* thou art young and handsom,
A Lady of a sweet complexion,
And such a flowing carriage, that it cannot
Chuse but inflame a Kingdom.

Evad. Gentle Brother!

Mel. 'Tis yet in thy remembrance, foolish woman,
To make me gentle.

Evad. How is this?

Mel. 'Tis base,
And I could blush at these years, thorough all
My honour'd scars, to come to such a parly.

Evad. I understand you not.

Mel. You dare not, Fool;
They that commit thy faults, fly the remembrance.

Evad. My faults, Sir! I would have you know I care not
If they were written here, here in my forehead.
Mel. Thy body is too little for the story,
The lusts of which would fill another woman,
Though she had Twins within her.
Evad. This is saucy;
Look you intrude no more, there lies your way.
Mel. Thou art my way, and I will tread upon thee,
Till I find truth out.
Evad. What truth is that you look for?
Mel. Thy long-lost honour: would the Gods had set me
One of their loudest bolts; come tell me quickly,
Do it without enforcement, and take heed
You swell me not above my temper.
Evad. How Sir? where got you this report?
Mel. Where there was people in every place.
Evad. They and the seconds of it are base people;
Believe them not, they lyed.
Mel. Do not play with mine anger, do not Wretch,
I come to know that desperate Fool that drew thee
From thy fair life; be wise, and lay him open.
Evad. Unhand me, and learn manners, such another
Forgetfulness forfeits your life.
Mel. Quench me this mighty humour, and then tell me
Whose Whore you are, for you are one, I know it.
Let all mine honours perish but I'le find him,
Though he lie lockt up in thy blood; be sudden;
There is no facing it, and be not flattered;
The burnt air, when the *Dog* raigns, is not fouler
Than thy contagious name, till thy repentance
(If the Gods grant thee any) purge thy sickness.
Evad. Be gone, you are my Brother, that's your safety.
Mel. I'le be a Wolf first; 'tis to be thy Brother
An infamy below the sin of a Coward:
I am as far from being part of thee,
As thou art from thy vertue: seek a kindred
'Mongst sensual beasts, and make a Goat thy Brother,
A Goat is cooler; will you tell me yet?
Evad. If you stay here and rail thus, I shall tell you,
I'le ha' you whipt; get you to your command,

And there preach to your Sentinels,
And tell them what a brave man you are; I shall laugh at you.

Mel. Y'are grown a glorious Whore; where be your Fighters? what mortal Fool durst raise thee to this daring,
And I alive? by my just Sword, h'ad safer
Bestride a Billow when the angry North
Plows up the Sea, or made Heavens fire his food;
Work me no higher; will you discover yet?

Evad. The Fellow's mad, sleep and speak sense.

Mel. Force my swollen heart no further; I would save thee; your great maintainers are not here, they dare not, would they were all, and armed, I would speak loud; here's one should thunder to 'em: will you tell me? thou hast no hope to scape; he that dares most, and damns away his soul to do thee service, will sooner fetch meat from a hungry Lion, than come to rescue thee; thou hast death about thee: h'as undone thine honour, poyson'd thy vertue, and of a lovely rose, left thee a canker.

Evad. Let me consider.

Mel. Do, whose child thou wert,
Whose honour thou hast murdered, whose grave open'd,
And so pull'd on the Gods, that in their justice
They must restore him flesh again and life,
And raise his dry bones to revenge his scandal.

Evad. The gods are not of my mind; they had better let 'em lie sweet still in the earth; they'l stink here.

Mel. Do you raise mirth out of my easiness?
Forsake me then all weaknesses of Nature,
That make men women: Speak you whore, speak truth,
Or by the dear soul of thy sleeping Father,
This sword shall be thy lover: tell, or I'le kill thee:
And when thou hast told all, thou wilt deserve it.

Evad. You will not murder me!

Mel. No, 'tis a justice, and a noble one,
To put the light out of such base offenders.

Evad. Help!

Mel. By thy foul self, no humane help shall help thee,
If thou criest: when I have kill'd thee, as I have
Vow'd to do, if thou confess not, naked as thou hast left
Thine honour, will I leave thee,

That on thy branded flesh the world may read
Thy black shame, and my justice; wilt thou bend yet?
Evad. Yes.
Mel. Up and begin your story.
Evad. Oh I am miserable.
Mel. 'Tis true, thou art, speak truth still.
Evad. I have offended, noble Sir: forgive me.
Mel. With what secure slave?
Evad. Do not ask me Sir.
Mine own remembrance is a misery too mightie for me.
Mel. Do not fall back again; my sword's unsheath'd yet.
Evad. What shall I do?
Mel. Be true, and make your fault less.
Evad. I dare not tell.
Mel. Tell, or I'le be this day a killing thee.
Evad. Will you forgive me then?
Mel. Stay, I must ask mine honour first, I have too much foolish nature in me; speak.
Evad. Is there none else here? (is't?
Mel. None but a fearful conscience, that's too many. Who
Evad. O hear me gently; it was the King.
Mel. No more. My worthy father's and my services
Are liberally rewarded! King, I thank thee,
For all my dangers and my wounds, thou hast paid me
In my own metal: These are Souldiers thanks.
How long have you liv'd thus *Evadne*?
Evad. Too long.
Mel. Too late you find it: can you be sorry?
Evad. Would I were half as blameless.
Mel. *Evadne*, thou wilt to thy trade again.
Evad. First to my grave.
Mel. Would gods th'hadst been so blest:
Dost thou not hate this King now? prethee hate him:
Couldst thou not curse him? I command thee curse him,
Curse till the gods hear, and deliver him
To thy just wishes: yet I fear *Evadne*,
You had rather play your game out.
Evad. No, I feel (after.
Too many sad confusions here to let in any loose flame here-
Mel. Dost thou not feel amongst all those one brave anger

That breaks out nobly, and directs thine arm to kill this base
(King?

Evad. All the gods forbid it.

Mel. No, all the gods require it, they are dishonoured in
(him.

Evad. 'Tis too fearful.

Mel. Y'are valiant in his bed, and bold enough
To be a stale whore, and have your Madams name
Discourse for Grooms and Pages, and hereafter
When his cool Majestie hath laid you by,
To be at pension with some needy Sir
For meat and courser clothes, thus far you know no fear.
Come, you shall kill him.

Evad. Good Sir!

Mel. And 'twere to kiss him dead, thou'd smother him;
Be wise and kill him: Canst thou live and know
What noble minds shall make thee see thy self
Found out with every finger, made the shame
Of all successions, and in this great ruine
Thy brother and thy noble husband broken?
Thou shalt not live thus; kneel and swear to help me
When I shall call thee to it, or by all
Holy in heaven and earth, thou shalt not live
To breath a full hour longer, not a thought:
Come 'tis a righteous oath; give me thy hand,
And both to heaven held up, swear by that wealth
This lustful thief stole from thee, when I say it,
To let his foul soul out.

Evad. Here I swear it,
And all you spirits of abused Ladies
Help me in this performance.

Mel. Enough; this must be known to none
But you and I *Evadne*; not to your Lord,
Though he be wise and noble, and a fellow
Dares step as far into a worthy action,
As the most daring, I as far as Justice.
Ask me not why. Farewell. [*Exit Mel.*

Evad. Would I could say so to my black disgrace.
Oh where have I been all this time! how friended,
That I should lose my self thus desperately,
And none for pity shew me how I wandred?
There is not in the compass of the light

A more unhappy creature: sure I am monstrous,
For I have done those follies, those mad mischiefs,
Would dare a woman. O my loaden soul,
Be not so cruel to me, choak not up [*Enter Amintor.*
The way to my repentance. O my Lord.
Amin. How now?
Evad. My much abused Lord! [*Kneels.*
Amin. This cannot be.
Evad. I do not kneel to live, I dare not hope it;
The wrongs I did are greater; look upon me
Though I appear with all my faults.
Amin. Stand up.
This is no new way to beget more sorrow;
Heaven knows I have too many; do not mock me;
Though I am tame and bred up with my wrongs,
Which are my foster-brothers, I may leap
Like a hand-wolf into my natural wilderness,
And do an out-rage: pray thee do not mock me.
Evad. My whole life is so leprous, it infects
All my repentance: I would buy your pardon
Though at the highest set, even with my life:
That slight contrition, that's no sacrifice
For what I have committed.
Amin. Sure I dazle:
There cannot be a faith in that foul woman
That knows no God more mighty than her mischiefs:
Thou dost still worst, still number on thy faults,
To press my poor heart thus. Can I believe
There's any seed of Vertue in that woman
Left to shoot up, that dares go on in sin
Known, and so known as thine is, O *Evadne*!
Would there were any safety in thy sex,
That I might put a thousand sorrows off,
And credit thy repentance: but I must not;
Thou hast brought me to the dull calamity,
To that strange misbelief of all the world,
And all things that are in it, that I fear
I shall fall like a tree, and find my grave,
Only remembring that I grieve.
Evad. My Lord,

Give me your griefs: you are an innocent,
A soul as white as heaven: let not my sins
Perish your noble youth: I do not fall here
To shadow by dissembling with my tears,
As all say women can, or to make less
What my hot will hath done, which heaven and you
Knows to be tougher than the hand of time
Can cut from mans remembrance; no I do not;
I do appear the same, the same *Evadne*,
Drest in the shames I liv'd in, the same monster.
But these are names of honour, to what I am;
I do present my self the foulest creature,
Most poysonous, dangerous, and despis'd of men,
Lerna e're bred, or *Nilus*; I am hell,
Till you, my dear Lord, shoot your light into me,
The beams of your forgiveness: I am soul-sick,
And [wither] with the fear of one condemn'd,
Till I have got your pardon.

Amin. Rise *Evadne*.
Those heavenly powers that put this good into thee,
Grant a continuance of it: I forgive thee;
Make thy self worthy of it, and take heed,
Take heed *Evadne* this be serious;
Mock not the powers above, that can and dare
Give thee a great example of their justice
To all ensuing eyes, if thou plai'st
With thy repentance, the best sacrifice.

Evad. I have done nothing good to win belief,
My life hath been so faithless; all the creatures
Made for heavens honours have their ends, and good ones,
All but the cousening *Crocodiles*, false women;
They reign here like those plagues, those killing sores
Men pray against; and when they die, like tales
Ill told, and unbeliev'd, they pass away,
And go to dust forgotten: But my Lord,
Those short dayes I shall number to my rest,
(As many must not see me) shall though too late,
Though in my evening, yet perceive a will,
Since I can do no good because a woman,
Reach constantly at some thing that is near it;

I will redeem one minute of my age,
Or like another *Niobe* I'le weep till I am water.

Amin. I am now dissolved:
My frozen soul melts: may each sin thou hast,
Find a new mercy: Rise, I am at peace:
Hadst thou been thus, thus excellently good,
Before that devil King tempted thy frailty,
Sure thou hadst made a star: give me thy hand;
From this time I will know thee, and as far
As honour gives me leave, be thy *Amintor*:
When we meet next, I will salute thee fairly,
And pray the gods to give thee happy dayes:
My charity shall go along with thee,
Though my embraces must be far from thee.
I should ha' kill'd thee, but this sweet repentance
Locks up my vengeance, for which thus I kiss thee,
The last kiss we must take; and would to heaven
The holy Priest that gave our hands together,
Had given us equal Vertues: go *Evadne*,
The gods thus part our bodies, have a care
My honour falls no farther, I am well then.

Evad. All the dear joyes here, and above hereafter
Crown thy fair soul: thus I take leave my Lord,
And never shall you see the foul *Evadne*
Till sh'ave tryed all honoured means that may
Set her in rest, and wash her stains away. [*Exeunt.*

Banquet. Enter King, Calianax. Hoboyes play within.

King. I cannot tell how I should credit this
From you that are his enemy.

Cal. I am sure he said it to me, and I'le justifie it
What way he dares oppose, but with my sword.

King. But did he break without all circumstance
To you his foe, that he would have the Fort
To kill me, and then escape?

Cal. If he deny it, I'le make him blush.

King. It sounds incredibly.

Cal. I, so does every thing I say of late.

King. Not so *Calianax*.

Cal. Yes, I should sit

Mute, whilst a Rogue with strong arms cuts your throat.
King. Well, I will try him, and if this be true
I'le pawn my life I'le find it; if't be false,
And that you clothe your hate in such a lie,
You shall hereafter doat in your own house, not in the Court.
Cal. Why if it be a lie,
Mine ears are false; for I'le be sworn I heard it:
Old men are good for nothing; you were best
Put me to death for hearing, and free him
For meaning of it; you would ha' trusted me
Once, but the time is altered. (world;
King. And will still where I may do with justice to the
You have no witness.
Cal. Yes, my self.
King. No more I mean there were that heard it.
Cal. How no more? would you have more? why am
Not I enough to hang a thousand Rogues?
King. But so you may hang honest men too if you please.
Cal. I may, 'tis like I will do so; there are a hundred will swear it for a need too, if I say it.
King. Such witnesses we need not. (knave.
Cal. And 'tis hard if my Word cannot hang a boysterous
King. Enough; where's *Strato*?
Stra. Sir!

Enter Strato.

King. Why where's all the company? call *Amintor* in.
Evadne, where's my Brother, and *Melantius*?
Bid him come too, and *Diphilus*; call all [*Exit Strato.*
That are without there: if he should desire
The combat of you, 'tis not in the power
Of all our Laws to hinder it, unless we mean to quit 'em.
Cal. Why if you do think
'Tis fit an old Man and a Counsellor,
To fight for what he sayes, then you may grant it.

Enter Amin. Evad. Mel. Diph. [*Lisip.*] *Cle. Stra. Diag.*

King. Come Sirs, *Amintor* thou art yet a Bridegroom,
And I will use thee so: thou shalt sit down;
Evadne sit, and you *Amintor* too;
This Banquet is for you, sir: Who has brought

A merry Tale about him, to raise a laughter
Amongst our wine? why *Strato*, where art thou?
Thou wilt chop out with them unseasonably
When I desire 'em not.
Strato. 'Tis my ill luck Sir, so to spend them then.
King. Reach me a boul of wine: *Melantius*, thou art sad.
Amin. I should be Sir the merriest here,
But I ha' ne're a story of mine own
Worth telling at this time.
King. Give me the Wine.
Melantius, I am now considering
How easie 'twere for any man we trust
To poyson one of us in such a boul.
Mel. I think it were not hard Sir, for a Knave.
Cal. Such as you are.
King. I' faith 'twere easie, it becomes us well
To get plain dealing men about our selves,
Such as you all are here: *Amintor*, to thee
And to thy fair *Evadne*.
Mel. Have you thought of this *Calianax*? [*Aside.*
Cal. Yes marry have I.
Mel. And what's your resolution?
Cal. Ye shall have it soundly?
King. Reach to *Amintor*, *Strato.*
Amin. Here my love,
This Wine will do thee wrong, for it will set
Blushes upon thy cheeks, and till thou dost a fault, 'twere pity.
King. Yet I wonder much
Of the strange desperation of these men,
That dare attempt such acts here in our State;
He could not escape that did it.
Mel. Were he known, unpossible.
King. It would be known, *Melantius.*
Mel. It ought to be, if he got then away
He must wear all our lives upon his sword,
He need not fly the Island, he must leave no one alive.
King. No, I should think no man
Could kill me and scape clear, but that old man.
Cal. But I! heaven bless me: I, should I my Liege?
King. I do not think thou wouldst, but yet thou might'st,

For thou hast in thy hands the means to scape,
By keeping of the Fort; he has, *Melantius*, and he has kept it (well.

Mel. From cobwebs Sir,
'Tis clean swept: I can find no other Art
In keeping of it now, 'twas ne're besieg'd since he commanded.

Cal. I shall be sure of your good word,
But I have kept it safe from such as you.

Mel. Keep your ill temper in,
I speak no malice; had my brother kept it I should ha' said as (much.

King. You are not merry, brother; drink wine,
Sit you all still! *Calianax*, [*Aside.*
I cannot trust thus: I have thrown out words
That would have fetcht warm blood upon the cheeks
Of guilty men, and he is never mov'd, he knows no such thing.

Cal. Impudence may scape, when feeble vertue is accus'd.

King. He must, if he were guilty, feel an alteration
At this our whisper, whilst we point at him,
You see he does not.

Cal. Let him hang himself,
What care I what he does; this he did say.

King. *Melantius*, you cannot easily conceive
What I have meant; for men that are in fault
Can subtly apprehend when others aime
At what they do amiss; but I forgive
Freely before this man; heaven do so too:
I will not touch thee so much as with shame
Of telling it, let it be so no more.

Cal. Why this is very fine.

Mel. I cannot tell
What 'tis you mean, but I am apt enough
Rudely to thrust into ignorant fault,
But let me know it; happily 'tis nought
But misconstruction, and where I am clear
I will not take forgiveness of the gods, much less of you.

King. Nay if you stand so stiff, I shall call back my mercy.

Mel. I want smoothness
To thank a man for pardoning of a crime I never knew.

King. Not to instruct your knowledge, but to shew you my ears are every where, you meant to kill me, and get the Fort to scape.

Mel. Pardon me Sir; my bluntness will be pardoned:
You preserve
A race of idle people here about you,
Eaters, and talkers, to defame the worth
Of those that do things worthy; the man that uttered this
Had perisht without food, be't who it will,
But for this arm that fenc't him from the foe.
And if I thought you gave a faith to this,
The plainness of my nature would speak more;
Give me a pardon (for you ought to do't)
To kill him that spake this.

Cal. I, that will be the end of all,
Then I am fairly paid for all my care and service.

Mel. That old man who calls me enemy, and of whom I
(Though I will never match my hate so low)
Have no good thought, would yet I think excuse me,
And swear he thought me wrong'd in this.

Cal. Who I, thou shameless fellow! didst thou not speak to me of it thy self?

Mel. O then it came from him.

Cal. From me! who should it come from but from me?

Mel. Nay, I believe your malice is enough,
But I ha' lost my anger. Sir, I hope you are well satisfied.

King. *Lisip.* Chear *Amintor* and his Lady; there's no sound
Comes from you; I will come and do't my self.

Amin. You have done already Sir for me, I thank you.

King. *Melantius*, I do credit this from him,
How slight so e're you mak't.

Mel. 'Tis strange you should.

Cal. 'Tis strange he should believe an old mans word,
That never lied in his life.

Mel. I talk not to thee;
Shall the wild words of this distempered man,
Frantick with age and sorrow, make a breach
Betwixt your Majesty and me? 'twas wrong
To hearken to him; but to credit him
As much, at least, as I have power to bear.
But pardon me, whilst I speak only truth,
I may commend my self—I have bestow'd
My careless blood with you, and should be loth

To think an action that would make me lose
That, and my thanks too: when I was a boy,
I thrust my self into my Countries cause,
And did a deed that pluckt five years from time,
And stil'd me man then: And for you my King,
Your subjects all have fed by vertue of my arm.
This sword of mine hath plow'd the ground,
And reapt the fruit in peace;
And your self have liv'd at home in ease:
So terrible I grew, that without swords
My name hath fetcht you conquest, and my heart
And limbs are still the same; my will is great
To do you service: let me not be paid
With such a strange distrust.

King. *Melantius*, I held it great injustice to believe
Thine Enemy, and did not; if I did,
I do not, let that satisfie: what struck
With sadness all? More Wine!

Cal. A few fine words have overthrown my truth:
Ah th'art a Villain.

Mel. Why thou wert better let me have the Fort,
Dotard, I will disgrace thee thus for ever; [*Aside.*
There shall no credit lie upon thy words;
Think better and deliver it.

Cal. My Liege, he's at me now agen to do it; speak,
Deny it if thou canst; examine him
Whilst he's hot, for he'l cool agen, he will forswear it.

King. This is lunacy I hope, *Melantius.*

Mel. He hath lost himself
Much since his Daughter mist the happiness
My Sister gain'd; and though he call me Foe, I pity him.

Cal. Pity! a pox upon you.

King. Mark his disordered words, and at the Mask.

Mel. *Diagoras* knows he raged, and rail'd at me,
And cal'd a Lady Whore, so innocent
She understood him not; but it becomes
Both you and me too, to forgive distraction,
Pardon him as I do.

Cal. I'le not speak for thee, for all thy cunning, if you

will be safe chop off his head, for there was never known so impudent a Rascal.

King. Some that love him, get him to bed: Why, pity should not let age make it self contemptible; we must be all old, have him away.

Mel. *Calianax*, the King believes you; come, you shall go
Home, and rest; you ha' done well; you'l give it up
When I have us'd you thus a moneth I hope.

Cal. Now, now, 'tis plain Sir, he does move me still;
He sayes he knows I'le give him up the Fort,
When he has us'd me thus a moneth: I am mad,
Am I not still?

Omnes. Ha, ha, ha!

Cal. I shall be mad indeed, if you do thus;
Why would you trust a sturdy fellow there
(That has no vertue in him, all's in his sword)
Before me? do but take his weapons from him,
And he's an Ass, and I am a very fool,
Both with him, and without him, as you use me.

Omnes. Ha, ha, ha!

King. 'Tis well *Calianax*; but if you use
This once again, I shall intreat some other
To see your Offices be well discharg'd.
Be merry Gentlemen, it grows somewhat late.
Amintor, thou wouldest be abed again.

Amin. Yes Sir.

King. And you *Evadne*; let me take thee in my arms, *Melantius*, and believe thou art as thou deservest to be, my friend still, and for ever. Good *Calianax*,
Sleep soundly, it will bring thee to thy self.

[*Exeunt omnes. Manent Mel.* and *Cal.*

Cal. Sleep soundly! I sleep soundly now I hope,
I could not be thus else. How dar'st thou stay
Alone with me, knowing how thou hast used me?

Mel. You cannot blast me with your tongue,
And that's the strongest part you have about you.

Cal. I do look for some great punishment for this,
For I begin to forget all my hate,
And tak't unkindly that mine enemy
Should use me so extraordinarily scurvily.

Mel. I shall melt too, if you begin to take
Unkindnesses: I never meant you hurt.
Cal. Thou'lt anger me again; thou wretched rogue,
Meant me no hurt! disgrace me with the King;
Lose all my Offices! this is no hurt,
Is it? I prethee what dost thou call hurt?
Mel. To poyson men because they love me not;
To call the credit of mens Wives in question;
To murder children betwixt me and land; this is all hurt.
Cal. All this thou think'st is sport;
For mine is worse: but use thy will with me;
For betwixt grief and anger I could cry.
Mel. Be wise then, and be safe; thou may'st revenge.
Cal. I o'th' King? I would revenge of thee.
Mel. That you must plot your self.
Cal. I am a fine plotter.
Mel. The short is, I will hold thee with the King
In this perplexity, till peevishness
And thy disgrace have laid thee in thy grave:
But if thou wilt deliver up the Fort,
I'le take thy trembling body in my arms,
And bear thee over dangers; thou shalt hold thy wonted state.
Cal. If I should tell the King, can'st thou deny't again?
Mel. Try and believe.
Cal. Nay then, thou can'st bring any thing about:
Thou shalt have the Fort.
Mel. Why well, here let our hate be buried, and
This hand shall right us both; give me thy aged breast to compass.
Cal. Nay, I do not love thee yet:
I cannot well endure to look on thee:
And if I thought it were a courtesie,
Thou should'st not have it: but I am disgrac'd;
My Offices are to be ta'ne away;
And if I did but hold this Fort a day,
I do believe the King would take it from me,
And give it thee, things are so strangely carried;
Nere thank me for't; but yet the King shall know
There was some such thing in't I told him of;
And that I was an honest man.
Mel. Hee'l buy that knowledge very dearly.

Enter Diphilus.

What news with thee?
Diph. This were a night indeed to do it in;
The King hath sent for her.
Mel. She shall perform it then; go *Diphilus*,
And take from this good man, my worthy friend,
The Fort; he'l give it thee.
Diph. Ha' you got that?
Cal. Art thou of the same breed? canst thou deny
This to the King too?
Diph. With a confidence as great as his.
Cal. Faith, like enough.
Mel. Away, and use him kindly.
Cal. Touch not me, I hate the whole strain: if thou follow me a great way off, I'le give thee up the Fort; and hang your selves.
Mel. Be gone.
Diph. He's finely wrought. [*Exeunt Cal. Diph.*
Mel. This is a night in spite of Astronomers
To do the deed in; I will wash the stain
That rests upon our House, off with his blood.

Enter Amintor.

Amin. *Melantius*, now assist me if thou beest
That which thou say'st, assist me: I have lost
All my distempers, and have found a rage so pleasing; help me.
Mel. Who can see him thus,
And not swear vengeance? what's the matter friend?
Amin. Out with thy sword; and hand in hand with me
Rush to the Chamber of this hated King,
And sink him with the weight of all his sins to hell for ever.
Mel. 'Twere a rash attempt,
Not to be done with safety: let your reason
Plot your revenge, and not your passion.
Amint. If thou refusest me in these extreams,
Thou art no friend: he sent for her to me;
By Heaven to me; my self; and I must tell ye
I love her as a stranger; there is worth
In that vile woman, worthy things, *Melantius*;

And she repents. I'le do't my self alone,
Though I be slain. Farewell.

Mel. He'l overthrow my whole design with madness:
Amintor, think what thou doest; I dare as much as valour;
But 'tis the King, the King, the King, *Amintor*,
With whom thou fightest; I know he's honest, [*Aside.*
And this will work with him.

Amint. I cannot tell
What thou hast said; but thou hast charm'd my sword
Out of my hand, and left me shaking here defenceless.

Mel. I will take it up for thee.

Amint. What a wild beast is uncollected man!
The thing that we call Honour, bears us all
Headlong unto sin, and yet it self is nothing.

Mel. Alas, how variable are thy thoughts!

Amint. Just like my fortunes: I was run to that
I purpos'd to have chid thee for.
Some Plot I did distrust thou hadst against the King
By that old fellows carriage: but take heed,
There is not the least limb growing to a King,
But carries thunder in it.

Mel. I have none against him.

Amint. Why, come then, and still remember we may not think revenge.

Mel. I will remember.

Actus Quintus.

Enter Evadne *and a* Gentleman.

EVAD. Sir, is the King abed?

Gent. Madam, an hour ago.

Evad. Give me the key then, and let none be near;
'Tis the Kings pleasure.

Gent. I understand you Madam, would 'twere mine.
I must not wish good rest unto your Ladiship.

Evad. You talk, you talk.

Gent. 'Tis all I dare do, Madam; but the King will wake, and then.

Evad. Saving your imagination, pray good night Sir.

Gent. A good night be it then, and a long one Madam; I am gone.

Evad. The night grows horrible, and all about me
Like my black purpose: O the Conscience [*King abed.*
Of a lost Virgin; whither wilt thou pull me?
To what things dismal, as the depth of Hell,
Wilt thou provoke me? Let no [woman] dare
From this hour be disloyal: if her heart
Be flesh, if she have blood, and can fear, 'tis a daring
Above that desperate fool that left his peace,
And went to Sea to fight: 'tis so many sins
An age cannot prevent 'em: and so great,
The gods want mercy for: yet I must through 'em.
I have begun a slaughter on my honour,
And I must end it there: he sleeps, good heavens!
Why give you peace to this untemperate beast
That hath so long transgressed you? I must kill him,
And I will do't bravely: the meer joy
Tells me I merit in it: yet I must not
Thus tamely do it as he sleeps: that were
To rock him to another world: my vengeance
Shall take him waking, and then lay before him
The number of his wrongs and punishments.
I'le shake his sins like furies, till I waken
His evil Angel, his sick Conscience:
And then I'le strike him dead: King, by your leave: [*Ties his armes to the bed.*
I dare not trust your strength: your Grace and I
Must grapple upon even terms no more:
So, if he rail me not from my resolution,
I shall be strong enough.
My Lord the King, my Lord; he sleeps
As if he meant to wake no more, my Lord;
Is he not dead already? Sir, my Lord.

King. Who's that?

Evad. O you sleep soundly Sir!

King. My dear *Evadne*,
I have been dreaming of thee; come to bed.

Evad. I am come at length Sir, but how welcome?

King. What pretty new device is this *Evadne*?
What do you tie me to you by my love?

This is a quaint one: Come my dear and kiss me;
I'le be thy *Mars* to bed my Queen of Love:
Let us be caught together, that the Gods may see,
And envy our embraces.
Evad. Stay Sir, stay,
You are too hot, and I have brought you Physick
To temper your high veins.
King. Prethee to bed then; let me take it warm,
There you shall know the state of my body better.
Evad. I know you have a surfeited foul body,
And you must bleed.
King. Bleed!
Evad. I, you shall bleed: lie still, and if the Devil,
Your lust will give you leave, repent: this steel
Comes to redeem the honour that you stole,
King, my fair name, which nothing but thy death
Can answer to the world.
King. How's this *Evadne*?
Evad. I am not she: nor bear I in this breast
So much cold Spirit to be call'd a Woman:
I am a Tyger: I am any thing
That knows not pity: stir not, if thou dost,
I'le take thee unprepar'd; thy fears upon thee,
That make thy sins look double, and so send thee
(By my revenge I will) to look those torments
Prepar'd for such black souls.
King. Thou dost not mean this: 'tis impossible:
Thou art too sweet and gentle.
Evad. No, I am not:
I am as foul as thou art, and can number
As many such hells here: I was once fair,
Once I was lovely, not a blowing Rose
More chastly sweet, till tho[u], thou, thou, foul Canker,
(Stir not) didst poyson me: I was a world of vertue,
Till your curst Court and you (hell bless you for't)
With your temptations on temptations
Made me give up mine honour; for which (King)
I am come to kill thee.
King. No.
Evad. I am.

King. Thou art not.
I prethee speak not these things; thou art gentle,
And wert not meant thus rugged.
Evad. Peace and hear me.
Stir nothing but your tongue, and that for mercy
To those above us; by whose lights I vow,
Those blessed fires that shot to see our sin,
If thy hot soul had substance with thy blood,
I would kill that too, which being past my steel,
My tongue shall teach: Thou art a shameless Villain,
A thing out of the overchange of Nature;
Sent like a thick cloud to disperse a plague
Upon weak catching women; such a tyrant
That for his Lust would sell away his Subjects,
I, all his heaven hereafter.
King. Hear *Evadne*,
Thou soul of sweetness! hear, I am thy King.
Evad. Thou art my shame; lie still, there's none about (you,
Within your cries; all promises of safety
Are but deluding dreams: thus, thus, thou foul man,
Thus I begin my vengeance. [*Stabs him.*
King. Hold *Evadne*!
I do command thee hold.
Evad. I do not mean Sir,
To part so fairly with you; we must change
More of these love-tricks yet.
King. What bloody villain
Provok't thee to this murther?
Evad. Thou, thou monster.
King. Oh!
Evad. Thou kept'st me brave at Court, and Whor'd me;
Then married me to a young noble Gentleman;
And Whor'd me still.
King. *Evadne*, pity me.
Evad. Hell take me then; this for my Lord *Amintor*;
This for my noble brother: and this stroke
For the most wrong'd of women. [*Kills him.*
King. Oh! I die.
Evad. Die all our faults together; I forgive thee. [*Exit.*

Enter two of the Bed-Chamber.

1. Come now she's gone, let's enter, the King expects it, and will be angry.

2. 'Tis a fine wench, we'l have a snap at her one of these nights as she goes from him.

1. Content: how quickly he had done with her! I see Kings can do no more that way than other mortal people.

2. How fast he is! I cannot hear him breathe.

1. Either the Tapers give a feeble light, or he looks very pale.

2. And so he does, pray Heaven he be well.
Let's look: Alas! he's stiffe, wounded and dead:
Treason, Treason!

1. Run forth and call. [*Exit Gent.*

2. Treason, Treason!

1. This will be laid on us: who can believe
A Woman could do this?

Enter Cleon *and* Lisippus.

Cleon. How now, where's the Traytor?

1. Fled, fled away; but there her woful act lies still.

Cle. Her act! a Woman!

Lis. Where's the body?

1. There.

Lis. Farewel thou worthy man; there were two bonds
That tyed our loves, a Brother and a King;
The least of which might fetch a flood of tears:
But such the misery of greatness is,
They have no time to mourn; then pardon me.
Sirs, which way went she? [*Enter Strato.*

Strat. Never follow her,
For she alas! was but the instrument.
News is now brought in, that *Melantius*
Has got the Fort, and stands upon the wall;
And with a loud voice calls those few that pass
At this dead time of night, delivering
The innocent of this act.

Lis. Gentlemen, I am your King.

Strat. We do acknowledge it.

Lis. I would I were not: follow all; for this must have a sudden stop. [*Exeunt*

Enter Melant. Diph. *and* Cal. *on the wall.*

Mel. If the dull people can believe I am arm'd,
Be constant *Diphilus*; now we have time,
Either to bring our banisht honours home,
Or create new ones in our ends.

Diph. I fear not;
My spirit lies not that way. Courage *Calianax.*

Cal. Would I had any, you should quickly know it.

Mel. Speak to the people; thou art eloquent.

Cal. 'Tis a fine eloquence to come to the gallows;
You were born to be my end; the Devil take you.
Now must I hang for company; 'tis strange
I should be old, and neither wise nor valiant.

Enter Lisip. Diag. Cleon, Strat. Guard.

Lisip. See where he stands as boldly confident,
As if he had his full command about him.

Strat. He looks as if he had the bet[t]er cause; Sir,
Under your gracious pardon let me speak it;
Though he be mighty-spirited and forward
To all great things; to all things of that danger
Worse men shake at the telling of; yet certainly
I do believe him noble, and this action
Rather pull'd on than sought; his mind was ever
As worthy as his hand.

Lis. 'Tis my fear too;
Heaven forgive all: summon him Lord *Cleon.*

Cleon. Ho from the walls there.

Mel. Worthy *Cleon*, welcome;
We could have wisht you here Lord; you are honest.

Cal. Well, thou art as flattering a knave, though I dare not tell you so. [*Aside.*

Lis. *Melantius!*

Mel. Sir.

Lis. I am sorry that we meet thus; our old love
Never requir'd such distance; pray Heaven
You have not left your self, and sought this safety
More out of fear than honour; you have lost
A noble Master, which your faith *Melantius*,
Some think might have preserv'd; yet you know best.

Cal. When time was I was mad; some that dares
Fight I hope will pay this Rascal.
Mel. Royal young man, whose tears look lovely on thee;
Had they been shed for a deserving one,
They had been lasting monuments. Thy Brother,
Whil'st he was good, I call'd him King, and serv'd him
With that strong faith, that most unwearied valour;
Pul'd people from the farthest Sun to seek him;
And by his friendship, I was then his souldier;
But since his hot pride drew him to disgrace me,
And brand my noble actions with his lust,
(That never cur'd dishonour of my Sister,
Base stain of Whore; and which is worse,
The joy to make it still so) like my self;
Thus have I flung him off with my allegiance,
And stand here mine own justice to revenge
What I have suffered in him; and this old man
Wrong'd almost to lunacy.
Cal. Who I? you'd draw me in: I have had no wrong,
I do disclaim ye all.
Mel. The short is this;
'Tis no ambition to lift up my self,
Urgeth me thus; I do desire again
To be a subject, so I may be freed;
If not, I know my strength, and will unbuild
This goodly Town; be speedy, and be wise, in a reply.
Strat. Be sudden Sir to tie
All again; what's done is past recal,
And past you to revenge; and there are thousands
That wait for such a troubled hour as this;
Throw him the blank.
Lis. *Melantius*, write in that thy choice,
My Seal is at it.
Mel. It was our honour drew us to this act,
Not gain; and we will only work our pardon.
Cal. Put my name in too.
Diph. You disclaim'd us but now, *Calianax*.
Cal. That's all one;
I'le not be hanged hereafter by a trick;
I'le have it in.

Mel. You shall, you shall;
Come to the back gate, and we'l call you King,
And give you up the Fort.
Lis. Away, away. [*Exeunt Omnes.*

Enter Aspatia *in mans apparel.*

Asp. This is my fatal hour; heaven may forgive
My rash attempt, that causelesly hath laid
Griefs on me that will never let me rest:
And put a Womans heart into my brest;
It is more honour for you that I die;
For she that can endure the misery
That I have on me, and be patient too,
May live, and laugh at all that you can do.
God save you Sir. [*Enter Servant.*
Ser. And you Sir; what's your business?
Asp. With you Sir now, to do me the Office
To help me to you[r] Lord.
Ser. What, would you serve him?
Asp. I'le do him any service; but to haste,
For my affairs are earnest, I desire to speak with him.
Ser. Sir, because you are in such haste, I would be loth delay you any longer: you cannot.
Asp. It shall become you tho' to tell your Lord.
Ser. Sir, he will speak with no body.
Asp. This is most strange: art thou gold proof? there's for thee; help me to him.
Ser. Pray be not angry Sir, I'le do my best. [*Exit.*
Asp. How stubbornly this fellow answer'd me!
There is a vile dishonest trick in man,
More than in women: all the men I meet
Appear thus to me, are harsh and rude,
And have a subtilty in every thing,
Which love could never know; but we fond women
Harbor the easiest and smoothest thoughts,
And think all shall go so; it is unjust
That men and women should be matcht together.

Enter Amintor *and his man.*

Amint. Where is he!

Ser. There my Lord.
Amint. What would you Sir?
Asp. Please it your Lordship to command your man
Out of the room; I shall deliver things
Worthy your hearing.
Amint. Leave us.
Asp. O that that shape should bury falshood in it. [*Aside.*
Amint. Now your will Sir.
Asp. When you know me, my Lord, you needs must guess
My business! and I am not hard to know;
For till the change of War mark'd this smooth face
With these few blemishes, people would call me
My Sisters Picture, and her mine; in short,
I am the brother to the wrong'd *Aspatia.*
Amint. The wrong'd *Aspatia*! would thou wert so too
Unto the wrong'd *Amintor*; let me kiss
That hand of thine in honour that I bear
Unto the wrong'd *Aspatia*: here I stand
That did it; would he could not; gentle youth,
Leave me, for there is something in thy looks
That calls my sins in a most hideous form
Into my mind; and I have grief enough
Without thy help.
Asp. I would I could with credit:
Since I was twelve years old I had not seen
My Sister till this hour; I now arriv'd;
She sent for me to see her Marriage,
A woful one: but they that are above,
Have ends in every thing; she us'd few words,
But yet enough to make me understand
The baseness of the injury you did her;
That little training I have had, is War;
I may behave my self rudely in Peace;
I would not though; I shall not need to tell you
I am but young; and you would be loth to lose
Honour that is not easily gain'd again;
Fairly I mean to deal; the age is strict
For single combats, and we shall be stopt
If it be publish't: if you like your sword,
Use it; if mine appear a better to you,

Change; for the ground is this, and this the time
To end our difference.
Amint. Charitable youth,
If thou be'st such, think not I will maintain
So strange a wrong; and for thy Sisters sake,
Know that I could not think that desperate thing
I durst not do; yet to enjoy this world
I would not see her; for beholding thee,
I am I know not what; if I have ought
That may content thee, take it and be gone;
For death is not so terrible as thou;
Thine eyes shoot guilt into me.
Asp. Thus she swore
Thou would'st behave thy self, and give me words
That would fetch tears into mine eyes, and so
Thou dost indeed; but yet she bade me watch,
Lest I were cousen'd, and be sure to fight ere I return'd.
Amint. That must not be with me;
For her I'le die directly, but against her will never hazard it.
Asp. You must be urg'd; I do not deal uncivilly with those
Dare to fight; but such a one as you (that
Must be us'd thus. [*She strikes him.*
Amint. Prethee youth take heed;
Thy Sister is a thing to me so much
Above mine honour, that I can endu[r]e
All this; good gods——a blow I can endure;
But stay not, lest thou draw a timely death upon thy self.
Asp. Thou art some prating fellow,
One that hath studyed out a trick to talk
And move soft-hearted people; to be kickt, [*She kicks him.*
Thus to be kickt——why should he be so slow [*Aside.*
In giving me my death?
Amint. A man can bear
No more and keep his flesh; forgive me then;
I would endure yet if I could; now shew
The spirit thou pretendest, and understand
Thou hast no honour to live: [*They fight.*
What dost thou mean? thou canst not fight:
The blows thou mak'st at me are quite besides;
And those I offer at thee, thou spread'st thine arms,

And tak'st upon thy breast, Alas! defenceless.
Asp. I have got enough,
And my desire; there's no place so fit for me to die as here.

Enter Evadne.

Evad. *Amintor*; I am loaden with events
That flie to make thee happy; I have joyes
That in a moment can call back thy wrongs,
And settle thee in thy free state again;
It is *Evadne* still that follows thee, but not her mischiefs.
[*Her hands bloody with a knife.*
Amint. Thou canst not fool me to believe agen;
But thou hast looks and things so full of news that I am staid.
Evad. Noble *Amintor*, put off thy amaze;
Let thine eyes loose, and speak, am I not fair?
Looks not *Evadne* beauteous with these rites now?
Were those hours half so lovely in thine eyes,
When our hands met before the holy man?
I was too foul within to look fair then;
Since I knew ill, I was not free till now.
Amint. There is presage of some important thing
About thee, which it seems thy tongue hath lost:
Thy hands are bloody, and thou hast a knife.
Evad. In this consists thy happiness and mine;
Joy to *Amintor*, for the King is dead.
Amint. Those have most power to hurt us that we love,
We lay our sleeping lives within their arms.
Why, thou hast rais'd up mischief to this height,
And found out one to out-name thy other faults;
Thou hast no intermission of thy sins,
But all thy life is a continual ill;
Black is thy colour now, disease thy nature.
Joy to *Amintor*! thou hast toucht a life,
The very name of which had power to chain
Up all my rage, and calm my wildest wrongs.
Evad. 'Tis done; and since I could not find a way
To meet thy love so clear, as through his life,
I cannot now repent it.
Amint. Could'st thou procure the Gods to speak to me,
To bid me love this woman, and forgive,
I think I should fall out with them; behold

Here lies a youth whose wounds bleed in my brest,
Sent by his violent Fate to fetch his death
From my slow hand: and to augment my woe,
You now are present stain'd with a Kings blood
Violently shed: this keeps night here,
And throws an unknown wilderness about me.
Asp. Oh, oh, oh!
Amint. No more, pursue me not.
Evad. Forgive me then, and take me to thy bed.
We may not part.
Amint. Forbear, be wise, and let my rage go this way.
Evad. 'Tis you that I would stay, not it.
Amint. Take heed, it will return with me.
Evad. If it must be, I shall not fear to meet it; take me
Amint. Thou monster of cruelty, forbear. (home.
Evad. For heavens sake look more calm;
Thine eyes are sharper than thou canst make thy sword.
Amint. Away, away, thy knees are more to me than violence.
I am worse than sick to see knees follow me
For that I must not grant; for heavens sake stand.
Evad. Receive me then.
Amint. I dare not stay thy language;
In midst of all my anger and my grief,
Thou dost awake something that troubles me,
And sayes I lov'd thee once; I dare not stay;
There is no end of womens reasoning. [*Leaves her.*
Evad. *Amintor*, thou shalt love me once again;
Go, I am calm; farewell; and peace for ever.
Evadne whom thou hat'st will die for thee. [*Kills her self.*
Amint. I have a little humane nature yet
That's left for thee, that bids me stay thy hand. [*Returns.*
Evad. Thy hand was welcome, but came too late;
Oh I am lost! the heavy sleep makes haste. [*She dies.*
Asp. Oh, oh, oh!
Amint. This earth of mine doth tremble, and I feel
A stark affrighted motion in my blood;
My soul grows weary of her house, and I
All over am a trouble to my self;
There is some hidden power in these dead things
That calls my flesh into'em; I am cold;

Be resolute, and bear'em company:
There's something yet which I am loth to leave.
There's man enough in me to meet the fears
That death can bring, and yet would it were done;
I can find nothing in the whole discourse
Of death, I durst not meet the boldest way;
Yet still betwixt the reason and the act,
The wrong I to *Aspatia* did stands up,
I have not such a fault to answer,
Though she may justly arm with scorn
And hate of me, my soul will part less troubled,
When I have paid to her in tears my sorrow:
I will not leave this act unsatisfied,
If all that's left in me can answer it.
Asp. Was it a dream? there stands *Amintor* still:
Or I dream still.
Amint. How dost thou? speak, receive my love, and help:
Thy blood climbs up to his old place again:
There's hope of thy recovery.
Asp. Did you not name *Aspatia*?
Amint. I did.
Asp. And talkt of tears and sorrow unto her?
Amint. 'Tis true, and till these happy signs in thee
Did stay my course, 'twas thither I was going.
Asp. Th'art there already, and these wounds are hers:
Those threats I brought with me, sought not revenge,
But came to fetch this blessing from thy hand, I am *Aspatia* yet.
Amint. Dare my soul ever look abroad agen?
Asp. I shall live *Amintor*; I am well:
A kind of healthful joy wanders within me.
Amint. The world wants lines to excuse thy loss:
Come let me bear thee to some place of help.
Asp. *Amintor* thou must stay, I must rest here,
My strength begins to disobey my will.
How dost thou my best soul? I would fain live,
Now if I could: would'st thou have loved me then?
Amint. Alas! all that I am's not worth a hair from thee.
Asp. Give me thy hand, mine hands grope up and down,
And cannot find thee; I am wondrous sick:
Have I thy hand *Amintor*?

Amint. Thou greatest blessing of the world, thou hast.

Asp. I do believe thee better than my sense.
Oh! I must go, farewell.

Amint. She swounds: *Aspatia* help, for Heavens sake water;
Such as may chain life for ever to this frame.
Aspatia, speak: what no help? yet I fool,
I'le chafe her temples, yet there's nothing stirs;
Some hidden Power tell her that *Amintor* calls,
And let her answer me: *Aspatia*, speak.
I have heard, if there be life, but bow
The body thus, and it will shew it self.
Oh she is gone! I will not leave her yet.
Since out of justice we must challenge nothing;
I'le call it mercy if you'l pity me,
You heavenly powers, and lend for some few years,
The blessed soul to this fair seat agen.
No comfort comes, the gods deny me too.
I'le bow the body once agen: *Aspatia*!
The soul is fled for ever, and I wrong
My self, so long to lose her company.
Must I talk now? Here's to be with thee love. [*Kills himself.*

Enter Servant.

Ser. This is a great grace to my Lord, to have the new King come to him; I must tell him, he is entring. O Heaven help, help;

Enter Lysip. Melant. Cal. Cleon, Diph. Strato.

Lys. Where's *Amintor*?

Strat. O there, there.

Lys. How strange is this!

Cal. What should we do here?

Mel. These deaths are such acquainted things with me,
That yet my heart dissolves not. May I stand
Stiff here for ever; eyes, call up your tears;
This is *Amintor*: heart he was my friend;
Melt, now it flows; *Amintor*, give a word
To call me to thee.

Amint. Oh!

Mel. *Melantius* calls his friend *Amintor*; Oh thy arms
Are kinder to me than thy tongue;

Speak, speak.
Amint. What?
Mel. That little word was worth all the sounds
That ever I shall hear agen.
Diph. O brother! here lies your Sister slain;
You lose your self in sorrow there.
Mel. Why *Diphilus*, it is
A thing to laugh at in respect of this;
Here was my Sister, Father, Brother, Son;
All that I had; speak once again;
What youth lies slain there by thee?
Amint. 'Tis *Aspatia*.
My senses fade, let me give up my soul
Into thy bosom.
Cal. What's that? what's that? *Aspatia*!
Mel. I never did repent the greatness of my heart till now;
It will not burst at need.
Cal. My daughter dead here too! and you have all fine new tricks to grieve; but I ne're knew any but direct crying.
Mel. I am a pratler, but no more.
Diph. Hold Brother.
Lysip. Stop him.
Diph. Fie; how unmanly was this offer in you!
Does this become our strain?
Cal. I know not what the mat[t]er is, but I am
Grown very kind, and am friends with you;
You have given me that among you will kill me
Quickly; but I'le go home, and live as long as I can.
Mel. His spirit is but poor that can be kept
From death for want of weapons.
Is not my hand a weapon good enough
To stop my breath? or if you tie down those,
I vow *Amintor* I will never eat,
Or drink, or sleep, or have to do with that
That may preserve life; this I swear to keep.
Lysip. Look to him tho', and bear those bodies in.
May this a fair example be to me,
To rule with temper: for on lustful Kings
Unlookt for sudden deaths from heaven are sent!
But curst is he that is their instrument.

PHILASTER:

OR,

Love lies a Bleeding.

The Scene being in Cicilie.

Persons Represented in the Play.

The King.
Philaster, *Heir to the Crown.*
Pharamond, *Prince of* Spain.
Dion, *a Lord.*
Cleremont } *Noble Gentlemen his*
Thrasiline } *Associates.*
Arethusa, *the Kings Daughter.*
Galatea, *a wise modest Lady attending the Princess.*
Megra, *a lascivious Lady.*
An old wanton Lady, or Croan.
Another Lady attending the Princess.
Eufrasia, *Daughter of* Dion, *but disguised like a Page, and called* Bellario.
An old Captain.
Five Citizens.
A Countrey fellow.
Two Woodmen.
The Kings Guard and Train.

Actus primus. Scena prima.

Enter Dion, Cleremont, *and* Thrasiline.

Cler. HEre's not Lords nor Ladies.

Dion. Credit me Gentlemen, I wonder at it. They receiv'd strict charge from the King to attend here: Besides it was boldly published, that no Officer should forbid any Gentlemen that desire to attend and hear.

Cle. Can you ghess the cause?

Di. Sir, it is plain about the *Spanish* Prince, that's come to marry our Kingdoms Heir, and be our Soveraign.

Thra. Many (that will seem to know much) say, she looks not on him like a Maid in Love.

Di. O Sir, the multitude (that seldom know any thing but their own opinions) speak that they would have; but the Prince, before his own approach, receiv'd so many confident messages from the State, that I think she's resolv'd to be rul'd.

Cle. Sir, it is thought, with her he shall enjoy both these Kingdoms of *Cicilie* and *Calabria*.

Di. Sir, it is (without controversie) so meant. But 'twill be a troublesome labour for him to enjoy both these Kingdoms, with safetie, the right Heir to one of them living, and living so vertuously, especially the people admiring the bravery of his mind, and lamenting his injuries.

Cle. Who, *Philaster*?

Di. Yes, whose Father we all know, was by our late King of *Calabria*, unrighteously deposed from his fruitful *Cicilie*. My self drew some blood in those Wars, which I would give my hand to be washed from.

Cle. Sir, my ignorance in State-policy, will not let me know why *Philaster* being Heir to one of these Kingdoms, the King should suffer him to walk abroad with such free liberty.

Di. Sir, it seems your nature is more constant than to enquire after State news. But the King (of late) made a hazard of both the Kingdoms, of *Cicilie* and his own, with offering but to imprison *Philaster*. At which the City was in arms, not to be charm'd down by any State-order or Proclamation, till they saw *Philaster* ride through the streets pleas'd, and without a guard; at which they threw their Hats, and their arms from them; some to make bonefires, some to drink, all for his deliverance. Which (wise men say) is the cause, the King labours to bring in the power of a Foreign Nation to aw his own with.

Enter Galatea, Megra, *and a Lady.*

Thra. See, the Ladies, what's the first?

Di. A wise and modest Gentlwoman that attends the (Princess.

Cle. The second?

Di. She is one that may stand still discreetly enough, and ill favour'dly Dance her Measure; simper when she is Courted by her Friend, and slight her Husband.

Cle. The last?

Di. Marry I think she is one whom the State keeps for the Agents of our confederate Princes: she'll cog and lie with a whole army before the League shall break: her name is common through the Kingdom, and the Trophies of her dishonour, advanced beyond *Hercules*-pillars. She loves to try the several constitutions of mens bodies; and indeed has destroyed the worth of her own body, by making experiment upon it, for the good of the Common-wealth.

Cle. She's a profitable member.

La. Peace, if you love me: you shall see these Gentlemen stand their ground, and not Court us.

Gal. What if they should?

Meg. What if they should?

La. Nay, let her alone; what if they should? why, if they should, I say, they were never abroad: what Foreigner would do so? it writes them directly untravel'd.

Gal. Why, what if they be?

Meg. What if they be?

La. Good Madam let her go on; what if they be? Why if they be I will justifie, they cannot maintain discourse with a judicious Lady, nor make a Leg, nor say Excuse me.

Gal. Ha, ha, ha.

La. Do you laugh Madam?

Di. Your desires upon you Ladies.

La. Then you must sit beside us.

Di. I shall sit near you then Lady.

La. Near me perhaps: But there's a Lady indures no stranger; and to me you appear a very strange fellow.

Meg. Me thinks he's not so strange, he would quickly be acquainted.

Thra. Peace, the King.

Enter King, Pharamond, Arethusa, *and Train.*

King. To give a stronger testimony of love
Than sickly promises (which commonly
In Princes find both birth and burial
In one breath) we have drawn you worthy Sir,
To make your fair indearments to [our] daughter,
And worthy services known to our subjects,
Now lov'd and wondered at. Next, our intent,

[illegible]

Whilst [illegible] hung off [illegible]

Thra. [illegible]

Cl. Wh[illegible]

Di. I [illegible]

Well, we sh[illegible] se[e], we [illegible]

Phi. Kissing your [illegible] Mistress [illegible]

To thank your Roy[al] Father [illegible]

To be my own free Trumpet. [illegible]

Great King, and these your [illegible] be,

(For so deserving you have spoke me [illegible]

And so deserving I dare speak my self)

[illegible]
[illegible]
[illegible] your Kingdoms
[illegible] Country,
[illegible]
[illegible] have been
[illegible]
[illegible]
[illegible] so I
[illegible] Gentlemen,
[illegible] Princes word,
[illegible] make up a Kingdom
[illegible] fear'd,
[illegible]
[illegible] my life I'le find it,
[illegible] And I vow
[illegible] to the subject,
[illegible] Prince himself,
[illegible] his Prince and law.)
[illegible] your dearest self
[illegible] of him, whose name and lustre
[illegible] and mightier) let me say,
[illegible] living; for sweet Princess,
[illegible] man of men, to be
[illegible] you shall make him yours, for whom
[illegible] must die.

[illegible]

[illegible] calls him *Spaniard*, being nothing but [illegible] of his own commendations.

Enter Philaster.

[illegible] wonder what's his price? For certainly he'll tell [illegible] so prais'd his shape: But here comes one more [illegible] large speeches, than the large speaker of them? [illegible] swallowed quick, if I can find, in all the Anatomy [illegible] vertues, one sinew sound enough to promise for [illegible] be Constable. By this Sun, he'll ne're make King [illegible] for trifles, in my poor judgment.

Phi. Right Noble Sir, as low as my obedience,
And with a heart as Loyal as my knee,

ud sails over,
tainted.
lready, for all the
blood: Be con-
hazard, although
offence,
fury
e;

To plant you deeply, our immediate Heir,
Both to our Blood and Kingdoms. For this Lady,
(The best part of your life, as you confirm me,
And I believe) though her few years and sex
Yet teach her nothing but her fears and blushes,
Desires without desire, discourse and knowledge
Only of what her self is to her self,
Make her feel moderate health: and when she sleeps,
In making no ill day, knows no ill dreams.
Think not (dear Sir) these undivided parts,
That must mould up a Virgin, are put on
To shew her so, as borrowed ornaments,
To speak her perfect love to you, or add
An Artificial shadow to her nature:
No Sir; I boldly dare proclaim her, yet
No Woman. But woo her still, and think her modesty
A sweeter mistress than the offer'd Language
Of any Dame, were she a Queen whose eye
Speaks common loves and comforts to her servants.
Last, noble son, (for so I now must call you)
What I have done thus publick, is not only
To add a comfort in particular
To you or me, but all; and to confirm
The Nobles, and the Gentry of these Kingdoms,
By oath to your succession, which shall be
Within this month at most.

Thra. This will be hardly done.

Cle. It must be ill done, if it be done.

Di. When 'tis at best, 'twill be but half done,
Whilst so brave a Gentleman's wrong'd and flung off.

Thra. I fear.

Cle. Who does not?

Di. I fear not for my self, and yet I fear too:
Well, we shall see, we shall see: no more.

Pha. Kissing your white hand (Mistress) I take leave,
To thank your Royal Father: and thus far,
To be my own free Trumpet. Understand
Great King, and these your subjects, mine that must be,
(For so deserving you have spoke me Sir,
And so deserving I dare speak my self)

To what a person, of what eminence,
Ripe expectation of what faculties,
Manners and vertues you would wed your Kingdoms?
You in me have your wishes. Oh this Country,
By more than all my hopes I hold it
Happy, in their dear memories that have been
Kings great and good, happy in yours, that is,
And from you (as a Chronicle to keep
Your Noble name from eating age) do I
Opine myself most happy. Gentlemen,
Believe me in a word, a Princes word,
There shall be nothing to make up a Kingdom
Mighty, and flourishing, defenced, fear'd,
Equall to be commanded and obey'd,
But through the travels of my life I'le find it,
And tye it to this Country. And I vow
My reign shall be so easie to the subject,
That every man shall be his Prince himself,
And his own law (yet I his Prince and law.)
And dearest Lady, to your dearest self
(Dear, in the choice of him, whose name and lustre
Must make you more and mightier) let me say,
You are the blessed'st living; for sweet Princess,
You shall enjoy a man of men, to be
Your servant; you shall make him yours, for whom
Great Queens must die.

Thra. Miraculous.

Cle. This speech calls him *Spaniard*, being nothing but
A large inventory of his own commendations.

Enter Philaster.

Di. I wonder what's his price? For certainly he'll tell himself he has so prais'd his shape: But here comes one more worthy those large speeches, than the large speaker of them? let me be swallowed quick, if I can find, in all the Anatomy of yon mans vertues, one sinew sound enough to promise for him, he shall be Constable. By this Sun, he'll ne're make King unless it be for trifles, in my poor judgment.

Phi. Right Noble Sir, as low as my obedience,
And with a heart as Loyal as my knee,

I beg your favour.
King. Rise, you have it Sir.
Di. Mark but the King how pale he looks with fear.
Oh! this same whorson Conscience, how it jades us!
King. Speak your intents Sir.
Phi. Shall I speak 'um freely?
Be still my royal Soveraign.
King. As a subject
We give you freedom.
Di. Now it heats.
Phi. Then thus I turn
My language to you Prince, you foreign man.
Ne're stare nor put on wonder, for you must
Indure me, and you shall. This earth you tread upon
(A dowry as you hope with this fair Princess,
Whose memory I bow to) was not left
By my dead Father (Oh, I had a Father)
To your inheritance, and I up and living,
Having my self about me and my sword,
The souls of all my name, and memories,
These arms and some few friends, besides the gods,
To part so calmly with it, and sit still,
And say I might have been! I tell thee *Pharamond*,
When thou art King, look I be dead and rotten,
And my name ashes; For, hear me *Pharamond*,
This very ground thou goest on, this fat earth,
My Fathers friends made fertile with their faiths,
Before that day of shame, shall gape and swallow
Thee and thy Nation, like a hungry grave,
Into her hidden bowels: Prince, it shall;
By *Nemesis* it shall.
Pha. He's mad beyond cure, mad.
Di. Here's a fellow has some fire in's veins:
The outlandish Prince looks like a Tooth-drawer.
Phi. Sir, Prince of Poppingjayes, I'le make it well appear
To you I am not mad.
King. You displease us.
You are too bold.
Phi. No Sir, I am too tame,
Too much a Turtle, a thing born without passion,

A faint shadow, that every drunken cloud sails over,
And makes nothing.

King. I do not fancy this,
Call our Physicians: sure he is somewhat tainted.

Thra. I do not think 'twill prove so.

Di. H'as given him a general purge already, for all the right he has, and now he means to let him blood: Be constant Gentlemen; by these hilts I'le run his hazard, although I run my name out of the Kingdom.

Cle. Peace, we are one soul.

Pha. What you have seen in me, to stir offence,
I cannot find, unless it be this Lady
Offer'd into mine arms, with the succession,
Which I must keep though it hath pleas'd your fury
To mutiny within you; without disputing
Your *Genealogies*, or taking knowledge
Whose branch you are. The King will leave it me;
And I dare make it mine; you have your answer.

Phi. If thou wert sole inheritor to him,
That made the world his; and couldst see no sun
Shine upon any but thine: were *Pharamond*
As truly valiant, as I feel him cold,
And ring'd among the choicest of his friends,
Such as would blush to talk such serious follies,
Or back such bellied commendations,
And from this present, spight of all these bugs,
You should hear further from me.

King. Sir, you wrong the Prince:
I gave you not this freedom to brave our best friends,
You deserve our frown: go to, be better temper'd.

Phi. It must be Sir, when I am nobler us'd.

Gal. Ladyes,
This would have been a pattern of succession,
Had he ne're met this mischief. By my life,
He is the worthiest the true name of man
This day within my knowledge.

Meg. I cannot tell what you may call your knowledge,
But the other is the man set in mine eye;
Oh! 'tis a Prince of wax.

Gal. A Dog it is.

King. *Philaster*, tell me,
The injuries you aim at in your riddles.
Phi. If you had my eyes Sir, and sufferance,
My griefs upon you and my broken fortunes,
My want's great, and now nought but hopes and fears,
My wrongs would make ill riddles to be laught at.
Dare you be still my King and right me not?
King. Give me your wrongs in private. [*They whisper.*
Phi. Take them, and ease me of a load would bow strong
Cle. He dares not stand the shock. (*Atlas.*
Di. I cannot blame him, there's danger in't. Every man in this age, has not a soul of Crystal for all men to read their actions through: mens hearts and faces are so far asunder, that they hold no intelligence. Do but view yon stranger well, and you shall see a Feaver through all his bravery, and feel him shake like a true Tenant; if he give not back his Crown again, upon the report of an Elder Gun, I have no augury.
King. Go to:
Be more your self, as you respect our favour:
You'l stir us else: Sir, I must have you know
That y'are and shall be at our pleasure, what fashion we
Will put upon you: smooth your brow, or by the gods.
Phi. I am dead Sir, y'are my fate: it was not I
Said I was not wrong'd: I carry all about me,
My weak stars led me to all my weak fortunes.
Who dares in all this presence speak (that is
But man of flesh and may be mortal) tell me
I do not most intirely love this Prince,
And honour his full vertues!
King. Sure he's possest.
Phi. Yes, with my Fathers spirit; It's here O King!
A dangerous spirit; now he tells me King,
I was a Kings heir, bids me be a King,
And whispers to me, these be all my Subjects.
'Tis strange, he will not let me sleep, but dives
Into my fancy, and there gives me shapes
That kneel, and do me service, cry me King:
But I'le suppress him, he's a factious spirit,
And will undo me: noble Sir, [your] hand, I am your servant.
King. Away, I do not like this:

I'le make you tamer, or I'le dispossess you
Both of life and spirit: For this time
I pardon your wild speech, without so much
As your imprisonment. [*Ex.* King, Pha. *and* Are.

Di. I thank you Sir, you dare not for the people.

Gal. Ladies, what think you now of this brave fellow?

Meg. A pretty talking fellow, hot at hand; but eye yon stranger, is not he a fine compleat Gentleman? O these strangers, I do affect them strangely: they do the rarest home things, and please the fullest! as I live, could love all the Nation over and over for his sake.

Gal. Pride comfort your poor head-piece Lady: 'tis a weak one, and had need of a Night-cap.

Di. See how his fancy labours, has he not spoke
Home, and bravely? what a dangerous train
Did he give fire to! How he shook the King,
Made his soul melt within him, and his blood
Run into whay! it stood upon his brow,
Like a cold winter dew.

Phi. Gentlemen,
You have no suit to me? I am no minion:
You stand (methinks) like men that would be Courtiers,
If you could well be flatter'd at a price,
Not to undo your Children: y'are all honest:
Go get you home again, and make your Country
A vertuous Court, to which your great ones may,
In their Diseased age, retire, and live recluse.

Cle. How do you worthy Sir?

Phi. Well, very well;
And so well, that if the King please, I find
I may live many years.

Di. The King must please,
Whilst we know what you are, and who you are,
Your wrongs and [injuries]: shrink not, worthy Sir,
But add your Father to you: in whose name,
We'll waken all the gods, and conjure up
The rods of vengeance, the abused people,
Who like to raging torrents shall swell high,
And so begirt the dens of these Male-dragons,
That through the strongest safety, they shall beg

For mercy at your swords point.
Phi. Friends, no more,
Our years may be corrupted: 'Tis an age
We dare not trust our wills to: do you love me?
Thra. Do we love Heaven and honour?
Phi. My Lord *Dion*, you had
A vertuous Gentlewoman call'd you Father;
Is she yet alive?
Di. Most honour'd Sir, she is:
And for the penance but of an idle dream,
Has undertook a tedious Pilgrimage.

Enter a Lady.

Phi. Is it to me, or any of these Gentlemen you come?
La. To you, brave Lord; the Princess would intreat
Your present company.
Phi. The Princess send for me! y'are mistaken.
La. If you be call'd *Philaster*, 'tis to you.
Phi. Kiss her hand, and say I will attend her.
Di. Do you know what you do?
Phi. Yes, go to see a woman.
Cle. But do you weigh the danger you are in?
Phi. Danger in a sweet face?
By *Jupiter* I must not fear a woman.
Thra. But are you sure it was the Princess sent?
It may be some foul train to catch your life.
Phi. I do not think it Gentlemen: she's noble,
Her eye may shoot me dead, or those true red
And white friends in her face may steal my soul out:
There's all the danger in't: but be what may,
Her single name hath arm'd me. [*Ex.* Phil.
Di. Go on:
And be as truly happy as thou art fearless:
Come Gentlemen, let's make our friends acquainted,
Lest the King prove false. [*Ex. Gentlemen.*

Enter Arethusa *and a* Lady.

Are. Comes he not?
La. Madam?
Are. Will *Philaster* come?

La. Dear Madam, you were wont
To credit me at first.
Are. But didst thou tell me so?
I am forgetful, and my womans strength
Is so o'recharg'd with danger like to grow
About my Marriage that these under-things
Dare not abide in such a troubled sea:
How look't he, when he told thee he would come?
La. Why, well.
Are. And not a little fearful?
La. Fear Madam? sure he knows not what it is.
Are. You are all of his Faction; the whole Court
Is bold in praise of him, whilst I
May live neglected: and do noble things,
As fools in strife throw gold into the Sea,
Drown'd in the doing: but I know he fears.
La. Fear? Madam (me thought) his looks hid more
Of love than fear.
Are. Of love? To whom? to you?
Did you deliver those plain words I sent,
With such a winning gesture, and quick look
That you have caught him?
La. Madam, I mean to you.
Are. Of love to me? Alas! thy ignorance
Lets thee not see the crosses of our births:
Nature, that loves not to be questioned
Why she did this, or that, but has her ends,
And knows she does well; never gave the world
Two things so opposite, so contrary,
As he and I am: If a bowl of blood
Drawn from this arm of mine, would poyson thee,
A draught of his would cure thee. Of love to me?
La. Madam, I think I hear him.
Are. Bring him in:
You gods that would not have your dooms withstood,
Whose holy wisdoms at this time it is,
To make the passion of a feeble maid
The way unto your justice, I obey. [*Enter* Phil.
La. Here is my Lord *Philaster*.
Are. Oh! 'tis well:

Withdraw your self.
Phi. Madam, your messenger
Made me believe, you wisht to speak with me.
Are. 'Tis true *Philaster*, but the words are such,
I have to say, and do so ill beseem
The mouth of woman, that I wish them said,
And yet am loth to speak them. Have you known
That I have ought detracted from your worth?
Have I in person wrong'd you? or have set
My baser instruments to throw disgrace
Upon your vertues?
Phi. Never Madam you.
Are. Why then should you in such a publick place,
Injure a Princess and a scandal lay
Upon my fortunes, fam'd to be so great:
Calling a great part of my dowry in question.
Phi. Madam, this truth which I shall speak, will be
Foolish: but for your fair and vertuous self,
I could afford my self to have no right
To any thing you wish'd.
Are. *Philaster*, know
I must enjoy these Kingdoms.
Phi. Madam, both?
Are. Both or I die: by Fate I die *Philaster*,
If I not calmly may enjoy them both.
Phi. I would do much to save that Noble life:
Yet would be loth to have posterity
Find in our stories, that *Philaster* gave
His right unto a Scepter, and a Crown,
To save a Ladies longing.
Are. Nay then hear:
I must, and will have them, and more.
Phi. What more?
Are. Or lose that little life the gods prepared,
To trouble this poor piece of earth withall.
Phi. Madam, what more?
Are. Turn then away thy face.
Phi. No.
Are. Do.
Phi. I cannot endure it: turn away my face?

I never yet saw enemy that lookt
So dreadful, but that I thought my self
As great a Basilisk as he; or spake
So horribly, but that I thought my tongue
Bore Thunder underneath, as much as his:
Nor beast that I could turn from: shall I then
Begin to fear sweet sounds? a Ladies voice,
Whom I do love? Say you would have my life,
Why, I will give it you; for it is of me
A thing so loath'd, and unto you that ask
Of so poor use, that I shall make no price
If you intreat, I will unmov'dly hear.
Are. Yet for my sake a little bend thy looks.
Phi. I do.
Are. Then know I must have them and thee.
Phi. And me?
Are. Thy love: without which, all the Land
Discovered yet, will serve me for no use,
But to be buried in.
Phi. Is't possible?
Are. With it, it were too little to bestow
On thee: Now, though thy breath doth strike me dead
(Which know it may) I have unript my breast.
Phi. Madam, you are too full of noble thoughts,
To lay a train for this contemned life,
Which you may have for asking: to suspect
Were base, where I deserve no ill: love you!
By all my hopes I do, above my life:
But how this passion should proceed from you
So violently, would amaze a man, that would be jealous.
Are. Another soul into my body shot,
Could not have fill'd me with more strength and spirit,
Than this thy breath: but spend not hasty time,
In seeking how I came thus: 'tis the gods,
The gods, that make me so; and sure our love
Will be the nobler, and the better blest,
In that the secret justice of the gods
Is mingled with it. Let us leave and kiss,
Lest some unwelcome guest should fall betwixt us,
And we should part without it.

Phi. 'Twill be ill
I should abide here long.
Are. 'Tis true, and worse
You should come often: How shall we devise
To hold intelligence? That our true lovers,
On any new occasion may agree, what path is best to tread?
Phi. I have a boy sent by the gods, I hope to this intent,
Not yet seen in the Court; hunting the Buck,
I found him sitting by a Fountain side,
Of which he borrow'd some to quench his thirst,
And paid the Nymph again as much in tears;
A Garland lay him by, made by himself,
Of many several flowers, bred in the bay,
Stuck in that mystick order, that the rareness
Delighted me: but ever when he turned
His tender eyes upon 'um, he would weep,
As if he meant to make 'um grow again.
Seeing such pretty helpless innocence
Dwell in his face, I ask'd him all his story;
He told me that his Parents gentle dyed,
Leaving him to the mercy of the fields,
Which gave him roots; and of the Crystal springs,
Which did not stop their courses: and the Sun,
Which still, he thank'd him, yielded him his light,
Then took he up his Garland and did shew,
What every flower as Country people hold,
Did signifie: and how all ordered thus,
Exprest his grief: and to my thoughts did read
The prettiest lecture of his Country Art
That could be wisht: so that, me thought, I could
Have studied it. I gladly entertain'd him,
Who was glad to follow; and have got
The trustiest, loving'st, and the gentlest boy,
That ever Master kept: Him will I send
To wait on you, and bear our hidden love.

Enter Lady.

Are. 'Tis well, no more.
La. Madam, the Prince is come to do his service.
Are. What will you do *Philaster* with your self?

Phi. Why, that which all the gods have appointed out for (me.

Are. Dear, hide thy self. Bring in the Prince.

Phi. Hide me from *Pharamond*!
When Thunder speaks, which is the voice of *Jove*,
Though I do reverence, yet I hide me not;
And shall a stranger Prince have leave to brag
Unto a forreign Nation, that he made *Philaster* hide himself?

Are. He cannot know it.

Phi. Though it should sleep for ever to the world,
It is a simple sin to hide my self,
Which will for ever on my conscience lie.

Are. Then good *Philaster*, give him scope and way
In what he saies: for he is apt to speak
What you are loth to hear: for my sake do.

Phi. I will.

Enter Pharamond.

Pha. My Princely Mistress, as true lovers ought,
I come to kiss these fair hands; and to shew
In outward Ceremonies, the dear love
Writ in my heart.

Phi. If I shall have an answer no directlier,
I am gone.

Pha. To what would he have an answer?

Are. To his claim unto the Kingdom.

Pha. Sirrah, I forbear you before the King.

Phi. Good Sir, do so still, I would not talk with you.

Pha. But now the time is fitter, do but offer
To make mention of right to any Kingdom,
Though it be scarce habitable.

Phi. Good Sir, let me go.

Pha. And by my sword.

Phi. Peace *Pharamond*: if thou—

Are. Leave us *Philaster*.

Phi. I have done.

Pha. You are gone, by heaven I'le fetch you back.

Phi. You shall not need.

Pha. What now?

Phi. Know *Pharamond*,
I loath to brawl with such a blast as thou,

Who art nought but a valiant voice: But if
Thou shalt provoke me further, men shall say
Thou wert, and not lament it.

Pha. Do you slight
My greatness so, and in the Chamber of the Princess!

Phi. It is a place to which I must confess
I owe a reverence: but wer't the Church,
I, at the Altar, there's no place so safe,
Where thou dar'st injure me, but I dare kill thee:
And for your greatness; know Sir, I can grasp
You, and your greatness thus, thus into nothing:
Give not a word, not a word back: Farewell. [*Exit* Phi.

Pha. 'Tis an odd fellow Madam, we must stop
His mouth with some Office, when we are married.

Are. You were best make him your Controuler.

Pha. I think he would discharge it well. But Madam,
I hope our hearts are knit; and yet so slow
The Ceremonies of State are, that 'twill be long
Before our hands be so: If then you please,
Being agreed in heart, let us not wait
For dreaming for me, but take a little stoln
Delights, and so prevent our joyes to come.

Are. If you dare speak such thoughts,
I must withdraw in honour. [*Exit* Are.

Pha. The constitution of my body will never hold out till the wedding; I must seek elsewhere. [*Exit* Pha.

Actus Secundus. Scena Prima.

Enter Philaster *and* Bellario.

Phi. AND thou shalt find her honourable boy,
Full of regard unto thy tender youth,
For thine own modesty; and for my sake,
Apter to give, than thou wilt be to ask, I, or deserve.

Bell. Sir, you did take me up when I was nothing;
And only yet am something, by being yours;
You trusted me unknown; and that which you are apt
To conster a simple innocence in me,
Perhaps, might have been craft; the cunning of a boy

Hardened in lies and theft; yet ventur'd you,
To part my miseries and me: for which,
I never can expect to serve a Lady
That bears more honour in her breast than you.
Phi. But boy, it will prefer thee; thou art young,
And bearest a childish overflowing love
To them that clap thy cheeks, and speak thee fair yet:
But when thy judgment comes to rule those passions,
Thou wilt remember best those careful friends
That plac'd thee in the noblest way of life;
She is a Princess I prefer thee to.
Bell. In that small time that I have seen the world,
I never knew a man hasty to part
With a servant he thought trusty; I remember
My Father would prefer the boys he kept
To greater men than he, but did it not,
Till they were grown too sawcy for himself.
Phi. Why gentle boy, I find no fault at all in thy behaviour.
Bell. Sir, if I have made
A fault of ignorance, instruct my youth;
I shall be willing, if not apt to learn;
Age and experience will adorn my mind
With larger knowledge: And if I have done
A wilful fault, think me not past all hope
For once; what Master holds so strict a hand
Over his boy, that he will part with him
Without one warning? Let me be corrected
To break my stubbornness if it be so,
Rather than turn me off, and I shall mend.
Phi. Thy love doth plead so prettily to stay,
That (trust me) I could weep to part with thee.
Alas! I do not turn thee off; thou knowest
It is my business that doth call thee hence,
And when thou art with her thou dwel'st with me:
Think so, and 'tis so; and when time is full,
That thou hast well discharged this heavy trust,
Laid on so weak a one, I will again
With joy receive thee; as I live, I will;
Nay weep not, gentle boy; 'Tis more than time
Thou didst attend the Princess.

Bell. I am gone;
But since I am to part with you my Lord,
And none knows whether I shall live to do
More service for you; take this little prayer;
Heaven bless your loves, your fights, all your designs.
May sick men, if they have your wish, be well;
And Heavens hate those you curse, though I be one. [*Exit.*

Phi. The love of boyes unto their Lords is strange,
I have read wonders of it; yet this boy
For my sake, (if a man may judge by looks,
And speech) would out-do story. I may see
A day to pay him for his loyalty. [*Exit* Phi.

Enter Pharamond.

Pha. Why should these Ladies stay so long? They must come this way; I know the Queen imployes 'em not, for the Reverend Mother sent me word they would all be for the Garden. If they should all prove honest now, I were in a fair taking; I was never so long without sport in my life, and in my conscience 'tis not my fault: Oh, for our Country Ladies! Here's one boulted, I'le hound at her.

Enter Galatea.

Gal. Your Grace!

Pha. Shall I not be a trouble?

Gal. Not to me Sir.

Pha. Nay, nay, you are too quick; by this sweet hand.

Gal. You'l be forsworn Sir, 'tis but an old glove. If you will talk at distance, I am for you: but good Prince, be not bawdy, nor do not brag; these two I bar, and then I think, I shall have sence enough to answer all the weighty *Apothegmes* your Royal blood shall manage.

Pha. Dear Lady, can you love?

Gal. Dear, Prince, how dear! I ne're cost you a Coach yet, nor put you to the dear repentance of a Banquet; here's no Scarlet Sir, to blush the sin out it was given for: This wyer mine own hair covers: and this face has been so far from being dear to any, that it ne're cost penny painting: And for the rest of my poor Wardrobe, such as you see, it leaves no hand behind it, to make the jealous Mercers wife curse our good doings.

Pha. You mistake me Lady.

[*Gal.*] Lord, I do so; would you or I could help it.

Pha. Do Ladies of this Country use to give no more respect to men of my full being?

Gal. Full being! I understand you not, unless your Grace means growing to fatness; and then your only remedy (upon my knowledge, Prince) is in a morning a Cup of neat White-wine brew'd with *Carduus*, then fast till supper, about eight you may eat; use exercise, and keep a Sparrow-hawk, you can shoot in a Tiller; but of all, your Grace must flie *Phlebotomie*, fresh Pork, Conger, and clarified Whay; They are all dullers of the vital spirits.

Pha. Lady, you talk of nothing all this while.

Gal. 'Tis very true Sir, I talk of you.

Pha. This is a crafty wench, I like her wit well, 'twill be rare to stir up a leaden appetite, she's a *Danae*, and must be courted in a showr of gold. Madam, look here, all these and more, than—

Gal. What have you there, my Lord? Gold? Now, as I live tis fair gold; you would have silver for it to play with the Pages; you could not have taken me in a worse time; But if you have present use my Lord, I'le send my man with silver and keep your gold for you.

Pha. Lady, Lady.

Gal. She's coming Sir behind, will take white mony. Yet for all this I'le match ye. [*Exit* Gal. *behind the hangings.*

Pha. If there be two such more in this Kingdom, and near the Court, we may even hang up our Harps: ten such *Camphire* constitutions as this, would call the golden age again in question, and teach the old way for every ill fac't Husband to get his own Children, and what a mischief that will breed, let all consider.

Enter Megra.

Here's another; if she be of the same last, the Devil shall pluck her on. Many fair mornings, Lady.

Meg. As many mornings bring as many dayes,
Fair, sweet, and hopeful to your Grace.

Pha. She gives good words yet; Sure this wench is free.
If your more serious business do not call you,

Let me hold quarter with you, we'll take an hour
Out quickly.

Meg. What would your Grace talk of?

Pha. Of some such pretty subject as your self.
I'le go no further than your eye, or lip,
There's theme enough for one man for an age.

Meg. Sir, they stand right, and my lips are yet even,
Smooth, young enough, ripe enough, red enough,
Or my glass wrongs me.

Pha. O they are two twin'd Cherries died in blushes,
Which those fair suns above, with their bright beams
Reflect upon, and ripen: sweetest beauty,
Bow down those branches, that the longing taste,
Of the faint looker on, may meet those blessings,
And taste and live.

Meg. O delicate sweet Prince;
She that hath snow enough about her heart,
To take the wanton spring of ten such lines off,
May be a Nun without probation.
Sir, you have in such neat poetry, gathered a kiss,
That if I had but five lines of that number,
Such pretty begging blanks, I should commend
Your fore-head, or your cheeks, and kiss you too.

Pha. Do it in prose; you cannot miss it Madam.

Meg. I shall, I shall.

Pha. By my life you shall not.
I'le prompt you first: Can you do it now?

Meg. Methinks 'tis easie, now I ha' don't before;
But yet I should stick at it.

Pha. Stick till to morrow.
I'le ne'r part you sweetest. But we lose time,
Can you love me?

Meg. Love you my Lord? How would you have me love you?

Pha. I'le teach you in a short sentence, cause I will not load your memory, that is all; love me, and lie with me.

Meg. Was it lie with you that you said? 'Tis impossible.

Pha. Not to a willing mind, that will endeavour; if I do not teach you to do it as easily in one night, as you'l go to bed, I'le lose my Royal blood for't.

Meg. Why Prince, you have a Lady of your own, that yet wants teaching.

Pha. I'le sooner teach a Mare the old measures, than teach her any thing belonging to the function; she's afraid to lie with her self, if she have but any masculine imaginations about her; I know when we are married, I must ravish her.

Meg. By my honour, that's a foul fault indeed, but time and your good help will wear it out Sir.

Pha. And for any other I see, excepting your dear self, dearest Lady, I had rather be Sir *Tim* the Schoolmaster, and leap a Dairy-maid.

Meg. Has your Grace seen the Court-star *Galatea*?

Pha. Out upon her; she's as cold of her favour as an apoplex: she sail'd by but now.

Meg. And how do you hold her wit Sir?

Pha. I hold her wit? The strength of all the Guard cannot hold it, if they were tied to it, she would blow 'em out of the Kingdom, they talk of *Jupiter*, he's but a squib cracker to her: (Look well about you, and you may find a tongue-bolt.) But speak sweet Lady, shall I be freely welcome?

Meg. Whither?

Pha. To your bed; if you mistrust my faith, you do me the unnoblest wrong.

Meg. I dare not Prince, I dare not.

Pha. Make your own conditions, my purse shall seal 'em, and what you dare imagine you can want, I'le furnish you withal: give two hours to your thoughts every morning about it. Come, I know you are bashful, speak in my ear, will you be mine? keep this, and with it me: soon I will visit you.

Meg. My Lord, my Chamber's most unsafe, but when 'tis night I'le find some means to slip into your lodging: till when—

Pha. Till when, this, and my heart go with thee.

[*Ex. several ways.*

Enter Galatea *from behind the hangings.*

Gal. Oh thou pernicious Petticoat Prince, are these your vertues? Well, if I do not lay a train to blow your sport up, I am no woman; and Lady Towsabel I'le fit you for't.

[*Exit* Gal.

Enter Arethusa *and a* Lady.

Are. Where's the boy?
La. Within Madam.
Are. Gave you him gold to buy him cloaths?
La. I did.
Are. And has he don't?
La. Yes Madam.
Are. 'Tis a pretty sad talking lad, is it not?
Askt you his name?
La. No Madam.

Enter Galatea.

Are. O you are welcome, what good news?
Gal. As good as any one can tell your Grace,
That saies she hath done that you would have wish'd.
Are. Hast thou discovered?
Gal. I have strained a point of modesty for you.
Are. I prethee how?
Gal. In listning after bawdery; I see, let a Lady live never so modestly, she shall be sure to find a lawful time, to harken after bawdery; your Prince, brave *Pharamond*, was so hot on't.
Are. With whom? (and place.
Gal. Why, with the Lady I suspect: I can tell the time
Are. O when, and where?
Gal. To night, his Lodging.
Are. Run thy self into the presence, mingle there again
With other Ladies, leave the rest to me:
If destiny (to whom we dare not say,
Why thou didst this) have not decreed it so
In lasting leaves (whose smallest Characters
Were never altered:) yet, this match shall break.
Where's the boy?
La. Here Madam.

Enter Bellario.

Are. Sir, you are sad to change your service, is't not so?
Bell. Madam, I have not chang'd; I wait on you,
To do him service.
Are. Thou disclaim'st in me;

Tell me thy name.
Bell. *Bellario.*
Are. Thou canst sing, and play?
Bell. If grief will give me leave, Madam, I can.
Are. Alas! what kind of grief can thy years know?
Hadst thou a curst master, when thou went'st to School?
Thou art not capable of other grief;
Thy brows and cheeks are smooth as waters be,
When no [b]reath troubles them: believe me boy,
Care seeks out wrinkled brows, and hollow eyes,
And builds himself caves to abide in them.
Come Sir, tell me truly, does your Lord love me?
Bell. Love Madam? I know not what it is.
Are. Canst thou know grief, and never yet knew'st love?
Thou art deceiv'd boy; does he speak of me
As if he wish'd me well?
Bell. If it be love,
To forget all respect of his own friends,
In thinking of your face; if it be love
To sit cross arm'd and sigh away the day,
Mingled with starts, crying your name as loud
And hastily, as men i'the streets do fire:
If it be love to weep himself away,
When he but hears of any Lady dead,
Or kill'd, because it might have been your chance;
If when he goes to rest (which will not be)
'Twixt every prayer he saies, to name you once
As others drop a bead, be to be in love;
Then Madam, I dare swear he loves you.
Are. O y'are a cunning boy, and taught to lie,
For your Lords credit; but thou knowest, a lie,
That bears this sound, is welcomer to me,
Than any truth that saies he loves me not.
Lead the way Boy: Do you attend me too;
'Tis thy Lords business hasts me thus; Away. [*Exeunt.*

Enter Dion, Cleremont, Thrasilin, Megra *and* Galatea.

Di. Come Ladies, shall we talk a round? As men
Do walk a mile, women should take an hour
After supper: 'Tis their exercise.

Gal. 'Tis late.
Meg. 'Tis all
My eyes will do to lead me to my bed.
Gal. I fear they are so heavy, you'l scarce find
The way to your lodging with 'em to night.

Enter Pharamond.

Thra. The Prince.
Pha. Not a bed Ladies? y'are good sitters up;
What think you of a pleasant dream to last
Till morning?
Meg. I should choose, my Lord, a pleasing wake before it.

Enter Arethusa *and* Bellario.

Are. 'Tis well my Lord y'are courting of Ladies.
Is't not late Gentlemen?
Cle. Yes Madam.
Are. Wait you there. [*Exit* Arethusa.
Meg. She's jealous, as I live; look you my Lord,
The Princess has a *Hilas*, an *Adonis*.
Pha. His form is Angel-like.
Meg. Why this is he, must, when you are wed,
Sit by your pillow, like young *Apollo*, with
His hand and voice, binding your thoughts in sleep;
The Princess does provide him for you, and for her self.
Pha. I find no musick in these boys.
Meg. Nor I.
They can do little, and that small they do,
They have not wit to hide.
Di. Serves he the Princess?
Thra. Yes.
Di. 'Tis a sweet boy, how brave she keeps him!
Pha. Ladies all good rest; I mean to kill a Buck
To morrow morning, ere y'ave done your dreams.
Meg. All happiness attend your Grace, Gentlemen good (rest,
Come shall we to bed?
Gal. Yes, all good night. [*Ex.* Gal. *and* Meg.
Di. May your dreams be true to you;
What shall we do Gallants? 'Tis late, the King

Is up still, see, he comes, a Guard along
With him.

Enter King, Arethusa *and* Guard.

King. Look your intelligence be true.
Are. Upon my life it is: and I do hope,
Your Highness will not tye me to a man,
That in the heat of wooing throws me off,
And takes another.
Di. What should this mean?
King. If it be true,
That Lady had been better have embrac'd
Cureless Diseases; get you to your rest, [*Ex.* Are. *and* Bel.
You shall be righted: Gentlemen draw near,
We shall imploy you: Is young *Pharamond*
Come to his lodging?
Di. I saw him enter there.
King. Haste some of you, and cunningly discover,
If *Megra* be in her lodging.
Cle. Sir,
She parted hence but now with other Ladies.
King. If she be there, we shall not need to make
A vain discovery of our suspicion.
You gods I see, that who unrighteously
Holds wealth or state from others, shall be curst,
In that, which meaner men are blest withall:
Ages to come shall know no male of him
Left to inherit, and his name shall be
Blotted from earth; If he have any child,
It shall be crossly matched: the gods themselves
Shall sow wild strife betwixt her Lord and her,
Yet, if it be your wills, forgive the sin
I have committed, let it not fall
Upon this understanding child of mine,
She has not broke your Laws; but how can I,
Look to be heard of gods, that must be just,
Praying upon the ground I hold by wrong?

Enter Dion.

Di. Sir, I have asked, and her women swear she is within,

but they I think are bawds; I told 'em I must speak with her: they laught, and said their Lady lay speechless. I said, my business was important; they said their Lady was about it: I grew hot, and cryed my business was a matter that concern'd life and death; they answered, so was sleeping, at which their Lady was; I urg'd again, she had scarce time to be so since last I saw her; they smil'd again, and seem'd to instruct me, that sleeping was nothing but lying down and winking: Answers more direct I could not get: in short Sir, I think she is not there.

King. 'Tis then no time to dally: you o'th' Guard,
Wait at the back door of the Princes lodging,
And see that none pass thence upon your lives.
Knock Gentlemen: knock loud: louder yet:
What, has their pleasure taken off their hearing?
I'le break your meditations: knock again:
Not yet? I do not think he sleeps, having this
Larum by him; once more, *Pharamond*, Prince.

Pharamond *above*.

Pha. What sawcy groom knocks at this dead of night?
Where be our waiters? By my vexed soul,
He meets his death, that meets me, for this boldness.

K. Prince, you wrong your thoughts, we are your friends,
Come down.

Pha. The King?

King. The same Sir, come down,
We have cause of present Counsel with you.

Pha. If your Grace please to use me, I'le attend you
To your Chamber. [Pha. *below*.

King. No, 'tis too late Prince, I'le make bold with yours.

Pha. I have some private reasons to my self,
Makes me unmannerly, and say you cannot;
Nay, press not forward Gentlemen, he must come
Through my life, that comes here.

King. Sir be resolv'd, I must and will come. Enter.

Pha. I will not be dishonour'd;
He that enters, enters upon his death;
Sir, 'tis a sign you make no stranger of me,
To bring these Renegados to my Chamber,

At these unseason'd hours.
King. Why do you
Chafe your self so? you are not wrong'd, nor shall be;
Onely I'le search your lodging, for some cause
To our self known: Enter I say.
Pha. I say no. [*Meg. Above.*
Meg. Let 'em enter Prince,
Let 'em enter, I am up, and ready; I know their business,
'Tis the poor breaking of a Ladies honour,
They hunt so hotly after; let 'em enjoy it.
You have your business Gentlemen, I lay here.
O my Lord the King, this is not noble in you
To make publick the weakness of a Woman.
King. Come down.
Meg. I dare my Lord; your whootings and your clamors,
Your private whispers, and your broad fleerings,
Can no more vex my soul, than this base carriage;
But I have vengeance yet in store for some,
Shall in the most contempt you can have of me,
Be joy and nourishment.
King. Will you come down?
Meg. Yes, to laugh at your worst: but I shall wrong you,
If my skill fail me not.
King. Sir, I must dearly chide you for this looseness,
You have wrong'd a worthy Lady; but no more,
Conduct him to my lodging, and to bed. (deed.
Cle. Get him another wench, and you bring him to bed in
Di. 'Tis strange a man cannot ride a Stagg
Or two, to breath himself, without a warrant:
If this geer hold, that lodgings be search'd thus,
Pray heaven we may lie with our own wives in safety,
That they be not by some trick of State mistaken.

Enter with Megra.

King. Now Lady of honour, where's your honour now?
No man can fit your palat, but the Prince.
Thou most ill shrowded rottenness; thou piece
Made by a Painter and a Pothecary;
Thou troubled sea of lust; thou wilderness,
Inhabited by wild thoughts; thou swoln cloud

Of Infection; thou ripe Mine of all Diseases;
Thou all Sin, all Hell, and last, all Devils, tell me,
Had you none to pull on with your courtesies,
But he that must be mine, and wrong my Daughter?
By all the gods, all these, and all the Pages,
And all the Court shall hoot thee through the Court,
Fling rotten Oranges, make ribald Rimes,
And sear thy name with Candles upon walls:
Do you laugh Lady *Venus*?

Meg. Faith Sir, you must pardon me;
I cannot chuse but laugh to see you merry.
If you do this, O King; nay, if you dare do it;
By all these gods you swore by, and as many
More of my own; I will have fellows, and such
Fellows in it, as shall make noble mirth;
The Princess, your dear Daughter, shall stand by me
On walls, and sung in ballads, any thing:
Urge me no more, I know her, and her haunts,
Her layes, leaps, and outlayes, and will discover all;
Nay will dishonour her. I know the boy
She keeps, a handsome boy; about eighteen:
Know what she does with him, where, and when.
Come Sir, you put me to a womans madness,
The glory of a fury; and if I do not
Do it to the height?

King. What boy is this she raves at?

Meg. Alas! good minded Prince, you know not these (things?
I am loth to reveal 'em. Keep this fault
As you would keep your health from the hot air
Of the corrupted people, or by heaven,
I will not fall alone: what I have known,
Shall be as publick as a print: all tongues
Shall speak it as they do the language they
Are born in, as free and commonly; I'le set it
Like a prodigious star for all to gaze at, (reign
And so high and glowing, that other Kingdoms far and For-
Shall read it there, nay travel with it, till they find
No tongue to make it more, nor no more people;
And then behold the fall of your fair Princess.

King. Has she a boy?

Cle. So please your Grace I have seen a boy wait
On her, a fair boy.
King. Go get you to your quarter:
For this time I'le study to forget you.
Meg. Do you study to forget me, and I'le study
To forget you. [*Ex.* King, Meg. *and* Guard.

Cle. Why here's a Male spirit for *Hercules*, if ever there be nine worthies of women, this wench shall ride astride, and be their Captain.

Di. Sure she hath a garrison of Devils in her tongue, she uttereth such balls of wild-fire. She has so netled the King, that all the Doctors in the Country will scarce cure him. That boy was a strange found out antidote to cure her infection: that boy, that Princess boy: that brave, chast, vertuous Ladies boy: and a fair boy, a well spoken boy: All these considered, can make nothing else—but there I leave you Gentlemen.

Thra. Nay we'l go wander with you. [*Exeunt.*

Actus Tertius. Scena Prima.

Enter Cle. Di. *and* Thra.

Cle. NAY doubtless 'tis true.
Di. I, and 'tis the gods
That rais'd this Punishment to scourge the King
With his own issue: Is it not a shame
For us, that should write noble in the land;
For us, that should be freemen, to behold
A man, that is the bravery of his age,
Philaster, prest down from his Royal right,
By this regardless King; and only look,
And see the Scepter ready to be cast
Into the hands of that lascivious Lady,
That lives in lust with a smooth boy, now to be
Married to yon strange Prince, who, but that people
Please to let him be a Prince, is born a slave,
In that which should be his most noble part,
His mind?
Thra. That man that would not stir with you,

To aid *Philaster*, let the gods forget,
That such a Creature walks upon the earth.
Cle. *Philaster* is too backward in't himself;
The Gentry do await it, and the people
Against their nature are all bent for him,
And like a field of standing Corn, that's mov'd
With a stiff gale, their heads bow all one way.
Di. The only cause that draws *Philaster* back
From this attempt, is the fair Princess love,
Which he admires and we can now confute.
Thra. Perhaps he'l not believe it.
Di. Why Gentlemen, 'tis without question so.
Cle. I 'tis past speech, she lives dishonestly.
But how shall we, if he be curious, work
Upon his faith?
Thra. We all are satisfied within our selves.
Di. Since it is true, and tends to his own good,
I'le make this new report to be my knowledge,
I'le say I know it, nay, I'le swear I saw it.
Cle. It will be best.
Thra. 'Twill move him.

Enter Philaster.

Di. Here he comes. Good morrow to your honour,
We have spent some time in seeking you.
Phi. My worthy friends,
You that can keep your memories to know
Your friend in miseries, and cannot frown
On men disgrac'd for vertue: A good day (tion?
Attend you all. What service may I do worthy your accepta-
Di. My good Lord,
We come to urge that vertue which we know
Lives in your breast, forth, rise, and make a head,
The Nobles, and the people are all dull'd
With this usurping King: and not a man
That ever heard the word, or knew such a thing
As vertue, but will second your attempts.
Phi. How honourable is this love in you
To me that have deserv'd none? Know my friends
(You that were born to shame your poor *Philaster*,

With too much courtesie) I could afford
To melt my self in thanks; but my designs
Are not yet ripe, suffice it, that ere long (would.
I shall imploy your loves: but yet the time is short of what I
Di. The time is fuller Sir, than you expect;
That which hereafter will not perhaps be reach'd
By violence, may now be caught; As for the King,
You know the people have long hated him;
But now the Princess, whom they lov'd.
Phi. Why, what of her?
Di. Is loath'd as much as he.
Phi. By what strange means?
Di. She's known a Whore.
Phi. Thou lyest.
Di. My Lord—
Phi. Thou lyest, [*Offers to draw and is held.*
And thou shalt feel it; I had thought thy mind
Had been of honour; thus to rob a Lady
Of her good name, is an infectious sin,
Not to be pardon'd; be it false as hell,
'Twill never be redeem'd, if it be sown
Amongst the people, fruitful to increase
All evil they shall hear. Let me alone,
That I may cut off falshood, whilst it springs.
Set hills on hills betwixt me and the man
That utters this, and I will scale them all,
And from the utmost top fall on his neck,
Like Thunder from a Cloud.
Di. This is most strange;
Sure he does love her.
Phi. I do love fair truth:
She is my Mistress, and who injures her,
Draws vengeance from me Sirs, let go my arms.
Thra. Nay, good my Lord be patient.
Cle. Sir, remember this is your honour'd friend,
That comes to do his service, and will shew you
Why he utter'd this.
Phi. I ask you pardon Sir,
My zeal to truth made me unmannerly:
Should I have heard dishonour spoke of you,

Behind your back untruly, I had been
As much distemper'd, and enrag'd as now.
Di. But this my Lord is truth.
Phi. O say not so, good Sir forbear to say so,
'Tis the truth that all womenkind is false;
Urge it no more, it is impossible;
Why should you think the Princess light?
Di. Why, she was taken at it.
Phi. 'Tis false, O Heaven 'tis false: it cannot be,
Can it? Speak Gentlemen, for love of truth speak;
Is't possible? can women all be damn'd?
Di. Why no, my Lord.
Phi. Why then it cannot be.
Di. And she was taken with her boy.
Phi. What boy?
Di. A Page, a boy that serves her.
Phi. Oh good gods, a little boy?
Di. I, know you him my Lord?
Phi. Hell and sin know him? Sir, you are deceiv'd;
I'le reason it a little coldly with you;
If she were lustful, would she take a boy,
That knows not yet desire? she would have one
Should meet her thoughts and knows the sin he acts,
Which is the great delight of wickedness;
You are abus'd, and so is she, and I.
Di. How you my Lord?
Phi. Why all the world's abus'd
In an unjust report.
Di. Oh noble Sir your vertues
Cannot look into the subtil thoughts of woman.
In short my Lord, I took them: I my self.
Phi. Now all the Devils thou didst flie from my rage,
Would thou hadst ta'ne devils ingendring plagues:
When thou didst take them, hide thee from my eyes,
Would thou hadst taken Thunder on thy breast,
When thou didst take them, or been strucken dumb
For ever: that this foul deed might have slept in silence.
Thra. Have you known him so ill temper'd?
Cle. Never before.
Phi. The winds that are let loose,

From the four several corners of the earth,
And spread themselves all over sea and land,
Kiss not a chaste one. What friend bears a sword
To run me through?

Di. Why, my Lord, are you so mov'd at this?

Phi. When any falls from vertue I am distract,
I have an interest in't.

Di. But good my Lord recal your self,
And think what's best to be done.

Phi. I thank you. I will do it;
Please you to leave me, I'le consider of it:
Tomorrow I will find your lodging forth,
And give you answer
The readiest way.

Di. All the gods direct you.

Thra. He was extream impatient.

Cle. It was his vertue and his noble mind.

[*Exeunt* Di. Cle. *and* Thra.

Phi. I had forgot to ask him where he took them,
I'le follow him. O that I had a sea
Within my breast, to quench the fire I feel;
More circumstances will but fan this fire;
It more afflicts me now, to know by whom
This deed is done, than simply that 'tis done:
And he that tells me this is honourable,
As far from lies, as she is far from truth.
O that like beasts, we could not grieve our selves,
With that we see not; Bulls and Rams will fight,
To keep their Females standing in their sight;
But take 'em from them, and you take at once
Their spleens away; and they will fall again
Unto their Pastures, growing fresh and fat,
And taste the waters of the springs as sweet,
As 'twas before, finding no start in sleep.
But miserable man; See, see you gods,

Enter Bellario.

He walks still; and the face you let him wear
When he was innocent, is still the same,
Not blasted; is this justice? Do you mean

To intrap mortality, that you allow
Treason so smooth a brow? I cannot now
Think he is guilty.

Bell. Health to you my Lord;
The Princess doth commend her love, her life,
And this unto you.

Phi. Oh *Bellario*,
Now I perceive she loves me, she does shew it
In loving thee my boy, she has made thee brave.

Bell. My Lord she has attired me past my wish,
Past my desert, more fit for her attendant,
Though far unfit for me, who do attend.

Phi. Thou art grown courtly boy. O let all women
That love black deeds, learn to dissemble here,
Here, by this paper she does write to me,
As if her heart were Mines of Adamant
To all the world besides, but unto me,
A maiden snow that melted with my looks.
Tell me my boy how doth the Princess use thee?
For I shall guess her love to me by that.

Bell. Scarce like her servant, but as if I were
Something allied to her; or had preserv'd
Her life three times by my fidelity.
As mothers fond do use their only sons;
As I'de use one, that's left unto my trust,
For whom my life should pay, if he met harm,
So she does use me.

Phi. Why, this is wondrous well:
But what kind language does she feed thee with?

Bell. Why, she does tell me, she will trust my youth
With all her loving secrets; and does call me
Her pretty servant, bids me weep no more
For leaving you: shee'l see my services
Regarded; and such words of that soft strain,
That I am nearer weeping when she ends
Than ere she spake.

Phi. This is much better still.

Bell. Are you ill my Lord?

Phi. Ill? No *Bellario*.

Bell. Me thinks your words

Fall not from off your tongue so evenly,
Nor is there in your looks that quietness,
That I was wont to see.
Phi. Thou art deceiv'd boy:
And she stroakes thy head?
Bell. Yes.
Phi. And she does clap thy cheeks?
Bell. She does my Lord.
Phi. And she does kiss thee boy? ha!
Bell. How my Lord?
Phi. She kisses thee?
Bell. Not so my Lord.
Phi. Come, come, I know she does.
Bell. No by my life.
Phi. Why then she does not love me; come, she does,
I bad her do it; I charg'd her by all charms
Of love between us, by the hope of peace
We should enjoy, to yield thee all delights
Naked, as to her bed: I took her oath
Thou should'st enjoy her: Tell me gentle boy,
Is she not paralleless? Is not her breath
Sweet as *Arabian* winds, when fruits are ripe?
Are not her breasts two liquid Ivory balls?
Is she not all a lasting Mine of joy?
Bell. I, now I see why my disturbed thoughts
Were so perplext. When first I went to her,
My heart held augury; you are abus'd,
Some villain has abus'd you; I do see
Whereto you tend; fall Rocks upon his head,
That put this to you; 'tis some subtil train,
To bring that noble frame of yours to nought.
Phi. Thou think'st I will be angry with thee; Come
Thou shalt know all my drift, I hate her more,
Than I love happiness, and plac'd thee there,
To pry with narrow eyes into her deeds;
Hast thou discover'd? Is she faln to lust,
As I would wish her? Speak some comfort to me.
Bell. My Lord, you did mistake the boy you sent:
Had she the lust of Sparrows, or of Goats;
Had she a sin that way, hid from the world,

Beyond the name of lust, I would not aid
Her base desires; but what I came to know
As servant to her, I would not reveal, to make my life last ages.
Phi. Oh my heart; this is a salve worse than the main (disease.
Tell me thy thoughts; for I will know the least
That dwells within thee, or will rip thy heart
To know it; I will see thy thoughts as plain,
As I do know thy face.
Bell. Why, so you do.
She is (for ought I know) by all the gods,
As chaste as Ice; but were she foul as Hell
And I did know it, thus; the breath of Kings,
The points of Swords, Tortures nor Bulls of Brass,
Should draw it from me.
Phi. Then 'tis no time to dally with thee;
I will take thy life, for I do hate thee; I could curse thee now.
Bell. If you do hate you could not curse me worse;
The gods have not a punishment in store
Greater for me, than is your hate.
Phi. Fie, fie, so young and so dissembling;
Tell me when and where thou di[d]st enjoy her,
Or let plagues fall on me, if I destroy thee not.
Bell. Heaven knows I never did: and when I lie
To save my life, may I live long and loath'd.
Hew me asunder, and whilst I can think
I'le love those pieces you have cut away,
Better than those that grow: and kiss these limbs,
Because you made 'em so.
Phi. Fearest thou not death?
Can boys contemn that?
Bell. Oh, what boy is he
Can be content to live to be a man (reason?
That sees the best of men thus passionate, thus without
Phi. Oh, but thou dost not know what 'tis to die.
Bell. Yes, I do know my Lord;
'Tis less than to be born; a lasting sleep,
A quiet resting from all jealousie;
A thing we all pursue; I know besides,
It is but giving over of a game that must be lost.
Phi. But there are pains, false boy,

For perjur'd souls; think but on these, and then
Thy heart will melt, and thou wilt utter all.
Bell. May they fall all upon me whilst I live,
If I be perjur'd, or have ever thought
Of that you charge me with; if I be false,
Send me to suffer in those punishments you speak of; kill me.
Phi. Oh, what should I do?
Why, who can but believe him? He does swear
So earnestly, that if it were not true,
The gods would not endure him. Rise *Bellario*,
Thy protestations are so deep; and thou
Dost look so truly, when thou utterest them,
That though I [know] 'em false, as were my hopes,
I cannot urge thee further; but thou wert
To blame to injure me, for I must love
Thy honest looks, and take no revenge upon
Thy tender youth; A love from me to thee
Is firm, what ere thou dost: It troubles me
That I have call'd the blood out of thy cheeks,
That did so well become thee: but good boy
Let me not see thee more; something is done,
That will distract me, that will make me mad,
If I behold thee: if thou tender'st me,
Let me not see thee.
Bell. I will fly as far
As there is morning, ere I give distaste
To that most honour'd mind. But through these tears
Shed at my hopeless parting, I can see
A world of Treason practis'd upon you,
And her and me. Farewel for evermore;
If you shall hear, that sorrow struck me dead,
And after find me Loyal, let there be
A tear shed from you in my memorie,
And I shall rest at peace. [*Exit* Bel.
Phi. Blessing be with thee,
What ever thou deserv'st. Oh, where shall I
Go bath thy body? Nature too unkind,
That made no medicine for a troubled mind! [*Ex.* Phi.

Enter Arethuse.

Are. I marvel my boy comes not back again;
But that I know my love will question him
Over and over; how I slept, wak'd, talk'd;
How I remembred him when his dear name
Was last spoke, and how, when I sigh'd, wept, sung,
And ten thousand such; I should be angry at his stay.

Enter King.

King. What are your meditations? who attends you?
Are. None but my single self, I need no Guard,
I do no wrong, nor fear none.
King. Tell me: have you not a boy?
Are. Yes Sir.
King. What kind of boy?
Are. A Page, a waiting boy.
King. A handsome boy?
Are. I think he be not ugly:
Well qualified, and dutiful, I know him,
I took him not for beauty.
King. He speaks, and sings and plays?
Are. Yes Sir.
King. About Eighteen?
Are. I never ask'd his age.
King. Is he full of service?
Are. By your pardon why do you ask?
King. Put him away.
Are. Sir?
King. Put him away, h'as done you that good service,
Shames me to speak of.
Are. Good Sir let me understand you.
King. If you fear me, shew it in duty; put away that boy.
Are. Let me have reason for it Sir, and then
Your will is my command.
King. Do not you blush to ask it? Cast him off,
Or I shall do the same to you. Y'are one
Shame with me, and so near unto my self,
That by my life, I dare not tell my self,
What you, my self have done.

Are. What have I done my Lord?
King. 'Tis a new language, that all love to learn,
The common people speak it well already,
They need no Grammer; understand me well,
There be foul whispers stirring; cast him off!
And suddenly do it: Farewel. [*Exit* King.
Are. Where may a Maiden live securely free,
Keeping her Honour safe? Not with the living,
They feed upon opinions, errours, dreams,
And make 'em truths: they draw a nourishment
Out of defamings, grow upon disgraces,
And when they see a vertue fortified
Strongly above the battery of their tongues;
Oh, how they cast to sink it; and defeated
(Soul sick with Poyson) strike the Monuments
Where noble names lie sleeping: till they sweat,
And the cold Marble melt.

Enter Philaster.

Phi. Peace to your fairest thoughts, dearest Mistress.
Are. Oh, my dearest servant I have a War within me.
Phi. He must be more than man, that makes these Crystals
Run into Rivers; sweetest fair, the cause;
And as I am your slave, tied to your goodness,
Your creature made again from what I was,
And newly spirited, I'le right your honours.
Are. Oh, my best love; that boy!
Phi. What boy?
Are. The pretty boy you gave me.
Phi. What of him?
Are. Must be no more mine.
Phi. Why?
Are. They are jealous of him.
Phi. Jealous, who?
Are. The King.
Phi. Oh, my fortune,
Then 'tis no idle jealousie. Let him go.
Are. Oh cruel, are you hard hearted too?
Who shall now tell you, how much I lov'd you;
Who shall swear it to you, and weep the tears I send?

Who shall now bring you Letters, Rings, Bracelets,
Lose his health in service? wake tedious nights
In stories of your praise? Who shall sing
Your crying Elegies? And strike a sad soul
Into senseless Pictures, and make them mourn?
Who shall take up his Lute, and touch it, till
He crown a silent sleep upon my eye-lid,
Making me dream and cry, Oh my dear, dear *Philaster*.

Phi. Oh my heart!
Would he had broken thee, that made thee know
This Lady was not Loyal. Mistress, forget
The boy, I'le get thee á far better.

Are. Oh never, never such a boy again, as my *Bellario*.

[*Phi.*] 'Tis but your fond affection.

Are. With thee my boy, farewel for ever,
All secrecy in servants: farewel faith,
And all desire to do well for it self:
Let all that shall succeed thee, for thy wrongs,
Sell and betray chast love.

Phi. And all this passion for a boy?

Are. He was your boy, and you put him to me,
And the loss of such must have a mourning for.

Phi. O thou forgetful woman!

Are. How, my Lord?

Phi. False *Arethusa*!
Hast thou a Medicine to restore my wits,
When I have lost 'em? If not, leave to talk, and do thus.

Are. Do what Sir? would you sleep?

Phi. For ever *Arethusa*. Oh you gods,
Give me a worthy patience; Have I stood
Naked, alone the shock of many fortunes?
Have I seen mischiefs numberless, and mighty
Grow li[k]e a sea upon me? Have I taken
Danger as stern as death into my bosom,
And laught upon it, made it but a mirth,
And flung it by? Do I live now like him,
Under this Tyrant King, that languishing
Hears his sad Bell, and sees his Mourners? Do I
Bear all this bravely, and must sink at length
Under a womans falshood? Oh that boy,

That cursed boy? None but a villain boy, to ease your lust?
Are. Nay, then I am betray'd,
I feel the plot cast for my overthrow; Oh I am wretched.
Phi. Now you may take that little right I have
To this poor Kingdom; give it to your Joy,
For I have no joy in it. Some far place,
Where never womankind durst set her foot,
For bursting with her poisons, must I seek,
And live to curse you;
There dig a Cave, and preach to birds and beasts,
What woman is, and help to save them from you.
How heaven is in your eyes, but in your hearts,
More hell than hell has; how your tongues like Scorpions,
Both heal and poyson; how your thoughts are woven
With thousand changes in one subtle webb,
And worn so by you. How that foolish man,
That reads the story of a womans face,
And dies believing it, is lost for ever.
How all the good you have, is but a shadow,
I'th' morning with you, and at night behind you,
Past and forgotten. How your vows are frosts,
Fast for a night, and with the next sun gone.
How you are, being taken all together,
A meer confusion, and so dead a *Chaos*,
That love cannot distinguish. These sad Texts
Till my last hour, I am bound to utter of you.
So farewel all my wo, all my delight. [*Exit* Phi.
Are. Be merciful ye gods and strike me dead;
What way have I deserv'd this? make my breast
Transparent as pure Crystal, that the world
Jealous of me, may see the foulest thought
My heart holds. Where shall a woman turn her eyes,
To find out constancy? Save me, how black, [*Enter* Bell.
And guilty (me thinks) that boy looks now?
Oh thou dissembler, that before thou spak'st
Wert in thy cradle false? sent to make lies,
And betray Innocents; thy Lord and thou,
May glory in the ashes of a Maid
Fool'd by her passion; but the conquest is
Nothing so great as wicked. Fly away,

Let my command force thee to that, which shame
Would do without it. If thou understoodst
The loathed Office thou hast undergone,
Why, thou wouldst hide thee under heaps of hills,
Lest men should dig and find thee.

Bell. Oh what God
Angry with men, hath sent this strange disease
Into the noblest minds? Madam this grief
You add unto me is no more than drops
To seas, for which they are not seen to swell;
My Lord had struck his anger through my heart,
And let out all the hope of future joyes,
You need not bid me fly, I came to part,
To take my latest leave, Farewel for ever;
I durst not run away in honesty,
From such a Lady, like a boy that stole,
Or made some grievous fault; the power of gods
Assist you in your sufferings; hasty time
Reveal the truth to your abused Lord,
And mine: That he may know your worth: whilst I
Go seek out some forgotten place to die. [*Exit* Bell.

Are. Peace guide thee, th'ast overthrown me once,
Yet if I had another *Troy* to lose,
Thou or another villain with thy looks,
Might talk me out of it, and send me naked,
My hair dishevel'd through the fiery streets.

Enter a Lady.

La. Madam, the King would hunt, and calls for you
With earnestness.

Are. I am in tune to hunt!
Diana if thou canst rage with a maid,
As with a man, let me discover thee
Bathing, and turn me to a fearful Hind,
That I may die pursu'd by cruel Hounds,
And have my story written in my wounds. [*Exeunt.*

Actus Quartus. Scena Prima.

Enter King, Pharamond, Arethusa, Galatea, Megra, Dion, Cleremont, Thrasilin, *and Attendants.*

K. WHat, are the Hounds before, and all the woodmen?
Our horses ready, and our bows bent?

Di. All Sir.

King. Y'are cloudy Sir, come we have forgotten
Your venial trespass, let not that sit heavy
Upon your spirit; none dare utter it.

Di. He looks like an old surfeited Stallion after his leaping, dull as a Dormouse: see how he sinks; the wench has shot him between wind and water, and I hope sprung a leak.

Thra. He needs no teaching, he strikes sure enough; his greatest fault is, he Hunts too much in the Purlues, would he would leave off Poaching.

Di. And for his horn, has left it at the Lodge where he lay late; Oh, he's a precious Lime-hound; turn him loose upon the pursuit of a Lady, and if he lose her, hang him up i'th' slip. When my Fox-bitch Beauty grows proud, I'le borrow him.

King. Is your Boy turn'd away?

Are. You did command Sir, and I obey you.

King. 'Tis well done: Hark ye further.

Cle. Is't possible this fellow should repent? Me thinks that were not noble in him: and yet he looks like a mortified member, as if he had a sick mans Salve in's mouth. If a worse man had done this fault now, some Physical Justice or other, would presently (without the help of an Almanack) have opened the obstructions of his Liver, and let him bloud with a Dog-whip.

Di. See, see, how modestly your Lady looks, as if she came from Churching with her Neighbour; why, what a Devil can a man see in her face, but that she's honest?

Pha. Troth no great matter to speak of, a foolish twinkling with the eye, that spoils her Coat; but he must be a cunning Herald that finds it.

Di. See how they Muster one another! O there's a Rank Regiment where the Devil carries the Colours, and his Dam

Drum major, now the world and the flesh come behind with the Carriage.

Cle. Sure this Lady has a good turn done her against her will: before she was common talk, now none dare say, Cantharides can stir her, her face looks like a Warrant, willing and commanding all Tongues, as they will answer it, to be tied up and bolted when this Lady means to let her self loose. As I live she has got her a goodly protection, and a gracious; and may use her body discreetly, for her healths sake, once a week, excepting Lent and Dog-days: Oh if they were to be got for mony, what a great sum would come out of the City for these Licences?

King. To horse, to horse, we lose the morning, Gentlemen. [*Exeunt.*

Enter two Woodmen.

1 *Wood.* What, have you lodged the Deer?

2 *Wood.* Yes, they are ready for the Bow.

1 *Wood.* Who shoots?

2 *Wood.* The Princess.

1 *Wood.* No she'l Hunt.

2 *Wood.* She'l take a Stand I say.

1 *Wood.* Who else?

2 *Wood.* Why the young stranger Prince.

1 *Wood.* He shall Shoot in a Stone-bow for me. I never lov'd his beyond-sea-ship, since he forsook the Say, for paying Ten shillings: he was there at the fall of a Deer, and would needs (out of his mightiness) give Ten groats for the Dowcers; marry the Steward would have had the Velvet-head into the bargain, to Turf his Hat withal: I think he should love Venery, he is an old Sir *Tristram*; for if you be remembred, he forsook the Stagg once, to strike a Rascal Milking in a Medow, and her he kill'd in the eye. Who shoots else?

2 *Wood.* The Lady *Galatea.*

1 *Wood.* That's a good wench, and she would not chide us for tumbling of her women in the Brakes. She's liberal, and by my Bow they say she's honest, and whether that be a fault, I have nothing to do. There's all?

2 *Wood.* No, one more, *Megra.*

1 *Wood.* That's a firker I' faith boy; there's a wench will Ride her Haunces as hard after a Kennel of Hounds, as a Hunting-saddle; and when she comes home, get 'em clapt, and all is well again. I have known her lose her self three times in one Afternoon (if the Woods had been answerable) and it has been work enough for one man to find her, and he has sweat for it. She Rides well, and she payes well. Hark, let's go. [*Exeunt.*

Enter Philaster.

Phi. Oh, that I had been nourished in these woods
With Milk of Goats, and Acorns, and not known
The right of Crowns, nor the dissembling Trains
Of Womens looks; but dig'd my self a Cave,
Where I, my Fire, my Cattel, and my Bed
Might have been shut together in one shed;
And then had taken me some Mountain Girl,
Beaten with Winds, chast as the hardened Rocks
Whereon she dwells; that might have strewed my Bed
With leaves, and Reeds, and with the Skins of beasts
Our Neighbours; and have born at her big breasts
My large course issue. This had been a life free from vexation.

Enter Bellario.

Bell. Oh wicked men!
An innocent man may walk safe among beasts,
Nothing assaults me here. See, my griev'd Lord
Sits as his soul were searching out a way,
To leave his body. Pardon me that must
Break thy last commandment; For I must speak;
You that are griev'd can pity; hear my Lord.
Phi. Is there a Creature yet so miserable,
That I can pity?
Bell. Oh my Noble Lord,
View my strange fortune, and bestow on me,
According to your bounty (if my service
Can merit nothing) so much as may serve
To keep that little piece I hold of life
From cold and hunger.
Phi. Is it thou? be gone:

Go sell those misbeseeming Cloaths thou wear'st,
And feed thy self with them.

Bell. Alas! my Lord, I can get nothing for them:
The silly Country people think 'tis Treason
To touch such gay things.

Phi. Now by my life this is
Unkindly done, to vex me with thy sight,
Th'art faln again to thy dissembling trade:
How should'st thou think to cozen me again?
Remains there yet a plague untri'd for me?
Even so thou wept'st and spok'st when first
I took thee up; curse on the time. If thy
Commanding tears can work on any other,
Use thy art, I'le not betray it. Which way
Wilt thou take, that I may shun thee;
For thine eyes are poyson to mine; and I
Am loth to grow in rage. This way, or that way?

Bell. Any will serve. But I will chuse to have
That path in chase that leads unto my grave.

[*Exeunt* Phil. *and* Bell. *severally.*

Enter Dion *and the* Woodmen.

Di. This is the strangest sudden change! You *Woodman.*

1 *Wood.* My Lord *Dion.*

Di. Saw you a Lady come this way on a Sable-horse stubbed with stars of white?

2 *Wood.* Was she not young and tall?

Di. Yes; Rode she to the wood, or to the plain?

2 *Wood.* Faith my Lord we saw none. [*Exeunt* Wood.

Enter Cleremont.

Di. Pox of your questions then. What, is she found?

Cle. Nor will be I think.

Di. Let him seek his Daughter himself; she cannot stray about a little necessary natural business, but the whole Court must be in Arms; when she has done, we shall have peace.

Cle. There's already a thousand fatherless tales amongst us; some say her Horse run away with her; some a Wolf pursued her; others, it was a plot to kill her; and that Armed men were seen in the Wood: but questionless, she rode away willingly.

Enter King, *and* Thrasiline.

King. Where is she?
Cle. Sir, I cannot tell.
King. How is that? Answer me so again.
Cle. Sir, shall I lie?
King. Yes, lie and damn, rather than tell me that;
I say again, where is she? Mutter not;
Sir, speak you where is she?
Di. Sir, I do not know.
King. Speak that again so boldly, and by Heaven
It is thy last. You fellows answer me,
Where is she? Mark me all, I am your King.
I wish to see my Daughter, shew her me;
I do command you all, as you are subjects,
To shew her me, what am I not your King?
If I, then am I not to be obeyed?
Di. Yes, if you command things possible and honest.
King. Things possible and honest! Hear me, thou,
Thou Traytor, that darest confine thy King to things
Possible and honest; shew her me,
Or let me perish, if I cover not all *Cicily* with bloud.
Di. Indeed I cannot, unless you tell me where she is.
King. You have betray'd me, y'have, let me lose
The Jewel of my life, go; bring her me,
And set her before me; 'tis the King —
Will have it so, whose breath can still the winds,
Uncloud the Sun, charm down the swelling Sea,
And stop the Flouds of Heaven; speak, can it not?
Di. No.
King. No, cannot the breath of Kings do this?
Di. No; nor smell sweet it self, if once the Lungs
Be but corrupted.
King. Is it so? Take heed.
Di. Sir, take you heed; how you dare the powers
That must be just.
King. Alas! what are we Kings?
Why do you gods place us above the rest;

To be serv'd, flatter'd, and ador'd till we
Believe we hold within our hands your Thunder,
And when we come to try the power we have,
There's not a leaf shakes at our threatnings.
I have sin'd 'tis true, and here stand to be punish'd;
Yet would not thus be punish'd; let me chuse
My way, and lay it on.

Di. He Articles with the gods; would some body would draw bonds, for the performance of Covenants betwixt them.

Enter Pha. Galatea, *and* Megra.

King. What, is she found?

Pha. No, we have ta'ne her Horse.
He gallopt empty by: there's some Treason;
You *Galatea* rode with her into the wood; why left you her?

Gal. She did command me.

King. Command! you should not.

Gal. 'Twould ill become my Fortunes and my Birth
To disobey the Daughter of my King.

King. Y'are all cunning to obey us for our hurt,
But I will have her.

Pha. If I have her not,
By this hand there shall be no more *Cicily*.

Di. What will he carry it to *Spain* in's pocket?

Pha. I will not leave one man alive, but the King,
A Cook and a Taylor.

Di. Yet you may do well to spare your Ladies Bed-fellow, and her you may keep for a Spawner.

King. I see the injuries I have done must be reveng'd.

Di. Sir, this is not the way to find her out.

King. Run all, disperse your selves: the man that finds her,
Or (if she be kill'd) the Traytor; I'le [make] him great.

Di. I know some would give five thousand pounds to find her.

Pha. Come let us seek.

King. Each man a several way, here I my self.

Di. Come Gentlemen we here.

Cle. Lady you must go search too.

Meg. I had rather be search'd my self. [*Exeunt omnes.*

Enter Arethusa.

Are. Where am I now? Feet find me out a way,

Without the counsel of my troubled head,
I'le follow you boldly about these woods,
O're mountains, thorow brambles, pits, and flouds:
Heaven I hope will ease me. I am sick.

Enter Bellario.

Bell. Yonder's my Lady; Heaven knows I want nothing;
Because I do not wish to live, yet I
Will try her Charity. Oh hear, you that have plenty,
From that flowing store, drop some on dry ground; see,
The lively red is gone to guard her heart;
I fear she faints. Madam look up, she breaths not;
Open once more those rosie twins, and send
Unto my Lord, your latest farewell; Oh, she stirs:
How is it Madam? Speak comfort.
Are. 'Tis not gently done,
To put me in a miserable life,
And hold me there; I pray thee let me go,
I shall do best without thee; I am well.

Enter Philaster.

Phil. I am to blame to be so much in rage,
I'le tell her coolely, when and where I heard
This killing truth. I will be temperate
In speaking, and as just in hearing.
Oh monstrous! Tempt me not ye gods, good gods
Tempt not a frail man, what's he, that has a heart
But he must ease it here?
Bell. My Lord, help the Princess.
Are. I am well, forbear.
Phi. Let me love lightning, let me be embrac'd
And kist by Scorpions, or adore the eyes
Of Basilisks, rather than trust to tongues,
And shrink these veins up; stick me here a stone
Lasting to ages in the memory
Of this damn'd act. Hear me you wicked ones,
You have put the hills on fire into this breast,
Not to be quench'd with tears, for which may guilt
Sit on your bosoms; at your meals, and beds,
Despair await you: what, before my face?

Poyson of Aspes between your lips; Diseases
Be your best issues; Nature make a Curse
And throw it on you.
Are. Dear *Philaster*, leave
To be enrag'd, and hear me.
Phi. I have done;
Forgive my passion, not the calm'd sea,
When *Æolus* locks up his windy brood,
Is less disturb'd than I, I'le make you know it.
Dear *Arethusa*, do but take this sword,
And search how temperate a heart I have;
Then you and this your boy, may live and raign
In lust without control; Wilt thou *Bellario*?
I prethee kill me; thou art poor, and maist
Nourish ambitious thoughts, when I am dead:
This way were freer; Am I raging now?
If I were mad I should desire to live;
Sirs, feel my pulse; whether have you known
A man in a more equal tune to die?
Bel. Alas my Lord, your pulse keeps madmans time,
So does your tongue.
Phi. You will not kill me then?
Are. Kill you?
Bell. Not for a world.
[*Phi.*] I blame not thee,
Bellario; thou hast done but that, which gods
Would have transform'd themselves to do; be gone,
Leave me without reply; this is the last
Of all our meeting. Kill me with this sword;
Be wise, or worse will follow: we are two
Earth cannot bear at once. Resolve to do, or suffer.
Are. If my fortunes be so good to let me fall
Upon thy hand, I shall have peace in death.
Yet tell me this, will there be no slanders,
No jealousies in the other world, no ill there?
Phi. No.
Are. Shew me then the way.
Phi. Then guide
My feeble hand, you that have power to do it,
For I must perform a piece of justice. If your youth

Have any way offended Heaven, let prayers
Short and effectual reconcile you to it.

Are. I am prepared.

Enter a Country-fellow.

Coun. I'le see the King if he be in the Forest, I have hunted him these two hours; if I should come home and not see him my Sisters would laugh at me; I can see nothing but people better horst than my self, that outride me; I can hear nothing but shouting. These Kings had need of good brains, this whooping is able to put a mean man out of his wits. There's a Courtier with his sword drawn, by this hand upon a woman, I think.

Phi. Are you at peace?

Are. With Heavens and Earth.

Phi. May they divide thy soul and body?

Coun. Hold dastard, strike a Woman! th'art a craven I warrant thee, thou wouldst be loth to play half a dozen of venies at wasters with a good fellow for a broken head.

Phi. Leave us good friend.

Are. What ill bred man art thou, to intrude thy self
Upon our private sports, our recreations?

Coun. God 'uds, I understand you not, but I know the Rogue has hurt you.

Phi. Pursue thy own affairs: it will be ill (to.
To multiply bloud upon my head; which thou wilt force me

Coun. I know not your Rhetorick, but I can lay it on if you touch the woman. [*They fight.*

Phi. Slave, take what thou deservest.

Are. Heavens guard my Lord.

Coun. Oh do you breath?

Phi. I hear the tread of people: I am hurt.
The gods take part against me, could this Boor
Have held me thus else? I must shift for life,
Though I do loath it. I would find a course,
To lose it, rather by my will than force. [*Exit* Phil.

Coun. I cannot follow the Rogue. I pray thee wench come and kiss me now.

Enter Phara. Dion, Cle. Thra. *and* Woodmen.

Pha. What art thou?

Coun. Almost kil'd I am for a foolish woman; a knave has hurt her. (Madam?

Pha. The Princess Gentlemen! Where's the wound Is it dangerous?

Are. He has not hurt me.

Coun. I'faith she lies, has hurt her in the breast, look else.

Pha. O sacred spring of innocent blood!

Di. 'Tis above wonder! who should dare this?

Are. I felt it not.

Pha. Speak villain, who has hurt the Princess?

Coun. Is it the Princess?

Di. I.

Coun. Then I have seen something yet.

Pha. But who has hurt her?

Coun. I told you a Rogue I ne're saw him before, I.

Pha. Madam who did it?

Are. Some dishonest wretch, Alas I know him not,
And do forgive him.

Coun. He's hurt too, he cannot go far, I made my Fathers old Fox flie about his ears.

Pha. How will you have me kill him?

Are. Not at all, 'tis some distracted fellow.

Pha. By this hand, I'le leave ne'er a piece of him bigger than a Nut, and bring him all in my Hat.

Are. Nay, good Sir;
If you do take him, bring him quick to me,
And I will study for a punishment,
Great as his fault.

Pha. I will.

Are. But swear.

Pha. By all my love I will: Woodmen conduct the Princess to the King, and bear that wounded fellow to dressing: Come Gentlemen, we'l follow the chase close.

[*Ex.* Are. Pha. Di. Cle. Thra. *and* 1 Woodman.

Coun. I pray you friend let me see the King.

2 *Wood.* That you shall, and receive thanks. [*Exeunt.*

Coun. If I get clear with this, I'le go see no more gay sights.

Enter Bellario.

Bell. A heaviness near death sits on my brow,

And I must sleep: Bear me thou gentle bank,
For ever if thou wilt: you sweet ones all,
Let me unworthy press you: I could wish
I rather were a Coarse strewed o're with you,
Than quick above you. Dulness shuts mine eyes,
And I am giddy; Oh that I could take
So sound a sleep, that I might never wake.

Enter Philaster.

Phi. I have done ill, my conscience calls me false,
To strike at her, that would not strike at me:
When I did fight, me thought I heard her pray
The gods to guard me. She may be abus'd,
And I a loathed villain: if she be,
She will conceal who hurt her; He has wounds,
And cannot follow, neither knows he me.
Who's this; *Bellario* sleeping? If thou beest
Guilty, there is no justice that thy sleep [*Cry within.*
Should be so sound, and mine, whom thou hast wrong'd,
So broken: Hark I am pursued: you gods
I'le take this offer'd means of my escape:
They have no mark to know me, but my wounds,
If she be true; if false, let mischief light
On all the world at once. Sword, print my wounds
Upon this sleeping boy: I ha' none I think
Are mortal, nor would I lay greater on thee. [*Wounds him.*
Bell. Oh death I hope is come, blest be that hand,
It meant me well; again, for pities sake.
Phi. I have caught my self, [Phi. *falls.*
The loss of bloud hath stayed my flight. Here, here,
Is he that stroke thee: take thy full revenge,
Use me, as I did mean thee, worse than death:
I'le teach thee to revenge this luckless hand
Wounded the Princess, tell my followers
Thou didst receive these hurts in staying me,
And I will second thee: Get a reward.
Bell. Fly, fly my Lord and save your self.
Phi. How's this?
Wouldst thou I should be safe?
Bell. Else it were vain

For me to live. These little wounds I have,
Ha' not bled much, reach me that noble hand,
I'le help to cover you.

Phi. Art thou true to me?

Bell. Or let me perish loath'd. Come my good Lord,
Creep in amongst those bushes: who does know
But that the gods may save your (much lov'd) breath?

Phi. Then I shall die for grief, if not for this,
That I have wounded thee: what wilt thou do?

Bell. Shift for my self well: peace, I hear 'em come.

Within. Follow, follow, follow; that way they went.

Bell. With my own wounds I'le bloudy my own sword.
I need not counterfeit to fall; Heaven knows,
That I can stand no longer.

Enter Pha. Dion, Cle. *and* Thra.

Pha. To this place we have tract him by his bloud.

Cle. Yonder, my Lord, creeps one away.

Di. Stay Sir, what are you?

Bell. A wretched creature wounded in these Woods
By Beasts; relieve me, if your names be men,
Or I shall perish.

Di. This is he my Lord,
Upon my soul that hurt her; 'tis the boy,
That wicked boy that serv'd her.

Pha. O thou damn'd in thy creation!
What cause could'st thou shape to hurt the Princess?

Bell. Then I am betrayed.

Di. Betrayed! no, apprehended.

Bell. I confess;
Urge it no more, that big with evil thoughts
I set upon her, and did take my aim
Her death. For charity let fall at once
The punishment you mean, and do not load
This weary flesh with tortures.

Pha. I will know who hir'd thee to this deed?

Bell. Mine own revenge.

Pha. Revenge, for what?

Bell. It pleas'd her to receive
Me as her Page, and when my fortunes ebb'd,

That men strid o're them carelesly, she did showr
Her welcome graces on me, and did swell
My fortunes, till they overflow'd their banks,
Threatning the men that crost 'em; when as swift
As storms arise at sea, she turn'd her eyes
To burning Suns upon me, and did dry
The streams she had bestowed, leaving me worse
And more contemn'd than other little brooks,
Because I had been great: In short, I knew
I could not live, and therefore did desire
To die reveng'd.
Pha. If tortures can be found,
Long as thy natural life, resolve to feel
The utmost rigour. [Philaster *creeps out of a bush.*
Cle. Help to lead him hence.
Phi. Turn back you ravishers of Innocence,
Know ye the price of that you bear away so rudely?
Pha. Who's that?
Di. 'Tis the Lord *Philaster.*
Phi. 'Tis not the treasure of all Kings in one,
The wealth of *Tagus*, nor the Rocks of Pearl,
That pave the Court of *Neptune*, can weigh down
That vertue. It was I that hurt the Princess.
Place me, some god, upon a *Piramis*,
Higher than hills of earth, and lend a voice
Loud as your Thunder to me, that from thence,
I may discourse to all the under-world,
The worth that dwells in him.
Pha. How's this?
Bell. My Lord, some man
Weary of life, that would be glad to die.
Phi. Leave these untimely courtesies *Bellario.*
Bell. Alas he's mad, come will you lead me on?
Phi. By all the Oaths that men ought most to keep:
And Gods do punish most, when men do break,
He toucht her not. Take heed *Bellario*,
How thou dost drown the vertues thou hast shown
With perjury. By all that's good 'twas I:
You know she stood betwixt me and my right.
Pha. Thy own tongue be thy judge.

Cle. It was *Philaster.*
Di. Is't not a brave boy?
Well Sirs, I fear we were all deceived.
Phi. Have I no friend here?
Di. Yes.
Phi. Then shew it;
Some good body lend a hand to draw us nearer.
Would you have tears shed for you when you die?
Then lay me gentle on his neck that there
I may weep flouds, and breath out my spirit:
'Tis not the wealth of *Plutus*, nor the gold
Lockt in the heart of earth, can buy away
This arm-full from me, this had been a ransom
To have redeem'd the great *Augustus Cæsar*,
Had he been taken: you hard-hearted men,
More stony than these Mountains, can you see
Such clear pure bloud drop, and not cut your flesh
To stop his life? To bind whose better wounds,
Queens ought to tear their hair, and with their tears, (*laster.*
Bath 'em. Forgive me, thou that art the wealth of poor *Phi-*

Enter King, Arethusa *and a* Guard.

King. Is the villain ta'ne? (*Philaster.*
Pha. Sir, here be two confess the deed; but say it was
Phi. Question it no more, it was.
King. The fellow that did fight with him will tell us.
Are. Ay me, I know he will.
King. Did not you know him?
Are. Sir, if it was he, he was disguised.
Phi. I was so. Oh my stars! that I should live still.
King. Thou ambitious fool;
Thou that hast laid a train for thy own life;
Now I do mean to do, I'le leave to talk, bear him to prison.
Are. Sir, they did plot together to take hence
This harmless life; should it pass unreveng'd,
I should to earth go weeping: grant me then
(By all the love a Father bears his Child)
Their custodies, and that I may appoint
Their tortures and their death.
Di. Death? soft, our Law will not reach that, for this fault.

King. 'Tis granted, take 'em to you, with a Guard.
Come Princely *Pharamond*, this business past,
We may with more security go on to your intended match.

Cle. I pray that this action lose not *Philaster* the hearts of the people.

Di. Fear it not, their overwise heads will think it but a trick.

[*Exeunt Omnes.*

Actus Quintus. Scena Prima.

Enter Dion, Cleremont, *and* Thrasiline.

Thra. HAS the King sent for him to death?

Di. Yes, but the King must know, 'tis not in his power to war with Heaven.

Cle. We linger time; the King sent for *Philaster* and the Headsman an hour ago.

Thra. Are all his wounds well?

Di. All they were but scratches; but the loss of bloud made him faint.

Cle. We dally Gentlemen.

Thra. Away.

Di. We'l scuffle hard before he perish. [*Exeunt.*

Enter Philaster, Arethusa, *and* Bellario.

Are. Nay dear *Philaster* grieve not, we are well.

Bell. Nay good my Lord forbear, we are wondrous well.

Phi. Oh *Arethusa*! O *Bellario*! leave to be kind:
I shall be shot from Heaven, as now from Earth,
If you continue so; I am a man,
False to a pair of the most trusty ones
That ever earth bore, can it bear us all?
Forgive and leave me, but the King hath sent
To call me to my death, Oh shew it me,
And then forget me: And for thee my boy,
I shall deliver words will mollifie
The hearts of beasts, to spare thy innocence.

Bell. Alas my Lord, my life is not a thing
Worthy your noble thoughts; 'tis not a life,

'Tis but a piece of child-hood thrown away:
Should I out-live, I shall then out-live
Vertue and honour. And when that day comes,
If ever I should close these eyes but once,
May I live spotted for my perjury,
And waste my limbs to nothing.
Are. And I (the woful'st maid as ever was,
Forc'd with my hands to bring my Lord to death)
Do by the honour of a Virgin swear,
To tell no hours beyond it.
Phi. Make me not hated so.
Are. Come from this prison, all joyful to our deaths.
Phi. People will tear me when they find you true
To such a wretch as I; I shall die loath'd.
Injoy your Kingdoms peaceably, whil'st I
For ever sleep forgotten with my faults,
Every just servant, every maid in love
Will have a piece of me if you be true.
Are. My dear Lord say not so.
Bell. A piece of you?
He was not born of women that can cut it and look on.
Phi. Take me in tears betwixt you,
For my heart will break with shame and sorrow.
Are. Why 'tis well.
Bell. Lament no more.
Phi. What would you have done
If you had wrong'd me basely, and had found
My life no price, compar'd to yours? For love Sirs,
Deal with me truly.
Bell. 'Twas mistaken, Sir.
Phi. Why if it were?
Bell. Then Sir we would have ask'd you pardon.
Phi. And have hope to enjoy it?
Are. Injoy it? I.
Phi. Would you indeed? be plain.
Bell. We would my Lord.
Phi. Forgive me then.
Are. So, so.
Bell. 'Tis as it should be now.
Phi. Lead to my death. [*Exeunt.*

Enter King, Dion, Cleremont, *and* Thrasiline.

King. Gentlemen, who saw the Prince?
Cle. So please you Sir, he's gone to see the City,
And the new Platform, with some Gentlemen
Attending on him.
King. Is the Princess ready
To bring her prisoner out?
Thra. She waits your Grace.
King. Tell her we stay.
Di. King, you may be deceiv'd yet:
The head you aim at cost more setting on
Than to be lost so slightly: If it must off
Like a wild overflow, that soops before him
A golden Stack, and with it shakes down Bridges,
Cracks the strong hearts of *Pines*, whose Cable roots
Held out a thousand Storms, a thousand Thunders,
And so made mightier, takes whole Villages
Upon his back, and in that heat of pride,
Charges strong Towns, Towers, Castles, Palaces,
And layes them desolate: so shall thy head,
Thy noble head, bury the lives of thousands
That must bleed with thee like a sacrifice,
In thy red ruines.

Enter Phil. Are. *and* Bell. *in a Robe and Garland.*

King. How now, what Mask is this?
Bell. Right Royal Sir, I should
Sing you an Epithalamium of these lovers,
But having lost my best ayres with my fortunes,
And wanting a celestial Harp to strike
This blessed union on; thus in glad story
I give you all. These two fair Cedar-branches,
The noblest of the Mountain, where they grew
Straightest and tallest, under whose still shades
The worthier beasts have made their layers, and slept
Free from the *Syrian* Star, and the fell Thunder-stroke,
Free from the Clouds, when they were big with humour,
And delivered in thousand spouts, their issues to the earth:
O there was none but silent quiet there!

Till never pleas'd fortune shot up shrubs,
Base under brambles to divorce these branches;
And for a while they did so, and did raign
Over the Mountain, and choakt up his beauty
With Brakes, rude Thornes and Thistles, till thy Sun
Scorcht them even to the roots, and dried them there:
And now a gentle gale hath blown again
That made these branches meet, and twine together,
Never to be divided: The god that sings
His holy numbers over marriage beds,
Hath knit their noble hearts, and here they stand
Your Children mighty King, and I have done.

King. How, how?

Are. Sir, if you love it in plain truth,
For there is no Masking in't; This Gentleman
The prisoner that you gave me is become
My keeper, and through all the bitter throws
Your jealousies and his ill fate have wrought him,
Thus nobly hath he strangled, and at length
Arriv'd here my dear Husband.

King. Your dear Husband! call in
The Captain of the Cittadel; There you shall keep
Your Wedding. I'le provide a Mask shall make
Your Hymen turn his Saffron into a sullen Coat,
And sing sad Requiems to your departing souls:
Bloud shall put out your Torches, and instead
Of gaudy flowers about your wanton necks,
An Ax shall hang like a prodigious Meteor
Ready to crop your loves sweets. Hear you gods:
From this time do I shake all title off,
Of Father to this woman, this base woman,
And what there is of vengeance, in a Lion
Cast amongst Dogs, or rob'd of his dear young,
The same inforc't more terrible, more mighty,
Expect from me.

Are. Sir,
By that little life I have left to swear by,
There's nothing that can stir me from my self.
What I have done, I have done without repentance,
For death can be no Bug-bear unto me,

So long as *Pharamond* is not my headsman.
Di. Sweet peace upon thy soul, thou worthy maid
When ere thou dyest; for this time I'le excuse thee,
Or be thy Prologue.
Phi. Sir, let me speak next,
And let my dying words be better with you
Than my dull living actions; if you aime
At the dear life of this sweet Innocent,
Y'are a Tyrant and a savage Monster;
Your memory shall be as foul behind you
As you are living, all your better deeds
Shall be in water writ, but this in Marble:
No Chronicle shall speak you, though your own,
But for the shame of men. No Monument
(Though high and big as *Pelion*) shall be able
To cover this base murther; make it rich
With Brass, with purest Gold, and shining Jasper,
Like the Pyramids, lay on Epitaphs,
Such as make great men gods; my little marble
(That only cloaths my ashes, not my faults)
Shall far out shine it: And for after issues
Think not so madly of the heavenly wisdoms,
That they will give you more, for your mad rage
To cut off, unless it be some Snake, or something
Like your self, that in his birth shall strangle you.
Remember, my Father King; there was a fault,
But I forgive it: let that sin perswade you
To love this Lady. If you have a soul,
Think, save her, and be saved, for my self,
I have so long expected this glad hour,
So languisht under you, and daily withered,
That heaven knows it is my joy to dye,
I find a recreation in't.

Enter a Messenger.

Mess. Where's the King?
King. Here.
Mess. Get you to your strength,
And rescue the Prince *Pharamond* from danger,
He's taken prisoner by the Citizens,

Fearing the Lord *Philaster*.

Di. Oh brave followers;
Mutiny, my fine dear Country-men, mutiny,
Now my brave valiant foremen, shew your weapons
In honour of your Mistresses.

Enter another Messenger.

Mess. Arm, arm, arm.

King. A thousand devils take 'em.

Di. A thousand blessings on 'em.

Mess. Arm O King, the City is in mutiny,
Led by an old Gray Ruffin, who comes on
In rescue of the Lord *Philaster*. [*Exit with* Are. Phi. Bell.

King. Away to the Cittadel, I'le see them safe,
And then cope with these Burgers: Let the Guard
And all the Gentlemen give strong attendance. [*Ex. King.*
[*Manent* Dion, Cleremont, Thrasiline.

Cle. The City up! this was above our wishes.

Di. I and the Marriage too; by my life,
This noble Lady has deceiv'd us all, a plague upon my self; a thousand plagues, for having such unworthy thoughts of her dear honour: O I could beat my self, or do you beat me and I'le beat you, for we had all one thought.

Cle. No, no, 'twill but lose time.

Di. You say true, are your swords sharp? Well my dear Country-men, what ye lack, if you continue and fall not back upon the first broken shin, I'le have you chronicled, and chronicled, and cut and chronicled and all to be prais'd, and sung in Sonnets, and bath'd in new brave Ballads, that all tongues shall troule you *in Sæcula Sæculorum* my kind Can-carriers.

Thra. What if a toy take 'em i'th' heels now, and they run all away, and cry the Devil take the hindmost?

Di. Then the same Devil take the foremost too, and sowce him for his breakfast; if they all prove Cowards, my curses fly amongst them and be speeding. May they have Murreins raign to keep the Gentlemen at home unbound in easie freez: May the Moths branch their Velvets, and their Silks only be worn before sore eyes. May their false lights undo 'em, and discover presses, holes, stains, and oldness in their Stuffs, and make them shop-rid: May they keep Whores and Horses, and break; and live mued up with necks of Beef and Turnips: May they have many children, and none like the Father: May they know no language but that gibberish they prattle to their Parcels, unless it be the goarish Latine they write in their bonds, and may they write that false, and lose their debts.

Enter the King.

King. Now the vengeance of all the gods confound them; how they swarm together! what a hum they raise; Devils choak your wilde throats; If a man had need to use their valours, he must pay a Brokage for it, and then bring 'em on, they will fight like sheep. 'Tis *Philaster*, none but *Philaster* must allay this heat: They will not hear me speak, but fling dirt at me, and call me Tyrant. Oh run dear friend, and bring the Lord *Philaster*: speak him fair, call him Prince, do him all the courtesie you can, commend me to him. Oh my wits, my wits! [*Exit* Cle.

Di. Oh my brave Countrymen! as I live, I will not buy a pin out of your walls for this; Nay, you shall cozen me, and I'le thank you; and send you Brawn and Bacon, and soil you every long vacation a brace of foremen, that at *Michaelmas* shall come up fat and kicking.

King. What they will do with this poor Prince, the gods know, and I fear.

Di. Why Sir: they'l flea him, and make Church Buckets on's skin to squench rebellion, then clap a rivet in's sconce, and hang him up for a sign.

Enter Cleremont *with* Philaster.

King. O worthy Sir forgive me, do not make
Your miseries and my faults meet together,
To bring a greater danger. Be your self,
Still sound amongst Diseases, I have wrong'd you,
And though I find it last, and beaten to it,
Let first your goodness know it. Calm the people,
And be what you were born to: take your love,
And with her my repentance, and my wishes,
And all my prayers, by the gods my heart speaks this:
And if the least fall from me not perform'd,
May I be struck with Thunder.

Phi. Mighty Sir,
I will not do your greatness so much wrong,
As not to make your word truth; free the Princess,
And the poor boy, and let me stand the shock
Of this mad Sea breach, which I'le either turn
Or perish with it.

King. Let your own word free them.

Phi. Then thus I take my leave kissing your hand,
And hanging on your Royal word: be Kingly,
And be not moved Sir, I shall bring your peace,
Or never bring my self back.

King. All the gods go with thee. [*Exeunt Omnes.*

Enter an old Captain and Citizens with Pharamond.

Cap. Come my brave Mirmidons let's fall on, let our caps
Swarm my boys, and you nimble tongues forget your mothers
Gibberish, of what do you lack, and set your mouths
Up Children, till your Pallats fall frighted half a
Fathom, past the cure of Bay-salt and gross Pepper.
And then cry *Philaster*, brave *Philaster*,
Let *Philaster* be deeper in request, my ding-dongs,
My pairs of dear Indentures, King of Clubs,
Than your cold water Chamblets or your paintings
Spitted with Copper; let not your hasty Silks,
Or your branch'd Cloth of Bodkin, or your Tishues,
Dearly belov'd of spiced Cake and Custard,
Your Robin-hoods scarlets and Johns, tie your affections
In darkness to your shops; no, dainty Duckers,
Up with your three pil'd spirits, your wrought valours.
And let your un-cut Coller make the King feel
The measure of your mightiness *Philaster.*
Cry my Rose nobles, cry.

All. Philaster, Philaster.

Cap. How do you like this my Lord Prince, these are mad boys, I tell you, these are things that will not strike their top-sayles to a Foist. And let a man of war, an Argosie hull and cry Cockles.

Pha. Why you rude slave, do you know what you do?

Cap. My Pretty Prince of Puppets, we do know,
And give your greatness warning, that you talk

No more such Bugs-words, or that soldred Crown
Shall be scratch'd with a Musket: Dear Prince Pippen,
Down with your noble bloud; or as I live,
I'le have you codled: let him lose my spirits,
Make us a round Ring with your Bills my Hectors,
And let us see what this trim man dares do.
Now Sir, have at you; here I [lie],
And with this swashing blow, do you swear Prince;
I could hulk your Grace, and hang you up cross-leg'd,
Like a Hare at a Poulters, and do this with this wiper.

Pha. You will not see me murder'd wicked Villains?

1 *Cit.* Yes indeed will we Sir, we have not seen one fo[r] a great while.

Capt. He would have weapons would he? give him a Broad-side my brave boyes with your pikes, branch me his skin in Flowers like a Satin, and between every Flower a mortal cut, your Royalty shall ravel, jag him Gentlemen, I'le have him cut to the kell, then down the seames, oh for a whip
To make him Galoone-Laces,
I'le have a Coach-whip.

Pha. O spare me Gentlemen.

Cap. Hold, hold, the man begins to fear and know himself,
He shall for this time only be seal'd up
With a Feather through his nose, that he may only see
Heaven, and think whither he's going,
Nay beyond-Sea Sir, we will proclaim you, you would be King
Thou tender Heir apparent to a Church-Ale,
Thou sleight Prince of single Sarcenet;
Thou Royal Ring-tail, fit to fly at nothing
But poor mens Poultry, and have every Boy
Beat thee from that too with his Bread and Butter.

Pha. Gods keep me from these Hell-hounds.

2 *Cit.* Shall's geld him Captain?

Cap. No, you shall spare his dowcets my dear Donsels,
As you respect the Ladies let them flourish; (Boys.
The curses of a longing woman kill as speedy as a Plague,

1 *Cit.* I'le have a Leg that's certain.

2 *Cit.* I'le have an Arm.

3 *Cit.* I'le have his Nose, and at mine own charge build a Colledge, and clap't upon the Gate.

4 *Cit.* I'le have his little Gut to string a Kit with, For certainly a Royal Gut will sound like silver. (once.

Pha. Would they were in thy belly, and I past my pain

5 *Cit.* Good Captain let me have his Liver to feed Ferrets.

Cap. Who will have parcels else? speak.

Pha. Good gods consider me, I shall be tortur'd.

1 *Cit.* Captain, I'le give you the trimming of your hand-sword, and let me have his Skin to make false Scabbards.

2. He had no horns Sir had he? (horns?

Cap. No Sir, he's a Pollard, what would'st thou do with

Cit. O if he had, I would have made rare Hafts and Whistles of 'em, but his Shin-bones if they be sound shall serve me.

Enter Philaster.

All. Long live *Philaster*, the brave Prince *Philaster*.

Phi. I thank you Gentlemen, but why are these
Rude weapons brought abroad, to teach your hands
Uncivil Trades?

Cap. My Royal Rosiclear,
We are thy Mirmidons, thy Guard, thy Rorers,
And when thy noble body is in durance,
Thus do we clap our musty Murrions on,
And trace the streets in terrour: Is it peace
Thou *Mars* of men? Is the King sociable,
And bids thee live? Art thou above thy foemen,
And free as *Phœbus*? Speak, if not, this stand
Of Royal blood shall be abroach, atilt, and run
Even to the lees of honour.

Phi. Hold and be satisfied, I am my self
Free as my thoughts are, by the gods I am.

Cap. Art thou the dainty darling of the King?
Art thou the *Hylas* to our *Hercules*?
Do the Lords bow, and the regarded scarlets,
Kiss their Gumd-gols, and cry, we are your servants?
Is the Court Navigable, and the presence struck
With Flags of friendship? if not, we are thy Castle
And this man sleeps.

Phi. I am what I desire to be, your friend,
I am what I was born to be, your Prince.

Pha. Sir, there is some humanity in you,
You have a noble soul, forget my name,
And know my misery, set me safe aboard
From these wild *Canibals*, and as I live,
I'le quit this Land for ever: there is nothing,
Perpetual prisonment, cold, hunger, sickness
Of all sorts, all dangers, and all together
The worst company of the worst men, madness, age,
To be as many Creatures as a woman,
And do as all they do, nay to despair;
But I would rather make it a new Nature,
And live with all those than endure one hour
Amongst these wild Dogs.

Phi. I do pity you: Friends discharge your fears,
Deliver me the Prince, I'le warrant you
I shall be old enough to find my safety.

3 *Cit.* Good Sir take heed he does not hurt you,
He's a fierce man I can tell you Sir.

Cap. Prince, by your leave I'le have a Sursingle,
And Male you like a Hawke. [*He stirs.*

Phi. Away, away, there is no danger in him:
Alas he had rather sleep to shake his fit off.
Look you friends, how gently he leads, upon my word
He's tame enough, he need[s] no further watching.
Good my friends go to your houses and by me have your pardons, and my love,
And know there shall be nothing in my power
You may deserve, but you shall have your wishes.
To give you more thanks were to flatter you,
Continue still your love, and for an earnest
Drink this.

All. Long maist thou live brave Prince, brave Prince, brave Prince. [*Exeunt* Phi. *and* Pha.

Cap. Thou art the King of Courtesie:
Fall off again my sweet youths, come and every man
Trace to his house again, and hang his pewter up, then to
The Tavern and bring your wives in Muffes: we will have
Musick and the red grape shall make us dance, and rise Boys. [*Exeunt.*

Enter King, Are. Gal. Meg. Cle. Dion, Thra. Bellario, *and Attendants.*

King. Is it appeas'd?
Di. Sir, all is quiet as this dead of night,
As peaceable as sleep, my Lord *Philaster*
Brings on the Prince himself.
King. Kind Gentlemen!
I will not break the least word I have given
In promise to him, I have heap'd a world
Of grief upon his head, which yet I hope
To wash away.

Enter Philaster *and* Pharamond.

Cle. My Lord is come.
King. My Son!
Blest be the time that I have leave to call
Such vertue mine; now thou art in mine arms,
Me thinks I have a salve unto my breast
For all the stings that dwell there, streams of grief
That I have wrought thee, and as much of joy
That I repent it, issue from mine eyes:
Let them appease thee, take thy right; take her,
She is thy right too, and forget to urge
My vexed soul with that I did before.
Phi. Sir, [it is] blotted from my memory,
Past and forgotten: For you Prince of *Spain*,
Whom I have thus redeem'd, you have full leave
To make an honourable voyage home.
And if you would go furnish'd to your Realm
With fair provision, I do see a Lady
Me thinks would gladly bear you company:
How like you this piece?
Meg. Sir, he likes it well,
For he hath tried it, and found it worth
His princely liking; we were ta'ne a bed,
I know your meaning, I am not the first
That Nature taught to seek a fellow forth:
Can shame remain perpetually in me,
And not in others? or have Princes salves

To cure ill names that meaner people want?
Phi. What mean you?
Meg. You must get another ship
To clear the Princess and the boy together.
Di. How now!
Meg. Others took me, and I took her and him
At that all women may be ta'ne sometimes:
Ship us all four my Lord, we can endure
Weather and wind alike.
King. Clear thou thy self, or know not me for Father.
Are. This earth, How false it is? what means is left for me
To clear my self? It lies in your belief,
My Lords believe me, and let all things else
Struggle together to dishonour me.
Bell. O stop your ears great King, that I may speak
As freedom would, then I will call this Lady
As base as be her actions, hear me Sir,
Believe [y]our hated bloud when it rebels
Against your reason sooner than this Lady.
Meg. By this good light he bears it hansomely.
Phi. This Lady? I will sooner trust the wind
With Feathers, or the troubled Sea with Pearl,
Than her with any thing; believe her not!
Why think you, if I did believe her words;
I would outlive 'em: honour cannot take
Revenge on you, then what were to be known
But death?
King. Forget her Sir, since all is knit
Between us: but I must request of you
One favour, and will sadly be denied.
Phi. Command what ere it be.
King. Swear to be true to what you promise.
Phi. By the powers above,
Let it not be the death of her or him,
And it is granted.
King. Bear away the boy
To Torture, I will have her clear'd or buried.
Phi. O let me call my words back, worthy Sir,
Ask something else, bury my life and right (once.
In one poor grave, but do not take away my life and fame at

King. Away with him, it stands irrevocable.
Phi. Turn all your eyes on me, here stands a man
The falsest and the basest of this world:
Set swords against this breast some honest man,
For I have liv'd till I am pitied,
My former deeds are hateful, but this last
Is pitifull, for I unwillingly
Have given the dear preserver of my life
Unto his Torture: is it in the power [*Offers to kill himself.*
Of flesh and blood, to carry this and live?
Are. Dear Sir be patient yet, or stay that hand.
King. Sirs, strip that boy.
Di. Come Sir, your tender flesh will try your constancie.
Bell. O kill me gentlemen.
Di. No, help Sirs.
Bell. Will you Torture me?
King. Hast there, why stay you?
Bell. Then I shall not break my vow,
You know just gods, though I discover all.
King. How's that? Will he confess?
Di. Sir, so he says.
King. Speak then.
Bell. Great King if you command
This Lord to talk with me alone, my tongue
Urg'd by my heart, shall utter all the thoughts
My youth hath known, and stranger things than these
You hear not often.
King. Walk aside with him.
Di. Why speak'st thou not?
Bell. Know you this face my Lord?
Di. No.
Bell. Have you not seen it, nor the like?
Di. Yes, I have seen the like, but readily
I know not where.
Bell. I have been often told
In Court, of one *Euphrasia*, a Lady
And Daughter to you; betwixt whom and me
(They that would flatter my bad face would swear)
There was such strange resemblance, that we two
Could not be known asunder, drest alike.

Di. By Heaven and so there is.
Bell. For her fair sake,
Who now doth spend the spring time of her life
In holy Pilgrimage, move to the King,
That I may scape this Torture.
Di. But thou speak'st
As like *Euphrasia* as thou dost look,
How came it to thy knowledge that she lives in Pilgrimage?
Bell. I know it not my Lord,
But I have heard it, and do scarce believe it.
Di. Oh my shame, is't possible? Draw near,
That I may gaze upon thee, art thou she?
Or else her Murderer? where wert thou born?
Bell. In *Siracusa.*
Di. What's thy name?
Bell. *Euphrasia.*
Di. O 'tis just, 'tis she now, I do know thee, Oh that thou (hadst died
And I had never seen thee nor my shame,
How shall I own thee? shall this tongue of mine
E're call thee Daughter more?
Bell. Would I had died indeed, I wish it too,
And so I must have done by vow, e're published
What I have told, but that there was no means
To hide it longer, yet I joy in this,
The Princess is all clear.
King. What have you done?
Di. All is discovered.
Phi. Why then hold you me?
Di. All is discovered, pray you let me go. {*He offers to stab himself.*
King. Stay him.
Are. What is discovered?
Di. Why my shame, it is a woman, let her speak the rest.
Phi. How! that again.
Di. It is a woman.
Phi. Blest be you powers that favour innocence.
King. Lay hold upon that Lady.
Phi. It is a woman Sir, hark Gentlemen!
It is a woman. *Arethusa* take
My soul into thy breast, that would be gone
With joy: it is a woman, thou art fair,

And vertuous still to ages, in despight of malice.
King. Speak you, where lies his shame?
Bell. I am his Daughter.
Phi. The Gods are just.
Di. I dare accuse none, but before you two
The vertue of our age, I bend my knee
For mercy.
Phi. Take it freely; for I know,
Though what thou didst were undiscreetly done,
'Twas meant well.
Are. And for me,
I have a power to pardon sins as oft
As any man has power to wrong me.
Cle. Noble and worthy.
Phi. But *Bellario*,
(For I must call thee still so) tell me why
Thou didst conceal thy Sex, it was a fault,
A fault *Bellario*, though thy other deeds
Of truth outweigh'd it: All these Jealousies
Had flown to nothing, if thou hadst discovered,
What now we know.
Bell. My Father would oft speak
Your worth and vertue, and as I did grow
More and more apprehensive, I did thirst
To see the man so rais'd, but yet all this
Was but a Maiden longing to be lost
As soon as found, till sitting in my window,
Printing my thoughts in Lawne, I saw a God
I thought (but it was you) enter our Gates,
My bloud flew out, and back again as fast
As I had puft it forth, and suck't it in
Like breath, then was I call'd away in hast
To entertain you. Never was a man
Heav'd from a Sheep-coat to a Scepter rais'd
So high in thoughts as I, you left a kiss
Upon these lips then, which I mean to keep
From you for ever, I did hear you talk
Far above singing; after you were gone,
I grew acquainted with my heart, and search'd
What stir'd it so, Alas I found it love,

Yet far from lust, for could I have but liv'd
In presence of you, I had had my end,
For this I did delude my noble Father
With a feign'd Pilgrimage, and drest my self
In habit of a boy, and, for I knew
My birth no match for you, I was past hope
Of having you. And understanding well
That when I made discovery of my Sex,
I could not stay with you, I made a vow
By all the most religious things a Maid
Could call together, never to be known,
Whilst there was hope to hide me from mens eyes,
For other than I seem'd; that I might ever
Abide with you, then sate I by the Fount
Where first you took me up.

King. Search out a match
Within our Kingdom where and when thou wilt,
And I will pay thy Dowry, and thy self
Wilt well deserve him.

Bell. Never Sir will I
Marry, it is a thing within my vow,
But if I may have leave to serve the Princess,
To see the vertues of her Lord and her,
I shall have hope to live.

Are. I *Philaster*,
Cannot be jealous, though you had a Lady
Drest like a Page to serve you, nor will I
Suspect her living here: come live with me,
Live free, as I do, she that loves my Lord,
Curst be the wife that hates her.

Phi. I grieve such vertues should be laid in earth
Without an Heir; hear me my Royal Father,
Wrong not the freedom of our souls so much,
To think to take revenge of that base woman,
Her malice cannot hurt us: set her free
As she was born, saving from shame and sin.

King. Set her at liberty, but leave the Court,
This is no place for such: you *Pharamond*
Shall have free passage, and a conduct home
Worthy so great a Prince, when you come there,

Remember 'twas your faults that lost you her,
And not my purpos'd will.

Pha. I do confess,
Renowned Sir.

King. Last joyn your hands in one, enjoy *Philaster*
This Kingdom which is yours, and after me
What ever I call mine, my blessing on you,
All happy hours be at your Marriage joyes,
That you may grow your selves over all Lands,
And live to see your plenteous branches spring
Where ever there is Sun. Let Princes learn
By this to rule the passions of their blood,
For what Heaven wills, can never be withstood.

[*Exeunt Omnes.*

A KING,

AND NO

KING.

Persons Represented in the Play.

Arbaces, *King of* Iberia.
Tigranes, *King of* Armenia.
Gobrias, *Lord Protector, and Father of* Arbaces.
Bacurius, *another Lord.*
Mardonius, } *Two Captains.*
Bessus, }
Ligo[n]es, *Father of* Spaconia.
Two Gentlemen.
Three Men and a Woman.
Philip, *a servant, and two Citizens Wives.*

A Messenger.
A Servant to Bacurius.
Two Sword-men.
A Boy.

Arane, *The [Queen-Mother].*
Panthea, *Her Daughter.*
Spaconia, *A Lady Daughter of* Ligones.
Mandane, *A waiting woman, and other attendants.*

Actus primus. Scena prima.

Enter Mardonius *and* Bessus, *two Captains.*

Mar. BEssus, the King has made a fair hand on't, he has ended the Wars at a blow, would my sword had a close basket hilt to hold Wine, and the blade would make knives, for we shall have nothing but eating and drinking.

Bes. We that are Commanders shall do well enough.

Mar. Faith *Bessus*, such Commanders as thou may; I had as lieve set thee Perdue for a pudding i'th' dark, as *Alexander* the Great.

Bes. I love these jests exceedingly.

Mar. I think thou lov'st 'em better than quarrelling *Bessus*, I'le say so much i'thy behalf, and yet thou 'rt valiant enough upon a retreat, I think thou wouldst kill any man that stopt thee if thou couldst.

Bes. But was not this a brave Combate *Mardonius*?

Mar. Why, didst thou see't?

Bes. You stood wi'me.

Mar. I did so, but me thought thou wink'dst every blow they strook.

Bes. Well, I believe there are better souldiers than I, that never saw two Princes fight in lists.

Mar. By my troth I think so too *Bessus*, many a thousand, but certainly all that are worse than thou have seen as much.

Bes. 'Twas bravely done of our King.

Mar. Yes, if he had not ended the wars: I'me glad thou dar'st talk of such dangerous businesses.

Bes. To take a Prince prisoner in the heart of's own Country in single combat.

Mar. See how thy blood curdles at this, I think thou couldst be contented to be beaten i'this passion.

Bes. Shall I tell you truly?

Mar. I.

Bes. I could willingly venture for't.

Mar. Um, no venture neither *Bessus*.

Bes. Let me not live, if I do not think 'tis a braver piece of service than that I'me so fam'd for.

Mar. Why, art thou fam'd for any valour?

Bes. Fam'd! I, I warrant you.

Ma. I'me e'en heartily glad on't, I have been with thee e're since thou cam'st to th'wars, and this is the first word that ever I heard on't, prethee who fames thee.

Bes. The Christian world.

Mar. 'Tis heathenishly done of'em in my conscience, thou deserv'st it not.

Bes. Yes, I ha' don good service.

Mar. I do not know how thou mayst wait of a man in's Chamber, or thy agility of shifting of a Trencher, but otherwise no service good *Bessus*.

Bes. You saw me do the service your self.

Mar. Not so hasty sweet *Bessus*, where was it, is the place vanish'd?

Bes. At *Bessus* desp'rate redemption.

Mar. At *Bessus* desp'rate redemption, where's that?

Bes. There where I redeem'd the day, the place bears my name.

Mar. Pray thee, who Christened it?

Bes. The Souldiers.

Mar. If I were not a very merrily dispos'd man, what would become of thee? one that had but a grain of choler in the whole composition of his body, would send thee of an errand to the worms for putting thy name upon that field: did not I beat thee there i'th' head o'th' Troops with a Trunchion, because thou wouldst needs run away with thy company, when we should charge the enemy?

Bes. True, but I did not run.

Mar. Right *Bessus*, I beat thee out on't.

Bes. But came I not up when the day was gone, and redeem'd all?

Mar. Thou knowest, and so do I, thou meanedst to flie, and thy fear making thee mistake, thou ranst upon the enemy, and a hot charge thou gav'st, as I'le do thee right, thou art furious in running away, and I think, we owe thy fear for our victory; If I were the King, and were sure thou wouldst mistake alwaies and run away upon th' enemy, thou shouldst be General by this light.

Bes. You'l never leave this till I fall foul.

Mar. No more such words dear *Bessus*, for though I have ever known thee a coward, and therefore durst never strike thee, yet if thou proceedest, I will allow thee valiant, and beat thee.

Bes. Come, our King's a brave fellow.

Mar. He is so *Bessus*, I wonder how thou cam'st to know it. But if thou wer't a man of understanding, I would tell thee, he is vain-glorious, and humble, and angry, and patient, and merry and dull, and joyful and sorrowful in extremity in an hour: Do not think me thy friend for this, for if I car'd who knew it, thou shouldst not hear it *Bessus*. Here he is with his prey in his foot.

Enter &c. Senet Flourish.

Enter Arbaces *and* Tigranes, *two Kings and two Gentlemen.*

Arb. Thy sadness brave *Tigranes* takes away
From my full victory, am I become
Of so small fame, that any man should grieve
When I o'recome him? They that plac'd me here,
Intended it an honour large enough, (though he
For the most valiant living, but to dare oppose me single,
Lost the day. What should afflict you, you are as free as I,
To be my prisoner, is to be more free
Than you were formerly, and never think
The man I held worthy to combate me
Shall be us'd servilely: Thy ransom is
To take my only Sister to thy Wife.
A heavy one *Tigranes*, for she is
A Lady, that the neighbour Princes send
Blanks to fetch home. I have been too unkind
To her *Tigranes*, she but nine years old
I left her, and ne're saw her since, your wars
Have held me long and taught me though a youth,
The way to victory, she was a pretty child,
Then I was little better, but now fame
Cries loudly on her, and my messengers
Make me believe she is a miracle;
She'l make you shrink, as I did, with a stroak
But of her eye *Tigranes.*

Tigr. Is't the course of *Iberia* to use their prisoners thus?
Had fortune thrown my name above *Arbace*,
I should not thus have talk'd Sir, in *Armenia*,
We hold it base, you should have kept your temper
Till you saw home again, where 'tis the fashion
Perhaps to brag.

Arb. Be you my witness earth, need I to brag,
Doth not this captive Prince speak
Me sufficiently, and all the acts
That I have wrought upon his suffering Land;
Should I then boast! where lies that foot of ground
Within his whole Realm, that I have not past,
Fighting and conquering; Far then from me

Be ostentation. I could tell the world
How I have laid his Kingdom desolate
By this sole Arm prop't by divinity,
Stript him out of his glories, and have sent
The pride of all his youth to people graves,
And made his Virgins languish for their Loves,
If I would brag, should I that have the power
To teach the Neighbour world humility,
Mix with vain-glory?
Mar. Indeed this is none.
Arb. *Tigranes*, Nay did I but take delight
To stretch my deeds as others do, on words,
I could amaze my hearers.
Mar. So you do.
Arb. But he shall wrong his and my modesty,
That thinks me apt to boast after any act
Fit for a good man to do upon his foe.
A little glory in a souldiers mouth
Is well-becoming, be it far from vain.
Mar. 'Tis pity that valour should be thus drunk.
Arb. I offer you my Sister, and you answer
I do insult, a Lady that no suite
Nor treasure, nor thy Crown could purchase thee,
But that thou fought'st with me.
Tigr. Though this be worse
Than that you spake before, it strikes me not;
But that you think to overgrace me with
The marriage of your Sister, troubles me.
I would give worlds for ransoms were they mine,
Rather than have her.
Arb. See if I insult
That am the Conquerour, and for a ransom
Offer rich treasure to the Conquered,
Which he refuses, and I bear his scorn:
It cannot be self-flattery to say,
The Daughters of your Country set by her,
Would see their shame, run home and blush to death,
At their own foulness; yet she is not fair,
Nor beautiful, those words express her not,
They say her looks have something excellent,

That wants a name: yet were she odious,
Her birth deserves the Empire of the world,
Sister to such a brother, that hath ta'ne
Victory prisoner, and throughout the earth,
Carries her bound, and should he let her loose,
She durst not leave him; Nature did her wrong,
To Print continual conquest on her cheeks,
And make no man worthy for her to taste
But me that am too near her, and as strangely
She did for me, but you will think I brag.

Mar. I do I'le be sworn. Thy valour and thy passions sever'd, would have made two excellent fellows in their kinds: I know not whether I should be sorry thou art so valiant, or so passionate, wou'd one of 'em were away.

Tigr. Do I refuse her that I doubt her worth?
Were she as vertuous as she would be thought,
So perfect that no one of her own sex
Could find a want, had she so tempting fair,
That she could wish it off for damning souls,
I would pay any ransom, twenty lives
Rather than meet her married in my bed.
Perhaps I have a love, where I have fixt
Mine eyes not to be mov'd, and she on me,
I am not fickle.

Arb. Is that all the cause?
Think you, you can so knit your self in love
To any other, that her searching sight
Cannot dissolve it? So before you tri'd,
You thought your self a match for me in [f]ight,
Trust me *Tigranes*, she can do as much
In peace, as I in war, she'l conquer too,
You shall see if you have the power to stand
The force of her swift looks, if you dislike,
I'le send you home with love, and name your ransom
Some other way, but if she be your choice,
She frees you: To *Iberia* you must.

Tigr. Sir, I have learn'd a prisoners sufferance,
And will obey, but give me leave to talk
In private with some friends before I go.

Arb. Some to await him forth, and see him safe,

But let him freely send for whom he please,
And none dare to disturb his conference,
I will not have him know what bondage is, [*Exit Tigranes.*
Till he be free from me. This Prince, *Mardonius*,
Is full of wisdom, valour, all the graces
Man can receive.

Mar. And yet you conquer'd him.

Arb. And yet I conquer'd him, and could have don't
Hadst thou joyn'd with him, though thy name in Arms
Be great; must all men that are vertuous
Think suddenly to match themselves with me?
I conquered him and bravely, did I not?

Bes. And please your Majesty, I was afraid at first.

Mar. When wert thou other?

Arb. Of what?

Bes. That you would not have spy'd your best advantages, for your Majesty in my opinion lay too high, methinks, under favour, you should have lain thus.

Mar. Like a Taylor at a wake.

Bes. And then, if please your Majesty to remember, at one time, by my troth I wisht my self wi'you.

Mar. By my troth thou wouldst ha' stunk 'em both out o'th' Lists.

Arb. What to do?

Bes. To put your Majesty in mind of an occasion; you lay thus, and *Tigranes* falsified a blow at your Leg, which you by doing thus avoided; but if you had whip'd up your Leg thus, and reach'd him on the ear, you had made the Blood-Royal run down his head.

Mar. What Country Fence-school learn'st thou at?

Arb. Pish, did not I take him nobly?

Mar. Why you did, and you have talked enough on't.

Arb. Talkt enough?
Will you confine my word? by heaven and earth,
I were much better be a King of beasts
Than such a people: if I had not patience
Above a God, I should be call'd a Tyrant
Throughout the world. They will offend to death
Each minute: Let me hear thee speak again,
And thou art earth again: why this is like

Tigranes speech that needs would say I brag'd.
Bessus, he said I brag'd.
Bes. Ha, ha, ha.
Arb. Why dost thou laugh?
By all the world, I'm grown ridiculous
To my own Subjects: Tie me in a Chair
And jest at me, but I shall make a start,
And punish some that others may take heed
How they are haughty; who will answer me?
He said I boasted, speak *Mardonius*,
Did I? He will not answer, O my temper!
I give you thanks above, that taught my heart
Patience, I can endure his silence; what will none
Vouchsafe to give me answer? am I grown
To such a poor respect, or do you mean
To break my wind? Speak, speak, some one of you,
Or else by heaven.
1 *Gent.* So please your.
Arb. Monstrous,
I cannot be heard out, they cut me off,
As if I were too saucy, I will live
In woods, and talk to trees, they will allow me
To end what I begin. The meanest Subject
Can find a freedom to discharge his soul
And not I, now it is a time to speak,
I hearken.
1 *Gent.* May it please.
Arb. I mean not you,
Did not I stop you once? but I am grown
To balk, but I defie, let another speak.
2 *Gent.* I hope your Majesty.
Arb. Thou drawest thy words,
That I must wait an hour, where other men
Can hear in instants; throw your words away,
Quick, and to purpose, I have told you this.
Bes. And please your Majesty.
Arb. Wilt thou devour me? this is such a rudeness
As you never shew'd me, and I want
Power to command too, else *Mardonius*
Would speak at my request; were you my King,

I would have answered at your word *Mardonius*,
I pray you speak, and truely, did I boast?
Mar. Truth will offend you.
Arb. You take all great care what will offend me,
When you dare to utter such things as these.
Mar. You told *Tigranes*, you had won his Land,
With that sole arm propt by Divinity:
Was not that bragging, and a wrong to us,
That daily ventured lives?
Arb. O that thy name
Were as great, as mine, would I had paid my wealth,
It were as great, as I might combate thee,
I would through all the Regions habitable
Search thee, and having found thee, wi'my Sword
Drive thee about the world, till I had met
Some place that yet mans curiosity
Hath mist of; there, there would I strike thee dead:
Forgotten of mankind, such Funeral rites
As beasts would give thee, thou shouldst have.
Bes. The King rages extreamly, shall we slink away?
He'l strike us.
2 *Gent.* Content.
Arb. There I would make you know 'twas this sole arm.
I grant you were my instruments, and did
As I commanded you, but 'twas this arm
Mov'd you like wheels, it mov'd you as it pleas'd.
Whither slip you now? what are you too good
To wait on me (*puffe*,) I had need have temper
That rule such people; I have nothing left
At my own choice, I would I might be private:
Mean men enjoy themselves, but 'tis our curse,
To have a tumult that out of their loves
Will wait on us, whether we will or no;
Go get you gone: Why here they stand like death,
My words move nothing.
1 *Gent.* Must we go?
Bes. I know not.
Arb. I pray you leave me Sirs, I'me proud of this,
That you will be intreated from my sight:
Why now the[y] leave me all: *Mardonius.* *Exeunt all but* Arb. *and* Mar.

Mar. Sir.

Arb. Will you leave me quite alone? me thinks
Civility should teach you more than this,
If I were but your friend: Stay here and wait.

Mar. Sir shall I speak?

Arb. Why, you would now think much
To be denied, but I can scar[c]e intreat
What I would have: do, speak.

Mar. But will you hear me out?

Arb. With me you Article to talk thus: well,
I will hear you out.

Mar. Sir, that I have ever lov'd you, my sword hath spoken for me; that I do, if it be doubted, I dare call an oath, a great one to my witness; and were you not my King, from amongst men, I should have chose you out to love above the rest: nor can this challenge thanks, for my own sake I should have done it, because I would have lov'd the most deserving man, for so you are.

Arb. Alas *Mardonius*, rise you shall not kneel,
We all are souldiers, and all venture lives:
And where there is no difference in mens worths,
Titles are jests, who can outvalue thee?
Mardonius thou hast lov'd me, and hast wrong,
Thy love is not rewarded, but believe
It shall be better, more than friend in arms,
My Father, and my Tutor, good *Mardonius*.

Mar. Sir, you did promise you would hear me out.

Arb. And so I will; speak freely, for from thee
Nothing can come but worthy things and true.

Mar. Though you have all this worth, you hold some qualities that do Eclipse your vertues.

Arb. Eclipse my vertues?

Mar. Yes, your passions, which are so manifold, that they appear even in this: when I commend you, you hug me for that truth: but when I speak your faults, you make a start, and flie the hearing but.

Arb. When you commend me? O that I should live
To need such commendations: If my deeds
Blew not my praise themselves about the earth,
I were most wretched: spare your idle praise:

If thou didst mean to flatter, and shouldst utter
Words in my praise, that thou thoughtst impudence,
My deeds should make 'em modest: when you praise I hug you? 'tis so [false], that wert thou worthy thou shouldst receive a death, a glorious death from me: but thou shalt understand thy lies, for shouldst thou praise me into Heaven, and there leave me inthron'd, I would despise thee though as much as now, which is as much as dust because I see thy envie.

Mar. However you will use me after, yet for your own promise sake, hear me the rest.

Arb. I will, and after call unto the winds, for they shall lend as large an ear as I to what you utter: speak.

Mar. Would you but leave these hasty tempers, which I do not say take from you all your worth, but darken 'em, then you will shine indeed.

Arb. Well.

Mar. Yet I would have you keep some passions, lest men should take you for a God, your vertues are such.

Arb. Why now you flatter.

Mar. I never understood the word, were you no King, and free from these moods, should I choose a companion for wit and pleasure, it should be you; or for honesty to enterchange my bosom with, it should be you; or wisdom to give me counsel, I would pick out you; or valour to defend my reputation, still I should find you out; for you are fit to fight for all the world, if it could come in question: Now I have spoke, consider to your self, find out a use; if so, then what shall fall to me is not material.

Arb. Is not material? more than ten such lives, as mine, *Mardonius*: it was nobly said, thou hast spoke truth, and boldly such a truth as might offend another. I have been too passionate and idle, thou shalt see a swift amendment, but I want those parts you praise me for: I fight for all the world? Give me a sword, and thou wilt go as far beyond me, as thou art beyond in years, I know thou dar'st and wilt; it troubles me that I should use so rough a phrase to thee, impute it to my folly, what thou wilt, so thou wilt par[d]on me: that thou and I should differ thus!

Mar. Why 'tis no matter Sir.

Arb. Faith but it is, but thou dost ever take all things I do, thus patiently, for which I never can requite thee, but with love, and that thou shalt be sure of. Thou and I have not been merry lately: pray thee tell me where hadst thou that same jewel in thine ear?

Mar. Why at the taking of a Town.

Arb. A wench upon my life, a wench *Mardonius* gave thee that jewel.

Mar. Wench! they respect not me, I'm old and rough, and every limb about me, but that which should, grows stiffer, I'those businesses I may swear I am truly honest: for I pay justly for what I take, and would be glad to be at a certainty.

Arb. Why, do the wenches encroach upon thee?

Mar. I by this light do they.

Arb. Didst thou sit at an old rent with 'em?

Mar. Yes faith.

Arb. And do they improve themselves?

Mar. I ten shillings to me, every new young fellow they come acquainted with.

Arb. How canst live on't?

Mar. Why I think I must petition to you.

Arb. Thou shalt take them up at my price.

Enter two Gentlemen and Bessus.

Mar. Your price?

Arb. I at the Kings price.

Mar. That may be more than I'me worth.

2 *Gent.* Is he not merry now?

1 *Gent.* I think not.

Bes. He is, he is: we'l shew our selves.

Arb. *Bessus*, I thought you had been in *Iberia* by this, I bad you hast; *Gobrias* will want entertainment for me.

Bes. And please your Majesty I have a sute.

Arb. Is't not lousie *Bessus*, what is't?

Bes. I am to carry a Lady with me.

Arb. Then thou hast two sutes.

Bes. And if I can prefer her to the Lady *Pentha* your Majesties Sister, to learn fashions, as her friends term it, it will be worth something to me.

Arb. So many nights lodgings as 'tis thither, wilt not?

Bes. I know not that Sir, but gold I shall be sure of.

Arb. Why thou shalt bid her entertain her from me, so thou wilt resolve me one thing.

Bes. If I can.

Arb. Faith 'tis a very disputable question, and yet I think thou canst decide it.

Bes. Your Majesty has a good opinion of my understanding.

Arb. I have so good an opinion of it: 'tis whether thou be valiant.

Bes. Some body has traduced me to you: do you see this sword Sir?

Arb. Yes.

Bes. If I do not make my back-biters eat it to a knife within this week, say I am not valiant.

Enter a Messenger.

Mes. Health to your Majesty.

Arb. From *Gobrias*?

Mes. Yes Sir.

Arb. How does he, is he well?

Mes. In perfect health.

Arb. Take that for thy good news. A trustier servant to his Prince there lives not, than is good *Gobrias*.

1 *Gent.* The King starts back.

Mar. His blood goes back as fast.

2 *Gent.* And now it comes again.

Mar. He alters strangely.

Arb. The hand of Heaven is on me, be it far from me to struggle, if my secret sins have pull'd this curse upon me, lend me tears now to wash me white, that I may feel a child-like innocence within my breast; which once perform'd, O give me leave to stand as fix'd as constancy her self, my eyes set here unmov'd, regardless of the world though thousand miseries incompass me.

Mar. This is strange, Sir, how do you?

Arb. *Mardonius*, my mother.

Mar. Is she dead?

Arb. Alas she's not so happy, thou dost know how she hath laboured since my Father died to take by treason hence this loathed life, that would but be to serve her, I have pardoned, and pardoned, and by that have made her fit to practise new sins, not repent the old: she now had stirr'd a slave to come from thence, and strike me here, whom *Gobrias* sifting out, took and condemn'd and executed there, the carefulst servant: Heaven let me but live to pay that man; Nature is poor to me, that will not let me have as many deaths as are the times that he hath sav'd my life, that I might dye 'em over all for him.

Mar. Sir let her bear her sins on her own head,
Vex not your self.

Arb. What will the world
Conceive of me? with what unnatural sins
Will they suppose me loaden, when my life
Is sought by her that gave it to the world?
But yet he writes me comfort here, my Sister,
He saies, is grown in beauty and in grace.
In all the innocent vertues that become
A tender spotless maid: she stains her cheeks
With morning tears to purge her mothers ill,
And 'mongst that sacred dew she mingles Prayers
Her pure Oblations for my safe return:
If I have lost the duty of a Son,
If any pomp or vanity of state
Made me forget my natural offices,
Nay farther, if I have not every night
Expostulated with my wandring thoughts,
If ought unto my parent they have err'd,
And call'd 'em back: do you direct her arm
Unto this foul dissembling heart of mine:
But if I have been just to her, send out
Your power to compass me, and hold me safe
From searching treason; I will use no means
But prayer: for rather suffer me to see
From mine own veins issue a deadly flood,
Than wash my danger off with mothers blood.

Mar. I n'ere saw such suddain extremities. [*Exeunt.*

Enter Tigranes *and* Spaconia.

Tigr. Why? wilt thou have me die *Spaconia*,
What should I do?

Spa. Nay let me stay alone,

And when you see *Armenia* again,
You shall behold a Tomb more worth than I;
Some friend that ever lov'd me or my cause,
Will build me something to distinguish me
From other women, many a weeping verse
He will lay on, and much lament those maids,
That plac'd their loves unfortunately high,
As I have done, where they can never reach;
But why should you go to *Iberia*?

Tigr. Alas, that thou wilt ask me, ask the man
That rages in a Fever why he lies
Distempered there, when all the other youths
Are coursing o're the Meadows with their Loves?
Can I resist it? am I not a slave
To him that conquer'd me?

Spa. That conquer'd thee *Tigranes*! he has won
But half of thee, thy body, but thy mind
May be as free as his, his will did never
Combate thine, and take it prisoner.

Tigr. But if he by force convey my body hence,
What helps it me or thee to be unwilling?

Spa. O *Tigranes*, I know you are to see a Lady there,
To see, and like I fear: perhaps the hope
Of her make[s] you forget me, ere we part,
Be happier than you know to wish; farewel.

Tigr. *Spaconia*, stay and hear me what I say:
In short, destruction meet me that I may
See it, and not avoid it, when I leave
To be thy faithful lover: part with me
Thou shalt not, there are none that know our love,
And I have given gold unto a Captain
That goes unto *Iberia* from the King,
That he will place a Lady of our Land
With the Kings Sister that is offered me;
Thither shall you, and being once got in
Perswade her by what subtil means you can
To be as backward in her love as I.

Spa. Can you imagine that a longing maid
When she beholds you, can be pull'd away
With words from loving you?

Tigr. Dispraise my health, my honesty, and tell her I am jealous.

Spa. Why, I had rather lose you: can my heart
Consent to let my tongue throw out such words,
And I that ever yet spoke what I thought,
Shall find it such a thing at first to lie?

Tigr. Yet do thy best.

Enter Bessus.

Bes. What, is your Majesty ready?

Tigr. There is the Lady, Captain.

Bes. Sweet Lady, by your leave, I co[u]ld wish my self more full of Courtship for your fair sake.

Spa. Sir I shall feel no want of that.

Bes. Lady, you must hast, I have received new letters from the King that require more hast than I expected, he will follow me suddenly himself, and begins to call for your Majesty already.

Tigr. He shall not do so long.

Bes. Sweet Lady, shall I call you my Charge hereafter?

Spa. I will not take upon me to govern your tongue Sir, you shall call me what you please.

Actus Secundus.

Enter Gobrias, Bacurius, Arane, Panthe, *and* Mandane, *Waiting-women with Attendants.*

Gob. MY Lord *Bacurius*, you must have regard unto the Queen, she is your prisoner, 'tis at your peril if she make escape.

Bac. My Lord, I know't, she is my prisoner from you committed; yet she is a woman, and so I keep her safe, you will not urge me to keep her close, I shall not shame to say I sorrow for her.

Gob. So do I my Lord; I sorrow for her, that so little grace doth govern her: that she should stretch her arm against her King, so little womanhood and natural goodness, as to think the death of her own Son.

Ara. Thou knowst the reason why, dissembling as thou art, and wilt not speak.

Gob. There is a Lady takes not after you,
Her Father is within her, that good man
Whose tears weigh'd down his sins, mark how she weeps,
How well it does become her, and if you
Can find no disposition in your self
To sorrow, yet by gracefulness in her
Find out the way, and by your reason weep:
All this she does for you, and more she needs
When for your self you will not lose a tear,
Think how this want of grief discredits you,
And you will weep, because you cannot weep.

Ara. You talk to me as having got a time fit for your purpose; but you know I know you speak not what you think. (should be urg'd

Pan. I would my heart were Stone, before my softness
Against my mother, a more troubled thought
No Virgin bears about; should I excuse
My Mothers fault, I should set light a life
In losing which, a brother and a King
Were taken from me, if I seek to save
That life so lov'd, I lose another life
That gave me being, I shall lose a Mother,
A word of such a sound in a childs ears
That it strikes reverence through it; may the will
Of heaven be done, and if one needs must fall,
Take a poor Virgins life to answer all.

Ara. But *Gobrias* let us talk, you know this fault
Is not in me as in another Mother.

Gob. I know it is not.

Ara. Yet you make it so.

Gob. Why, is not all that's past beyond your help?

Ara. I know it is.

Gob. Nay should you publish it before the world,
Think you 'twould be believ'd?

Ara. I know it would not.

Gob. Nay should I joyn with you, should we not both be torn and yet both die uncredited?

Ara. I think we should.

Gob. Why then take you such violent courses? As for me I do but right in saving of the King from all your plots.

Ara. The King?

Gob. I bad you rest with patience, and a time
Would come for me to reconcile all to
Your own content, but by this way you take
Away my power, and what was done unknown,
Was not by me but you: your urging being done
I must preserve my own, but time may bring
All this to light, and happily for all.

Ara. Accursed be this over curious brain
That gave that plot a birth, accurst this womb
That after did conceive to my disgrace.

Bac. My Lord Protector, they say there are divers Letters come from *Armenia*, that *Bessus* has done good service, and brought again a day, by his particular valour, receiv'd you any to that effect?

Gob. Yes, 'tis most certain.

Bac. I'm sorry for't, not that the day was won,
But that 'twas won by him: we held him here
A Coward, he did me wrong once, at which I laugh'd,
And so did all the world, for nor I,
Nor any other held him worth my sword.

Enter Bessus *and* Spaconia.

Bes. Health to my Protector; from the King
These Letters; and to your grace Madam, these.

Gob. How does his Majesty?

Bes. As well as conquest by his own means and his valiant C[o]mmanders can make him; your letters will tell you all.

Pan. I will not open mine till I do know
My Brothers health: good Captain is he well?

Bes. As the rest of us that fought are.

Pan. But how's that? is he hurt?

Bes. He's a strange souldier that gets not a knock.

Pan. I do not ask how strange that souldier is
That gets no hurt, but whether he have one.

Bes. He had divers.

Pan. And is he well again?

Bes. Well again, an't please your Grace: why I was run

twice through the body, and shot i'th' head with a cross-arrow, and yet am well again.

Pan. I do not care how thou do'st, is he well?

Bes. Not care how I do? Let a man out of the mightiness of his spirit, fructifie Foreign Countries with his blood for the good of his own, and thus he shall be answered: Why I may live to relieve with spear and shield, such a Lady as you distressed.

Pan. Why, I will care, I'me glad that thou art well, I prethee is he so?

Gob. The King is well and will be here to morrow.

Pan. My prayer is heard, now will I open mine.

Gob. *Bacurius*, I must ease you of your charge:
Madam, the wonted mercy of the King,
That overtakes your faults, has met with this,
And struck it out, he has forgiven you freely,
Your own will is your law, be where you please.

Ara. I thank him. (row?

Gob. You will be ready to wait upon his Majesty to mor-

Ara. I will. [*Exit* Arane.

Bac. Madam be wise hereafter; I am glad I have lost this Office.

Gob. Good Captain *Bessus*, tell us the discourse betwixt *Tigranes* and our King, and how we got the victory.

Pan. I prethee do, and if my Brother were
In any danger, let not thy tale make
Him abide there long before thou bring him off,
For all that while my heart will beat.

Bes. Madam let what will beat, I must tell the truth, and thus it was; they fought single in lists, but one to one; as for my own part, I was dangerously hurt but three days before, else, perhaps, we had been two to two, I cannot tell, some thought we had, and the occasion of my hurt was this, the enemy had made Trenches.

Gob. Captain, without the manner of your hurt be much material to this business, we'l hear't some other time.

Pan. I prethee leave it, and go on with my Brother.

Bes. I will, but 'twould be worth your hearing: To the Lists they came, and single-sword and gantlet was their fight.

Pan. Alas!

Bes. Without the Lists there stood some dozen Captains of either side mingled, all which were sworn, and one of those was I: and 'twas my chance to stand next a Captain o'th' enemies side, called *Tiribasus*; Valiant they said he was; whilst these two Kings were streaching themselves, this *Tiribasus* cast something a scornful look on me, and ask't me who I thought would overcome: I smil'd and told him if he would fight with me, he should perceive by the event of that whose King would win: something he answered, and a scuffle was like to grow, when one *Zipetus* offered to help him, I—

Pan. All this is of thy self, I pray thee *Bessus* tell something of my Brother, did he nothing?

Bes. Why yes, I'le tell your Grace, they were not to fight till the word given, which for my own part, by my troth I confess I was not to give.

Pan. See for his own part.

Bac. I fear yet this fellow's abus'd with a good report.

Bes. But I—

Pan. Still of himself.

Bes. Cri'd give the word, when as some of them say, *Tigranes* was stooping, but the word was not given then, yet one *Cosroes* of the enemies part, held up his finger to me, which is as much with us Martialists, as I will fight with you: I said not a word, nor made sign during the combate, but that once done.

Pan. He slips o're all the fight.

Bes. I call'd him to me, *Cosroes* said I.

Pan. I will hear no more.

Bes. No, no, I lie.

Bac. I dare be sworn thou dost.

Bes. Captain said I, so it was.

Pan. I tell thee, I will hear no further.

Bes. No? Your Grace will wish you had.

Pan. I will not wish it, what is this the Lady
My brother writes to me to take?

Bes. And please your Grace this is she: Charge, will you come near the Princess?

Pan. You'r welcome from your Country, and this land shall shew unto you all the kindness that I can make it; what's your name?

Spa. *Thalectris.*

Pan. Y'are very welcome, you have got a letter to put you to me, that has power enough to place mine enemy here; then much more you that are so far from being so to me that you ne're saw me.

Bes. Madam, I dare pass my word for her truth.

Spa. My truth?

Pan. Why Captain, do you think I am afraid she'l steal?

Bes. I cannot tell, servants are slippery, but I dare give my word for her, and for honesty, she came along with me, and many favours she did me by the way, but by this light none but what she might do with modesty, to a man of my rank.

Pan. Why Captain, here's no body thinks otherwise.

Bes. Nay, if you should, your Grace may think your pleasure; but I am sure I brought her from *Armenia*, and in all that way, if ever I touch'd any bare of her above her knee, I pray God I may sink where I stand.

Spa. Above my knee?

Bes. No, you know I did not, and if any man will say, I did, this sword shall answer; Nay, I'le defend the reputation of my charge whilst I live, your Grace shall understand I am secret in these businesses, and know how to defend a Ladies honour.

Spa. I hope your Grace knows him so well already, I shall not need to tell you he's vain and foolish.

Bes. I you may call me what you please, but I'le defend your good name against the world; and so I take my leave of your Grace, and of you my Lord Protector; I am likewise glad to see your Lordship well.

Bac. O Captain *Bessus*, I thank you, I would speak with you anon.

Bes. When you please, I will attend your Lordship.

Bac. Madam, I'le take my leave too.

Pan. Good *Bacurius.* [*Exeunt* Bes. *and* Bac.

Gob. Madam what writes his Majesty to you?

Pan. O my Lord, the kindest words, I'le keep 'em whilst I live, here in my bosom, there's no art in 'em, they lie disordered in this paper, just as hearty nature speaks 'em.

Gob. And to me he writes what tears of joy he shed to

hear how you were grown in every vertues way, and yields all thanks to me, for that dear care which I was bound to have in training you, there is no Princess living that enjoys a brother of that worth.

Pan. My Lord, no maid longs more for any thing,
And feels more heat and cold within her breast,
Than I do now, in hopes to see him.

Gob. Yet I wonder much
At this he writes, he brings along with him
A husband for you, that same Captive Prince,
And if he loves you as he makes a shew,
He will allow you freedom in your choice.

Pan. And so he will my Lord, I warrant you, he will but offer and give me the power to take or leave.

Gob. Trust me, were I a Lady, I could not like that man were bargain'd with before I choose him.

Pan. But I am not built on such wild humours, if I find him worthy, he is not less because he's offer'd.

Spa. 'Tis true, he is not, would he would seem less.

Gob. I think there's no Lady can affect
Another Prince, your brother standing by;
He doth Eclipse mens vertues so with his.

Spa. I know a Lady may, and more I fear
Another Lady will.

Pan. Would I might see him.

Gob. Why so you shall, my businesses are great,
I will attend you when it is his pleasure to see you.

Pan. I thank you good my Lord.

Gob. You will be ready Madam. [*Exit Gob.*

Pan. Yes.

Spa. I do beseech you Madam, send away
Your other women, and receive from me
A few sad words, which set against your joyes
May make 'em shine the more.

Pan. Sirs, leave me all. [*Exeunt Women.*

Spa. I kneel a stranger here to beg a thing
Unfit for me to ask, and you to grant,
'Tis such another strange ill-laid request,
As if a begger should intreat a King
To leave his Scepter, and his Throne to him

And take his rags to wander o're the world
Hungry and cold.

Pan. That were a strange request.

Spa. As ill is mine.

Pan. Then do not utter it.

Spa. Alas 'tis of that nature, that it must
Be utter'd, I, and granted, or I die:
I am asham'd to speak it; but where life
Lies at the stake, I cannot think her woman
That will not take something unreasonably to hazard saving of it: I shall seem a strange Petitioner, that wish all ill to them I beg of, e're they give me ought; yet so I must: I would you were not fair, nor wise, for in your ill consists my good: if you were foolish, you would hear my prayer, if foul, you had not power to hinder me: he would not love you.

Pan. What's the meaning of it.

Spa. Nay, my request is more without the bounds
Of reason yet: for 'tis not in the power
Of you to do, what I would have you grant.

Pan. Why then 'tis idle, pray thee speak it out.

Spa. Your brother brings a Prince into this land,
Of such a noble shape, so sweet a grace,
So full of worth withal, that every maid
That looks upon him, gives away her self
To him for ever; and for you to have
He brings him: and so mad is my demand
That I desire you not to have this man,
This excellent man, for whom you needs must die,
If you should miss him. I do now expect
You should laugh at me.

Pan. Trust me I could weep rather, for I have found
In all thy words a strange disjoynted sorrow.

Spa. 'Tis by me his own desire so, that you would not love (him.

Pan. His own desire! why credit me *Thalestris*,
I am no common wooer: if he shall wooe me, his worth may be such, that I dare not swear I will not love him; but if he will stay to have me wooe him, I will promise thee, he may keep all his graces to himself, and fear no ravishing from me.

Spa. 'Tis yet his own desire, but when he sees your face, I fear it will not be; therefore I charge you as you have pity, stop these tender ears from his enchanting voice, close up those eyes, that you may neither catch a dart from him, nor he from you; I charge you as you hope to live in quiet; for when I am dead, for certain I will walk to visit him if he break promise with me: for as fast as Oaths without a formal Ceremony can make me, I am to him.

Pan. Then be fearless;
For if he were a thing 'twixt God and man,
I could gaze on him; if I knew it sin
To love him without passion: Dry your eyes,
I swear you shall enjoy him still for me,
I will not hinder you; but I perceive
You are not what you seem, rise, rise *Thalestris*,
If your right name be so.

Spa. Indeed it is not, *Spaconia* is my name; but I desire not to be known to other.

Pan. Why, by me you shall not, I will never do you wrong, what good I can, I will, think not my birth or education such, that I should injure a stranger Virgin; you are welcome hither, in company you wish to be commanded, but when we are alone, I shall be ready to be your servant.

[*Exeunt.*

Enter three Men and a Woman.

1 Come, come, run, run, run.

2 We shall out-go her.

3 One were better be hang'd than carry out women fidling to these shews.

Wom. Is the King hard by?

1 You heard he with the Bottles said, he thought we should come too late: What abundance of people here is!

Wom. But what had he in those Bottles?

3 I know not.

2 Why, Ink goodman fool.

3 Ink, what to do?

1 Why the King look you, will many times call for these Bottles, and break his mind to his friends.

Wom. Let's take our places, we shall have no room else.

2 The man told us he would walk o' foot through the people.

3 I marry did he.
1 Our shops are well look't to now.
2 'Slife, yonder's my Master, I think.
1 No 'tis not he.

Enter a man with two Citizens-wives.

1 *Cit.* Lord how fine the fields be, what sweet living 'tis in the Country!

2 *Cit.* I poor souls, God help 'em; they live as contentedly as one of us.

1 *Cit.* My husbands Cousin would have had me gone into the Country last year, wert thou ever there?

2 *Cit.* I, poor souls, I was amongst 'em once.

1 *Cit.* And what kind of creatures are they, for love of God?

2 *Cit.* Very good people, God help 'em.

1 *Cit.* Wilt thou go down with me this Summer when I am brought to bed?

2 *Cit.* Alas, it is no place for us.

1 *Cit.* Why, pray thee?

2 *Cit.* Why you can have nothing there, there's no body cryes brooms.

1 *Cit.* No?

2 *Cit.* No truly, nor milk.

1 *Cit.* Nor milk, how do they?

2 *Cit.* They are fain to milk themselves i'th' Country.

1 *Cit.* Good Lord! but the people there, I think, will be very dutiful to one of us.

2 *Cit.* I God knows will they, and yet they do not greatly care for our husbands.

1 *Cit.* Do they not? Alas! I'good faith I cannot blame them: for we do not greatly care for them our selves. *Philip*, I pray choose us a place.

Phil. There's the best forsooth.

1 *Cit.* By your leave good people a little.

3 What's the matter?

Phil. I pray you my friend, do not thrust my Mistress so, she's with Child.

2 Let her look to her self then, has she not had showing enough yet? if she stay shouldring here, she may haps go home with a cake in her belly.

3 How now, goodman squitter-breech, why do you lean on me?

Phi. Because I will.

3 Will you Sir sawce-box?

1 *Cit.* Look if one ha'not struck *Philip*, come hither *Philip*, why did he strike thee?

Phil. For leaning on him.

1 *Cit.* Why didst thou lean on him?

Phil. I did not think he would have struck me.

1 *Cit.* As God save me la thou'rt as wild as a Buck, there's no quarel but thou'rt at one end or other on't.

3 It's at the first end then, for he'l ne'r stay the last.

1 *Cit.* Well slip-string, I shall meet with you.

3 When you will.

1 *Cit.* I'le give a crown to meet with you.

3 At a Bawdy-house.

1 *Cit.* I you're full of your Roguery; but if I do meet you it shall cost me a fall.

Flourish. Enter one running.

4 The King, the King, the King. Now, now, now, now.

Flourish. Enter Arb. Tigr. *the two Kings and* Mardonius.

All. God preserve your Majesty.

Arb. I thank you all, now are my joyes at full, when I behold you safe, my loving Subjects; by you I grow, 'tis your united love that lifts me to this height: all the account that I can render you for all the love you have bestowed on me, all your expences to maintain my war, is but a little word, you will imagine 'tis slender paiment, yet 'tis such a word, as is not to be bought but with your bloods, 'tis Peace.

All. God preserve your Majesty.

Arb. Now you may live securely i'your Towns,
Your Children round about you; may sit
Under your Vines, and make the miseries
Of other Kingdoms a discourse for you,
And lend them sorrows; for your selves, you may
Safely forget there are such things as tears,
And you may all whose good thoughts I have gain'd,
Hold me unworthy, where I think my life

A sacrifice too great to keep you thus
In such a calm estate.

All. God bless your Majesty.

Arb. See all good people, I have brought the man whose very name you fear'd, a captive home; behold him, 'tis *Tigranes*; in your heart sing songs of gladness, and deliverance.

1 *Cit.* Out upon him.

2 *Cit.* How he looks.

3 *Wom.* Hang him, hang him.

Mar. These are sweet people.

Tigr. Sir, you do me wrong, to render me a scorned spectacle to common people.

Arb. It was so far from me to mean it so: if I have ought deserv'd, my loving Subjects, let me beg of you, not to revile this Prince, in whom there dwells all worth of which the name of a man is capable, valour beyond compare, the terrour of his name has stretcht it self where ever there is sun; and yet for you I fought with him single, and won him too; I made his valour stoop, and brought that name soar'd to so unbeliev'd a height, to fall beneath mine: this inspir'd with all your loves, I did perform, and will for your content, be ever ready for a greater work.

All. The Lord bless your Majesty.

Tigr. So he has made me amends now with a speech in commendation of himself: I would not be so vain-glorious.

Arb. If there be any thing in which I may
Do good to any creature, here speak out;
For I must leave you: and it troubles me,
That my occasions for the good of you,
Are such as call me from you: else, my joy
Would be to spend my days among you all.
You shew your loves in these large multitudes
That come to meet me, I will pray for you,
Heaven prosper you, that you may know old years,
And live to see your childrens children sit
At your boards with plenty: when there is
A want of any thing, let it be known
To me, and I will be a Father to you:
God keep you all.

[*Flourish. Exeunt Kings and their Train.*

All. God bless your Majesty, God bless your Majesty.

1 Come, shall we go? all's done.

Wom. I for God sake, I have not made a fire yet.

2 Away, away, all's done.

3 Content, farewel *Philip*.

1 *Cit.* Away you halter-sack you.

2 *Philip* will not fight, he's afraid on's face.

Phil. I marry am I afraid of my face.

3 Thou wouldst be *Philip* if thou sawst it in a glass; it looks so like a Visour. [*Exeunt* 2, 3, *and Woman.*

1 *Cit.* You'l be hang'd sirra: Come *Philip* walk before us homewards; did not his Majesty say he had brought us home Pease for all our money?

2 *Cit.* Yes marry did he.

1 *Cit.* They're the first I heard of this year by my troth, I longed for some of 'em: did he not say we should have some?

2 *Cit.* Yes, and so we shall anon I warrant you have every one a peck brought home to our houses.

Actus Tertius.

Enter Arbaces *and* Gobrias.

Arb. MY Sister take it ill?

Gob. Not very ill,
Something unkindly she does take it Sir to have
Her Husband chosen to her hands.

Arb. Why *Gobrias* let her, I must have her know, my will and not her own must govern her: what will she marry with some slave at home?

Gob. O she is far from any stubbornness, you much mistake her, and no doubt will like where you would have her, but when you behold her, you will be loth to part with such a jewel.

Arb. To part with her? why *Gobrias*, art thou mad? she is my Sister.

Gob. Sir, I know she is: but it were pity to make poor our Land, with such a beauty to enrich another.

Arb. Pish will she have him?

Gob. I do hope she will not, I think she will Sir.

Arb. Were she my Father and my Mother too, and all the names for which we think folks friends, she should be forc't to have him when I know 'tis fit: I will not hear her say she's loth.

Gob. Heaven bring my purpose luckily to pass, you know 'tis just, she will not need constraint she loves you so.

Arb. How does she love me, speak?

Gob. She loves you more than people love their health, that live by labour; more than I could love a man that died for me, if he could live again.

Arb. She is not like her mother then.

Gob. O no, when you were in *Armenia*,
I durst not let her know when you were hurt:
For at the first on every little scratch,
She kept her Chamber, wept, and could not eat,
Till you were well, and many times the news
Was so long coming, that before we heard
She was as near her death, as you your health.

Arb. Alas poor soul, but yet she must be rul'd;
I know not how I shall requite her well.
I long to see her, have you sent for her,
To tell her I am ready?

Gob. Sir I have.

Enter 1 Gent. *and* Tigranes.

1 *Gent.* Sir, here is the *Armenian* King.

Arb. He's welcome.

1 *Gent.* And the Queen-mother, and the Princess wait without.

Arb. Good *Gobrias* bring 'em in.
Tigranes, you will think you are arriv'd
In a strange Land, where Mothers cast to poyson
Their only Sons; think you you shall be safe?

Tigr. Too safe I am Sir.

Enter Gobrias, Arane, Panthea, Spaconia, Bacurius, Mardonius *and* Bessus, *and two Gentlemen.*

Ara. As low as this I bow to you, and would
As low as is my grave, to shew a mind
Thankful for all your mercies.

Arb. O stand up,
And let me kneel, the light will be asham'd
To see observance done to me by you.
Ara. You are my King.
Arb. You are my Mother, rise;
As far be all your faults from your own soul,
As from my memory; then you shall be
As white as innocence her self.
Ara. I came
Only to shew my duty, and acknowledge
My sorrows for my sins; longer to stay
Were but to draw eyes more attentively
Upon my shame, that power that kept you safe
From me, preserve you still.
Arb. Your own desires shall be your guide. [*Exit* Arane.
Pan. Now let me die, since I have seen my Lord the King
Return in safetie, I have seen all good that life
Can shew me; I have ne're another wish
For Heaven to grant, nor were it fit I should;
For I am bound to spend my age to come,
In giving thanks that this was granted me.
Gob. Why does not your Majesty speak?
Arb. To whom?
Gob. To the Princess.
Pan. Alas Sir, I am fearful, you do look
On me, as if I were some loathed thing
That you were finding out a way to shun.
Gob. Sir, you should speak to her.
Arb. Ha?
Pan. I know I am unworthy, yet not ill arm'd, with which innocence here I will kneel, till I am one with earth, but I will gain some words and kindness from you.
Tigr. Will you speak Sir?
Arb. Speak, am I what I was?
What art thou that dost creep into my breast,
And dar'st not see my face? shew forth thy self:
I feel a pair of fiery wings displai'd
Hither, from hence; you shall not tarry there,
Up, and be gone, if thou beest Love be gone:
Or I will tear thee from my wounded breast,

Pull thy lov'd Down away, and with thy Quill
By this right arm drawn from thy wonted wing,
Write to thy laughing Mother i'thy bloud,
That you are powers bely'd, and all your darts
Are to be blown away, by men resolv'd,
Like dust; I know thou fear'st my words, away.

Tigr. O misery! why should he be so slow?
There can no falshood come of loving her;
Though I have given my faith; she is a thing
Both to be lov'd and serv'd beyond my faith:
I would he would present me to her quickly.

Pan. Will you not speak at all? are you so far
From kind words? yet to save my modesty,
That must talk till you answer, do not stand
As you were dumb, say something, though it be
Poyson'd with anger, that it may strike me dead.

Mar. Have you no life at all? for man-hood sake
Let her not kneel, and talk neglected thus;
A tree would find a tongue to answer her,
Did she but give it such a lov'd respect.

Arb. You mean this Lady: lift her from the earth; why do you let her kneel so long? Alas, Madam, your beauty uses to command, and not to beg. What is your sute to me? it shall be granted, yet the time is short, and my affairs are great: but where's my Sister? I bade she should be brought.

Mar. What, is he mad?

Arb. *Gobrias*, where is she?

Gob. Sir.

Arb. Where is she man?

Gob. Who, Sir?

Arb. Who, hast thou forgot my Sister?

Gob. Your Sister, Sir?

Arb. Your Sister, Sir? some one that hath a wit, answer, where is she?

Gob. Do you not see her there?

Arb. Where?

Gob. There.

Arb. There, where?

Mar. S'light, there, are you blind?

Arb. Which do you mean, that little one?

Gob. No Sir.
Arb. No Sir? why, do you mock me? I can see
No other here, but that petitioning Lady.
Gob. That's she.
Arb. Away.
Gob. Sir, it is she.
Arb. 'Tis false.
Gob. Is it?
Arb. As hell, by Heaven, as false as hell,
My Sister: is she dead? if it be so,
Speak boldly to me; for I am a man,
And dare not quarrel with Divinity;
And do not think to cozen me with this:
I see you all are mute and stand amaz'd,
Fearful to answer me; it is too true,
A decreed instant cuts off ev'ry life,
For which to mourn, is to repine; she dy'd
A Virgin, though more innocent than sheep,
As clear as her own eyes, and blessedness
Eternal waits upon her where she is:
I know she could not make a wish to change
Her state for new, and you shall see me bear
My crosses like a man; we all must die,
And she hath taught us how.
Gob. Do not mistake,
And vex your self for nothing; for her death
Is a long life off, I hope: 'Tis she,
And if my speech deserve not faith, lay death
Upon me, and my latest words shall force
A credit from you.
Arb. Which, good *Gobrias*? that Lady dost thou mean?
Gob. That Lady Sir,
She is your Sister, and she is your Sister
That loves you so, 'tis she for whom I weep,
To see you use her thus.
Arb. It cannot be.
Tigr. Pish, this is tedious,
I cannot hold, I must present my self,
And yet the sight of my *Spaconia*
Touches me, as a sudden thunder-clap

Does one that is about to sin.
Arb. Away,
No more of this; here I pronounce him Traytor,
The direct plotter of my death, that names
Or thinks her for my Sister, 'tis a lie,
The most malicious of the world, invented
To mad your King; he that will say so next,
Let him draw out his sword and sheath it here,
It is a sin fully as pardonable:
She is no kin to me, nor shall she be;
If she were ever, I create her none:
And which of you can question this? My power
Is like the Sea, that is to be obey'd,
And not disputed with: I have decreed her
As far from having part of blood with me,
As the nak'd *Indians*; come and answer me,
He that is boldest now; is that my Sister?
Mar. O this is fine.
Bes. No marry, she is not, an't please your Majesty,
I never thought she was, she's nothing like you.
Arb. No 'tis true, she is not.
Mar. Thou shou'dst be hang'd.
Pan. Sir, I will speak but once; by the same power
You make my blood a stranger unto yours,
You may command me dead, and so much love
A stranger may importune, pray you do;
If this request appear too much to grant,
Adopt me of some other Family,
By your unquestion'd word; else I shall live
Like sinfull issues that are left in streets
By their regardless Mothers, and no name
Will be found for me.
Arb. I will hear no more,
Why should there be such musick in a voyce,
And sin for me to hear it? All the world
May take delight in this, and 'tis damnation
For me to do so: You are fair and wise
And vertuous I think, and he is blest
That is so near you as my brother is;
But you are nought to me but a disease;

Continual torment without hope of ease;
Such an ungodly sickness I have got,
That he that undertakes my cure, must first
O'rethrow Divinity, all moral Laws,
And leave mankind as unconfin'd as beasts,
Allowing 'em to do all actions
As freely as they drink when they desire.
Let me not hear you speak again; yet see
I shall but lang[u]ish for the want of that,
The having which, would kill me: No man here
Offer to speak for her; for I consider
As much as you can say; I will not toil
My body and my mind too, rest thou there,
Here's one within will labour for you both.

Pan. I would I were past speaking.

Gob. Fear not Madam,
The King will alter, 'tis some sudden rage,
And you shall see it end some other way.

Pan. Pray heaven it do.

Tig. Though she to whom I swore, be here, I cannot
Stifle my passion longer; if my father
Should rise again disquieted with this,
And charge me to forbear, yet it would out.
Madam, a stranger, and a pris'ner begs
To be bid welcome.

Pan. You are welcome, Sir,
I think, but if you be not, 'tis past me
To make you so: for I am here a stranger,
Greater than you; we know from whence you come,
But I appear a lost thing, and by whom
Is yet uncertain, found here i'th' Court,
And onely suffer'd to walk up and down,
As one not worth the owning.

Spa. O, I fear
Tigranes will be caught, he looks, me-thinks,
As he would change his eyes with her; some help
There is above for me, I hope.

Tigr. Why do you turn away, and weep so fast,
And utter things that mis-become your looks,
Can you want owning?

Spa. O 'tis certain so.
Tigr. Acknowledge your self mine.
Arb. How now?
Tigr. And then see if you want an owner.
Arb. They are talking.
Tigr. Nations shall owne you for their Queen.
Arb. *Tigranes*, art not thou my prisoner?
Tigr. I am.
Arb. And who is this?
Tigr. She is your Sister.
Arb. She is so.
Mar. Is she so again? that's well.
Arb. And then how dare you offer to change words with (her?
Tigr. Dare do it! Why? you brought me hither Sir,
To that intent.
Arb. Perhaps I told you so,
If I had sworn it, had you so much folly
To credit it? The least word that she speaks
Is worth a life; rule your disordered tongue,
Or I will temper it.
Spa. Blest be the breath.
Tigr. Temper my tongue! such incivilities
As these, no barbarous people ever knew:
You break the lawes of Nature, and of Nations,
You talk to me as if I were a prisoner
For theft: my tongue be temper'd? I must speak
If thunder check me, and I will.
Arb. You will?
Spa. Alas my fortune.
Tigr. Do not fear his frown, dear Madam, hear me.
Arb. Fear not my frown? but that 'twere base in me
To fight with one I know I can o'recome,
Again thou shouldst be conquer'd by me.
Mar. He has one ransome with him already; me-thinks
'T were good to fight double, or quit.
Arb. Away with him to prison: Now Sir, see
If my frown be regardless; Why delay you?
Seise him *Bacurius*, you shall know my word
Sweeps like a wind, and all it grapples with,
Are as the chaffe before it.

Tigr. Touch me not.
Arb. Help there.
Tigr. Away.
1 *Gent.* It is in vain to struggle.
2 *Gent.* You must be forc'd.
Bac. Sir, you must pardon us, we must obey.
Arb. Why do you dally there? drag him away
By any thing.
Bac. Come Sir.
Tigr. Justice, thou ought'st to give me strength enough
To shake all these off; This is tyrannie,
Arbaces, sutler than the burning Bulls,
Or that fam'd *Titans* bed. Thou mightst as well
Search i'th' deep of Winter through the snow
For half starv'd people, to bring home with thee,
To shew 'em fire, and send 'em back again,
As use me thus.
Arb. Let him be close, *Bacurius*. [*Exeunt* Tigr. *and* Bac.
Spa. I ne're rejoyc'd at any ill to him,
But this imprisonment: what shall become
Of me forsaken?
Gob. You will not let your Sister
Depart thus discontented from you, Sir?
Arb. By no means *Gobrias*, I have done her wrong,
And made my self believe much of my self,
That is not in me: You did kneel to me,
Whilest I stood stubborn and regardless by,
And like a god incensed, gave no ear
To all your prayers: behold, I kneel to you,
Shew a contempt as large as was my own,
And I will suffer it, yet at the last forgive me.
Pan. O you wrong me more in this,
Than in your rage you did: you mock me now.
Arb. Never forgive me then, which is the worst
Can happen to me.
Pan. If you be in earnest,
Stand up and give me but a gentle look,
And two kind words, and I shall be in heaven.
Arb. Rise you then to hear; I acknowledge thee
My hope, the only jewel of my life,

The best of Sisters, dearer than my breath,
A happiness as high as I could think;
And when my actions call thee otherwise,
Perdition light upon me.

Pan. This is better
Than if you had not frown'd, it comes to me,
Like mercie at the block, and when I leave
To serve you with my life, your curse be with me.

Arb. Then thus I do salute thee, and again,
To make this knot the stronger, Paradise
Is there: It may be you are yet in doubt,
This third kiss blots it out, I wade in sin,
And foolishly intice my self along;
Take her away, see her a prisoner
In her own chamber closely, *Gobrias.*

Pan. Alas Sir, why?

Arb. I must not stay the answer, doe it.

Gob. Good Sir.

Arb. No more, doe it I say.

Mard. This is better and better.

Pan. Yet hear me speak.

Arb. I will not hear you speak,
Away with her, let no man think to speak
For such a creature; for she is a witch,
A prisoner, and a Traitor.

Gob. Madam, this office grieves me.

Pan. Nay, 'tis well the king is pleased with it.

Arb. *Bessus*, go you along too with her; I will prove
All this that I have said, if I may live
So long; but I am desperately sick,
For she has given me poison in a kiss;
She had't betwixt her lips, and with her eyes
She witches people: go without a word.

[*Exeunt* Gob. Pan. Bes. *and* Spaconia.

Why should you that have made me stand in war
Like fate it self, cutting what threds I pleas'd,
Decree such an unworthy end of me,
And all my glories? What am I, alas,
That you oppose me? if my secret thoughts
Have ever harbour'd swellings against you,

They could not hurt you, and it is in you
To give me sorrow, that will render me
Apt to receive your mercy; rather so,
Let it be rather so, than punish me
With such unmanly sins: Incest is in me
Dwelling already, and it must be holy
That pulls it thence, where art *Mardonius*?

Mar. Here Sir.

Arb. I pray thee bear me, if thou canst,
Am I not grown a strange weight?

Mar. As you were.

Arb. No heavier?

Mar. No Sir.

Arb. Why, my legs
Refuse to bear my body; O *Mardonius*,
Thou hast in field beheld me, when thou knowst
I could have gone, though I could never run.

Mar. And so I shall again.

Arb. O no, 'tis past.

Mar. Pray you go rest your self.

Arb. Wilt thou hereafter when they talk of me,
As thou shalt hear nothing but infamy,
Remember some of those things?

Mar. Yes I will.

Arb. I pray thee do: for thou shalt never see me so again.
[*Exeunt.*

Enter Bessus alone.

Bes. They talk of fame, I have gotten it in the wars; and will afford any man a reasonable penny-worth: some will say, they could be content to have it, but that it is to be atchiev'd with danger; but my opinion is otherwise: for if I might stand still in Cannon-proof, and have fame fall upon me, I would refuse it: my reputation came principally by thinking to run away, which no body knows but *Mardonius*, and I think he conceals it to anger me. Before I went to the warrs, I came to the Town a young fellow, without means or parts to deserve friends; and my empty guts perswaded me to lie, and abuse people for my meat, which I did, and they beat me: then would I fast two days, till my hunger cri'd out on me, rail still, then me-thought I had a monstrous stomach to abuse 'em again, and did it. I, this state I continu'd till they hung me up by th' heels, and beat me wi' hasle sticks, as if they would have baked me, and have cousen'd some body wi'me for Venison: After this I rail'd, and eat quietly: for the whole Kingdom took notice of me for a baffl'd whipt fellow, and what I said was remembred in mirth but never in anger, of which I was glad; I would it were at that pass again. After this, heaven calls an Aunt of mine, that left two hundred pound in a cousins hand for me, who taking me to be a gallant young spirit, raised a company for me with the money and sent me into *Armenia* with'em: Away I would have run from them, but that I could get no company, and alone I durst not run. I was never at battail but once, and there I was running, but *Mardonius* cudgel'd me; yet I got loose at last, but was so fraid, that I saw no more than my shoulders doe, but fled with my whole company amongst my Enemies, and overthrew'em: Now the report of my valour is come over before me, and they say I was a raw young fellow, but now I am improv'd, a Plague on their eloquence, 't will cost me many a beating; And *Mardonius* might help this too, if he would; for now they think to get honour on me, and all the men I have abus'd call me freshly worthily, as they call it by the way of challenge.

Enter a Gent.

3 *Gent.* Good morrow, Captain *Bessus.*

Bes. Good morrow Sir.

3 *Gent.* I come to speak with you.

Bes. You're very welcome.

3 *Gent.* From one that holds himself wrong'd by you some three years since: your worth he says is fam'd, and he doth nothing doubt but you will do him right, as beseems a souldier.

Bes. A pox on'em, so they cry all.

3 *Gent.* And a slight note I have about me for you, for the delivery of which you must excuse me; it is an office that friendship calls upon me to do, and no way offensive to you; since I desire but right on both sides.

Bes. 'Tis a challenge Sir, is it not?

3 *Gent.* 'Tis an inviting to the field.

Bes. An inviting? O Sir your Mercy, what a Complement he delivers it with? he might as agreeable to my nature present me poison with such a speech: um um um reputation, um um um call you to account, um um um forc'd to this, um um um with my Sword, um um um like a Gentleman, um um um dear to me, um um um satisfaction: 'Tis very well Sir, I do accept it, but he must await an answer this thirteen weeks.

3 *Gent.* Why Sir, he would be glad to wipe off his stain as soon as he could.

Bes. Sir upon my credit I am already ingag'd to two hundred, and twelve, all which must have their stains wip'd off, if that be the word, before him.

3 *Gent.* Sir, if you be truly ingag'd but to one, he shall stay a competent time.

Bes. Upon my faith Sir, to two hundred and twelve, and I have a spent body, too much bruis'd in battel, so that I cannot fight, I must be plain, above three combats a day: All the kindness I can shew him, is to set him resolvedly in my rowle, the two hundred and thirteenth man, which is something, for I tell you, I think there will be more after him, than before him, I think so; pray you commend me to him, and tell him this.

3 *Gent.* I will Sir, good morrow to you.

[*Exit* 3 *Gent.*

Bes. Good morrow good Sir. Certainly my safest way were to print my self a coward, with a discovery how I came by my credit, and clap it upon every post; I have received above thirty challenges within this two hours, marry all but the first I put off with ingagement, and by good fortune, the first is no madder of fighting than I, so that that's referred, the place where it must be ended, is four days journey off, and our arbitratours are these: He has chosen a Gentleman in travel, and I have a special friend with a quartain ague, like to hold him this five years, for mine: and when his man comes home, we are to expect my friends health: If they would finde me challenges thus thick, as long as I liv'd, I would have no other living; I can make seven shillings a day o'th' paper to the Grocers: yet I learn nothing by all these but a little skill in comparing of stiles. I do finde evidently, that there is some one Scrivener in this Town, that has a great hand in writing of Challenges, for they are all of a cut, and six of 'em in a hand; and they all end, my reputation is dear to me, and I must require satisfaction: Who's there? more paper I hope, no, 'tis my Lord *Bacurius*, I fear all is not well betwixt us.

Enter Bacurius.

Bac. Now Captain *Bessus*, I come about a frivolous matter, caus'd by as idle a report: you know you were a coward.

Bes. Very right.

Bac. And wronged me.

Bes. True my Lord.

Bac. But now people will call you valiant, desertlesly I think, yet for their satisfaction, I will have you fight with me.

Bes. O my good Lord, my deep Engagements.

Bac. Tell not me of your Engagements, Captain *Bessus*, it is not to be put off with an excuse: for my own part, I am none of the multitude that believe your conversion from Coward.

Bes. My Lord, I seek not Quarrels, and this belongs not to me, I am not to maintain it.

Bac. Who then pray?

Bes. *Bessus* the Coward wrong'd you.

Bac. Right.

Bes. And shall *Bessus* the Valiant, maintain what *Bessus* the Coward did?

Bac. I pray thee leave these cheating tricks, I swear thou shalt fight with me, or thou shalt be beaten extreamly, and kick'd.

Bes. Since you provoke me thus far, my Lord, I will fight with you, and by my Sword it shall cost me twenty pound, but I will have my Leg well a week sooner purposely.

Bac. Your Leg? Why, what ailes your Leg? i'le do a cure on you, stand up.

Bes. My Lord, this is not Noble in you.

Bac. What dost thou with such a phrase in thy mouth? I will kick thee out of all good words before I leave thee.

Bes. My Lord, I take this as a punishment for the offence I did when I was a Coward.

Bac. When thou wert? Confess thy self a Coward still, or by this light, I'le beat thee into Spunge.

Bes. Why I am one.

Bac. Are you so Sir? And why do you wear a Sword then? Come unbuckle.

Bes. My Lord.

Bac. Unbuckle I say, and give it me, or as I live, thy head will ake extreamly.

Bes. It is a pretty Hilt, and if your Lordship take an affection to it, with all my heart I present it to you for a New-years-gift.

Bac. I thank you very heartily, sweet Captain, farewel.

Bes. One word more, I beseech your Lordship to render me my knife again.

Bac. Marry by all means Captain; cherish your self with it, and eat hard, good Captain; we cannot tell whether we shall have any more such: Adue dear Captain. [*Exit* Bac.

Bes. I will make better use of this, than of my Sword: A base spirit has this vantage of a brave one, it keeps alwayes at a stay, nothing brings it down, not beating. I remember I promis'd the King in a great Audience, that I would make my back-biters eat my sword to a knife; how to get another sword I know not, nor know any means left for me to maintain my credit, but impudence: therefore I will out-swear him and all his followers, that this is all that's left uneaten of my sword. [*Exit* Bessus.

Enter Mardonius.

Mar. I'le move the King, he is most strangely alter'd; I guess the cause I fear too right, Heaven has some secret end in't, and 'tis a scourge no question justly laid upon him: he has followed me through twenty Rooms; and ever when I stay to wait his command, he blushes like a Girl, and looks upon me, as if modesty kept in his business: so turns away from me, but if I go on, he follows me again.

Enter Arbaces.

See, here he is. I do not use this, yet I know not how, I cannot chuse but weep to see him; his very Enemies I think, whose wounds have bred his fame, if they should see him now, would find tears i'their eyes.

Arb. I cannot utter it, why should I keep
A breast to harbour thoughts? I dare not speak.
Darkness is in my bosom, and there lie
A thousand thoughts that cannot brook the light:
How wilt thou vex 'em when this deed is done,
Conscience, that art afraid to let me name it?

Mar. How do you Sir?

Arb. Why very well *Mardonius*, how dost thou do?

Mar. Better than you I fear.

Arb. I hope thou art; for to be plain with thee,
Thou art in Hell else, secret scorching flames
That far transcend earthly material fires
Are crept into me, and there is no cure.
Is it not strange *Mardonius*, there's no cure?

Mar. Sir, either I mistake, or there is something hid
That you would utter to me.

Arb. So there is, but yet I cannot do it.

Mar. Out with it Sir, if it be dangerous, I will not shrink to do you service, I shall not esteem my life a weightier matter than indeed it is, I know it is subject to more chances than it has hours, and I were better lose it in my Kings cause, than with an ague, or a fall, or sleeping, to a Thief; as all these are probable enough: let me but know what I shall do for you.

Arb. It will not out: were you with *Gobrias*,
And bad him give my Sister all content
The place affords, and give her leave to send
And speak to whom she please?

Mar. Yes Sir, I was.

Arb. And did you to *Bacurius* say as much
About *Tigranes*?

Mar. Yes.

Arb. That's all my business.

Mar. O say not so,
You had an answer of this before;
Besides I think this business might
Be utter'd more carelesly.

Arb. Come thou shalt have it out, I do beseech thee
By all the love thou hast profest to me,
To see my Sister from me.

Mar. Well, and what?

Arb. That's all.

Mar. That's strange, I shall say nothing to her?

Arb. Not a word;
But if thou lovest me, find some subtil way
To make her understand by signs.

Mar. But what shall I make her understand?

Arb. O *Mardonius*, for that I must be pardon'd.

Mar. You may, but I can only see her then.

Arb. 'Tis true;
Bear her this Ring then, and
One more advice, thou shalt speak to her:
Tell her I do love My kindred all: wilt thou?

Mar. Is there no more?

Arb. O yes and her the best;
Better than any Brother loves his Sister: That's all.

Mar. Methinks this need not have been delivered with such a caution; I'le do it.

Arb. There is more yet,
Wilt thou be faith[f]ul to me?

Mar. Sir, if I take upon me to deliver it, after I hear it, I'le pass through fire to do it.

Arb. I love her better than a Brother ought;
Dost thou conceive me?

Mar. I hope you do not Sir.

Arb. No, thou art dull, kneel down before her,
And ne'r rise again, till she will love me.

Mar. Why, I think she does.

Arb. But better than she does, another way;
As wives love Husbands.

Mar. Why, I think there are few Wives that love their Husbands better than she does you.

Arb. Thou wilt not understand me: is it fit
This should be uttered plainly? take it then
Naked as it is: I would desire her love
Lasciviously, lewdly, incestuously,
To do a sin that needs must damn us both,
And thee too: dost thou understand me now?

Mar. Yes, there's your Ring again; what have I done
Dishonestly in my whole life, name it,
That you should put so base a business to me?

Arb. Didst thou not tell me thou wouldst do it?

Mar. Yes; if I undertook it, but if all
My hairs were lives, I would not be engag'd
In such a case to save my last life.

Arb. O guilt! ha how poor and weak a thing art thou!
This man that is my servant, whom my breath
Might blow upon the world, might beat me here
Having this cause, whil'st I prest down with sin
Could not resist him: hear *Mardonius*,
It was a motion mis-beseeming man,
And I am sorry for it.

Mar. Heaven grant you may be so: you must understand, nothing that you can utter, can remove my love and service from my Prince. But otherwise, I think I shall not love you more. For you are sinful, and if you do this crime, you ought to have no Laws. For after this, it will be great injustice in you to punish any offender for any crime. For my self I find my heart too big: I feel I have not patience to look on whilst you run these forbidden courses. Means I have none but your favour, and I am rather glad that I shall lose 'em both together, than keep 'em with such conditions; I shall find a dwelling amongst some people, where though our Garments perhaps be courser, we shall be richer far within, and harbour no such vices in 'em: the Gods preserve you, and mend.

Arb. *Mardonius*, stay *Mardonius*, for though
My present state requires nothing but knaves
To be about me, such as are prepar'd
For every wicked act, yet who does know
But that my loathed Fate may turn about,
And I have use for honest men again?
I hope I may, I prethee leave me not.

Enter Bessus.

Bes. Where is the King?

Mar. There.

Bes. An't please your Majesty, there's the knife.

Arb. What knife?

Bes. The Sword is eaten.

Mar. Away you fool, the King is serious,

And cannot now admit your vanities.

Bes. Vanities! I'me no honest man, if my enemies have not brought it to this, what, do you think I lie?

Arb. No, no, 'tis well *Bessus*, 'tis very well I'm glad on't.

Mar. If your enemies brought it to this, your enemies are Cutlers, come leave the King.

Bes. Why, may not valour approach him?

Mar. Yes, but he has affairs, depart, or I shall be something unmannerly with you.

Arb. No, let him stay *Mardonius*, let him stay,
I have occasion with him very weighty,
And I can spare you now.

Mar. Sir?

Arb. Why I can spare you now.

Bes. *Mardonius* give way to these State affairs.

Mar. Indeed you are fitter for this present purpose.

[*Exit* Mar.

Arb. *Bessus*, I should imploy thee, wilt thou do't?

Bes. Do't for you? by this Air I will do any thing without exception, be it a good, bad, or indifferent thing.

Arb. Do not swear.

Bes. By this light but I will, any thing whatsoever.

Arb. But I shall name the thing,
Thy Conscience will not suffer thee to do.

Bes. I would fain hear that thing.

Arb. Why I would have thee get my Sister for me?
Thou understandst me, in a wicked manner.

Bes. O you would have a bout with her?
I'le do't, I'le do't, I'faith.

Arb. Wilt thou, do'st thou make no more on't?

Bes. More? no, why is there any thing else? if there be, it shall be done too.

Arb. Hast thou no greater sense of such a sin?
Thou art too wicked for my company,
Though I have hell within me, thou may'st yet
Corrupt me further: pray thee answer me,
How do I shew to thee after this motion?

Bes. Why your Majesty looks as well in my opinion, as ever you did since you were born.

Arb. But thou appear'st to me after thy grant,

The ugliest, loathed detestable thing
That I ever met with. Thou hast eyes
Like the flames of *Sulphur*, which me thinks do dart
Infection on me, and thou hast a mouth
Enough to take me in where there do stand
Four rows of Iron Teeth.

Bes. I feel no such thing, but 'tis no matter how I look, I'le do my business as well as they that look better, and when this is dispatch'd, if you have a mind to your Mother, tell me, and you shall see I'le set it hard.

Arb. My Mother! Heaven forgive me to hear this,
I am inspir'd with horrour: now I hate thee
Worse than my sin, which if I could come by
Should suffer death Eternal ne're to rise
In any breast again. Know I will die
Languishing mad, as I resolve, I shall,
E're I will deal by such an instrument:
Thou art too sinful to imploy in this;
Out of the World, away.

Bes. What do you mean, Sir?

Arb. Hung round with Curses, take thy fearful flight
Into the Desarts, where 'mongst all the Monsters
If thou find'st one so beastly as thy self,
Thou shalt be held as innocent.

Bes. Good Sir.

Arb. If there were no such instruments as thou,
We Kings could never act such wicked deeds:
Seek out a man that mocks Divinity,
That breaks each precept both of God and man,
And natures too, and does it without lust,
Meerly because it is a law, and good,
And live with him: for him thou canst not spoil.
Away I say, I will not do this sin. [*Exit* Bessus.
I'le press it here, till it do break my breast,
It heaves to get out, but thou art a sin,
And spight of torture I will keep thee in.

Actus Quartus.

Enter Gobrias, Panthea, *and* Spaconia.

Gob. HAve you written Madam?
Pan. Yes, good *Gobrias.*
Gob. And with a kindness, and such winning words
As may provoke him, at one instant feel
His double fault, your wrong, and his own rashness?
Pan. I have sent words enough, if words may win him
From his displeasure; and such words I hope,
As shall gain much upon his goodness, *Gobrias.*
Yet fearing they are many, and a womans,
A poor belief may follow, I have woven
As many truths within 'em to speak for me,
That if he be but gracious, and receive 'em—
Gob. Good Lady be not fearful, though he should not
Give you your present end in this, believe it,
You shall feel, if your vertue can induce you
To labour on't, this tempest which I know,
Is but a poor proof 'gainst your patience:
All those contents, your spirit will arrive at,
Newer and sweeter to you; your Royal brother,
When he shall once collect himself, and see
How far he has been asunder from himself;
What a meer stranger to his golden temper:
Must from those roots of vertue, never dying,
Though somewhat stopt with humour, shoot again
Into a thousand glories, bearing his fair branches
High as our hopes can look at, straight as justice,
Loaden with ripe contents; he loves you dearly,
I know it, and I hope I need not farther
Win you to understand it.
Pan. I believe it.
But howsoever, I am sure I love him dearly:
So dearly, that if any thing I write
For my enlarging should beget his anger,
Heaven be a witness with me and my faith,
I had rather live intomb'd here.
Gob. You shall not feel a worse stroke than your grief,

I am sorry 'tis so sharp, I kiss your hand,
And this night will deliver this true story,
With this hand to your Brother.

Pan. Peace go with you, you are a good man. [*Exit* Gob.
My *Spaconia*, why are you ever sad thus?

Spa. O dear Lady.

Pan. Prethee discover not a way to sadness,
Nearer than I have in me, our two sorrows
Work like two eager Hawks, who shall get highest;
How shall I lessen thine? for mine I fear
Is easier known than cur'd.

Spa. Heaven comfort both,
And give you happy ends, however I
Fall in my stubborn fortunes.

Pan. This but teaches
How to be more familiar with our sorrows,
That are too much our masters: good *Spaconia*
How shall I do you service?

Spa. Noblest Lady,
You make me more a slave still to your goodness,
And only live to purchase thanks to pay you,
For that is all the business of my life: now
I will be bold, since you will have it so,
To ask a noble favour of you.

Pan. Speak it, 'tis yours, for from so sweet a vertue,
No ill demand has issue.

Spa. Then ever vertuous, let me beg your will
In helping me to see the Prince *Tigranes*,
With whom I am equal prisoner, if not more.

Pan. Reserve me to a greater end *Spaconia*;
Bacurius cannot want so much good manners
As to deny your gentle visitation,
Though you came only with your own command.

Spa. I know they will deny me gracious Madam,
Being a stranger, and so little fam'd,
So utter empty of those excellencies
That tame Authority; but in you sweet Lady,
All these are natural; beside, a power
Deriv'd immediate from your Royal brother,
Whose least word in you may command the Kingdom.

Pan. More than my word *Spaconia*, you shall carry,
For fear it fail you.
Spa. Dare you trust a Token?
Madam I fear I am grown too bold a begger.
Pan. You are a pretty one, and trust me Lady
It joyes me, I shall do a good to you,
Though to my self I never shall be happy:
Here, take this Ring, and from me as a Token
Deliver it; I think they will not stay you:
So all your own desires go with you Lady.
Spa. And sweet peace to your Grace.
Pan. Pray Heaven I find it. [*Exeunt.*

Enter Tigranes, *in prison.*

Tigr. Fool that I am, I have undone my self,
And with my own hand turn'd my fortune round,
That was a fair one: I have childishly
Plaid with my hope so long, till I have broke it,
And now too late I mourn for't; O *Spaconia*!
Thou hast found an even way to thy revenge now,
Why didst thou follow me like a faint shadow,
To wither my desires? But wretched fool,
Why did I plant thee 'twixt the Sun and me,
To make me freeze thus? Why did I prefer her
To the fair Princess? O thou fool, thou fool,
Thou family of fools, live like a slave still,
And in thee bear thine own hell and thy torment,
Thou hast deserv'd: Couldst thou find no Lady
But she that has thy hopes to put her to,
And hazard all thy peace? None to abuse,
But she that lov'd thee ever? poor *Spaconia*,
And so much lov'd thee, that in honesty
And honour thou art bound to meet her vertues:
She that forgot the greatness of her grief
And miseries, that must follow such mad passions,
Endless and wild as women; she that for thee
And with thee left her liberty, her name,
And Country, you have paid me equal, Heavens,
And sent my own rod to correct me with;
A woman: for inconstancy I'le suffer,

Lay it on justice, till my soul melt in me
For my unmanly, beastly, sudden doting
Upon a new face: after all my oaths
Many and strange ones,
I feel my old fire flame again and burn
So strong and violent, that should I see her
Again, the grief and that would kill me.

Enter Bacurius *and* Spaconia.

Bac. Lady, your token I acknowledge, you may pass;
There is the King.

Spa. I thank your Lordship for it. [*Exit* Bac.

Tigr. She comes, she comes, shame hide me ever from her,
Would I were buried, or so far remov'd
Light might not find me out, I dare not see her.

Spa. Nay never hide your self; or were you hid
Where earth hides all her riches, near her Center;
My wrongs without more day would light me to you:
I must speak e're I die; were all your greatness
Doubled upon you, y'are a perjur'd man,
And only mighty in your wickedness
Of wronging women. Thou art false, false Prince;
I live to see it, poor *Spaconia* lives
To tell thee thou art false; and then no more;
She lives to tell thee thou art more unconstant,
Than all ill women ever were together.
Thy faith is firm as raging over-flowes,
That no bank can command; as lasting
As boyes gay bubbles, blown i'th' Air and broken:
The wind is fixt to thee: and sooner shall
The beaten Mariner with his shrill whistle
Calm the loud murmur of the troubled main,
And strike it smooth again; than thy soul fall
To have peace in love with any: Thou art all
That all good men must hate; and if thy story
Shall tell succeeding ages what thou wert,
O let it spare me in it, lest true lovers
In pity of my wrong, burn thy black Legend,
And with their curses, shake thy sleeping ashes.

Tigr. Oh! oh!

Spa. The destinies, I hope, have pointed out
Our ends, that thou maist die for love,
Though not for me; for this assure thy self,
The Princess hates thee deadly, and will sooner
Be won to marry with a Bull, and safer
Than such a beast as thou art: I have struck,
I fear, too deep; beshrow me for't; Sir,
This sorrow works me like a cunning friendship,
Into the same piece with it; 'tis asham'd,
Alas, I have been too rugged: Dear my Lord,
I am sorry I have spoken any thing,
Indeed I am, that may add more restraint
To that too much you have: good Sir, be pleas'd
To think it was a fault of love, not malice;
And do as I will do, forgive it Prince.
I do, and can forgive the greatest sins
To me you can repent of; pray believe.

Tigr. O my *Spaconia*! O thou vertuous woman!

Spa. Nay, more, the King Sir.

Enter Arbaces, Bacurius, Mardonius.

Arb. Have you been carefull of our noble Prisoner,
That he want nothing fitting for his greatness?

Bac. I hope his grace will quit me for my care Sir.

Arb. 'Tis well, royal *Tigranes*, health.

Tigr. More than the strictness of this place can give Sir,
I offer back again to great *Arbaces*.

Arb. We thank you worthy Prince, and pray excuse us,
We have not seen you since your being here,
I hope your noble usage has been equall
With your own person: your imprisonment,
If it be any, I dare say is easie,
And shall not last t[w]o dayes.

Tigr. I thank you;
My usage here has been the same it was,
Worthy a royal Conqueror. For my restraint,
It came unkindly, because much unlook'd for;
But I must bear it.

Arb. What Lady's that? *Bacurius*?

Bac. One of the Princess women, Sir.

Arb. I fear'd it, why comes she hither?
Bac. To speak with the Prince *Tigranes*.
Arb. From whom, *Bacurius*?
Bac. From the Princess, Sir.
Arb. I knew I had seen her.
Mar. His fit begins to take him now again,
'Tis a strange Feaver, and 'twill shake us all anon, I fear,
Would he were well cur'd of this raging folly:
Give me the warrs, where men are mad, and may talk what they list, and held the bravest fellows; This pelting prating peace is good for nothing: drinking's a vertue to't.
Arb. I see there's truth in no man, nor obedience,
But for his own ends, why did you let her in?
Bac. It was your own command to barr none from him,
Besides, the Princess sent her ring Sir, for my warrant.
Arb. A token to *Tigranes*, did she not?
Sir tell truth.
Bac. I do not use to lie Sir,
'Tis no way I eat or live by, and I think,
This is no token Sir.
Mar. This combat has undone him: if he had been well beaten, he had been temperate; I shall never see him handsome again, till he have a Horse-mans staffe yok'd thorow his shoulders, or an arm broken with a bullet.
Arb. I am trifled with.
Bac. Sir?
Arb. I know it, as I know thee to be false.
Mar. Now the clap comes.
Bac. You never knew me so, Sir I dare speak it,
And durst a worse man tell me, though my better—
Mar. 'Tis well said, by my soul.
Arb. Sirra, you answer as you had no life.
Bac. That I fear Sir to lose nobly.
Arb. I say Sir, once again.
Bac. You may say what yo[u] please, Sir,
Would I might do so.
Arb. I will, Sir, and say openly, this woman carries letters,
By my life I know she carries letters, this woman does it.
Mar. Would *Bessus* were here to take her aside and search her, He would quickly tell you what she carried Sir.

Arb. I have found it out, this woman carries letters.

Mar. If this hold, 'twill be an ill world for Bawdes, Chamber-maids and Post-boyes, I thank heaven I have none but his letters patents, things of his own enditing.

Arb. Prince, this cunning cannot do't.

Tigr. Doe, What Sir? I reach you not.

Arb. It shall not serve your turn, Prince.

Tigr. Serve my turn Sir?

Arb. I Sir, it shall not serve your turn.

Tigr. Be plainer, good Sir.

Arb. This woman shall carry no more letters back to your Love *Panthea*, by Heaven she shall not, I say she shall not.

Mar. This would make a Saint swear like a souldier.

Tigr. This beats me more, King, than the blowes you gave me.

Arb. Take'em away both, and together let them prisoners be, strictly and closely kept, or Sirra, your life shall answer it, and let no body speak with'em hereafter.

Tigr. Well, I am subject to you,
And must indure these passions:
This is the imprisonment I have look'd for always.
And the dearer place I would choose.

[*Exeunt* Tigr. Spa. Bac.

Mar. Sir, you have done well now.

Arb. Dare you reprove it?

Mar. No.

Arb. You must be crossing me.

Mar. I have no letters Sir to anger you,
But a dry sonnet of my Corporals
To an old Suttlers wife, and that I'll burn, Sir.
'Tis like to prove a fine age for the Ignorant.

Arb. How darst thou so often forfeit thy life?
Thou know'st 'tis in my power to take it.

Mar. Yes, and I know you wo'not, or if you doe, you'll miss it quickly.

Arb. Why?

Mar. Who shall tell you of these childish follies
When I am dead? who shall put to his power
To draw those vertues out of a flood of humors,
When they are drown'd, and make'em shine again?

No, cut my head off:
Then you may talk, and be believed, and grow worse,
And have your too self-glorious temper rot
Into a deep sleep, and the Kingdom with you,
Till forraign swords be in your throats, and slaughter
Be every where about you like your flatterers.
Do, kill me.

Arb. Prethee be tamer, good *Mardonius*,
Thou know'st I love thee, nay I honour thee,
Believe it good old Souldier, I am thine;
But I am rack'd clean from my self, bear with me,
Woot thou bear with me my *Mardonius*?

Enter Gobrias.

Mar. There comes a good man, love him too, he's tempe-
You may live to have need of such a vertue, (rate,
Rage is not still in fashion.

Arb. Welcome good *Gobrias*.

Gob. My service and this letter to your Grace.

Arb. From whom?

Gob. From the rich Mine of vertue and beauty,
Your mournfull Sister.

Arb. She is in prison, *Gobrias*, is she not?

Gob. She is Sir, till your pleasure to enlarge her,
Which on my knees I beg. Oh 'tis not fit,
That all the sweetness of the world in one,
The youth and vertue that would tame wild Tygers,
And wilder people, that have known no manners,
Should live thus cloistred up; for your loves sake,
If there be any in that noble heart,
To her a wretched Lady, and forlorn,
Or for her love to you, which is as much
As nature and obedience ever gave,
Have pity on her beauties.

Arb. Pray thee stand up; 'Tis true, she is too fair,
And all these commendations but her own,
Would thou had'st never so commended her,
Or I nere liv'd to have heard it *Gobrias*;
If thou but know'st the wrong her beautie does her,
Thou wouldst in pity of her be a lyar,

Thy ignorance has drawn me wretched man,
Whither my self nor thou canst well tell: O my fate!
I think she loves me, but I fear another
Is deeper in her heart: How thinkst thou *Gobrias*?

Gob. I do beseech your Grace believe it not,
For let me perish if it be not false. Good Sir, read her Letter.

Mar. This Love, or what a devil it is I know not, begets more mischief than a Wake. I had rather be well beaten, starv'd, or lowsie, than live within the Air on't. He that had seen this brave fellow Charge through a grove of Pikes but t'other day, and look upon him now, will ne'r believe his eyes again: if he continue thus but two days more, a Taylor may beat him with one hand tied behind him.

Arb. Alas, she would be at liberty.
And there be a thousand reasons *Gobrias*,
Thousands that will deny't:
Which if she knew, she would contentedly
Be where she is: and bless her vertues for it,
And me, though she were closer, she would, *Gobrias*,
Good man indeed she would.

Gob. Then good Sir, for her satisfaction,
Send for her and with reason make her know
Why she must live thus from you.

Arb. I will; go bring her to me. [*Exeunt all.*

Enter Bessus, *and two Sword-men, and a Boy.*

Bes. Y'are very welcome both; some stools boy,
And reach a Table; Gentlemen o'th' Sword,
Pray sit without more complement; be gone child.
I have been curious in the searching of you,
Because I understand you wise and valiant persons.

1 We understand our selves Sir.

Bes. Nay Gentlemen, and dear friends o'th' Sword,
No complement I pray, but to the cause
I hang upon, which in few, is my honour.

2 You cannot hang too much Sir, for your honour,
But to your cause.

Bes. Be wise, and speak truth, my first doubt is,
My beating by my Prince.

1 Stay there a little Sir, do you doubt a beating?

Or have you had a beating by your Prince?

Bes. Gentlemen o'th' Sword, my Prince has beaten me.

2 Brother, what think you of this case?

1 If he has beaten him, the case is clear.

2 If he have beaten him, I grant the case;
But how? we cannot be too subtil in this business,
I say, but how?

Bes. Even with his Royal hand.

1 Was it a blow of love, or indignation?

Bes. 'Twas twenty blows of indignation, Gentlemen,
Besides two blows o'th' face.

2 Those blows o'th' face have made a new cause on't,
The rest were but an horrible rudeness.

1 Two blows o'th' face, and given by a worse man, I must confess, as the Sword-men say, had turn'd the business: Mark me brother, by a worse man; but being by his Prince, had they been ten, and those ten drawn teeth, besides the hazard of his nose for ever; all this had been but favours: this is my flat opinion, which I'le die in.

2 The King may do much Captain, believe it; for had he crackt your Scull through, like a bottle, or broke a Rib or two with tossing of you, yet you had lost no honour: This is strange you may imagine, but this is truth now Captain.

Bes. I will be glad to embrace it Gentlemen;
But how far may he strike me?

1 There is another: a new cause rising from the time and distance, in which I will deliver my opinion: he may strike, beat, or cause to be beaten: for these are natural to man: your Prince, I say, may beat you, so far forth as his dominion reacheth, that's for the distance; the time, ten miles a day, I take it.

2 Brother, you err, 'tis fifteen miles a day,
His stage is ten, his beatings are fifteen.

Bes. 'Tis the longest, but we subjects must—

1 Be subject to it; you are wise and vertuous.

Bes. Obedience ever makes that noble use on't,
To which I dedicate my beaten body;
I must trouble you a little further, Gentlemen o'th' Sword.

2 No trouble at all to us Sir, if we may
Profit your understanding, we are bound

By vertue of our calling to utter our opinions,
Shortly, and discreetly.

Bes. My sorest business is, I have been kick'd.

2 How far Sir?

Bes. Not to flatter my self in it, all over, my sword forc'd but not lost; for discreetly I rendred it to save that imputation.

1 It shew'd discretion, the best part of valour.

2 Brother, this is a pretty cause, pray ponder on't;
Our friend here has been kick'd.

1 He has so, brother.

2 Sorely he saies: Now, had he set down here
Upon the meer kick, 't had been Cowardly.

1 I think it had been Cowardly indeed.

2 But our friend has redeem'd it in delivering
His sword without compulsion; and that man
That took it of him, I pronounce a weak one,
And his kicks nullities.
He should have kick'd him after the delivering
Which is the confirmation of a Coward.

1 Brother, I take it, you mistake the question;
For, say that I were kick'd.

2 I must not say so;
Nor I must not hear it spoke by the tongue of man.
You kick'd, dear brother! you're merry.

1 But put the case I were kick'd?

2 Let them put it that are things weary of their lives, and know not honour; put the case you were kick'd?

1 I do not say I was kickt.

2 Nor no silly creature that wears his head without a Case, his soûl in a Skin-coat: You kickt dear brother?

Bes. Nay Gentlemen, let us do what we shall do,
Truly and honest[l]y; good Sirs to the question.

1 Why then I say, suppose your Boy kick't, Captain?

2 The Boy may be suppos'd is liable.

1 A foolish forward zeal Sir, in my friend;
But to the Boy, suppose the Boy were kickt.

Bes. I do suppose it.

1 Has your Boy a sword?

Bes. Surely no; I pray suppose a sword too.

1 I do suppose it; you grant your Boy was kick't then.

2 By no means Captain, let it be supposed still; the word grant, makes not for us.

1 I say this must be granted.

2 This must be granted brother?

1 I, this must be granted.

2 Still this must?

1 I say this must be granted.

2 I, give me the must again, brother, you palter.

1 I will not hear you, wasp.

2 Brother, I say you palter, the must three times together; I wear as sharp Steel as another man, and my Fox bites as deep, musted, my dear brother.
But to the cause again.

Bes. Nay look you Gentlemen.

2 In a word, I ha' done.

1 A tall man but intemperate, 'tis great pity;
Once more suppose the Boy kick'd.

2 Forward.

1 And being thorowly kick'd, laughs at the kicker.

2 So much for us; proceed.

1 And in this beaten scorn, as I may call it,
Delivers up his weapon; where lies the error?

Bes. It lies i'th' beating Sir, I found it four dayes since.

2 The error, and a sore one as I take it,
Lies in the thing kicking.

Bes. I understand that well, 'tis so indeed Sir.

1 That is according to the man that did it.

2 There springs a new branch, whose was the foot?

Bes. A Lords.

1 The cause is mighty, but had it been two Lords,
And both had kick'd you, if you laugh, 'tis clear.

Bes. I did laugh,
But how will that help me, Gentlemen?

2 Yes, it shall help you if you laught aloud.

Bes. As loud as a kick'd man could laugh, I laught Sir.

1 My reason now, the valiant man is known
By suffering and contemning; you have
Enough of both, and you are valiant.

2 If he be sure he has been kick'd enough:

For that brave sufferance you speak of brother,
Consists not in a beating and away,
But in a cudgell'd body, from eighteen
To eight and thirty; in a head rebuk'd
With pots of all size, degrees, stools, and bed-staves,
This showes a valiant man.

Bes. Then I am valiant, as valiant as the proudest,
For these are all familiar things to me;
Familiar as my sleep, or want of money,
All my whole body's but one bruise with beating,
I think I have been cudgell'd with all nations,
And almost all Religions.

2 Embrace him brother, this man is valiant,
I know it by my self, he's valiant.

1 Captain, thou art a valiant Gentleman,
To bide upon, a very valiant man.

Bes. My equall friends o'th'Sword, I must request your hands to this.

2 'Tis fit it should be.

Bes. Boy, get me some wine, and pen and Ink within: Am I clear, Gentlemen?

1 Sir, the world has taken notice what we have done,
Make much of your body, for I'll pawn my steel,
Men will be coyer of their legs hereafter.

Bes. I must request you goe along and testife to the Lord *Bacurius*, whose foot has struck me, how you find my cause.

2 We will, and tell that Lord he must be rul'd,
Or there are those abroad, will rule his Lordship. [*Exeunt.*

Enter Arbaces *at one door, and* Gob. *and* Panthea *at another.*

Gob. Sir, here's the Princess.

Arb. Leave us then alone,
For the main cause of her imprisonment
Must not be heard by any but her self. [*Exit* Gob.
You're welcome Sister, and would to heaven
I could so bid you by another name:
If you above love not such sins as these,
Circle my heart with thoughts as cold as snow
To quench these rising flames that harbour here.

[*P*]*an.* Sir, does it please you I should speak?

Arb. Please me?
I, more than all the art of musick can,
Thy speech doth please me, for it ever sounds,
As thou brought'st joyfull unexpected news;
And yet it is not fit thou shouldst be heard.
I pray thee think so.
Pan. Be it so, I will.
Am I the first that ever had a wrong
So far from being fit to have redress,
That 'twas unfit to hear it? I will back
To prison, rather than disquiet you,
And wait till it be fit.
Arb. No, do not goe;
For I will hear thee with a serious thought:
I have collected all that's man about me
Together strongly, and I am resolv'd
To hear thee largely, but I do beseech thee,
Do not come nearer to me, for there is
Something in that, that will undoe us both.
Pan. Alas Sir, am I venome?
Arb. Yes, to me;
Though of thy self I think thee to be
In equall degree of heat or cold,
As nature can make: yet as unsound men
Convert the sweetest and the nourishing'st meats
Into diseases; so shall I distemper'd,
Do thee, I pray thee draw no nearer to me.
Pan. Sir, this is that I would: I am of late
Shut from the world, and why it should be thus,
Is all I wish to know.
Arb. Why credit me *Panthea*,
Credit me that am thy brother,
Thy loving brother, that there is a cause
Sufficient, yet unfit for thee to know,
That might undoe thee everlastingly,
Only to hear, wilt thou but credit this?
By Heaven 'tis true, believe it if thou canst.
Pan. Children and fools are ever credulous,
And I am both, I think, for I believe;
If you dissemble, be it on your head;

I'le back unto my prison: yet me-thinks
I might be kept in some place where you are;
For in my self, I find I know not what
To call it, but it is a great desire
To see you often.

Arb. Fie, you come in a step, what do you mean?
Dear sister, do not so: Alas *Panthea*,
Where I am would you be? Why that's the cause
You are imprison'd, that you may not be
Where I am.

Pan. Then I must indure it Sir, Heaven keep you.

Arb. Nay, you shall hear the case in short *Panthea*,
And when thou hear'st it, thou wilt blush for me,
And hang thy head down like a Violet
Full of the mornings dew: There is a way
To gain thy freedome, but 'tis such a one
As puts thee in worse bondage, and I know,
Thou wouldst encounter fire, and make a proof
Whether the gods have care of innocence,
Rather than follow it: Know that I have lost,
The only difference betwixt man and beast,
My reason.

Pan. Heaven forbid.

Arb. Nay 'tis gone;
And I am left as far without a bound,
As the wild Ocean, that obeys the winds;
Each sodain passion throwes me where it lists,
And overwhelms all that oppose my will:
I have beheld thee with a lustfull eye;
My heart is set on wickedness to act
Such sins with thee, as I have been afraid
To think of, if thou dar'st consent to this,
Which I beseech thee do not, thou maist gain
Thy liberty, and yield me a content;
If not, thy dwelling must be dark and close,
Where I may never see thee; For heaven knows
That laid this punishment upon my pride,
Thy sight at some time will enforce my madness
To make a start e'ne to thy ravishing;
Now spit upon me, and call all reproaches

Thou canst devise together, and at once
Hurle'em against me: for I am a sickness
As killing as the plague, ready to seize thee.
Pan. Far be it from me to revile the King:
But it is true, that I shall rather choose
To search out death, that else would search out me,
And in a grave sleep with my innocence,
Than welcome such a sin: It is my fate,
To these cross accidents I was ordain'd,
And must have patience; and but that my eyes
Have more of woman in 'em than my heart,
I would not weep: Peace enter you again.
Arb. Farwell, and good *Panthea* pray for me,
Thy prayers are pure, that I may find a death
However soon before my passions grow
That they forget what I desire is sin;
For thither they are tending: if that happen,
Then I shall force thee tho' thou wert a Virgin
By vow to Heaven, and shall pull a heap
Of strange yet uninvented sin upon me.
Pan. Sir, I will pray for you, yet you shall know
It is a sullen fate that governs us,
For I could wish as heartily as you
I were no sister to you, I should then
Imbrace your lawfull love, sooner than health.
Arb. Couldst thou affect me then?
Pan. So perfectly,
That as it is, I ne're shall sway my heart,
To like another.
Arb. Then I curse my birth,
Must this be added to my miseries
That thou art willing too? is there no stop
To our full happiness, but these meer sounds
Brother and Sister?
Pan. There is nothing else,
But these alas will separate us more
Than twenty worlds betwixt us.
Arb. I have liv'd
To conquer men and now am overthrown
Only by words Brother and Sister: where

Have those words dwelling? I will find 'em out,
And utterly destroy 'em; but they are
Not to be grasp'd: let 'em be men or beasts,
And I will cut 'em from the Earth, or Towns,
And I will raze 'em, and the[n] blow 'em up:
Let 'em be Seas, and I will drink 'em off,
And yet have unquencht fire left in my breast:
Let 'em be any thing but meerly voice.

Pan. But 'tis not in the power of any force,
Or policy to conquer them.

Arb. *Panthea*, What shall we do?
Shall we stand firmly here, and gaze our eyes out?

Pan. Would I could do so,
But I shall weep out mine.

Arb. Accursed man,
Thou bought'st thy reason at too dear a rate,
For thou hast all thy actions bounded in
With curious rules, when every beast is free:
What is there that acknowledges a kindred
But wretched man? Who ever saw the Bull
Fearfully leave the Heifer that he lik'd
Because they had one Dam?

Pan. Sir, I disturb you and my self too;
'Twere better I were gone.

Arb. I will not be so foolish as I was,
Stay, we will love just as becomes our births,
No otherwise: Brothers and Sisters may
Walk hand in hand together; so will we,
Come nearer: is there any hurt in this?

Pan. I hope not.

Arb. Faith there is none at all:
And tell me truly now, is there not one
You love above me?

Pan. No by Heaven.

Arb. Why yet you sent unto *Tigranes*, Sister.

Pan. True, but for another: for the truth—

Arb. No more,
I'le credit thee, thou canst not lie,
Thou art all truth.

Pan. But is there nothing else,

That we may do, but only walk? methinks
Brothers and Sisters lawfully may kiss.

Arb. And so they may *Panthea*, so will we,
And kiss again too; we were too scrupulous,
And foolish, but we will be so no more.

Pan. If you have any mercy, let me go
To prison, to my death, to any thing:
I feel a sin growing upon my blood,
Worse than all these, hotter than yours.

Arb. That is impossible, what shou'd we do?

Pan. Flie Sir, for Heavens sake.

Arb. So we must away,
Sin grows upon us more by this delay.

[*Exeunt several wayes.*

Actus Quintus.

Enter Mardonius *and* Lygones.

Mar. SIR, the King has seen your Commission, and believes it, and freely by this warrant gives you power to visit Prince *Tigranes*, your Noble Master.

Lygr. I thank his Grace and kiss his hand.

Mar. But is the main of all your business ended in this?

Lyg. I have another, but a worse, I am asham'd, it is a business.

Mar. You serve a worthy person, and a stranger I am sure you are; you may imploy me if you please without your purse, such Offices should ever be their own rewards.

Lyg. I am bound to your Nobleness.

Mar. I may have need of you, and then this courtesie,
If it be any, is not ill bestowed;
But may I civilly desire the rest?
I shall not be a hurter if no helper.

Lyg. Sir you shall know I have lost a foolish Daughter,
And with her all my patience, pilfer'd away
By a mean Captain of your Kings.

Mar. Stay there Sir:
If he have reacht the Noble worth of Captain,
He may well claim a worthy Gentlewoman,
Though she were yours, and Noble.

Lyg. I grant all that too: but this wretched fellow
Reaches no further than the empty name
That serves to feed him; were he valiant,
Or had but in him any noble nature
That might hereafter promise him a good man,
My cares were so much lighter, and my grave
A span yet from me.
Mar. I confess such fellows
Be in all Royal Camps, and have and must be,
To make the sin of Coward more detested
In the mean souldier that with such a foil
Sets off much valour. By description
I should now guess him to you, it was *Bessus*,
I dare almost with confidence pronounce it.
Lyg. 'Tis such a scurvie name as *Bessus*, and now I think ('tis he.
Mar. Captain do you call him?
Believe me Sir, you have a misery
Too mighty for your age: A pox upon him,
For that must be the end of all his service:
Your Daughter was not mad Sir?
Lyg. No, would she had been,
The fault had had more credit: I would do something.

Mar. I would fain counsel you, but to what I know not, he's so below a beating, that the Women find him not worthy of their Distaves, and to hang him were to cast away a Rope; he's such an Airie, thin unbodyed Coward, that no revenge can catch him: I'le tell you Sir, and tell you truth; this Rascal fears neither God nor man, he has been so beaten: sufferance has made him Wainscot: he has had since he was first a slave, at least three hundred Daggers set in's head, as little boys do new Knives in hot meat, there's not a Rib in's body o' my Conscience that has not been thrice broken with dry beating: and now his sides look like two Wicker Targets, every way bended; Children will shortly take him for a Wall, and set their Stone-bows in his forehead, he is of so base a sense, I cannot in a week imagine what shall be done to him.

Lyg. Sure I have committed some great sin
That this fellow should be made my Rod,
I would see him, but I shall have no patience.
Mar. 'Tis no great matter if you have not: if a Laming

of him, or such a toy may do you pleasure Sir, he has it for you, and I'le help you to him: 'tis no news to him to have a Leg broken, or Shoulder out, with being turn'd o'th' stones like a Tansie: draw not your Sword if you love it; for on my Conscience his head will break it: we use him i'th' Wars like a Ram to shake a wall withal. Here comes the very person of him, do as you shall find your temper, I must leave you: but if you do not break him like a Bisket, you are much to blame Sir. [*Exit* Mar.

Enter Bessus *and the Sword men.*

Lyg. Is your name *Bessus*?

Bes. Men call me Captain *Bessus.*

Lyg. Then Ca[p]tain *Bessus*, you are a rank rascall, without more exordiums, a durty frozen slave; and with the favor of your friends here I will beat you.

2 *Sword.* Pray use your pleasure Sir,
You seem to be a Gentleman.

Lyg. Thus Captain *Bessus*, thus; thus twing your nose, thus kick, thus tread you.

Bes. I do beseech you yield your cause Sir quickly.

Lyg. Indeed I should have told that first.

Bes. I take it so.

1 *Sword.* Captain, he should indeed, he is mistaken.

Lyg. Sir, you shall have it quickly, and more beating, you have stoln away a Lady, Captain coward, and such an one. *beats him.*

Bes. Hold, I beseech you, hold Sir, I never yet stole any living thing that had a tooth about it.

Lyg. I know you dare lie.

Bes. With none but Summer Whores upon my life Sir, my means and manners never could attempt above a hedge or hay-cock.

Lyg. Sirra, that quits not me, where is this Lady? do that you do not use to do; tell truth, or by my hand, I'le beat your Captains brains out, wash'em, and put 'em in again, that will I.

Bes. There was a Lady Sir, I must confess, once in my charge: the Prince *Tigranes* gave her to my guard for her safety, how I us'd her, she may her self report, she's with the

Prince now: I did but wait upon her like a groom, which she will testife I am sure: if not, my brains are at your service when you please Sir, and glad I have 'em for you.

Lyg. This is most likely, Sir, I ask you pardon, and am sorry I was so intemperate.

Bes. Well I can ask no more, you will think it strange not to have me beat you at first sight.

Lyg. Indeed I would, but I know your goodness can forget twenty beatings, you must forgive me.

Bes. Yes there's my hand, go where you will, I shall think you a valiant fellow for all this.

Lyg. My da[u]ghter is a Whore, I feel it now too sensible; yet I will see her, discharge my self from being father to her, and then back to my Country, and there die, farwell Captain. [*Exit* Lygo.

Bes. Farwell Sir, farwell, commend me to the gentlewoman I pray.

1 *Sword.* How now Captain? bear up man.

Bes. Gentlemen o'th'sword, your hands once more; I have been kickt agen, but the foolish fellow is penitent, has askt me Mercy, and my honour's safe.

2 *Sword.* We knew that, or the foolish fellow had better have kickt his grandsir.

Bes. Confirm, confirm I pray.

1 *Sword.* There be our hands agen, now let him come and say he was not sorry, and he sleeps for it.

Bes. Alas good ignorant old man, let him go, let him go, these courses will undo him. [*Exeunt clear.*

Enter Lygones *and* Bacurius.

Bac. My Lord, your authority is good, and I am glad it is so, for my consent would never hinder you from seeing your own King, I am a Minister, but not a governor of this State, yonder is your King, I'le leave you. [*Exit.*

Enter Tigranes *and* Spaconia.

Lyg. There he is indeed, and with him my disloyal child.

Tigr. I do perceive my fault so much, that yet me thinks thou shouldst not have forgiven me.

Lyg. Health to your Majesty.

Tigr. What? good *Lygones* welcome, what business brought thee hither?

Lyg. Several businesses. My publick businesses will appear by this, I have a message to deliver, which if it please you so to authorize, is an embassage from the Armenian State, unto *Arbaces* for your liberty: the offer's there set down, please you to read it.

Tigr. There is no alteration happened since I came thence?

Lyg. None Sir, all is as it was.

Tigr. And all our friends are well?

Lyg. All very well.

Spa. Though I have done nothing but what was good, I dare not see my Father, it was fault enough not to acquaint him with that good.

Lyg. Madam I should have seen you.

Spa. O good Sir forgive me.

Lyg. Forgive you, why? I am no kin to you, am I?

Spa. Should it be measur'd by my mean deserts, indeed you are not.

Lyg. Thou couldest prate unhappily ere thou couldst go, would thou couldst do as well, and how does your custome hold out here?

Spa. Sir?

Lyg. Are you in private still, or how?

Spa. What do you mean?

Lyg. Do you take mony? are you come to sell sin yet? perhaps I can help you to liberal Clients: or has not the King cast you off yet? O thou vile creature, whose best commendation is, that thou art a young whore, I would thy Mother had liv'd to see this, or rather that I had died ere I had seen it; why didst not make me acquainted when thou wert first resolv'd to be a whore, I would have seen thy hot lust satisfied more privately: I would have kept a dancer and a whole consort of musicians in my own house only to fiddle thee.

Spa. Sir, I was never whore.

Lyg. If thou couldst not say so much for thy self, thou shouldst be carted.

Tigr. *Lygones*, I have read it, and I like it, you shall deliver it.

Lyg. Well Sir, I will: but I have private business with you.

Tigr. Speak, what is't?

Lyg. How has my age deserv'd so ill of you, that you can pick no strumpets i'th' land, but out of my breed?

Tigr. Strumpets, good *Lygones*?

Lyg. Yes, and I wish to have you know, I scorn to get a whore for any prince alive, and yet scorn will not help methinks: my Daughter might have been spar'd, there were enow besides.

Tigr. May I not prosper but she's innocent as morning light for me, and I dare swear for all the world.

Lyg. Why is she with you then? can she wait on you better than your man, has she a gift in plucking off your stockings, can she make Cawdles well or cut your cornes? Why do you keep her with you? For a Queen I know you do contemn her, so should I, and every subject else think much at it.

Tigr. Let 'em think much, but 'tis more firm than earth: thou see'st thy Queen there.

Lyg. Then have I made a fair hand, I call'd her Whore. If I shall speak now as her Father, I cannot chuse but greatly rejoyce that she shall be a Queen: but if I shall speak to you as a States-man, she were more fit to be your whore.

Tigr. Get you about your business to *Arbaces*, now you talk idlely.

Lyg. Yes Sir, I will go, and shall she be a Queen? she had more wit than her old Father, when she ran away: shall she be Queen? now by my troth 'tis fine, I'le dance out of all measure at her wedding: shall I not Sir?

Tigr. Yes marry shalt thou.

Lyg. I'le make these withered kexes bear my body two hours together above ground.

Tigr. Nay go, my business requires hast.

Lyg. Good Heaven preserve you, you are an excellent King.

Spa. Farwell good Father.

Lyg. Farwell sweet vertuous Daughter, I never was so joyfull in all my life, that I remember: shall she be a Queen? Now I perceive a man may weep for joy, I had thought they had lyed that said so. [*Exit* Lygones.

Tigr. Come my dear love.

Spa. But you may see another may alter that again.

Tigr. Urge it no more, I have made up a new strong constancy, not to be shook with eyes: I know I have the passions of a man, but if I meet with any subject that should hold my eyes more firmly than is fit, I'le think of thee, and run away from it: let that suffice. [*Exeunt all.*

Enter Bacurius *and his Servant.*

Bac. Three Gentlemen without to speak with me?

Ser. Yes Sir.

Bac. Let them come in.

Enter Bessus *with the two Sword-men.*

Ser. They are entred Sir already.

Bac. Now fellows your business? are these the Gentlemen?

Bes. My Lord, I have made bold to bring these Gentlemen, my friends o'th' Sword along with me.

Bac. I am afraid you'l fight then.

Bes. My good Lord, I will not, your Lordship is much mistaken, fear not Lord.

Bac. Sir, I am sorry for't.

Bes. I ask no more in honour, Gentlemen you hear my Lord is sorry.

Bac. Not that I have beaten you, but beaten one that will be beaten: one whose dull body will require a laming, as Surfeits do the diet, spring and fall; now to your Sword-men; what come they for, good Captain Stock-fish?

Bes. It seems your Lordship has forgot my name.

Bac. No, nor your nature neither, though they are things fitter I must confess for any thing, than my remembrance, or any honest mans: what shall these Billets do; be pil'd up in my wood-yard?

Bes. Your Lordship holds your mirth still, Heaven continue it: but for these Gentlemen, they come—

Bac. To swear you are a Coward, spare your book, I do believe it.

Bes. Your Lordship still draws wide, they come to vouch under their valiant hands I am no Coward.

Bac. That would be a show indeed worth seeing: sirra be wise, and take Mony for this motion, travel with it, and where the name of *Bessus* has been known or a good Coward stirring, 'twill yield more than a tilting. This will prove more beneficial to you, if you be thrifty, than your Captainship, and more natural: men of most valiant hands is this true?

2 *Sword.* It is so, most renowned.

Bac. 'Tis somewhat strange.

1 *Sword.* Lord, it is strange, yet true; we have examined from your Lordships foot there, to this mans head, the nature of the beatings; and we do find his honour is come off clean and sufficient: this as our swords shall help us.

Bac. You are much bound to your Bil-bow-men, I am glad you are straight again Captain; 'twere good you would think on some way to gratifie them, they have undergone a labour for you, *Bessus*, would have puzl'd *Hercules* with all his valour.

2 *Sword.* Your Lordship must understand we are no men o'th' Law, that take pay for our opinions: it is sufficient we have clear'd our friend.

Bac. Yet there is something due, which I as toucht in Conscience will discharge Captain; I'le pay this Rent for you.

Bes. Spare your self my good Lord; my brave friends aim at nothing but the vertue.

Bac. That's but a cold discharge Sir for the pains.

2 *Sword.* O Lord, my good Lord.

Bac. Be not so modest, I will give you something.

Bes. They shall dine with your Lordship, that's sufficient.

Bac. Something in hand the while, you Rogues, you Apple-squires: do you come hither with your botled valour, your windy froth, to limit out my beatings?

1 *Sword.* I do beseech your Lordship.

2 *Sword.* O good Lord.

Bac. S'foot what a beavy of beaten slaves are here! get me a Cudgel sirra, and a tough one.

2 *Sword.* More of your foot, I do beseech your Lordship.

Bac. You shall, you shall dog, and your fellow-beagle.

1 *Sword.* O' this side good my Lord.

Bac. Off with your swords, for if you hurt my foot, I'le have you flead you Rascals.

1 *Sword.* Mine's off my Lord.

2 *Sword.* I beseech your Lordship stay a little, my strap's tied to my Cod piece-point: now when you please.

Bac. Captain these are your valiant friends, you long for a little too?

Bes. I am very well, I humbly thank your Lordship.

Bac. What's that in your pocket, hurts my Toe you Mungril? Thy Buttocks cannot be so hard, out with it quickly.

2 *Sword.* Here 'tis Sir, a small piece of Artillery, that a Gentleman a dear friend of your Lordships sent me with, to get it mended Sir, for if you mark, the nose is somewhat loose.

Bac. A friend of mine you Rascal? I was never wearier of doing any thing, than kicking these two Foot-balls.

Enter Servant.

Serv. Here is a good Cudgel Sir.

Bac. It comes too late I'me weary, pray thee do thou beat them.

2 *Sword.* My Lord, this is foul play i'faith, to put a fresh man upon us, men are but men Sir.

Bac. That jest shall save your bones; Captain, Rally up your rotten Regiment and be gone: I had rather thrash than be bound to kick these Rascals, till they cry'd ho; *Bessus* you may put your hand to them now, and then you are quit. Farewel, as you like this, pray visit me again, 'twill keep me in good health. [*Exit* Bac.

2 *Sword.* H'as a devilish hard foot, I never felt the like.

1 *Sword.* Nor I, and yet I am sure I have felt a hundred.

2 *Sword.* If he kick thus i'th' Dog-daies, he will be dry foundred: what cure now Captain besides Oyl of Baies?

Bes. Why well enough I warrant you, you can go.

2 *Sword.* Yes, heaven be thanked; but I feel a shrowd ach, sure h'as sprang my huckle-bone.

1 *Sword.* I ha' lost a hanch.

Bes. A little butter, friend a little butter, butter and parseley and a soveraign matter: *probatum est.*

2 *Sword.* Captain we must request your hand now to our honours.

Bes. Yes marry shall ye, and then let all the world come, we are valiant to our selves, and there's an end.

1 *Sword.* Nay then we must be valiant; O my ribs.

2 *Sword.* O my small guts, a plague upon these sharp-toed shooes, they are murtherers. [*Exeunt clear.*

Enter Arbaces *with his sword drawn.*

Arb. It is resolv'd, I bare it whilst I could, I can no more, I must begin with murther of my friends, and so go on to that incestuous ravishing, and end my life and sins with a forbidden blow, upon my self.

Enter Mardonius.

Mar. What Tragedy is near? That hand was never wont to draw a sword, but it cry'd dead to something.

Arb. *Mardonius*, have you bid *Gobrias* come?

Mar. How do you Sir?

Arb. Well, is he coming?

Mar. Why Sir, are you thus? why do your hands proclaim a lawless War against your self?

Arb. Thou answerest me one question with an other, is *Gobrias* coming?

Mar. Sir he is.

Arb. 'Tis well, I can forbear your questions then, be gone.

Mar. Sir, I have mark't.

Arb. Mark less, it troubles you and me.

Mar. You are more variable than you were.

Arb. It may be so.

Mar. To day no Hermit could be humbler than you were to us all.

Arb. And what of this?

Mar. And now you take new rage into your eyes, as you would look us all out of the Land.

Arb. I do confess it, will that satisfie? I prethee get thee gone.

Mar. Sir, I will speak.

Arb. Will ye?

Mar. It is my duty. I fear you will kill your self: I am a subject, and you shall do me wrong in't: 'tis my cause, and I may speak.

Arb. Thou art not train'd in sin, it seems *Mardonius*: kill my self! by Heaven I will not do it yet; and when I will, I'le tell thee then: I shall be such a creature, that thou wilt give me leave without a word. There is a method in mans wickedness, it grows up by degrees: I am not come so high as killing of my self, there are a hundred thousand sins 'twixt me and it, which I must doe, and I shall come to't at last; but take my oath not now, be satisfied, and get thee hence.

Mar. I am sorry 'tis so ill.

Arb. Be sorry then, true sorrow is alone, grieve by thy self.

Mar. I pray you let me see your Sword put up before I go: I'le leave you then.

Arb. Why so? what folly is this in thee, is it not as apt to mischief as it was before? can I not reach it thinkst thou? these are toyes for Children to be pleas'd with, and not men, now I am safe you think: I would the book of fate were here, my Sword is not so sure but I would get it out and mangle that, that all the destinies should quite forget their fixt decrees, and hast to make us new, for other fortunes, mine could not be worse, wilt thou now leave me?

Mar. Heaven put into your bosome temperate thoughts, I'le leave you though I fear.

Arb. Go, thou art honest, why should the hasty error of my youth be so unpardonable to draw a sin helpless upon me?

Enter Gobrias.

Gob. There is the King, now it is ripe.

Arb. Draw near thou guilty man, that art the authour of the loathedst crime five ages have brought forth, and hear me speak; curses more incurable, and all the evils mans body or his Spirit can receive be with thee.

Gob. Why Sir do you curse me thus?

Arb. Why do I curse thee? if there be a man subtil in curses, that exceeds the rest, his worst wish on thee, thou hast broke my heart.

Gob. How Sir, have I preserv'd you from a child, from all the arrows, malice, or ambition could shoot at you, and have I this for my pay?

Arb. 'Tis true, thou didst preserve me, and in that wert crueller than hardned murtherers of infants and their Mothers! thou didst save me only till thou hadst studied out a way how to destroy me cunningly thy self: this was a curious way of torturing.

Gob. What do you mean?

Arb. Thou knowst the evils thou hast done to me; dost thou remember all those witching letters thou sent'st unto me to *Armenia*, fill'd with the praise of my beloved Sister, where thou extol'st her beauty, what had I to do with that? what could her beauty be to me? and thou didst write how well she lov'd me, dost thou remember this? so that I doted something before I saw her.

Gob. This is true.

Arb. Is it? and when I was return'd thou knowst thou didst pursue it, till thou woundst me into such a strange and unbeliev'd affection, as good men cannot think on.

Gob. This I grant, I think I was the cause.

Arb. Wert thou? Nay more, I think thou meant'st it.

Gob. Sir, I hate to lie, as I love Heaven and honesty, I did, it was my meaning.

Arb. Be thine own sad judge, a further condemnation will not need, prepare thy self to dy.

Gob. Why Sir to dy?

Arb. Why shouldst thou live? was ever yet offender so impudent, that had a thought of Mercy after confession of a crime like this? get out I cannot where thou hurl'st me in, but I can take revenge, that's all the sweetness left for me.

Gob. Now is the time, hear me but speak.

Arb. No, yet I will be far more mercifull than thou wert to me; thou didst steal into me and never gav'st me warning: so much time as I give thee now, had prevented thee for ever. Notwithstanding all thy sins, if thou hast hope, that there is yet a prayer to save thee, turn and speak it to thy self.

Gob. Sir, you shall know your sins before you do'em, if you kill me.

Arb. I will not stay then.

Gob. Know you kill your Father.

Arb. How?

Gob. You kill your Father.

Arb. My Father? though I know't for a lie, made out of fear to save thy stained life; the very reverence of the word comes cross me, and ties mine arm down.

Gob. I will tell you that shall heighten you again, I am thy Father, I charge thee hear me.

Arb. If it should be so, as 'tis most false, and that I should be found a Bastard issue, the despised fruit of lawless lust, I should no more admire all my wild passions: but another truth shall be wrung from thee: if I could come by the Spirit of pain, it should be poured on thee, till thou allow'st thy self more full of lies than he that teaches thee.

Enter Arane.

Ara. Turn thee about, I come to speak to thee thou wicked man, hear me thou tyrant.

Arb. I will turn to thee, hear me thou Strumpet; I have blotted out the name of Mother, as thou hast thy shame.

Ara. My shame! thou hast less shame than any thing; why dost thou keep my Daughter in a prison? why dost thou call her Sister, and do this?

Arb. Cease thy strange impudence, and answer quickly if thou contemnest me, this will ask an answer, and have it.

Ara. Help me Gentle *Gobrias.*

Arb. Guilt [dare] not help guilt though they grow together in doing ill, yet at the [punishment] they sever, and each flies the noise of other, think not of help, answer.

Ara. I will, to what?

Arb. To such a thing, as if it be a truth think what a creature thou hast made thy self, that didst not shame to do, what I must blush only to ask thee: tell me who I am, whose son I am without all circumstance, be thou as hasty as my Sword will be if thou refusest.

Ara. Why, you are his son.

Arb. His Son? swear, swear, thou worse than woman damn'd.

Ara. By all that's good you are.

Arb. Then art thou all that ever was known bad, now is the cause of all my strange mis-fortunes come to light: what reverence expectest thou from a child, to bring forth which thou hast offended heaven, thy husband, and the Land? adulterous witch, I know now why thou wouldst have poyson'd me, I was thy lust which thou wouldst have forgot: then wicked Mother of my sins, and me, show me the way to the inheritance I have by thee: which is a spacious world of impious acts, that I may soon possess it: plagues rot thee, as thou liv'st, and such diseases, as use to pay lust, recompence thy deed.

Gob. You do not know why you curse thus.

Arb. Too well; you are a pair of Vipers; and behold the Serpent you have got; there is no beast but if he knew it, has a pedigree as brave as mine, for they have more descents, and I am every way as beastly got, as far without the compass of Law as they.

Ara. You spend your rage and words in vain, and rail upon a guess; hear us a little.

Arb. No, I will never hear, but talk away my breath, and die.

Gob. Why, but you are no Bastard.

Arb. How's that?

Ara. Nor child of mine.

Arb. Still you go on in wonders to me.

Gob. Pray you be more patient, I may bring comfort to you.

Arb. I will kneel, and hear with the obedience of a child; good Father speak, I do acknowledge you, so you bring comfort.

Gob. First know, our last King, your supposed Father was old and feeble when he married her, and almost all the Land thought she was past hope of issue from him.

Arb. Therefore she took leave to play the whore, because the King was old: is this the comfort?

Ara. What will you find out to give me satisfaction, when you find how you have injur'd me? let fire consume me, if ever I were a whore.

Gob. For-bear these starts, or I will leave you wedded to despair, as you are now: if you can find a temper, my breath shall be a pleasant western wind that cools and blasts not.

Arb. Bring it out good Father. I'le lie, and listen here as reverently as to an Angel: if I breath too loud, tell me; for I would be as still as night.

Gob. Our King I say, was old, and this our Queen desir'd to bring an heir, but yet her husband she thought was past it, and to be dishonest I think she would not: if she would have been, the truth is, she was watcht so narrowly, and had so slender opportunities, she hardly could have been: but yet her cunning found out this way; she feign'd her self with child, and posts were sent in hast throughout the Land, and humble thanks was given in every Church, and prayers were made for her safe going and delivery: she feign'd now to grow bigger, and perceiv'd this hope of issue made her fear'd, and brought a far more large respect from every man, and saw her power increase, and was resolv'd, since she believ'd, she could not hav't indeed, at least she would be thought to have a child.

Arb. Do I not hear it well? nay I will make no noise at all; but pray you to the point, quickly as you can.

Gob. Now when the time was full, she should be brought to bed, I had a Son born, which was you, this the Queen hearing of mov'd me to let her have you; and such reasons she shewed me, as she knew would tie my secrecie, she swore you should be King, and to be short, I did deliver you unto her, and pretended you were dead, and in mine own house kept a funeral, and had an empty coffin put in Earth, that night this Queen feign'd hastily to labour and by a pair of women of her own, which she had charm'd, she made the world believe she was delivered of you. You grew up as the Kings Son, till you were six years old; then did the King dye, and did leave to me Protection of the Realm; and contrary to his own expectation, left this Queen truely with child indeed, of the fair Princess *Panthea*: then she could have torn her hair and did alone to me, yet durst not speak in publick, for she knew she should be found a traytor: and her tale would have been thought madness, or any thing rather than truth. This was the only cause why she did seek to poyson you, and I to keep you safe; and this the reason, why I sought to kindle some sparks of love in you to fair *Panthea*, that she might get part of her right again.

Arb. And have you made an end now? is this all? if not, I will be still till I be aged, till all my hairs be Silver.

Gob. This is all.

Arb. And is it true say you too Madam?

Ara. Yes heaven knows it is most true.

Arb. *Panthea* then is not my Sister?

Gob. No.

Arb. But can you prove this?

Gob. If you will give consent, else who dares go about it?

Arb. Give consent? why I will have 'em all that know it rackt, to get this from 'em, all that wait without, come in, what ere you be, come in and be partakers of my joy, O you are welcome.

Enter Bessus, Gentlemen, Mardonius, *and other attendants.*

Arb. The best news, nay draw no nearer, they all shall hear it, I am found no King.

Mar. Is that so good news?

Arb. Yes the happiest news that ere was heard.

Mar. Indeed 'twere well for you if you might be a little less obey'd.

Arb. One call the Queen.

Mar. Why she is there.

Arb. The Queen *Mardonius*, *Panthea* is the Queen and I am plain *Arbaces*; go some one, she is in *Gobrias* house, since I saw you there are a thousand things delivered to me, you little dream of. [*Exit a Gent.*

Mar. So it should seem my Lord, what fury's this?

Gob. Believe me 'tis no fury, all that he saies is truth.

Mar. 'Tis very strange.

Arb. Why do you keep your hats off Gentlemen? is it to me? I swear it must not be; nay, trust me, in good faith it must not be; I cannot now command you, but I pray you for the respect you bare me, when you took me for your King, each man clap on his hat at my desire.

Mar. We will, you are not found so mean a man, but that you may be cover'd as well as we, may you not?

Arb. O not here, you may, but not I, for here is my Father in presence.

Mar. Where?

Arb. Why there: O the whole story would be a wilderness to lose thy self for ever: O pardon me dear Father for all the idle and unreverent words that I have spoke in idle moods to you: I am *Arbaces*, we all fellow-subjects, nor is the Queen *Panthea* now my Sister.

Bes. Why if you remember fellow-subject *Arbaces*; I told

you once she was not your sister: I, and she lookt nothing like you.

Arb. I think you did, good Captain *Bessus.*

Bes. Here will arise another question now amongst the Sword-men, whether I be to call him to account for beating me, now he is proved no King.

Enter Lygones.

Mar. Sir here's *Lygones,* the agent for the *Armenian* State.

Arb. Where is he? I know your business good *Lygones.*

Lyg. We must have our King again, and will.

Arb. I knew that was your business: you shall have your King again, and have him so again as never King was had, go one of you and bid *Bacurius* bring *Tigranes* hither; and bring the Lady with him, that *Panthea,* the Queen *Panthea* sent me word this [morning], was brave *Tigranes* mistress.

[*Ex. two Gent.*

Lyg. 'Tis *Spaconia.*

Arb. I, I, *Spaconia.*

Lyg. She is my Daughter.

Arb. She is so: I could now tell any thing I never heard: your King shall go so home, as never man went.

Mar. Shall he go on's head?

Arb. He shall have chariots easier than air that I will have invented; and ne're think one shall pay any ransome, and thy self that art the messenger, shalt ride before him on a horse cut out of an intire Diamond, that shall be made to go with golden wheeles, I know not how yet.

Lyg. Why I shall be made for ever? they beli'd this King with us, and said he was unkind.

Arb. And then thy Daughter, she shall have some strange thing, wee'l have the Kingdom sold utterly, and put into a toy which she shall wear about her carelesly some where or other. See the vertuous Queen; behold the humblest subject that you have kneel here before you.

Enter Panthea *and* 1 *Gent.*

Pan. Why kneel you to me that am your Vassal?

Arb. Grant me one request.

Pan. Alas what can I grant you? what I can, I will.

Arb. That you will please to marry me if I can prove it lawfull.

Pan. Is that all? more willingly than I would draw this air.

Arb. I'le kiss this hand in earnest.

2 *Gent.* Sir, *Tigranes* is coming though he made it strange at first, to see the Princess any more.

Enter Tigranes *and* Spaconia.

Arb. The Queen thou meanest, O my *Tigranes.* Pardon me, tread on my neck, I freely offer it, and if thou beest so given take revenge, for I have injur'd thee.

Tigr. No, I forgive, and rejoyce more that you have found repentance, than I my liberty.

Arb. Mayest thou be happy in thy fair choice, for thou art temperate. You owe no ransom to the state, know that I have a thousand joyes to tell you of, which yet I dare not utter till I pay my thanks to Heaven for 'em: Will you go with me and help me? pray you do.

Tigr. I will.

Arb. Take then your fair one with you; and you Queen of goodness and of us, O give me leave to take your arm in mine: come every one that takes delight in goodness, help to sing loud thanks for me, that I am prov'd no King.

THE

SCORNFUL LADY,

A

COMEDY.

Persons Represented in the Play.

Elder Loveless, *a Sutor to the Lady.*
Young Loveless, *a Prodigal.*
Savil, *Steward to Elder* Loveless.
Lady *and* Martha, } *Two Sisters.*
Younglove, *or* Abigal, *a waiting Gentlewoman.*
Welford, *a Sutor to the Lady.*
Sir Roger, *Curate to the Lady.*
A { Captain, Travailer, Poet, Tabaco-man, } *Hangers on to Young* Loveless.
Wenches.
Fidlers.
Morecraft, *an Usurer.*
A Rich Widow.
Attendants.

Actus primus. Scena prima.

Enter the two Lovelesses, Savil *the Steward, and a Page.*

Elder Love. BRother, is your last hope past to mollifie *More-crafts* heart about your Morgage?

Young Love. Hopelesly past: I have presented the Usurer with a richer draught than ever *Cleopatra* swallowed; he hath suckt in ten thousand pounds worth of my Land, more than he paid for at a gulp, without Trumpets.

El. Lo. I have as hard a task to perform in this house.

Yo. Lo. Faith mine was to make an Usurer honest, or to lose my Land.

El. Lo. And mine is to perswade a passionate woman, or to leave the Land. Make the boat stay, I fear I shall begin my unfortunate journey this night, though the darkness of the night and the roughness of the waters might easily disswade an unwilling man.

Savil. Sir, your Fathers old friends hold it the sounder course for your body and estate to stay at home and marry, and propagate and govern in our Country, than to Travel and die without issue.

El. Lo. *Savil*, you shall gain the opinion of a better servant, in seeking to execute, not alter my will, howsoever my intents succeed.

Yo. Lo. Yonder's Mistres *Younglove*, Brother, the grave rubber of your Mistresses toes.

Enter Mistres Younglove *the waiting woman.*

El. Lo. Mistres *Younglove.*

Young. Master *Loveless*, truly we thought your sails had been hoist: my Mistres is perswaded you are Sea-sick ere this.

El. Lo. Loves she her ill taken up resolution so dearly? Didst thou move her from me?

Young. By this light that shines, there's no removing her, if she get a stiffe opinion by the end. I attempted her to day when they say a woman can deny nothing.

El. Lo. What critical minute was that?

Young. When her smock was over her ears: but she was no more pliant than if it hung about her heels.

El. Lo. I prethee deliver my service, and say, I desire to see the dear cause of my banishment; and then for *France.*

Young. I'le do't: hark hither, is that your Brother?

El. Lo. Yes, have you lost your memory?

Young. As I live he's a pretty fellow. [*Exit.*

Yo. Lo. O this is a sweet *Brache.*

El. Lo. Why she knows not you.

Yo. Lo. No, but she offered me once to know her: to this day she loves youth of Eighteen; she heard a tale how *Cupid* struck her in love with a great Lord in the Tilt-yard, but he never saw her; yet she in kindness would needs wear a Willow-garland at his Wedding. She lov'd all the Players in the last Queens time once over: she was struck when they acted Lovers, and forsook some when they plaid Murthers. She has nine *Spur-royals*, and the servants say she hoards old gold; and she her self pronounces angerly, that the Farmers eldest son, or her Mistres Husbands Clerk shall be, that Marries her, shall make her a joynture of fourscore pounds a year; she tells tales of the serving-men.

El. Lo. Enough, I know her Brother. I shall intreat you only to salute my Mistres, and take leave, we'l part at the Stairs.

Enter Lady *and waiting women.*

Lady. Now Sir, this first part of your will is performed: what's the rest?

El. Lo. First, let me beg your notice for this Gentleman my Brother.

Lady. I shall take it as a favour done to me, though the Gentleman hath received but an untimely grace from you, yet my charitable disposition would have been ready to have done him freer courtesies as a stranger, than upon those cold commendations.

Yo. Lo. Lady, my salutations crave acquaintance and leave at once.

Lady. Sir I hope you are the master of your own occasions. [*Exit* Yo. Lo. *and* Savil.

El. Lo. Would I were so. Mistris, for me to praise over again that worth, which all the world, and you your self can see.

Lady. It's a cold room this, Servant.

El. Lo. Mistris.

La. What think you if I have a Chimney for't, out here?

El. Lo. Mistris, another in my place, that were not tyed to believe all your actions just, would apprehend himself wrong'd: But I whose vertues are constancy and obedience.

La. *Younglove*, make a good fire above to warm me after my servants *Exordiums*.

El. Lo. I have heard and seen your affability to be such, that the servants you give wages to may speak.

La. 'Tis true, 'tis true; but they speak to th' purpose.

El. Lo. Mistris, your will leads my speeches from the purpose. But as a man—

La. A *Simile* servant? This room was built for honest meaners, that deliver themselves hastily and plainly, and are gone. Is this a time or place for *Exordiums*, and *Similes* and *Metaphors*? If you have ought to say, break into't: my answers shall very reasonably meet you.

El. Lo. Mistris I came to see you.

La. That's happily dispatcht, the next.

El. Lo. To take leave of you.

La. To be gone?

El. Lo. Yes.

La. You need not have despair'd of that, nor have us'd so many circumstances to win me to give you leave to perform my command; is there a third?

El. Lo. Yes, I had a third had you been apt to hear it.

La. I? Never apter. Fast (good servant) fast.

El. Lo. 'Twas to intreat you to hear reason.

La. Most willingly, have you brought one can speak it?

El. Lo. Lastly, it is to kindle in that barren heart love and forgiveness.

La. You would stay at home?

El. Lo. Yes Lady.

La. Why you may, and doubtlesly will, when you have debated that your commander is but your Mistris, a woman, a weak one, wildly overborn with passions: but the thing by her commanded, is to see *Dovers* dreadful cliffe, passing in a poor Water-house; the dangers of the merciless Channel 'twixt that and *Callis*, five long hours sail, with three poor weeks victuals.

El. Lo. You wrong me.

La. Then to land dumb, unable to enquire for an English hoast, to remove from City to City, by most chargeable Post-horse, like one that rode in quest of his Mother tongue.

El. Lo. You wrong me much.

La. And all these (almost invincible labours) performed for your Mistris, to be in danger to forsake her, and to put on new allegeance to some *French* Lady, who is content to change language with your laughter, and after your whole year spent in Tennis and broken speech, to stand to the hazard of being laught at, at your return, and have tales made on you by the Chamber-maids.

El. Lo. You wrong me much.

La. Louder yet.

El. Lo. You know your least word is of force to make me seek out dangers, move me not with toyes: but in this banishment, I must take leave to say, you are unjust: was one kiss forc't from you in publick by me so unpardonable? Why all the hours of day and night have seen us kiss.

La. 'Tis true, and so you told the company that heard me chide.

Elder Lov. Your own eyes were not dearer to you than I.

Lady. And so you told 'em.

Elder Lo. I did, yet no sign of disgrace need to have stain'd your cheek: you your self knew your pure and simple heart to be most unspotted, and free from the least baseness.

Lady. I did: But if a Maids heart doth but once think that she is suspected, her own face will write her guilty.

Elder Lo. But where lay this disgrace? The world that knew us, knew our resolutions well: And could it be hop'd that I should give away my freedom; and venture a perpetual bondage with one I never kist? or could I in strict wisdom take too much love upon me, from her that chose me for her Husband?

Lady. Believe me; if my Wedding-smock were on,
Were the Gloves bought and given, the Licence come,
Were the Rosemary-branches dipt, and all
The Hipochrist and Cakes eat and drunk off,
Were these two armes incompast with the hands
Of Bachelors to lead me to the Church,
Were my feet in the door, were I *John*, said,
If *John* should boast a favour done by me,
I would not wed that year: And you I hope,
When you have spent this year commodiously,
In atchieving Languages, will at your return
Acknowledge me more coy of parting with mine eyes,
Than such a friend: More talk I hold not now
If you dare go.

Elder Lo. I dare, you know: First let me kiss.

Lady. Farewel sweet Servant, your task perform'd,

On a new ground as a beginning Sutor,
I shall be apt to hear you.

Elder Lo. Farewel cruel Mistres. [*Exit* Lady.

Enter Young Loveless, *and* Savil.

Young Lo. Brother you'l hazard the losing your tide to *Gravesend*: you have a long half mile by Land to *Greenewich*?

Elder Lo. I go: but Brother, what yet unheard of course to live, doth your imagination flatter you with? Your ordinary means are devour'd.

Young Lo. Course? why Horse-coursing I think. Consume no time in this: I have no Estate to be mended by meditation: he that busies himself about my fortunes may properly be said to busie himself about nothing.

Elder Lo. Yet some course you must take, which for my satisfaction resolve and open; if you will shape none, I must inform you that that man but perswades himself he means to live, that imagines not the means.

Young Lo. Why live upon others, as others have lived upon me.

Elder Lo. I apprehend not that: you have fed others, and consequently dispos'd of 'em: and the same measure must you expect from your maintainers, which will be too heavy an alteration for you to bear.

Young Lo. Why I'le purse; if that raise me not, I'le bet at Bowling-alleyes, or man Whores; I would fain live by others: but I'le live whilst I am unhang'd, and after the thought's taken.

Elder Love. I see you are ty'd to no particular imploiment then?

Young Lo. Faith I may choose my course: they say nature brings forth none but she provides for them: I'le try her liberality.

Elder Lo. Well, to keep your feet out of base and dangerous paths, I have resolved you shall live as Master of my House. It shall be your care *Savil* to see him fed and cloathed, not according to his present Estate, but to his birth and former fortunes.

Young Lo. If it be refer'd to him, if I be not found in

Carnation Jearsie-stockins, blew devils breeches, with the gards down, and my pocket i'th' sleeves, I'le n'er look you i'th' face again.

Sa. A comelier wear I wuss it is than those dangling slops.

Elder Lo. To keep you readie to do him all service peaceably, and him to command you reasonably, I leave these further directions in writing, which at your best leasure together open and read.

Enter Younglove *to them with a Jewell.*

Abig. Sir, my Mistress commends her love to you in this token, and these words; it is a Jewell (she sayes) which as a favour from her she would request you to wear till your years travel be performed: which once expired, she will hastily expect your happy return.

Elder Lo. Return my service with such thanks, as she may imagine the heart of a suddenly over-joyed man would willingly utter, and you I hope I shall with slender arguments perswade to wear this Diamond, that when my Mistris shall through my long absence, and the approach of new Suitors, offer to forget me; you may cast your eye down to your finger, and remember and speak of me: She will hear thee better than those allied by birth to her; as we see many men much swayed by the Grooms of their Chambers, not that they have a greater part of their love or opinion on them, than on others, but for that they know their secrets.

Abi. O' my credit I swear, I think 'twas made for me: Fear no other Suitors.

Elder Love. I shall not need to teach you how to discredit their beginning, you know how to take exception at their shirts at washing, or to make the maids swear they found plasters in their beds.

Abi. I know, I know, and do not you fear the Suitors.

Elder Lo. Farewell, be mindfull, and be happie; the night calls me. [*Exeunt omnes præter Younglove.*

Abi. The Gods of the Winds befriend you Sir; a constant and a liberal Lover thou art, more such God send us.

Enter Welford.

Wel. Let'em not stand still, we have rid.

Abi. A suitor I know by his riding hard, I'le not be seen.

Wel. A prettie Hall this, no Servant in't? I would look freshly.

Abi. You have delivered your errand to me then: there's no danger in a hansome young fellow: I'le shew my self.

Wel. Lady, may it please you to bestow upon a stranger the ordinary grace of salutation: Are you the Lady of this house?

Abi. Sir, I am worthily proud to be a Servant of hers.

Wel. Lady, I should be as proud to be a Servant of yours, did not my so late acquaintance make me despair.

Abi. Sir, it is not so hard to atchieve, but nature may bring it about.

Wel. For these comfortable words, I remain your glad Debtor. Is your Lady at home?

Abi. She is no stragler Sir.

Wel. May her occasions admit me to speak with her?

Abi. If you come in the way of a Suitor, No.

Wel. I know your affable vertue will be moved to perswade her, that a Gentleman benighted and strayed, offers to be bound to her for a nights lodging.

Abi. I will commend this message to her; but if you aim at her body, you will be deluded: other women of the household of good carriage and government; upon any of which if you can cast your affection, they will perhaps be found as faithfull and not so coy. [*Exit* Younglove.

Wel. What a skin full of lust is this? I thought I had come a wooing, and I am the courted partie. This is right Court fashion: Men, Women, and all woo, catch that catch may. If this soft hearted woman have infused any of her tenderness into her Lady, there is hope she will be plyant. But who's here?

Enter Sir Roger *the Curate.*

Roger. Gad save you Sir. My Lady lets you know she desires to be acquainted with your name, before she confer with you?

Wel. Sir, my name calls me *Welford.*

Roger. Sir, you are a Gentleman of a good name. I'le try his wit.

Wel. I will uphold it as good as any of my Ancestors had this two hundred years Sir.

Roger. I knew a worshipfull and a Religious Gentleman of your name in the Bishoprick of *Durham.* Call you him Cousen?

Wel. I am only allyed to his vertues Sir.

Roger. It is modestly said: I should carry the badge of your Christianity with me too.

Wel. What's that, a Cross? there's a tester.

Roger. I mean the name which your God-fathers and God-mothers gave you at the Font.

Wel. 'Tis *Harry*: but you cannot proceed orderly now in your Catechism: for you have told me who gave me that name. Shall I beg your name?

Roger. *Roger.*

Wel. What room fill you in this house?

Roger. More rooms than one.

Wel. The more the merrier: but may my boldness know, why your Lady hath sent you to decypher my name?

Roger. Her own words were these: To know whether you were a formerly denyed Suitor, disguised in this message: for I can assure you she delights not in *Thalame*: *Hymen* and she are at variance, I shall return with much hast.

[*Exit* Roger.

Wel. And much speed Sir, I hope: certainly I am arrived amongst a Nation of new found fools, on a Land where no Navigator has yet planted wit; if I had foreseen it, I would have laded my breeches with bells, knives, copper, and glasses, to trade with women for their virginities: yet I fear, I should have betrayed my self to a needless charge then: here's the walking night-cap again.

Enter Roger.

Roger. Sir, my Ladies pleasure is to see you: who hath commanded me to acknowledge her sorrow, that you must take the pains to come up for so bad entertainment.

Wel. I shall obey your Lady that sent it, and acknowledge you that brought it to be your Arts Master.

Rog. I am but a Batchelor of Art, Sir; and I have the mending of all under this roof, from my Lady on her down-bed, to the maid in the Pease-straw.

Wel. A Cobler, Sir?

Roger. No Sir, I inculcate Divine Service within these Walls.

Wel. But the Inhabitants of this house do often imploy you on errands without any scruple of Conscience.

Rog. Yes, I do take the air many mornings on foot, three or four miles for eggs: but why move you that?

Wel. To know whether it might become your function to bid my man to neglect his horse a little to attend on me.

Roger. Most properly Sir.

Wel. I pray you doe so then: the whilst I will attend your Lady. You direct all this house in the true way?

Roger. I doe Sir.

Wel. And this door I hope conducts to your Lady?

Rog. Your understanding is ingenious. [*Ex. severally.*

Enter young Loveless *and* Savil, *with a writing.*

Sa. By your favour Sir, you shall pardon me?

Yo. Lo. I shall bear your favour Sir, cross me no more; I say they shall come in.

Savil. Sir, you forget who I am?

Yo. Lo. Sir, I do not; thou art my Brothers Steward, his cast off mill-money, his Kitchen Arithmetick.

Sa. Sir, I hope you will not make so little of me?

Yo. Lo. I make thee not so little as thou art: for indeed there goes no more to the making of a Steward, but a fair *Imprimis*, and then a reasonable *Item* infus'd into him, and the thing is done.

Sa. Nay then you stir my duty, and I must tell you?

Young Lo. What wouldst thou tell me, how Hopps grow, or hold some rotten discourse of Sheep, or when our Lady-day falls? Prethee farewel, and entertain my friends, be drunk and burn thy Table-books: and my dear spark of velvet, thou and I.

Sa. Good Sir remember?

Young Lo. I do remember thee a foolish fellow, one that

did put his trust in Almanacks, and Horse-fairs, and rose by Hony and Pot-butter. Shall they come in yet?

Sa. Nay then I must unfold your Brothers pleasure, these be the lessons Sir, he left behind him.

Young Lo. Prethee expound the first.

Sa. I leave to maintain my house three hundred pounds a year; and my Brother to dispose of it.

Young Lo. Mark that my wicked Steward, and I dispose of it?

Sav. Whilest he bears himself like a Gentleman, and my credit falls not in him. Mark that my good young Sir, mark that.

Young Lo. Nay, if it be no more I shall fulfil it, whilst my Legs will carry me I'le bear my self Gentleman-like, but when I am drunk, let them bear me that can. Forward dear Steward.

Sav. Next it is my will, that he be furnished (as my Brother) with Attendance, Apparel, and the obedience of my people.

Young Lo. Steward this is as plain as your old Minikin-breeches. Your wisdom will relent now, will it not? Be mollified or—you understand me Sir, proceed?

Sav. Next, that my Steward keep his place, and power, and bound my Brother's wildness with his care.

Young Lo. I'le hear no more of this *Apocrypha*, bind it by it self Steward.

Sav. This is your Brothers will, and as I take it, he makes no mention of such company as you would draw unto you. Captains of Gallyfoists, such as in a clear day have seen *Callis*, fellows that have no more of God, than their Oaths come to: they wear swords to reach fire at a Play, and get there the oyl'd end of a Pipe, for their Guerdon: then the remnant of your Regiment, are wealthy Tobacco-Marchants, that set up with one Ounce, and break for three: together with a Forlorn hope of Poets, and all these look like Carthusians, things without linnen: Are these fit company for my Masters Brother?

Young Lo. I will either convert thee (O thou Pagan Steward) or presently confound thee and thy reckonings, who's there? Call in the Gentlemen.

Sav. Good Sir.

Young Lo. Nay, you shall know both who I am, and where I am.

Sav. Are you my Masters Brother?

Young Lo. Are you the sage Master Steward, with a face like an old *Ephemerides*?

Enter his Comrades, Captain, Traveller, *&c.*

Sav. Then God help us all I say.

Young Lo. I, and 'tis well said my old peer of *France*: welcome Gentlemen, welcome Gentlemen; mine own dear Lads y'are richly welcome. Know this old *Harry* Groat.

Cap. Sir I will take your love.

Sav. Sir, you will take my Purse.

Cap. And study to continue it.

Sav. I do believe you.

Trav. Your honorable friend and Masters Brother, hath given you to us for a worthy fellow, and so we hugg you Sir.

Sav. Has given himself into the hands of Varlets, not to be carv'd out. Sir, are these the pieces?

Young Lo. They are the Morals of the Age, the vertues, men made of gold.

Sav. Of your gold you mean Sir.

Young Lo. This is a man of War, and cryes go on, and wears his colours.

Sav. In's nose.

Young Lo. In the fragrant field. This is a Traveller Sir, knows men and manners, and has plow'd up the Sea so far till both the Poles have knockt, has seen the Sun take Coach, and can distinguish the colour of his Horses, and their kinds, and had a *Flanders*-Mare leapt there.

Sav. 'Tis much.

Tra. I have seen more Sir.

Sav. 'Tis even enough o' Conscience; sit down, and rest you, you are at the end of the world already. Would you had as good a Living Sir, as this fellow could lie you out of, he has a notable gift in't.

Young Lo. This ministers the smoak, and this the Muses.

Sav. And you the Cloaths, and Meat, and Money, you have a goodly generation of 'em, pray let them multiply, your

Brother's house is big enough, and to say truth, h'as too much Land, hang it durt.

Young Lo. Why now thou art a loving stinkard. Fire off thy Annotations and thy Rent-books, thou hast a weak brain *Savil*, and with the next long Bill thou wilt run mad. Gentlemen, you are once more welcome to three hundred pounds a year; we will be freely merry, shall we not?

Capt. Merry as mirth and wine, my lovely *Loveless.*

Poet. A serious look shall be a Jury to excommunicate any man from our company.

Tra. We will not talk wisely neither?

Young Lo. What think you Gentlemen by all this Revenue in Drink?

Capt. I am all for Drink.

Tra. I am dry till it be so.

Poet. He that will not cry Amen to this, let him live sober, seem wise, and dye o'th' *Coram.*

Young Lo. It shall be so, we'l have it all in Drink, let Meat and Lodging go, they are transitory, and shew men meerly mortal: then we'l have Wenches, every one his Wench, and every week a fresh one: we'l keep no powdered flesh: all these we have by warrant, under the title of things necessary. Here upon this place I ground it, The obedience of my people, and all necessaries: your opinions Gentlemen?

Capt. 'Tis plain and evident that he meant Wenches.

Sav. Good Sir let me expound it?

Capt. Here be as sound men, as your self Sir.

Poet. This do I hold to be the i[n]terpretation of it: In this word Necessary, is concluded all that be helps to Man; Woman was made the first, and therefore here the chiefest.

Young Lo. Believe me 'tis a learned one; and by these words, The obedience of my people, you Steward being one, are bound to fetch us Wenches.

Capt. He is, he is.

Young Lo. Steward, attend us for instructions.

Sav. But will you keep no house Sir?

Young Lo. Nothing but drink Sir, three hundred pounds in drink.

Sav. O miserable house, and miserable I that live to see it! Good Sir keep some meat.

Young Lo. Get us good Whores, and for your part, I'le board you in an Alehouse, you shall have Cheese and Onions.

Sav. What shall become of me, no Chimney smoaking? Well Prodigal, your Brother will come home. [*Exit.*

Young Lo. Come Lads, I'le warrant you for Wenches, three hundred poūnds in drink. [*Exeunt omnes.*

Actus Secundus. Scena Prima.

Enter Lady, *her Sister* Martha, Welford, Younglove, *and others.*

Lady. SIR, now you see your bad lodging, I must bid you good night.

Wel. Lady if there be any want, 'tis in want of you.

Lady. A little sleep will ease that complement. Once more good night.

Wel. Once more dear Lady, and then all sweet nights.

Lady. Dear Sir be short and sweet then.

Wel. Shall the morrow prove better to me, shall I hope my sute happier by this nights rest?

Lady. Is your sute so sickly that rest will help it? Pray ye let it rest then till I call for it. Sir as a stranger you have had all my welcome: but had I known your errand ere you came, your passage had been straiter. Sir, good night.

Welford. So fair, and cruel, dear unkind good night. [*Exit* Lady.

Nay Sir, you shall stay with me, I'le press your zeal so far.

Roger. O Lord Sir.

Wel. Do you love *Tobacco*?

Rog. Surely I love it, but it loves not me; yet with your reverence I'le be bold.

Wel. Pray light it Sir. How do you like it?

Rog. I promise you it is notable stinging geer indeed. It is wet Sir, Lord how it brings down Rheum!

Wel. Handle it again Sir, you have a warm text of it.

Rog. Thanks ever promised for it. I promise you it is very powerful, and by a Trope, spiritual; for certainly it moves in sundry places.

Wel. I, it does so Sir, and me especially to ask Sir, why you wear a Night-cap.

Rog. Assuredly I will speak the truth unto you: you shall understand Sir, that my head is broken, and by whom; even by that visible beast the Butler.

Wel. The Butler? certainly he had all his drink about him when he did it. Strike one of your grave Cassock? The offence Sir?

Rog. Reproving him at Tra-trip Sir, for swearing; you have the total surely.

Wel. You told him when his rage was set a tilt, and so he crackt your Canons. I hope he has not hurt your gentle reading: But shall we see these Gentlewomen to night.

Rog. Have patience Sir until our fellow *Nicholas* be deceast, that is, asleep: for so the word is taken: to sleep to dye, to dye to sleep, a very figure Sir.

Wel. Cannot you cast another for the Gentlewomen?

Rog. Not till the man be in his bed, his grave: his grave, his bed: the very same again Sir. Our Comick Poet gives the reason sweetly; *Plenus rimarum est*, he is full of loope-holes, and will discover to our Patroness.

Wel. Your comment Sir has made me understand you.

Enter Martha *the* Ladies *Sister, and* Younglove, *to them with a Posset.*

Rog. Sir be addrest, the graces do salute you with the full bowl of plenty. Is our old enemy entomb'd?

Abig. He's safe.

Rog. And does he snore out supinely with the Poet?

Mar. No, he out-snores the Poet.

Wel. Gentlewoman, this courtesie shall bind a stranger to you, ever your servant.

Mar. Sir, my Sisters strictness makes not us forget you are a stranger and a Gentleman.

Abig. In sooth Sir, were I chang'd into my Lady, a Gentleman so well indued with parts, should not be lost.

Wel. I thank you Gentlewoman, and rest bound to you. See how this foul familiar chewes the Cud: From thee, and three and fifty good Love deliver me.

Mar. Will you sit down Sir, and take a spoon?

Wel. I take it kindly, Lady.

Mar. It is our best banquet Sir.

Rog. Shall we give thanks?

Wel. I have to the Gentlewomen already Sir.

Mar. Good Sir *Roger*, keep that breath to cool your part o'th' Posset, you may chance have a scalding zeal else; and you will needs be doing, pray tell your twenty to your self. Would you could like this Sir?

Wel. I would your Sister would like me as well Lady.

Mar. Sure Sir, she would not eat you: but banish that imagination; she's only wedded to her self, lyes with her self, and loves her self; and for another Husband than herself, he may knock at the gate, but ne're come in: be wise Sir, she's a Woman, and a trouble, and has her many faults, the least of which is, she cannot love you.

Abig. God pardon her, she'l do worse, would I were worthy his least grief, Mistris *Martha*.

Wel. Now I must over-hear her.

Mar. Faith would thou hadst them all with all my heart; I do not think they would make thee a day older.

Abig. Sir, will you put in deeper, 'tis the sweeter.

Mar. Well said old sayings.

Wel. She looks like one indeed. Gentlewoman you keep your word, your sweet self has made the bottom sweeter.

Abig. Sir, I begin a frolick, dare you change Sir?

Wel. My self for you, so please you. That smile has turn'd my stomach: this is right the old Embleme of the Moyle cropping of Thistles: Lord what a hunting head she carries, sure she has been ridden with a Martingale. Now love deliver me.

Rog. Do I dream, or do I wake? surely I know not: am I rub'd off? Is this the way of all my morning Prayers? Oh *Roger*, thou art but grass, and woman as a flower. Did I for this consume my quarters in Meditation, Vowes, and wooed her in *Heroical Epistles*? Did I expound the Owl, and undertook with labour and expence the recollection of those thousand Pieces, consum'd in Cellars, and Tabacco-shops of that our honour'd *Englishman Ni. Br.*? Have I done this, and am I done thus too? I will end with the wise man, and say; He that holds a Woman, has an Eel by the tail.

Mar. Sir 'tis so late, and our entertainment (meaning our Posset) by this is grown so cold, that 'twere an unmannerly part longer to hold you from your rest: let what the house has be at your command Sir.

Wel. Sweet rest be with you Lady; and to you what you desire too.

Abig. It should be some such good thing like your self then. [*Exeunt.*

Wel. Heaven keep me from that curse, and all my issue. Good night Antiquity.

Rog. *Solamen Miseris socios habuisse Doloris*: but I alone.

Wel. Learned Sir, will you bid my man come to me? and requesting a greater measure of your learning, good night, good Master *Roger.*

Rog. Good Sir, peace be with you. [*Exit* Roger.

Wel. Adue dear *Domine.* Half a dozen such in a Kingdom would make a man forswear confession: for who that had but half his wits about him, would commit the Counsel of a serious sin to such a cruel Night-cap? Why how now shall we have an Antick? [*Enter Servant.* Whose head do you carry upon your shoulders, that you jole it so against the Post? Is't for your ease? Or have you seen the Celler? Where are my slippers Sir?

Ser. Here Sir.

Wel. Where Sir? have you got the pot Verdugo? have you seen the Horses Sir?

Ser. Yes Sir.

Wel. Have they any meat?

Ser. Faith Sir, they have a kind of wholesome Rushes, Hay I cannot call it.

Wel. And no Provender?

Ser. Sir, so I take it.

Wel. You are merry Sir, and why so?

Ser. Faith Sir, here are no Oats to be got, unless you'l have 'em in Porredge: the people are so mainly given to spoon-meat: yonder's a cast of Coach-mares of the Gentlewomans, the strangest Cattel.

Wel. Why?

Ser. Why, they are transparent Sir, you may see through them: and such a house!

Wel. Come Sir, the truth of your discovery.

Ser. Sir, they are in tribes like Jewes: the Kitchin and the Dayrie make one tribe, and have their faction and their fornication within themselves; the Buttery and the Landry are another, and there's no love lost; the chambers are intire, and what's done there, is somewhat higher than my knowledge: but this I am sure, between these copulations, a stranger is kept vertuous, that is, fasting. But of all this the drink Sir.

Wel. What of that Sir?

Ser. Faith Sir, I will handle it as the time and your patience will give me leave. This drink, or this cooling Julip, of which three spoonfuls kills the Calenture, a pint breeds the cold Palsie.

Wel. Sir, you bely the house.

Ser. I would I did Sir. But as I am a true man, if 'twere but one degree colder, nothing but an Asses hoof would hold it.

Wel. I am glad on't Sir, for if it had proved stronger, you had been tongue ti'd of these commendations. Light me the candle Sir, I'le hear no more. [*Exeunt.*

Enter young Loveless *and his* Comrades, *with wenches, and two Fidlers.*

Yo. Lo. Come my brave man of war, trace out thy darling,
And you my learned Council, sit and turn boyes,
Kiss till the Cow come home, kiss close, kiss close knaves.
My Modern Poet, thou shalt kiss in couplets.

Enter with Wine.

Strike up you merry varlets, and leave your peeping,
This is no pay for Fidlers.

Capt. O my dear boy, thy *Hercules*, thy Captain
Makes thee his *Hylas*, his delight, his solace.
Love thy brave man of war, and let thy bounty
Clap him in *Shamois*: Let there be deducted out of our main (potation
Five Marks in hatchments to adorn this thigh,
Crampt with this rest of peace, and I will fight
Thy battels.

Yo. Lo. Thou shalt hav't boy, and fly in Feather, Lead on a March you Michers.

Enter Savill.

Savill. O my head, O my heart, what a noyse and change is here! would I had been cold i'th' mouth before this day, and ne're have liv'd to see this dissolution. He that lives within a mile of this place, had as good sleep in the perpetual noyse of an Iron Mill. There's a dead Sea of drink i'th' Seller, in which goodly vessels lye wrackt, and in the middle of this deluge appear the tops of flagons and black jacks, like Churches drown'd i'th' marshes.

Yo. Lo. What, art thou come? My sweet Sir *Amias* welcome to *Troy*. Come thou shalt kiss my *Helen*, and court her in a dance.

Sav. Good Sir consider?

Yo. Lo. Shall we consider Gentlemen? How say you?

Capt. Consider? that were a simple toy i'faith, consider? whose moral's that? The man that cryes consider is our foe: let my steel know him.

Young Lo. Stay thy dead doing hand, he must not die yet: prethee be calm my *Hector*.

Capt. Peasant slave, thou groom compos'd of grudgings, live and thank this Gentleman, thou hadst seen *Pluto* else. The next consider kills thee.

Trav. Let him drink down his word again in a gallon of Sack.

Poet. 'Tis but a snuffe, make it two gallons, and let him doe it kneeling in repentance.

Savil. Nay rather kill me, there's but a lay-man lost. Good Captain doe your office.

Young Lo. Thou shalt drink Steward, drink and dance my Steward. Strike him a horn-pipe squeakers, take thy striver, and pace her till she stew.

Savil. Sure Sir, I cannot dance with your Gentlewomen, they are too light for me, pray break my head, and let me goe.

Capt. He shall dance, he shall dance.

Young Lo. He shall dance, and drink, and be drunk and dance, and be drunk again, and shall see no meat in a year.

Poet. And three quarters?

Young Lo. And three quarters be it.

Capt. Who knocks there? let him in.

Enter Elder Loveless *disguised.*

Savill. Some to deliver me I hope.

Elder Lo. Gentlemen, God save you all, my business is to one Master *Loveless*?

Capt. This is the Gentleman you mean; view him, and take his Inventorie, he's a right one.

Elder Lo. He promises no less Sir.

Young Lo. Sir, your business?

Elder Lo. Sir, I should let you know, yet I am loth, yet I am sworn to't, would some other tongue would speak it for me.

Young Lo. Out with it i' Gods name.

Elder Lo. All I desire Sir is, the patience and sufferance of a man, and good Sir be not mov'd more.

Young Lo. Then a pottle of sack will doe, here's my hand, prethee thy business?

Elder Lo. Good Sir excuse me, and whatsoever you hear, think must have been known unto you, and be your self discreet, and bear it nobly.

Young Lo. Prethee dispatch me.

Elder Lo. Your Brother's dead Sir.

Young Lo. Thou dost not mean dead drunk?

Elder Lo. No, no, dead and drown'd at sea Sir.

Young Lo. Art sure he's dead?

Elder Lo. Too sure Sir.

Young Lo. I but art thou very certainly sure of it?

Elder Lo. As sure Sir, as I tell it.

Young Lo. But art thou sure he came not up again?

Elder Lo. He may come up, but ne're to call you Brother.

Young Lo. But art sure he had water enough to drown him?

Elder Lo. Sure Sir, he wanted none.

Young Lo. I would not have him want, I lov'd him better; here I forgive thee: and i'faith be plain, how do I bear it?

Elder Lo. Very wisely Sir.

Young Lo. Fill him some wine. Thou dost not see me mov'd, these transitorie toyes ne're trouble me, he's in a better place, my friend I know't. Some fellows would have cryed now, and have curst thee, and faln out with their meat, and kept a pudder; but all this helps not, he was too good for us, and let God keep him: there's the right use on't friend. Off with thy drink, thou hast a spice of sorrow makes thee dry: fill him another. *Savill*, your Master's dead, and who am I now *Savill*? Nay, let's all bear it well, wipe *Savill* wipe, tears are but thrown away: we shall have wenches now, shall we not *Savill*?

Savill. Yes Sir.

Young Lo. And drink innumerable.

Savil. Yes forsooth.

Young Lo. And you'll strain curtsie and be drunk a little?

Savil. I would be glad, Sir, to doe my weak endeavour.

Yo. Lo. You may be brought in time to love a wench too.

Savil. In time the sturdie Oak Sir.

Young Lo. Some more wine for my friend there.

Elder Lo. I shall be drunk anon for my good news: but I have a loving Brother, that's my comfort.

Youn[g] Lo. Here's to you Sir, this is the worst I wish you for your news: and if I had another elder Brother, and say it were his chance to feed Haddocks, I should be still the same you see me now, a poor contented Gentleman. More wine for my friend there, he's dry again.

Elder Lo. I shall be if I follow this beginning. Well my dear Brother, if I scape this drowning, 'tis your turn next to sink, you shall duck twice before I help you. Sir I cannot drink more; pray let me have your pardon.

Young Lo. O Lord Sir, 'tis your modestie: more wine, give him a bigger glass; hug him my Captain, thou shalt be my chief mourner.

Capt. And this my pennon: Sir, a full carouse to you, and to my Lord of Land here.

Elder Lo. I feel a buzzing in my brains, pray God they bear this out, and I'le ne're trouble them so far again. Here's to you Sir.

Young Lo. To my dear Steward, down o' your knees you infidel, you Pagan; be drunk and penitent.

Savil. Forgive me Sir, and I'le be any thing.

Young Lo. Then be a Baud, I'le have thee a brave Baud.

Elder Lo. Sir, I must take my leave of you, my business is so urgent.

Young Lo. Let's have a bridling cast before you go. Fill's a new stoupe.

Elder Lo. I dare not Sir, by no means.

Young Lo. Have you any mind to a wench? I would fain gratifie you for the pains you took Sir.

Elder Lo. As little as to the t'other.

Young Lo. If you find any stirring do but say so.

Elder Lo. Sir, you are too bounteous, when I feel that itching, you shall asswage it Sir, before another: this only and Farewell Sir. Your Brother when the storm was most extream, told all about him, he left a will which lies close behind a Chimney in the matted Chamber: and so as well Sir, as you have made me able, I take my leave.

Young Lo. Let us imbrace him all: if you grow drie before you end your business, pray take a baite here, I have a fresh hogshead for you.

Savil. You shall neither will nor chuse Sir. My Master is a wonderfull fine Gentleman, has a fine state, a very fine state Sir, I am his Steward Sir, and his man.

Elder Lo. Would you were your own sir, as I left you. Well I must cast about, or all sinks.

Savil. Farewell Gentleman, Gentleman, Gentleman.

Elder Lo. What would you with me sir?

Savil. Farewell Gentleman.

Elder Lo. O sleep Sir, sleep. [*Exit* Elder Lo.

Young Lo. Well boyes, you see what's faln, let's in and drink, and give thanks for it.

Capt. Let's give thanks for it.

Young Lo. Drunk as I live.

Savil. Drunk as I live boyes.

Young Lo. Why, now thou art able to discharge thine office, and cast up a reckoning of some weight; I will be knighted, for my state will bear it, 'tis sixteen hundred boyes: off with your husks, I'le skin you all in Sattin.

Capt. O sweet *Loveless*!

Savil. All in Sattin? O sweet *Loveless*!

Young Lo. March in my noble Compeeres: and this my Countess shall be led by two: and so proceed we to the Will. [*Exeunt.*

Enter Morecraft *the* Usurer, *and* Widow.

Morec. And Widow as I say be your own friend: your husband left you wealthy, I and wise, continue so sweet duck, continue so. Take heed of young smooth Varlets, younger Brothers: they are worms that will eat through your bags: they are very Lightning, that with a flash or two will melt your money, and never singe your purse-strings: they are Colts, wench Colts, heady and dangerous, till we take 'em up, and make 'em fit for Bonds: look upon me, I have had, and have yet matter of moment girle, matter of moment; you may meet with a worse back, I'le not commend it.

Wid. Nor I neither Sir.

Mor. Yet thus far by your favour Widow, 'tis tuffe.

Wid. And therefore not for my dyet, for I love a tender one.

Mor. Sweet Widow leave your frumps, and be edified: you know my state, I sell no Perspectives, Scarfs, Gloves, nor Hangers, nor put my trust in Shoe-ties; and where your Husband in an age was rising by burnt figs, dreg'd with meal and powdered sugar, saunders, and grains, wormeseed and rotten Raisins, and such vile Tobacco, that made the footmen mangie; I in a year have put up hundreds inclos'd, my Widow, those pleasant Meadows, by a forfeit morgage: for which the poor Knight takes a lone chamber, owes for his Ale, and dare not beat his Hostess: nay more—

Wid. Good Sir no more, what ere my Husband was, I know what I am, and if you marry me, you must bear it bravely off Sir.

Mor. Not with the head, sweet Widow.

Wid. No sweet Sir, but with your shoulders: I must have you dub'd, for under that I will not stoop a feather. My husband was a fellow lov'd to toyle, fed ill, made gain his exercise, and so grew costive, which for that I was his wife, I gave way to, and spun mine own smocks course, and sir, so little: but let that pass, time, that wears all things out, wore out this husband, who in penitence of such fruitless five years marriage, left me great with his wealth, which if you'le be a worthie gossip to, be knighted Sir. [*Enter* Savil.

Morec. Now, Sir, from whom come you? whose man are you Sir?

Savil. Sir, I come from young Master *Loveless*.

Mor. Be silent Sir, I have no money, not a penny for you, he's sunk, your Master's sunk, a perisht man Sir.

Savil. Indeed his Brother's sunk sir, God be with him, a perisht man indeed, and drown'd at Sea.

Morec. How saidst thou, good my friend, his Brother (drown'd?

Savil. Untimely sir, at Sea.

Morec. And thy young Master left sole Heir?

Savil. Yes Sir.

Morec. And he wants money?

Sav. Yes, and sent me to you, for he is now to be knighted.

Mor. Widow be wise, there's more Land coming, widow be very wise, and give thanks for me widow.

Widow. Be you very wise, and be knighted, and then give thanks for me Sir.

Savil. What sayes your worship to this mony?

Mor. I say he may have mony if he please.

Savil. A thousand Sir?

Mor. A thousand Sir, provided any wise Sir, his Land lye for the payment, otherwise—

Enter Young Loveless *and* Comrades *to them.*

Savil. He's here himself Sir, and can better tell you.

Mor. My notable dear friend, and worthy Master *Loveless*, and now right worshipfull, all joy and welcom.

Yo. Lo. Thanks to my dear incloser Master *Morecraft*, prethee old Angel gold, salute my family, I'le do as much for yours; this, and your own desires, fair Gentlewoman.

Wid. And yours Sir, if you mean well; 'tis a hansome Gentleman.

Young Lo. Sirrah, my Brother's dead.

More. Dead?

Yo. Lo. Dead, and by this time soust for Ember Week.

Morecraft. Dead?

Young Lo. Drown'd, drown'd at sea man, by the next fresh Conger that comes we shall hear more.

Mor. Now by my faith of my body it moves me much.

Yo. Lo. What, wilt thou be an Ass, and weep for the dead? why I thought nothing but a general inundation would have mov'd thee, prethe be quiet, he hath left his land behind him.

Morecraft. O has he so?

Young Lo. Yes faith, I thank him for't, I have all boy, hast any ready mony?

Morecraft. Will you sell Sir?

Young Lo. No not out right good Gripe; marry, a morgage or such a slight securitie.

More. I have no mony, Sir, for Morgage; if you will sell, and all or none, I'le work a new Mine for you.

Sav. Good Sir look before you, he'l work you out of all else: if you sell all your Land, you have sold your Country, and then you must to Sea, to seek your Brother, and there lye pickled in a Powdering tub, and break your teeth with Biskets and hard Beef, that must have watering Sir: and where's your 300 pounds a year in drink then? If you'l tun up the Straights you may, for you have no calling for drink there, but with a Canon, nor no scoring but on your Ships sides, and then if you scape with life, and take a Faggot boat and a bottle of *Usquebaugh*, come home poor men, like a tipe of Thames-street stinking of Pitch and Poor-John. I cannot tell Sir, I would be loth to see it.

Capt. Steward, you are an Ass, a meazel'd mungril, and were it not again the peace of my soveraign friend here, I would break your fore-casting Coxcomb, dog I would even with my staffe of Office there. Thy Pen and Inkhorn Noble boy, the God of gold here has fed thee well, take mony for thy durt: hark and believe, thou art cold of constitution, thy eat unhealthful, sell and be wise; we are three that will adorn thee, and live according to thine own heart child; mirth shall be only ours, and only ours shall be the black eyed beauties of the time. Mony makes men Eternal.

Poet. Do what you will, 'tis the noblest course, then you may live without the charge of people, only we four will make a Family, I and an Age that will beget new *Annals*, in which I'le write thy life my son of pleasure, equal with *Nero* and *Caligula*.

Young Lo. What men were they Captain?

Capt. Two roaring Boys of *Rome*, that made all split.

Young Lo. Come Sir, what dare you give?

Sav. You will not sell Sir?

Young Lo. Who told you so Sir?

Sav. Good Sir have a care.

Young Lo. Peace, or I'le tack your Tongue up to your Roof. What money? speak.

More. Six thousand pound Sir.

Capt. Take it, h'as overbidden by the Sun: bind him to his bargain quickly.

Young Lo. Come strike me luck with earnest, and draw the writings.

More. There's a Gods peny for thee.

Sav. Sir for my old Masters sake let my Farm be excepted, if I become his Tenant I am undone, my Children beggers, and my Wife God knows what: consider me dear Sir.

More. I'le have all or none.

Young Lo. All in, all in: dispatch the writings.

[*Exit with Com.*

Wid. Go, thou art a pretty forehanded fellow, would thou wert wiser.

Sav. Now do I sensibly begin to feel my self a Rascal; would I could teach a School, or beg, or lye well, I am utterly undone; now he that taught thee to deceive and cousen, take thee to his mercy; so be it. [*Exit* Savil.

More. Come Widow come, never stand upon a Knighthood, 'tis a meer paper honour, and not proof enough for a Serjeant. Come, Come, I'le make thee—

Wid. To answer in short, 'tis this Sir. No Knight no Widow, if you make me any thing, it must be a Lady, and so I take my leave.

More. Farewel sweet Widow, and think of it. [*Ex.* Wid.

Wid. Sir, I do more than think of it, it makes me dream Sir.

More. She's rich and sober, if this itch were from her: and say I be at the charge to pay the Footmen, and the Trumpets, I and the Horsemen too, and be a Knight, and she refuse me then; then am I hoist into the subsidy, and so by consequence should prove a Coxcomb: I'le have a care of that. Six thousand pound, and then the Land is mine, there's some refreshing yet. [*Exit.*

Actus Tertius. Scena Prima.

Enter Abigal, *and drops her Glove.*

Abigal. IF he but follow me, as all my hopes tell me, he's man enough, up goes my rest, and I know I shall draw him.

Enter Welford.

Wel. This is the strangest pampered piece of flesh towards fifty, that ever frailty copt withal, what a trim *lennoy* here she has put upon me; these women are a proud kind of Cattel, and love this whorson doing so directly, that they will not stick to make their very skins Bawdes to their flesh. Here's Dogskin and Storax sufficient to kill a Hawk: what to do with it, besides nailing it up amongst *Irish* heads of Teere, to shew the mightiness of her Palm, I know not: there she is. I must enter into Dialogue. Lady you have lost your Glove.

Abig. Not Sir, if you have found it.

Wel. It was my meaning Lady to restore it.

Abig. 'Twill be uncivil in me to take back a favour, Fortune hath so well bestowed Sir, pray wear it for me.

Wel. I had rather wear a Bell. But hark you Mistres, what hidden vertue is there in this Glove, that you would have me wear it? Is't good against sore eyes, or will it charm the Toothach? Or these red tops; being steept in white wine soluble, wil't kill the Itch? Or has it so conceal'd a providence to keep my hand from Bonds? If it have none of these and prove no more but a bare Glove of half a Crown a pair, 'twill be but half a courtesie, I wear two alwayes, faith let's draw cuts, one will do me no pleasure.

Abig. The tenderness of his years keeps him as yet in ignorance, he's a well moulded fellow, and I wonder his bloud should stir no higher; but 'tis his want of company: I must grow nearer to him.

Enter Elder Loveless *disguised.*

Elder Lo. God save you both.

Abig. And pardon you Sir; this is somewhat rude, how came you hither?

Elder Lo. Why through the doors, they are open.

Wel. What are you? And what business have you here?

Elder Lo. More I believe than you have.

Abig. Who would this fellow speak with? Art thou sober?

Elder Lo. Yes, I come not here to sleep.

Wel. Prethee what art thou?

Elder Lo. As much (gay man) as thou art, I am a Gentle-(man.

Wel. Art thou no more?

Elder Lo. Yes more than thou dar'st be; a Souldier.

Abig. Thou dost not come to quarrel?

Elder Lo. No, not with women; I come to speak here with a Gentlewoman.

Abig. Why, I am one.

Elder Lo. But not with one so gentle.

Wel. This is a fine fellow.

Elder Lo. Sir, I am not fine yet. I am but new come over, direct me with your ticket to your Taylor, and then I shall be fine Sir. Lady if there be a better of your Sex within this house, say I would see her.

Abig. Why am not I good enough for you Sir?

Elder Lo. Your way you'l be too good, pray end my business. This is another Sutor, O frail Woman!

Wel. This fellow with his bluntness hopes to do more than the long sutes of a thousand could; though he be sowre he's quick, I must not trust him. Sir, this Lady is not to speak with you, she is more serious: you smell as if you were new calkt; go and be hansome, and then you may sit with her Servingmen.

El. Lo. What are you Sir?

Wel. Guess by my outside.

Elder Lo. Then I take you Sir, for some new silken thing wean'd from the Country, that shall (when you come to keep good company) be beaten into better manners. Pray good proud Gentlewoman, help me to your Mistress.

Abig. How many lives hast thou, that thou talk'st thus rudely?

Elder Lo. But one, one, I am neither Cat nor Woman.

Wel. And will that one life, Sir, maintain you ever in such bold sawciness?

Elder Lo. Yes, amongst a Nation of such men as you are, and be no worse for wearing, shall I speak with this Lady?

Abig. No by my troth shall you not.
Elder Lo. I must stay here then?
Wel. That you shall not neither.
Elder Lo. Good fine thing tell me why?
Wel. Good angry thing I'le tell you:
This is no place for such companions,
Such lousie Gentlemen shall find their business
Better i'th' Suburbs, there your strong pitch perfume,
Mingled with lees of Ale, shall reek in fashion:
This is no Thames-street, Sir.
Abig. This Gentleman informs you truly:
Prethee be satisfied, and seek the Suburbs,
Good Captain, or what ever title else,
The Warlike Eele-boats have bestowed upon thee,
Go and reform thy self, prethee be sweeter,
And know my Lady speaks with no Swabbers.
Elder Lo. You cannot talk me out with your tradition
Of wit you pick from Plays, go to, I have found ye:
And for you, Sir, whose tender gentle blood
Runs in your Nose, and makes you snuff at all,
But three pil'd people, I do let you know,
He that begot your worships Sattin-sute,
Can make no men Sir: I will see this Lady,
And with the reverence of your silkenship,
In these old Ornaments.
Wel. You will not sure?
Elder Lo. Sure Sir I shall.
Abig. You would be beaten out?
Elder Lo. Indeed I would not, or if I would be beaten,
Pray who shall beat me? this good Gentleman
Looks as if he were o'th' peace.
Wel. Sir you shall see that: will you get you out?
Elder Lo. Yes, that, that shall correct your boys tongue.
Dare you fight, I will stay here still. [*They draw.*
Abig. O their things are out, help, help for Gods sake,
Madam; Jesus they foin at one another.

Enter Lady.

Madam, why, who is within there?
Lady. Who breeds this rudeness?

Wel. This uncivil fellow;
He saies he comes from Sea, where I believe,
H'as purg'd away his manners.
Lady. Why what of him?
Wel. Why he will rudely without once God bless you,
Press to your privacies, and no denial
Must stand betwixt your person and his business;
I let go his ill Language.
Lady. Sir, have you business with me?
Elder Lo. Madam some I have,
But not so serious to pawn my life for't:
If you keep this quarter, and maintain about you
Such Knights o'th' *Sun* as this is, to defie
Men of imployment to ye, you may live,
But in what fame?
Lady. Pray stay Sir, who has wrong'd you?
Elder Lo. Wrong me he cannot, though uncivilly
He flung his wild words at me: but to you
I think he did no honour, to deny
The hast I come withal, a passage to you,
Though I seem course.
Lady. Excuse me gentle Sir, 'twas from my knowledge,
And shall have no protection. And to you Sir,
You have shew'd more heat than wit, and from your self
Have borrowed power, I never gave you here,
To do these vile unmanly things: my house
Is no blind street to swagger in; and my favours
Not doting yet on your unknown deserts
So far, that I should make you Master of my business;
My credit yet stands fairer with the people
Than to be tried with swords; and they that come
To do me service, must not think to win me
With hazard of a murther; if your love
Consist in fury, carry it to the Camp:
And there in honour of some common Mistress,
Shorten your youth, I pray be better temper'd:
And give me leave a while Sir.
Wel. You must have it. [*Exit* Welford.
Lady. Now Sir, your business?
El. Lo. First, I thank you for schooling this young fellow,

Whom his own follies, which he's prone enough
Daily to fall into, if you but frown,
Shall level him a way to his repentance:
Next, I should rail at you, but you are a Woman,
And anger's lost upon you.

Lady. Why at me Sir?
I never did you wrong, for to my knowledge
This is the first sight of you.

Elder Lo. You have done that,
I must confess I have the least curse in
Because the least acquaintance: But there be
(If there be honour in the minds of men)
Thousands when they shall know what I deliver,
(As all good men must share in't) will to shame
Blast your black memory.

Lady. How is this good Sir?

Elder Lo. 'Tis that, that if you have a soul will choak it:
Y'ave kill'd a Gentleman.

Lady. I kill'd a Gentleman!

Elder Lo. You and your cruelty have kill'd him Woman,
And such a man (let me be angry in't)
Whose least worth weighed above all womens vertues
That are; I spare you all to come too: guess him now?

Lady. I am so innocent I cannot Sir.

Elder Lo. Repent you mean, you are a perfect Woman,
And as the first was, made for mans undoing.

Lady. Sir, you have mist your way, I am not she.

Elder Lo. Would he had mist his way too, though he had
Wandered farther than Women are ill spoken of,
So he had mist this misery, you Lady.

Lady. How do you do, Sir?

Elder Lo. Well enough I hope.
While I can keep my self out from temptations.

Lady. Leap into this matter, whither would ye?

Elder Lo. You had a Servant that your peevishness
Injoined to Travel.

Lady. Such a one I have
Still, and shall be griev'd 'twere otherwise.

El. Lo. Then have your asking, and be griev'd he's dead;
How you will answer for his worth, I know not,

But this I am sure, either he, or you, or both
Were stark mad, else he might have liv'd
To have given a stronger testimony to th' world
Of what he might have been. He was a man
I knew but in his evening, ten Suns after,
Forc'd by a Tyrant storm our beaten Bark
Bulg'd under us; in which sad parting blow,
He call'd upon his Saint, but not for life,
On you unhappy Woman, and whilest all
Sought to preserve their Souls, he desperately
Imbrac'd a Wave, crying to all that saw it,
If any live, go to my Fate that forc'd me
To this untimely end, and make her happy:
His name was *Loveless*: And I scap't the storm,
And now you have my business.

Lady. 'Tis too much.
Would I had been that storm, he had not perisht.
If you'l rail now I will forgive you Sir.
Or if you'l call in more, if any more
Come from this ruine, I shall justly suffer
What they can say, I do confess my self
A guiltie cause in this. I would say more,
But grief is grown too great to be delivered.

Elder Lo. I like this well: these women are strange things.
'Tis somewhat of the latest now to weep,
You should have wept when he was going from you,
And chain'd him with those tears at home.

La. Would you had told me then so, these two arms had been his Sea.

Elder Lo. Trust me you move me much: but say he lived, these were forgotten things again.

Lady. I, say you so? Sure I should know that voice: this is knavery. I'le fit you for it. Were he living Sir, I would perswade you to be charitable, I, and confess we are not all so ill as your opinion holds us. O my friend, what penance shall I pull upon my fault, upon my most unworthy self for this?

Elder Lo. Leave, to love others, 'twas some jealousie
That turn'd him desperate.

Lady. I'le be with you straight: are you wrung there?

Elder Lo. This works amain upon her.

Lady. I do confess there is a Gentleman
Has born me long good will.

Elder Lo. I do not like that.

Lady. And vow'd a thousand services to me; to me, regardless of him: But since Fate, that no power can withstand, has taken from me my first, and best love, and to weep away my youth is a mere folly, I will shew you what I determine sir: you shall know all: Call M. *Welford* there: That Gentleman I mean to make the model of my Fortunes, and in his chast imbraces keep alive the memory of my lost lovely *Loveless*: he is somewhat like him too.

Elder Lo. Then you can love.

Lady. Yes certainly Sir?
Though it please you to think me hard and cruel,
I hope I shall perswade you otherwise.

Elder Lo. I have made my self a fine fool.

Enter Welford.

Wel. Would you have spoke with me Madam?

Lady. Yes M. *Welford*, and I ask your pardon before this Gentleman for being froward: this kiss, and henceforth more affection.

Elder Lo. So, 'tis better I were drown'd indeed.

Wel. This is a sudden passion, God hold it.
This fellow out of his fear sure has
Perswaded her. I'le give him a new suit on't.

La. A parting kiss, and good Sir, let me pray you
To wait me in the Gallerie.

Wel. I am in another world, Madam where you please.
[*Exit* Welford.

Elder Lo. I will to Sea, and 't shall goe hard but I'le be drown'd indeed.

La. Now Sir you see I am no such hard creature,
But time may win me.

Elder Lo. You have forgot your lost Love.

La. Alas Sir, what would you have me do? I cannot call him back again with sorrow; I'le love this man as dearly, and beshrow me I'le keep him far enough from Sea, and 'twas told me, now I remember me, by an old wise woman, that my first Love should be drown'd, and see 'tis come about.

Elder Lo. I would she had told you your second should be hang'd too, and let that come about: but this is very strange.

La. Faith Sir, consider all, and then I know you'le be of my mind: if weeping would redeem him, I would weep still.

Elder Lo. But say that I were *Loveless*,
And scap'd the storm, how would you answer this?

Lady. Why for that Gentleman I would leave all the world.

Elder Lo. This young thing too?

Lady. That young thing too,
Or any young thing else: why, I would lose my state.

Elder Lo. Why then he lives still, I am he, your *Loveless.*

Lady. Alas I knew it Sir, and for that purpose prepared this Pageant: get you to your task. And leave these Players tricks, or I shall leave you, indeed I shall. Travel, or know me not.

Elder Lo. Will you then marry?

Lady. I will not promise, take your choice. Farewell.

Elder Lo. There is no other Purgatorie but a Woman.
I must doe something. [*Exit* Loveless.

Enter Welford.

Wel. Mistress I am bold.

Lady. You are indeed.

Wel. You so overjoyed me Lady.

Lady. Take heed you surfeit not, pray fast and welcom.

Wel. By this light you love me extreamly.

Lady. By this, and to morrows light, I care not for you.

Wel. Come, come, you cannot hide it.

Lady. Indeed I can, where you shall never find it.

Wel. I like this mirth well Lady.

Lady. You shall have more on't.

Wel. I must kiss you.

Lady. No Sir.

Wel. Indeed I must.

Lady. What must be, must be; I'le take my leave, you have your parting blow: I pray commend me to those few friends you have, that sent you hither, and tell them when you travel next, 'twere fit you brought less bravery with you, and more wit, you'le never get a wife else.

Wel. Are you in earnest?

Lady. Yes faith. Will you eat Sir, your horses will be readie straight, you shall have a napkin laid in the butterie for ye.

Wel. Do not you love me then?

Lady. Yes, for that face.

Wel. It is a good one Ladie.

Lady. Yes, if it were not warpt, the fire in time may mend it.

Wel. Me thinks yours is none of the best Ladie.

Lady. No by my troth Sir; yet o' my conscience,
You would make shift with it.

Wel. Come pray no more of this.

Lady. I will not: Fare you well. Ho, who's within there? bring out the Gentlemans horses, he's in haste; and set some cold meat on the Table.

Wel. I have too much of that I thank you Ladie: take your Chamber when you please, there goes a black one with you Ladie.

Lady. Farewell young man. [*Exit* Ladie.

Wel. You have made me one, Farewell: and may the curse of a great house fall upon thee, I mean the Butler. The devil and all his works are in these women, would all of my sex were of my mind, I would make 'em a new Lent, and a long one, that flesh might be in more reverence with them.

Enter Abigal *to him.*

Abig. I am sorry M. *Welford.*

Wel. So am I, that you are here.

Abig. How does my Ladie use you?

Wel. As I would use you, scurvilie.

Abig. I should have been more kind Sir.

Wel. I should have been undone then. Pray leave me, and look to your sweet-meats; hark, your Ladie calls.

Abig. Sir, I shall borrow so much time without offence.

Wel. Y'are nothing but offence, for Gods love leave me.

Abig. 'Tis strange my Ladie should be such a tyrant?

Wel. To send you to me, 'Pray goe stitch, good doe, y'are more trouble to me than a Term.

Abig. I do not know how my good will, if I said love I lied not, should any way deserve this?

Wel. A thousand waies, a thousand waies; sweet creature let me depart in peace.

Abig. What Creature Sir? I hope I am a woman.

Wel. A hundred I think by your noise.

Abig. Since you are angrie Sir, I am bold to tell you that I am a woman, and a rib.

Wel. Of a roasted horse.

Abig. Conster me that?

Wel. A Dog can doe it better; Farwell Countess, and commend me to your Ladie, tell her she's proud, and scurvie, and so I commit you both to your tempter.

Abig. Sweet Mr. *Welford.*

Wel. Avoid old Satanus: Go daub your ruines, your face looks fouler than a storm: the Foot-man stayes for you in the Lobby Lady.

Abig. If you were a Gentleman, I should know it by your gentle conditions: are these fit words to give a Gentlewoman?

Wel. As fit as they were made for ye: Sirrah, my horses. Farwell old Adage, keep your nose warm, the Rheum will make it horn else— [*Exit* Welford.

Abig. The blessings of a Prodigal young heir be thy companions *Welford*, marry come up my Gentleman, are your gums grown so tender they cannot bite? A skittish Filly will be your fortune *Welford*, and fair enough for such a packsaddle. And I doubt not (if my aim hold) to see her made to amble to your hand. [*Exit Abigal.*

Enter Young Loveless, *and* Comrades, Morecraft, Widow, Savil, *and the rest.*

Captain. Save thy brave shoulder, my young puissant Knight, and may thy back Sword bite them to the bone that love thee not, thou art an errant man, go on. The circumcis'd shall fall by thee. Let Land and labour fill the man that tills, thy sword must be thy plough, and *Jove* it speed. *Mecha* shall sweat, and *Mahomet* shall fall, and thy dear name fill up his monument.

Yo. L. It shall Captain, I mean to be a Worthy.

Cap. One Worthy is too little, thou shalt be all.

Mor. Captain I shall deserve some of your love too.

Capt. Thou shalt have heart and hand too, noble *More-*

craft, if thou wilt lend me mony. I am a man of Garrison, be rul'd, and open to me those infernal gates, whence none of thy evil Angels pass again, and I will stile thee noble, nay *Don Diego*. I'le woo thy *Infanta* for thee, and my Knight shall feast her with high meats, and make her apt.

Mor. Pardon me Captain, y'are beside my meaning.

Young Lo. No M^r. *Morecraft*, 'tis the Captains meaning I should prepare her for ye.

Capt. Or provok her. Speak my modern man, I say provoke her.

Poet. Captain, I say so too, or stir her to it. So say the Criticks.

Young Lo. But howsoever you expound it sir, she's very welcom, and this shall serve for witness. And Widow, since y'are come so happily, you shall deliver up the keyes, and free possession of this house, whilst I stand by to ratifie.

Wid. I had rather give it back again believe me,
'Tis a miserie to say you had it. Take heed?

Young Lo. 'Tis past that Widow, come, sit down, some wine there, there is a scurvie banquet if we had it. All this fair house is yours Sir *Savil*?

Savil. Yes Sir.

Young Lo. Are your keyes readie, I must ease your burden.

Sav. I am readie Sir to be undone, when you shall call me to't.

Young Lo. Come come, thou shalt live better.

Sav. I shall have less to doe, that's all, there's half a dozen of my friends i'th' fields sunning against a bank, with half a breech among 'em, I shall be with 'em shortly. The care and continuall vexation of being rich, eat up this rascall. What shall become of my poor familie, they are no sheep, and they must keep themselves.

Young Lo. Drink Master *Morecraft*, pray be merrie all:
Nay and you will not drink there's no societie,
Captain speak loud, and drink: widow, a word.

Cap. Expou[n]d her throughly Knight. Here God o' gold, here's to thy fair possessions; Be a Baron and a bold one: leave off your tickling of young heirs like Trouts, and let thy Chimnies smoke. Feed men of war, live and be honest, and be saved yet.

Mor. I thank you worthie Captain for your counsel. You keep your Chimnies smoking there, your nostrils, and when you can, you feed a man of War, this makes you not a Baron, but a bare one: and how or when you shall be saved, let the Clark o'th' companie (you have commanded) have a just care of.

Poet. The man is much moved. Be not angrie Sir, but as the Poet sings, let your displeasure be a short furie, and goe out. You have spoke home, and bitterly, to me Sir. Captain take truce, the Miser is a tart and a wittie whorson—

Cap. Poet, you feign perdie, the wit of this man lies in his fingers ends, he must tell all; his tongue fills his mouth like a neats tongue, and only serves to lick his hungrie chaps after a purchase: his brains and brimstone are the devils diet to a fat usurers head: To her Knight, to her: clap her aboard, and stow her. Where's the brave Steward?

Savil. Here's your poor friend, and *Savil* Sir.

Capt. Away, th'art rich in ornaments of nature. First in thy face, thou hast a serious face, a betting, bargaining, and saving face, a rich face, pawn it to the Usurer; a face to kindle the compassion of the most ignorant and frozen Justice.

Savil. 'Tis such I dare not shew it shortly sir.

Capt. Be blithe and bonny steward: Master *Morecraft*, Drink to this man of reckoning?

Mor. Here's e'ne to him.

Savil. The Devil guide it downward: would there were in't an acre of the great broom field he bought, to sweep your durtie Conscience, or to choak ye, 'tis all one to me, Usurer.

Young Lo. Consider what I told you, you are young, unapt for worldly business: Is it fit one of such tenderness, so delicate, so contrarie to things of care, should stir and break her better meditations, in the bare brokage of a brace of Angels? or a new Kirtel, though it be Satten? eat by the hope of surfeits, and lie down only in expectation of a morrow, that may undo some easie hearted fool, or reach a widows curses? Let out mony, whose use returns the principal? and get out of these troubles, a consuming heir: For such a one must follow necessarily, you shall die hated, if not old and miserable; and that possest wealth that you got with pining, live to see tumbled to anothers hands, that is no more a kin to you, than you to his couzenage.

Widow. Sir you speak well, would God that charity had first begun here.

Young Lo. 'Tis yet time. Be merrie, me thinks you want wine there, there's more i'th' house. Captain, where rests the health?

Captain. It shall goe round boy.

Young Lo. Say you can suffer this, because the end points at much profit, can you so far bow below your blood, below your too much beautie, to be a partner of this fellowes bed, and lie with his diseases? if you can, I will no[t] press you further: yet look upon him: there's nothing in that hide-bound Usurer, that man of mat, that all decai'd, but aches, for you to love, unless his perisht lungs, his drie cough, or his scurvie. This is truth, and so far I dare speak yet: he has yet past cure of Physick, spaw, or any diet, a primitive pox in his bones; and o' my Knowledge he has been ten times rowell'd: ye may love him; he had a bastard, his own toward issue, whipt, and then cropt for washing out the roses, in three farthings to make 'em pence.

Widow. I do not like these Morals.

Young Lo. You must not like him then.

Enter Elder Love.

Elder Lo. By your leave Gentlemen?

Young Lo. By my troth sir you are welcom, welcom faith: Lord what a stranger you are grown; pray know this Gentlewoman, and if you please these friends here: we are merry, you see the worst on't; your house has been kept warm Sir.

Elder Lo. I am glad to hear it Brother, pray God you are wise too.

Young Lo. Pray Mr *Morecraft* know my elder Brother, and Captain do you complement. *Savil* I dare swear is glad at heart to see you; Lord, we heard Sir you were drown'd at Sea, and see how luckily things come about!

More. This mony must be paid again Sir.

Young Lo. No Sir, pray keep the Sale, 'twill make good Tailors measures; I am well I thank you.

Wid. By my troth the Gentleman has stew'd him in his own Sawce, I shall love him for't.

Sav. I know not where I am, I am so glad: your worship

is the welcom'st man alive; upon my knees I bid you welcome home: here has been such a hurry, such a din, such dismal Drinking, Swearing and Whoring, 'thas almost made me mad: we have all liv'd in a continual *Turnbal-street*; Sir, blest be Heaven, that sent you safe again, now shall I eat and go to bed again.

Elder Lo. Brother dismiss these people.

Young Lo. Captain be gone a while, meet me at my old *Randevouse* in the evening, take your small Poet with you. Mr *Morecraft* you were best go prattle with your learned Counsel, I shall preserve your mony, I was couzen'd when time was, we are quit Sir.

Wid. Better and better still.

Elder Lo. What is this fellow, Brother?

Young Lo. The thirsty Usurer that supt my Land off.

Elder Lo. What does he tarry for?

Young Lo. Sir to be Landlord of your House and State: I was bold to make a little sale Sir.

More. Am I overreach'd? if there be Law I'le hamper ye.

Elder Lo. Prethee be gone, and rave at home, thou art so base a fool I cannot laugh at thee: Sirrah, this comes of couzening, home and spare, eat Reddish till you raise your sums again. If you stir far in this, I'le have you whipt, your ears nail'd for intelligencing o'the Pillory, and your goods forfeit: you are a stale couzener, leave my house: no more.

More. A pox upon your house. Come Widow, I shall yet hamper this young Gamester.

Wid. Good twelve i'th' hundred keep your way, I am not for your diet, marry in your own Tribe *Jew*, and get a Broker.

Young Lo. 'Tis well said Widow: will you jog on Sir?

More. Yes, I will go, but 'tis no matter whither:
But when I trust a wild Fool, and a Woman,
May I lend Gratis, and build Hospitals.

Young Lo. Nay good Sir, make all even, here's a Widow wants your good word for me, she's rich, and may renew me and my fortunes.

Elder Lo. I am glad you look before you. Gentlewoman, here is a poor distressed younger Brother.

Wid. You do him wrong Sir, he's a Knight.

Elder Lo. I ask you mercy: yet 'tis no matter, his Knighthood is no inheritance I take it: whatsoever he is, he is your Servant, or would be, Lady. Faith be not merciless, but make a man; he's young and handsome, though he be my Brother, and his observances may deserve your Love: he shall not fail for means.

Wid. Sir you speak like a worthy Brother: and so much I do credit your fair Language, that I shall love your Brother: and so love him, but I shall blush to say more.

Elder Lo. Stop her mouth. I hope you shall not live to know that hour when this shall be repented. Now Brother I should chide, but I'le give no distaste to your fair Mistress. I will instruct her in't and she shall do't: you have been wild and ignorant, pray mend it.

Young Lo. Sir, every day now Spring comes on.

Elder Lo. To you good Mr *Savil* and your Office, thus much I have to say: Y'are from my Steward become, first your own Drunkard, then his Bawd: they say y'are excellent grown in both, and perfect: give me your keys Sir *Savil.*

Savil. Good Sir consider whom you left me to.

Elder Lo. I left you as a curb for, not to provoke my Brothers follies: where's the best drink, now? come, tell me *Savil*; where's the soundest Whores? Ye old he Goat, ye dried Ape, ye lame Stallion, must you be leading in my house your Whores, like Fairies dance their night rounds, without fear either of King or Constable, within my walls? Are all my Hangings safe; my Sheep unfold yet? I hope my Plate is currant, I ha' too much on't. What say you to 300 pounds in drink now?

Sav. Good Sir forgive me, and but hear me speak?

Elder Lo. Me thinks thou shouldst be drunk still, and not speak, 'tis the more pardonable.

Sav. I will Sir, if you will have it so.

Elder Lo. I thank ye: yes, e'ne pursue it Sir: do you hear? get a Whore soon for your recreation: go look out Captain *Broken-breech* your fellow, and Quarrel if you dare: I shall deliver these Keys to one shall have more honesty, though not so much fine wit Sir. You may walk and gather *Cresses* fit to cool your Liver; there's something for you to begin a Diet, you'l have the Pox else. Speed you well, Sir *Savil*: you may eat at my house to preserve life; but keep no Fornication in the Stables. [*Ex. om. pr.* Savil.

Sav. Now must I hang my self, my friends will look for't.
Eating and sleeping, I do despise you both now:
I will run mad first, and if that get not pitty,
I'le drown my self, to a most dismal ditty. [*Exit* Savil.

Actus Quartus. Scena Prima.

Enter Abigal *sola.*

Abigal. ALas poor Gentlewoman, to what a misery hath Age brought thee: to what a scurvy Fortune! Thou that hast been a Companion for Noblemen, and at the worst of those times for Gentlemen: now like a broken Servingman, must beg for favour to those, that would have crawl'd like Pilgrims to my Chamber but for an Apparition of me. You that be coming on, make much of fifteen, and so till five and twenty: use your time with reverence, that your profits may arise: it will not tarry with you, *Ecce signum*: here was a face, but time that like a surfeit eats our youth, plague of his iron teeth, and draw 'em for't, has been a little bolder here than welcome: and now to say the truth, I am fit for no man. Old men i'th' house of fifty, call me Granum; and when they are drunk, e'ne then, when *Jone* and my Lady are all one, not one will do me reason. My little Levite hath forsaken me, his silver sound of Cittern quite abolish[t], [h]is doleful *hymns* under my Chamber window, digested into tedious learning: well fool, you leapt a Haddock when you left him: he's a clean man, and a good edifier, and twenty nobles is his state *de claro*, besides his pigs in *posse*. To this good *Homilist* I have been ever stubborn, which God forgive me for, and mend my manners: and Love, if ever thou hadst care of forty, of such a piece of lape ground, hear my prayer, and fire his zeal so far forth that my faults in this renued impression of my love may shew corrected to our gentle reader.

Enter Roger.

See how negligently he passes by me: with what an Equipage Canonical, as though he had broken the heart of *Bellarmine*, or added something to the singing Brethren. 'Tis scorn, I know it, and deserve it, M[r] *Roger*.

Rog. Fair Gentlewoman, my name is *Roger*.

Abig. Then gentle *Roger*?

Rog. Ungentle *Abigal.* (womans?

Abig. Why Mr *Roger* will you set your wit to a weak

Rog. You are weak indeed: for so the Poet sings.

Abig. I do confess my weakness, sweet Sir *Roger.*

Rog. Good my Ladies Gentlewoman, or my good Ladies Gentlewoman (this trope is lost to you now) leave your prating, you have a season of your first mother in ye: and surely had the Devil been in love, he had been abused too: go *Dalilah*, you make men fools, and wear Fig-breeches.

Abi. Well, well, hard hearted man; dilate upon the weak infirmities of women: these are fit texts, but once there was a time, would I had never seen those eyes, those eyes, those orient eyes.

Rog. I they were pearls once with you.

Abi. Saving your reverence Sir, so they are still.

Rog. Nay, nay, I do beseech you leave your cogging, what they are, they are, they serve me without Spectacles I thank 'em.

Abig. O will you kill me?

Rog. I do not think I can,
Y'are like a Copy-hold with nine lives in't.

Abig. You were wont to bear a Christian fear about you: For your own worships sake.

Rog. I was a Christian fool then: Do you remember what a dance you led me? how I grew qualm'd in love, and was a dunce? could expound but once a quarter, and then was out too: and then out of the stinking stir you put me in, I prayed for my own issue. You do remember all this?

Abig. O be as then you were!

Rog. I thank you for it, surely I will be wiser *Abigal*: and as the Ethnick Poet sings, I will not lose my oyl and labour too. Y'are for the worshipfull I take it *Abigal.*

Abig. O take it so, and then I am for thee!

Rog. I like these tears well, and this humbling also, they are Symptomes of contrition. If I should fall into my fit again, would you not shake me into a quotidian Coxcombe? Would you not use me scurvily again, and give me possets with purging Confets in't? I tell thee Gentlewoman, thou hast been harder to me, than a long pedigree.

Abig. O Curate cure me: I will love thee better, dearer, longer: I will do any thing, betray the secrets of the main house-hold to thy reformation. My Ladie shall look lovingly on thy learning, and when true time shall point thee for a Parson, I will convert thy egges to penny custards, and thy tith goose shall graze and multiply.

Rog. I am mollified, as well shall testifie this faithfull kiss, and have a great care Mistris *Abigal* how you depress the Spirit any more with your rebukes and mocks: for certainly the edge of such a follie cuts it self.

Abigal. O Sir, you have pierc'd me thorow. Here I vow a recantation to those malicious faults I ever did against you. Never more will I despise your learning, never more pin cards and cony tails upon your Cassock, never again reproach your reverend nightcap, and call it by the mangie name of murrin, never your reverend person more, and say, you look like one of *Baals* Priests in a hanging, never again when you say grace laugh at you, nor put you out at prayers: never cramp you more, nor when you ride, get Sope and Thistles for you. No my *Roger*, these faults shall be corrected and amended, as by the tenour of my tears appears.

Rog. Now cannot I hold if I should be hang'd, I must crie too. Come to thine own beloved, and do even what thou wilt with me sweet, sweet *Abigal.* I am thine own for ever: here's my hand, when *Roger* proves a recreant, hang him i'th' Bel-ropes.

Enter Lady, *and* Martha.

Lady. Why how now Master *Roger*, no prayers down with you to night? Did you hear the bell ring? You are courting: your flock shall fat well for it.

Rog. I humbly ask your pardon: I'le clap up Prayers, but stay a little, and be with you again. [*Exit* Roger.

Enter Elder Love.

Lady. How dare you, being so unworthie a fellow,
Presume to come to move me any more?

Elder Lo. Ha, ha, ha.

Lady. What ails the fellow?

Elder Lo. The fellow comes to laugh at you, I tell you

Ladie I would not for your Land, be such a Coxcomb, such a whining Ass, as you decreed me for when I was last here.

Lady. I joy to hear you are wise, 'tis a rare Jewel
In an Elder Brother: pray be wiser yet.

Elder Lo. Me thinks I am very wise: I do not come a wooing. Indeed I'le move no more love to your Ladiship.

Lady. What makes you here then?

Elder Lo. Only to see you and be merry Ladie: that's all my business. Faith let's be very merry. Where's little *Roger*? he's a good fellow: an hour or two well spent in wholsome mirth, is worth a thousand of these puling passions. 'Tis an ill world for Lovers.

Lady. They were never fewer.

Elder Lo. I thank God there's one less for me Ladie.

Lady. You were never any Sir.

Elder Lo. Till now, and now I am the prettiest fellow.

Lady. You talk like a Tailor Sir.

Elder Lo. Me thinks your faces are no such fine things now.

Lady. Why did you tell me you were wise? Lord what a lying age is this, where will you mend these faces?

Elder Lo. A Hogs face soust is worth a hundred of 'em.

Lady. Sure you had a Sow to your Mother.

Elder Lo. She brought such fine white Pigs as you, fit for none but Parsons Ladie.

Lady. 'Tis well you will allow us our Clergie yet.

Elder Lo. That shall not save you. O that I were in love again with a wish.

Lady. By this light you are a scurvie fellow, pray be gone.

Elder Lo. You know I am a clean skin'd man.

Lady. Do I know it?

Elder Lo. Come, come, you would know it; that's as good: but not a snap, never long for't, not a snap dear Ladie.

Lady. Hark ye Sir, hark ye, get ye to the Suburbs, there's horse flesh for such hounds: will you goe Sir?

Elder Lo. Lord how I lov'd this woman, how I worshipt this prettie calf with the white face here: as I live, you were the prettiest fool to play withall, the wittiest little varlet, it would talk: Lord how it talk't! and when I angred it, it would cry out, and scratch, and eat no meat, and it would say, goe hang.

Lady. It will say so still, if you anger it.

Elder Lo. And when I askt it, if it would be married, it sent me of an errand into *France*, and would abuse me, and be glad it did so.

Lady. Sir this is most unmanly, pray by gon.

Elder Lo. And swear (even when it twitter'd to be at me) I was unhansome.

Lady. Have you no manners in you?

Elder Lo. And say my back was melted, when God he knows, I kept it at a charge: Four *Flaunders* Mares would have been easier to me, and a Fencer.

Lady. You think all this is true now?

Elder Lo. Faith whether it be or no, 'tis too good for you. But so much for our mirth: Now have at you in earnest.

L[a]. There is enough Sir, I desire no more.

El. Lo. Yes faith, wee'l have a cast at your best parts now. And then the Devil take the worst.

Lady. Pray Sir no more, I am not so much affected with your commendations, 'tis almost dinner, I know they stay for you at the Ordinary.

Elder Lo. E'ne a short Grace, and then I am gone; You are a woman, and the proudest that ever lov'd a Coach: the scornfullest, scurviest, and most senceless woman; the greediest to be prais'd, and never mov'd though it be gross and open; the most envious, that at the poor fame of anothers face, would eat your own, and more than is your own, the paint belonging to it: of such a self opinion, that you think none can deserve your glove: and for your malice, you are so excellent, you might have been your Tempters tutor: nay, never cry.

Lady. Your own heart knows you wrong me: I cry for ye?

Elder Lo. You shall before I leave you.

Lady. Is all this spoke in earnest?

Elder Lo. Yes and more as soon as I can get it out.

Lady. Well out with't.

Elder Lo. You are, let me see.

Lady. One that has us'd you with too much respect.

Elder Lo. One that hath us'd me (since you will have it so) the basest, the most Foot-boy-like, without respect of what I was, or what you might be by me; you have us'd me, as

I would use a jade, ride him off's legs, then turn him to the Commons; you have us'd me with discretion, and I thank ye. If you have many more such pretty Servants, pray build an Hospital, and when they are old, pray keep 'em for shame.

Lady. I cannot think yet this is serious.

Elder Lo. Will you have more on't?

Lady. No faith, there's enough if it be true:
Too much by all my part; you are no Lover then?

Elder Lo. No, I had rather be a Carrier.

Lady. Why the Gods amend all.

Elder Lo. Neither do I think there can be such a fellow found i'th' world, to be in love with such a froward woman, if there be such, they're mad, *Jove* comfort 'em. Now you have all, and I as new a man, as light, and spirited, that I feel my self clean through another creature. O 'tis brave to be ones own man, I can see you now as I would see a Picture, sit all day by you and never kiss your hand: hear you sing, and never fall backward: but with as set a temper, as I would hear a Fidler, rise and thank you. I can now keep my mony in my purse, that still was gadding out for Scarfes and Wast-coats: and keep my hand from Mercers sheep-skins finely. I can eat mutton now, and feast my self with my two shillings, and can see a play for eighteen pence again: I can my Ladie.

Lady. The carriage of this fellow vexes me. Sir, pray let me speak a little private with you, I must not suffer this.

Elder Lo. Ha, ha, ha, what would you with me?
You will not ravish me? Now, your set speech?

Lady. Thou perjur'd man.

Elder Lo. Ha, ha, ha, this is a fine *exordium.*
And why I pray you perjur'd?

Lady. Did you not swear a thousand thousand times you lov'd me best of all things?

Elder Lo. I do confess it: make your best of that.

Lady. Why do you say you do not then?

Elder Lo. Nay I'le swear it,
And give sufficient reason, your own usage.

Lady. Do you not love me then?

Elder Lo. No faith.

Lady. Did you ever think I lov'd you dearly?

Elder Lo. Yes, but I see but rotten fruits on't.

Lady. Do not denie your hand for I must kiss it, and take my last farewell, now let me die so you be happy.

El. Lo. I am too foolish: Ladie speak dear Ladie.

Lady. No let me die. *She swounds.*

Mar. Oh my Sister!

Abi. O my Ladie help, help.

Mar. Run for some *Rosalis*!

Elder Lo. I have plaid the fine ass: bend her bodie, Lady, best, dearest, worthiest Lady, hear your Servant, I am not as I shew'd: O wretched fool, to fling away the Jewel of thy life thus. Give her more air, see she begins to stir, sweet Mistress hear me!

Lady. Is my Servant well?

Elder Lo. In being yours I am so.

Lady. Then I care not.

Elder Lo. How do ye, reach a chair there; I confess my fault not pardonable, in pursuing thus upon such tenderness my wilfull error; but had I known it would have wrought thus with ye, thus strangely, not the world had won me to it, and let not (my best Ladie) any word spoke to my end disturb your quiet peace: for sooner shall you know a general ruine, than my faith broken. Do not doubt this Mistris, for by my life I cannot live without you. Come, come, you shall not grieve, rather be angrie, and heap infliction upon me: I will suffer. O I could curse my self, pray smile upon me. Upon my faith it was but a trick to trie you, knowing you lov'd me dearlie, and yet strangely that you would never shew it, though my means was all humilitie.

All. Ha, ha.

Elder Lo. How now?

Lady. I thank you fine fool for your most fine plot; this was a subtile one, a stiff device to have caught Dottrels with. Good senceless Sir, could you imagine I should swound for you, and know your self to be an arrant ass? I, a discovered one. 'Tis quit I thank you Sir. Ha, ha, ha.

Mar. Take heed Sir, she may chance to swound again.

All. Ha, ha, ha.

Abi. Step to her Sir, see how she changes colour.

Elder Lo. I'le goe to hell first, and be better welcom.
I am fool'd, I do confess it, finely fool'd,
Ladie, fool'd Madam, and I thank you for it.

Lady. Faith 'tis not so much worth Sir:
But if I knew when you come next a burding,
I'le have a stronger noose to hold the Woodcock.

All. Ha, ha, ha.

Elder Lo. I am glad to see you merry, pray laugh on.

Mar. H'ad a hard heart that could not laugh at you Sir, ha, ha, ha.

Lady. Pray Sister do not laugh, you'le anger him,
And then hee'l rail like a rude Costermonger,
That School-boys had couzened of his Apples,
As loud and senceless.

Elder Lo. I will not rail.

Mar. Faith then let's hear him Sister.

Elder Lo. Yes, you shall hear me.

Lady. Shall we be the better by it then?

Eld. L. No, he that makes a woman better by his words,
I'le have him Sainted: blows will not doe it.

Lady. By this light hee'll beat us.

Elder Lo. You do deserve it richly,
And ‸may live to have a Beadle doe it.

Lady. Now he rails.

Elder Lo. Come scornfull Folly,
If this be railing, you shall hear me rail.

Lady. Pray put it in good words then.

Elder Lo. The worst are good enough for such a trifle,
Such a proud piece of Cobweblawn.

Lady. You bite Sir?

Elder Lo. I would till the bones crackt, and I had my will.

Mar. We had best muzzel him, he grows mad.

Elder Lo. I would 'twere lawfull in the next great sickness to have the Dogs spared, those harmless creatures, and knock i'th' head these hot continual plagues, women, that are more infectious. I hope the State will think on't.

Lady. Are you well Sir?

Mar. He looks as though he had a grievous fit o'th' Colick.

Elder Lo. Green-ginger will cure me.

Abig. I'le heat a trencher for him.

Elder Lo. Durty *December* doe, Thou with a face as old

as *Erra Pater*, such a Prognosticating nose: thou thing that ten years since has left to be a woman, outworn the expectation of a Baud; and thy dry bones can reach at nothing now, but gords or ninepins, pray goe fetch a trencher goe.

Lady. Let him alone, he's crack't.

Abig. I'le see him hang'd first, is a beastly fellow to use a woman of my breeding thus; I marry is he: would I were a man, I'de make him eat his Knaves words!

Elder Lo. Tie your she Otter up, good Lady folly, she stinks worse than a Bear-baiting.

Lady. Why will you be angry now?

Elder Lo. Goe paint and purge, call in your kennel with you: you a Lady?

Abi. Sirra, look to't against the quarter Sessions, if there be good behaviour in the world, I'le have thee bound to it.

Elder Lo. You must not seek it in your Ladies house then; pray send this Ferret home, and spin good *Abigal.* And Madam, that your Ladiship may know, in what base manner you have us'd my service, I do from this hour hate thee heartily; and though your folly should whip you to repentance, and waken you at length to see my wrongs, 'tis not the endeavour of your life shall win me; not all the friends you have, intercession, nor your submissive letters, though they spoke as many tears as words; not your knees grown to th' ground in penitence, nor all your state, to kiss you; nor my pardon, nor will to give you Christian burial, if you dye thus; so farewell. When I am married and made sure, I'le come and visit you again, and vex you Ladie. By all my hopes I'le be a torment to you, worse than a tedious winter. I know you will recant and sue to me, but save that labour: I'le rather love a fever and continual thirst, rather contract my youth to drink and sacerdote upon quarrels, or take a drawn whore from an Hospital, that time, diseases, and *Mercury* had eaten, than to be drawn to love you.

Lady. Ha, ha, ha, pray do, but take heed though.

Elder Lo. From thee, false dice, jades, Cowards, and plaguy Summers, good Lord deliver me. [*Exit* Elder Love.

Lady. But hark you Servant, hark ye: is he gon? call him again.

Abigal. Hang him Paddock.

Lady. Art thou here still? flie, flie, and call my Servant, flie or ne'r see me more.

Abigal. I had rather knit again than see that rascall, but I must doe it. [*Exit* Abigal.

Lady. I would be loth to anger him too much; what fine foolery is this in a woman, to use those men most frowardly they love most? If I should lose him thus, I were rightly served. I hope he's not so much himself, to take it to th'heart: how now? will he come back?

Enter Abigal.

Abig. Never, he swears, whilst he can hear men say there's any woman living: he swore he would ha' me first.

Lady. Didst thou intreat him wench?

Abigal. As well as I could Madam. But this is still your way, to love being absent, and when he's with you, laugh at him and abuse him. There's another way if you could hit on't.

Lady. Thou saist true, get me paper, pen and ink, I'le write to him, I'de be loth he should sleep in's anger.
Women are most fools when they think th'are wisest.

[*Ex. Omnes.*

Musick. Enter Young Loveless, *and* Widow, *going to be Married, with them his* Comrades.

Widow. Pray Sir cast off these fellows, as unfitting for your bare knowledge, and far more your companie: is't fit such Ragamuffins as these are should bear the name of friends? and furnish out a civil house? ye're to be married now, and men that love you must expect a course far from your old carrier: if you will keep 'em, turn 'em to th' stable, and there make 'em grooms: and yet now consider it, such beggars once set o' horse back, you have heard will ride, how far you had best to look.

Captain. Hear you, you that must be Ladie, pray content your self and think upon your carriage soon at night, what dressing will best take your Knight, what wastcote, what cordial will do well i'th' morning for him, what triers have you?

Widow. What do you mean Sir?

Capt. Those that must switch him up: if he start well,

fear not but cry Saint *George*, and bear him hard: when you perceive his wind growes hot and wanting, let him a little down, he's fleet, ne're doubt him, and stands sound.

Widow. Sir, you hear these fellows?

Young Love. Merrie companions, wench, Merry companions.

Widow. To one another let 'em be companions, but good Sir not to you: you shall be civil and slip off these base trappings.

Cap. He shall not need, my most swee[t] Ladie Grocer, if he be civil, not your powdered Sugar, nor your Raisins shall perswade the Captain to live a Coxcomb with him; let him be civil and eat i'th' *Arches*, and see what will come on't.

Poet. Let him be civil, doe: undo him; I, that's the next way. I will not take (if he be civil once) two hundred pound a year to live with him; be civil? there's a trim perswasion.

Capt. If thou beest civil Knight, as *Jove* defends it, get thee another nose, that will be pull'd off by the angry boyes for thy conversion: the children thou shalt get on this Civillian cannot inherit by the law, th'are *Ethnicks*, and all thy sport meer Moral leacherie: when they are grown, having but little in 'em, they may prove Haberdashers, or gross Grocers, like their dear Damm there: prethee be civil Knight, in time thou maist read to thy houshold, and be drunk once a year: this would shew finely.

Young Lo. I wonder sweet heart you will offer this, you do not understand these Gentlemen: I will be short and pithy: I had rather cast you off by the way of charge: these are Creatures, that nothing goes to the maintenance of but Corn and Water. I will keep these fellows just in the competencie of two Hens.

Wid. If you can cast it so Sir, you have my liking. If they eat less, I should not be offended: But how these Sir, can live upon so little as Corn and Water, I am unbelieving.

Young Lo. Why prethee sweet heart what's your Ale? is not that Corn and Water, my sweet Widow?

Wid. I but my sweet Knight where's the meat to this, and cloaths that they must look for?

Young Lo. In this short sentence Ale, is all included:

Meat, Drink, and Cloth; These are no ravening Footmen, no fellows, that at Ordinaries dare eat their eighteen pence thrice out before they rise, and yet goe hungry to play, and crack more nuts than would suffice a dozen Squirrels; besides the din, which is damnable: I had rather rail, and be confin'd to a *Boatmaker*, than live amongst such rascals; these are people of such a clean discretion in their diet, of such a moderate sustenance, that they sweat if they but smell hot meat. *Porredge* is poison, they hate a Kitchin as they hate a Counter, and show 'em but a Feather-bed they swound. Ale is their eating and their drinking surely, which keeps their bodies clear, and soluble. Bread is a binder, and for that abolisht even in their Ale, whose lost room fills an apple, which is more airy and of subtiler nature. The rest they take is little, and that little is little easie: For like strict men of order, they do correct their bodies with a bench, or a poor stubborn table; if a chimny offer it self with some few broken rushes, they are in down: when they are sick, that's drunk, they may have fresh straw, else they do despise these worldly pamperings. For their poor apparel, 'tis worn out to the diet; new they seek none, and if a man should offer, they are angrie, scarce to be reconcil'd again with him: you shall not hear 'em ask one a cast doublet once in a year, which is modesty befitting my poor friends: you see their *Wardrobe*, though slender, competent: For shirts I take it, they are things worn out of their remembrance. Lousie they will be when they list, and *mangie*, which shows a fine variety: and then to cure 'em, a *Tanners* limepit, which is little charge, two dogs, and these; these two may be cur'd for 3. pence.

Wid. You have half perswaded me, pray use your pleasure: and my good friends since I do know your diet, I'le take an order, meat shall not offend you, you shall have Ale.

Capt. We ask no more, let it be, mighty Lady: and if we perish, then our own sins on us.

Young Lo. Come forward Gentlemen, to Church my boys, when we have done, I'le give you cheer in bowles. [*Exeunt.*

Actus Quintus. Scena Prima.

Enter Elder Loveless.

Elder Lo. THis senseless woman vexes me to th' heart, she will not from my memory: would she were a man for one two hours, that I might beat her. If I had been unhansome, old or jealous, 'thad been an even lay she might have scorn'd me; but to be young, and by this light I think as proper as the proudest; made as clean, as straight, and strong backt; means and manners equal with the best cloth of silver Sir i'th' kingdom: But these are things at some time of the Moon, below the cut of Canvas: sure she has some Meeching Rascal in her house, some Hind, that she hath seen bear (like another *Milo*) quarters of Malt upon his back, and sing with't, Thrash all day, and i'th' evening in his stockings, strike up a Hornpipe, and there stink two hours, and ne're a whit the worse man; these are they, these steel chin'd Rascals that undo us all. Would I had been a Carter, or a Coachman, I had done the deed e're this time.

Enter Servant.

Ser. Sir, there's a Gentleman without would speak with you.

Elder Lo. Bid him come in.

Enter Welford.

Wel. By your leave Sir.

Elder Lo. You are welcome, what's your will Sir?

Wel. Have you forgotten me?

Elder Lo. I do not much remember you.

Wel. You must Sir. I am that Gentleman you pleas'd to wrong, in your disguise, I have inquired you out.

Elder Lo. I was disguised indeed Sir if I wrong'd you, pray where and when?

Wel. In such a Ladies house, I need not name her.

Elder Lo. I do remember you, you seem'd to be a Sutor to that Lady?

Wel. If you remember this, do not forget how scurvily you us'd me: that was no place to quarrel in, pray you think of it; if you be honest you dare fight with me, without more urging, else I must provoke ye.

Elder Lo. Sir I dare fight, but never for a woman, I will not have her in my cause, she's mortal, and so is not my anger: if you have brought a nobler subject for our Swords, I am for you; in this I would be loth to prick my Finger. And where you say I wrong'd you, 'tis so far from my profession, that amongst my fears, to do wrong is the greatest: credit me we have been both abused, (not by our selves, for that I hold a spleen, no sin of malice, and may with man enough be best forgoten,) but by that willfull, scornful piece of hatred, that much forgetful Lady: for whose sake, if we should leave our reason, and run on upon our sense, like *Rams*, the little world of good men would laugh at us, and despise us, fixing upon our desperate memories the never-worn out names of Fools and Fencers. Sir 'tis not fear, but reason makes me tell you; in this I had rather help you Sir, than hurt you, and you shall find it, though you throw your self into as many dangers as she offers, though you redeem her lost name every day, and find her out new honours with your Sword, you shall but be her mirth as I have been.

Wel. I ask you mercy Sir, you have ta'ne my edge off: yet I would fain be even with this Lady.

Elder Lo. In which I'le be your helper: we are two, and they are two: two Sisters, rich alike, only the elder has the prouder Dowry: In troth I pity this disgrace in you, yet of mine own I am senceless: do but follow my Counsel, and I'le pawn my spirit, we'l overreach 'em yet; the means is this—

Enter Servant.

Ser. Sir there's a Gentlewoma[n] will needs speak with you, I cannot keep her out, she's entred Sir.

Elder Lo. It is the waiting woman, pray be not seen: sirrah hold her in discourse a while: hark in your ear, go and dispatch it quickly, when I come in, I'le tell you all the project.

Wel. I care not which I have. [*Exit* Welford.

Elder Lo. Away, 'tis done, she must not see you: now Lady *Guiniver* what news with you?

Enter Abigal.

Abig. Pray leave these frumps Sir, and receive this letter.

Elder Lo. From whom good vanity?

Abig. 'Tis from my Lady Sir: Alas good soul, she cries and takes on!

Elder Lo. Do's she so good Soul? wou'd she not have a Cawdle? do's she send you with your fine Oratory goody *Tully* to tye me to believe again? bring out the Cat-hounds, I'le make you take a tree Whore, then with my tiller bring down your *Gibship*, and then have you cast, and hung up i'th' Warren.

Abig. I am no beast Sir, would you knew it.

Elder Lo. Wou'd I did, for I am yet very doubtful; what will you say now?

Abig. Nothing not I.

Elder Lo. Art thou a woman, and say nothing?

Abig. Unless you'l hear me with more moderation, I can speak wise enough.

Elder Lo. And loud enough? will your Lady love me?

Abig. It seems so by her letter, and her lamentations; but you are such another man.

Elder Lo. Not such another as I was, Mumps; nor will not be: I'le read her fine Epistle: ha, ha, ha, is not thy Mistress mad?

Abig. For you she will be, 'tis a shame you should use a poor Gentlewoman so untowardly; she loves the ground you tread on; and you (hard heart) because she jested with you, mean to kill her; 'tis a fine conquest as they say.

Elder Lo. Hast thou so much moisture in the Whitleather hide yet, that thou canst cry? I wou'd have sworn thou hadst been touchwood five year since; nay let it rain, thy face chops for a shower like a dry Dunghil.

Abig. I'le not indure this Ribauldry; farewel i'th' Devils name; if my Lady die, I'le be sworn before a Jury, thou art the cause on't.

Elder Lo. Do Maukin do, deliver to your Lady from me this: I mean to see her, if I have no other business: which before I'le want to come to her, I mean to go seek birds nests: yet I may come too: but if I come, from this door till I see her, will I think how to rail vildly at her; how to vex her, and make her cry so much, that the Physician if she fall sick upon't, shall find the cause to be want of Urine, and she remediless dye in her Heresie: Farewell old Adage, I hope to see the Boys make Potguns on thee.

Abig. Th'art a vile man, God bless my issue from thee.

Elder Lo. Thou hast but one, and that's in thy left crupper, that makes thee hobble so; you must be ground i'th' breach like a Top, you'l ne're spin well else: Farewell Fytchock. [*Exeunt.*

Enter Lady *alone.*

Lady. Is it not strange that every womans will should track out new wayes to disturb her self? if I should call my reason to account, it cannot answer why I keep my self from mine own wish, and stop the man I love from his; and every hour repent again, yet still go on: I know 'tis like a man, that wants his natural sleep, and growing dull would gladly give the remnant of his life for two hours rest; yet through his frowardness, will rather choose to watch another man, drowsie as he, than take his own repose. All this I know: yet a strange peevishness and anger, not to have the power to do things unexpected, carries me away to mine own ruine: I had rather die sometimes than not disgrace in public him whom people think I love, and do't with oaths, and am in earnest then: O what are we! Men, you must answer this, that dare obey such things as we command. How now? what newes?

Enter Abigal.

Abi. Faith Madam none worth hearing.

Lady. Is he not come?

Abi. No truly.

Lady. Nor has he writ?

Abigal. Neither. I pray God you have not undone your self.

Lady. Why, but what saies he?

Abi. Faith he talks strangely.

Lady. How strangely?

Abi. First at your Letter he laught extremely.

Lady. What, in contempt?

Abi. He laught monstrous loud, as he would die, and when you wrote it I think you were in no such merry mood, to provoke him that way: and having done he cried Alas for her, and violently laught again.

Lady. Did he?

Abi. Yes, till I was angry.

Lady. Angry, why? why wert thou angry? he did doe but well, I did deserve it, he had been a fool, an unfit man for any one to love, had he not laught thus at me: you were angry, that show'd your folly; I shall love him more for that, than all that ere he did before: but said he nothing else?

Abi. Many uncertain things: he said though you had mockt him, because you were a woman, he could wish to do you so much favour as to see you: yet he said, he knew you rash, and was loth to offend you with the sight of one, whom now he was bound not to leave.

Lady. What one was that?

Abi. I know not, but truly I do fear there is a making up there: for I heard the servants, as I past by some, whisper such a thing: and as I came back through the hall, there were two or three Clarks writing great conveyances in hast, which they said were for their Mistris joynture.

Lady. 'Tis very like, and fit it should be so, for he does think, and reasonably think, that I should keep him with my idle tricks for ever ere he be married.

Abi. At last he said, it should go hard but he would see you for your satisfaction.

Lady. All we that are called Women, know as well as men, it were a far more noble thing to grace where we are grace't, and give respect there where we are respected: yet we practise a wilder course, and never bend our eyes on men with pleasure, till they find the way to give us a neglect: then we, too late, perceive the loss of what we might have had, and dote to death.

Enter Martha.

Mar. Sister, yonder's your Servant, with a Gentlewoman with him.

Lady. Where?

Mar. Close at the door.

Lady. Alas I am undone, I fear he is be[t]roth'd, What kind of woman is she?

Mar. A most ill favoured one, with her Masque on: And how her face should mend the rest I know not.

La. But yet her mind was of a milder stuff than mine was.

Enter Elder Loveless, *and* Welford *in Womans apparel.*

Lady. Now I see him, if my heart swell not again (away thou womans pride) so that I cannot speak a gentle word to him, let me not live.

Elder Lo. By your leave here.

Lady. How now, what new trick invites you hither? Ha'you a fine device again?

Elder Lo. Faith this is the finest device I have now: How dost thou sweet heart?

Wel. Why very well, so long as I may please
You my dear Lover. I nor can, nor will
Be ill when you are well, well when you are ill.

Elder Lo. O thy sweet temper! what would I have given, that Lady had been like thee: seest thou her? that face (my love) join'd with thy humble mind, had made a wench indeed.

Wel. Alas my love, what God hath done, I dare not think to mend. I use no paint, nor any drugs of Art, my hands and face will shew it.

La. Why what thing have you brought to shew us there? do you take mony for it?

Elder Lo. A Godlike thing, not to be bought for mony: 'tis my Mistris: in whom there is no passion, nor no scorn: what I will is for law; pray you salute her.

Lady. Salute her? by this good light, I would not kiss her for half my wealth.

Elder Lo. Why? why pray you?
You shall see me do't afore you; look you.

Lady. Now fie upon thee, a beast would not have don't.
I would not kiss thee of a month to gain a Kingdom.

Elder Lo. Marry you shall not be troubled.

Lady. Why was there ever such a *Meg* as this?
Sure thou art mad.

Elder Lo. I was mad once, when I lov'd pictures; for what are shape and colours else, but pictures? in that tawnie hide there lies an endless mass of vertues, when all your red and white ones want it.

Lady. And this is she you are to marry, is't not?

Elder Lo. Yes indeed is't.

Lady. God give you joy.

Elder Lo. Amen.

Wel. I thank yo[u], as unknown for your good wish.
The like to you when ever you shall wed.

Elder Lo. O gentle Spirit!

Lady. You thank me? I pray
Keep your breath nearer you, I do not like it.

Wel. I would not willingly offend at all,
Much less a Lady of your worthie parts.

Elder Lo. Sweet, Sweet!

La. I do not think this woman can by nature be thus,
Thus ugly; sure she's some common Strumpet,
Deform'd with exercise of sin?

Wel. O Sir believe not this, for Heaven so comfort me as I am free from foul pollution with any man; my honour ta'ne away, I am no woman.

Elder Lo. Arise my dearest Soul; I do not credit it. Alas, I fear her tender heart will break with this reproach; fie that you know no more civility to a weak Virgin. 'Tis no matter Sweet, let her say what she will, thou art not worse to me, and therefore not at all; be careless.

Wel. For all things else I would, but for mine honor; Me thinks.

Elder Lo. Alas, thine honour is not stain'd,
Is this the business that you sent for me about?

Mar. Faith Sister you are much to blame, to use a woman, whatsoe're she be, thus; I'le salute her: You are welcom hither.

Wel. I humbly thank you.

Elder Lo. Milde yet as the Dove, for all these injuries. Come shall we goe, I love thee not so ill to keep thee here a jesting stock.
Adue to the worlds end.

Lady. Why whither now?

Elder Lo. Nay you shall never know, because you shall not find me.

Lady. I pray let me speak with you.

Elder Lo. 'Tis very well: come.

Lady. I pray you let me speak with you.

Elder Lo. Yes for another mock.

Lady. By Heaven I have no mocks: good Sir a word.

Elder Lo. Though you deserve not so much at my hands, yet if you be in such earnest, I'le speak a word with you; but I beseech you be brief: for in good faith there's a Parson and a licence stay for us i'th' Church all this while: and you know 'tis night.

Lady. Sir, give me hearing patiently, and whatsoever I have heretofore spoke jestingly, forget: for as I hope for mercy any where, what I shall utter now is from my heart, and as I mean.

Elder Lo. Well, well, what do you mean?

Lady. Was not I once your Mistress, and you my Servant?

Elder Lo. O 'tis about the old matter.

Lady. Nay good Sir stay me out; I would but hear you excuse your self, why you should take this woman, and leave me.

Elder Lo. Prethee why not, deserves she not as much as you?

Lady. I think not, if you will look
With an indifferency upon us both.

Elder Lo. Upon your faces, 'tis true: but if judiciously we shall cast our eyes upon your minds, you are a thousand women of her in worth: she cannot swound in jest, nor set her lover tasks, to shew her peevishness, and his affection, nor cross what he saies, though it be Canonical. She's a good plain wench, that will do as I will have her, and bring me lusty Boys to throw the Sledge, and lift at Pigs of Lead: and for a Wife, she's far beyond you: what can you do in a houshold to provide for your issue, but lye i' bed and get 'em? your business is to dress you, and at idle hours to eat; when she can do a thousand profitable things: she can do pretty well in the Pastry, and knows how Pullen should be cram'd, she cuts Cambrick at a thread, weaves Bone-lace, and quilts Balls; and what are you good for?

Lady. Admit it true, that she were far beyond me in all respects, does that give you a licence to forswear your self?

Elder Lo. Forswear my self, how?

Lady. Perhaps you have forgotten the innumerable oaths you have utter'd in disclaiming all for Wives but me: I'le not remember you: God give you joy.

Elder Lo. Nay but conceive me, the intent of oaths is ever understood: Admit I should protest to such a friend, to see him at his Lodging to morrow: Divines would never hold me perjur'd if I were struck blind, or he hid him where my diligent search could not find him: so there were no cross act of mine own in't. Can it be imagined I mean to force you to Marriage, and to have you whether you will or no?

Lady. Alas you need not. I make already tender of my self, and then you are forsworn.

Elder Lo. Some sin I see indeed must necessarily fall upon me, as whosoever deals with Women shall never utterly avoid it: yet I would chuse the least ill; which is to forsake you, that have done me all the abuses of a malignant Woman, contemn'd my service, and would have held me prating about Marriage, till I had been past getting of Children: then her that hath forsaken her Family, and put her tender body in my hand, upon my word—

Lady. Which of us swore you first to?

Elder Lo. Why to you.

Lady. Which oath is to be kept then?

Elder Lo. I prethee do not urge my sins unto me,
Without I could amend 'em.

Lady. Why you may by wedding me.

Elder Lo. How will that satisfie my word to her?

Lady. 'Tis not to be kept, and needs no satisfaction,
'Tis an error fit for repentance only.

Elder Lo. Shall I live to wrong that tender hearted Virgin so? It may not be.

Lady. Why may it not be?

Elder Lo. I swear I would rather marry thee than her: but yet mine honesty?

Lady. What honesty? 'Tis more preserv'd this way:
Come, by this light, servant, thou shalt, I'le kiss thee on't.

Elder Lo. This kiss indeed is sweet, pray God no sin lie under it.

Lady. There is no sin at all, try but another.

Wel. O my heart!

Mar. Help Sister, this Lady swounds.

Elder Lo. How do you?

Wel. Why very well, if you be so.

Elder Lo. Since a quiet mind lives not in any Woman, I shall do a most ungodly thing. Hear me one word more, which by all my hopes I will not alter, I did make an oath when you delai'd me so, that this very night I would be married. Now if you will go without delay, suddenly, as late as it is, with your own Minister to your own Chapel, I'le wed you and to bed.

Lady. A match dear servant.

Elder Lo. For if you should forsake me now, I care not, she would not though for all her injuries, such is her spirit. If I be not ashamed to kiss her now I part, may I not live.

Wel. I see you go, as slily as you think to steal away: yet I will pray for you; all blessings of the world light on you two, that you may live to be an aged pair. All curses on me if I do not speak what I do wish indeed.

Elder Lo. If I can speak to purpose to her, I am a villain.

Lady. Servant away.

Mar. Sister, will you Marry that inconstant man? think you he will not cast you off to morrow, to wrong a Lady thus, lookt she like dirt, 'twas basely done. May you ne're prosper with him.

Wel. Now God forbid. Alas I was unworthy, so I told him.

Mar. That was your modesty, too good for him.
I would not see your wedding for a world.

Lady. Chuse chuse, come *Younglove.*

[*Exit* La. Elder Lo. *and* Young.

Mar. Dry up your eyes forsooth, you shall not think we are all such uncivil beasts as these. Would I knew how to give you a revenge.

Wel. So would not I: No let me suffer truly, that I desire.

Mar. Pray walk in with me, 'tis very late, and you shall stay all night: your bed shall be no worse than mine; I wish I could but do you right.

Wel. My humble thanks:
God grant I may but live to quit your love. [*Exeunt.*

Enter Young Loveless *and* Savil.

Young Lo. Did your Master send for me *Savil*?

Sav. Yes, he did send for your worship Sir.

Young Lo. Do you know the business?

Sav. Alas Sir, I know nothing, nor am imployed beyond my hours of eating. My dancing days are done Sir.

Young Lo. What art thou now then?

Sav. If you consider me in little, I am with your worships reverence Sir, a Rascal: one that upon the next anger of your Brother, must raise a sconce by the high way, and sell switches; my wife is learning now Sir, to weave inkle.

Young Lo. What dost thou mean to do with thy Children *Savil*?

Sav. My eldest boy is half a Rogue already, he was born bursten, and your worship knows, that is a pretty step to mens compassions. My youngest boy I purpose Sir to bind for ten years to a G[ao]ler, to draw under him, that he may shew us mercy in his function.

Young Lo. Your family is quartered with discretion: you are resolved to Cant then: where *Savil* shall your scene lie?

Sav. Beggers must be no chusers.
In every place (I take it) but the stocks.

Young Lo. This is your drinking, and your whoring *Savil*, I told you of it, but your heart was hardened.

Sav. 'Tis true, you were the first that told me of it I do remember yet in tears, you told me you would have Whores, and in that passion Sir, you broke out thus; Thou miserable man, repent, and brew three Strikes more in a Hogshead. 'Tis noon e're we be drunk now, and the time can tarry for no man.

Young Lo. Y'are grown a bitter Gentleman. I see misery can clear your head better than Mustard, I'le be a sutor for your Keys again Sir.

Sav. Will you but be so gracious to me Sir? I shall be bound.

Young Lo. You shall Sir
To your bunch again, or I'le miss foully.

Enter Morecraft.

Mor. Save you Gentleman, save you.

Young Lo. Now Polecat, what young Rabets nest have you to draw?

Mor. Come, prethee be familiar Knight.

Young Lo. Away Fox, I'le send for Terriers for you.

Mor. Thou art wide yet: I'le keep thee companie.

Young Lo. I am about some business; Indentures,
If ye follow me I'le beat you: take heed,
A[s] I live I'le cancel your Coxcomb.

Mor. Thou art cozen'd now, I am no usurer:
What poor fellow's this?

Savil. I am poor indeed Sir.

Mor. Give him mony Knight.

Young Lo. Do you begin the offering.

Mor. There poor fellow, here's an Angel for thee.

Young Lo. Art thou in earnest *Morecraft*?

Mor. Yes faith Knight, I'le follow thy example: thou hadst land and thousands, thou spendst, and flungst away, and yet it flows in double: I purchased, wrung, and wierdraw'd, for my wealth, lost, and was cozen'd: for which I make a vow, to trie all the waies above ground, but I'le find a constant means to riches without curses.

Young Lo. I am glad of your conversion Master *Morecraft*:
Y'are in a fair course, pray pursue it still.

Mor. Come, we are all gallants now, I'le keep thee company; Here honest fellow, for this Gentlemans sake, there's two Angels more for thee.

Savil. God quite you Sir, and keep you long in this mind.

Young Lo. Wilt thou persevere?

Mor. Till I have a penny. I have brave cloathes a making, and two horses; canst thou not help me to a match Knight, I'le lay a thousand pound upon my crop-ear.

Yo. Lo. Foot, this is stranger than an *Africk* monster,
There will be no more talk of the *Cleve* wars
Whilst this lasts, come, I'le put thee into blood.

Sav. Would all his damn'd tribe were as tender hearted. I beseech you let this Gentleman join with you in the recovery of my Keyes; I like his good beginning Sir, the whilst I'le pray for both your worships.

Young Lo. He shall Sir.

Mor. Shall we goe noble Knight? I would fain be acquainted.

Young Lo. I'le be your Servant Sir. [*Exeunt.*

Enter Elder Loveless, *and* Lady.

Elder Lo. Faith my sweet Lady, I have caught you now, maugre your subtilties, and fine devices, be coy again now.

Lady. Prethee sweet-heart tell true.

Elder Lo. By this light, by all the pleasures I have had this night, by your lost maidenhead, you are cozened meerly. I have cast beyond your wit. That Gentleman is your retainer *Welford.*

Lady. It cannot be so.

Elder Lo. Your Sister has found it so, or I mistake, mark how she blushes when you see her next. Ha, ha, ha, I shall not travel now, ha, ha, ha.

Lady. Prethee sweet heart be quiet, thou hast angred me at heart.

Elder Lo. I'le please you soon again.

La. Welford?

Elder Lo. I *Welford,* hee's a young handsome fellow, well bred and landed, your Sister can instruct you in his good parts, better than I by this time.

Lady. Uds foot am I fetcht over thus?

Elder Lo. Yes i'faith.
And over shall be fetcht again, never fear it.

Lady. I must be patient, though it torture me:
You have got the Sun Sir.

Elder Lo. And the Moon too, in which I'le be the man.

Lady. But had I known this, had I but surmiz'd it, you should have hunted three trains more, before you had come to th' course, you should have hankt o'th' bridle, Sir, i'faith.

El. Lo. I knew it, and min'd with you, and so blew you up. Now you may see the Gentlewoman: stand close.

Enter Welford, *and* Martha.

Mar. For Gods sake Sir, be private in this business,
You have undone me else. O God, what have I done?

Wel. No harm I warrant thee.

Mar. How shall I look upon my friends again?
With what face?

Wel. Why e'ne with that: 'tis a good one, thou canst not find a better: look upon all the faces thou shalt see there, and you shall find 'em smooth still, fair still, sweet still, and to your thinking honest; those have done as much as you have yet, or dare doe Mistris, and yet they keep no stir.

Mar. Good Sir goe in, and put your womans cloaths on: If you be seen thus, I am lost for ever.

Wel. I'le watch you for that Mistris: I am no fool, here will I tarry till the house be up and witness with me.

Mar. Good dear friend goe in.

Wel. To bed again if you please, else I am fixt here till there be notice taken what I am, and what I have done: if you could juggle me into my woman-hood again, and so cog me out of your company, all this would be forsworn, and I again an *asinego*, as your Sister left me. No, I'le have it known and publisht; then if you'le be a whore, forsake me and be asham'd: and when you can hold no longer, marry some cast *Cleve Captain*, and sell Bottle-ale.

Mar. I dare not stay Sir, use me modestly, I am your wife.

Wel. Goe in, I'le make up all.

Elder Lo. I'le be a witness of your naked truth Sir: this is the Gentlewoman, prethee look upon him, that is he that made me break my faith sweet: but thank your Sister, she hath soder'd it.

Lady. What a dull ass was I, I could not see this wencher from a wench: twenty to one, if I had been but tender like my Sister, he had served me such a slippery trick too.

Wel. Twenty to one I had.

Elder Lo. I would have watcht you Sir, by your good patience, for ferreting in my ground.

Lady. You have been with my Sister.

Wel. Yes to bring.

Elder Lo. An heir into the world he means.

Lady. There is no chafing now.

Wel. I have had my part on't: I have been chaft this three hours, that's the least, I am reasonable cool now.

Lady. Cannot you fare well, but you must cry roast-meat?

Wel. He that fares well, and will not bless the founders, is either surfeited, or ill taught, Lady, for mine own part,

I have found so sweet a diet, I can commend it, though I cannot spare it.

Elder Lo. How like you this dish, *Welford*, I made a supper on't, and fed so heartily, I could not sleep.

Lady. By this light, had I but scented out your [train], ye had slept with a bare pillow in your arms and kist that, or else the bed-post, for any wife ye had got this twelve-month yet: I would have vext you more than a try'd post-horse; and been longer bearing, than ever after-game at *Irish* was. Lord, that I were unmarried again.

Elder Lo. Lady I would not undertake ye, were you again a *Haggard*, for the best cast of four Ladys i'th' Kingdom: you were ever tickle-footed, and would not truss round.

Wel. Is she fast?

Elder Lo. She was all night lockt here boy.

Wel. Then you may lure her without fear of losing: take off her Cranes. You have a delicate Gentlewoman to your Sister: Lord what a prettie furie she was in, when she perceived I was a man: but I thank God I satisfied her scruple, without the Parson o'th' town.

Elder Lo. What did ye?

Wel. Madam, can you tell what we did?

Elder Lo. She has a shrewd guess at it I see it by her.

Lady. Well you may mock us: but my large Gentlewoman, my *Mary Ambre*, had I but seen into you, you should have had another bed-fellow, fitter a great deal for your itch.

Wel. I thank you Lady, me thought it was well,
You are so curious.

Enter Young Loveless, *his* Lady, Morecraft, Savil, *and two Servingmen.*

El. Lo. Get on your doublet, here comes my Brother.

Yo. Lo. Good morrow Brother, and all good to your Lady.

Mor. God save you and good morrow to you all.

El. Lo. Good morrow. Here's a poor brother of yours.

Lady. Fie how this shames me.

Mor. Prethee good fellow help me to a cup of beer.

Ser. I will Sir.

Yo. Lo. Brother what makes you here? will this Lady do? Will she? is she not nettl'd still?

Elder Lo. No I have cur'd her.
Mr. *Welford*, pray know this Gentleman is my Brother.

Wel. Sir I shall long to love him.

Yo. Lo. I shall not be your debter Sir. But how is't with you?

Elder Lo. As well as may be man: I am married: your new acquaintance hath her Sister, and all's well.

Yo. Lo. I am glad on't. Now my prettie Lady Sister,
How do you find my Brother?

Lady. Almost as wild as you are.

Yo. Lo. He will make the better husband: you have tried him?

Lady. Against my will Sir.

Yo. Lo. Hee'l make your will amends soon, do not doubt it.
But Sir I must intreat you to be better known
To this converted *Jew* here.

Ser. Here's Beer for you Sir.

Mor. And here's for you an Angel:
Pray buy no Land, 'twill never prosper Sir.

Elder Lo. How's this?

Yo. Lo. Bless you, and then I'le tell: He's turn'd Gallant.

Elder Lo. Gallant?

Yo. Lo. I Gallant, and is now called, *Cutting Morecraft*:
The reason I'le inform you at more leisure.

Wel. O good Sir let me know him presently.

Young Lo. You shall hug one another.

Mor. Sir I must keep you company.

Elder Lo. And reason.

Young Lo. Cutting *Morecraft* faces about, I must present another.

Mor. As many as you will Sir, I am for 'em.

Wel. Sir I shall do you service.

Mor. I shall look for't in good faith Sir.

Elder Lo. Prethee good sweet heart kiss him.

Lady. Who, that fellow?

Savil. Sir will it please you to remember me: my keys good Sir.

Young Lo. I'le doe it presently.

El. Lo. Come thou shalt kiss him for our sport sake.

La. Let him come on then; and do you hear, do not instruct me in these tricks, for you may repent it.

El. Lo. That at my peril. Lusty M^r^. *Morecraft*,
Here is a Lady would salute you.
Mor. She shall not lose her longing Sir: what is she?
Elder Lo. My wife Sir.
Mor. She must be then my Mistres.
Lady. Must I Sir?
Elder Lo. O yes, you must.
Mor. And you must take this ring, a poor pawn
Of some fiftie pound.
El. Lo. Take it by any means, 'tis lawfull prize.
Lady. Sir I shall call you servant.
Mor. I shall be proud on't: what fellow's that?
Young Lo. My Ladies Coachman.
Mor. There's something, (my friend) for you to buy whips,
And for you Sir, and you Sir.
Elder Lo. Under a miracle this is the strangest
I ever heard of.
Mor. What, shall we play, or drink? what shall we doe?
Who will hunt with me for a hundred pounds?
Wel. Stranger and Stranger!
Sir you shall find sport after a day or two.
Young Lo. Sir I have a sute unto you
Concerning your old servant *Savil.*
Elder Lo. O, for his keys, I know it.
Savil. Now Sir, strike in.
Mor. Sir I must have you grant me.
Elder Lo. 'Tis done Sir, take your keys again:
But hark you *Savil*, leave off the motions
Of the flesh, and be honest, or else you shall graze again:
I'le try you once more.
Savil. If ever I be taken drunk, or whoring,
Take off the biggest key i'th' bunch, and open
My head with it Sir: I humbly thank your worships.
Elder Lo. Nay then I see we must keep holiday.

Enter Roger, *and* Abigal.

Here's the last couple in hell.
Roger. Joy be among you all.
Lady. Why how now Sir, what is the meaning of this emblem?

Roger. Marriage an't like your worship.

Lady. Are you married?

Roger. As well as the next Priest could doe it, Madam.

Elder Lo. I think the sign's in *Gemini*, here's such coupling.

Wel. Sir *Roger*, what will you take to lie from your sweet-heart to night?

Roger. Not the best benefice in your worships gift Sir.

Wel. A whorson, how he swells.

Young Lo. How many times to night Sir *Roger*?

Roger. Sir you grow scurrilous:
What I shall do, I shall do: I shall not need your help.

Young Lo. For horse flesh *Roger*.

Elder Lo. Come prethee be not angry, 'tis a day
Given wholly to our mirth.

Lady. It shall be so Sir: Sir *Roger* and his Bride,
We shall intreat to be at our charge.

El. Lo. *Welford* get you to the Church: by this light,
You shall not lie with her again, till y'are married.

Wel. I am gone.

Mor. To every Bride I dedicate this day
Six healths a piece, and it shall goe hard,
But every one a jewell: Come be mad boys.

El. Lo. Th'art in a good beginning: come who leads?
Sir *Roger*, you shall have the *Van*: lead the way:
Would every dogged wench had such a day. [*Exeunt.*

The Custom of the Country.

Persons Represented in the Play.

Count Clodio, *Governour and a dishonourable pursuer of* Zenocia.
Manuel du Sosa, *Governour of* Lisbon, *and Brother to* Guiomar.
Arnoldo, *A Gentleman contracted to* Zenocia.
Rutilio, *A merry Gentleman Brother to* Arnoldo.
Charino, *Father to* Zenocia.
Duarte, *Son to* Guiomar, *a Gentleman well qualified but vain glorious.*
Alonzo, *a young* Portugal *Gentleman, enemy to* Duarte.
Leopold, *a Sea Captain Enamour'd on* Hippolyta.
Zabulon, *a* Jew, *servant to* Hippolyta.
Jaques, *servant to* Sulpitia.
Doctor.
Chirurgion.
Officers.
Guard.
Page.
Bravo.
Knaves, *of the Male Stewes.*
Servants.

WOMEN.

Zenocia, *Mistress to* Arnoldo, *and a chaste Wife.*
Guiomar, *a vertuous Lady, Mother to* Duarte.
Hippolyta, *a rich Lady, wantonly in Love with* Arnoldo.
Sulpitia, *a Bawd, Mistress of the Male Stewes.*

The Scene sometimes Lisbon, *sometimes* Italy.

The principal Actors were

Joseph Taylor.	*Robert Benfeild.*
John Lowin.	*William Eglestone.*
Nicholas Toolie.	*Richard Sharpe.*
John Underwood.	*Thomas Holcomb.*

Actus primus. Scena prima.

Enter Rutilio, *and* Arnold[o].

Rut. WHY do you grieve thus still?
Arn. 'Twould melt a Marble,
And tame a Savage man, to feel my fortune.

Rut. What fortune? I have liv'd this thirty years,
And run through all these follies you call fortunes,
Yet never fixt on any good and constant,
But what I made myself: why should I grieve then
At that I may mould any way?
Arn. You are wide still.
Rut. You love a Gentlewoman, a young handsom woman,
I have lov'd a thosand, not so few.
Arn. You are dispos'd.
Rut. You hope to Marry her; 'tis a lawful calling
And prettily esteem'd of, but take heed then,
Take heed dear Brother of a stranger fortune
Than e're you felt yet; fortune my foe is a friend to it.
Arn. 'Tis true I love, dearly, and truly love,
A noble, vertuous, and most beauteous Maid,
And am belov'd again.
Rut. That's too much o' Conscience,
To love all these would run me out o' my wits.
Arn. Prethee give ear, I am to Marry her.
Rut. Dispatch it then, and I'le go call the Piper.
Arn. But O the wicked Custom of this Country,
The barbarous, most inhumane, damned Custom.
Rut. 'Tis true, to marry is a Custom
I' the world; for look you Brother,
Wou'd any man stand plucking for the Ace of Harts,
With one pack of Cards all dayes on's life?
Arn. You do not
Or else you purpose not to understand me.
Rut. Proceed, I will give ear.
Arn. They have a Custom
In this most beastly Country, out upon't.
Rut. Let's hear it first.
Arn. That when a Maid is contracted
And ready for the tye o'th' Church, the Governour,
He that commands in chief, must have her Maiden-head,
Or Ransom it for mony at his pleasure.
Rut. How might a man atchieve that place? a rare Custom!
An admirable rare Custom: and none excepted?
Arn. None, none.
Rut. The rarer still: how could I lay about me,

In this rare Office? are they born to it, or chosen?
Arn. Both equal damnable.
Rut. Me thinks both excellent,
Would I were the next heir.
Arn. To this mad fortune
Am I now come, my Marriage is proclaim'd,
And nothing can redeem me from this mischief.
Rut. She's very young.
Arn. Yes.
Rut. And fair I dare proclaim her,
Else mine eyes fail.
Arn. Fair as the bud unblasted.
Rut. I cannot blame him then, if 'twere mine own case,
I would not go an Ace less.
Arn. Fye *Rutilio*,
Why do you make your brothers misery
Your sport and game?
Rut. There is no pastime like it.
Arn. I look'd for your advice, your timely Counsel,
How to avoid this blow, not to be mockt at,
And my afflictions jeer'd.
Rut. I tell thee *Arnoldo*,
An thou wert my Father, as thou art but my Brother,
My younger Brother too, I must be merry.
And where there is a wench yet can, a young wench,
A handsome wench, and sooner a good turn too,
An I were to be hang'd, thus must I handle it.
But you shall see Sir, I can change this habit
To do you any service; advise what you please,
And see with what Devotion I'le attend it?
But yet me thinks, I am taken with this Custom,

Enter Charino *and* Zenocia.

And could pretend to th' place.
Arn. Draw off a little;
Here comes my Mistress and her Father.
Rut. A dainty wench!
Wou'd I might farm his Custom.
Char. My dear Daughter,
Now to bethink your self of new advice

Will be too late, later this timeless sorrow,
No price, nor prayers, can infringe the fate
Your beauty hath cast on yo[u], my best *Zenocia*,
Be rul'd by me, a Fathers care directs ye,
Look on the Count, look chearfully and sweetly;
What though he have the power to possess ye,
To pluck your Maiden honour, and then slight ye
By Custom unresistible to enjoy you;
Yet my sweet Child, so much your youth and goodness,
The beauty of your soul, and Saint-like Modesty,
Have won upon his mild mind, so much charm'd him,
That all power laid aside, what Law allows him,
Or sudden fires, kindled from those bright eyes,
He sues to be your servant, fairly, nobly
For ever to be tyed your faithful Husband:
Consider my best child.

Zeno. I have considered.

Char. The blessedness that this breeds too, consider
Besides your Fathers Honour, your own peace,
The banishment for ever of this Custom,
This base and barbarous use, for after once
He has found the happiness of holy Marriage,
And what it is to grow up with one Beauty,
How he will scorn and kick at such an heritage
Left him by lust and lewd progenitors.
All Virgins too, shall bless your name, shall Saint it,
And like so many Pilgrims go to your shrine,
When time has turn'd your beauty into ashes,
Fill'd with your pious memory.

Zeno. Good Father
Hide not that bitter Pill I loath to swallow
In such sweet words.

Char. The Count's a handsome Gentleman,
And having him, y'are certain of a fortune,
A high and noble fortune to attend you:
Where if you fling your Love upon this stranger
This young *Arnoldo*, not knowing from what place
Or honourable strain of blood he is sprung, you venture
All your own sweets, and my long cares to nothing,
Nor are you certain of his faith; why may not that

Wander as he does, every where?
Zen. No more Sir;
I must not hear, I dare not hear him wrong'd thus,
Vertue is never wounded, but I suffer.
'Tis an ill Office in your age, a poor one,
To judge thus weakly: and believe your self too,
A weaker, to betray your innocent Daughter,
To his intemp'rate, rude, and wild embraces,
She hates as Heaven hates falshood.
Rut. A good wench,
She sticks close to you Sir.
Zeno. His faith uncertain?
The nobleness his vertue springs from, doubted?
D'ye doubt it is day now? or when your body's perfect,
Your stomach's well dispos'd, your pulse's temperate,
D'ye doubt you are in health? I tell you Father,
One hour of this mans goodness, this mans Nobleness
Put in the Scale, against the Counts whole being,
Forgive his lusts too, which are half his life,
He could no more endure to hold weight with him;
Arnoldo's very looks, are fair examples;
His common and indifferent actions,
Rules and strong ties of vertue: he has my first love,
To him in sacred vow I have given this body,
In him my mind inhabits.
Rut. Good wench still.
Zeno. And till he fling me off, as undeserving,
Which I confess I am, of such a blessing,
But would be loth to find it so—
Arn. O never;
Never my happy Mistress, never, never,
When your poor servant lives but in your favour,
One foot i'th' grave the other shall not linger.
What sacrifice of thanks, what age of service,
What danger, of more dreadful look than death,
What willing Martyrdom to crown me constant
May merit such a goodness, such a sweetness?
A love so Nobly great, no power can ruine;
Most blessed Maid go on, the Gods that gave this,
This pure unspotted love, the Child of Heaven,

In their own goodness, must preserve and save it,
And raise you a reward beyond our recompence.
Zeno. I ask but you, a pure Maid to possess,
And then they have crown'd my wishes: If I fall then
Go seek some better love, mine will debase you.
Rut. A pretty innocent fool; well, Governour,
Though I think well of your custom, and could wish my self
For this night in your place, heartily wish it:
Yet if you play not fair play and above board too,
I have a foolish gin here, I say no more;
I'le tell you what, and if your honours guts are not inchanted.
Arn. I should now chide you Sir, for so declining
The goodness and the grace you have ever shew'd me,
And your own vertue too, in seeking rashly
To violate that love Heaven has appointed,
To wrest your Daughters thoughts, part that affection
That both our hearts have tyed, and seek to give it
Rut. To a wild fellow, that would weary her;
A Cannibal, that feeds on the heads of Maids,
Then flings their bones and bodies to the Devil,
Would any man of discretion venture such a gristle,
To the rude clawes of such a *Cat-a-mountain*?
You had better tear her between two Oaks, a Town Bull
Is a meer *Stoick* to this fellow, a grave Philosopher,
And a *Spanish* Jennet, a most vertuous Gentleman.
Arn. Does this seem handsome Sir?
Rut. Though I confess
Any man would desire to have her, and by any means,
At any rate too, yet that this common Hangman,
That hath whipt off the heads of a thousand maids already,
That he should glean the Harvest, sticks in my stomach:
This Rogue breaks young wenches to the Saddle,
And teaches them to stumble ever after;
That he should have her? for my Brother now
That is a handsome young fellow; and well thought on,
And will deal tenderly in the business;
Or for my self that have a reputation,
And have studied the conclusions of these causes,
And know the perfect manage, I'le tell you old Sir,
If I should call you wise Sir, I should bely you,

This thing, you study to betray your child to,
This Maiden-monger. When you have done your best,
And think you have fixt her in the point of honour,
Who do you think you have tyed her to? a Surgeon,
I must confess an excellent dissector,
One that has cut up more young tender Lamb-pies—
Char. What I spake Gentlemen, was meer compulsion,
No Fathers free-will, nor did I touch your person
With any edge of spight; or strain your loves
With any base, or hir'd perswasions;
Witness these tears, how well I wisht your fortunes. [*Exit.*
Rut. There's some grace in thee yet, you are determined
To marry this Count, Lady.
Zen. Marry him *Rutilio*?
Rut. Marry him, and lye with him I mean.
Zen. You cannot mean that,
If you be a true Gentleman, you dare not,
The Brother to this man, and one that loves him;
I'le marry the Devil first.
Rut. A better choice
And lay his horns by, a handsomer bed-fellow,
A cooler o' my conscience.
Arn. Pray let me ask you;
And my dear Mistris, be not angry with me
For what I shall propound, I am confident,
No promise, nor no power, can force your love,
I mean in way of marriage, never stir you,
Nor to forget my faith, no state can wound you.
But for this Custom, which this wretched country
Hath wrought into a law, and must be satisfied;
Where all the pleas of honour are but laught at,
And modesty regarded as a may-game,
What shall be here considered? power we have none,
To make resistance, nor policie to cross it:
'Tis held Religion too, to pay this duty.
Zeno. I'le dye an *Atheist* then.
Arn. My noblest Mistris,
Not that I wish it so, but say it were so,
Say you did render up part of your honour,
For whilst your will is clear, all cannot perish;

Say for one night you entertain'd this monster,
Should I esteem you worse, forc'd to this render?
Your mind I know is pure, and full as beauteous;
After this short eclipse, you would rise again,
And shaking off that cloud, spread all your lustre.

Zeno. Who made you witty, to undoe your self, Sir?
Or are you loaden, with the love I bring you,
And fain would fling that burthen on another?
Am I grown common in your eyes *Arnoldo*?
Old, or unworthy of your fellowship?
D'ye think because a woman, I must err,
And therefore rather wish that fall before-hand
Coloured with Custom, not to be resisted?
D'ye love as painters doe, only some pieces,
Some certain handsome touches of your Mistris,
And let the mind pass by you, unexamined?
Be not abus'd; with what the maiden vessel
Is seasoned first, you understand the proverb.

Rut. I am afraid, this thing will make me vertuous.

Zeno. Should you lay by the least part of that love
Y'ave sworn is mine, your youth and faith has given me,
To entertain another, nay a fairer,
And make the case thus desp'rate, she must dy else;
D'ye think I would give way, or count this honest?
Be not deceiv'd, these eyes should never see you more,
This tongue forget to name you, and this heart
Hate you, as if you were born, my full *Antipathie.*
Empire and more imperious love, alone
Rule, and admit no rivals: the purest springs
When they are courted by lascivious land-floods,
Their maiden pureness, and their coolness perish.
And though they purge again to their first beauty,
The sweetness of their taste is clean departed.
I must have all or none; and am not worthy
Longer the noble name of wife, *Arnoldo*,
Than I can bring a whole heart pure and handsom.

Arnol. I never shall deserve you: not to thank you;
You are so heavenly good, no man can reach you:
I am sorrie I spake so rashly, 'twas but to try you.

Rut. You might have tryed a thousand women so,

And 900, fourscore and 19 should ha' followed your counsel.
Take heed o' clapping spurrs to such free cattell.
Arn. We must bethink us suddenly and constantly,
And wisely too, we expect no common danger.
Zen. Be most assur'd, I'le dye first.

Enter Clodio, *and* Guard.

Rut. An't come to that once,
The Devil pick his bones, that dyes a coward,
I'le jog along with you, here comes the Stallion,
How smug he looks upon the imagination
Of what he hopes to act! pox on your kidneys;
How they begin to melt! how big he bears,
Sure he will leap before us all: what a sweet company
Of rogues and panders wait upon his lewdness!
Plague of your chops, you ha' more handsome bitts,
Than a hundred honester men, and more deserving.
How the dogg leers.
Clod. You need not now be jealous,
I speak at distance to your wife, but when the Priest has done,
We shall grow nearer, and more familiar.
Rut. I'le watch you for that trick, baboon, I'le
Smoke you: the rogue sweats, as if he had eaten
Grains, he broyles, if I do come to the
Basting of you.
Arno. Your Lordship
May happily speak this, to fright a stranger,
But 'tis not in your honour, to perform it;
The Custom of this place, if such there be,
At best most damnable, may urge you to it,
But if you be an honest man you hate it,
How ever I will presently prepare
To make her mine, and most undoubtedly
Believe you are abus'd, this custome feign'd too,
And what you now pretend, most fair and vertuous.
Clod. Go and believe, a good belief does well Sir;
And you Sir, clear the place, but leave her here.
Arn. Your Lordships pleasure.
Clod. That anon *Arnoldo*,
This is but talk.

Rut. Shall we goe off?
Arn. By any means,
I know she has pious thoughts enough to guard her:
Besides, here's nothing due to him till the tye be done,
Nor dare he offer.
Rut. Now do I long to worry him:
Pray have a care to the main chance.
Zen. Pray Sir, fear not. [*Exit* Ar. *and* Rut.
Clod. Now, what say you to me?
Zen. Sir it becomes
The modestie, that maids are ever born with,
To use few words.
Clod. Do you see nothing in me?
Nothing to catch your eyes, nothing of wonder
The common mould of men, come short, and want in?
Do you read no future fortune for your self here?
And what a happiness it may be to you,
To have him honour you, all women aim at?
To have him love you Lady, that man love you,
The best, and the most beauteous have run mad for?
Look and be wise, you have a favour offer'd you
I do not every day propound to women;
You are a prettie one; and though each hour
I am glutted with the sacrifice of beautie,
I may be brought, as you may handle it,
To cast so good a grace and liking on you.
You understand, come kiss me, and be joyfull,
I give you leave.
Zen. Faith Sir, 'twill not shew handsome;
Our sex is blushing, full of fear, unskil'd too
In these alarms.
Clod. Learn then and be perfect.
Zen. I do beseech your honour pardon me,
And take some skilfull one can hold you play,
I am a fool.
Clod. I tell thee maid I love thee,
Let that word make thee happie, so far love thee,
That though I may enjoy thee without ceremony,
I will descend so low, to marry thee,
Me thinks I see the race that shall spring from us,

Some Princes, some great Souldiers.
Zen. I am afraid
Your honour's couzen'd in this calculation;
For certain, I shall ne're have a child by you.
Clod. Why?
Zen. Because I must not think to marry you,
I dare not Sir, the step betwixt your honour,
And my poor humble State.
Clod. I will descend to thee,
And buoy thee up.
Zen. I'le sink to th' Center first.
Why would your Lordship marry, and confine that pleasure
You ever have had freely cast upon you?
Take heed my Lord, this marrying is a mad matter,
Lighter a pair of shackles will hang on you,
And quieter a quartane feaver find you.
If you wed me I must enjoy you only,
Your eyes must be called home, your thoughts in cages,
To sing to no ears then but mine; your heart bound,
The custom, that your youth was ever nurst in,
Must be forgot, I shall forget my duty else,
And how that will appear—
Clod. Wee'l talk of that more.
Zen. Besides I tell ye, I am naturally,
As all young women are, that shew like handsome,
Exceeding proud, being commended, monstrous.
Of an unquiet temper, seldom pleas'd,
Unless it be with infinite observance,
Which you were never bred to; once well angred,
As every cross in us, provokes that passion,
And like a Sea, I roule, toss, and chafe a week after.
And then all mischief I can think upon,
Abusing of your bed the least and poorest,
I tell you what you'le finde, and in these fitts,
This little beauty you are pleased to honour,
Will be so chang'd, so alter'd to an ugliness,
To such a vizard, ten to one, I dye too,
Take't then upon my death you murder'd me.
Clod. Away, away fool, why dost thou proclame these
To prevent that in me, thou hast chosen in another?

Zen. Him I have chosen, I can rule and master,
Temper to what I please, you are a great one
Of a strong will to bend, I dare not venture.
Be wise my Lord, and say you were well counsel'd,
Take mony for my ransom, and forget me,
'Twill be both safe, and noble for your honour,
And wheresoever my fortunes shall conduct me,
So worthy mentions I shall render of you,
So vertuous and so fair.

Clod. You will not marrie me?

Zen. I do beseech your honour, be not angry
At what I say, I cannot love ye, dare not;
But set a ransom, for the flowr you covet.

Clod. No mony, nor no prayers, shall redeem that,
Not all the art you have.

Zen. Set your own price Sir.

Clod. Goe to your wedding, never kneel to me,
When that's done, you are mine, I will enjoy you:
Your tears do nothing, I will not lose my custom
To cast upon my self an Empires fortune.

Zen. My mind shall not pay this custom, cruel man. [*Ex.*

Clod. Your body will content me: I'le look for you. [*Ex.*

Enter Charino, *and servants in blacks. Covering the place with blacks.*

Char. Strew all your withered flowers, your Autumn (sweets
By the hot Sun ravisht of bud and beauty
Thus round about her Bride-bed, hang those blacks there
The emblemes of her honour lost; all joy
That leads a Virgin to receive her lover,
Keep from this place, all fellow-maids that bless her,
And blushing do unloose her Zone, keep from her:
No merry noise nor lusty songs be heard here,
Nor full cups crown'd with wine make the rooms giddy;
This is no masque of mirth, but murdered honour.
Sing mournfully that sad Epithalamion
I gave thee now: and prethee let thy lute weep.

Song, Dance. *Enter* Rutilio.

Rut. How now, what livery's this? do you call this (a wedding?
This is more like a funeral.

Char. It is one,
And my poor Daughter going to her grave,
To his most loath'd embraces that gapes for her.
Make the Earles bed readie, is the marriage done Sir?
Rut. Yes they are knit; but must this slubberdegullion
Have her maiden-head now?
[*Char.*] There's no avoiding it.
Rut. And there's the scaffold where she must lose it.
[*Char.*] The bed Sir.
Rut. No way to wipe his mouldy chaps?
Char. That we know.
Rut. To any honest well-deserving fellow,
And 'twere but to a merry Cobbler, I could sit still now,
I love the game so well; but that this puckfist,
This universal rutter—fare ye well Sir;
And if you have any good prayers, put 'em forward,
There may be yet a remedie.
Char. I wish it, [*Exit* Rut.
And all my best devotions offer to it.

Enter Clodio, *and* Guard.

Clod. Now is this tye dispatch'd?
Char. I think it be Sir.
Clod. And my bed ready?
Char. There you may quickly find Sir,
Such a loath'd preparation.
Clod. Never grumble,
Nor fling a discontent upon my pleasure,
It must and shall be done: give me some wine,
And fill it till it leap upon my lips: [*wine*
Here's to the foolish maidenhead you wot of,
The toy I must take pains for.
Char. I beseech your Lordship
Load not a Fathers love.
Clod. Pledge it *Charino*,
Or by my life I'le make thee pledge thy last,
And be sure she be a maid, a perfect Virgin,
(I will not have my expectation dull'd)
Or your old pate goes off. I am hot and fiery,
And my bloud beats alarms through my body,

And fancie high. You of my guard retire,
And let me hear no noise about the lodging
But musick and sweet ayres, now fetch your Daughter,
And bid the coy wench put on all her beauties,
All her enticements, out-blush damask Roses,
And dim the breaking East with her bright Crystals.
I am all on fire, away.

Char. And I am frozen. [*Exit.*

Enter Zenocia *with Bow and Quiver, an Arrow bent,*
Arnoldo *and* Rutilio *after her, arm'd.*

Zen. Come fearless on.

Rut. Nay an I budge from thee
Beat me with durty sticks.

Clod. What Masque is this?
What pretty fancy to provoke me high?
The beauteous Huntress, fairer far, and sweeter;
Diana shewes an *Ethiop* to this beauty
Protected by two Virgin Knights.

Rut. That's a lye,
A loud one, if you knew as much as I do,
The Guard's dispers'd.

Arn. Fortune I hope invites us.

Clod. I can no longer hold, she pulls my heart from me.

Zen. Stand, and stand fixt, move not a foot, nor speak not,
For if thou doest, upon this point thy death sits.
Thou miserable, base, and sordid lecher,
Thou scum of noble blood, repent and speedily,
Repent thy thousand thefts, from helpless Virgins,
Their innocence betrayed to thy embraces.

Arn. The base dishonour, that thou doest to strangers,
In glorying to abuse the Laws of Marriage,
Thy Infamy thou hast flung upon thy Country,
In nourishing this black and barbarous Custom.

Clod. My Guard.

Arn. One word more, and thou diest.

Rut. One syllable
That tends to any thing, but I beseech you,
And as y'are Gentlemen tender my case,
And I'le thrust my Javeling down thy throat.

Thou Dog-whelp, thou, pox upon thee, what
Should I call thee, Pompion,
Thou kiss my Lady? thou scour her Chamber-pot:
Thou have a Maiden-head? a mottly Coat,
You great blind fool, farewel and be hang'd to ye,
Lose no time Lady.

Arn. Pray take your pleasure Sir,
And so we'l take our leaves.

Zen. We are determined,
Dye, before yield.

Arn. Honour, and a fair grave.

Zen. Before a lustful Bed, so for our fortunes.

Rut. *Du cat awbee*, good Count, cry, prethee cry,
O what a wench hast thou lost! cry you great booby. [*Exe.*

Enter Charino.

Clod. And is she gone then, am I dishonoured thus,
Cozened and baffl'd? my Guard there, no man answer?
My Guard I say, sirrah you knew of this plot;
Where are my Guard? I'le have your life you villain,
You politick old Thief.

Char. Heaven send her far enough,

Enter Guard.

And let me pay the ransom.

Guard. Did your honour call us?

Clod. Post every way, and presently recover
The two strange Gentlemen, and the fair Lady.

Guard. This day was Married Sir?

Clod. The same.

Guard. We saw 'em.
Making with all main speed to th' Port.

Clod. Away villains. [*Exit Guard.*
Recover her, or I shall dye; deal truly,
Didst not thou know?

Char. By all that's good I did not.
If your honour mean their flight, to say I grieve for that,
Will be to lye; you may handle me as you please.

Clod. Be sure, with all the cruelty, with all the rigor,
For thou hast rob'd me villain of a treasure.

Enter Guard.

How now?

Guard. They're all aboard, a Bark rode ready for 'em,
And now are under Sail, and past recovery.

Clod. Rig me a Ship with all the speed that may be,
I will not lose her: thou her most false Father,
Shalt go along; and if I miss her, hear me,
A whole day will I study to destroy thee.

Char. I shall be joyful of it; and so you'l find me.

[*Exeunt omnes.*

Actus Secundus. Scena Prima.

Enter Manuel du Sosa, *and* Guiomar.

Man. I Hear and see too much of him, and that
Compels me Madam, though unwillingly,
To wish I had no Uncles part in him,
And much I fear, the comfort of a Son
You will not long enjoy.

Gui. 'Tis not my fault,
And therefore from his guilt my innocence
Cannot be tainted, since his Fathers death,
(Peace to his soul) a Mothers prayers and care
Were never wanting, in his education.
His Child-hood I pass o're, as being brought up
Under my wing; and growing ripe for study,
I overcame the tenderness, and joy
I had to look upon him, and provided
The choicest Masters, and of greatest name
Of *Salamanca*, in all liberal Arts.

Man. To train his youth up.
I must witness that.

Gui. How there he prospered to the admiration
Of all that knew him, for a general Scholar,
Being one of note, before he was a man,
Is still remembred in that *Academy*,
From thence I sent him to the Emperours Court,
Attended like his Fathers Son, and there

Maintain'd him, in such bravery and height,
As did become a Courtier.
Man. 'Twas that spoil'd him, my Nephew had been happy.
The Court's a School indeed, in which some few
Learn vertuous principles, but most forget
What ever they brought thither good and honest.
Trifling is there in practice, serious actions
Are obsolete and out of use, my Nephew
Had been a happy man, had he ne're known
What's there in grace and fashion.
Gui. I have heard yet,
That while he liv'd in Court, the Emperour
Took notice of his carriage and good parts,
The Grandees did not scorn his company,
And of the greatest Ladies he was held
A compleat Gentleman.
Man. He indeed Daunc'd well;
A turn o'th' Toe, with a lofty trick or two,
To argue nimbleness, and a strong back,
Will go far with a Madam: 'tis most true,
That he's an excellent Scholar, and he knows it;
An exact Courtier, and he knows that too;
He has fought thrice, and come off still with honour,
Which he forgets not.
Gui. Nor have I much reason,
To grieve his fortune that way.
Man. You are mistaken,
Prosperity does search a Gentlemans temper,
More than his adverse fortune: I have known
Many, and of rare parts from their success
In private Duels, rais'd up to such a pride,
And so transform'd from what they were, that all
That lov'd them truly, wish'd they had fallen in them.
I need not write examples, in your Son
'Tis too apparent; for e're *Don Duarte*
Made tryal of his valour, he indeed was
Admired for civil courtesie, but now
He's swoln so high, out of his own assurance,
Of what he dares do, that he seeks occasions,
Unjust occasions, grounded on blind passion,

Ever to be in quarrels, and this makes him
Shunn'd of all fair Societies.
Gui. Would it were
In my weak power to help it: I will use
With my entreaties th' Authority of a Mother,
As you may of an Uncle, and enlarge it
With your command, as being a Governour
To the great King in *Lisbon.*

Enter Duarte *and his Page.*

Man. Here he comes.
We are unseen, observe him.
Dua. Boy.
Page. My Lord.
Dua. What saith the *Spanish* Captain that I struck,
To my bold challenge?
Page. He refus'd to read it.
Dua. Why didst not leave it there?
Page. I did my Lord,
But to no purpose, for he seems more willing
To sit down with the wrongs, than to repair
His honour by the sword; he knows too well,
That from your Lordship nothing can be got
But more blows, and disgraces.
Dua. He's a wretch,
A miserable wretch, and all my fury
Is lost upon him; holds the Mask, appointed
I'th' honour of *Hippolyta*?
Page. 'Tis broke off.
Dua. The reason?
Page. This was one, they heard your Lordship
Was by the Ladies choice to lead the Dance,
And therefore they, too well assur'd how far
You would outshine 'em, gave it o're and said,
They would not serve for foiles to set you off.
Dua. They at their best are such, and ever shall be
Where I appear.
Man. Do you note his modesty?
Dua. But was there nothing else pretended?
Page. Yes,

Young Don *Alonzo*, the great Captains Nephew,
Stood on comparisons.
Dua. With whom?
Page. With you,
And openly profess'd that all precedence,
His birth and state consider'd, was due to him,
Nor were your Lordship to contend with one
So far above you.
Dua. I look down upon him
With such contempt and scorn, as on my slave,
He's a name only, and all good in him
He must derive from his great grandsires Ashes,
For had not their victorious acts bequeath'd
His titles to him, and wrote on his forehead,
This is a Lord, he had liv'd unobserv'd
By any man of mark, and died as one
Amongst the common route. Compare with me?
'Tis Gyant-like ambition; I know him,
And know my self, that man is truly noble,
And he may justly call that worth his own,
Which his deserts have purchas'd, I could wish
My birth were more obscure, my friends and kinsmen
Of lesser power, or that my provident Father
Had been like to that riotous Emperour
That chose his belly for his only heir;
For being of no family then, and poor
My vertues wheresoe'r I liv'd, should make
That kingdom my inheritance.
Gui. Strange self Love!
Dua. For if I studied the Countries Laws,
I should so easily sound all their depth,
And rise up such a wonder, that the pleaders,
That now are in most practice and esteem,
Should starve for want of Clients: if I travell'd,
Like wise *Ulysses* to see men and manners,
I would return in act, more knowing, than
Homer could fancy him; if a Physician,
So oft I would restore death-wounded men,
That where I liv'd, *Galen* should not be nam'd,
And he that joyn'd again the scatter'd limbs

Of torn *Hippolytus* should be forgotten.
I could teach *Ovid* courtship, how to win
A *Julia*, and enjoy her, though her Dower
Were all the Sun gives light to: and for arms
Were the *Persian* host that drank up Rivers, added
To the *Turks* present powers, I could direct,
Command, and Marshal them.
Man. And yet you know not
To rule your self, you would not to a boy else
Like *Plautus* Braggart boast thus.
Dua. All I speak,
In act I can make good.
Gui. Why then being Master
Of such and so good parts do you destroy them,
With self opinion, or like a rich miser,
Hoard up the treasures you possess, imparting
Nor to your self nor others, the use of them?
They are to you but like inchanted viands,
On which you seem to feed, yet pine with hunger;
And those so rare perfections in my Son
Which would make others happy, render me
A wretched Mother.
Man. You are too insolent.
And those too many excellencies, that feed
Your pride, turn to a Pleurisie, and kill
That which should nourish vertue; dare you think
All blessings are confer'd on you alone?
Y'are grosly cousen'd; there's no good in you,
Which others have not: are you a Scholar? so
Are many, and as knowing: are you valiant?
Waste not that courage then in braules, but spend it
In the Wars, in service of your King and Country.
Dua. Yes, so I might be General, no man lives
That's worthy to command me.
Man. Sir, in *Lisbon*
I am: and you shall know it; every hour
I am troubled with complaints of your behaviour
From men of all conditions, and all sexes.
And my authority, which you presume
Will bear you out, in that you are my Nephew,

No longer shall protect you, for I vow
Though all that's past I pardon, I will punish
The next fault with as much severity
As if you were a stranger, rest assur'd on't.

Gui. And by that love you should bear, or that duty
You owe a Mother, once more I command you
To cast this haughtiness off; which if you do,
All that is mine, is yours, if not, expect
My prayers, and vows, for your conversion only,
But never means nor favour. [*Ex.* Manuel *and* Guiomar.

Dua. I am Tutor'd
As if I were a child still, the base Peasants
That fear, and envy my great worth, have done this;
But I will find them out, I will o'boord
Get my disguise; I have too long been idle,
Nor will I curb my spirit, I was born free,
And will pursue the course best liketh me. [*Exeunt.*

Enter Leopold, Sailers, *and* Zenocia.

Leop. Divide the spoil amongst you, this fair Captive
I only challenge for my self.

Sail. You have won her
And well deserve her: twenty years I have liv'd
A Burgess of the Sea, and have been present
At many a desperate fight, but never saw
So small a Bark with such incredible valour
So long defended, and against such odds,
And by two men scarce arm'd too.

Leop. 'Twas a wonder.
And yet the courage they exprest being taken,
And their contempt of death wan more upon me
Than all they did, when they were free: me thinks
I see them yet when they were brought aboard us,
Disarm'd and ready to be put in fetters
How on the suddain, as if they had sworn
Never to taste the bread of servitude,
Both snatching up their swords, and from this Virgin,
Taking a farewel only with their eyes,
They leapt into the Sea.

Sail. Indeed 'twas rare.

Leop. It wrought so much on me, that but I fear'd
The great ship that pursued us, our own safety
Hindring my charitable purpose to 'em,
I would have took 'em up, and with their lives
They should have had their liberties.
Zen. O too late,
For they are lost, for ever lost.
Leop. Take comfort
'Tis not impossible, but that they live yet,
For when they left the ships, they were within
A League o'th' shore, and with such strength and cunning
They swimming, did delude the rising Billows,
With one hand making way, and with the other,
Their bloudy swords advanced, threatning the Sea-gods
With war, unless they brought them safely off,
That I am almost confident they live,
And you again may see them.
Zen. In that hope
I brook a wretched being, till I am
Made certain of their fortunes; but they dead,
Death hath so many doors to let out life,
I will not long survive them.
Leop. Hope the best,
And let the courteous usage you have found,
Not usual in men of War perswade you
To tell me your condition.
Zen. You know it,
A Captive, my fate and your power have made me,
Such I am now, but what I was it skills not:
For they being dead, in whom I only live,
I dare not challenge Family, or Country,
And therefore Sir enquire not, let it suffice,
I am your servant, and a thankful servant
(If you will call that so, which is but duty)
I ever will be, and my honour safe,
Which nobly hitherto ye have preserv'd,
No slavery can appear in such a form,
Which with a masculine constancy I will not
Boldly look on and suffer.
Leop. You mistake me:

That you are made my prisoner, may prove
The birth of your good fortune. I do find
A winning language in your tongue and looks;
Nor can a suit by you mov'd be deni'd,
And therefore of a prisoner you must be
The Victors advocate.

Zen. To whom?

Leop. A Lady:
In whom all graces that can perfect beauty
Are friendly met. I grant that you are fair:
And had I not seen her before, perhaps
I might have sought to you.

Zen. This I hear gladly.

Leop. To this incomparable Lady I will give you,
(Yet being mine, you are already hers)
And to serve her is more than to be free,
At least I think so; and when you live with her,
If you will please to think on him that brought you
To such a happiness, for so her bounty
Will make you think her service, you shall ever
Make me at your devotion.

Zen. All I can do,
Rest you assur'd of.

Leop. At night I'le present you,
Till when I am your Guard.

Zen. Ever your servant. [*Exeunt.*

Enter Arnoldo *and* Rutilio.

Arn. To what are we reserv'd?

Rut. Troth 'tis uncertain,
Drowning we have scap'd miraculously, and
Stand fair for ought I know for hanging; mony
We have none, nor e're are like to have,
'Tis to be doubted: besides we are strangers,
Wondrous hungry strangers; and charity
Growing cold, and miracles ceasing,
Without a Conjurers help, cannot find
When we shall eat again.

Arn. These are no wants
If put in ballance with *Zenocias* loss;

In that alone all miseries are spoken:
O my *Rutilio*, when I think on her,
And that which she may suffer, being a Captive,
Then I could curse my self, almost those powers
That send me from the fury of the Ocean.

Rut. You have lost a wife indeed, a fair and chast one,
Two blessings, not found often in one woman;
But she may be recovered, questionless
The ship that took us was of *Portugal*,
And here in *Lisbon*, by some means or other
We may hear of her.

Arn. In that hope I live.

Rut. And so do I, but hope is a poor Sallad
To dine and sup with, after a two dayes fast too,
Have you no mony left?

Arn. Not a Denier.

Rut. Nor any thing to pawn? 'tis now in fashion,
Having a Mistress, sure you should not be
Without a neat Historical shirt.

Arn. For shame
Talk not so poorly.

Rut. I must talk of that
Necessity prompts us to, for beg I cannot,
Nor am I made to creep in at a window,
To filch to feed me, something must be done,
And suddenly resolve on't.

Enter Zabulon *and a Servant.*

Arn. What are these?

Rut. One by his habit is a *Jew*.

Zab. No more:
Thou art sure that's he.

Ser. Most certain.

Zab. How long is it
Since first she saw him?

Ser. Some two hours.

Zab. Be gone—let me alone to work him. [*Exit* Ser.

Rut. How he eyes you!
Now he moves towards us, in the Devils name
What would he with us?

Arn. Innocence is bold:
Nor can I fear.
Zab. That you are poor and strangers,
I easily perceive.
Rut. But that you'l help us,
Or any of your tribe, we dare not hope Sir.
Zab. Why think you so?
Rut. Because you are a *Jew* Sir,
And courtesies come sooner from the Devil
Than any of your Nation.
Zab. We are men,
And have like you, compassion when we find
Fit subjects for our bounty, and for proof
That we dare give, and freely, not to you Sir,
Pray spare your pains, there's gold, stand not amaz'd,
'Tis current I assure you.
Rut. Take it man,
Sure thy good Angel is a *Jew*, and comes
In his own shape to help thee: I could wish now
Mine would appear too like a *Turk*.
Arn. I thank you,
But yet must tell you, if this be the Prologue
To any bad act, you would have me practise,
I must not take it.
Zab. This is but the earnest
Of [t]hat which is to follow, and the bond
Which you must seal to for't, is your advancement,
Fortune with all that's in her power to give,
Offers her self up to you: entertain her,
And that which Princes have kneel'd for in vain
Presents it self to you.
Arn. 'Tis above wonder.
Zab. But far beneath the truth, in my relation
Of what you shall possess, if you emb[r]ace it.
There is an hour in each mans life appointed
To make his happiness if then he seize it,
And this, (in which, beyond all expectation,
You are invited to your good) is yours,
If you dare follow me, so, if not, hereafter
Expect not the like offer. [*Exit.*

Arn. 'Tis no vision.
Rut. 'Tis gold I'm sure.
Arn. We must like brothers share;
There's for you.
Rut. By this light I'm glad I have it:
There are few Gallants, (for men may be such
And yet want gold, yea and sometimes silver)
But would receive such favours from the Devil,
Though he appear'd like a Broker, and demanded
Sixty i'th' hundred.
Arn. Wherefore should I fear
Some plot upon my life? 'tis now to me
Not worth the keeping. I will follow him,
Farewel, wish me good fortune, we shall meet
Again I doubt not.
Rut. Or I'le ne're trust *Jew* more, [*Exit* Arnoldo.
Nor Christian for his sake—plague o' my stars,
How long might I have walkt without a Cloak,
Before I should have met with such a fortune?
We elder Brothers, though we are proper men,
Ha' not the luck, ha' too much beard, that spoils us;
The smooth Chin carries all: what's here to do now?
[*Manet* Rutilio.

Enter Duarte, Alonzo, *and a* Page.

Dua. I'le take you as I find you.
Alon. That were base—you see I am unarm'd.
Dua. Out with your Bodkin
Your Pocket-dagger, your Steletto, out with it,
Or by this hand I'le kill you: such as you are
Have studied the undoing of poor Cutlers,
And made all manly weapons out of fashion:
You carry Poniards to murder men,
Yet dare not wear a sword to guard your Honour.
Rut. That's true indeed: upon my life this gallant
Is brib'd to repeal banisht swords.
Dua. I'le shew you
The difference now between a *Spanish* Rapier
And your pure Pisa.
Alon. Let me fetch a sword,

Upon mine honour I'le return.

Dua. Not so Sir.

Alon. Or lend me yours I pray you, and take this.

Rut. To be disgrac'd as you are, no I thank you
Spight of the fashion, while I live, I am
Instructed to go arm'd: what folly 'tis
For you that are a man, to put your self
Into your enemies mercy.

Dua. Yield it quickly
Or I'le cut off your hand, and now disgrace you,
Thus kick and baffle you: as you like this,
You may again prefer complaints against me
To my Uncle and my Mother, and then think
To make it good with a Poniard.

Alon. I am paid
For being of the fashion.

Dua. Get a sword,
Then if you dare redeem your reputation:
You know I am easily found: I'le add this to it
To put you in mind.

Rut. You are too insolent,
And do insult too much on the advantage
Of that which your unequal weapon gave you,
More than your valour.

Dua. This to me, you Peasant?
Thou art not worthy of my foot poor fellow,
'Tis scorn, not pity, makes me give thee life:
Kneel down and thank me for't: how, do you stare?

Rut. I have a sword Sir, you shall find, a good one;
This is no stabbing guard.

Dua. Wert thou thrice arm'd,
Thus yet I durst attempt thee.

Rut. Then have at you, [*Fight.*
I scorn to take blows.

Dua. O I am slain. [*Falls.*

Page. Help! murther, murther!

Alon. Shift for your self you are dead else,
You have kill'd the Governou[r]s Nephew.

Page. Raise the streets there.

Alon. If once you are beset you cannot scape,

Will you betray your self?
Rut. Undone for ever. [*Exit* Rut. *and* Alonzo.

Enter Officers.

1 *Offi.* Who makes this out-cry?
Page. O my Lord is murdered;
This way he took, make after him,
Help help there. [*Exit* Page.
2 *Offi.* 'Tis *Don Duarte.*
1 *Offi.* Pride has got a fall,
He was still in quarrels, scorn'd us Peace-makers,
And all our Bill-authority, now h'as paid for't.
You ha' met with your match Sir now, bring off his body
And bear it to the Governour. Some pursue
The murderer; yet if he scape, it skills not;
Were I a Prince, I would reward him for't,
He has rid the City of a turbulent beast,
There's few will pity him: but for his Mother
I truly grieve indeed, she's a good Lady. [*Exeunt.*

Enter Guiomar *and* Servants.

Gui. He's not i'th' house?
Ser. No Madam.
Gui. Haste and seek him,
Go all and every where, I'le not to bed
Till you return him, take away the lights too,
The Moon lends me too much, to find my fears
And those devotions I am to pay
Are written in my heart, not in this book, [*Kneel.*
And I shall read them there without a Taper. [*Ex.* Ser.

Enter Rutilio.

Rut. I am pursued; all the Ports are stopt too;
Not any hope to escape, behind, before me,
On either side I am beset, cursed fortune
My enemie on the Sea, and on the Land too,
Redeem'd from one affliction to another:
Would I had made the greedy waves my tomb
And dyed obscure, and innocent, not as *Nero*
Smear'd o're with blood. Whither have my fears brought me?
I am got into a house, the doors all open,

This, by the largeness of the room, the hangings,
And other rich adornments, glistring through
The sable masque of night, sayes it belongs
To one of means and rank: no servant stirring?
Murmur nor whisper?
Guio. Who's that?
Rut. By the voice,
This is a woman.
Guio. *Stephano*, *Jaspe*, *Julia*,
Who waits there?
Rut. 'Tis the Lady of the house,
I'le flie to her protection.
Guio. Speak, what are you?
Rut. Of all that ever breath'd, a man most wretched.
Guio. I am sure you are a man of most ill manners,
You could not with so little reverence else
Press to my private chamber. Whither would you,
Or what do you seek for?
Rut. Gracious woman hear me;
I am a stranger, and in that I answer
All your demands, a most unfortunate stranger,
That call'd unto it by my enemies pride,
Have left him dead i'th' streets, Justice pursues me,
And for that life I took unwillingly,
And in a fair defence, I must lose mine,
Unless you in your charity protect me.
Your house is now my sanctuary, and the Altar,
I gladly would take hold of your sweet mercy.
By all that's dear unto you, by your vertues,
And by your innocence, that needs no forgiveness,
Take pity on me.
Guio. Are you a *Castillian*?
Rut. No Madam, *Italy* claims my birth.
Guio. I ask not
With purpose to betray you, if you were
Ten thousand times a Spaniard, the nation
We Portugals most hate, I yet would save you
If it lay in my power: lift up these hangings;
Behind my Beds head there's a hollow place,
Into which enter; so, but from this stir not

If the Officers come, as you expect they will doe,
I know they owe such reverence to my lodgings,
That they will easily give credit to me
And search no further.
    Rut. The blest Saints pay for me
The infinite debt I owe you.
    Guio. How he quakes!
Thus far I feel his heart beat, be of comfort,
Once more I give my promise for your safety,
All men are subject to such accidents,
Especially the valiant; and who knows not,
But that the charity I afford this stranger
My only Son else where may stand in need of?

Enter Officers, *and* Servants, *with the body of* Duarte—*Page.*

    1 *Ser.* Now Madam, if your wisedom ever could
Raise up defences against floods of sorrow
That haste to overwhelm you, make true use of
Your great discretion.
    2 *Ser.* Your only son
My Lord *Duart's* slain.
    1 *Off.* His murtherer, pursued by us
Was by a boy discovered
Entring your house, and that induced us
To press into it for his apprehension.
    Guio. Oh!
    1 *Ser.* Sure her heart is broke.
    Off. Madam.
    Guio. Stand off.
My sorrow is so dear and pretious to me,
That you must not partake it, suffer it
Like wounds that do breed inward to dispatch me.
O my *Duart*, such an end as this
Thy pride long since did prophesie; thou art dead,
And to encrease my misery, thy sad Mother
Must make a wilfull shipwrack of her vow
Or thou fall unreveng'd. My Soul's divided,
And piety to a son, and true performance
Of hospitable duties to my guest,
That are to others Angels, are my furies.

Vengeance knocks at my heart, but my word given
Denies the entrance, is no *Medium* left,
But that I must protect the murderer,
Or suffer in that faith he made his altar?
Motherly love give place, the fault made this way,
To keep a vow, to which high Heaven is witness,
Heaven may be pleas'd to pardon.

Enter Manuel, Doctors, Surgeons.

Man. 'Tis too late,
Hee's gone, past all recovery: now reproof
Were but unseasonable when I should give comfort,
And yet remember Sister.
Guio. O forbear,
Search for the murtherer, and remove the body,
And as you think fit, give it burial.
Wretch that I am, uncapable of all comfort,
And therefore I intreat my friends and kinsfolk,
And you my Lord, for some space to forbear
Your courteous visitations.
Man. We obey you. [*Exeunt omnes with the body.* Manet Guiomar.
Rut. My Spirits come back, and now despair resigns
Her place again to hope.
Guio. What ere thou art
To whom I have given means of life, to witness
With what Religion I have kept my promise,
Come fearless forth, but let thy face be cover'd,
That I hereafter be not forc't to know thee,
For motherly affection may return
My vow once paid to heaven. Thou hast taken from me
The respiration of my heart, the light
Of my swoln eyes, in his life that sustain'd me:
Yet my word given to save you, I make good,
Because what you did, was not done with malice,
You are not known, there is no mark about you
That can discover you; let not fear betray you.
With all convenient speed you can, flie from me
That I may never see you; and that want
Of means may be no let unto your journie,

There are a hundred Crownes: you are at the door now,
And so Farewell for ever.
Rut. Let me first fall
Before your feet, and on them pay the duty
I owe your goodness; next all blessings to you,
And Heaven restore the joyes I have bereft you,
With full increase hereafter, living be
The Goddess stil'd of Hospitalitie.

Actus Tertius. Scena Prima.

Enter Leopold, *and* Zenocia.

Leo. FLing off these sullen clouds, you are enter'd now
Into a house of joy and happiness,
I have prepar'd a blessing for ye.
Zen. Thank ye, my state would rather ask a curse.
Leo. You are peevish
And know not when ye are friended, I have us'd those means,
The Lady of this house, the noble Lady,
Will take ye as her own, and use ye graciously:
Make much of what you are, Mistris of that beautie,
And expose it not to such betraying sorrows,
When ye are old, and all those sweets hang wither'd,

Enter Servant.

Then sit and sigh.
Zen. My *Autumn* is not far off.
Leo. Have you told your Lady?
Ser. Yes Sir, I have told her
Both of your noble service, and your present,
Which she accepts.
Leo. I should be blest to see her.
Ser. That now you cannot doe: she keeps the Chamber
Not well dispos'd; and has denied all visits,
The maid I have in charge to receive from ye,
So please you render her.
Leo. With all my service,
But fain I would have seen.
Ser. 'Tis but your patience;
No doubt she cannot but remember nobly.

Leo. These three years I have lov'd this scornfull Lady,
And follow'd her with all the truth of service,
In all which time, but twice she has honour'd me
With sight of her blest beauty: when you please Sir,
You may receive your charge, and tell your Lady;
A Gentleman whose life is only dedicated
To her commands, kisses her beauteous hands;
And Faire-one, now your help, you may remember
The honest courtesies, since you are mine,
I ever did your modestie: you shall be near her,
And if sometimes you name my service to her,
And tell her with what nobleness I love her,
'Twill be a gratitude I shall remember.
Zen. What in my poor power lyes, so it be honest.
Leo. I ask no more.
Ser. You must along with me (Fair.)
Leo. And so I leave you two: but a fortune
Too happy for my fate: you shall enjoy her.

Scena Secunda.

Enter Zabulon *and* Servants.

Zab. Be quick, be quick, out with the banquet there,
These scents are dull; cast richer on, and fuller;
Scent every place, where have you plac'd the musick?
Ser. Here they stand ready Sir.
Zab. 'Tis well, be sure
The wines be lusty, high, and full of Spirit,
And Amber'd all.
Ser. They are.
Zab. Give fair attendance.
In the best trim, and state, make ready all. [*Banquet set*
I shall come presently again. *forth. Exit.*
2 *Ser.* We shall Sir,
What preparation's this?
Some new device
My Lady has in hand.
1 *Ser.* O, prosper it
As long as it carries good wine in the mouth,
And good meat with it, where are all the rest?
2 *Ser.* They are ready to attend. [*Musick.*

1 *Ser.* Sure some great person,
They would not make this hurry else.
2 *Ser.* Hark the Musick.

Enter Zabulon, *and* Arnoldo.

It will appear now certain, here it comes.
Now to our places.
Arn. Whither will he lead me?
What invitation's this? to what new end
Are these fair preparations? a rich Banquet,
Musick, and every place stuck with adornment,
Fit for a Princes welcome; what new game
Has Fortune now prepar'd to shew me happy?
And then again to sink me? 'tis no illusion,
Mine eyes are not deceiv'd, all these are reall;
What wealth and state!
Zab. Will you sit down and eat Sir?
These carry little wonder, they are usual;
But you shall see, if you be wise to observe it,
That that will strike dead, strike with amazement,
Then if you be a man: this fair health to you.
Ar. What shall I see? I pledge ye Sir, I was never
So buried in amazement—
Zab. You are so still:
Drink freely.
Ar. The very wines are admirable:
Good Sir, give me leave to ask this question,
For what great worthy man are these prepar'd?
And why do you bring me hither?
Zab. They are for you, Sir;
And under-value not the worth you carry,
You are that worthy man: think well of these,
They shall be more, and greater.
Ar. Well, blind fortune
Thou hast the prettiest changes when thou art pleas'd,
To play thy game out wantonly—
Zab. Come be lusty,
And awake your Spirits. [*Cease Musick.*
Ar. Good Sir, do not wake me.
For willingly I would dye in this dream, pray whose Servants

Are all these that attend here?
Zab. They are yours;
They wait on you.
Ar. I never yet remember
I kept such faces, nor that I was ever able
To maintain so many.
Zab. Now you are, and shall be.
Ar. You'l say this house is mine too?
Zab. Say it? swear it.
Ar. And all this wealth?
Zab. This is the least you see Sir.
Ar. Why, where has this been hid these thirtie years?
For certainly I never found I was wealthie
Till this hour, never dream'd of house, and Servants.
I had thought I had been a younger Brother, a poor Gent.
I may eat boldly then.
Zab. 'Tis prepar'd for ye.
Ar. The taste is perfect, and most delicate:
But why for me? give me some wine, I do drink;
I feel it sensibly, and I am here,
Here in this glorious place: I am bravely us'd too,
Good Gentle Sir, give me leave to think a little,
For either I am much abus'd—
Zab. Strike Musick
And sing that lusty Song. [*Musick. Song.*
Ar. Bewitching harmony!
Sure I am turn'd into another Creature.

Enter Hippolyta.

Happy and blest, *Arnoldo* was unfortunate;
Ha! bless mine eyes; what pretious piece of nature
To pose the world?
Zab. I told you, you would see that
Would darken these poor preparations;
What think ye now? nay rise not, 'tis no vision.
Ar. 'Tis more: 'tis miracle.
Hip. You are welcom Sir.
Ar. It speaks, and entertains me still more glorious;
She is warm, and this is flesh here: how she stirs me!
Bless me what stars are there?

Hip. May I sit near ye?
Ar. No, you are too pure an object to behold,
Too excellent to look upon, and live;
I must remove.
Zab. She is a woman Sir,
Fy, what faint heart is this?
Arn. The house of wonder.
Zab. Do not you think your self now truly happy?
You have the abstract of all sweetness by ye,
The precious wealth youth labours to arrive at;
Nor is she less in honour, than in beauty,
Ferrara's Royal Duke is proud to call her
His best, his Noblest, and most happy Sister,
Fortune has made her Mistress of herself,
Wealthy, and wise, without a power to sway her,
Wonder of *Italy*, of all hearts Mistress.
Arn. And all this is—
Zab. *Hippolyta* the beauteous.
Hip. You are a poor relator of my fortunes,
Too weak a Chronicle to speak my blessings,
And leave out that essential part of story
I am most high and happy in, most fortunate,
The acquaintance, and the noble fellowship
Of this fair Gentleman: pray ye do not wonder,
Nor hold it strange to hear a handsome Lady
Speak freely to ye: with your fair leave and courtesie
I will sit by ye.
Arn. I know not what to answer,
Nor where I am, nor to what end consider;
Why do you use me thus?
Hip. Are ye angry Sir,
Because ye are entertain'd with all humanity?
Freely and nobly us'd?
Arn. No gentle Lady,
That were uncivil, but it much amazes me
A stranger, and a man of no desert
Should find such floods of courtesie.
Hip. I love ye,
I honour ye, the first and best of all men,
And where that fair opinion leads, 'tis usual

These trifles that but serve to set off, follow.
I would not have you proud now, nor disdainful
Because I say I love ye, though I swear it,
Nor think it a stale favour I fling on ye,
Though ye be handsome, and the only man
I must confess I ever fixt mine eye on,
And bring along all promises that please us,
Yet I should hate ye then, despise ye, scorn ye,
And with as much contempt pursue your person,
As now I do with love. But you are wiser,
At least I think, more master of your fortune,
And so I drink your health.

Arn. Hold fast good honesty,
I am a lost man else.

Hip. Now you may kiss me,
'Tis the first kiss, I ever askt, I swear to ye.

Arn. That I dare do sweet Lady.

Hip. You do it well too;
You are a Master Sir, that makes you coy.

Arn. Would you would send your people off.

Hip. Well thought on.
Wait all without. [*Exit* Zab. *and Servants.*

Zab. I hope she is pleas'd throughly.

Hip. Why stand ye still? here's no man to detect ye,
My people are gone off: come, come, leave conjuring,
The Spirit you would raise, is here already,
Look boldly on me.

Arn. What would you have me do?

Hip. O most unmanly question! have you do?
Is't possible your years should want a Tutor?
I'le teach ye: come, embrace me.

Arn. Fye stand off;
And give me leave, more now than e're, to wonder,
A building of so goodly a proportion,
Outwardly all exact, the frame of Heaven,
Should hide within so base inhabitants?
You are as fair, as if the morning bare ye,
Imagination never made a sweeter;
Can it be possible this frame should suffer,
And built on slight affections, fright the viewer?

Be excellent in all, as you are outward,
The worthy Mistress of those many blessings
Heaven has bestowed, make 'em appear still nobler,
Because they are trusted to a weaker keeper.
Would ye have me love ye?

Hip. Yes.

Arn. Not for your beauty;
Though I confess, it blowes the first fire in us,
Time as he passes by, puts out that sparkle;
Nor for your wealth, although the world kneel to it,
And make it all addition to a woman,
Fortune that ruines all, makes that his conquest;
Be honest, and be vertuous, I'le admire ye,
At least be wise, and where ye lay these nets,
Strow over 'em a little modesty,
'Twill well become your cause, and catch more Fools.

Hip. Could any one that lov'd this wholesome counsel
But love the giver more? you make me fonder:
You have a vertuous mind, I want that ornament;
Is it a sin I covet to enjoy ye?
If ye imagine I am too free a Lover,
And act that part belongs to you, I am silent:
Mine eyes shall speak my blushes, parly with ye;
I will not touch your hand, but with a tremble
Fitting a Vestal Nun; not long to kiss ye,
But gently as the Air, and undiscern'd too,
I'le steal it thus: I'le walk your shadow by ye,
So still and silent that it shall be equal,
To put me off, as that, and when I covet,
To give such toyes as these—

Arn. A new temptation—

Hip. Thus like the lazie minutes will I drop 'em,
Which past once are forgotten.

Arn. Excellent vice!

Hip. Will ye be won? look stedfastly upon me,
Look manly, take a mans affections to you;
Young women, in the old world were not wont, Sir,
To hang out gaudy bushes for their beauties,
To talk themselves into young mens affections;
How cold and dull you are!

Arn. How I stagger!
She is wise, as fair; but 'tis a wicked wisdom;
I'le choak before I yield.
Hip. Who waits within there? [Zabulon *within.*
Make ready the green Chamber.
Zab. It shall be Madam.
Arn. I am afraid she will injoy me indeed.
Hip. What Musick do ye love?
Arn. A modest tongue.
Hip. We'l have enough of that: fye, fye, how lumpish!
In a young Ladyes arms thus dull?
Arn. For Heaven sake
Profess a little goodness.
Hip. Of what Country?
Arn. I am of *Rome.*
Hip. Nay then I know you mock me,
The *Italians* are not frighted with such bug-bears,
Prethee go in.
Arn. I am not well.
Hip. I'le make thee,
I'le kiss thee well.
Arn. I am not sick of that sore.
Hip. Upon my Conscience, I must ravish thee,
I shall be famous for the first example:
With this I'le tye ye first, then try your strength Sir.
Arn. My strength? away base woman, I abhor thee.
I am not caught with stales, disease dwell with thee. [*Exit.*
Hip. Are ye so quick? and have I lost my wishes?
Hoe, *Zabulon*; my servants.

Enter Zabulon *and* Servants.

Zab. Call'd ye Madam?
Hip. Is all that beauty scorned, so many su'd for;
So many Princes? by a stranger too?
Must I endure this?
Zab. Where's the Gentleman?
Hip. Go presently, pursue the stranger, *Zabulon.*
He has broke from me, Jewels I have given him:
Charge him with theft: he has stoln my love, my freedome,
Draw him before the Governour, imprison him,

Why dost thou stay?
Zab. I'le teach him a new dance,
For playing fast and loose with such a Lady.
Come fellows, come: I'le execute your anger,
And to the full.
Hip. His scorn shall feel my vengeance.— [*Exeunt.*

Scena Tertia.

Enter Sulpicia *and* Jaques.

Sul. Shall I never see a lusty man again?
Ja. Faith Mistress
You do so over-labour 'em when you have 'em,
And so dry-founder 'em, they cannot last.
Sul. Where's the *French*-man?
Ja. Alas, he's all to fitters,
And lyes, taking the height of his fortune with a Syringe.
He's chin'd, he's chin'd good man, he is a mourner.
Sul. What's become of the *Dane*?
Ja. Who? goldy-locks?
He's foul i'th' touch-hole; and recoils again,
The main Spring's weaken'd that holds up his cock,
He lies at the sign of the *Sun*, to be new breech'd.
Sul. The Rutter too, is gone.
Ja. O that was a brave Rascal,
He would labour like a Thrasher: but alas
What thing can ever last? he has been ill mew'd,
And drawn too soon; I have seen him in the Hospital.
Sul. There was an *English*-man.
Ja. I there was an *English*-man;
You'l scant find any now, to make that name good:
There were those *English* that were men indeed,
And would perform like men, but now they are vanisht:
They are so taken up in their own Country,
And so beaten of their speed by their own women,
When they come here, they draw their legs like Hackneys:
Drink, and their own devices have undone 'em.
Sul. I must have one that's strong, no life in *Lisbon* else,
Perfect and young: my Custom with young Ladies,
And high fed City dames, will fall, and break else.

I want my self too, in mine age to nourish me:
They are all sunk I mantain'd: now what's this business,
What goodly fellow's that?

Enter Rutilio *and* Officers.

Rut. Why do you drag me?
Pox o' your justice; let me loose.
1 *Offi.* Not so Sir.
Rut. Cannot a man fall into one of your drunken Cellars,
And venture the breaking on's neck, your trap-doors open,
But he must be us'd thus rascally?
1 *Offi.* What made you wandring
So late i'th' night? you know that is imprisonment.
Rut. May be I walk in my sleep.
2 *Offi.* May be we'l walk ye.
What made you wandring Sir, into that vault
Where all the City store, and the Munition lay?
Rut. I fell into it by chance, I broke my shins for't:
Your worships feel not that: I knockt my head
Against a hundred posts, would you had had it.
Cannot I break my neck in my own defence?
2 *Offi.* This will not serve: you cannot put it off so,
Your coming thither was to play the villain,
To fire the Powder, to blow up that part o'th' City.
Rut. Yes, with my nose: why were the trap-doors open?
Might not you fall, or you, had you gone that way?
I thought your City had sunk.
1 *Offi.* You did your best Sir,
We must presume, to help it into th' Air,
If you call that sinking: we have told you what's the law,
He that is taken there, unless a Magistrate,
And have command in that place, presently
If there be nothing found apparent near him
Worthy his torture, or his present death,
Must either pay his fine for his presumption,
(Which is six hundred Duckets) or for six years
Tug at an Oar i'th' Gallies: will ye walk Sir,
For we presume you cannot pay the penalty.
Rut. Row in the Gallies, after all this mischief?
2 *Offi.* May be you were drunk, they'l keep you sober there.

Rut. Tug at an Oar? you are not arrant rascals,
To catch me in a pit-fall, and betray me?
Sul. A lusty minded man.
Ja. A wondrous able.
Sul. Pray Gentlemen, allow me but that liberty
To speak a few words with your prisoner,
And I shall thank you.
1 *Offi.* Take your pleasure Lady.
Sul. What would you give that woman should redeem ye,
Redeem ye from this slavery?
Rut. Besides my service
I would give her my whole self, I would be her vassal.
Sul. She has reason to expect as much, considering
The great sum she pays for't, yet take comfort,
What ye shall do to merit this, is easie,
And I will be the woman shall befriend ye,
'Tis but to entertain some handsome Ladies,
And young fair Gentlewomen: you guess the way:
But giving of your mind—
Rut. I am excellent at it:
You cannot pick out such another living.
I understand ye: is't not thus?
Sul. Ye have it.
Rut. Bring me a hundred of 'em: I'le dispatch 'em.
I will be none but yours: should another offer
Another way to redeem me, I should scorn it.
What women you shall please: I am monstrous lusty:
Not to be taken down: would you have Children?
I'le get you those as fast, and thick as flie-blows.
Sul. I admire him: wonder at him!
Rut. Hark ye Lady,
You may require sometimes—
Sul. I by my faith.
Rut. And you shall have it by my faith, and handsomly:
This old Cat will suck shrewdly: you have no Daughters?
I flye at all: now am I in my Kingdom.
Tug at an Oar? no, tug in a Feather-bed,
With good warm Caudles; hang your bread and water,
I'le make you young again, believe that Lady.
I will so frubbish you.

Sul. Come, follow Officers,
This Gentleman is free: I'le pay the Duckets.
Rut. And when you catch me in your City-powdring-tub
Again, boil me with Cabbidge.
1 *Offi.* You are both warn'd and arm'd Sir. [*Exeunt.*

Scena Quarta.

Enter Leopold, Hippolyta, Zenocia.

Zen. Will your Ladyship wear this Dressing?
Hip. Leave thy prating:
I care not what I wear.
Zen. Yet 'tis my duty
To know your pleasure, and my worst affliction
To see you discontented.
Hip. Weeping too?
Prethee forgive me: I am much distemper'd,
And speak I know not what: to make thee amends
The Gown that I wore yesterday, is thine;
Let it alone awhile.
Leo. Now you perceive,
And taste her bounty.
Zen. Much above my merit.
Leo. But have you not yet found a happy time
To move for me.
Zen. I have watched all occasions,
But hitherto, without success: yet doubt not
But I'le embrace the first means.
Leo. Do, and prosper:
Excellent creature, whose perfections make
Even sorrow lovely, if your frowns thus take me,
What would your smiles doe?
Hip. Pox o' this stale Courtship:
If I have any power.
Leo. I am commanded,
Obedience is the Lovers sacrifice
Which I pay gladly.
Hip. To be forc'd to wooe,
Being a woman, could not but torment me,
But bringing for my advocates, youth and beauty,

Set off with wealth, and then to be deni'd too
Do's comprehend all tortures. They flatter'd me,
That said my looks were charms, my touches fetters,
My locks soft chains, to bind the arms of Princes,
And make them in that wish'd for bondage, happy.
I am like others of a coarser feature,
As weak to allure, but in my dotage, stronger:
I am no *Circe*; he, more than *Ulysses*,
Scorns all my offer'd bounties, slights my favours,
And, as I were some new Egyptian, flyes me,
Leaving no pawn, but my own shame behind him.
But he shall finde, that in my fell revenge,
I am a woman: one that never pardons
The rude contemner of her proffered sweetness.

Enter Zabulon.

Zab. Madam, 'tis done.
Hip. What's done?
Zab. The uncivill stranger
Is at your suite arrested.
Hip. 'Tis well handled.
Zab. And under guard sent to the Governour,
With whom my testimony, and the favour
He bears your Ladiship, have so prevail'd
That he is sentenc'd.
Hip. How?
Zab. To lose his head.
Hip. Is that the means to quench the scorching heat
Of my inrag'd desires? must innocence suffer,
'Cause I am faulty? or is my Love so fatall
That of necessity it must destroy
The object it most longs for? dull *Hippolyta*,
To think that injuries could make way for love,
When courtesies were despis'd: that by his death
Thou shouldst gain that, which only thou canst hope for
While he is living: My honour's at the stake now,
And cannot be preserv'd, unless he perish,
The enjoying of the thing I love, I ever
Have priz'd above my fame: why doubt I now then?
One only way is left me, to redeem all:
Make ready my Caroch.

Leo. What will you Madam?
Hip. And yet I am impatient of such stay:
Bind up my hair: fye, fye, while that is doing
The Law may seise his life: thus as I am then,
Not like *Hippolyta*, but a *Bacchanall*
My frantique Love transports me. [*Exit.*
Leo. Sure she's distracted.
Zab. Pray you follow her: I will along with you:
I more than ghess the cause: women that love
Are most uncertain, and one minute crave,
What in another they refuse to have. [*Exit.*

Scena Quinta.

Enter Clodio, Charino.

Clo. Assure thy self *Charino*, I am alter'd
From what I was; the tempests we have met with
In our uncertain voyage, were smooth gales
Compar'd to those, the memory of my lusts
Rais'd in my Conscience: and if ere again
I live to see *Zenocia*, I will sue,
And seek to her as a Lover, and a Servant,
And not command affection, like a Tyrant.
Char. In hearing this, you make me young again,
And Heaven, it seems, favouring this good change in you
In setting of a period to our dangers
Gives us fair hopes to find that here in *Lisbon*
Which hitherto in vain we long have sought for.
I have receiv'd assur'd intelligence,
Such strangers have been seen here: and though yet
I cannot learn their fortunes, nor the place
Of their abode, I have a Soul presages
A fortunate event here.
Clo. There have pass'd
A mutual enterchange of courtesies
Between me, and the Governour; therefore boldly
We may presume of him, and of his power
If we finde cause to use them, otherwise
I would not be known here, and these disguises
Will keep us from discovery.

Enter Manuel, Doctor, Arnoldo, Guard.

Char. What are these?
Clo. The Governour: with him my Rival, bound.
Char. For certain 'tis *Arnoldo.*
Clo. Let's attend
What the success will be.
Mar. Is't possible
There should be hope of his recovery,
His wounds so many and so deadly?
Doct. So they appear'd at first, but the blood stop'd,
His trance forsook him, and on better search
We found they were not mortal.
Man. Use all care
To perfect this unhop'd for cure: that done
Propose your own rewards: and till you shall
Hear farther from me, for some ends I have,
Conceal it from his Mother.
Doct. Wee'l not fail Sir. [*Exit.*
Man. You still stand confident on your innocence.
Arn. It is my best and last guard, which I will not
Leave, to relye on your uncertain mercy.

Enter Hippolyta, Zabulon, Leopold, Zenocia, 2 Servants.

Hip. Who bad you follow me! Goe home, and you Sir,
As you respect me, goe with her.
Arn. *Zenocia!*
And in her house a Servant!
Char. 'Tis my Daughter.
Clo. My love? Contain your joy, observe the sequel. [*Zen.*
Man. Fye Madam, how undecent 'tis for you, (*passes.*
So far unlike your self to bee seen thus
In th' open streets? why do you kneel? pray you rise,
I am acquainted with the wrong, and loss
You have sustain'd, and the Delinquent now
Stands ready for his punishment.
Hip. Let it fall, Sir,
On the offender: he is innocent,
And most unworthy of these bonds he wears,
But I made up of guilt.

Man. What strange turn's this?
Leo. This was my prisoner once.
Hip. If chastity
In a young man, and tempted to the height too
Did ere deserve reward, or admiration,
He justly may claim both. Love to his person
(Or if you please give it a fouler name)
Compel'd me first to train him to my house,
All engines I rais'd there to shake his vertue,
Which in the assault were useless; he unmov'd still
As if he had no part of humane frailty.
Against the nature of my Sex, almost
I plaid the Ravisher. You might have seen
In our contention, young *Apollo* fly
And love-sick *Daphne* follow, all arts failing,
By flight he wan the victory, breaking from
My scorn'd embraces: the repulse (in women
Unsufferable) invited me to practise
A means to be reveng'd: and from this grew
His Accusation, and the abuse
Of your still equall justice: My rage ever
Thanks heaven, though wanton, I found not my self
So far engag'd to Hell, to prosecute
To the death what I had plotted, for that love
That made me first desire him, then accuse him,
Commands me with the hazard of my self
First to entreat his pardon, then acquit him.
Man. What ere you are, so much I love your vertue,
That I desire your friendship: do you unloose him
From those bonds, you are worthy of: your repentance
Makes part of satisfaction; yet I must
Severely reprehend you.
Leo. I am made
A stale on all parts: But this fellow shall
Pay dearly for her favour.
Arn. My life's so full
Of various changes, that I now despair
Of any certain port; one trouble ending,
A new, and worse succeeds it: what should *Zenocia*
Do in this womans house? Can chastity

And hot Lust dwell together without infection?
I would not be or jealous, or secure,
Yet something must be done, to sound the depth on't:
That she lives is my bliss, but living there,
A hell of torments; there's no way to her
In whom I live, but by this door, through which
To me 'tis death to enter, yet I must,
And will make tryal.

Man. Let me hear no more
Of these devices, Lady: this I pardon,
And at your intercession I forgive
Your instrument the Jew too: get you home.
The hundred thousand crowns you lent the City
Towards the setting forth of the last Navy
Bound for the Islands, was a good then, which
I ballance with your ill now.

Char. Now Sir, to him,
You know my Daughter needs it.

Hip. Let me take
A farewell with mine eye, Sir, though my lip
Be barr'd the Ceremonie, courtesie
And Custom too allows of.

Arn. Gentle Madam,
I neither am so cold, nor so ill bred
But that I dare receive it: you are unguarded,
And let me tell you that I am asham'd
Of my late rudeness, and would gladly therefore
If you please to accept my ready service
Wait on you to your house.

Hip. Above my hope:
Sir, if an Angel were to be my convoy,
He should not be more welcom.— [*Ex.* Arn. *and* Hip.

Clo. Now you know me.

Man. Yes Sir, and honour you: ever remembring
Your many bounties, being ambitious only
To give you cause to say by some one service
That I am not ungratefull.

Clod. 'Tis now offer'd:
I have a suit to you, and an easie one,
Which e're long you shall know.

Man. When you think fit Sir,
And then as a command I will receive it,
Till when, most welcom: you are welcom too Sir,
'Tis spoken from the heart, and therefore needs not
Much protestation: at your better leisure
I will enquire the cause that brought you hither:
In the mean time serve you.
Clod. You out-doe me Sir. [*Exeunt.*

Actus Quartus. Scena Prima.

Enter Duarte, Doctor.

Dua. YOU have bestow'd on me a second life,
For which I live your creature, and have better'd
What nature fram'd unperfect, my first being
Insolent pride made monstrous; but this later
In learning me to know my self, hath taught me
Not to wrong others.
Doct. Then we live indeed,
When we can goe to rest without alarm
Given every minute to a guilt-sick conscience
To keep us waking, and rise in the morning
Secure in being innocent: but when
In the remembrance of our worser actions
We ever bear about us whips and furies,
To make the day a night of sorrow to us,
Even life's a burthen.
Dua. I have found and felt it;
But will endeavour having first made peace
With those intestine enemies my rude passions,
To be so with man-kind: but worthy Doctor,
Pray if you can resolve me; was the Gentleman
That left me dead, ere brought unto his tryal?
Doct. Not known, nor apprehended.
Dua. That's my grief.
Doct. Why, do you wish he had been punished?
Dua. No,
The stream of my swoln sorrow runs not that way:
For could I find him, as I vow to Heaven

It shall be my first care to seek him out,
I would with thanks acknowledge that his sword,
In opening my veins, which proud bloud poison'd,
Gave the first symptoms of true health.
Doct. 'Tis in you
A Christian resolution: that you live
Is by the Governours, your Uncles charge
As yet conceal'd. And though a sons loss never
Was solemniz'd with more tears of true sorrow
Than have been paid by your unequal'd Mother
For your supposed death, she's not acquainted
With your recovery.
Dua. For some few dayes
Pray let her so continue: thus disguis'd
I may abroad unknown.
Doct. Without suspicion
Of being discovered
Dua. I am confident
No moisture sooner dies than womens tears,
And therefore though I know my Mother vertuous,
Yet being one of that frail sex I purpose
Her farther tryal.
Doct. That as you think fit—I'le not betray you.
Dua. To find out this stranger
This true Physician of my mind and manners
Were such a blessing. He seem'd poor, and may
Perhaps be now in want; would I could find him.
The Innes I'le search first, then the publick Stewes;
He was of *Italy*, and that Country breeds not
Precisians that way, but hot Libertines;
And such the most are: 'tis but a little travail:
I am unfurnisht too, pray M^r^. Doctor,
Can you supply me?
Doct. With what summ you please.
Dua. I will not be long absent.
Doct. That I wish too;
For till you have more strength, I would not have you
To be too bold.
Dua. Fear not, I will be carefull. [*Exeunt.*

Enter Leopold, Zabulon, Bravo.

Zab. I have brought him Sir, a fellow that will do it
Though Hell stood in his way, ever provided
You pay him for't.
Leop. He has a strange aspect,
And looks much like the figure of a hang-man
In a table of the Passion.
Zab. He transcends
All precedents, believe it, a flesh'd ruffian,
That hath so often taken the Strappado,
That 'tis to him but as a lofty trick
Is to a tumbler: he hath perused too
All Dungeons in *Portu*[*g*]*al*, thrice seven years
Rowed in the Galleys for three several murthers,
Though I presume that he has done a hundred,
And scap't unpunisht.
Leop. He is much in debt to you,
You set him off so well. What will you take Sir
To beat a fellow for me, that thus wrong'd me?
Bra. To beat him say you?
Leop. Yes, beat him to lameness,
To cut his lips or nose off; any thing,
That may disfigure him.
Bra. Let me consider?
Five hundred pistolets for such a service
I think were no dear penniworth.
Zab. Five hundred!
Why there are of your Brother-hood in the City,
I'le undertake, shall kill a man for twenty.
Bra. Kill him? I think so; I'le kill any man
For half the mony.
Leop. And will you ask more
For a sound beating than a murther?
Bra. I Sir,
And with good reason, for a dog that's dead,
The Spanish proverb says, will never bite:
But should I beat or hurt him only, he may
Recover, and kill me.
Leo. A good conclusion,

The obduracie of this rascal makes me tender.
I'le run some other course, there's your reward
Without the employment.

Bra. For that as you please Sir;
When you have need to kill a man, pray use me,
But I am out at beating. [*Exit.*

Zab. What's to be done then?

Leop. I'le tell thee *Zabulon*, and make thee privy
To my most near designs: this stranger, which
Hippolyta so dotes on, was my prisoner
When the last Virgin, I bestowed upon her,
Was made my prize; how he escaped, hereafter
I'le let thee know; and it may be the love
He bears the servant, makes him scorn the Mistris.

Zab. 'Tis not unlike; for the first time he saw her
His looks exprest so much, and for more proof
Since he came to my Ladys house, though yet
He never knew her, he hath practis'd with me
To help him to a conference, without
The knowledge of *Hippolyta*; which I promis'd.

Leop. And by all means perform it for their meeting,
But work it so, that my disdainful Mistris
(Whom, notwithstanding all her injuries,
'Tis my hard fate to love) may see and hear them.

Zab. To what end Sir?

Leop. This *Zabulon*: when she sees
Who is her rival, and her Lovers baseness
To leave a Princess for her bondwoman,
The sight will make her scorn, what now she dotes on,
I'le double thy reward.

Zab. You are like to speed then:
For I confess what you will soon believe,
We serve them best that are most apt to give.
For you, I'le place you where you shall see all, and yet be (unobserv'd.

Leop. That I desire too. [*Exeunt.*

Enter Arnoldo.

Arn. I cannot see her yet, how it afflicts me
The poyson of this place should mix it self
With her pure thoughts? 'Twas she that was commanded,

Or my eyes failed me grosly; that youth, that face
And all that noble sweetness. May she not live here,
And yet be honest still?

Enter Zenocia.

Zen. It is *Arnoldo*,
From all his dangers free; fortune I bless thee.
My noble husband! how my joy swells in me,
But why in this place? what business hath he here?
He cannot hear of me, I am not known here.
I left him vertuous; how I shake to think now!
And how that joy I had, cools, and forsakes me!

Enter above Hippolyta *and* Zabulon.

This Lady is but fair, I have been thought so
Without compare admired; She has bewitched him
And he forgot—
Arn. 'Tis she again, the same—the same *Zenocia.*
Zab. There they are together.—Now you may mark.
Hip. Peace, let 'em parly.
Arn. That you are well *Zenocia*, and once more
Bless my despairing eyes, with your wisht presence,
I thank the gods; but that I meet you here—
Hip. They are acquainted.
Zab. I found that secret Madam,
When you co[m]manded her go home: pray hear 'em.
Zen. That you meet me here, ne're blush at that *Arnoldo.*
Your coming comes too late: I am a woman,
And one woman with another may be trusted;
Do you fear the house?
Arn. More than a fear, I know it,
Know it not good, not honest.
Zen. What do you here then?
I'th' name of vertue why do you approach it?
Will you confess the doubt and yet pursue it?
Where have your eyes been wandring, my *Arnoldo*?
What constancy, what faith do you call this? Fie,
Aim at one wanton mark, and wound another?

I do confess, the Lady fair, most beauteous,
And able to betray a strong mans liberty,
But you that have a love, a wife—you do well
To deal thus wisely with me: yet *Arnoldo*,
Since you are pleas'd to study a new beauty,
And think this old and ill, beaten with misery,
Study a nobler way for shame to love me,
Wrong not her honesty.

Leopold places himself unseen below.

Arn. You have confirm'd me.

Zen. Who though she be your wife, will never hinder (you,
So much I rest a servant to your wishes,
And love your Loves, though they be my destructions,
No man shall know me, nor the share I have in thee,
No eye suspect I am able to prevent you,
For since I am a slave to this great Lady,
Whom I perceive you follow,

Arn. Be not blinded.

Zen. Fortune shall make me useful to your service,
I will speak for you.

Arn. Speak for me? you wrong me.

Zen. I will endeavour all the wayes I am able
To make her think well of you; will that please?
To make her dote upon you, dote to madness,
So far against my self I will obey you.
But when that's done, and I have shewed this duty,
This great obedience, few will buy it at my price,
Thus will I shake hands with you, wish you well,
But never see you more, nor receive comfort
From any thing, *Arnoldo*.

Arn. You are too tender;
I neither doubt you, nor desire longer
To be a man, and live, than I am honest
And only yours; our infinite affections
Abus'd us both.

Zab. Where are your favours now?
The courtesies you shew'd this stranger, Madam?

Hip. Have I now found the cause?

Zab. Attend it further.

Zen. Did she invite you, do you say?

Arn. Most cunningly,

And with a preparation of that state
I was brought in and welcom'd.
Zen. Seem'd to love you?
Arn. Most infinitely, at first sight, most dotingly.
Zen. She is a goodly Lady.
Arn. Wondrous handsom:
At first view, being taken unprepar'd,
Your memory not present then to assist me,
She seem'd so glorious sweet, and so far stir'd me,
Nay be not jealous, there's no harm done.
Zen. Prethee—didst thou not kiss, *Arnoldo*?
Arn. Yes faith did I.
Zen. And then—
Arn. I durst not, did not—
Zen. I forgive you,
Come tell the truth.
Arn. May be I lay with her.
Hip. He mocks me too, most basely.
Zen. Did ye faith? did ye forget so far?
Arn. Come, come, no weeping;
I would have lyen first in my grave, believe that.
Why will you ask those things you would not hear?
She is too untemperate to betray my vertues,
Too openly lascivious: had she dealt
But with that seeming modesty she might,
And flung a little Art upon her ardor,
But 'twas forgot, and I forgot to like her,
And glad I was deceiv'd. No my *Zenocia*,
My first love here begun, rests here unreapt yet,
And here for ever.
Zen. You have made me happy,
Even in the midst of bondage blest.
Zab. You see now
What rubs are in your way.
Hip. And quickly *Zabulon*
I'le root 'em out.—Be sure you do this presently.
Zab. Do not you alter then.
Hip. I am resolute. [*Exit* Zabulon.
Arn. To see you only I came hither last,
Drawn by no love of hers, nor base allurements,

For by this holy light I hate her heartily.

Leop. I am glad of that, you have sav'd me so much
And so much fear, (vengeance
From this hour fair befal you.

Arn. Some means I shall make shortly to redeem you,
Till when, observe her well, and fit her temper,
Only her lust contemn.

Zen. When shall I see you?

Arn. I will live hereabouts, and bear her fair still,
Till I can find a fit hour to redeem you.

Hip. Shut all the doors.

Arn. Who's that?

Zen. We are betray'd,
The Lady of the house has heard our parly,
Seen us, and seen our Loves.

Hip. You courteous Gallant,
You that scorn all I can bestow, that laugh at
The afflictions, and the groans I suffer for you,
That slight and jeer my love, contemn the fortune
My favours can fling on you, have I caught you?
Have I now found the cause? ye fool my wishes;
Is mine own slave, my bane? I nourish that
That sucks up my content. I'le pray no more,
Nor wooe no more; thou shalt see foolish man,
And to thy bitter pain and anguish, look on
The vengeance I shall take, provok'd and slighted;
Redeem her then, and steal her hence: ho *Zabulon*
Now to your work.

Enter Zabulon, *and* Servants, *some holding* Arnoldo, *some ready with a cord to strangle Zenocia.*

Arn. Lady, but hear me speak first,
As you have pity.

Hip. I have none. You taught me,
When I even hung about your neck, you scorn'd me.

Zab. Shall we pluck yet?

Hip. No, hold a little *Zabulon*,
I'le pluck his heart-strings first: now am I worthy
A little of your love?

Arn. I'le be your Servant,

Command me through what danger you shall aime at,
Let it be death.
Hip. Be sure Sir, I shall fit you.
Arn. But spare this Virgin.
Hip. I would spare that villain first,
Had cut my Fathers throat.
Arn. Bounteous Lady,
If in your sex there be that noble softness,
That tenderness of heart, women are crown'd for—
Zen. Kneel not *Arnoldo*, doe her not that honour,
She is not worthy such submission,
I scorn a life depends upon her pity.
Proud woman do thy worst, and arm thy anger
With thoughts as black as Hell, as hot and bloody,
I bring a patience here, shall make 'em blush,
An innocence, shall outlook thee, and death too.
Arn. Make me your slave, I give my freedom to ye,
For ever to be fetter'd to your service;
'Twas I offended, be not so unjust then,
To strike the innocent, this gentle maid
Never intended fear and doubt against you:
She is your Servant, pay not her observance
With cruel looks, her duteous faith with death.
Hip. Am I fair now? now am I worth your liking?
Zen. Not fair, not to be liked, thou glorious Devil,
Thou vernisht piece of lust, thou painted fury.
Arn. Speak gently sweet, speak gently.
Zen. I'le speak nobly.
'Tis not the saving of a life I aim at,
Mark me lascivious woman, mark me truly,
And then consider, how I weigh thy anger.
Life is no longer mine, nor dear unto me,
Than usefull to his honour I preserve it.
If thou hadst studied all the courtesies
Humanity and noble blood are linkt to,
Thou couldst not have propounded such a benefit,
Nor heapt upon me such unlookt for honour
As dying for his sake, to be his Martyr,
'Tis such a grace.
Hip. You shall not want that favour,

Let your bones work miracles.
Arn. Dear Lady
By those fair eyes—
Hip. There is but this way left ye
To save her life.—
Arn. Speak it, and I embrace it.
Hip. Come to my private chamber presently,
And there, what love and I command—
Arn. I'le doe it,
Be comforted *Zenocia.*
Zen. Do not do this
To save me, do not lose your self I charge you,
I charge you by your love, that love [you] bear me;
That love, that constant love you have twin'd to me,
By all your promises, take heed you keep 'em,
Now is your constant tryal. If thou dost this,
Or mov'st one foot, to guide thee to her lust,
My curses and eternal hate pursue thee.
Redeem me at the base price of dis-loyalty?
Must my undoubted honesty be thy Bawd too?
Go and intwine thy self about that body;
Tell her, for my life thou hast lost thine honour,
Pull'd all thy vows from heaven, basely, most basely
Stoop'd to the servile flames of that foul woman,
To add an hour to me that hate thee for it,
Know thee not again, nor name thee for a Husband.
Arn. What shall I do to save her?
Hip. How now, what hast there?

Enter a Servant.

Ser. The Governour, attended with some Gentlemen,
Are newly entred, to speak with your Ladiship.
Hip. Pox o' their business, reprieve her for this hour,
I shall have other time.
Arn. Now fortune help us.
Hip. I'le meet 'em presently: retire awhile all. [*Exeunt.*
Zab. You rise to day upon your right side Lady;
You know the danger too, and may prevent it,
And if you suffer her to perish thus,
As she must do, and suddenly, believe it,

Unless you stand her friend; you know the way on't,
I guess you poorly love her, less your fortune.
Let her know nothing, and perform this matter,
There are hours ordained for several businesses,
You understand.

Arn. I understand you Bawd Sir,
And such a Counsellour I never car'd for.

Enter the Governour, Clodio, Leopold, Charino *and* Attendants *at one door*, Hippolyta *at the other*.

Hip. Your Lordship does me honour.

Gover. Fair *Hippolyta*,
I am come to ease you of a charge.

Hip. I keep none
I count a burthen Sir: and yet I lye too.

Gover. Which is the Maid; is she here?

Clod. Yes Sir,
This is she, this is *Zenocia*,
The very same I sued to your Lordship for.

Zen. *Clodio* again? more misery? more ruin?
Under what angry star is my life govern'd?

Gov. Come hither Maid, you are once more a free woman,
Here I discharge your bonds.

Arn. Another smile,
Another trick of fortune to betray us!

Hip. Why does your Lordship use me so unnobly?
Against my will to take away my bond-woman?

Gov. She was no lawful prize, therefore no bond-woman:
She's of that Country we hold friendship with,
And ever did, and therefore to be used
With entertainment, fair and courteous.
The breach of League in us gives foul example,
Therefore you must be pleas'd to think this honest;
Did you know what she was?

Leop. Not till this instant;
For had I known her, she had been no prisoner.

Gov. There, take the Maid, she is at her own dispose now,
And if there be ought else to do your honour
Any poor service in—

Clod. I am vowed your servant.

Arn. Your Father's here too, that's our only comfort,
And in a Country now, we stand free people,
Where *Clodio* has no power, be comforted.

Zen. I fear some trick yet.

Arn. Be not so dejected.

Gover. You must not be displeas'd; so farewel Lady.
Come Gentlemen; Captain, you must with me too,
I have a little business.

Leop. I attend your Lordship:
Now my way's free, and my hope's Lord again.

[*Exeunt all but* Hip. *and* Zab.

Hip. D'ye jeer me now ye are going?
I may live yet—to make you howl both.

Zab. You might have done; you had power then,
But now the chains are off, the command lost,
And such a story they will make of this
To laugh out lazie time.

Hip. No means yet left me?
For now I burst with anger: none to satisfie me?
No comfort? no revenge?

Zab. You speak too late;
You might have had all these, your useful servants,
Had you been wise, and suddain: what power, or will
Over her beauty, have you now? by violence
To constrain his love; she is as free as you are,
And no law can impeach her liberty,
And whilst she is so, *Arnoldo* will despise you.

Hip. Either my love or anger must be satisfied,
Or I must dye.

Zab. I have a way wou'd do it,
Wou'd do it yet, protect me from the Law.

Hip. From any thing; thou knowest what power I have,
What mony, and what friends.

Zab. 'Tis a devilish one:
But such must now be us'd: walk in, I'le tell you;
And if you like it, if the Devil can do any thing—

Hip. Devil, or what thou wilt, so I be satisfied. [*Ex.*

Enter Sulpitia, *and* Jaques.

Sulp. This is the rarest and the lustiest fellow,

And so bestirs himself—
Jaq. Give him breath Mistress,
You'l melt him else.
Sulp. He does perform such wonders—
The women are mad on him.
Jaq. Give him breath I say;
The man is but a man, he must have breath.
Sulp. How many had he yesterday?
And they paid bravely too.
Jaq. About fourteen,
But still I cry give breath, spare him and have him.
Sulp. Five Dames to day; this was a small stage,
He may endure five more.
Jaq. Breath, breath I cry still;
Body o' me give breath, the man's a lost man else.
Feed him and give him breath.

Enter 2 Gentlewomen.

Sulp. Welcome Gentlewomen,
Y'are very welcome. (fellow
1 *Gen.* We hear you have a lusty and well complexion'd
That does rare tricks; my Sister and my self here,
Would trifle out an hour or two, so please you.
Sulp. *Jaques*, conduct 'em in.
Both. There's for your courtesie. [*Ex.* Jaq. *and* Gent.
Sulp. Good pay still, good round pay, this happy fellow
Will set me up again; he brings in gold
Faster than I have leisure to receive it.
O that his body were not flesh and fading;
But I'le so pap him up—nothing too dear for him;
What a sweet scent he has?—Now what news *Jaques*?
Jaq. He cannot last, I pity the poor man,
I suffer for him; two Coaches of young City dames,
And they drive as the Devil were in the wheels,
Are ready now to enter: and behind these
An old dead-palsied Lady in a Litter,
And she makes all the haste she can: the man's lost,
You may gather up his dry bones to make Nine-pins,
But for his flesh.
Sulp. These are but easie labours

Yet, for I know he must have rest.
Ja. He must—you'll beat him off his legs else presently.
Sul. Go in, and bid him please himself, I am pleas'd too:
To morrow's a new day; but if he can
I would have him take pity o' the old Lady.
Alas 'tis charity.
Jaq. I'le tell him all this,
And if he be not too fool-hardy.

Enter Zabulon.

Sulp. How now?
What news with you?
Zab. You must presently
Shew all the art you have, and for my Lady.
Sulp. She may command.
Zab. You must not dream nor trifle.
Sulp. Which way?
Zab. A spell you must prepare, a powerful one,
Peruse but these directions, you shall find all;
There is the picture too, be quick, and faithful,
And do it with that strength—when 'tis perform'd,
Pitch your reward at what you please, you have it.
Sul. I'le do my best, and suddenly: but hark ye,
Will you never lye at home again?
Zab. Excuse me,
I have too much business yet.
Sulp. I am right glad on't.
Zab. Think on your business, so farewel.
Sulp. I'le do it.
Zab. Within this hour I'le visit you again
And give you greater lights.
Sulp. I shall observe ye;
This brings a brave reward, bravely I'le do it,
And all the hidden art I have, express in't.
[*Exeunt at both doors.*

Enter Rutilio *with a Night-cap.*

Rut. Now do I look as if I were Crow-trodden,
Fye, how my hams shrink under me! O me,
I am broken-winded too; is this a life?

Is this the recreation I have aim'd at?
I had a body once, a handsome body,
And wholesome too. Now I appear like a rascal,
That had been hung a year or two in Gibbets.
Fye how I faint! women? keep me from women;
Place me before a Cannon, 'tis a pleasure;
Stretch me upon a Rack, a recreation;
But women? women? O the Devil! women?
Curtius Gulf was never half so dangerous.
Is there no way to find the Trap-door again,
And fall into the Cellar, and be taken?
No lucky fortune to direct me that way?
No Gallies to be got, nor yet no Gallows?
For I fear nothing now, no earthly thing
But these unsatisfied Men-leeches, women.
How devilishly my bones ake! O the old Lady!
I have a kind of waiting-woman lyes cross my back too,
O how she stings! no treason to deliver me?
Now what are you? do you mock me?

Enter 3. *with Night-caps very faintly.*

1 No Sir, no;
We were your Predecessors in this place.
2 And come to see you bear up.
Rut. Good Gentlemen;
You seem to have a snuffing in your head Sir,
A parlous snuffing, but this same dampish air—
2 A dampish air indeed.
Rut. Blow your face tenderly,
Your nose will ne're endure it: mercy o' me,
What are men chang'd to here? is my nose fast yet?
Me thinks it shakes i'th' hilts: pray tell me gentlemen,
How long is't since you flourisht here?
3 Not long since.
Rut. Move your self easily, I see you are tender,
Nor long endured.
2 The labour was so much Sir,
And so few to perform it—
Rut. Must I come to this?
And draw my legs after me like a lame Dog?

I cannot run away, I am too feeble:
Will you sue for this place again Gentlemen? (plexions.
1 No truly Sir, the place has been too warm for our com-
2 We have enough on't, rest you merry Sir,
We came but to congratulate your fortune,
You have abundance.
3 Bear your fortune soberly,
And so we leave you to the next fair Lady. [*Ex. the* 3.
Rut. Stay but a little, and I'le meet you Gentlemen,
At the next Hospital: there's no living thus,
Nor am I able to endure it longer,
With all the helps and heats that can be given me,
I am at my trot already: they are fair and young
Most of the women that repair unto me,
But they stick on like Burs, shake me like Feathers.

Enter Sulpitia.

More Women yet?
Would I were honestly married
To any thing that had but half a face,
And not a groat to keep her, nor a smock,
That I might be civilly merry when I pleased,
Rather than labouring in these Fulling-mills.
Sul. By this the spell begins to work: you are lusty,
I see you bear up bravely yet.
Rut. Do you hear Lady,
Do not make a game-bear of me, to play me hourly,
And fling on all your whelps; it would not hold;
Play me with some discretion; to day one course,
And two dayes hence another.
Sulp. If you be so angry
Pay back the mony I redeem'd you at
And take your course, I can have men enough:
You have cost me a hundred crowns since you came hither,
In Broths and strength[n]ing Caudles; till you do pay me,
If you will eat and live, you shall endeavour,
I'le chain you to't else.
Rut. Make me a Dog-kennel,
I'le keep your house and bark, and feed on bare bones,
And be whipt out o' doors,

Do you mark me Lady? whipt,
I'le eat old shoes.

Enter Duarte.

Dua. In this house I am told
There is a stranger, of a goodly person,
And such a one there was; if I could see him,
I yet remember him.
Sulp. Your business Sir,
If it be for a woman, ye are couzen'd,
I keep none here. [*Exit.*
Dua. Certain this is the Gentleman;
The very same.
Rut. Death, if I had but mony,
Or any friend to bring me from this bondage,
I would Thresh, set up a Cobler's shop, keep Hogs,
And feed with 'em, sell Tinder-boxes,
And Knights of Ginger-bread, Thatch for three
Half pence a day, and think it Lordly,
From this base Stallion trade: why does he eye me,
Eye me so narrowly?
Dua. It seems you are troubled Sir,
I heard you speak of want.
Rut. 'Tis better hearing
Far, than relieving Sir.
Dua. I do not think so, you know me not.
Rut. Not yet that I remember.
Dua. You shall, and for your friend: I am beholding to ye,
Greatly beholding Sir; if you remember,
You fought with such a man, they call'd *Duarte*,
A proud distemper'd man: he was my enemy,
My mortal foe, you slew him fairly, nobly.
Rut. Speak softly Sir, you do not mean to betray me,
I wisht the Gallows, now th'are coming fairly.
Dua. Be confident, for as I live, I love you,
And now you shall perceive it: for that service,
Me, and my purse command: there, take it to ye,
'Tis gold, and no small sum, a thousand Duckets,
Supply your want.
Rut. But do you do this faithfully?

Dua. If I mean ill, spit in my face and kick me:
In what else I may serve you, Sir—
Rut. I thank you,
This is as strange to me as Knights adventures.
I have a project, 'tis an honest one,
And now I'le tempt my fortune.
Dua. Trust me with it.
Rut. You are so good and honest I must trust ye,
'Tis but to carry a letter to a Lady
That sav'd my life once.
Dua. That will be most thankful,
I will do't with all care.
Rut. Where are you, white-broth?
Now lusty blood,
Come in, and tell your mony:
'Tis ready here, no threats, nor no orations,
Nor prayers now.
Sulp. You do not mean to leave me.
Rut. I'le live in Hell sooner than here, and cooler.
Come quickly come, dispatch, this air's unwho[l]som:
Quickly good Lady, quickly to't.
Sulp. Well, since it must be,
The next I'le fetter faster sure, and closer.
Rut. And pick his bones, as y'have done mine, pox take ye.
Dua. At my lodging for a while, you shall be quartered,
And there take Physick for your health.
Rut. I thank ye,
I have found my angel now too, if I can keep him.
[*Exeunt omnes.*

Actus Quintus. Scena Prima.

Enter Rutilio *and* Duarte.

Rut. YOU like the Letter?
Dua. Yes, but I must tell you
You tempt a desperate hazard, to sollicite
The mother, (and the grieved one too, 'tis rumor'd)
Of him you slew so lately.
Rut. I have told you

Some proofs of her affection, and I know not
A nearer way to make her satisfaction
For a lost Son, than speedily to help her
To a good Husband; one that will beget
Both Sons and Daughters, if she be not barren.
I have had a breathing now, and have recovered
What I lost in my late service, 'twas a hot one:
It fired and fired me; but all thanks to you Sir,
You have both freed and cool'd me.

Dua. What is done Sir,
I thought well done, and was in that rewarded,
And therefore spare your thanks.

Rut. I'le no more Whoring:
This fencing 'twixt a pair of sheets, more wears one
Than all the exercise in the world besides.
To be drunk with good Canary, a meer Julip
Or like gourd-water to't; twenty Surfeits
Come short of one nights work there. If I get this Lady
As ten to one I shall, I was ne're denied yet,
I will live wondrous honestly; walk before her
Gravely and demurely
And then instruct my family; you are sad,
What do you muse on Sir?

Dua. Truth I was thinking
What course to take for the delivery of your letter,
And now I have it: but faith did this Lady
(For do not gull your self) for certain know,
You kill'd her Son?

Rut. Give me a Book I'le swear't;
Denyed me to the Officers, that pursued me,
Brought me her self to th' door, then gave me gold
To bear my charges, and shall I make doubt then
But that she lov'd me? I am confident
Time having ta'ne her grief off, that I shall be
Most welcome to her: for then to have wooed her
Had been unseasonable.

Dua. Well Sir, there's more mony,
To ma[ke] you handsome; I'le about your business:
You know where you must stay?

Rut. There you shall find me:

Would I could meet my Brother now, to know,
Whether the Jew, his Genius, or my Christian,
Has prov'd the better friend. [*Exit.*

Dua. O who would trust
Deceiving woman! or believe that one
The best, and most Canoniz'd ever was
More than a seeming goodness? I could rail now
Against the sex, and curse it; but the theam
And way's too common: yet that *Guiomar*
My Mother; (nor let that forbid her to be
The wonder of our nation) she that was
Mark'd out the great example, for all Matrons
Both Wife and Widow; she that in my breeding
Exprest the utmost of a Mothers care,
And tenderness to a Son; she that yet feigns
Such sorrow for me; good God, that this mother,
After all this, should give up to a stranger,
The wreak she ow'd her Son; I fear her honour.
That he was sav'd, much joyes me, and grieve only
That she was his preserver. I'le try further,
And by this Engine, find whether the tears,
Of which she is so prodigal, are for me,
Or us'd to cloak her base hypocrisie. [*Exit.*

Enter Hippolyta *and* Sulpitia.

Hip. Are you assur'd the charm prevails?

Sulp. Do I live?
Or do you speak to me? Now this very instant
Health takes its last leave of her; meager paleness
Like winter, nips the Roses and the Lilies,
The Spring that youth, and love adorn'd her face with.
To force affection, is beyond our art,
For I have prov'd all means that hell has taught me,
Or the malice of a woman, which exceeds it,
To change *Arnoldo*'s love, but to no purpose:
But for your bond-woman—

Hip. Let her pine and dye;
She remov'd, which like a brighter Sun,
Obscures my beams, I may shine out again,
And as I have been, be admir'd and sought to:

How long has she to live?
Sulp. Lady, before
The Sun twice rise and set, be confident,
She is but dead; I know my Charm hath found her.
Nor can the Governours Guard; her lovers tears;
Her Fathers sorrow, or his power that freed her,
Defend her from it.

Enter Zabulon.

Zab. All things have succeeded,
As you could wish; I saw her brought sick home;
The image of pale death, stampt on her fore-head.
Let me adore this second Hecate,
This great Commandress, of the fatal Sisters,
That as she pleases, can cut short, or lengthen
The thread of life.
Hip. Where was she when the inchantment
First seis'd upon her?
Zab. Taking the fresh air,
In the company of the Governour, and Count *Clodio*,
Arnoldo too, was present with her Father,
When, in a moment (so the servants told me)
As she was giving thanks to the Governour,
And *Clodio*, for her unexpected freedom,
As if she had been blasted, she sunk down,
To their amazement.
Hip. 'Tis thy master-piece
Which I will so reward, that thou shalt fix here,
And with the hazard of thy life, no more
Make tryal of thy powerful Art; which known
Our Laws call death: off with this Magical Robe,
And be thy self.

Enter Governour, Clodio, *and* Charino.

Sulp. Stand close, you shall hear more.
Man. You must have patience; all rage is vain now,
And piety forbids, that we should question
What is decreed above, or ask a reason
Why heaven determines this or that way of us.
Clod. Heaven has no hand in't; 'tis a work of hell.

Her life hath been so innocent, all her actions
So free from the suspicion of crime,
As rather she deserves a Saints place here,
Than to endure, what now her sweetness suffers.
Char. Not for her fault, but mine Sir, *Zenocia* suffers:
The sin I made, when I sought to rase down
Arnoldo's love, built on a Rock of truth,
Now to the height is punish'd. I profess,
Had he no birth, nor parts, the present sorrow
He now expresses for her, does deserve her
Above all Kings, though such had been his rivals.
Clod. All ancient stories, of the love of Husbands
To vertuous Wives, be now no more remembred.
Char. The tales of *Turtles*, ever be forgotten,
Or, for his sake believ'd.
Man. I have heard, there has been
Between some married pairs, such sympathy,
That th' Husband has felt really the throws
His Wife then teeming suffers, this true grief
Confirms, 'tis not impossible.
Clod. We shall find
Fit time for this hereafter; let's use now
All possible means to help her.
Man. Care, nor cost,
Nor what Physicians can do, shall be wanting;
Make use of any means or men.
Char. You are noble. [*Exeunt* Man. Clod. *and* Char.
Sulp. Ten Colledges of Doctors shall not save her.
Her fate is in your hand.
Hip. Can I restore her?
Sulp. If you command my Art.
Hip. I'le dye my self first.
And yet I'le go visit her, and see
This miracle of sorrow in *Arnoldo*:
And 'twere for me, I should change places with her,
And dye most happy, such a lovers tears
Were a rich monument, but too good for her,
Whose misery I glory in: come *Sulpitia*,
You shall along with me, good *Zabulon*
Be not far off.

Zab. I will attend you Madam. [*Exeunt.*

Enter Duarte, *and a* Servant.

Ser. I have serv'd you from my youth, and ever
You have found me faithful: that you live's a treasure
I'le lock up here; nor shall it be let forth,
But when you give me warrant.
Dua. I rely
Upon thy faith; nay, no more protestations,
Too many of them will call that in question,
Which now I doubt not: she is there?
Ser. Alone too,
But take it on my life, your entertainment,
Appearing as you are, will be but course,
For the displeasure I shall undergo
I am prepar'd.
Dua. Leave me, I'le stand the hazard. [*Exit* Servant.
The silence that's observ'd, her close retirements,
No visitants admitted, not the day;
These sable colours, all signs of true sorrow,
Or hers is deeply counterfeit. I'le look nearer,
Manners give leave—she sits upon the ground;
By heaven she weeps; my picture in her hand too;
She kisses it and weeps again.

Enter Guiomar.

Gui. Who's there?
Dua. There is no starting back now Madam.
Gui. Ha, another murderer! I'le not protect thee,
Though I have no more Sons.
Dua. Your pardon Lady,
There's no such foul fact taints me.
Gui. What makes thou here then?
Where are my servants, do none but my sorrows
Attend upon me? speak, what brought thee hither?
Dua. A will to give you comfort.
Gui. Thou art but a man.
And 'tis beyond a humane reach to do it,
If thou could raise the dead out of their graves,
Bid time run back, make me now what I was,

A happy Mother; gladly I would hear thee,
But that's impossible.
Dua. Please you but read this;
You shall know better there, why I am sent,
Than if I should deliver it.
Gui. From whom comes it?
Dua. That will instruct you. I suspect this stranger,
Yet she spake something that holds such alliance
With his reports; I know not what to think on't;
What a frown was there? she looks me through, & through,
Now reads again, now pauses, and now smiles;
And yet there's more of anger in't than mirth,
These are strange changes; oh I understand it,
She's full of serious thoughts.
Gui. You are just, you Heavens,
And never do forget to hear their prayers,
That truly pay their vows, the defer'd vengeance,
For you, and my words sake so long defer'd,
Under which as a mountain my heart groans yet
When 'twas despair'd of, now is offer'd to me;
And if I lose it, I am both wayes guilty.
The womans mask, dissimulation help me.
Come hither friend, I am sure you know the Gentleman,
That sent these charms.
Dua. Charms Lady?
Gui. These charms;
I well may call them so, they've won upon me,
More than ere letter did; thou art his friend,
(The confidence he has in thee, confirms it)
And therefore I'le be open breasted to thee;
To hear of him, though yet I never saw him,
Was most desir'd of all men; let me blush,
And then I'le say I love him.
Dua. All men see,
In this a womans vertue.
Gui. I expected
For the courtesie I did, long since to have seen him,
And though I then forbad it, you men know,
Between our hearts and tongues there's a large distance;
But I'le excuse him, may be hitherto

He has forborn it, in respect my Son
Fell by his hand.
Dua. And reason Lady.
Gui. No, he did me a pleasure in't, a riotous fellow,
And with that insolent, not worth the owning;
I have indeed kept a long solemn sorrow,
For my friends sake partly; but especially
For his long absence.
Dua. O the Devil.
Guio. Therefore
Bid him be speedy; a Priest shall be ready
To tye the holy knot; this kiss I send him,
Deliver that and bring him.
Dua. I am dumb:
A good cause I have now, and a good sword,
And something I shall do, I wait upon you. [*Exeunt.*

Enter Manuel, Charino, Arnoldo, Zenocia, *born in a chair.* 2 Doctors, Clodio.

Doct. Give her more air, she dyes else.
Arn. O thou dread power,
That mad'st this all, and of thy workmanship
This virgin wife, the Master piece, look down on her;
Let her minds virtues, cloth'd in this fair garment,
That worthily deserves a better name
Than flesh and bloud, now sue, and prevail for her.
Or if those are denyed, let innocence,
To which all passages in Heaven stand open,
Appear in her white robe, before thy throne;
And mediate for her: or if this age of sin
Be worthy of a miracle, the Sun
In his diurnal progress never saw
So sweet a subject to imploy it on.
Man. Wonders are ceas'd Sir, we must work by means.
Arno. 'Tis true, and such reverend Physicians are;
To you thus low I fall then; so may you ever
Be stil'd the hands of Heaven, natures restorers;
Get wealth and honours; and by your success,
In all your undertakings, propagate
Your great opinion in the world, as now

You use your saving art; for know good Gentlemen,
Besides the fame, and all that I possess,
For a reward, posterity shall stand
Indebted to you, for (as Heaven forbid it)
Should my *Zenocia* dye, robbing this age
Of all that's good or gracefull, times succeeding,
The story of her pure life not yet perfect,
Will suffer in the want of her example.

Doct. Were all the world to perish with her, we
Can do no more, than what art and experience
Give us assurance of, we have us'd all means
To find the cause of her disease, yet cannot;
How should we then, promise the cure?

Arn. Away,
I did bely you, when I charg'd you with
The power of doing, ye are meer names only,
And even your best perfection, accidental;
What ever malady thou art, or Spirit,
As some hold all diseases that afflict us,
As love already makes me sensible
Of half her sufferings, ease her of her part,
And let me stand the butt of thy fell malice,
And I will swear th'art mercifull.

Doct. Your hand Lady;
What a strange heat is here! bring some warm water.

Arn. She shall use nothing that is yours; my sorrow
Provides her of a better bath, my tears
Shall do that office.

Zeno. O my best *Arnoldo*!
The truest of all lovers! I would live
Were heaven so pleas'd, but to reward your sorrow
With my true service; but since that's denied me,
May you live long and happy: do not suffer
(By your affection to me I conjure you)
My sickness to infect you; though much love
Makes you too subject to it.

Arn. In this only
Zenocia wrongs her servant; can the body
Subsist, the Soul departed? 'tis as easie
As I to live without you; I am your husband,

And long have been so, though our adverse fortune,
Bandying us from one hazard to another,
Would never grant me so much happiness,
As to pay a husbands debt; despite of fortune,
In death I'le follow you, and guard mine own;
And there enjoy what here my fate forbids me.
Clod. So true a sorrow, and so feelingly
Exprest, I never read of.
Man. I am struck
With wonder to behold it, as with pity.
Char. If you that are a stranger, suffer for them,
Being tied no further than humanity
Leads you to soft compassion; think great Sir,
What of necessity I must endure,
That am a Father?

Hippolyta, Zabulon, *and* Sulpitia *at the door.*

Zab. Wait me there, I hold it
Unfit to have you seen; as I find cause,
You shall proceed.
Man. You are welcom Lady.
Hip. Sir, I come to do a charitable office,
How does the patient?
Clod. You may enquire
Of more than one; for two are sick, and deadly,
He languishes in her, her health's despair'd of,
And in hers, his.
Hip. 'Tis a strange spectacle,
With what a patience they sit unmov'd!
Are they not dead already?
Doct. By her pulse,
She cannot last a day.
Arn. Oh by that summons,
I know my time too!
Hip. Look to the man.
Clod. Apply
Your Art, to save the Lady, preserve her,
A town is your reward.
Hip. I'le treble it,
In ready gold, if you restore *Arnoldo*;

For in his death I dye too.
Clod. Without her
I am no more.
Arn. Are you there Madam? now
You may feast on my miseries; my coldness
In answering your affections, or hardness,
Give it what name you please, you are reveng'd of,
For now you may perceive, our thred of life
Was spun together, and the poor *Arnoldo*
Made only to enjoy the best *Zenocia*,
And not to serve the use of any other;
And in that she may equal; my Lord *Clodio*
Had long since else enjoyed her, nor could I
Have been so blind, as not to see your great
And many excellencies far, far beyond
Or my deservings, or my hopes; we are now
Going our latest journey, and together,
Our only comfort we desire, pray give it,
Your charity to our ashes, such we must be,
And not to curse our memories.
Hip. I am much mov'd.
Clod. I am wholly overcome, all love to women
Farewell for ever; ere you dye, your pardon;
And yours Sir; had she many years to live,
Perhaps I might look on her, as a Brother,
But as a lover never; and since all
Your sad misfortunes had original
From the barbarous Custom practis'd in my Country,
Heaven witness, for your sake I here release it;
So to your memory, chaste Wives and Virgins
Shall ever pay their vowes. I give her to you;
And wish, she were so now, as when my lust
Forc'd you to quit the Country.
Hip. It is in vain
To strive with destiny, here my dotage ends,
Look up *Zenocia*, health in me speaks to you;
She gives him to you, that by divers ways,
So long has kept him from you: and repent not,
That you were once my servant, for which health
In recompence of what I made you suffer,

The hundred thousand Crowns, the City owes me,
Shall be your dower.

Man. 'Tis a magnificent gift,
Had it been timely given.

Hip. It is believe it, *Sulpitia.*

Enter a Servant, *and* Sulpitia.

Sulp. Madam.

Hip. Quick, undoe the charm;
Ask not a reason why; let it suffice,
It is my will.

Sulp. Which I obey and gladly. [*Exit.*

Man. Is to be married, sayest thou?

Ser. So she sayes Sir,
And does desire your presence. [*They are born off in chairs.*

Man. And tell her I'le come.

Hip. Pray carry them to their rest; for though already,
They do appear as dead, let my life pay for't,
If they recover not.

Man. What you have warranted,
Assure your self, will be expected from you;
Look to them carefully; and till the tryal,—

Hip. Which shall not be above four hours.

Man. Let me
Intreat your companies: there is something
Of weight invites me hence.

All. We'll wait upon you. [*Exeunt.*

Enter Guiomar, *and* Servants.

Guio. You understand what my directions are,
And what they guide you to; the faithfull promise
You have made me all.

All. We do and will perform it.

Guio. The Governour will not fail to be here presently;
Retire a while, till you shall find occasion,
And bring me word, when they arrive.

All. Wee shall Madam.

Guio. Only stay you to entertain.

1 *Ser.* I am ready.

Guio. I wonder at the bold, and practis'd malice,

Men ever have o' foot against our honours,
That nothing we can do, never so vertuous,
No shape put on so pious, no not think
What a good is, be that good ne're so noble,
Never so laden with admir'd example,
But still we end in lust; our aims, our actions,
Nay, even our charities, with lust are branded;
Why should this stranger else, this wretched stranger,
Whose life I sav'd at what dear price sticks here yet,
Why should he hope? he was not here an hour,
And certainly in that time, I may swear it
I gave him no loose look, I had no reason;
Unless my tears were flames, my curses courtships;
The killing of my Son, a kindness to me.
Why should he send to me, or with what safety
(Examining the ruine he had wrought me)
Though at that time, my pious pity found him,
And my word fixt; I am troubled, strongly troubled.

Enter a Servant.

Ser. The Gentlemen are come.
Guio. Then bid 'em welcome—I must retire. [*Exit.*

Enter Rutilio, *and* Duarte.

Ser. You are welcom Gentlemen.
Rut. I thank you friend, I would speak with your Lady.
Ser. I'le let her understand.
Rut. It shall befit you.
How do I look Sir, in this handsome trim? [*Exit* Servant.
Me thinks I am wondrous brave.
Duar. You are very decent.
Rut. These by themselves, without more helps of nature,
Would set a woman hard; I know 'em all,
And where their first aims light; I'le lay my head on't,
I'le take her eye, as soon as she looks on me,
And if I come to speak once, woe be to her,
I have her in a nooze, she cannot scape me;
I have their several lasts.
Dua. You are throughly studied,
But tell me Sir, being unacquainted with her,

As you confess you are—
Rut. That's not an hours work,
I'le make a Nun forget her beads in two hours.
Dua. She being set in years, next none of those lusters
Appearing in her eye, that warm the fancy;
Nor nothing in her face, but handsom ruines.
Rut. I love old stories: those live believ'd, Authentique,
When 20. of your modern faces are call'd in,
For new opinion, paintings, and corruptions;
Give me an old confirm'd face; besides she sav'd me,
She sav'd my life, have I not cause to love her?
She's rich and of a constant state, a fair one,
Have I not cause to wooe her? I have tryed sufficient
All your young Phillies, I think this back has try'd 'em,
And smarted for it too: they run away with me,
Take bitt between the teeth, and play the Devils;
A staied pace now becomes my years; a sure one,
Where I may sit and crack no girths.
Dua. How miserable,
If my Mother should confirm, what I suspect now,
Beyond all humane cure were my condition!
Then I shall wish, this body had been so too.
Here comes the Lady Sir.

Enter Guiomar.

Rut. Excellent Lady,
To shew I am a creature, bound to your service,
And only yours—
Guio. Keep at that distance Sir;
For if you stir—
Rut. I am obedient.
She has found already, I am for her turn;
With what a greedy hawks eye she beholds me!
Mark how she musters all my parts.
Guio. A goodly Gentleman,
Of a more manly set, I never look'd on. (of 'em.
Rut. Mark, mark her eyes still; mark but the carriage
Guio. How happy am I now, since my Son fell,
He fell not by a base unnoble hand!
As that still troubled me; how far more happy

Shall my revenge be, since the Sacrifice,
I offer to his grave, shall be both worthy
A Sons untimely loss, and a Mothers sorrow!
Rut. Sir, I am made believe it; she is mine own,
I told you what a spell I carried with me,
All this time does she spend in contemplation
Of that unmatch'd delight: I shall be thankfull to ye;
And if you please to know my house, to use it;
To take it for your own.
Guio. Who waits without there?

Enter Guard, *and* Servants, *they seize upon* Rut. *and bind him.*

Rut. How now? what means this, Lady?
Guio. Bind him fast.
Rut. Are these the bride-laces you prepare for me?
The colours that you give?
Dua. Fye Gentle Lady,
This is not noble dealing.
Guio. Be you satisfied,
I[t] seems you are a stranger to this meaning,
You shall not be so long.
Rut. Do you call this wooing—Is there no end of (womens persecutions?
Must I needs fool into mine own destruction?
Have I not had fair warnings, and enough too?
Still pick the Devils teeth? you are not mad Lady;
Do I come fairly, and like a Gentleman,
To offer you that honour?
Guio. You are deceiv'd Sir,
You come besotted, to your own destruction:
I sent not for you; what honour can ye add to me,
That brake that staff of honour, my age lean'd on?
That rob'd me of that right, made me a Mother?
Hear me thou wretched man, hear me with terrour,
And let thine own bold folly shake thy Soul,
Hear me pronounce thy death, that now hangs o're thee,
Thou desperate fool; who bad thee seek this ruine?
What mad unmanly fate, made thee discover
Thy cursed face to me again? was't not enough
To have the fair protection of my house,
When misery and justice close pursued thee?

When thine own bloudy sword, cryed out against thee,
Hatcht in the life of him? yet I forgave thee.
My hospitable word, even when I saw
The goodliest branch of all my blood lopt from me,
Did I not seal still to thee?

Rut. I am gone.

Guio. And when thou went'st, to Imp thy miserie,
Did I not give thee means? but hark ungratefull,
Was it not thus? to hide thy face and fly me?
To keep thy name for ever from my memory?
Thy cursed blood and kindred? did I not swear then,
If ever, (in this wretched life thou hast left me,
Short and unfortunate,) I saw thee again,
Or came but to the knowledge, where thou wandredst,
To call my vow back, and pursue with vengeance
With all the miseries a Mother suffers?

Rut. I was born to be hang'd, there's no avoiding it.

Guio. And dar'st thou with this impudence appear here?
Walk like the winding sheet my Son was put in,
Stand with those wounds?

Dua. I am happy now again;
Happy the hour I fell, to find a Mother,
So pious, good, and excellent in sorrows.

Enter a Servant.

Ser. The Governour's come in.

Guio. O let him enter.

Rut. I have fool'd my self a fair thred of all my fortunes,
This strikes me most; not that I fear to perish,
But that this unmannerly boldness has brought me to it.

Enter Governour, Clodio, Charino.

Gov. Are these fit preparations for a wedding Lady?
I came prepar'd a guest.

Guio. O give me justice;
As ever you will leave a vertuous name,
Do justice, justice, Sir.

Gove. You need not ask it,
I am bound to it.

Guio. Justice upon this man
That kill'd my Son.
Gove. Do you confess the act?
Rut. Yes Sir.
Clod. *Rutilio*?
Char. 'Tis the same.
Clod. How fell he thus?
Here will be sorrow for the good *Arnoldo.*
Gove. Take heed Sir what you say.
Rut. I have weigh'd it well,
I am the man, nor is it life I start at;
Only I am unhappy I am poor,
Poor in expence of lives, there I am wretched,
That I have not two lives lent me for his sacrifice;
One for her Son, another for her sorrows.
Excellent Lady, now rejoyce again,
For though I cannot think, y'are pleas'd in blood,
Nor with that greedy thirst pursue your vengeance;
The tenderness, even in those tears denies that;
Yet let the world believe, you lov'd *Duarte*;
The unmatcht courtesies you have done my miseries;
Without this forfeit to the law, would charge me
To tender you this life, and proud 'twould please you.
Guio. Shall I have justice?
Gover. Yes.
Rut. I'le ask it for ye,
I'le follow it my self, against my self.
Sir, 'Tis most fit I dye; dispatch it quickly,
The monstrous burthen of that grief she labours with
Will kill her else, then blood on blood lyes on me;
Had I a thousand lives, I'd give 'em all,
Before I would draw one tear more from that vertue.
Guio. Be not too cruel Sir, and yet his bold sword—
But his life cannot restore that, he's a man too—
Of a fair promise, but alas my Son's dead;
If I have justice, must it kill him?
Gov. Yes.
Guio. If I have not, it kills me, strong and goodly!
Why should he perish too?
Gover. It lies in your power,

You only may accuse him, or may quit him.
Clod. Be there no other witnesses?
Guio. Not any.
And if I save him, will not the world proclaim,
I have forgot a Son, to save a murderer?
And yet he looks not like one, he looks manly.
Hip. Pity so brave a Gentleman should perish.
She cannot be so hard, so cruel hearted.
Guio. Will you pronounce? yet stay a little Sir.
Rut. Rid your self, Lady, of this misery;
And let me go, I do but breed more tempests,
With which you are already too much shaken.
Guio. Do now, pronounce; I will not hear.
Dua. You shall not,
Yet turn and see good Madam.
Gove. Do not wonder.
'Tis he, restor'd again, thank the good Doctor,
Pray do not stand amaz'd, it is *Duarte*;
Is well, is safe again.
Guio. O my sweet Son,
I will not press my wonder now with questions—
Sir, I am sorry for that cruelty,
I urg'd against you.
Rut. Madam, it was but justice.
Dua. 'Tis [t]rue, the Doctor heal'd this body again,
But this man heal'd my soul, made my minde perfect,
The good sharp lessons his sword read to me, sav'd me;
For which, if you lov'd me, dear Mother,
Honour and love this man.
Guio. You sent this letter?
Rut. My boldness makes me blush now.
Guio. I'le wipe off that,
And with this kiss, I take you for my husband,
Your wooing's done Sir; I believe you love me,
And that's the wealth I look for now.
Rut. You have it.
Dua. You have ended my desire to all my wishes.
Gov. Now 'tis a wedding again. And if *Hippolyta*
Make good, what with the hazard of her life,
She undertook, the evening will set clear

Enter Hippolyta, *leading* Leopold, Arnoldo, Zenocia, *in either hand*, Zabulon, Sulpitia.

After a stormy day.
Char. Here comes the Lady.
Clod. With fair *Zenocia*,
Health with life again
Restor'd unto her.
Zen. The gift of her goodness.
Rut. Let us embrace, I am of your order too,
And though I once despair'd of women, now
I find they relish much of Scorpions,
For both have stings, and both can hurt, and cure too;
But what have been your fortunes?
Arn. Wee'l defer
Our story, and at time more fit, relate it.
Now all that reverence vertue, and in that
Zenocias constancy, and perfect love,
Or for her sake *Arnoldo*, join with us
In th' honour of this Lady.
Char. She deserves it.
Hip. *Hippolytas* life shall make that good hereafter,
Nor will I alone better my self but others:
For these whose wants perhaps have made their actions
Not altogether innocent, shall from me
Be so supplied, that need shall not compel them,
To any course of life, but what the law
Shall give allowance to.
Zab. *Sulpitia*, Your Ladiships creatures.
Rut. Be so, and no more you man-huckster.
Hip. And worthy *Leopold*, you that with such fervour,
So long have sought me, and in that deserv'd me,
Shall now find full reward for all your travels,
Which you have made more dear by patient sufferance.
And though my violent dotage did transport me,
Beyond those bounds, my modesty should have kept in,
Though my desires were loose, from unchast art
Heaven knows I am free.
Leop. The thought of that's dead to me;
I gladly take your offer.

Rut. Do so Sir,
A piece of crackt gold ever will weigh down
Silver that's whole.
Gov. You shall be all my guests,
I must not be denyed.
Arn. Come my *Zenocia.*
Our bark at length has found a quiet harbour;
And the unspotted progress of our loves
Ends not alone in safety, but reward,
To instruct others, by our fair example;
That though good purposes are long withstood,
The hand of Heaven still guides such as are good.
[*Ex. omnes.*

The Prologue.

SO free this work is, Gentlemen, from offence,
That we are confident, it needs no defence
From us, or from the Poets—we dare look
On any man, that brings his Table-book
To write down, what again he may repeat
At some great Table, to deserve his meat.
Let such come swell'd with malice, to apply
What is mirth here, there for an injurie.
Nor Lord, nor Lady we have tax'd; nor State,
Nor any private person, their poor hate
Will be starv'd here, for envy shall not finde
One touch that may be wrested to her minde.
And yet despair not, Gentlemen, The play
Is quick and witty; so the Poets say,
And we believe them; the plot neat, and new,
Fashion'd like those, that are approv'd by you.
Only 'twill crave attention, in the most;
Because one point unmark'd, the whole is lost.
Hear first then, and judge after, and be free,
And as our cause is, let our censure be.

Epilogue.

WHY there should be an Epilogue to a play,
I know no cause: the old and usuall way,
For which they were made, was to entreat the grace
Of such as were spectators in this place,
And time, 'tis to no purpose; for I know
What you resolve already to bestow,
Will not be alter'd, what so e're I say,
In the behalf of us, and of the Play;
Only to quit our doubts, if you think fit,
You may, or cry it up, or silence it.

Another Prologue for the Custom of the Country.

WE wish, if it were possible, you knew
What we would give for this nights look, if new.
It being our ambition to delight
Our kind spectators with what's good, and right.
Yet so far know, and credit me, 'twas made
By such, as were held work-men in their Trade,
At a time too, when they as I divine,
Were truly merrie, and drank lusty wine,
The nectar of the Muses; Some are here
I dare presume, to whom it did appear
A well-drawn piece, which gave a lawfull birth
To passionate Scenes mixt with no vulgar mirth.
But unto such to whom 'tis known by fame
From others, perhaps only by the name,
I am a suitor, that they would prepare
Sound palats, and then judge their bill of fare.
It were injustice to decry this now
For being like'd before, you may allow
(Your candor safe) what's taught in the old schools,
All such as liv'd before you, were not fools.

The Epilogue.

I Spake much in the Prologue for the Play,
To its desert I hope, yet you might say
Should I change now from that, which then was meant,
Or in a syllable grow less confident,
I were weak-hearted. I am still the same
In my opinion, and forbear to frame
Qualification, or excuse: If you
Concur with me, and hold my judgement true,
Shew it with any sign, and from this place,
Or send me off exploded, or with grace.

APPENDIX.

In the following references to the text the lines are numbered from the top of the page, including titles, acts, stage directions, &c., but not, of course, the headline. Where, as in the lists of Persons Represented, there are double columns, the right-hand column is numbered after the left.

It has not been thought necessary to record the correction of every turned letter nor the substitution of marks of interrogation for marks of exclamation and *vice versâ*: the original compositor's stock of each running low occasionally, he used the two signs somewhat indiscriminately. Full-stops have been silently inserted at the ends of speeches and each fresh speaker has been given the dignity of a fresh line: in the double-columned folio the speeches are frequently run on. Only misprints of interest in the Quartos are recorded.

THE EPISTLE DEDICATORIE. p. x, l. 8. 1st Folio *prints a comma after*] not.

TO THE READER. p. xi, l. 6. 1st F *omits the bracket*.

THE STATIONER TO THE READERS. p. xiv, l. 33. 1st F *prints*] confessed it,

COMMENDATORY VERSES. p. xvii, l. 33. 1st F *misprints*] theirs. l. 41. 1st F *misprints*] Ii. l. 42. 1st F *misprints*] hist.

p. xx, l. 34. 1st F *misprints*] F!e.

p. xxiii, l. 1. 2nd F] sprung.

p. xxvi, l. 21. 1st F *misprints*] Fletcer.

p. xxxvi, l. 10. 1st F *misprints*] solemue.

p. xxxvii, l. 39. 1st F *misprints*] aud. l. 43. 2nd F] delights.

p. xxxviii, l. 4. 2nd F] And these. l. 20. 2nd F *gives signature*] William Cartwright.

p. xxxix, l. 27. 1st F *misprints*] sucb.

p. xliii, l. 13. 2nd F] wert. l. 35. 2nd F] knowst.

p. xlviii, l. 33. 2nd F] receive the full god in. l. 35. 2nd F] Francis Palmer.

p. lii, l. 40. 1st F *misprints*] Fletcer.

p. lv, l. 19. 1st F *misprints*] ehe.

THE MAIDS TRAGEDY. The editions prior to the Folio of 1679 are as follows:

(A) The Maides Tragedy. | As it hath beene | divers times Acted at the Blacke-friers by | the Kings Majesties Servants. | London | Printed for Francis Constable and are to be sold | at the white Lyon over against the great North | doore of Pauls Church. 1619.

(B) The Maids Tragedie. | As it hath beene | divers times Acted at the Black-Friers by | the Kings Majesties Servants. | Newly perused, augmented, and inlarged, This second Impression. | London, | Printed for Francis Constable, and are | to be sold at the White Lion in | Pauls Church-yard. 1622.

(C) The Maids Tragedie | As it hath beene | divers times Acted at the Black-Friers by | the Kings Majesties Servants. | Written by Francis Beaumont, and John Fletcher Gentlemen. | The third Impression, Revised and Refined. | London, | Printed by A. M. for Richard Hawkins, and are to bee | sold at his Shop in Chancery-Lane neere | Serjeants-Inne. 1630.

(D) The Maides Tragedie: | as it hath beene | divers times Acted at the Black-Friers by | the Kings Majesties Servants. | Written by Francis Beaumont, and John Fletcher | Gentlemen. | The fourth Impression, Revised and Refined. | Printed by E. G. for Henry Shepherd, and are to be sold at the | signe of the Bible in Chancery lane. 1638.

(E) The Maids Tragedie. | As it hath beene | Divers times Acted at the Black- | Friers, by the Kings | Majesties Servants. | Written by Francis Beaumont, and | John Fletcher Gentlemen. | The fifth Impression, Revised and Refined. | London Printed by E. P. for William Leake, and are to be sold at his | shop in Chancery-lane, neare the Rowles. 1641.

(F) The | Maids Tragedy, | as it hath been divers times Acted at the Black- | Friers, by the Kings Majesties Servants: | written by Francis Beaumont and | John Fletcher, Gentlemen. | The sixth Impression, Revised and Corrected exactly by the Original. | London Printed for William Leake, at the Crown in Fleet-street, be | tween the two Temple Gates. 1650.

(G) The | Maids Tragedy, | as it hath been divers times | Acted | at the Black-Friers, | by the | Kings Majesties Servants. | Written by Francis Beaumont, | and John Fletcher, Gentlemen. | The sixth Impression, Revised and Corrected exactly | by the Original. | London, | Printed in the Year 1661.

In the following notes each of these quartos is referred to by the capital letter prefixed to it in the above list. A—F contain a wood-cut representing Amintor stabbing Aspatia.

p. 1, l. 3. A—G] Speakers. l. 6. A and B *omit*] a Noble Gentleman. C after the list of Speakers *adds* the following verses, repeated with variations of spelling in D—G]

The Stationers Censure.

Good Wine requires no Bush, they say,
And I, No Prologue such a Play:
The Makers therefore did forbeare
To have that Grace prefixed here.
But cease here (Censure) least the Buyer
Hold thee in this a vaine Supplyer.
My office is to set it forth
When Fame applauds it's reall worth.

l. 26. A possibly correctly gives this speech to Lysippus. l. 27. A] You are brother. l. 30. B, C and D *omit*] thou. ll. 31 and 32. A and B] masks. l. 33. A *omits*] their King. l. 34. A] groome. l. 38. A *omits*] to Rhodes. l. 39. A] blowes abroad bringst us our peace at home.

p. 2, l. 1. A *omits*] too. l. 2. A] welcome. A—E] above his or. l. 3. A] world. l. 16. A] straight. l. 18. A] most true. l. 19. A] solemnities. l. 22. A] Yes, and have given cause to those, that here. l. 29. A *omits*] with armes. l. 33. A *omits*] my friend. l. 34. A *omits*] and temperate.

p. 3, l. 3. A] weighes. l. 5. A] Enter Aspatia passing with attendance. ll. 14 and 15. Printed as one line in G and the Folio. The *Exit Aspatia* has been printed in the text at the end of Aspatia's speech, as in A—F. l. 16. A] You are mistaken sir, she is not married. A full-stop has been substituted for a comma at the end of the line here, and elsewhere in similar cases. l. 21. G *omits*] he. l. 25. A] has. l. 27. B] about. l. 28. G *omits*] the fair. l. 37. A] 'a should not thinke. l. 38. A] Could I but call it backe. l. 39. A] such base revenges. l. 40. A *omits*] holds he still his greatness with the King.

p. 4, l. 1. A] O t'were pittie for this Lady sir. l. 2. A] sits. l. 3. A] in unfrequented woods. l. 4. A] where when. l. 5. A] flowers, Then she will sit, and sigh, and tell. l. 8. A] and strow them over her like a corse. l. 12. A] And swound, and sing againe. l. 13. A] your young. l. 14. A] fils. l. 27. G *omits*] much. l. 36. A, B and C] thine innocence. l. 39. A, B and C] I am poore in words. l. 40. A] could do no more but weep. G] could no more weep.

p. 5, l. 2. A—G] fetcht. l. 4. A and B] that. l. 7. A] these. l. 9. A] too cruell. B] too fickle. l. 14. A and B] about. l. 18. A *omits* this line, and gives the following speech to Amintor. l. 20. A *adds*] Exeunt Lysippus, Cleon, Strato, Diphilus. l. 25. A] In sports, il'e. l. 26. A and B] But I have. l. 30. A] challenge gentlemen. A and B *omit*] in't. l. 32. A] and Diagoras. l. 34. A] will be angry with me.

p. 6, l. 1. A] One must sweat out his heart with. B—G] One may swear his heart out. l. 3. A and B] I shall never. l. 4. A *omits*] Pray stay. l. 5. A] you coxcomely asse, ile be. l. 6. A and B] judge. l. 10. A] through in my office. l. 11. A—D] they ha. l. 12. A] But now. l. 15. A] hark, hark, whose there, codes, codes. l. 18. A] Who is't. l. 20. A *omits*] with you. l. 25. A] there is no room. l. 28. A *adds*] Exit Melantius Lady other dore. l. 31. A] let the dores shut agen, no; do your heads itch. [The reader will note that here, and elsewhere in the text, 'I' frequently='Ay.'] l. 32. A *omits*] for you. l. 33. A] giving way. l. 35. A] a dozen heads in the twinckling. l. 37. A—G] I pray you can you. l. 40. A *omits*] to Melantius.

p. 7, l. 2. A—G] a must. l. 3. A *adds*] Enter Melantius. l. 7. A and B] mine. l. 12. A *omits*] but. l. 13. A *omits*] so near the presence of the King. l. 18. G] a woman. l. 20. A] so womanish. l. 23. A *omits*] Why. l. 24. A] quite forget. l. 28. A] Bate me the King, and be of flesh and blood. l. 29. A—G] A lies. l. 32. D and E] pluckt. l. 35. A and B] braved. C—G] bran'd. l. 37. A] the blood. l. 40. A] and able.

p. 8, l. 3. A] talke your pleasure. l. 4. A] What vilde wrong. l. 6. A] hands. l. 21. A] thy love. l. 22. A] with me. l. 24. A—D] mine hand. l. 33. A *omits*] can be unto me. l. 34. A *omits*] The. l. 36. A] Our raigne is now, for in the quenching sea.

p. 9, l. 4. A—D] hornes quite through. E] horne quite through. l. 7. A] persons that have many longing eies. l. 9. A] can I not finde. l. 10. A] am I so blinde. l. 12. F and G] break. l. 18. A and B] reines. l. 19. A] upon those, that appeare. l. 23. B] keepe our places. l. 26. G *omits*] but. ll. 28—37. These lines do not appear in A. l. 38. A] that power. l. 39. A] to fill this happy houre. l. 40. A] and let.

p. 10, l. 2. A *omits*] then call. l. 3. A] flowrie banck. l. 4. A] *Latmus* brow. l. 5. A] thy day. B] this day. l. 6. A] darke power. l. 7. A] and winde. l. 9. A] Turnes. l. 11. A] nobler. l. 17. A] hath force me hither. l. 24. A and B] goe from. l. 25. A] his subjects. l. 26. A and B] intentions. l. 31. A] Bid them draw neere to have thy watrie race. l. 32. A] Led on in couples, we are pleas'd to grace. l. 34. A] vessels. l. 37. A] See the winde. B] Oh, the wind.

p. 11, l. 5. A *omits*] too. l. 7. A *omits*] great. l. 8. G] commands. l. 15. A] I will not be long thence, goe hence againe. l. 16. A] And bid the other call out of the Maine. l. 19. A—D] The beaten. E] beating. l. 27. Folio *misprints*] mid-might. l. 29. A and B] and thee. l. 34. A and G] rights.

p. 12, l. 6. A] old night. l. 8. C] cause thee. l. 9. A] their losses. l. 14. A] loud cryings. l. 17. A] if she call. After this song A *adds*] Maskers daunce, *Neptune* leads it. ll. 18—34. These lines do not appear in A. l. 37. A—D] The sea goes hie.

p. 13, l. 1. A] has raised. l. 4. Folio] call. l. 5. A] We thanke you for this houre, | My favour to you all to gratulate. l. 7. G] may floods. l. 8. A] and no eb shall dare. l. 10. A] governments. l. 11. A] proud waters should. l. 13. In place of stage-direction A *reads*] *Exeunt Maskers*. Descend. l. 21. A] Kingdome. l. 22. A—D] all fall drencht...forget. l. 23. A] I dare no more. l. 24. A] Once heave thy drowsie head agen and see. l. 26. A] lash. l. 27. A—E] and yon. A] sun flaring stream. B—E] same flashing streame. l. 30. A] *Cinth*. Adew. A *omits*] Finis Mask. l. 31. A] light their. l. 34. Folio *misprints*] may case. l. 36. A and B] Kingdomes.

p. 14, l. 5. A *omits*] very. After l. 7 A adds] Evad. Howes that? Dul. That I might goe to bed with him with credit that you doe. l. 18. A] Madame. l. 19. In A these four words are given to '1. Lad.' l. 21. A] Tis best. l. 25. A *omits*] high. l. 28. A, B and C] livelier. l. 31. A] We all will take it I hope that are here. l. 34. A—E *omit*] to. l. 35. A] Wilt lie in my place.

p. 15, l. 3. A] Doe I prethee. l. 13. G] timely. l. 18. A] My right. l. 29. A—D] lost none. l. 31. A and B] I should. l. 32. A] Loe if you have not. l. 35. A] unto. l. 36. A] and I. l. 38. A] must be.

p. 16, ll. 1—20. These lines do not appear in A. l. 10. C] Fie out. l. 23. A] may not discontent. l. 26. A and B] And teach you. l. 30. G] should look.

p. 17, l. 6. A] Heele finde. l. 7. A *omits*] yet. l. 19. A and B *omit*] my. l. 22. A gives this line to '1. Lad.' l. 25. A] A griefe. l. 26. A] mine eyes raine. l. 28. A] why did I. l. 32. A] breake. l. 33. A] the King inforst me. l. 35. A] is she. l. 39. A] shall.

p. 18, l. 1. A] rights. l. 30. A] look will like. l. 39. A] and by thy selfe sweete love. l. 40. A] revenge it.

p. 19, l. 2. A] to me. ll. 4, 5. A] The world can yeeld, are light as aire. l. 8. A] the sun of thy lips. l. 9. A, B and C] wonnot. l. 10. A *omits*] do. l. 12. A and B] wrongst. l. 16. A *omits*] then. l. 17. A] should'st. l. 18. A] cannot. l. 26. A] Her natural temper. l. 29. A] Neither of these, what thinke you I am mad. l. 31. A] Is this the Truth, wil you not lie with me to night. l. 32. A *omits*] To night. A] You talke as if you thought I would hereafter. l. 37. A] your bed. A, B and C *omit*] for. l. 40. A] would.

p. 20, l. 4. A] the kisses of a bride. l. 13. A] Shall know this, not an altar then will smoake. l. 20. A] She cannot jest. l. 23. A] the paine of death. l. 37. A] Instant me with it. l. 40. G] the Night.

p. 21, l. 2. A] their voyce. l. 7. A] as that. l. 12. G] man. l. 15. A and B *omit*] out. l. 17. A—D] woman. l. 18. A and B] doe dwell.

p. 22, l. 4. A *omits*] in practice. l. 22. A] It is not. l. 25. A] sacred word. l. 32. A and B] hath put. l. 37. A and G *omit*] a. l. 38. A *omits*] Evad.

p. 23, l. 1. A] shall love. l. 4. A] in thy breast. l. 8. A] could. l. 23. A, B and C] know. l. 26. A] e'ne to his heart. l. 27. A] I have left. l. 36. A] I did. l. 39. A] longing.

p. 24, l. 2. A *omits*] Amint. l. 6. A *omits*] sad. l. 7. A] Good good. l. 14. A *omits* this line. l. 15. A] Did you ere. ll. 16 and 17. A *omits* these lines. l. 18. A] a mettled temper. l. 21. A] Nere I. ll. 23—31. These lines from 'and be sure' to the end of l. 31 are omitted in A. l. 24. B] gives life. l. 34. A] faind sorrow. l. 35. A] Oenes. B, C and E] Ænones. l. 37. A] expressing furie.

p. 25, l. 1. A *omits*] and. l. 2. A and B] Just as thine does. C] Just as thine eyes does. l. 12. A] looke black. l. 19. A] None of all. l. 20. A] exprest well. l. 23. A repeats this line. l. 25. A] Doe that feare bravely wench. l. 27. A full-stop at end of line has been taken away. l. 30. A] there. l. 34. A] poore Ladies. l. 37. For this line A *reads*] Suppose I stand upon Sea, breach now. l. 39. A] Wilde as the place she was in, let all about me. l. 40. A] Be teares of my story, doe my face.

p. 26, l. 2. A] thus make me looke good girle. l. 3. A] sorrowes mount. l. 6. A] see, see wenches. l. 11. A and B] a dumbe silence. l. 18. A] You'l lie downe shortly, in and whine there. l. 19. A] rustie. B, C and D] reasty. A and B] want heates. C, D and E] heares. l. 20. A] We shall have some of the Court boyes heat you shortly. ll. 21 and 22. A] Good my Lord be not angry, we doe nothing | But what my Ladies pleasure is, we are thus in griefe. l. 25. A] A slie dissembling slave. l. 28. A *omits*] what, made an Ass. l. 29. A] must be.

p. 27, l. 4. A] Our brides. l. 9. A] None, its ods. l. 24. A] I faith I did not. l. 26. A] We have ventured. l. 27. A—G] A shall command. After 'Rhodes' A—D *add*] Shall we be merry. l. 28. A prints 'Aside' at the end of l. 31, B—E at the end of l. 29. l. 34. A] doth. l. 35. A] the headsman. l. 36. A *omits*] again.

p. 28, l. 1. A] does hee not mocke mee. l. 2. A *omits*] use to. l. 4. A] that wilde breach. C—G and Folio] what wild breath. l. 5. A—G] was so rude. A *omits*] Aside. l. 20. A] this sudden. l. 23. A *omits*] But.

l. 24. A] Say, stay my friend. l. 34. A] shoot. l. 35. A—G] A carries. l. 37. A *omits*] But.

p. 29, l. 1. A—D] This is complement. E] Beleeve me, this complement too cunning for me. l. 4. G] that she may. l. 18. A *omits*] I done. l. 25. A—D] Nor I. A *omits*] Aside. l. 38. A] heighned.

p. 30, l. 7. A] Well? can you be other. l. 9. A *omits*] Amintor. l. 12. A *omits*] too. l. 25. A, B and C] indeed. l. 30. A] how then shewes the sport to you.

p. 31, l. 7. A—G] do hope. l. 13. A *adds*] Aside. ll. 15 and 16. A *omits*] with you. l. 17. A—G] A will not tell. ll. 18 and 19. For these lines A *reads*] For it is apt to thrust this arme of mine to acts unlawfull. l. 21. A] have jealous pangs. l. 23. A] When she dares. l. 27. A *omits*] will and. l. 35. A and B] great, that me thought. A and B] they did misbecome.

p. 32, l. 5. A—G] my. l. 6. G] Touch. ll. 14 and 15. A—G read 'A' for 'He.' l. 17. A—D] not onely shun. l. 20. A—D] I am. E] I no man. l. 21. A *omits*] me. l. 24. A—G] desire. l. 32. A] This is dissembling. ll. 33—36. A *omits* these lines. l. 34. B—D] thee with, look. l. 39. A] shouldst.

p. 33, l. 5. A] The King and I. l. 6. A and B] Oh God. l. 7. G] Who shall. l. 19. A] lies. ll. 24 and 25. In place of these lines A *reads*] Unless I show how nobly I have freed my selfe. l. 26. G] thou cannot fear.

p. 34, l. 4. A] treacherous sword. l. 7. A] there are. A—F] thousands. A *omits*] fools. l. 8. A] the Land. l. 13. A] my fault. l. 25. A—G] hold, hold. l. 28. A] Seconded like that. l. 30. A] Plagues here. l. 31. A *omits*] not. l. 32. A—D] And so I leave you. l. 33. A, B and C] You must needs be prating.

p. 35, l. 5. A] her part. l. 6. A *omits*] treacherous slave. l. 9. A] office. l. 12. A *omits*] Leave. l. 22. A—D] where you. l. 25. A—D] you'l give ground. l. 28. A] hast strength. l. 36. A] I had mongst cowards, but durst never fight. l. 39. A—D] hold him. l. 40. A] askt.

p. 36, l. 2. A *omits*] go home, and. l. 9. A] Mans eyes. A *omits*] so. l. 27. A] strives. l. 29. A] yow weare. l. 31. A] your tongue.

p. 37, l. 1. A] Immutable colour. l. 11. A] and tis not like. l. 18. G *omits*] an. l. 21. A—G] a lied. l. 27. A] See how you plead. l. 29. A, B and C] what I ha done. l. 30. A] with miseries.

p. 38, l. 3. A and B] mine old armour. l. 9. A—E] scape. l. 18. A—D] How's this. l. 27. A] tane. l. 29. A] and stick. ll. 37 and 38. A and B] goe as high As troubled waters.

p. 39, l. 6. A] to be knowne. l. 7. A] be blessed. l. 12. A] fix a farewell. l. 25. A] didst make. l. 37. A—G] foule act on my selfe.

p. 40, l. 1. A] ease of. l. 10. A and B] my horrid point. l. 20. A] thy heart. l. 24. A—E] all that this world. l. 27. A] this bosome. l. 32. A] I call it frõ thee. l. 33. A *omits*] and shame me To posterity. l. 39. A *omits*] be.

p. 41, l. 19. A] speake it. l. 25. A] but have a care. l. 28. A] your house. l. 32. A *omits*] and no more.

p. 42, l. 4. A and B] As well as I could, and sent him. l. 20. A *omits*] to mine.

p. 43, l. 9. G] See what starrs you make. A] your idle hatred. A *omits*] to my love and freedom to you. l. 11. A] I am come. l. 17. A—E *omit*] that. l. 26. A *omits*] or. l. 27. A] The last is spoke, refuse my offerd love.

p. 44, l. 11. A—E] commendations. l. 13. A] your dores. l. 20. A—E] commendations. l. 21. A—E] has made. l. 23. A *omits*] it *after* has. l. 30. A and B] thy repentance. l. 36. A and B] I understand ye not.

p. 45, l. 1. G] ye know. l. 5. D] wins within her. l. 7. A and B] theres your way. l. 11. After this line A—G *add*] Rather to grapple with the plague, or stand. l. 18. A] theile lie. l. 27. A] Though he lie lockt up in thy blood, come tell me. l. 34. A—E *omit*] a. l. 37. A] thy father.

p. 46, l. 7. A] his foe. l. 13. The conclusion of this speech from 'thou hast no hope' is omitted in A. l. 15. B] snatch meat. l. 17. B—G] has undone. l. 23. F *omits* this line. l. 24. A—E] this scandall. l. 27. C—G] raise much out. l. 32. G] thou will deserve it.

p. 47, l. 19. A] Is there no more here. l. 21. A *omits*] O hear me gently; it was. l. 22. A *omits*] no more. ll. 27 and 28. A] *Evad.* Too long, too late I finde it. *Mel.* Can you be very sorry. l. 30. A] Woman thou wilt not to thy trade againe. l. 32. A, B and G] thou hadst. l. 34. A] Has sunk thy faire soule, I command thee curse him.

p. 48, l. 10. A] you had no feare. B and C] you knew no feare. l. 13. A—E] thoudst. l. 37. A and B] Gods where have I beene.

p. 49, l. 13. A] This is a new way to beget more sorrows. l. 17. A—E] naturall wildnesse. l. 22. A and B] that; no sacrifice. C and D] thats; no sacrifice. l. 35. A—E] that dull calamity.

p. 50, l. 8. A] Shall cut. l. 17. Folio *misprints*] whither. F and G] whether. l. 28. A] get beleife. l. 38. G] I will.

p. 51, l. 3. A *omits*] now. l. 6. G] been thus excellently good. l. 25. A, B and C] she have. l. 34. A—D] scape.

p. 52, l. 7. A] I besworne. l. 10. A—D *omit*] of. A—G] a trusted. l. 35. C—G and Folio *misprint*] *Lipsi.* A *omits*] *Diag.*

p. 53, l. 1. F] raise laughter. l. 7. A] *Mel.* l. 12. G] to trust. l. 23. A—D] Ye shall have it soundly I warrant you. l. 31. A—F] scape.

p. 54, l. 16. A—G] A must. l. 21. A—D] can easily. l. 22. A] faults.

p. 55, l. 4. A] Facers, and talkers to defame the world. l. 18. A] Who I, thou shamelesse Fellow that hast spoke to me of it thy Selfe. l. 25. E, F and G] Come from you. l. 29. F gives this speech to Calianax and the next two to Melantius. l. 30. A, B and C] a should. l. 31. A, B and C] in's life.

p. 56, ll. 7 and 8. A *omits* these lines. l. 9. A—G] you your selfe. l. 12. A—E] will as great. l. 16. A *omits*] not. l. 21. G *omits*] better. l. 22. A *omits*] *Aside.* l. 24. G] belive it. l. 27. A—D] Whilst he is hot, for if hee coole agen. E] Whilst he hot, for he coole agen. l. 33. A and B] A pittie. l. 34. A and B] *Mel.* Marke his disordered words, and at the Maske. l. 38. A and B *omit*] too.

p. 57, l. 8. F] When I has. l. 15. A, B and C] Why should. l. 16. D and E] him, alas in his sword. l. 21. A] Too well. G] 'Tis we. l. 28. A *omits*] and believe. ll. 37 and 38. A] Dost not thou looke for some great punishment for this? I feele | My selfe beginne to forget all my hate. l. 40. A] so extremely.

p. 58, l. 1. A] I shall meet. l. 2. A] Unkindnesse. l. 4. A] no wrong. l. 9. A and B] this I call hurt. l. 19. A] his disgrace. l. 26. A] *Melantius*, thou shalt have the fort. l. 40. A—G add at the end of the line] *Diph.*

p. 59, l. 19. A—D *omit*] in. l. 34. G] refused. l. 38. A and B] vild.

p. 60, l. 11. G *omits*] up. l. 20. A—E] Theres not. l. 21. A—E] in 't. l. 23. Folio] Why? The sign has been changed to a comma here and elsewhere in similar cases. l. 25. A and B *add*] *Exeunt.* l. 36. A] and then me thinkes.

p. 61, l. 2. A and B *add*] *Exit.* l. 5. A] lost virtue. l. 7. F, G and Folio] no man dare. l. 9. A] tis a madnesse. l. 10. A] that desperate mans. B and C] fooles. l. 12. A] repent 'em. l. 15. A—G] a sleepes. A] a sleepes, oh God. l. 17. A] That has so farre transgrest you. l. 18. G *omits*] And. l. 19. A] Confirmes me that I merit. l. 21. A] To rake him. l. 22. A] Shall seaze him. l. 23. G] punishment. l. 24. A and B] Ile shape. l. 26. A] I strike. l. 30. In place of this line A *reads*] As I beleeve I shall not, I shall fit him. l. 31. A—G] a sleepes.

p. 62, l. 3. A] may looke. l. 5. F] Say Sir, stay. l. 9. A] Here thou shalt. B and C] thou shalt. D] you shalt. l. 18. A] How *Evadne*? l. 33. Folio] thon.

p. 63, l. 10. A—E] reach. l. 11. A—E] overcharge. l. 15. D] is heaven. l. 16. F] Here Evadne. l. 21. A *omits*] *Stabs him.* l. 29. A *adds*] *Stabs him.* l. 31. A—E add at end of line] King. In F and G the word 'king' is printed by mistake and wrongly spaced at the end of the following line.

p. 64, l. 10. A omits this line. l. 12. A *omits one*] Treason. l. 35. A—E] innocence.

p. 65, l. 1. F *omits*] and. l. 5. A and B] Or to create. l. 17. Folio] beter. l. 21. A] certaine. l. 29. A—E] We could a wisht. l. 31. A—G] thee. l. 35. A] pray to heaven. l. 37. E] then of honor. l. 39. In place of this line A *reads*] I'm sure might have preserved.

p. 66, ll. 1 and 2. A omits these lines. l. 3. A and B] those tears. l. 9. A] And begge. B and C] buy. l. 15. A—E] I have. l. 16. A] for revenge. l. 19. A—G] you wud. l. 24. A—D] free. l. 28. A—E] All up againe. l. 34. A—E] honours. l. 35. A—E] No gaine. A—D] pardons. l. 37. A—D] us all but.

p. 67, l. 2. A] call the King. l. 9. G *omits*] a. l. 10. A] that I doe. l. 16. A—E] the faire office. l. 17. Folio] you. l. 21. A and B] loth to delay. l. 22. A—D *omit*] any. l. 24. A] Sir he will speake with no body, but in particular, I have in charge about no waightie matters. l. 29. A, B and C] vild. l. 30. G] woman. l. 34. A—E] and the smoothest.

p. 68, l. 7. G] O that shape. l. 11. A—E] chance of warre. D and E] marke. l. 21. A] odious. l. 31. A—E] injuries. l. 35. A—E] and would be loth.

p. 69, l. 23. A—E] I prethee. l. 25. Folio] endute. l. 27. A—E] timelesse. l. 29. A—G] has. l. 37. A—D] No houre to live.

p. 70, l. 3. A—D] there is no place. l. 4. B—F print as one stage-direction] Enter Evadne. Her hands bloudy with a knife. A *omits*] Her hands bloudy with a knife. l. 11. A] stald. l. 26. A—E] his height.

l. 27. A—E] found one. l. 29. A—D] continued. l. 33. A] tame my wildest wrongs.

p. 71, ll. 3—5. A omits the words from 'and' to 'shed.' l. 17. A] crueller. l. 20. A and B] for Gods sake. l. 26. A—F] womans. l. 27. A—D] me now againe. l. 32. A—E] but it came. l. 40. A] my selfe unto 'em. E] unto.

p. 72, l. 9. A—E] such another fault. l. 10. A—E] arme her selfe with scorne. l. 24. A and B] Staid my course, it was. l. 25. A and B] Thou art. l. 29. A and B] I shall sure live. C and D] I shall surely live. l. 38. A, B and C] thine hand. A] mine eyes grow up and downe.

p. 73, l. 4. A and B] for Gods sake. l. 5. A—E *omit*] for. l. 7. A, B and C] there nothing stirs. l. 8. A—E *omit*] that. l. 10. A—D] be any life. l. 15. A and B] lend forth some. l. 24. A and B] Oh God. l. 26. A *omits*] Cleon.

p. 74, l. 13. A and B] My last is said, let me give up my soule. l. 16. A *omits*] my. l. 25. Folio] mater. l. 26. A] with you all now. l. 28. A *adds*] *Exit*. l. 31. A—E] hands. A, B and C] sharpe enough. l. 39. A and B] from God.

A—G *add*] Finis.

THE MAIDS TRAGEDY. VERSE AND PROSE VARIATIONS[1].

p. 1, ll. 29 and 30. A, C, D and E] 2 ll. *Poetrie, well.*

p. 2, ll. 7 and 8. A—E] 3 ll. *worth, goe, it.* l. 14. A—E] 2 ll. *Diphilus, ill.*

p. 3, l. 28. A—E] 2 ll. *Evadne, sister.* l. 29. A—E] 2 ll. *them, strange.*

p. 4, ll. 1—5. A and B] 5 ll. *walkes,* [A *sir,* see note to p. 4 *ante*] *earth, delight, flowers, tell.* l. 29. A—E] *speech, love.*

p. 5, l. 20. A—E] 2 ll. *gone, Diphilus.*

p. 8, l. 28. A—E] 2 ll. *home, maske.*

p. 10, l. 17. A—E] 2 ll. *know, ascend.*

p. 13, l. 4. A—E] 2 ll. *powre, calme.*

p. 15, ll. 33—35. A] 3 ll. *caught, fire, thee.* ll. 34 and 35. B—E] 2 ll. *fire, thee.* ll. 36 and 37. A—E] 2 ll. *thing, not.*

p. 19, l. 8. A—E] 2 ll. *sin, lips.* ll. 9 and 10. A] 1 line. l. 23. A—E] 2 ll. *done, meanes.*

p. 20, l. 24. A—E] 2 ll. *oath, true.* ll. 30 and 31. F and G] 1 line.

p. 21, ll. 1 and 2. F and G] 1 line. l. 24. A—D] 2 ll. *hell, me.* ll. 25—27. A and D] 4 ll. *bed, locks, weare, armes.*

p. 22, ll. 28 and 29. A—E] 2 ll. *us, waite.* F and G] 1 line. l. 36. A—E] 2 ll. *be, honourable.* l. 38. A—E] 2 ll. *self, for.*

p. 25, ll. 21 and 22. A] 2 ll. *so, quick-sand.*

p. 28, ll. 16 and 17. A—E] 2 ll. *here, thine.* F and G] 1 line.

[1] In these notes the words printed in italics are the last words of the lines indicated in the various texts.

p. 30, ll. 10 and 11. A—G] 1 line. ll. 27 and 28. A—G] 1 line.

p. 31, ll. 15 and 16. A] 2 ll. *may, well.*

p. 32, l. 7. A—E] 2 ll. *royaltie, stain.* l. 8. A—E] 2 ll. *me, thee.*

p. 33, ll. 27 and 28. A] 2 ll. *weight, rage.* ll. 38 and 39. A and B] 2 ll. *of, you.*

p. 34, l. 8. A] 2 ll. *enough, Land.* B—E] 2 ll. *enough, Island.* l. 21. A—E] 2 ll. *King, it.* ll. 20 and 21. G] 2 ll. *for, it.*

p. 35, l. 25. A—E] 2 ll. *feare, draw.* ll. 35 and 36. A] 2 ll. *tricke, fight.*

p. 36, l. 15. A—E] 2 ll. *rarenesse, now.* l. 32. A—E] 2 ll. *be, it.*

p. 37, l. 8. A—E] *indeed, another.* l. 28. A—E] 2 ll. *say, friend.*

p. 38, l. 6. A—E] 2 ll. *innocence, it.*

p. 39, l. 1. A—E] 2 ll. *base, lies.*

p. 40, l. 29. A—E] 2 ll. *way, backe.*

p. 41, l. 2. A—E] 2 ll. *thine, stir.* l. 8. A] 2 ll. *word, quick.* ll. 39 and 40. A] 2 ll. *why I, else.* B—G] 2 ll. *why, else.*

p. 42, ll. 19—21. A] 3 ll. *hands, I, thee.* l. 21. B—E] 2 ll. *I, thee.*

p. 43, l. 11. A—E] 2 ll. *sute, you.* l. 16. A—E] 2 ll. *it, hands.*

p. 44, ll. 15 and 16. A—E] 3 ll. *daunce, skins, businesse.*

p. 47, l. 10. A—E] *miserie, me.* l. 20. A—E] 2 ll. *many, ist.* l. 39. A—E] *in, hereafter.*

p. 48, l. 1. A—E] 2 ll. *arme, King.*

p. 51, l. 2. A—E] 2 ll. *weepe, water.*

p. 52, l. 5. A—E] 2 ll. *house, Court.* l. 31. A—E] 2 ll. *unlesse, 'em.*

p. 53, l. 27. A—E] 2 ll. *dost, pitty.* l. 36. A—E] 2 ll. *leave, alive.*

p. 54, l. 2. A—E] 2 ll. *Melantius, well.* l. 5. A—E] 2 ll. *besieg'd, commanded.* l. 9. A—E] 2 ll. *it, much.* l. 14. A—E] 2 ll. *mov'd, thing.* l. 34. A—E] 2 ll. *gods, you.* l. 37. A—E] 2 ll. *crime, knew.*

p. 55, l. 23. A—E] 2 ll. *hope, satisfied.*

p. 56, l. 27. A—E] 2 ll. *agen, it.* ll. 31 and 32. A—E] 2 ll. *Foe, him.*

p. 57, ll. 35 and 36. A] 3 ll. *thats, strongest, ye.*

p. 58, l. 9. A—E] 2 ll. *Land, hurt.* l. 22. A—E] 2 ll. *hold, state.* l. 28. A—G] 2 ll. *brest, compasse.*

p. 59, l. 25. A—E] 2 ll. *rage, me.* l. 30. A—E] 2 ll. *sins, ever.*

p. 60, l. 10. A—E] 2 ll. *here, defencelesse.* ll. 17 and 18. A] 2 ll. *plot, King.* ll. 35 and 36. B—D] 2 ll. *will, then.*

p. 64, l. 19. A—E] 2 ll. *act, still.*

p. 67, l. 20. A—E] 2 ll. *desire, him.*

p. 69, l. 17. A—E] 2 ll. *fight, returnd.* l. 19. A—E] 2 ll. *against her, it.* ll. 20 and 21. A—E] 2 ll. *with, you.* l. 27. A—E] 2 ll. *death, selfe.* ll. 37—40 and p. 70, l. 1. A] 5 ll. *meane, me, thee, brest, defencelesse.*

p. 70, l. 3. A—E] 2 ll. *fit, here.* l. 9. A—E] 2 ll. *thee, mischiefes.* l. 11. A—E] 2 ll. *newes, staid* (A *stald*).

p. 71, l. 14. A—E] 2 ll. *it, home.*

p. 72, l. 27. A—E] 2 ll. *hand, yet.* l. 37. A—E] 2 ll. *haire, thee.*

PHILASTER.

(A) Phylaster. | Or, | Love lyes a Bleeding. | Acted at the Globe by his Majesties Servants. | Written by Francis Baymont and John Fletcher. Gent. | Printed at London for Thomas Walkley, and are to be sold at his | shop at the Eagle and Child, in Brittaines Bursse. 1620.

This edition contains, on the title-page, a wood-cut representing 'The Princes' (The Princess) and 'A Cuntrie Gentellman' seated on the ground, and 'Phielaster' leaving them. See the scene in Act IV (*ante*, p. 125).

(B) Philaster. | Or, | Love lies a Bleeding. | As it hath beene diverse times Acted, | at the Globe, and Blacke-Friers, by | his Majesties Servants. | Written by Francis Beaumont. and John Fletcher. Gent. | The second Impression, corrected, and | amended. | London, | Printed for Thomas Walkley, and are to | be solde at his shoppe, at the signe of the | Eagle and Childe, in Brittaines Bursse. | 1622.

(C) Philaster, | or | Love lies a Bleeding. | Acted at the Globe, and Black-friers. By his Majesties Servants. | The Authors being Francis Beaumont, and John Fletcher. | Gentlemen. | The third Impression. | London, | Printed by A. M. for Richard Hawkins, and are to | be sold at his Shop in Chancery-lane, adjoyning | to Sarjeants Inne gate. 1628.

(D) Philaster, | or | Love lies a Bleeding. | Acted at the Globe, and Black-friers. By his Majesties Servants. | The Authors being Francis Beaumont, and John Fletcher. Gentlemen. | The fourth Impression. | London, | Printed by W. J. for Richard Hawkins, and are to | be sold at his Shop in Chancery-lane, adjoyning | to Sarjeants Inne gate. 1634.

(E) Philaster | or | Love lies a Bleeding. | Acted at the Globe, and Black-friers. By his Majesties Servants. | The Authors being Francis Beaumont, and John Fletcher. Gent. | The fourth Impression. | London, | Printed by E. Griffin for William Leak, and are to | be sold at his shop in Chancerie Lane neere | the Rowles. 1639.

(F) Philaster: | or, | Love lies a bleeding. | Acted at the Globe, and Blackfriers, By his Majesties Servants. | The Authors being Francis Beaumont, and John Fletcher, Gent. | The fifth Impression. | London: | Printed for William Leake, and are to be sold at his shop at the | Sign of the Crown in Fleetstreet, between the two | Temple Gates. 1652.

This edition contains on the title-page a small device of fleurs-de-lis.

(G) Philaster | or, | Love lies a bleeding. | Acted at the Globe, and Black-friers, By his Majesties Servants. | The Authors being Francis Beaumont. and John Fletcher, Gent. | The fifth Impression. | London: | Printed for William Leake, and are to be sold at his shop at the | signe of the Crown in Fleet street, between the two | Temple Gates. 1652.

On the back of the title-page (which contains the device of a crown) is a list of books printed or sold by William Leake.

(H) Philaster | or, | Love lies a Bleeding: | Acted at the Globe, and Black-friers, By his Majesties servants. | The Authors being Francis Beaumont, and John Fletcher, Gent. | The sixth Impression. | London, | Printed for William Leake, and are to be sold at his shop at the | signe of the Crown in Fleet street, between the two | Temple Gates.

This edition, conjecturally dated 1660 in the British Museum Catalogue, contains, on the back of the title-page and at the foot of the list of persons represented, lists of books printed or sold by William Leake at the Crown in Fleet Street.

A The first few pages and the last few pages of the play as printed in A vary so completely from the other texts that it has been necessary to print them separately. See *post*, pp. 401—3, 413—17.

B contains the following Address to the Reader:

'*To the Reader*.

'Courteous Reader. *Philaster*, and *Arethusa* his love, have laine so long a bleeding, by reason of some dangerous and gaping wounds, which they received in the first Impression, that it is wondered how they could goe abroad so long, or travaile so farre as they have done. Although they were hurt neither by me, nor the Printer; yet I knowing and finding by experience, how many well-wishers they have abroad, have adventured to bind up their wounds, & to enable them to visite upon better tearmes, such friends of theirs, as were pleased to take knowledge of them, so mained [? maimed] and deformed, as they at the first were; and if they were then gracious in your sight, assuredly they will now finde double favour, being reformed, and set forth suteable, to their birth, and breeding.

By your serviceable
Friend,
Thomas Walkley.'

C prefixes to the play the following Address repeated with variations of spelling in the five later quartos:

'The Stationer, To the Understanding Gentrie.

'This play so affectionatly taken, and approoved by the Seeing Auditors, or Hearing Spectators, (of which sort, I take, or conceive you to bee the greatest part) hath received (as appeares by the copious vent of two [D and E three; F, G and H four] Editions,) no lesse acceptance with improovement of you likewise the Readers, albeit the first Impression swarm'd with Errors, prooving it selfe like pure Gold, which the more it hath beene tried and refined, the better is esteemed; the best Poems of this kind, in the first presentation, resemble [D—H resembling] that all tempting Minerall newly digged up, the Actors being onely the labouring Miners, but you the skilfull Triers and Refiners: Now considering [D—H consider] how currant this hath passed, under the infallible stampe of your judicious censure, and applause, and (like a gainefull Office in this Age) eagerly sought for, not onely by those that have heard & seene it, [F—H *omit* heard and] but by others that have meerely heard thereof: here you behold me acting the Merchant-adventurers part, yet as well for their satisfaction, as mine owne benefit, and if my hopes (which I hope, shall never lye like this LOVE A BLEEDING,) doe fairely arrive at their intended Haven, I shall then be ready to lade a new Bottome, and [D—H *omit* and] set foorth againe, to gaine the good-will both of you and them. To whom respectively I convey this hearty greeting: ADIEU.'

p. 75, l. 3. A and B *omit*] or, Love lies a Bleeding. ll. 4 *et seq.* A]

THE ACTORS NAMES.

King of Cecely	Callatea, a Lady of Honor.
Arathusa, the Princesse.	Megra, another Lady.
Phylaster.	A Waiting Gentlewoman.
Pharamont, a Spanish Prince,	Two Woodmen.
Leon, a Lord.	A Countrey Gallant.
Gleremon } Trasilin } Two Noble Gentlemen	An Old Captaine. And Souldiers.
Bellario a Page, Leon's daughter.	A Messenger.

B *omits* the list of Persons Represented in the Play and also *The Scene*, etc. l. 5. C—H] The persons presented are these, viz.

In A the play, down to l. 26 of p. 78, begins as follows]

Actus I. Scoen. I.

Enter at severall doores Lord Lyon, Trasiline, *followes him*, Clerimon *meetes them.*

TRASILINE.

Well ore tane my Lord.

LYON. Noble friend welcome, and see who encounters us, honourable good *Clerimon.*

CLE. My good Lord *Lyon*, most happily met worthy *Trasiline*,
Come gallants, what's the newes,
the season affoords us variety,
the novilsts of our time runnes on heapes,
to glut their itching eares with airie sounds,
trotting to'th burse; and in the Temple walke
with greater zeale to heare a novall lye,
than a pyous Anthum tho chanted by Cherubins.

TRANS. True Sir:
and holds set counsels, to vent their braine sicke opinions
with presagements what all states shall designe.

CLE. Thats as their intelligence serves.

LYON. And that shall serve as long as invention lastes,
there dreames they relate, as spoke from Oracles,
or if the gods should hold a synod, and make them their secritaries,
they will divine and prophecie too: but come and speake your
thoughts of the intended marriage with the Spanish Prince,
He is come you see, and bravely entertainde.

TRAS. Hee is so, but not married yet.

CLE. But like to be, and shall have in dowry with the Princesse this Kingdome of *Cycele.*

LEON. Soft and faire, there is more will forbid the baines, then say amen to the marriage: though the King usurped the Kingdome during the non-age of the Prince *Phylaster*, hee must not thinke to bereave him of it quite; hee is now come to yeares to claime the Crowne.

TRA. And lose his head i' the asking.

LEON. A diadem worn by a headlesse King wold be wonderous, *Phylaster* is too weake in power.

CLE. He hath many friends.
LEON. And few helpers.
TRA. The people love him.
LEON. I grant it, that the King knowes too well,
And makes this Contract to make his faction strong:
Whats a giddy-headed multitude,
That's not Disciplinde nor trainde up in Armes,
To be trusted unto? No, he that will
Bandy for a Monarchie, must provide
Brave marshall troopes with resolution armde,
To stand the shock of bloudy doubtfull warre,
Not danted though disastrous Fate doth frowne,
And spit all spightfull fury in their face:
Defying horror in her ugliest forme,
And growes more valiant, the more danger threats;
Or let leane famine her affliction send,
Whose pining plagues a second hel doth bring,
Thei'le hold their courage in her height of spleene,
Till valour win plenty to supply them,
What thinke ye, would yer feast-hunting Citizens
Indure this?

TRA. No sir, a faire march a mile out of town that their wives may bring them their dinners, is the hottest service that they are trained up to.

CLE. I could wish their experience answered their loves,
Then should the much too much wrongd *Phylaster*,
Possesse his right in spight of Don and the divell.
TRA. My heart is with your wishes.
LEON. And so is mine,
And so should all that loves their true borne Prince,
Then let us joyne our Forces with our mindes,
In whats our power to right this wronged Lord,
And watch advantage as best may fit the time
To stir the murmuring people up,
Who is already possest with his wrongs,
And easily would in rebellion rise,
Which full well the King doth both know and feare,
But first our service wee'le proffer to the Prince,
And set our projects as he accepts of us;
But husht, the King is comming.

sound musicke within.

Enter the King, Pharamont, *the Princesse, the Lady* Gallatea, *the Lady* Megra, *a Gentlewoman, with Lords attending, the King takes his seate.*

KING. Faire Prince,
Since heavens great guider furthers our intents,
And brought you with safety here to arrive
Within our Kingdome and Court of *Cycele*,
We bid you most welcome, Princely *Pharamont*,
And that our Kingly bounty shall confirme,
Even whilst the Heavens hold so propitious aspect
Wee'le crowne your wisht desires (with our owne)

Lend me your hand sweet Prince, hereby enjoy
A full fruition of your best contents,
The interest I hold I doe possesse you with,
Onely a fathers care, and prayers retaine,
That heaven may heape on blessings, take her Prince,
A sweeter Mistrisse then the offered Language of any dame,
were she a Queene whose eye speakes common Loves,
and comfort to her servants: Last Noble son, for so I now must call you, what I have done thus publik, is not to add a comfort in particular to you or mee, but all, and to confirme the Nobles and the Gentrie of our Kingdome by oath to your succession: which shall be within this moneth at most.

l. 28. B—E] nor Lords, nor Ladyes. l. 33. B and C] desired. l. 34. Folio] ghess.

p. 76, l. 1. B and C] Faith sir. l. 8. F] for me.

p. 77, l. 1. B and C] Faith, I thinke. l. 29. B] quickly to bee. l. 33. D—H] To give a stranger. l. 35. In B—H bracket ends with this line. l. 37. F, G, H and the Folio *misprint*] your daughter. l. 38. C, D and E] your subjects.

p. 78, l. 9. E—H] I making. l. 13. B] To talke of her. l. 22. B *omits*] a. l. 29. A] when it is. l. 30. A—E] is wrong'd.

p. 79, l. 4. A] And in me. l. 5. A, B and C] By more then all the gods, I hold it happy. D and E] By more then all my hopes I hold it happy (A—E *repeat happy at beginning of next line*). l. 9. A] rotting age. l. 10. A—H] Open. l. 15. A] finde it out. l. 16. A, B and C] And tye it to this Countrey. By all the gods. l. 17. A] as easie to the subjects. l. 27. A] Miracles. l. 30. A prints this stage-direction after the word 'shape' in l. 32. l. 31. A] he'le sell him, he has so be praised his shape. B—G] sell himself. l. 33. A] large praises. ll. 34 and 35. A] Let mee bee swallowed quicke, if I can finde all the Anatomy of yon mans vertues unseene to sound enough. l. 37. A, B and C] of trifles. l. 39. A *omits*] And.

p. 80, l. 1. A] for favour. l. 3. A, B and C] how pale he lookes, he feares. l. 4. A] And this same whoresone conscience, ah how it jades us. l. 5. B] intent. l. 6. A] speak on. l. 11. F and G] turn'd. l. 15. A] sweet Princesse. l. 25. A, B and C *add after*] ashes, as I. l. 26. F] goes. l. 30. A] his hidden bowels. l. 31. A, B and C] By the just gods it shall. l. 35. A] I Prince of popines, I will make it well appeare. l. 40. A] Turcle.

p. 81, l. 2. A] make. ll. 3 and 4. A] I doe not fancy this choller, Sure hee's somewhat tainted. l. 8. A] be constant gentle heavens, I'le run. B and C] Be constant Gentlemen, by heaven I'le run. l. 10. A—D] we are all one. l. 17. A] leave it to me. l. 19. D, E and G] were. l. 21. A—F] any thing but thine. G] any thine. l. 25. A and B] belied. l. 26. A] and from his presence. Spit all those bragges. B—E] presence. B *omits*] all. ll. 29 and 30. A *omits*] to brave our best friends. You deserve our frown. l. 31. A] noblier. l. 32. A gives this speech to Leon, i.e., Dion. l. 34. A] never. l. 35. A] This is. l. 37. A *omits*] your. l. 38. A] but i'm sure tothers the man set in my eye. A—G] my eye.

p. 82, l. 4. A] griefe. l. 5. A] My wants. A, B and C] now nothing hopes and feares. l. 7. A and B *omit*] not. l. 8. A] Phy: whispers the King. l. 9. A *omits* this line. ll. 12 and 13. A] has a soule of Christall, to read their actions, though mens faces. l. 14. A *omits*] Do. A] but view the stranger well. F] your stranger. l. 15. A] throw all. A] braveries. l. 16. A] a true truant. l. 17. A] I am no augery. l. 21. A] you are. l. 22. A] smooth your selfe. l. 24. A, B and C *omit*] not. l. 25. A—E] my weake starres lead me too; [A:] all my weake fortunes. l. 26. A] dare. A *omits* parenthesis. B] presence (speake, that is. l. 30. A *omits*] Sure. l. 31. A] Yes, with my fathers spirit is heare O King. l. 32. A] and now. l. 34. A—E] these are. l. 39. The Folio *misprints*] hour hand.

p. 83, l. 2. A] of your life. l. 4. A *omits*] your. A *omits*] Ex. King, Pha. and Are. B—H *omit*] and. l. 6. A gives this speech to 'Tra.,' i.e., Thrasiline. l. 8. A—G] is he not. l. 10. A—G] I could. A] their nation. l. 12. A gives this speech to 'Lad.,' i.e., Lady. A, B and C] Gods comfort. A *omits*] Lady. l. 13. A] has. A, B and C with variations of spelling *add*] Exet Ladies. l. 27. A] recluses. l. 28. A] How doe your worth sir. l. 30. A *omits*] I find. l. 32. A] Sir, the King must please. l. 33. A] who you are, and what you are. F] what we are and who you are. l. 34. The Folio *misprints*] juriuries. A] your wrongs and vertues. l. 35. A] but call your father to you. l. 38. A *omits*] to.

p. 84, l. 2. A] Friend. l. 3. A—D] our eares. l. 5. F] Do you love. l. 6. A] Lyon. l. 10. A] a penance. l. 12. For this line A after l. 8 *reads*] Enter a Gentlewoman. l. 13. A] I'st to me, or to any of these Gentlemen you come. l. 14. Here and at l. 17 for 'La.' A *reads*] Gent-Woo. l. 16. A] you are. l. 17. A *omits*] to. l. 18. A, B and C] her faire hand. l. 19. A *adds*] Exit Gent-Woo. l. 21. F] But do weigh. l. 28. A] and white fiend frends in her cheekes. l. 30. In D—H the stage-direction 'Ex. Phil.' is printed at the end of l. 29. l. 32. B—G] th' art. l. 35. A] Enter Princesse and her Gentlewoman. ll. 36 and 37. For 'Are.' A *reads* throughout the scene 'Prin.,' and for 'La.' *reads* 'Woo.'

p. 85, l. 2. A] at the first. l. 5. A—H] dangers. l. 7. A] dares. l. 12. A, B and C] You all are. l. 17. A *omits*] Fear. A] mee thoughts. l. 21. A] with such a woing jesture and puicke looks. l. 22. A *omits*] him. l. 27. A] his ends. l. 29. A] To things so opposite, so bound to put. l. 31. A *omits*] of mine. l. 32. A *omits*] Of. l. 35. A] that will not have your dens withstood. l. 37. A, B and C] passions. l. 38. A] into. l. 40. A and B] Oh it is well.

p. 86, l. 5. A] dos so ill become. l. 14. A] Injury. l. 15. A] found to be so great. l. 24. A] Both, or I do. A, B and C] by heaven. l. 25. A] if I not calmely die injoy them both. l. 28. H] give. l. 40. A and B] I can indure it.

p. 87, l. 1. A] saw yet. l. 2. A—H] dreadfully. l. 3. A] speake. l. 4. A—D] horrible. l. 7. A] a womans tongue. l. 10. A] you that beg. l. 11. F and G] unprice. l. 17. F] The love. l. 22. A *omits*] doth. B—E] doe. l. 26. A] might have. l. 35. A *omits*] The gods. l. 36. A] the worthier, and the better blest. l. 39. A] unwelcom'd.

p. 88, l. 5. A—G] true loves. l. 9. B—H] fountaines. l. 11. A] as much againe. l. 13. A] bred in the vayle. l. 16. A] eye. l. 17. A] make them. l. 23. A] the course. l. 24. A] it yeelded him his life. l. 30. A] me thoughts. l. 32. A] whom was glad. l. 33. F and G] The truliest. F] gentle. l. 36. A] Enter woman. In A and B this stage-direction occurs after l. 37. l. 38. A for 'La.' *reads*] Woo. l. 39. A] Phylaster doe.

p. 89, l. 4. A, B and C] the voyce of God. l. 5. A] yet I doe not hide my selfe. l. 13. Folio has a full-stop at end of line. l. 14. A *omits*] for my sake do. l. 16. A] Enter Pharamont and a woman. ll. 19 and 20. A] the deare love within my heart. l. 21. A] if I shall have an answer or no, derectly I am gone. l. 23. A] To what? what would he have answer. B—E *omit*] an. l. 25. A—D] forbare. l. 29. A] though it lie. l. 31. A, B and C] And by the gods. l. 32. A] if then. l. 35. A *omits* this line, though the words '*Pha.* You' are printed as turn-over words at the foot of the page.

p. 90, l. 1. A] nothing. l. 5. A] so much. ll. 7 and 8. A] but wert the Church at the high Altar. l. 9. A] injurie. l. 10. A *omits*] Sir. l. 12. A and B *omit*] Phi. l. 16. A *omits*] But. l. 17. A, B and C] but yet. l. 19. A] before our hearts bee so, then if you please. l. 21. A—E] dreaming forme. l. 23. A] your thoughts. l. 28. A] and his boy, called Bellario. l. 31. A] thy owne. l. 33. A *reads* 'Boy' for 'Bell.' here and throughout the play. l. 34. A] And I am onely yet some thing. l. 35. A—H] were apt. l. 37. A] crafty.

p. 91, l. 6. A] bear'st. l. 7. A] claps. A *omits*] yet. l. 8. A] but when judgement comes no rule those passions. l. 17. A *omits*] grown. l. 30. A] dos plead. l. 32. A] knowst. l. 33. A] dos call. l. 34. B] dwellest.

p. 92, l. 5. A] your loves, your sighes. l. 7. B—H] heaven. A] Exit boy. l. 8. C] Lord. l. 11. A] I must see. l. 12. A *omits*] Phi. l. 18. A] before in my life. l. 20. A] I'le hound at her. Madame. F] Heer's on boulted, I'le bound at her. l. 21. In A the words 'Enter Gallatea' occur after the word 'fault' in l. 19. l. 25. A] y'are. l. 26. A *omits*] but. l. 28. A] those two I onely barre. l. 32. A] Couch. l. 33. A] a play and a banquet. ll. 34 and 35. A] to make you blush, this is my owne hayre, and this face. l. 36. A—D and F] a peny painting. l. 37. A and H] wardrop. G] wardrope. l. 38. A] the jealous silke-mans wife curse our doing.

p. 93, l. 1. A] You much mistake me Lady. l. 2. Folio *misprints Pha.* for *Gal.* After this line A *adds*] *Pha.* Y'are very dangerous bitter, like a potion. *Gal.* No sir, I do not mean to purge you, though I meane to purge a little time on you. l. 8. A and B] Cardus. A] about five. l. 11. A] and Conger. A] they are dullers. l. 12. A] the vitall anymales. l. 13. A] all this time. ll. 16 and 17. A] Shee's daintie, and must be courted with a shewer of gold. l. 19. A] What ha you. l. 20. A] you'd have silver fort. l. 21. A] a worse time sir. l. 23. A] gold safe for you. A *adds*] She slips behind the Orras. ll. 25 and 26. In place of these two lines A] *Gal.* Shes comming sir behind, Will ye take white money yet for all this. *Exit.* l. 27. A] If there be but two such in this Kingdome more. B—H] If there be but two such more in this Kingdome. l. 28. A] ene. l. 31. A] would breed. l. 39. A] doe not call you Lady.

p. 94, l. 1. A—G] talke an houre. l. 5. A] your lip. l. 6. A] time enough. l. 8. A—D] and red enough. l. 10. A] twend Cherries dyde in blush. l. 11. A] deepe beames. l. 14. A] sweete looker on. A] these blessings. l. 15. A *adds as a stage-direction*] They kisse. l. 18. A *omits*] off. l. 19. A] it may be a number without Probatum. l. 20. A] by such neate Poetrie. l. 26. A] but you. l. 28. A] now you ha dont before me. l. 29. A] And yet. l. 31. A] never. l. 34. A] ye. l. 36. A—H and Folio] this is all.

p. 95, l. 5. A] my masculine imagination. l. 7. B] mine honor. l. 9. A] my other. l. 10. A] Sir *Timen* a schoolemaister. l. 11. A] keepe. B and C *add*] Madam. l. 14. Folio] apoplex? l. 15. A *omits* 'And' and 'Sir.' l. 17. A] tied toot. l. 19. A *omits*] Look well about you, and you may find a tongue-bolt. l. 21. A and B] whether. l. 24. A *omits* the second 'I dare not.' l. 27. A] give worship to you thoughts. l. 28. A] y'are. l. 29. A] I shall visit you. l. 30. A] most uncertaine. l. 34. A] Exit ambo. B] Exeunt. l. 35. A] the Orras. l. 38. A] Dowsabell. A] for it. l. 39. A *omits*] Gal.

p. 96, l. 1. A] Enter Princesse and her Gentlewoman. These characters are in A indicated by 'Prin.' and 'Wo.' throughout the scene. l. 3. A *omits*] Madam. l. 8. A—H and Folio] boy. A] i'st not. l. 11. In A this stage-direction occurs after l. 7. l. 14. A—G] has done. l. 19. A] they shall be. l. 23. A, B and C] suspected. l. 26. A] presents. l. 31. A—H] was never. l. 34. A] Enter Boy. He is called 'Boy' throughout the scene. l. 35. A] your sad. l. 38. A] Then trust in me.

p. 97, l. 6. A] a crosse schoole-maister. l. 8. A] water. l. 9. H and Folio *misprint*] dreath. F, G and H] trouble. l. 10. A *omits*] out. l. 11. A] it selfe. l. 12. A, B and C] doth. l. 13. A] *Boy*. I know not Madame, what it is. l. 18. A, B and C] respect to. l. 19. A, B and C] with thinking. l. 20. A, B and C] thinke away. l. 21. A] with mingling starts, and crying. l. 22. A *omits*] and hastily. A] in streetes. l. 24. A] any woman. l. 28. A] drop beades. ll. 30 and 31. A] taught to your Lords credit. l. 35. A] thus away. l. 36. A] Enter the three Gentlewomen, Megra, Gallatea, and another Lady. B—H *omit*] and. l. 37. A gives this speech to 'Tra.,' i.e., Thrasiline. l. 38. A—G] talke an hour.

p. 98, l. 4. A] theyre. B] theile scarce find. l. 5. A and B] your owne lodging. l. 6. A] Enter Pharamont, the Princesse boy, and a woman. l. 9. A] pleasing. l. 11. A] I shall choose. l. 12. A *omits* this stage-direction. l. 13. Here and throughout the scene 'Are.' is 'Prin.' in A. A *omits*] my Lord. A and B] these Ladyes. l. 15. A gives this speech to Galatea. l. 17. A *omits*] you. l. 18. A *omits*] has. A] Hilus. l. 20. A] Why this is that. l. 27. A] to hide it. l. 32. A] you have. G] y'are. l. 34. A *omits*] Come. l. 35. A *omits*] Ex. Gal. and Meg. B—H *omit*] and.

p. 99, l. 3. A as stage-direction after the word 'late' on p. 98, l. 37 *reads*] Enter the King, the Princesse, and a guard. l. 4. C *omits*] your. l. 11. A *omits*] have. l. 12. A *omits*] Ex. Are. and Bel. B—H *omit*] and. l. 19. A gives this speech to 'Leon,' i.e., Dion, and *adds*] Exit Leon. l. 28. A] from the earth. l. 33. A] undeserving child. A *omits*] of mine. l. 34. A] if she has not broke your lawes, but how could I. l. 36. A] in wrong.

p. 100, l. 9. A] get from them. A *omits*] I think. A] shee's. l. 11. F] not time. l. 14. A *omits*] louder yet. l. 15. A] your pleasure...your hearing. l. 16. A] meditation. Folio] meditations? ll. 17 and 18. A] and lowder, not yet, I do not thinke he sleepes, having such larumes by him, once more, Pharamont. *They knock*. ll. 17 and 18. B] his Larum. l. 19. A] Enter Pharamont above. l. 23. A] Prince, Prince. l. 26. A] The same, sir. Come downe sir. l. 29. A *omits*] Pha. below. l. 31. A] I have certain private reasons to my selfe sir. ll. 31 and 32. A as a marginal direction] They prease to come in. l. 33. A *omits*] Gentlemen. l. 35. A] I must come, and will come enter. D—H and Folio print 'Enter' after a space at the end of preceding line. l. 36. A] dishonoured thus. l. 39. A] runagates.

p. 101, l. 3. A *omits*] so. l. 4. A *omits*] I'le. l. 5. A *omits*] known. l. 6. A] I so no. A *omits*] Meg. Above. l. 8. A *omits*] and ready. l. 9. A] tis a poore. l. 15. A] whoting. l. 18. A] still in store. l. 22. A—E and G] wring. l. 24. A] chide you dearly. l. 25. A *omits*] worthy. l. 26. A] his lodging. l. 28. A] Stage. l. 31. A, B and C] Pray God. ll. 31 and 32. A has marginal stage-direction] they come downe to the King. l. 33. A *omits* this stage-direction. l. 37. A] Apothecaries.

p. 102, l. 2. A] all sinne and hell. l. 5. A *omits*] and. l. 7. A] reball rymes. l. 9. B, C and D] ye. l. 13. A—G] those gods. l. 15. A] that shall make. l. 17. A] Upon wals. A] or any thing. l. 19. A] her fayre leaps And out-lying, and will discover all, and will dishonour her. l. 22. A *omits*] and. l. 31. A] sinke alone. l. 32. A] in print. ll. 33 and 34. A] they're. l. 37. A *omits*] nay.

p. 103, l. 1. A gives this speech to 'Leon,' i.e., Dion. l. 3. A] quarters. ll. 5 and 6. A] Do so, and i'le forget your ——. l. 6. A] and the Guard. B—H *omit*] and. l. 7. A *omits*] Why. A and B] fit for Hercules. l. 8. A] worthy. C] woman. A] aside. l. 10. A—H] has. l. 11. A—H] uttered. B and C] metled. l. 12. A] will not cure him. l. 13. A, B and C] infections. l. 14. A] chast, brave. l. 16. A] leave yee. l. 18. A] Exit three Gentlemen. l. 20. A] Enter three Gentlemen. B—H *omit*] and. l. 21. A] And doubtlesse. l. 25. A] for all us. A *omits*] should. l. 33. A] strange thing.

p. 104, l. 3. A *omits* this line. l. 5. A *omits*] bent. l. 6. A *omits*] that's. l. 8. A] draweth. l. 10. A] and we can now comfort. l. 11. A *omits*] it. l. 12. A gives this speech to Cleremont. l. 13. A gives this speech to 'Leon,' i.e., Dion. l. 15. A] on his beleefe. l. 17. A] Lords to his owne good. l. 19. A *omits*] nay. l. 23. A gives this speech to Cleremont. ll. 27 and 28. A] frame on men disgrace for vertue. l. 30. A *omits*] good. l. 33. A] dull. l. 35. A *omits*] or. A] knowes. B] knowne. l. 38. A] deserved more.

p. 105, l. 2. A and B] to thankes. l. 3. A] sufficient. l. 5. A *omits*] Sir. l. 6. A *omits*] will not. l. 8. A] long have. l. 11. A gives this speech to 'Tra.,' i.e., Thrasiline. l. 14. B by mistake gives this speech to Di. l. 16. A] He offers to draw his sword, and is held. l. 18. A] then to rob. l. 22. A] faithfull to increase. l. 24. A] cut out falsehood where it growes. l. 25. A] that man. l. 32. A] injuries. l. 38. A] your pardon. l. 39. A] makes.

p. 106, l. 1. A] backs. l. 5. A] tis then truth that women all are false. B and C] Tis then truth that woman-kind is false. D] thee truth. D—G] woman-kind. l. 6. A] tis. l. 9. A, B and C] by heaven. ll. 10 and 11. A *omits*] for love of truth speak; Is't possible? l. 10. B and C] for God's love speake. l. 12. A *omits* this line. l. 13. A gives this line to 'Tra.,' i.e., Thrasiline. l. 14. A gives this speech to Cleremont. l. 20. A] a little milder. l. 22. A] desires. l. 23. A] and know the sinne she acts. B and C] know. l. 26. A gives this speech to Cleremont. l. 30. A] women. l. 34. A and B] mine eyes. l. 35. A] daggers in thy breast. B] tane. l. 36. A] stuacke dumb. C] did. l. 37. A] this fault might. ll. 38 and 39. In A the speakers are transposed.

p. 107, l. 1. A *omits*] several. l. 2. A] and spreads them selfe. l. 3. A] Meetes not a fayre on. What, etc. l. 4. A] thorow. l. 5. A gives this speech to 'Tra.,' i.e., Thrasiline. l. 6. A—D] fall. A, B and C] distracted. l. 10. A] do 't. l. 12. A] lodgings. A *omits*] forth. ll. 14 and 15. A] Omnes. All the gods direct you the readiest way. B, C and D] Di. All the gods direct you The readiest way. A *adds*] Exit three Gent. ll. 16—18. A *omits* these lines. l. 18. B—H *omit*] and. l. 19. A] aske um where he tooke her. l. 22. A] would but flame. l. 24. A] the deede. A] it is. l. 30. A] take them. l. 33. F] spring. l. 36. A prints after the words 'miserable man'] Enter boy. l. 39. A] not blush.

p. 108, l. 4. In A throughout the scene Bellario is indicated by 'Boy.' l. 6. A adds stage-direction] He gives him a letter. l. 10. A *omits*] my. l. 12. A] But far unfit for me that doe attend. l. 13. A] my boy. l. 15. A] with this paper. l. 16. A] twines of Adamant. l. 19. A] How dos. l. 20. A *omits* this line. l. 26. A] meet. l. 28. A] Why, tis. l. 31. A] with al her maiden store. l. 33. A] service. l. 34. A] rewarded. l. 36. A] speakes. l. 38. A] not well. B—G] not ill.

p. 109, l. 1. A] fall out from your tongue, so unevenly. l. 2. A] quicknesse. l. 12. A, B and C] Never my Lord, by heaven. l. 13. A, B and C] That's strange, I know, etc. l. 16. A] I bid her do 't. l. 18. A] delight. l. 19. A] as to her Lord. l. 21. A] paradise. B] parrallesse. C and D] parallesse. l. 25. A] Yes, now I see why my discurled thoughts. l. 27. A] augeries. l. 29. A] where you tend. l. 31. A] noble friend. l. 35. A] with sparrowes eyes. l. 39. A] and of goates. l. 40. A] that weighed from.

p. 110, l. 2. A] come. l. 4. A] main deceit. l. 8. A—H] As I do now thy face. l. 14. A] wrack it. l. 17. A] hate me. l. 19. A *omits*] Greater. A] to me. l. 21. Folio] dist. l. 22. A] upon me. A *adds* stage-direction] He drawes his sword. l. 23. A, B and C] By heaven I never did. l. 27. A—G] kiss those limbs. l. 29. A—D] Fear'st. l. 32. A] could be. l. 34. A *omits*] but. B] doest. l. 39. A] giving ore againe, That must be lost.

p. 111, l. 1. A, B and C] those. l. 2. A] and then thou wilt. l. 7. B by mistake *omits*] *Phi*. l. 12. B—E] doest. B] utterst. H] uttrest. l. 13. Folio *misprints*] known. l. 17. A] Thy honest lookes. l. 18. B] doest. l. 19. A] thy blood. l. 23. A] tenderest. l. 27. A] honord frame. l. 28. A] haplesse. l. 31. A] sorrowes. l. 33. Folio has full-stop at end of line. l. 34. A *omits*] Exit Bel. l. 36. A] what ere. A, B and C] deservest. F] deserv'd. l. 37. A and B] bathe. A—G] this body. l. 38. A] mad'st no medicine to.

p. 112, l. 1. A] Enter Princesse. l. 2. For 'Are.' A prints throughout scene] Prin. A *omits*] again. l. 4. A] slept, make talke. l. 5. A] remember. l. 6. A] was last spoken, And how spoke when I sight song. l. 9. A] What, in your. B—E and G] What, at your. F] What of your. l. 17. A] ugly Sir. l. 28. A and B] Put him away I say. l. 32. A *omits*] Sir. l. 33. A] a command. l. 35. A] that shame to you, ye are one. l. 36. A *omits*] unto. l. 37. A] by the gods.

p. 113, l. 1. B] I have. A *omits*] my Lord. l. 7. A] maid. l. 8. A, B and C] honour faire. l. 10. A] truth. l. 14. A] Oh how they mind to. l. 15. A] foule sicke. A] stricke the mountaines. l. 16. A] be sleeping. l. 25. E—H *misprint*] He right. A—G] honour. l. 35. A] Oh my misfortune. B, a space being left between the 'i' and the 'f'] My mi fortune. C] Oh my my fortune. l. 36. F] Let me go.

p. 114, l. 1. H] your letters. l. 2. A] make. l. 3. A] Who shall now sing. l. 5. A] and make them warme. l. 7. A, B and C] eye-lids. l. 8. A] Make me. D, E, G and H] Philast. l. 12. A] get you. l. 14. Folio *misprints*] Bell. l. 16. A] All service in servants. l. 17. A] and all desires to doe well, for thy sake. l. 21. A] unto. l. 29. A by mistake *omits*] Phi. A] O ye gods, ye gods. l. 30. A] a wealthy patience. l. 31. A] above the shocke. l. 32. A] mischiefe. l. 33. Folio *misprints*] live. l. 34. A] as deepe as. l. 36. A] And flowing it by. l. 38. A] heare. l. 39. A *omits*] must.

p. 115, l. 8. A] poyson. l. 10. A] and there dig. A] beasts and birds. l. 11. A] women are. A *omits*] and help to save them from you. l. 16. A *omits*] so. A] men. l. 17. A] reade. l. 21. A] frost. l. 28. A] you gods. F *omits*] ye. l. 30. A *omits*] as pure Crystal. C] a pure Christall. l. 32. A] shall women turne their eies. l. 33. A after 'constancy'] Enter boy. l. 34. A] And vile. B] And guiltily. l. 35. A] spokst. H] speak'st. l. 37. A] And to betray innocence. l. 38. A] Maist.

p. 116, l. 3. A] undertooke. l. 5. A] Lest we should. l. 7. A] angry with me. l. 11. A] has. B—H] hath. l. 17. A] some greater fault. l. 18. A] suffering. l. 21. A] Exit Boy. l. 22. A] thou hast. l. 23. A] But if I had another time to lose. l. 25. A] Might take. l. 30. A *omits*] a Lady. l. 35. A] Exit Princesse.

p. 117, ll. 2 and 3. A] Enter the King, Pharamont, Princesse, Megra, Gallatea, Leon, Cle., Tra. and two Wood-men. l. 7. A] you are. l. 8. A] trespasses. l. 9. A, B and C] here's none. A] dares. l. 12. A] lake. l. 17. A] pernitious. A *omits*] loose. l. 18. A, B and C] pursue. A] any Lady. l. 22. A—H] obeyed. l. 23. A and B] furder. l. 24. A gives this speech to 'Leon,' i.e., Dion, and the following speech to 'Tra.' l. 31. A—G] yon Lady. l. 32. A and B] neighbours. l. 33. A] can you see. l. 34. A gives this speech to Cleremont, B and C to 'Tra.' A, B and C] Faith no great. l. 37. A gives this speech to 'Tra.,' and the following speech to 'Leon,' i.e., Dion. l. 38. A] regient. A] damn'd.

p. 118, l. 1. A] the flesh and the world. l. 3. A] done against. l. 4. A] dares. l. 8. A *omits*] her. l. 9. A—D] health. l. 10. A] except. l. 11. A and B] large summe. ll. 14 and 15. A] Exit King and Lords, Manet Wood-men. l. 16. A] the Deere below. l. 23. A] strange. l. 28. A] docets. B, C and D] Dowcets. A] his steward. A—E *omit*] had. l. 30. A] he and old Sir Tristrum. A] ye. l. 31. A] a Stagge. l. 37. A, B and C] by the gods. A *omits*] she's. A] a fault or no.

p. 119, l. 2. A—G] haunches. l. 5. B—G] have been. l. 8. A] harke else. A *omits*] Exeunt. l. 9. A] Enter Philaster solus. l. 10. A] the woods. l. 11. A] acrons. B—H] akrons. l. 13. A] of cruell love. ll. 17 and 18. A] chaste as the rocke whereon she dwelt. l. 20. A] borne out her. l. 22. A] Enter Boy. l. 24. A—H *omit*] man. l. 25. A] I see. ll. 27 and 28. A] that brake. l. 33. A] fortunes. l. 38. A *omits* this and the five succeeding lines.

p. 120, l. 1. B, C and D] wearest. l. 6. A, B and C] by the gods. l. 8. A] thou art. l. 11. A, B and C] Even so thou wepst, and lookst, and spokst. A] when I first tooke thee. l. 12. A *omits*] up. l. 17. A *adds*] Exit Phylaster. l. 20. A] Exit Boy. B—H *omit*] and. l. 21. A] Enter Leon, Cle. and Wood-men. l. 22. A—G] chance. l. 23. A] Cle. My Lord Leon. C and D] My Lord Don. l. 25. A] starre-dyed with stars. B—G] studded with. l. 26. A] 1 Wood. l. 28. A *omits*] Exeunt Wood.

l. 29. A *omits*] Enter Cleremont. l. 30. B] you questions. C] you. l. 36. B—G] ran. l. 37. A and B] twas.

p. 121, l. 3. A] Enter the King, Tra. and other Lords. l. 5. A gives this speech to 'Leon,' i.e., Dion. l. 6. A and B] Howe's that. l. 7. A gives this speech to 'Leon,' i.e., Dion. l. 18. A] why then. ll. 20 and 21. A] heare me then, thou traytor. l. 21. A] darst. B—H] dar'st. ll. 21 and 22. A] possible and honest, things. l. 24. A, B and C] Faith I cannot. A] you'le. l. 25. A] you have let me. l. 27. A—G] her here before me. l. 32. A] a King. l. 33. A gives this speech to Cleremont. A] no more smell. l. 35. A *omits* Is it so *and reads* Take you heed. l. 36. A *omits*] Sir.

p. 122, l. 1. A] still we. l. 3. A] power we thinke we have. l. 5. A] here I stand. l. 6. A] these be punisht. l. 9. A] covenant. l. 10. A *omits*] and. l. 14. A] into the Wood with her. l. 19. A] O y'are all. A and B] hurts. l. 22. A] by this sword. l. 26. A, B and C] Yes, you may. A] to leave. A—G] Lady bedfellow. ll. 26 and 27. A] bedfellow here for a spincer. l. 31. Folio] may. l. 32. A] I, some would. ll. 33 and 34. A gives these two speeches to the King and Pharamont respectively. l. 37. A gives this speech to Galatea. A] the search my selfe. l. 38. A] Enter the Princesse solus. l. 39. A] finde out the way.

p. 123, l. 3. A] or mountaines. A—C] through. l. 4. A *adds* stage-direction] She sits downe. l. 5. A] Enter Boy. l. 6. A] Yonder my Lady is. A] gods knowes. B and C] god knowes. l. 9. A] grounds. l. 12. A *omits*] more. A] twines. l. 13. F, G] I oh. H] he stirres. l. 14. A] i'st. l. 18. A *omits*] I am well. l. 24. A—H] you gods. l. 25. A] Who's hee. l. 26. A] ease it with his tongue. l. 27. A, B and C] helpe, helpe. l. 29. A] lightnings. l. 31. A, B and C] trust the tongues. A, B and C with variations of spelling *add*] of hell-bred women [B woman]. Some good god looke downe. l. 33. A *omits*] ages in the. l. 35. A—G] put hills of fire. A] my breast.

p. 124, l. 2. D—G] makes. l. 3. B] through. l. 5. A] to inrage. l. 8. D, E and G] looks up. l. 9. A *omits*] it. B] know't. l. 10. A *omits*] do but. l. 16. A] thy way. l. 18. A] you have. l. 19. A] in more. l. 20. A gives this speech to 'Prin.,' i.e., Arethusa. A] madmens. l. 23. A gives this speech to 'Boy,' and the following speech to 'Prin.' l. 24. A, B and C] the world. l. 25. Folio *misprints*] *Pha.* l. 28. A *adds* stage-direction] Exit Boy. B] Exit Bell. l. 29. A] meetings. l. 32. B—H] fortune. l. 33. A] peace with earth. l. 34. A and B] there will. l. 35. A—E] jealousie. A] no il here. l. 37. A] Shew me the way to joy.

p. 125, l. 2. A] to 't. l. 4. A] Countrey Gallant. l. 5. A] I will. l. 6. A] this two houres. C, D and E] these two houre. l. 8. B] then then. E, G and H] out rid. l. 9. A] strong braines. l. 10. A] The whooping would put a man. l. 12. A *adds*] Phy. wounds her. l. 13. A—H] heaven. l. 14. A] Nay, they. l. 16. A] thoud'st. C—H] wouldest. A, B and C *omit*] of. l. 17. B and C] veines. A] with a man. l. 21. A] God judge me. B and C] God uds me. l. 25. A] Rethrack. l. 26. A prints 'They fight' at the end of the following line. l. 28. A] Gods guard. B and C] Heaven. l. 31. A] would this bore. l. 33. A] though I doe lose it. l. 34. A prints 'Exit Phy.' after the word 'Rogue' in the following line. l. 36. A *omits*] and.

p. 126, l. 3. A gives this speech to 'Leon,' i.e., Dion. l. 6. A and B]

By God she lies. A] i' the breast. l. 7. A] Oh secret spring. l. 12. A] Omnes. I. l. 14. A] But who has done it. l. 16. A gives this speech to 'Leon,' i.e., Dion. l. 19. A] I let. l. 20. A] about 's eares. l. 23. A] By this ayre. A—E] never. A *omits*] of him. l. 24. B and C] all to you in my hat. l. 28. A] sinne. l. 29. F] I will. I will. l. 31. A, B and C] Woodman. l. 32. A] unto the King. l. 34. A prints simply] Exit. l. 36. A gives this speech to Cleremont. l. 37. A, B and C] of this. A] I'le see. B—H] goe to see. l. 38. A] Enter the Boy. l. 39. A] O heavens! heavy death sits on my brow.

p. 127, l. 2. A] sweete on all. l. 5. A] my eyes. l. 6. A *omits*] Oh. l. 17. A prints stage-direction after the word 'broken' in l. 19. l. 21. A] but my blood. l. 24. A] upon his sleeping body, he has none. l. 25. A] He wounds him. l. 27. A] it wisht. A] for pittie. l. 28. A prints after the first 'here' in following line] Phy. falls downe. l. 36. A] Hide, hide. l. 39. B—G] were it.

p. 128, l. 1. A *omits*] little. l. 2. A] has not. l. 4. A] Art thou then true to me. l. 5. A *omits*] good. l. 6. A] these. l. 7. A] your breeth in't, Shromd. l. 11. A *omits* one 'follow.' l. 14. A *omits*] That. A *adds*] Boy falls downe. l. 15. B—H *omit*] and. l. 16. A] I tract. l. 17. A gives this speech to 'Leon,' i.e., Dion, and the next to Cleremont. l. 22. A gives this speech to Thrasiline. l. 23. A] it is. l. 25. F] the creation. l. 26. A and B] to strike. l. 31. A, B and C] did make. l. 34. A] tortour. l. 36. A] My. l. 37. A gives this speech to Cleremont.

p. 129, l. 1. A, B and C] carelesse. l. 4. A] them. l. 6. A] Sines. l. 14. A] vigour. A prints the stage-direction at the end of the following line. l. 16. A] innocents. l. 17. A] know you the price of what. l. 19. A] My Lord Phylaster. A *omits*] Tis. l. 23. H] as hurt. l. 24. A] on a Pyramades. l. 26. A] as you. l. 27. A] teach the under-world. l. 32. A] this untimely courtesie. l. 33. C—H] he is. A] you beare me hence. l. 35. A] to punish. l. 38. A, B and C] by all the gods.

p. 130. A gives the first five speeches to Dion, Thrasiline, Bellario, Dion and Bellario respectively. l. 2. C] Is it. l. 3. A] Well, I feare me sir, we. B—H] fear me, we. A *omits*] all. l. 9. A] gentlie. B—G] gently. l. 10. A and B] breath forth my. l. 11. A] Not all the wealth of Pluto. l. 17. A] a cleere. l. 18. A, B and C] bitter. l. 19. A] haires. l. 20. A] bathe them. l. 21. A] Enter the King, Princesse, and a guard. l. 23. A gives this speech to Dion. A] but sute it was Phylaster. l. 24. A gives this speech to the King, and the following one to Pharamond. l. 25. A—D] will tell us that. l. 26. A] Ay me, I know him well. l. 28. A] Sir, if it were he. l. 32. beare them. l. 35. A *omits*] go. l. 36. A] loves. l. 37. A *omits*] and. l. 38. A—G] deaths. l. 39. A] your law.

p. 131, l. 3. A] We shall. A] on with our intended match. A *adds*] Exit King and Pharamont. l. 4. A gives this speech to 'Leon,' i.e., Dion, and the following one to Cleremont. l. 7. A *omits*] Omnes. B—H *add*] Finis Actus quarti. l. 10. This speech and the seven succeeding ones are given by A to 'Leon' (Dion), Cleremont, Thrasiline, 'Leon,' Thrasiline, Cleremont, 'Leon' and Thrasiline respectively. l. 19. A *omits*] Exeunt. l. 20. A] shufle. A *omits*] Exeunt. l. 21. A] Enter Phylaster, Princesse, Boy, in prison. B—H *omit*] and. l. 22. A, B and C] Nay faith Philaster. l. 23. B] forbeare, were wondrous well. l. 24. A] and Bellario. l. 25. A] shut. A *omits*] as now from Earth. l. 27. A] the truest ones. l. 29. A] forgive me, and.

p. 132, l. 2. A—G] Should I outlive you. A] I should out live. B—H] I should then outlive. l. 3. A] come. l. 4. A—H] shall close. l. 6. A] waste by time. B] waste by limbs. l. 7. A—G] that ever. A] ever liv'd. l. 10. A] houre behind it. l. 15. A] Kingdome. l. 17. A] Every just maiden. l. 19. A] My deerest, say not so. l. 21. A] woman. l. 26. A] Why? what. l. 28. A] life no whit compared. l. 32. B] your pardon. l. 36. A gives this speech to 'Prin.,' i.e., Arethusa.

p. 133, l. 1. A] Enter the King, Leon, Cle., Tra. and a guard. B—H *omit*] and. l. 3. A gives this speech to 'Leon,' i.e., Dion. l. 4. A] Plotforme. l. 8. A gives this speech to Cleremont. l. 9. A *adds*] Exit Tra. l. 12. A] to lose it. A—E] lightly. A after the word 'lightly' adds stage-direction] aside. l. 14. A] stocke. l. 17. A] weightier. l. 18. A] the heate. l. 20. A] and leaves them desolate. l. 24. A] Enter Phi., Princesse, Boy, with a garland of flowers on's head. B—H *omit* the first 'and.' l. 26. A] shal. l. 27. A] Epethelamon. A *omits*] of these lovers. l. 28. F] But have lost. l. 30. A *omits*] on. l. 31. A] Cædor. l. 32. A] mountaines. l. 35. A] free from the firver of the Serian starre. B—G] Sirian. l. 37. A, B and C] deliver. A] that issues.

p. 134, l. 1. A—D] pleased. l. 2. A] base, under branches, to devour. l. 4. A] did choake. B—D] choake. l. 5. A] brakes, rud, thornes. A—G] the Sun. l. 6. A *omits*] even. A] roote. A] um there. l. 7. F *omits*] a. B and C] gentler. A] has. l. 9. A] never to be unarmde. l. 10. A, B and C] number. A *omits*] holy. A] ore. l. 11. A] has. F *omits*] noble. l. 12. A] worthy king. l. 15. A, B and C] For now there. l. 17. A] bitter threats. l. 19. A—E] struggled. l. 22. A] where you. l. 28. A] Metour. l. 32. A] of venge-in. l. 33. A] chaft amongst. B—E] Chast. B—G] among. l. 35. A] looke from me. l. 37. A] that I have left. l. 38. F] There is. A *omits*] that. l. 40. A] For death to me can be life.

p. 135, l. 1. A] as long as. l. 4. A] ore by. l. 8. A *omits*] dear. l. 9. A] you are. A after this line *adds*] That feedes upon the blood you gave a life to. l. 14. A] a shame. l. 15. F] Pelican. l. 17. A *omits*] with purest. l. 32. A, B and C] that by the gods it is a joy. l. 37. A *omits*] you.

p. 136, l. 1. A *omits*] Fearing. A] For the Lord Phylaster. l. 2. A] fellowes. l. 6. A *omits* this line. l. 7. A] 2 Mes. B and C] Arme, arme, arme, arme. l. 8. A] take these Citizens. l. 9. A] them. l. 12. A *omits*] Exit with Are., Phi., Bell. l. 16. A] Exit King, Manet Leon, Cle. and Tra. l. 18. A] by al the gods. l. 25. A] you lackes. B] ye lacks. l. 26. A] Skin. A] see you. B] have ye. l. 28. A] brave new. l. 29. A] My kinde Countrimen. l. 33. A] sawce. l. 34. A] flush amongst um, and ill speeding. ll. 34 and 35. A] have injurious raine. A *omits*] unbound. ll. 35 and 36. A] in rafine freeze. A] moth. l. 38. A] preases.

p. 137, l. 1. F] neck. l. 3. A] And know. l. 4. A] gotish. B and C] goatish. l. 10. A] wide. A] your valours. l. 11. A] we must. A] for 't. A *omits*] 'em. l. 12. A] and you will. B—E] and they. l. 15. A] speake him well. l. 16. A] courtesies. l. 17. A *omits*] Exit Cle. l. 18. A] Citizens. l. 20. A *omits*] and soil you. ll. 21 and 22. A] Every long vocation; and foule shall come up fat And in brave liking. l. 21. B] ever long. l. 23. A] that poore. l. 24. A *omits*] and. l. 25. A *omits*] Sir. l. 26. A—G] quench. l. 28. A] Enter Phylaster. l. 33. A] to 't. l. 34.

A] Let me your goodnesse know. l. 36. A, B and C] All my wishes. l. 37. A] speakes all this.

p. 138, l. 4. A *omits*] poor. l. 7. A] free her. l. 9. A] noble word. l. 10. A] you peace. l. 12. A] Now all the. A *omits*] Exeunt Omnes. l. 13. A] Enter an olde Captaine, with a crew of Citizens leading Pharamont prisoner. l. 15. B and C] your nimble. B—G] mother. l. 21. B and C] Kings. l. 22. E and G] you paintings. l. 25. B] beloved. B and C] Custards. l. 29. B—D] Collers.

p. 139, l. 1. B] solder'd. l. 6. B] me see. l. 7. For 'lie' G prints 'ie' with a space at the beginning where the 'l' should be. H and the Folio *misprint*] here I it. l. 8. B] washing. B] do you see sweete Prince. C] do you sweet Prince. D, E, G and H] sweat. F] swet. l. 12. B—H and Folio] foe. l. 26. B—G] Nay my beyond, etc. l. 28. B—H] scarcenet. l. 33. B and C] 1 Cit. l. 36. B—H] kills.

p. 140, l. 4. D, E and G] God Captaine. l. 7. B and C] of your 2-hand sword. l. 9. B—E, G and H] 2 Ci. F] 2 Cit. l. 11. B—E, G and H] 2 Ci. F] 2 Cit. B and C] had had. l. 12. C—G] skin bones. l. 35. B, C and D] stucke. E] stuck. l. 38. B—H] I do desire to be.

p. 141, l. 2. F] thy name. l. 7. B—H] of all dangers. B—H] altogether. l. 12. B and C] all these. l. 20. B—G] And make. B and F] He strives. l. 23. H] your friends. l. 34. B and C] Go thy wayes, thou art.

p. 142, l. 2. B and C] attendance. l. 24. Folio *misprints*] is it. l. 33. B] and hath found. l. 35. F] knew.

p. 143, l. 4. B—G with variations in spelling] To bear. B] her boy. l. 7. B—G] sometime. l. 9. D] wine. l. 17. B] As base as are. C *omits*] be. l. 18. Folio *misprints*] hour. B] heated. l. 36. B—H] that boy. l. 38. B and C] word. l. 39. F—H] life and rig.

p. 144, l. 6. B—G] were hateful. l. 11. B and C] oh stay. l. 12. F] Sir. l. 13. B] tire your constancy.

p. 145, l. 9. F *omits*] it. l. 22. B and C *omit*] I. l. 27. B—G] All's. l. 29. B—D make this line the conclusion of Philaster's speech, and consequently apply the marginal stage-direction to him.

p. 146, l. 22. B—E] oft would.

p. 147, l. 1. B—G] but have. l. 17. F *omits*] thou wilt. l. 31. B—H] vertue. l. 35. F] set us free.

p. 148, l. 9. F] your self. l. 10. B—E] And like to see. l. 14. After this line B—F, H *add*] Finis.

From p. 138, l. 13, to end of Play, A reads]

Enter an olde Captaine, with a crew of Citizens, leading PHARAMONT *prisoner.*

CAP. Come my brave Mermedons, fal on, let your caps swarm, & your nimble tongues forget your gibrish, of what you lack, and set your mouthes ope' children, till your pallats fall frighted halfe a fathom past the cure of bay-salt & grosse pepper; and then crie *Phylaster*, brave *Phylaster*. Let *Phylaster* be deep in request, my ding-a-dings, my paire of deare Indentures: King of clubs, thẽ your cut-water-chamlets, and your painting: let not your hasty silkes, deerly belovers of Custards & Cheescakes, or your branch cloth of bodkins, or your tyffenies, your robbin-hood scarlet and Johns, tie your affections in durance to your shops, my dainty duckers, up with your three pil'd spirits, that rightvalourous, and let your accute colours make the King to feele the measure of your mightinesse; *Phylaster*, cry, myrose nobles, cry.

OMNES. *Phylaster*, *Phylaster*.

CAP. How doe you like this, my Lord prisoner?
These are mad boyes I can tell you,
These bee things that will not strike top-sayle to a Foyst,
And let a Man of warre, an Argosea,
Stoope to carry coales.

PHAR. Why, you damn'd slaves, doe you know who I am?

CAP. Yes, my pretie Prince of puppits, we do know, and give you gentle warning, you talke no more such bugs words, lest that sodden Crowne should be scracht with a musket; deare Prince pippin, I'le have you codled, let him loose my spirits, and make a ring with your bils my hearts: Now let mee see what this brave man dares doe: note sir, have at you with this washing blow, here I lie, doe you huffe sweete Prince? I could hock your grace, and hang you crosse leg'd, like a Hare at a Poulters stall; and do thus.

PHAR. Gentlemen, honest Gentlemen—

1 SOUL. A speakes treason Captaine, shal's knock him downe?

CAP. Hold, I say.

2 SOUL. Good Captaine let me have one mal at's mazard, I feele my stomacke strangely provoked to bee at his Spanish pot-nowle, shal's kill him?

OMNES. I, kill him, kill him.

CAP. Againe I say hold.

3 SOUL. O how ranke he lookes, sweete Captaine let's geld him, and send his dowsets for a dish to the Burdello.

4 SOUL. No, let's rather sell them to some woman Chymist, that extractions, shee might draw an excellent provocative oyle from useth them, that might be very usefull.

CAP. You see, my scurvy Don, how precious you are in esteem amongst us, had you not beene better kept at home, I thinke you had: must you needes come amongst us, to have your saffron hide taw'd as wee intend it: My Don, *Phylaster* must suffer death to satisfie your melancholly spleene, he must my Don, he must; but we your Physitians, hold it fit that you bleede for it: Come my robusticks, my brave regiment of rattle makers, let's cal a common cornuted counsell, and like grave Senators, beare up our brancht crests, in sitting upon the severall tortures we shall put him to, and with as little sense as may be, put your wils in execution.

SOME CRIES. Burne him, burne him.

OTHERS. Hang him, hang him. *Enter* PHYLASTER.

CAP. No, rather let's carbinade his cods-head, and cut him to collops: shall I begin?

PHI. Stay your furies my loving Countrimen.

OMNES. *Phylaster* is come, *Phylaster*, *Phylaster*.

CAP. My porcupines of spite, make roome I say, that I may salute my brave Prince: and is Prince *Phylaster* at liberty?

PHI. I am, most loving countrimen.

CAP. Then give me thy Princely goll, which thus I kisse, to whom I crouch and bow; But see my royall sparke, this head-strong swarme that follow me humming like a master Bee, have I led forth their Hives, and being on wing, and in our heady flight, have seazed him shall suffer for thy wrongs.

OMNES. I, I, let's kill him, kill him.

PHI. But heare me, Countrimen.

CAP. Heare the Prince, I say, heare *Phylaster.*

OMNES. I, I, heare the Prince, heare the Prince.

PHI. My comming is to give you thanks, my deere Countrimen, whose powerfull sway hath curb'd the prossecuting fury of my foes.

OMNES. We will curb um, we will curb um.

PHI. I finde you will,
But if my intrest in your loves be such,
As the world takes notice of, Let me crave
You would deliver *Pharamont* to my hand,
And from me accept this *Gives um his purse.*
Testimonie of my love.
Which is but a pittance of those ample thankes,
Which shall redowne with showred courtesies.

CAP. Take him to thee brave Prince, and we thy bounty thankefully accept, and will drinke thy health, thy perpetuall health my Prince, whilst memory lasts amongst us, we are thy Mermidons, my *Achillis*: we are those will follow thee, and in thy service will scowre our rusty murins and our bill-bow-blades, most noble *Phylaster*, we will: Come my rowtists let's retyer till occasion calls us to attend the noble *Phylaster.*

OMNES. *Phylaster, Phylaster, Phylaster.*

Exit CAPTAINE, *and Citizens.*

PHAR. Worthy sir, I owe you a life,
For but your selfe theres nought could have prevail'd.

PHI. Tis the least of service that I owe the King,
Who was carefull to preserve ye. *Exit.*

Enter LEON, TRASILINE, *and* CLERIMON.

TRA. I ever thought the boy was honest.

LEON. Well, tis a brave boy Gentlemen.

CLE. Yet you'ld not beleeve this.

LEON. A plague on my forwardnesse, what a villaine was I, to wrong um so; a mischiefe on my muddy braines, was I mad?

TRA. A little frantick in your rash attempt, but that was your love to *Phylaster*, sir.

LEON. A pox on such love, have you any hope my countinance will ere serve me to looke on them?

CLE. O very well Sir.

LEON. Very ill Sir, uds death, I could beate out my braines, or hang my selfe in revenge.

CLE. There would be little gotten by it, ene keepe you as ye are.

LEON. An excellent boy, Gentlemen beleeve it, harke the King is comming, *Cornets sounds.*

Enter the King, Princesse, GALLATEA, MEGRA, BELLARIO, *a Gentlewoman, and other attendants.*

K. No newes of his returne,
Will not this rable multitude be appeas'd?
I feare their outrage, lest it should extend
With dangering of *Pharamonts* life.

Enter PHILASTER *with* PHARAMONT.

LEON. See Sir, *Phylaster* is return'd.

PHI. Royall Sir,
Receive into your bosome your desired peace,
Those discontented mutineares be appeasde,
And this fortaigne Prince in safety.
K. How happie am I in thee *Phylaster*?
Whose excellent vertues begets a world of love,
I am indebted to thee for a Kingdome.
I here surrender up all Soveraignetie,
Raigne peacefully with thy espoused Bride, *Delivers his Crowne to him.*
Ashume my Son to take what is thy due.
PHA. How Sir, yer son, what am I then, your Daughter you gave to me.
KIN. But heaven hath made asignement unto him,
And brought your contract to anullity:
Sir, your entertainment hath beene most faire,
Had not your hell-bred lust dride up the spring,
From whence flow'd forth those favours that you found:
I am glad to see you safe, let this suffice,
Your selfe hath crost your selfe.
LEON. They are married sir.
PHAR. How married? I hope your highnesse will not use me so,
I came not to be disgraced, and returne alone.
KING. I cannot helpe it sir.
LEON. To returne alone, you neede not sir,
Here is one will beare you company.
You know this Ladies proofe, if you
Fail'd not in the say-taging.
ME. I hold your scoffes in vildest base contempt,
Or is there said or done, ought I repent,
But can retort even to your grinning teeths,
Your worst of spights, tho Princesse lofty steps
May not be tract, yet may they tread awry,
That boy there——
BEL. If to me ye speake Lady,
I must tell you, youhave lost your selfe
In your too much forwardnesse, and hath forgot
Both modesty and truth, with what impudence
You have throwne most damnable aspertions
On that noble Princesse and my selfe: witnesse the world;
Behold me sir. *Kneeles to* LEON, *and discovers her haire.*
LEON. I should know this face; my daughter.
BEL. The same sir.
PRIN. How, our sometime Page, *Bellario*, turn'd woman?
BEL. Madame, the cause induc't me to transforme my selfe,
Proceeded from a respective modest
Affection I bare to my my Lord,
The Prince *Phylaster*, to do him service,
As farre from any lacivious thought,
As that Lady is farre from go odnesse,
And if my true intents may be beleeved,
And from your Highnesse Madame, pardon finde,
You have the truth.
PRIN. I doe beleeve thee, *Bellario* I shall call thee still.

PHI. The faithfullest servant that ever gave attendance.
LEON. Now Lady lust, what say you to'th boy now;
Doe you hang the head, do ye, shame would steale
Into your face, if ye had grace to entertaine it,
Do ye slinke away?

Exit MEGRA *hiding her face.*

KING. Give present order she be banisht the Court,
And straightly confinde till our further
Pleasure is knowne.

PHAR. Heres such an age of transformation, that I doe not know how to trust my selfe, I'le get me gone to: Sir, the disparagement you have done, must be cald in question. I have power to right my selfe, and will.

Exit PHARAMONT.

KING. We feare ye not Sir.
PHI. Let a strong convoy guard him through the Kingdome,
With him, let's part with all our cares and feare,
And Crowne with joy our happy loves successe.
KING. Which to make more full, Lady *Gallatea*,
Let honour'd *Clerimont* acceptance finde
In your chast thoughts.
PHI. Tis my sute too.
PRIN. Such royall spokes-men must not be deni'd.
GAL. Nor shall not, Madame.
KING. Then thus I joyne your hands.
GAL. Our hearts were knit before. *They kisse.*
PHI. But tis you Lady, must make all compleat,
And gives a full perod to content,
Let your loves cordiall againe revive,
The drooping spirits of noble *Trasiline*.
What saies Lord *Leon* to it?
LEON. Marry my Lord I say, I know she once lov'd him.
At least made shew she did,
But since tis my Lord *Phylasters* desire,
I'le make a surrender of all the right
A father has in her; here take her sir,
With all my heart, and heaven give you joy.
KING. Then let us in these nuptuall feastes to hold,
Heaven hath decreed, and Fate stands uncontrold.

FINIS.

PHILASTER. VERSE AND PROSE VARIATIONS.

The variations are those of A except where otherwise stated.

p. 78, l. 35. A prints this speech as prose.

p. 79, l. 39, and p. 80, l. 1. A reads as one line.

p. 80, ll. 6 and 7. One line. ll. 8 and 9. One line. l. 11. A gives this speech as prose. ll. 37—40, and p. 81, l. 1. Four lines ending *bold*, *Turcle*, *shaddow*, *over*.

p. 81, ll. 12—17. Five lines ending *armes*, *hath*, *disputing*, *are*, *me*. l. 19. Eight lines ending *him*, *his*, *thine*, *cold*, *such*, *follies*, *presence*, *me*.

l. 28. This speech in two lines ending *freedome*, *temperde*. l. 32. This speech in four lines ending *succession*, *is*, *within*, *knowledge*.

p. 82, ll. 1 and 2. One line. l. 9. C, D, E] two lines, *them*, *Atlas*. l. 18. This speech and the next as prose. l. 33. The rest of the speech in seven lines, ending *whispers*, *will*, *there*, *service*, *factious*, *hand*, *servant*. l. 39. B, C, D, E] two lines, *hand*, *servant*.

p. 83, ll. 1—4. Prose. l. 14. This speech and the next prose. ll. 29—31. Two lines ending *please* and *yeares*. l. 33. The rest of the speech in prose.

p. 84, ll. 2—4. Two lines ending *Age* and *me*. ll. 6—11. Four lines ending *Gentlewoman*, *alive*, *idle*, *pilgrimage*. ll. 22 and 23. Prose. l. 26. This speech and the next in prose.

p. 85, ll. 1 and 2. One line. ll. 3—32. Prose. ll. 34—38. Four lines ending *with-*, *make*, *your*, *obay*. l. 40 and p. 86, l. 1. One line.

p. 86, ll. 4—11. Seven lines ending *say*, *woman*, *them*, *detracted*, *you*, *disgrace*, *vertues*. ll. 14—16. Two lines ending *fortunes*, *question*. ll. 18—20. Two lines ending *affoord*, *wisht*. ll. 21 and 22. One line. ll. 27—32. Four lines ending *stories*, *Crowne*, *longing*, *more*.

p. 87, ll. 1—12. Ten lines ending *dreadfully*, *he*, *tongue*, *his*, *begin*, *love*, *you*, *beg*, *price*, *heare*. ll. 17—19. Two lines ending *yet*, *in*. ll. 21—23. Prose. ll. 26—30. Prose. ll. 34—40. Six lines ending *so*, *better*, *gods*, *some*, *us*, *it*. l. 30. B, C, D, E] two lines, *man*, *jealous*.

p. 88, ll. 1—6. Five lines ending *long*, *often*, *intelligence*, *agree*, *tread*. l. 6. B, C, D, E] two lines, *agree*, *tread*. l. 7. B, C, D, E] two lines, *boy*, *intent*. l. 7. This speech in prose.

p. 89, l. 2. B, C, D, E] two lines, *selfe*, *Prince*. l. 7. B, D, E] two lines, *made*, *himselfe*. l. 7. Two lines ending *Phylaster* and *himselfe*. ll. 10 and 11. Two lines ending *ever*, *lie*. ll. 18—20. Two lines ending *ceremonies* and *heart*. ll. 21 and 22. One line. ll. 27—29. Prose. l. 38. This speech in prose.

p. 90, ll. 4 and 5. Two lines ending *much*, *Princesse*. l. 6. This speech and the next in prose. l. 16. This speech beginning from 'Madam' and the next speech in prose. ll. 29—34. Six lines ending *regard*, *modesty*, *aske*, *deserve*, *nothing*, *yours*. l. 32. B, C, D, E] two lines, *aske*, *deserve*. l. 35. The rest of the speech in prose.

p. 91, ll. 6—11. Prose. ll. 13—17. Prose. l. 18 and B, C, D, E] two lines ending *all*, *behaviour*. ll. 19—29. Ten lines ending *ignorance*, *learne*, *larger*, *fault*, *once*, *boy*, *warning*, *stubborneness*, *off*, *mend*. ll. 32—40. Seven lines ending *businesse*, *her*, *full*, *trust*, *joy*, *weepe*, *Princesse*.

p. 92, ll. 1—12. Prose. ll. 14—20. Nine lines ending *must*, *not*, *word*, *all*, *taking*, *life*, *fault*, *boulted*, *Madame*.

p. 93, ll. 5—12. Nine lines ending *grace*, *remedy*, *morning*, *Cardus*, *exercise*, *Tiller*, *Flebotomie*, *whay*, *anymales*. ll. 15—18. Four lines ending *well*, *appetite*, *gold*, *then*. ll. 25 and 26. Two lines ending *behind*, *this*.

p. 94, ll. 5 and 6. Two lines ending *enough*, *Age*. ll. 7 and 8. Two lines ending *smooth*, *enough*. ll. 16—23. Prose. l. 24. Two lines ending *prose*, *Madame*. l. 27. Two lines ending *first*, *now*. ll. 30—32. Two lines ending *sweetest*, *me*. ll. 35 and 36. Three lines ending *sentence*, *memory*, *me*. ll. 38—40. Three lines ending *endeavour*, *night*, *for't*.

p. 95, ll. 1—20. Twenty-one lines ending *owne*, *teaching*, *measures*, *function*, *selfe*, *her*, *her*, *indeed*, *sir*, *selfe*, *schoolemaister*, *maid*, *Gallatea*, *favour*, *now*, *wit*, *guard*, *toot*, *Jubiter*, *Lady*, *welcome*. ll. 25—29. Six lines ending *um*, *want*, *thoughts*, *bashfull*, *with*, *you*.

p. 96, ll. 8 and 9. One line. ll. 26—32. Prose. ll. 36 and 37. Prose.

p. 97, ll. 17—29. Prose. ll. 30—35. Five lines ending *credit*, *sound*, *sayes*, *too*, *away*. ll. 37—39. Prose.

p. 98, ll. 1—5. Prose (probably). ll. 8—10. Prose. ll. 20—23. Four lines ending *by*, *hand*, *Princesse*, *selfe*. ll. 25 and 26. One line. ll. 33 and 34. Two lines ending *grace*, *bed*. l. 37 and p. 99, ll. 1 and 2. Three lines ending *late*, *comes*, *him*.

p. 99, ll. 5—16. Prose. ll. 19—36. Prose.

p. 100, ll. 11—18. Prose. ll. 20—22. Prose. ll. 26 and 27. Two lines ending *sir*, *you*. ll. 33 and 34. Two lines ending *life*, *heere*. ll. 36—39 and p. 101, l. 1. Prose.

p. 101, ll. 2—5. Three lines ending *wrongd*, *lodging*, *say*. ll. 8—23. Prose. ll. 28—32. Five lines ending *two*, *hold*, *lye*, *not*, *mistaken*. ll. 37—39 and p. 102, ll. 1—9. Ten lines ending *lust*, *thoughts*, *diseases*, *me*, *courtesies*, *daughter*, *Court*, *orrenges*, *candles*, *Venus*.

p. 102, ll. 10—25. Thirteen lines ending *laugh*, *King*, *by*, *fellowes*, *mirth*, *me*, *more*, *leaps*, *her*, *eighteene*, *when*, *madness*, *height*. ll. 32—39. Seven lines ending *it*, *commonly*, *at*, *forraigne*, *tongue*, *people*, *Princesse*.

p. 103, ll. 1 and 2. Two lines ending *her*, *boy*. ll. 10—17. Eight lines ending *tongue*, *King*, *him*, *infections*, *brave*, *boy*, *else*, *Gentlemen*. ll. 24—36. Eleven lines ending *us*, *freemen*, *age*, *right*, *Scepter*, *Lady*, *boy*, *thing*, *Prince*, *part*, *mind*. l. 37 and p. 104, ll. 1 and 2. Three lines ending *Phylaster*, *Creature*, *earth*.

p. 104, ll. 4—7. Three lines ending *people*, *corne*, *way*. ll. 25—29. Prose. l. 29. B, C, D] two lines, *doe*, *acceptation*. ll. 30—38. Seven lines ending *know*, *head*, *king*, *word*, *attempts*, *me*, *friends*.

p. 105, l. 4. B, C, D, E] two lines, *time*, *would*. ll. 1—9. Nine lines ending *selfe*, *sufficient*, *loves*, *would*, *expect*, *violence*, *know*, *now*, *lov'd*. ll. 16—28. Ten lines ending *thought*, *Lady*, *pardon'd*, *redeem'd*, *increase*, *I*, *hils*, *all*, *necke*, *clowde*. ll. 29 and 30. One line. ll. 31—37. Prose. l. 40 and p. 106, ll. 1 and 2. Prose.

p. 106, l. 4 (from 'Good Sir')—7. Prose. ll. 21—25. Prose. ll. 27 and 28. One line. ll. 29—31. Three lines ending *looke*, *Lord*, *selfe*. ll. 36 and 37. Three lines ending *them*, *fault*, *silence*. l. 37. B, C, D, E] two lines, *slept*, *silence*. l. 40 and p. 107, ll. 1 and 2. Two lines ending *corners*, *land*.

p. 107, ll. 12 and 13. One line. ll. 19—39 and p. 108, ll. 1—3. Twenty lines ending *her*, *breast*, *circumstances*, *now*, *simply*, *honourable*, *truth*, *selves*, *fight*, *sight*, *once*, *againe*, *fat*, *before*, *man*, *weare*, *blush*, *mortalitie*, *brow*, *guilty*. l. 35. B] two lines, *man*, *gods*.

p. 108, ll. 7—9. Three lines ending *me*, *boy*, *brave*. ll. 13 and 14. Two lines ending *boy*, *here*. ll. 17—19. Three lines ending *snow*, *boy*, *thee*. ll. 22—27. Five lines ending *life*, *fond*, *trust*, *pay*, *me*. ll. 30—36. Prose. l. 40 and p. 109, ll. 1—3. Prose.

p. 109, ll. 4 and 5. One line. ll. 15 (from 'Come she dos')—37. Prose. l. 40 and p. 110, ll. 1—3. Four lines ending *lust*, *desires*, *her*, *ages*.

APPENDIX

p. 110, l. 3. B, C, D, E] two lines, *reveale, ages.* l. 4. B, C, D, E] two lines, *heart, disease.* l. 4. Two lines ending *heart, deceit.* ll. 9 and 10. One line. ll. 15 and 16. Two lines ending *life, now.* l. 16. B, C, D] two lines, *hate thee, now.* ll. 20—22. Three lines ending *where, me, not.* ll. 23—26. Three lines ending *life, asunder, away.* ll. 29 and 30. One line. ll. 31—33. Three lines ending *live, passionate, reason.* l. 33. B, C, D, E] two lines, *passionate, reason.* ll. 35—39. Four lines ending *borne, jealousie, againe, lost.* l. 39. B, C, D, E] two lines, *game, lost.*

p. 111, ll. 1 and 2. Two lines ending *melt, all.* ll. 4—6. Three lines ending *with, of, me.* l. 6. B, C, D, E] two lines, *punishments, me.* ll. 7—24. Prose. ll. 26—34. Prose. ll. 35—37. Two lines ending *deservest, unkind.*

p. 112, ll. 3—7. Five lines ending *over, him, spoken, such, stay.* l. 7. B, C, D, E] two lines, *angry, stay.* ll. 17 and 18. Two lines ending *well, him.* l. 31. B, C, D, E] two lines, *me, boy.* ll. 32 and 33. One line. ll. 35—38. Four lines ending *me, gods, selfe, done.*

p. 113, ll. 4—6. Three lines ending *foule, it, farewell.* ll. 9—15. Six lines ending *truth, defamings, fortified, tongues, foule, mountains.* l. 20. Two lines ending *servant, me.* ll. 21—25. Prose.

p. 114, ll. 6—8. Four lines ending *it, eye-lids, crie, Phylaster.* l. 8. B, C, D, E] my deere | deare *Philaster.* ll. 9—12. Three lines ending *thee, loyal, better.* l. 13. B, C, D, E] two lines, *againe, Bellario.* ll. 16—18. Three lines ending *all, that, wrongs.* l. 27. Two lines ending *not, thus.* l. 27. B, C, D, E] two lines, *talke, thus.* ll. 30—40 and p. 115, l. 1. Ten lines ending *naked, mischiefe, me, bosome, mirth, King, Mourners, length, cursed boy, lust.*

p. 115, l. 1. B, C, D, E] two lines, *boy, lust.* l. 3 and B, C, D, E] two lines ending *overthrow, wretched.* ll. 4—23. Sixteen lines ending *this, it, foote, seeke, Cave, are, hell, Scorpyons, woven, you, face, have, you, night, are, altogether.* ll. 29—34. Five lines ending *transparant, me, holds, constancie, now.* ll. 38—40 and p. 116, l. 2. Four lines ending *passion, wicked, that, understoodst.*

p. 116, ll. 6—10. Three lines ending *desease, me, swell.* ll. 14—21. Eight lines ending *leave, ever, Lady, fault, suffering, mine, seeke, die.* ll. 28 and 29. Two lines ending *hunt, earnestnesse.* ll. 30—32. Two lines ending *canst, thee.*

p. 117, ll. 7—9. Three lines ending *veniall, spirit, it.* ll. 13—15. Three lines ending *enough, purlewes, poaching.* ll. 24—30. Nine lines ending *repent, him, member, mouth, now, presently, Almanacke, liver, dog-whip.* ll. 31—33. Four lines ending *lookes, neighbours, face, honest.*

p. 119, ll. 17—21. Five lines ending *dwelt, reedes, borne, issue, vexation.* l. 21. B, C, D, E] two lines, *life, vexation.* ll. 23—37. Ten lines ending *beasts, as, body, speake, Lord, pittie, fortunes, bounty, keepe, hunger.*

p. 120, ll. 6—17. Ten lines ending *me, trade, againe, so, thee, worke, way, are, rage, way.* ll. 32—37 and p. 121, ll. 1 and 2. Eight lines ending *stray, businesse, armes, peace, us, her, seene, willingly.*

p. 121, ll. 12—18. Prose. l. 23. C, D, E] two lines, *not, blood.* ll. 20—34. Prose. ll. 38 and 39 and p. 122, ll. 1 and 2. Three lines ending *gods, adord, Thunder.*

p. 122, ll. 6 and 7. Two lines ending *way*, *on*. ll. 12—14. Prose l. 14. B, C, D, E] two lines, *wood*, *her*. ll. 21 and 22. Prose. ll. 24 and 25. Two lines ending *alive*, *Taylor*. ll. 30 and 31. Prose. l. 39 and p. 123, ll. 1—18. Prose.

p. 123, ll. 22—26. Two lines ending *speaking*, *not*, and Prose. l. 29 and p. 124, ll. 1—3. Eleven lines ending *kist*, *Basaliskes*, *women*, *up*, *act*, *fire*, *teares*, *beds*, *face*, *issues*, *you*.

p. 124, ll. 4—19. Thirteen lines ending *me*, *done*, *Eolus*, *I*, *sword*, *you*, *controule*, *me*, *thoughts*, *now*, *pulse*, *more*, *die*. ll. 25—35. Ten lines ending *that*, *do*, *last*, *wise*, *resolve*, *suffer*, *hand*, *earth*, *other*, *here*. l. 31. B, C, D, E] two lines, *doe*, *suffer*. ll. 38—40 and p. 125, ll. 1 and 2. Four lines ending *power*, *Justice*, *heaven*, *to't*.

p. 125, ll. 5—10. Seven lines ending *Forrest*, *home*, *me*, *selfe*, *shouting*, *braines*, *wits*. ll. 19 and 20. Prose. ll. 21 and 22. Two lines ending *not*, *ye*. ll. 23 and 24. Prose. l. 24. B, C, D, E] two lines, *head*, *to*. ll. 30—32. Prose. ll. 35 and 36. Two lines ending *rogue*, *now*.

p. 126, ll. 1 and 2. Two lines ending *woman*, *her*. ll. 25—28. Prose.

p. 127, ll. 5—7. Three lines ending *giddy*, *sleepe*, *wake*. ll. 13—25. Fourteen lines ending *conceale*, *follow*, *sleeping*, *sleepe*, *wrong'd*, *broken*, *take*, *escape*, *blood*, *mischiefe*, *once*, *body*, *mortall*, *thee*. ll. 26 and 27. Prose. l. 29. Line ends with first *here*. ll. 33 and 34. Two lines ending *thou*, *me*. ll. 37 and 38. One line. l. 39 and p. 128, ll. 1—3. Three lines ending *live*, *much*, *you*.

p. 128, ll. 19 and 20. Two lines ending *beasts*, *men*. ll. 22—24. Two lines ending *her*, *her*. ll. 25 and 26. Prose. ll. 29—34. Four lines ending *thoughts*, *death*, *meane*, *tortour*. l. 38 and p. 129, ll. 1—11. Eleven lines ending *Page*, *carelesse*, *me*, *over-flowde*, *them*, *turnde*, *streames*, *contem'd*, *great*, *live*, *revenged*.

p. 129, ll. 12—14. Two lines ending *life*, *vigor*. l. 17 and B, C, D] two lines ending *away*, *rudely*. ll. 24—28. Four lines ending *then*, *you*, *teach*, *him*. ll. 30 and 31. One line.

p. 130, ll. 6—20. Prose. l. 20. B, C, D, E] two lines, *wealth*, *Philaster*. l. 23. B, C, D, E] two lines, *two*, *Philaster*. ll. 30—38. Prose. l. 32. B, C, D, E] two lines, *talke*, *prison*.

p. 131, l. 3 and B, C, D, E] two lines ending *on*, *match*. l. 6. Two lines ending *heads*, *trick*. ll. 24—33. Nine lines ending *Bellario*, *heaven*, *paire*, *bore*, *me*, *death*, *boy*, *beasts*, *innocence*. l. 34 and p. 132, ll. 1—6. Seven lines ending *worthy*, *peece*, *you*, *honour*, *close*, *perjurie*, *nothing*.

p. 132, ll. 15—17. Two lines ending *sleepe*, *love*. ll. 20 and 21. Prose. l. 21. B, C, D, E] two lines, *it*, *on*. ll. 28 and 29. Two lines ending *love*, *truely*.

p. 133, ll. 6 and 7. One line. ll. 10—23. Twelve lines ending *at*, *lightly*, *him*, *bridges*, *rootes*, *thunders*, *back*, *Townes*, *desolate*, *lives*, *sacrifice*, *ruines*. ll. 26—38 and p. 134, ll. 1—12. Prose.

p. 134, ll. 14—35. Prose. ll. 36 and 37. One line. l. 40 and p. 135, l. 1. Two lines ending *Pharamont*, *heads-man*.

p. 135, ll. 3 and 4. Prose. ll. 7—33. Twenty-three lines ending *life*, *monster*, *to*, *living*, *writ*, *you*, *men*, *Pelion*, *brasse*, *Pyramides*, *gods*, *faults*, *issues*, *wisedomes*, *off*, *self*, *King*, *sinne*, *soule*, *long*, *you*, *die*, *in't*.

p. 136, ll. 2 and 3. One line. ll. 24—29. Seven lines ending *deere*, *not*, *Chronicled*, *prais'd*, *ballads*, *seculorum*, *Countrimen*.

p. 137, ll. 8—22. Sixteen lines ending *them*, *raise*, *neede*, *for't*, *sheepe*, *heate*, *me*, *Lord*, *Prince*, *him*, *wits*, *pin*, *me*, *bakon*, *fat*, *liking*. ll. 29—39 and p. 138, ll. 1—6. Thirteen lines ending *miseries*, *danger*, *you*, *to't*, *be*, *repentance*, *gods*, *me*, *thunder*, *wrong*, *boy*, *sea-breach*, *it*.

p. 138, ll. 33—36. B—G] four lines ending *boyes*, *top-sailes*, *Argosie*, *Cockels*. F and G print last 2 ll. as one.

p. 139, l. 26. B, C, D, E] two lines ending *you* and *King*. l. 36. B, C, D, E] two lines ending *kils*, *Boyes*.

p. 143, l. 11. B, C, D, E] two lines ending *earth*, *me*. l. 40. B, C, D, E] two lines ending *away*, *once*.

p. 145, l. 8. B, C, D, E] two lines ending *lives*, *Pilgrimage*. l. 17. B, C, D, E] two lines ending *she*, *dyed*. l. 32. B, C, D, E] two lines ending *shame*, *rest*.

A KING AND NO KING.

(A) A King and no King. | Acted at the Globe, by his Maje|sties Servants. | Written by Francis Beamount, and John Flecher. | At London | Printed for Thomas Walkley, and are to bee sold | at his shoppe at the Eagle and Childe in | Brittans-Bursse. 1619.

(B) A King | and | No King. | Acted at the Blacke-Fryars, by his | Majesties Servants. | And now the second time Printed, according | to the true Copie. | Written by Francis Beamount and | John Flecher. | London, | Printed for Thomas Walkley, and are to be sold at | his shop at the Eagle and Childe in | Brittans-Burse. 1625.

(C) A King, | and | No King. | Acted at the Blacke-Fryars, by his | Majesties Servants. | And now the third time Printed, according | to the true Copie. | Written by Francis Beamont & John Fletcher Gent. | The Stationer to | Dramatophilus. | A Play and no Play, who this Booke shall read, | Will judge, and weepe, as if 'twere done indeed. | London, | Printed by A. M. for Richard Hawkins, and are to bee sold | at his Shop in Chancerie Lane, neere | Serjeants Inne. 1631.

(D) A King | and | No King. | Acted at the Black-Fryars, by his | Majesties Servants. | And now the fourth time printed, according | to the true Copie. | Written by Francis Beaumont & John Fletcher Gent. | The Stationer to | Dramatophilus. | A Play and no Play, who this Booke shall read, | Will judge, and weepe, as if 'twere done indeed. | London, | Printed by E. G. for William Leake, and are to be sold | at his shop in Chancery-lane, neere unto the | Rowles. 1639.

(E) A King | and | No King. | Acted at the Black-Fryers, by his | Majesties Servants. | And now the fifth time Printed, according | To the true Copie. | Written by Francis Beaumont & John Fletcher Gent. | The Statinor to | Dramatophilus. | A Play and no Play, who this Book shall read, | Will judge, and weep, as if 'twere done indeed | London, | Printed for William

Leak, and are to be sold | at his shop at the signe of the Crown in Fleet- | street, between the two temple Gates. 1655.

On the back of the last page is printed a list of books printed or sold by William Leake.

(F) A | King, | and | No King. | Acted at the Black-Fryars, by his | Majesties Servants. | And now the fourth time Printed, according to | the true Copie. | Written by Francis Beaumont and John Fletcher Gent. | The Stationer to | Dramatophilus. | A Play and no Play, who this Book shall read, | Will judge, and weep, as if 'twere done indeed. | London, Printed in the Year, 1661.

(G) A | King | and | No King. | As it is now Acted at the | Theatre Royal, | By | His Majesties Servants. | Written by Francis Beaumont and John Fletcher Gent. | London: | Printed by Andr. Clark, for William and John Leake at the | Crown in Fleetstreet, betwixt the two Temple-gates. | M.DC.LXXVI.

A contains on the title-page a wood-cut representing Arbaces with his crown partly lifted from his head by a hand emerging from a cloud.

A prefixes the following dedication]

To the Right Worshipfull and Worthie Knight, Sir Henrie Nevill. Worthy Sir, I Present, or rather returne unto your view, that which formerly hath beene received from you, hereby effecting what you did desire: To commend the worke in my unlearned method, were rather to detract from it, then to give it any luster. It sufficeth it hath your Worships approbation and patronage, to the commendation of the Authors, and incouragement of their further labours: and thus wholy committing my selfe and it to your Worships dispose I rest, ever readie to doe you service, not onely in the like, but in what I may.

Thomas Walkley.

p. 149, l. 4. A and B *omit* the List of Persons Represented in the Play. C—F] The Personated Persons. G] The Persons Represented. G *omits*] in the Play. G includes in its List of The Persons Represented the names of the players of the chief parts, viz.] Arbaces, Mr Hart; Tigranes, Mr Kynaston; Gobrias, Mr Wintershall; Bacurius, Mr Lydall; Mardonius, Mr Mohun; Bessus, Mr Lacy, or Mr Shottrell; Lygones, Mr Cartwright; Two Sword-men, Mr Watson, Mr Haynes; Arane, Mrs Corey; Panthea, Mrs Cox; Spaconia, Mrs Marshall. l. 12. Folio *misprints*] Ligoces. l. 21. C—G and Folio] The Queenes Mother. l. 27. A—G *omit*] Actus primus. Scena prima. G] Act 1. l. 29. A *omits*] he. ll. 35 and 36. B] had's.

p. 150, l. 2. A] them. l. 3. A] thou art. l. 5. A] and thou couldst. l. 8. A] with me. l. 9. A—F] winkst. G] winkedst. l. 10. A] strake. l. 17. A] I am glad. l. 19. A] of his owne. l. 21. A] cruddles. B and G] crudles. l. 22. A] wouldst. A] in this passion. l. 25. A] for it. l. 26. A] neither good Bessus. l. 27. A] it is. l. 30. A] I famed, I, I warrant you. l. 31. A] I am verie heartily. l. 32. A] ever. A] ath' warres. B—G *omit*] is. l. 39. A, B and G] in shifting a.

p. 151, ll. 4 and 5. A] desperate. l. 5. A *omits*] At. l. 8. A] Prethee. l. 9. A, B and G] The Souldier. l. 10. A] meerely. l. 12. E] compasion. F] compassion. l. 14. B—F] a'th. l. 19. A, B and G] not I. l. 21. A] mean'st. B, C and G] meant'st. D, E and F] meanest. l. 26. A] the enemie. B] shouldest. l. 31. A—G] proceedst. l. 33. A] Come, come. l. 34. A] comst. l. 37. A] extreamities. l. 40. A] the prey.

p. 152, ll. 1 and 2. In place of these lines A] Enter Arbaces and Tigranes, with attendants. l. 2. B and G] two Kings, &c. The two Gentlemen. l. 4. A] fall victorie. l. 9. A—G] are free as I. l. 18. A, B, C and G] yeare. l. 27. A *omits*] Tigr. l. 28. A—D and G] Arbaces. l. 29. A] talkt: for in Armenia.

p. 153, l. 11. A] Tigranes, no. l. 16. A] an Act. l. 17. A and G] Fit for a God. B—F *omit*] man. l. 20. A] Its. l. 26. A] spoke. A] not mee. l. 40. A] are something.

p. 154, l. 8. A] to take. B and G] her for to take. l. 17. A] no owne of. l. 18. A] Would finde. l. 19. A] off her damning. l. 20. A] twenty times. l. 29. Folio] sight. l. 40. A] Some two.

p. 155, l. 3. For *Exit Tigranes* A] Exe. l. 8. B and G *omit*] don't. A] don. l. 20. A] ift. l. 21. A and G] with you. l. 22. A] sunke. l. 28. A] th' eare. l. 29. B and G] runne about his head. A] bloud runne abouts head. l. 30. A] didst thou learn that at. B—F] learn'st that at. G] learn'st thou that at. l. 31. A] Puft, did I not. l. 33. A—F] Talke. l. 34. A] While you. A—G] words.

p. 156, l. 6. A] to a chaire. l. 8. A—F] other. A] will take. l. 14. A] give mee audience. G *omits*] me. l. 16. A] soone one of you. ll. 29 and 30. G *omits*] but I am grown To balk, but I defie. l. 30. A] but I desire, let. l. 32. B, C and G] draulst. D] drawlst. l. 34. G] in an instant. l. 36. A] An't. l. 38. A, B and G] As yet you. l. 39. A] command mee else.

p. 157, l. 11. B, C and G] Were great as. l. 12. A] that I might. l. 14. A] with. l. 28. A *omits*] puffe. B and G *omit* the bracket, and print 'puffe' in roman type as part of the speech. l. 29. D, E and F] rules. l. 34. A] Will you be gone. l. 35. A] My word mooves. C—F] My words moves. l. 36. A] 2 Gent. l. 39. A] That they will. B *omits*] you. A *omits*] Exeunt all but Arb. and Mar. l. 40. Folio] the.

p. 158, l. 7. Folio] scare. l. 17. A] doted, because. B—F *omit*] it. l. 35. A *omits*] but. A] of your faults. l. 39. A] above the earth.

p. 159, l. 4. Folio] safe. l. 15. A, B and G] would. l. 21. A] these wilde moodes. l. 22. A] honest. l. 23. A, B and G] would. l. 25. A] would. l. 34. A, B, C and G] Give thee. l. 37. Folio *misprints*] paron. l. 40. C] doest. F *omits*] I.

p. 160, l. 4. B, C and D] i' thine eare. F] thy eare. l. 10. A] Ith those. G] in those. l. 12. B] they wenches. l. 18. B by mistake *adds*] Enter Bessus, and the two Gent. l. 22. A *omits* this stage-direction. l. 25. A] I am. l. 26. A] 1 Gent. l. 27. A] 2 Gent. l. 30. A] I bad you; halfe. l. 31. A] An't. l. 35. A] Panthan. l. 38. A] will not. l. 39. A *omits*] Sir.

p. 161, l. 6. E and F] a good an opinion. l. 15. A *omits*] a. G] Enter a Messenger, with a Packet. l. 21. A] Thanke thee for. l. 29. A] teares enough. B—F] tears I'now. G] tears Enow. l. 32. C—F] set her.

p. 162, l. 2. A] now has hired. l. 7. F] them. l. 12. A] laden. l. 16. E and F] that come. l. 18. A—D and G] mourning. l. 19. A] her sacred dew. l. 32. A] prayers. l. 34. A] dangers. l. 35. A *omits*] Exeunt.

p. 163, l. 3. A, B and G] either loves. l. 7. A—G] place. A] unfortunately too light. l. 17. A *omits*] thee. l. 24. Folio] make. l. 31. B and G] gi'n. A, B and G] to. l. 33. A] would place.

p. 164, l. 11. Folio *misprints*] conld. l. 15. A—G] requires. A] more speed. l. 18. B] He shall not doe so Lord. l. 21. A *adds*] Finis Actus Primi. B and C *add*] The end of the First Act. l. 24. A] attendance. G *adds*] and Guards.

p. 165, l. 5. A] paid downe. l. 20. A] let light. l. 25. A—D] eare. l. 30. A] another woman. l. 36. A] twill. F] 'twood not. l. 37. F *omits*] not.

p. 166, l. 9. A] mine own. l. 21. B—F] a did. l. 23. A] held time. l. 25. A—G with variations in spelling] my Lord Protectour. l. 29. Folio *misprints*] Cammanders.

p. 167, l. 7. A *omits*] as you. l. 12. A, B and G] prayers are. A] I will. l. 20. A *omits*] Arane. l. 23. A] Betweene. l. 36. A] heare it. l. 37. A] I, I prethee.

p. 168, l. 1. F] Captain. l. 3. A] neere a Captaine. l. 4. A] of the. l. 7. A—G] whom. l. 11. A] prethee. l. 14. F] was given. l. 18. A] I, but I. l. 20. A] saide. ll. 21 and 22. A] when one. l. 23. A] Marshallists. l. 30. F] doest. l. 31. A] twas so. B—G] so 'twas. l. 36. A] An't. l. 37. A and B] neerer. G] nearer. l. 39. A] kindnesses.

p. 169, l. 1. A and G] Thalestris. l. 10. A] for her honestie. l. 17. A] on her. l. 33. A *adds*] Exit. B—G with various abbreviations *add*] Exit Bessus. l. 34. A, B and G *add*] Exit. l. 35. A—G *omit* stage-direction. l. 39. F] speeks them.

p. 170, l. 1. A] vertuous. l. 6. A] or feeles. l. 7. A—G] hope. l. 11. A—D and G] love. l. 16. E and F] where bargain'd. l. 18. A] find time worthy. l. 20. A, B and G] there is. l. 22. A] with this. l. 27. A] to see you Madam. l. 29. A *omits*] Gob. l. 35. A *omits*] Exeunt Women.

p. 171, l. 9. F] a stake. l. 14. F] if foole. l. 20. A] prethee. l. 22. F] noble sharp. l. 33. A] desire too. E and F] his one desire.

p. 172, l. 1. A—D and G] those tender. l. 4. A, B and G] I shall. l. 13. B, C and F] Thalectris. l. 16. B, C and G] others. l. 26. A, B and G] women out. l. 29. A] say. l. 35. A—D and G] those. l. 37. A] places quickly. l. 38. A, D and F] a foote. B, C and E] afoote. G] afoot.

p. 173, l. 2. A] looke. l. 5. A] Enter two Citizens wives, and Philip. l. 15. A, B and G] with me downe. l. 16. A] abed. l. 17. A] tis. l. 18. A] prethee. l. 29. A] In good faith. l. 34. A] I. l. 35. A *omits*] you. l. 37. A] had thrusting. G] shoving. l. 38. A] hap to go.

p. 174, l. 2. A] so on me. l. 5. A] have not. l. 10. A] law, thou art. A] there is. l. 11. A] thou art. A] of it. l. 12. A] he will never. l. 13. A] stripling. l. 17. A] you are. l. 18. B—F] cast. l. 19. A *omits* this line. l. 20. A—D and G] The King, the King, the King, the King. l. 21. A *omits*] Flourish. A] Enter Arbaces, Tigranes, Mardonius, and others. l. 23. E and F] I think. l. 29. A] without our bloods. B and G] but with our. G] bloud. l. 31. A] in your Townes. l. 32. A—D and G] about you; you may sit. l. 37. A, B and G] may you. F] you may fall. l. 38. A, B and G] when I.

p. 175, l. 5. E and F] beheld. l. 6. A] hearts. l. 9. A] Hang him, hang him, hang him. l. 13. A, B and G] was farre. l. 14. E and F] nor to revile. l. 15. A—D and G] the nature. l. 19. A] made that name. l. 21. C and D] and well for. l. 22. B—G] word. l. 25. A] commendations. l. 29. A] Thus my. l. 30. A] calles. l. 36. A] Eate at. l. 40. In place of this line A] Exeunt.

p. 176, l. 1. A *omits* one 'God bless your Majesty.' l. 7. A] 1. l. 10. A *omits*] so. B, C, D and G] women. A] Exeunt 1, 2, 3, and Women. l. 11. A—G] afore. l. 12. A] homeward. l. 13. A *omits*] all. l. 15. A] They are. A—G] heard on. l. 18. A *adds*] Finis Actus Secundi. B and C *add*] The end of the Second Act. l. 19. A] Actus Tertii Scaena Prima. l. 23. A] doth. l. 29. A—D and G] where you will have her. l. 37. A *omits*] I do hope she will not.

p. 177, l. 6. A] Sir, sheele not. l. 15. B and G] would. l. 18. C—F *omit*] you. l. 24. A *omits*] 1 Gent. and. l. 25. A] here's. l. 29. A] them. B and G *add*] Exit Gobrias. l. 35. A *omits*] and two Gentlemen. G *adds*] Attendants, and Guards.

p. 178, l. 11. A, B and G] sorrow. l. 14. A *adds*] Exit. l. 15. A *omits*] Exit Arane. l. 32. G] words and kind ones. l. 35. C] doest. l. 36. D] forth my selfe. l. 38. A and G] thence. l. 40. A] wounded flesh.

p. 179, l. 1. A, B and G] a quill. l. 2. A, B, C and G] wanton wing. l. 3. A] in thy bloud. l. 16. A, B and G *omit*] it. l. 33. A by mistake gives the words 'some one that hath [A has] a wit, answer, where is she' to Gobrias, with the result that the names of the speakers of the following four speeches are transposed.

p. 180, l. 18. A] sleepe. l. 27. A] Is a long life of yet, I hope. l. 31. C, D and E] doest. ll. 33—35. A *omits* these lines.

p. 181, l. 11. A] If shee were any. l. 14. D] dispute. l. 16. F and G] naked. l. 19. A, B and G] is she not. l. 39. A, B and G] your brother.

p. 182, l. 6. A] them. l. 8. A] yet so. l. 9. Folio *prints*] langish. l. 17. A] sudden change. l. 19. A, B and G] Pray God it doe. l. 24. A] prisoner. l. 31. A] in the.

p. 183, l. 13. A, B and G] And how dare you then. C and D] And how then dare you. l. 21. A, B and G] that breath. l. 24. A] law.

p. 184, l. 12. A] subtiller. G] subtiler. l. 13. A and G] Tyrants. B] Tirants. F] mightest. l. 14. A] in the depth. B] i' the depth. C and G] i' the deepe. l. 18. A *omits*] Exeunt Tigr. and Bac. l. 21. G *adds*] Exit Spaconia. l. 39. A and B] then to; here I. G] then too; here I.

p. 185, l. 11. A] still in doubt. l. 12. A] This, this third. l. 25. A, B, C and G] A poysoner. l. 26. A by mistake gives this speech to Bacurius and the following one to Gobrias. l. 32. A] had it twixt. A] Exeunt omnes, prae. Ar. Mar. G] Exeunt Gob. Pan. and Bes.

p. 186, l. 9. A] I prethee. l. 10. B and G] Am not I. l. 19. F] O do. l. 25. A] I prethee. l. 26. A *adds*] *Mar.* I warrant ye. l. 28. G] of game. l. 30. B and G *omit*] it.

p. 187, l. 2. A] them. l. 3. A] In this state (*omits* I). B, C, D and G] I' this state. l. 4. B—F] b' the. A] with. l. 5. A] with. l. 10. A, B and G with variations of spelling] God cald. C and D] heaven cald. l. 11. A] pounds. l. 17. A and G] afraid. l. 21. G] A pox. A—G] of their. l. 23. A] of me. l. 24. A] freshly to account, worthily. l. 25. B and G *omit*] the. l. 26. A *omits*] a. l. 27. Here and throughout the scene '3 Gent' is in A described as 'Gent.' l. 30. A] you are. l. 32. A] he nothing doubts.

p. 188, l. 2. A—D, F and G with variations of spelling] O cry you mercie. E] O cir you mercy. l. 3. A, B, C and G with variations of spelling] agreeablie. l. 4. Here and in the following three lines A reads only one 'um' in place of three. l. 12. A by mistake *omits*] *Bes.* l. 19. A] plaine with you. l. 20. A] can doe him. A] resolutely. l. 21. B and C] hundreth. l. 22. F] no more. l. 23. A] pray ye. l. 26. A simply] Exit. l. 30. D] these two houres. l. 32. F *omits*] that. A] reserv'd. l. 34. A] are there. l. 35. A] likely to hold him this time here for mine. l. 36. B, C and G] yeare. D] these five yeares. l. 37. A] send me.

p. 189, l. 27. A] I prethee. l. 28. A—D and G] beate. l. 31. A] pounds. l. 32. A *omits*] well. F] well and walk sooner. l. 33. C] I do. l. 36. C] doest.

p. 190, l. 5. A—G] Come, unbuckle, quicke. l. 7. C—F] Unbuckle say. l. 17. A *omits*] Bac. l. 24. A] will I. l. 25. A] that this is all is left. G] that is left. l. 26. A *omits*] Bessus. l. 28. G] he's. l. 32. A, B and G] await. l. 35. A *omits* this stage-direction. l. 39. A] in their eyes.

p. 191, l. 3. A—G] lies. l. 5. A—G] vex me. l. 6. G] thou art. l. 8. A *omits*] do. l. 12. F] fire. l. 14. A, B and G] is not that. G] there is. l. 18. A, B and G] I shall not. l. 20. A—G] I know 'tis. l. 21. A] hath. l. 22. A] or fall. l. 34. A] of all this.

p. 192, l. 2. A, B and G] shall I. l. 6. A] But what, what should. B and G] should. l. 11. A, B and G] on more advice. l. 17. A *omits*] a. l. 19. Folio *misprints*] faithul. l. 21. F] doe't. l. 23. C—F] doest. l. 24. A, B and G] I hope I. l. 37. E and F] doest.

p. 193, l. 4. A, B and G] cause. l. 5. A, B, C and G *omit*] ha. l. 7. A, B, C and G] blow about the world. l. 8. A, B and G] his cause. l. 9. A] deare Mardonius. l. 12. A, B and G] Pray God you. l. 24. A, B and G] God preserve you, and mend you. l. 26. A, B and G] require. l. 30. A, B and G] use of. l. 32. A *adds*] to them.

p. 194, l. 2. A] I am. l. 4. A, B, F and G] I am. A includes the words 'I am glad'on't' in the following speech of Mardonius. l. 5. A, B and G] to that. ll. 7—9. A *omits* these lines. l. 11. A, B and G] occasions. l. 15. A, B, C and G] to the. l. 16. A—D and G] for his. l. 17. A *omits*] Mar. l. 19. A] Doe for. The letters 'ith' are in C cut off at the end of the line. l. 23. A, B and G] a thing. l. 26. G] would fain have thee. l. 27. A] understands. G] understandest. l. 30. A] dost make. l. 32. A, B and G] tell me, it shall. C has the same reading, though the word 'tell' is by mistake cut off from the end of the line. A *omits*] too. l. 35. A, B and C] and mayst yet.

p. 195, l. 2. A—D and G] that I have ever. l. 3. A, B and G *omit*] the. l. 8. A, B, C and G] your businesse. l. 12. A, B and G *omit*] now. l. 29. A—F] Gods and mans. l. 30. G] nature. l. 36. A *adds*] Finis Actus Tertii. B and C *add*] The end of the Third Act.

p. 196, l. 1. A] Actus Quarti Scaena Prima. l. 2. A—G *omit*] and. l. 11. A, B, C and G] Yet fearing since they. A] th' are many. l. 13. F] them. l. 14. F] them. l. 15. A] fearefull; if he. l. 18. A] labour out this. l. 19. A] against. ll. 25 and 26. A encloses the words 'never... humour' within brackets. l. 26. D, E and F] shot. l. 30. F] no farther. l. 33. A *omits*] But.

p. 197, l. 3. A *adds*] Exit. l. 4. A *omits*] Exit Gob. l. 13. A] yours. l. 29. G] I'm. A] if no more. l. 36. B—G] these. l. 37. A] That have Authority. l. 38. F] besides.

p. 198, l. 1. A] words. l. 4. A] Ime. l. 12. A, B and G] Pray God. l. 13. A *omits*] in prison. l. 15. A and F] mine. A] turne. l. 27. A, B and G] deserv'd it. l. 33. A] griefes. l. 35. A] womans. F] woman. l. 36. A] lost. l. 39. G] unconstancy.

p. 199, l. 7. A] kill me Ladie. l. 9. A *omits*] Lady. l. 15. A] for were. l. 20. A] in the. l. 26. A, B and G] is as firme. l. 27. A] and as lasting. l. 28. A, B and G] in the. C] in th' ayre. l. 31. A] murmurs. l. 37. A—D and G] wrongs.

p. 200, l. 1. A by mistake *omits*] Spa. l. 2. A, B, C and G] Our ends alike. l. 9. A] hee's asham'd. l. 17. A] pray believe me. l. 19. A, B and G] No more. l. 20. A] and Mardonius. l. 32. A—G] outlast. Folio *misprints*] too. l. 38. A] is that.

p. 201, l. 5. A] know. l. 10. A] pratling. l. 11. A] to it. l. 15. A—G] Beside. l. 17. A] Sirra. l. 23. A] Staffe poak't. A, B, C and G] through. F] throw. l. 24. A—D and G] broke. l. 25. D, E and F] stifled with. l. 30. F] worst. l. 35. A] you may say Sir what. Folio *misprints*] yon. l. 36. A gives this line to Mardonius.

p. 202, l. 3. A, B and G] I thank God. l. 5. A] doe it. l. 6. A *omits*] Doe. l. 13. A *adds*] and a Souldier like a termogant. l. 16. A] let um be prisoners. l. 18. F] them. ll. 19 and 20. A gives these lines to Bacurius. ll. 21 and 22. A and G give these lines to Spaconia. l. 22. A, B, C and G] deare. l. 23. A] Ex. Bacu. with Tig. and Spa. l. 24. A, B, C and G] have you. l. 25. F] prove. l. 30. A] Sadlers. l. 32. A, D and F] darest. l. 33. A] knowest. l. 34. G] will not. l. 37. A] shall then tell. B] of this. l. 40. A] Where. F] them.

p. 203, l. 1. A *adds after* off] doe, kill me. l. 2. A *omits*] worse. l. 4. A, B, C and G] a dead sleepe. l. 5. A] Like forraigne swords. l. 10. A] all thine. l. 12. G] Wilt. A] with me good Mardonius. l. 20. A, B and G] and all beautie. l. 22. F] she is not. l. 23. A] doe enlarge her. l. 26. A] that would have. l. 29. E and F] heat. l. 30. E] To here wretched. F *omits*] a. l. 38. A] knew of. B, C and D] knewst the.

p. 204, l. 7. A] is it. l. 15. A—D and G *omit*] a. l. 16. A *omits*] Thousands. E and F] Thousand. A] denie it. l. 18. A, B and G] vertue. l. 24. A *omits*] all. l. 26. A—G] stooles there boy. l. 32. A, B and G] and my deare. l. 33. B, C and G] to th' cause. l. 35. F *omits* this line. l. 37. A prints the words 'be wise, and speake truth' as the conclusion of the second Sword-man's speech.

p. 205, l. 4. A] If he have. l. 5. B—E] If a have. F] If I have. l. 12. A] case. l. 13. A, B and G] an honourable. l. 15. A, B and G] we Sword-men. l. 17. A, B and G] drawne ten teeth. A—G] beside. l. 18. A] all these. l. 21. B—E] a crackt. l. 22. A] with crossing. l. 26. A—G] There's. l. 30. A, B, C and G] mile. l. 32. A—G] mile. l. 34. A, B and C] 'Tis a the longest. G] o' the longest. l. 35. A by mistake gives this line to Bessus and the following speech to the first Sword-man.

p. 206, ll. 5 and 6. F] word forc'd. l. 9. A—D and G] case. l. 12. A] sit. G] sat. l. 13. A] it had. l. 15. E and F] delivery. l. 19. B—E] A should. F] And should. A—D and G] deliverie. l. 24. A] by th'. l. 25. A] you are. l. 28. A *omits*] the. l. 32. B and G] that we. l. 33. Folio *misprints*] honesty. A] good Sir to th'. l. 35. A] The boy may be supposd, hee's lyable; but kicke my brother.

p. 207, l. 7. A] Still the must. l. 9. A—D and G *omit*] I. A] againe, againe. l. 12. F *omits*] my. l. 20. A] at the kicke. l. 22. F] baren scorn, as I will call it. l. 27. A—G] sore indeed Sir. l. 29. A] the foole. l. 30. A] Ah Lords. l. 32. A, B, C and G] laught.

p. 208, l. 5. A—G] size, daggers. F] sizes. l. 16. A] To abide upon't. l. 20. A, B, C and G *omit*] me. F] Both get me. l. 21. F] cleane. l. 22. G] what you have done. l. 27. F] Go will, and tell. l. 28. A—D] Or there be. l. 29. A *omits* and *before* Gob. l. 33. A *omits*] Exit Gob. l. 34. A] you are. A, B, C and G] and I would. A, B and G] to God. l. 38. G] the rising. l. 39. B, C and G] I shall. l. 40. Folio *misprints*] Ban.

p. 209, l. 3. A] does. l. 6. A] I prethee. l. 8. A, B and G] I am. l. 23. A, B and G] In as equal a degree. C and D] In equal a degree. l. 27. A] I prethee. l. 33. C, D and E] and there is. E] no cause. F] and there is none can see.

p. 210, l. 6. D, E and F] stop. l. 11. A, B and G] God keepe you. l. 12. A, B and G] cause. l. 19. A] innocents. l. 20. A, B and G *omit*] that. l. 24. A, B and G] it is. l. 27. A, B and G] as it lists. l. 33. A encloses 'Which I beseech thee doe not' within brackets. l. 36. A, B and G] For God knows. l. 39. A] start eye to.

p. 211, l. 2. F] them. l. 5. A] should. l. 11. F] them. l. 20. A, B and G] sinnes. l. 32. A] no steppe.

p. 212, ll. 1—6 and 8. F] them. l. 2. A] them. l. 5. Folio] and them. l. 6. A] drinke them off. l. 25. A gives this line to Panthea. l. 27. D, E and F] brother. l. 29. B] i' this. l. 35. A *omits*] Why. l. 38. A, B and G] I know thou.

p. 213, l. 4. A, B and G *omit* too *before* scrupulous. ll. 8 and 9. In place of these lines G *reads*] I dare no longer stay. l. 9. A and B] hotter I feare then yours. l. 11. A, B and G] for God's sake. l. 14. A *omits* stage-direction. B and G *omit*] several wayes. A *adds*] Finis Actus Quarti. B and C *add*] The end of the Fourth Act. l. 15. A] Actus Quinti Scaena Prima. l. 19. A] leave to visit. l. 20. A] hands. l. 26. A] officers.

p. 214, l. 3. B—F] were a valiant. l. 6. A] something lighter. l. 28. A—D *omit*] he. G] h'as. l. 29. B—F] a was. l. 30. A] in his. E and F] in in's. l. 31. A—E] a my. F] in my. G] i' my. l. 33. A, B and G] like to wicker Targets. l. 35. A *omits*] he. A] so low a sence. l. 36. A] should. l. 38. A, B and G] That this strange fellow.

p. 215, l. 3. A—D and G] broke. A—G] or a shoulder out. A—F] ath' stones. l. 4. A] of my. l. 10. A *omits*] the. l. 13. Folio *misprints*] Catain. l. 16. A *omits*] Sword. l. 19. A] thus kicke you, and thus. B and G] thus kicke, and thus. l. 21. A—D and G] told you that. l. 23. A *omits*] Sword. A—F] a should. l. 25. A, B, C and G] a one. l. 26. A *omits*] beats him. l. 29. A, B and G] Sir I know. l. 30. A *prints* 'Bes.' at the beginning of the following line, thus making this line part of Lygones' speech.

p. 216, l. 6. A, B and G] you would. l. 7. A, B, C and G] strange now to have. l. 12. Folio *misprints*] danghter. l. 13. A, B and G] of being. l. 15. A *omits*] Lygo. l. 18. A *omits*] Sword. l. 19. A] ath' sword. l. 20. G] h'as. l. 23. A] a kick't. l. 24. A *omits* 'Bes.,' thus making this line part of the second Sword-man's speech. l. 25. A *omits*] Sword. A gives the words 'Now let him come and say he was not sorry, And he sleepes for it' to '2,' i.e., the second Sword-man. l. 26. B—F] a was not. B—F] a sleepes. l. 28. A *omits*] clear. G] Exeunt omnes. l. 34. A prints this stage-direction after the words 'There he is indeed' in l. 35.

p. 217, l. 3. A, B, C and G] businesse will. l. 5. B] the Armenia state. l. 9. F *omits*] is. l. 20. A—G] couldst prate. l. 28. A] vild. B and C] vilde. B—F] commendations. l. 30. A, B and G] or rather would I. l. 34. A and F] mine own. l. 38. A] and like it.

p. 218, l. 3. A] in the. B, C, D and G] i' the. l. 6. B *misprints*] my Prince. l. 8. A] beside. l. 12. A] men. l. 13. C] Cawdle. l. 14. A] your Queene. l. 21. A] should speake. l. 27. A] a Queene. l. 33. A, B and G] Good God. l. 37. A, B and G *omit*] all.

p. 219, l. 4. A] that shall. l. 6. A *omits*] all. l. 7. A] a servant. l. 11. A] and Swordmen. In A this stage-direction is printed after the following line. l. 15. A—F] ath' sword. l. 17. A—D and G *omit*] much. l. 20. A] I can aske. l. 23. A] will require launcing. l. 24. A] and full. l. 28. A *omits*] must. l. 31. A, B and G] God continue it. l. 32. F *misprints*] they to it.

p. 220, l. 5. The two Sword-men are throughout the scene referred to in A as '2' or '1.' l. 6. A *omits* 'Bac.,' thus giving the line to the second Sword-man. l. 13. A—G *omit*] on. F] them, that have. l. 16. A—F] ath' law. l. 22. F] That is. A] their paines. l. 26. A] ye rogues, ye apple-squiers. l. 31. A] a many of. F] a beautie of. l. 33. E] I do do beseech. l. 35. A—F] A this side.

p. 221, l. 4. A] in your pocket slave, my key you. B and G] in your pocket slave, my toe. l. 5. A] with't. l. 11. A—G] doing nothing. l. 12. A *omits* this stage-direction. B] Enter Servant, Will. Adkinson. l. 13. A—D] Here's. l. 14. A] I am. A] prethee. l. 15. A] beate um. l. 17. A *omits*] Sir. l. 18. A *omits*] Captain, Rally. A] up with your. F] rally upon. l. 20. A] cride hold. l. 22. E and F] vit me. l. 23. A, B and G] breath. A *omits*] Exit Bac. l. 25. A] Ime sure I ha. l. 26. B—F] a kicke. B—F] a will. l. 27. C—F] beside. l. 29. A, B and G] yes, God be thanked. l. 33. A, B, C and G] is a. l. 34. A] hands.

p. 222, l. 2. A *omits*] clear. G] Exeunt omnes. l. 4. A—D and G] bore. After this line A *adds*]

——————Hell open all thy gates,
And I will thorough them; if they be shut,

Ile batter um, but I will find the place
Where the most damn'd have dwelling; ere I end,
Amongst them all they shall not have a sinne,
But I will call it mine:

l. 5. A—D and G] friend. A, B and G] to an. l. 13. B, C and D] a comming. l. 14. A—G] does your hand. l. 19. This line from 'I can' and the next line are given by A to Mardonius. l. 24. A] humblier.

p. 223, l. 4. A, B and G *omit*] and. l. 12. A] thinkest. l. 13. G] these are tales. l. 15. A—D and G] should get. l. 17. A] Farre other Fortunes. l. 19. A, B and G] God put. G] temporall. l. 20. A *adds*] Exit. B and G *add*] Exit Mar. l. 21. A—D and G] errors. l. 27. A, B and G *omit*] more. l. 35. A—D and G *omit*] my.

p. 224, l. 4. F] knowest. l. 9. A] doest. l. 12. A] and I when I. F] knowest. l. 16. B and F] meanst. l. 17. A, B, C and G] a lie. A, B and G] God and. l. 22. A, B and G] wouldst. l. 28. A] gavest. l. 31. A] your selfe. B and G] it thy selfe. l. 38. A and G] know it. l. 39. E and F] staind.

p. 225, l. 7. A, B, C and G] allowest. l. 15. C—F] doest...doest. l. 17. A—D and G] Cease thou strange. l. 18. A] contemn'st. ll. 20 and 21. Folio *misprints*] dear...punishnment. l. 35. A and C] expects. B] expectes. D] expectst. G] expect'st. l. 39. A] thou wicked.

p. 226, l. 10. A, B, C and G] of a law. l. 19. A *omits*] you. ll. 25 and 26. A—G] Land as she. l. 29. A *misprints*] *Arb.* l. 31. A—D and G *omit*] a.

p. 227, l. 2. A] opportunitie. ll. 4 and 5. A, B and G] and God was humbly thankt in every Church, That so had blest the Queene, and prayers etc. l. 12. A—D and G] quicke. l. 14. A] abed. l. 16. A] sware. l. 20. A] the Queene. l. 23. A—G] yeare. l. 28. A] her talke. l. 32. A] sparke. l. 35. A, B and G] till I am. A] are silver. l. 37. A *omits*] too. l. 38. A, B and G] yes God knowes.

p. 228, l. 2. A by mistake *omits*] *Gob.* A] dare. l. 3. A] them. l. 4. A—G] waites. l. 7. A] Ent. Mar. Bessus, and others. l. 8. A *omits*] *Arb.* A] Mardonius, the best. B *misprints*] *Mar.* l. 11. E and F] happie. l. 14. A] On, call. l. 19. A *omits*] *Exit a Gent.* l. 24. A *omits*] I swear it must not be; nay, trust me. l. 26. B and C] beare. l. 28. A] but you are not.

p. 229, l. 1. A] I say she. l. 8. A] Armenian king. l. 15. Folio *misprints*] morning. l. 16. A *omits* this stage-direction. l. 24. A and G] He shall. B] A shall. C] An shall. l. 25. A—G] shall. l. 26. F *omits*] that. l. 31. A *misprints*] thinke. l. 35. In place of this stage-direction A after the word 'Queen' in l. 33 *reads*] Enter Pan.

p. 230, l. 6. A gives this speech to Mardonius. l. 7. A *omits*] at first. l. 8. In A this stage-direction occurs after 'Queen' in the following line. l. 14. A and F] Maist. G] May'st. l. 17. F] them. l. 20. A—G] your Queene. l. 23. A—G *add*] Finis.

APPENDIX

A KING AND NO KING. VERSE AND PROSE VARIATIONS[1].

p. 152, ll. 8 and 9. A—D and G] 3 ll. *dare, day, I.* l. 27. A] 2 ll. *of, thus.* ll. 33—35. A] 3 ll. *Earth, Prince, Acts.*

p. 157, l. 20. A] 2 ll. *King, away.*

p. 159, ll. 3—8. A—D and G] 8 ll. *praise, worthy, death, lies, there, though, dust, envy.* ll. 11 and 12. A—D and G] 3 ll. *windes, I, speake.* ll. 29—38. A—D and G] 14 ll. *lives, said, truth, bin, see, parts, world, farre, yeares, mee, thee, wilt, I, thus.* l. 40 and p. 160, ll. 1—4. A—D and G] 6 ll. *take, which, love, I, mee, eare.*

p. 160, ll. 6 and 7. A, B and G] 2 ll. *Mardonius, Jewell.*

p. 161, ll. 21 and 22. A—D and G] 3 ll. *newes, not, Gobrias.* ll. 27—33. A—D and G] 9 ll. *farre, sinnes, teares, feele, brest, stand, eyes, world, me.* ll. 37—39 and p. 162, ll. 1—7. A—D and G] 14 ll. *know, died, life, pardon'd, fit, olde, thence, out, there, live, me, deathes, life, him.*

p. 163, ll. 16—22. A, B, C and G] 9 ll. *of* (C = *halfe*), *free, thine, prisoner, force, me, unwilling, Tigranes, there.* D] 7 ll. *halfe, free, thine, force, me, Tigranes, there.*

p. 164, ll. 1 and 2. A—D and G] 2 ll. *health, jealous.* ll. 25—35 and p. 165, ll. 1 and 2. A—D and G] 16 ll. *regard, prisoner, escape, prisoner, woman, me, say, her, Lord, grace, arme, womanhood, death, sonne, why, speake.*

p. 165, ll. 14—17. A—D and G] 5 ll. *time, know, thinke, heart, urgd.* ll. 35 and 36. A—D and G] 2 ll. *it, believ'd.* ll. 38 and 39. A—D and G] 3 ll. *you, die, uncredited* (D = *should*).

p. 166, ll. 1 and 2. A—D and G] 4 ll. *then, me, King, plots* (D adds l. 3). ll. 5—8. A—D and G] 5 ll. *me, content, power, me, done.* ll. 19—23. A—D and G] Prose. ll. 25 and 26. A] *these, these.*

p. 167, ll. 9 and 10. A] 2 ll. *well, so.* l. 19. A—D and G] 2 ll. *readie, morrow.* ll. 21—28. A] 10 ll. *hereafter, office, discourse, how, victorie, doe, danger, long, while, beate.* ll. 21—24. B—D and G] 4 ll. *hereafter, office, discourse, victory.* ll. 25—28. B—D and G] Prose.

p. 168, ll. 11 and 12. A—D and G] 2 ll. *Bessus, nothing.* ll. 39 and 40. A—D and G] 2 ll. *kindnesses, name.*

p. 169, ll. 2—5. A—D and G] 5 ll. *letter, enough, you, me, me.* ll. 25 and 26. A and G] 2 ll. *already, foolish.* ll. 37—40 and p. 170, ll. 1—4. A—D and G] 12 ll. *Lord, live, um, Just, um, mee, heare, way, care, you, enjoyes, worth.*

p. 170, ll. 5—10. A—D and G] Prose. ll. 13—18. A—D and G] 8 ll. *you, power, leave, like, him, humours, lesse, offer'd.* ll. 27—29. A] 2 ll. *pleasure, Madam.*

p. 171, ll. 10—15. A—D and G] 9 ll. *unreasonably, seeme, ill, ought, faire, good, prayer, me, you.* ll. 31—40 and p. 172, ll. 1—6. A—D] 24 ll. *weepe, words, sorrow, me, him, Thalestris, me, sweare, stay, thee, himselfe, me, yet, face, you, eares, eyes, him, hope, dead, him, fast, ceremony, him.*

p. 172, ll. 15—21. A—D and G] 11 ll. *not, desire, others, me* (or *not*), *wrong, birth, injure, hither, commanded, ready, servand.*

p. 174, l. 20. A—D] 2 ll. *King, now.* ll. 23—29. A—D and G] 11 ll. *full, subjects, love, height, you, me, warre, imagine, word, blouds, peace.*

[1] The prose printings of E and F have not been recorded.

p. 175, ll. 4—6. A—D and G] 4 ll. *man, home, hearts, deliverance.* ll. 11—22. A—D and G] 17 ll. *wrong, spectacle, people, me, deserved, you, dwels, man, compare, selfe, you, too, name, fall, loves, content, worke.* ll. 35 and 36. A—D and G] 2 ll. *Children, is.*

p. 176, ll. 23—35. A—D and G] 14 ll. *Sir, hands, know, her, home, stubbornnesse, like, her, Jewell, mad, sister, is, Land, another.*

p. 177, ll. 1—10. A—D and G] 11 ll. *too, friends, know, loth, passe, constraint, so, speake, health, love, againe.*

p. 178, ll. 16 and 17. A—D and G] 3 ll. *die, returne, life.* ll. 30—32. A—D and G] 4 ll. *ill, kneele, gaine, you.*

p. 179, ll. 21—25. A—D and G] 7 ll. *earth, alas, command, me, short, sister, brought.*

p. 180, l. 31. A—D and G] 2 ll. *Gobrias, meane.*

p. 191, ll. 35 and 36. A—D and G] 2 ll. *utterd, careleslie.*

p. 192, ll. 9—12. E and F] 3 ll. *and, love, thou.* ll. 10—12. A—D and G] 3 ll. *advice, love, thou.* ll. 16 and 17. A—D and G] 3 ll. *this, caution, it* (G *adds* l. 18). ll. 20 and 21. A—D and G] 2 ll. *it, it.*

p. 194, ll. 5 and 6. A] 2 ll. *cutlers, King.* l. 22. A] 2 ll. *will, whatsoever.*

p. 195, ll. 21 and 22. A] 2 ll. *in-, Monsters.*

p. 196, l. 38, and p. 197, ll. 1—3. A] Prose.

p. 197, ll. 4 and 5. A] 3 ll. *you, Spaconia, thus.*

p. 199, ll. 9 and 10. B—D and G] 3 ll. *Ladie, passe, King.* ll. 12 and 13. A and G] 2 ll. *from, remov'd.*

p. 201, ll. 7 and 8. A] 2 ll. *all, folly.* l. 15. A] 2 ll. *Sir, warrant.* ll. 39 and 40.

p. 202, ll. 19—22. A] Prose.

p. 204, l. 6. A—D and G] 2 ll. *false, letter.* ll. 36—38. A] 2 ll. *truth, Prince.*

p. 205, ll. 26 and 27. A—D and G] 3 ll. *another, distance, opinion.*

p. 207, ll. 11—13. A—D and G] 3 ll. *toge-, man, brother.* l. 24. A—D and G] 2 ll. *Sir, since.*

p. 209, ll. 31 and 32. A] 2 ll. *me, brother.*

p. 212, ll. 11 and 12. A] 3 ll. *Panthea, gaze, out.* ll. 23 and 24. A] 2 ll. *you, gone.*

Act 5 is in verse in Quartos A, B, C and D, in prose in Quartos E and F from p. 214, l. 22. As the Second Folio also prints it in prose it has been decided to give here the verse of Quarto A (1619) in full.

Actus Quinti Scaena Prima.

Enter Mardonius, and Ligones.

Mar. Sir, the King has seene your Commission, and beleeves it, and freely by this warrant gives you leave to visit Prince *Tigranes* your noble Master.

Lig. I thanke his Grace, and kisse his hands.

Mar. But is the maine of all your businesse
Ended in this?

Lig. I have another, but a worse; I am asham'd, it is a businesse.—

Mar. You serve a worthy person, and a stranger I am sure you are; you may imploy mee if you please, without your purse, such Officers should ever be their owne rewards.

Lig. I am bound to your noblenesse.

Mar. I may have neede of you, and then this curtesie,
If it be any, is not ill bestowed:
But may I civilly desire the rest?
I shall not be a hurter, if no helper.

Lig. Sir, you shall know I have lost a foolish daughter,
And with her all my patience; pilferd away
By a meane Captaine of your Kings.

Mar. Stay there Sir:
If he have reacht the noble worth of Captaine,
He may well claime a worthy gentlewoman,
Though shee were yours, and noble.

Lig. I grant all that too: but this wretched fellow
Reaches no further then the emptie name,
That serves to feede him; were he valiant,
Or had but in him any noble nature,
That might hereafter promise him a good man;
My cares were something lighter, and my grave
A span yet from me.

Mar. I confesse such fellowes
Be in all royall Campes, and have, and must be
To make the sinne of coward more detested
In the meane Souldier, that with such a foyle
Sets of much valour: By description
I should now guesse him to you. It was *Bessus*,
I dare almost with confidence pronounce it.

Lig. Tis such a scurvy name as *Bessus*, and now I thinke tis hee.

Mar. Captaine, doe you call him?
Beleeve me Sir, you have a miserie
Too mighty for your age: A pox upon him,
For that must be the end of all his service:
Your daughter was not mad Sir?

Lig. No, would shee had beene,
The fault had had more credit: I would doe something.

Mar. I would faine counsell you; but to what I know not:
Hee's so below a beating, that the women
Find him not worthy of their distaves; and
To hang him, were to cast away a rope,
Hee's such an ayrie thin unbodied coward,
That no revenge can catch him:
Ile tell you Sir, and tell you truth; this rascall
Feares neither God nor man, has beene so beaten:
Sufferance has made him wanscote; he has had
Since hee was first a slave, at least three hundred daggers

Set in his head, as little boyes doe new knives in hot meat;
Ther's not a rib in's bodie a my conscience,
That has not beene thrice broken with drie beating;
And now his sides looke like to wicker targets,
Everie way bended:
Children will shortly take him for a wall,
And set their stone-bowes in his forhead: is of so low a sence,
I cannot in a weeke imagine what should be done to him.

Lig. Sure I have committed some great sinne,
That this strange fellow should be made my rod:
I would see him, but I shall have no patience:

Mar. Tis no great matter if you have not, if a laming of him, or such a toy may doe you pleasure Sir, he has it for you, and Ile helpe you to him: tis no newes to him to have a leg broke, or a shoulder out, with being turnd ath' stones like a Tanzie: Draw not your sword, if you love it; for my conscience his head will breake it: we use him ith' warres like a Ramme to shake a wall withall; here comes the verie person of him, doe as you shall find your temper I must leave you: but if you doe not breake him like a bisket, you are much too blame Sir. *Ex. Mardo. Enter Bessus and Sword-men.*

Lig. Is your name *Bessus?*

Bes. Men call me Captaine *Bessus.*

Lig. Then Captaine *Bessus* you are a ranke rascall, without more exordiums, a durty frozen slave; and with the favour of your friends here, I will beate you.

2. Pray use your pleasure Sir, you seem to be a gentleman.

Lig. Thus Captaine *Bessus*, thus; thus twinge your nose, thus kicke you, and thus tread you.

Bess. I doe beseech you yeeld your cause Sir quickly.

Lig. Indeed I should have told you that first.

Bess. I take it so.

1. Captaine, a should indeed, he is mistaken:

Lig. Sir you shall have it quickly, and more beating,
You have stolne away a Lady Captaine Coward,
And such a one.

Bes. Hold, I beseech you, hold Sir,
I never yet stole any living thing
That had a tooth about it.

Lig. Sir I know you dare lie
With none but Summer Whores upon my life Sir.

Bes. My meanes and manners never could attempt
Above a hedge or hey-cocke.

Lig. Sirra that quits not me, where is this Ladie,
Doe that you doe not use to doe, tell truth,
Or by my hand Ile beat your Captaines braines out.
Wash um, and put um in againe, that will I.

Bes. There was a Ladie Sir, I must confesse
Once in my charge: the Prince *Tigranes* gave her
To my guard for her safetie, how I usd her
She may her selfe report, shee's with the Prince now:
I did but waite upon her like a Groome,
Which she will testifie I am sure: If not,
My braines are at your service when you please Sir,
And glad I have um for you?

Lig. This is most likely, Sir I aske your pardon,
And am sorrie I was so intemperate.
Bes. Well, I can aske no more, you would thinke it strange
Now to have me beat you at first sight.
Lig. Indeed I would but I know your goodnes can forget
Twentie beatings. You must forgive me.
Bes. Yes, ther's my hand, goe where you will, I shall thinke
You a valiant fellow for all this.
Lig. My daughter is a Whore,
I feele it now too sencible; yet I will see her,
Discharge my selfe of being Father to her,
And then backe to my Countrie, and there die;
Farewell Captaine. *Exit.*
Bes. Farewell Sir, farewell, commend me to the Gentlewoman I praia.
1. How now Captaine, beare up man.
Bes. Gentlemen ath' sword your hands once more, I have
Beene kickt againe, but the foolish fellow is penitent,
Has ask't me mercy, and my honor's safe.
2. We knew that, or the foolish fellow had better a kick't
His Grandsire.
Confirme, confirme I pray.
1. There be our hands againe.
2. Now let him come, and say he was not sorry,
And he sleepes for it.
Bes. Alas good ignorant old man, let him goe,
Let him goe, these courses will undoe him. *Exeunt.*

Enter Ligones, and Bacurius.

Bac. My Lord your authoritie is good, and I am glad it is so, for my consent would never hinder you from seeing your owne King. I am a Minister, but not a governour of this state; yonder is your King, Ile leave you. *Exit.*
Lig. There he is indeed, *Enter Tig. and Spaco.*
And with him my disloyall childe.
Tig. I doe perceive my fault so much, that yet
Me thinkes thou shouldst not have forgiven me.
Lig. Health to your Maiestie.
Tig. What? good *Ligones*, welcome; what businesse
brought thee hether?
Lig. Severall Businesses.
My publique businesse will appeare by this:
I have a message to deliver, which
If it please you so to authorise, is
An embassage from the Armenian state,
Unto *Arbaces* for your libertie:
The offer's there set downe, please you to read it.
Tig. There is no alteration happened
Since I came thence?
Lig. None Sir, all is as it was.
Tig. And all our friends are well.
Lig. All verie well.
Spa. Though I have done nothing but what was good,
I dare not see my Father: it was fault
Enough not to acquaint him with that good.

Lig. Madam I should have seene you.
Spa. O good Sir forgive me.
Lig. Forgive you, why I am no kin to you, am I?
Spa. Should it be measur'd by my meane deserts,
Indeed you are not.
Lig. Thou couldst prate unhappily
Ere thou couldst goe, would thou couldst doe as well.
And how does your custome hold out here. *Spa.* Sir.
Lig. Are you in private still, or how?
Spa. What doe you meane?
Lig. Doe you take money? are you come to sell sinne yet? perhaps I c helpe you to liberall Clients: or has not the King cast you off yet? O th vild creature, whose best commendation is, that thou art a young Who I would thy Mother had liv'd to see this: or rather would I had dyed ere I h seene it: why did'st not make me acquainted when thou wert first resolv'd be a Whore? I would have seene thy hot lust satisfied more privately. I wou have kept a dancer, and a whole consort of Musitions in mine owne hous onely to fiddle thee. *Spa.* Sir I was never whore.
Lig. If thou couldst not say so much for thy selfe thou shouldst be Carte
Tig. *Ligones* I have read it, and like it,
You shall deliver it.
Lig. Well Sir I will: but I have private busines with you.
Tig. Speake, what ist?
Lig. How has my age deserv'd so ill of you,
That you can picke no strumpets in the Land,
But out of my breed.
Tig. Strumpets good *Ligones*?
Lig. Yes, and I wish to have you know, I scorne
To get a Whore for any Prince alive,
And yet scorne will not helpe me thinkes: My daughter
Might have beene spar'd, there were enough beside.
Tig. May I not prosper, but Shee's innocent
As morning light for me, and I dare sweare
For all the world.
Lig. Why is she with you then?
Can she waite on you better then your men,
Has she a gift in plucking off your stockings,
Can she make Cawdles well, or cut your Cornes,
Why doe you keepe her with you? For your Queene
I know you doe contemne her, so should I
And every Subject else thinke much at it.
Tig. Let um thinke much, but tis more firme then earth
Thou seest thy Queene there.
Lig. Then have I made a faire hand, I cald her Whore,
If I shall speake now as her Father, I cannot chuse
But greatly rejoyce that she shall be a Queene: but if
I should speake to you as a Statesman shee were more fit
To be your Whore.
Tig. Get you about your businesse to *Arbaces*,
Now you talke idlie.
Lig. Yes Sir, I will goe.
And shall she be a Queene, she had more wit
Then her old Father when she ranne away:

Shall shee be a Queene, now by my troth tis fine,
Ile dance out of all measure at her wedding:
Shall I not Sir?

Tigr. Yes marrie shalt thou.

Lig. Ile make these witherd Kexes beare my bodie
Two houres together above ground.

Tigr. Nay, goe, my businesse requires haste.

Lig. Good God preserve you, you are an excellent King.

Spa. Farewell good Father.

Lig. Farewell sweete vertuous Daughter;
I never was so joyfull in my life,
That I remember: shall shee be a Queene?
Now I perceive a man may weepe for joy,
I had thought they had lied that said so. *Exit.*

Tig. Come my deare love.

Spa. But you may see another
May alter that againe.

Tigr. Urge it no more;
I have made up a new strong constancie,
Not to be shooke with eyes; I know I have
The passions of a man, but if I meete
With any subject that shall hold my eyes
More firmely then is fit; Ile thinke of thee,
And runne away from it: let that suffice. *Exeunt.*

Enter Bacurius, and a servant.

Bac. Three gentlemen without to speake with me?

Ser. Yes Sir. *Bac*. Let them come in.

Ser. They are enterd Sir already.

Enter Bessus, and Swordmen.

Bac. Now fellowes, your busines, are these the Gentlemen.

Bess. My Lord I have made bold to bring these Gentlemen my Friends ath' sword along with me.

Bac. I am afraid youle fight then.

Bes. My good Lord I will not, your Lordship is mistaken,
Feare not Lord.

Bac. Sir I am sorrie fort.

Bes. I can aske no more in honor, Gentlemen you heare my Lord is sorrie.

Bac. Not that I have beaten you, but beaten one that will be beaten: one whose dull bodie will require launcing: As surfeits doe the diet, spring and full. Now to your swordmen, what come they for good Captaine Stock-fish?

Bes. It seemes your Lordship has forgot my name.

Bac. No, nor your nature neither, though they are things fitter I confesse for anything, then my remembrance, or anie honestmans, what shall these billets doe, be pilde up in my Wood-yard?

Bes. Your Lordship holds your mirth still, God continue it: but for these Gentlemen they come.

Bac. To sweare you are a Coward, spare your Booke, I doe beleeve it.

Bes. Your Lordship still drawes wide, they come to vouch under their valiant hands, I am no Coward.

Bac. That would be a shew indeed worth seeing: sirra be wise and take money for this motion, travell with it, and where the name of *Bessus* has been knowne, or a good Coward stirring, twill yeeld more then a tilting. This will prove more beneficiall to you, if you be thriftie, then your Captaineship, and more naturall; Men of most valiant hands is this true?

2. It is so most renowned,
Tis somewhat strange.

1. Lord, it is strange, yet true; wee have examined from your Lordships foote there to this mans head, the nature of the beatings; and we doe find his honour is come off cleane, and sufficient: This as our swords shall helpe us.

Bac. You are much bound to you bilbow-men, I am glad you are straight again Captaine: twere good you would thinke some way to gratifie them, they have undergone a labour for you *Bessus*, would have puzzled *Hercules*, with all his valour.

2. Your Lordship must understand we are no men ath' Law, that take pay for our opinions: it is sufficient wee have cleer'd our friend.

Bac. Yet here is something due, which I as toucht in conscience will discharge Captaine; Ile pay this rent for you.

Bess. Spare your selfe my good Lord; my brave friends aime at nothing but the vertue.

Bac. Thats but a cold discharge Sir for their paines.

2. O Lord, my good Lord.

Bac. Be not so modest, I will give you something.

Bes. They shall dine with your Lordship, that's sufficient.

Bac. Something in hand the while; ye rogues, ye apple-squiers: doe you come hether with your botled valour, your windie frothe, to limit out my beatings.

1. I doe beseech your Lordship.

2. O good Lord.

Bac. Sfoote, what a many of beaten slaves are here? get me a cudgel sirra, and a tough one.

2. More of your foot, I doe beseech your Lordship.

Bac. You shall, you shall dog, and your fellow beagle.

1. A this side good my Lord.

Bac. Off with your swords, for if you hurt my foote, Ile have you flead you rascals.

1. Mines off my Lord.

2. I beseech your Lordship stay a little, my strap's tied to my codpiec point: Now when you please.

Bac. Captaine, these are your valiant friends, you long for a little too?

Bess. I am verie well, I humblie thanke your Lordship.

Bac. Whats that in your pocket slave, my key you mungrell? thy buttock cannot be so hard, out with't quicklie.

2. Here tis Sir, a small piece of Artillerie, that a gentleman a deare frien of your Lordships sent me with to get it mended Sir; for it you marke, th nose is somewhat loose.

Bac. A friend of mine you rascall, I was never wearier of doing nothing then kicking these two foote-bals.

Ser. Heres a good cudgell Sir.

Bac. It comes too late; I am wearie, prethee doe thou beate um.

2. My Lord this is foule play ifaith, to put a fresh man upon us; Men are but men.

Bac. That jest shall save your bones, up with your rotten regiment, an be gone; I had rather thresh, then be bound to kicke these raskals, till the cride hold: *Bessus* you may put your hand to them now, and then you are qui

Farewell, as you like this, pray visit mee againe, twill keepe me in good breath.

2. Has a divellish hard foote, I never felt the like.

1. Nor I, and yet Ime sure I ha felt a hundred.

2. If he kicke thus ith dog-daies, he will be drie founderd: what cure now Captaine, besides oyle of bayes?

Bess. Why well enough I warrant you, you can goe.

2. Yes, God be thanked; but I feele a shrewd ach, sure he has sprang my huckle bone.

1. I ha lost a haunch.

Bess. A little butter friend, a little butter; butter and parselie is a soveraigne matter: *probatum est.*

2. Captaine, we must request your hands now to our honours.

Bess. Yes marrie shall ye, and then let all the world come, we are valiant to our selves, and theres an end.

1. Nay, then we must be valiant; O my ribbes.

2. O my small guts, a plague upon these sharpe toe'd shooes, they are murderers. *Exeunt.*

Enter Arbaces with his Sword drawne.

Arb. It is resolv'd, I bore it whilst I could,
I can no more, Hell open all thy gates,
And I will thorough them; if they be shut,
Ile batter um, but I will find the place
Where the most damn'd have dwelling; ere I end,
Amongst them all they shall not have a sinne,
But I may call it mine: I must beginne
With murder of my friend, and so goe on
To an incestuous ravishing, and end
My life and sinnes with a forbidden blow
Upon my selfe. *Enter Mardonius.*

Mardo. What Tragedie is nere?
That hand was never wont to draw a Sword,
But it cride dead to something:

Arb. *Mar.* have you bid *Gobrius* come?

Mar. How doe you Sir?

Arb. Well, is he comming?

Mar. Why Sir are you thus?
Why does your hand proclaime a lawlesse warre
Against your selfe?

Arb. Thou answerest me one question with another,
Is *Gobrius* comming?

Mar. Sir he is. *Arb.* Tis well.

Mar. I can forbeare your questions then, be gone
Sir, I have markt.

Arb. Marke lesse, it troubles you and me.

Mar. You are more variable then you were.

Arb. It may be so.

Mar. To day no Hermit could be humblier
Then you were to us all.

Arb. And what of this?

Mar. And now you take new rage into your eies,
As you would looke us all out of the Land.

Arb. I doe confesse it, will that satisfie,
I prethee get thee gone.
Mar. Sir I will speake. *Arb.* Will ye?
Mar. It is my dutie,
I feare you will kill your selfe: I am a subject,
And you shall doe me wrong in't: tis my cause,
And I may speake.
Arb. Thou art not traind in sinne,
It seemes *Mardonius*: kill my selfe, by heaven
I will not doe it yet; and when I will,
Ile tell thee then: I shall be such a creature,
That thou wilt give me leave without a word.
There is a method in mans wickednesse,
It growes up by degrees; I am not come
So high as killing of my selfe, there are
A hundred thousand sinnes twixt me and it,
Which I must doe, I shall come toot at last;
But take my oath not now, be satisfied,
And get thee hence.
Mar. I am sorrie tis so ill.
Arb. Be sorrie then,
True sorrow is alone, grieve by thy selfe.
Mar. I pray you let mee see your sword put up
Before I goe; Ile leave you then.
Arb. Why so?
What follie is this in thee? is it not
As apt to mischiefe as it was before?
Can I not reach it thinkest thou? these are toyes
For children to be pleas'd with, and not men;
Now I am safe you thinke: I would the booke
Of Fate were here, my sword is not so sure,
But I should get it out, and mangle that
That all the destinies should quite forget
Their fix't decrees, and hast to make us new
Farre other Fortunes mine could not be worse,
Wilt thou now leave me?
Mar. God put into your bosome temperate thoughts,
Ile leave you though I feare. *Exi*
Arb. Goe, thou art honest,
Why should the hastie errors of my youth
Be so unpardonable, to draw a sinne
Helpelesse upon me? *Enter Gobriu*
Gob. There is the King, now it is ripe.
Arb. Draw neere thou guiltie man,
That are the author of the loathedst crime
Five ages have brought forth, and heare me speake
Curses incurable, and all the evils
Mans bodie or his spirit can receive
Be with thee.
Gob. Why Sir doe you curse me thus?
Arb. Why doe I curse thee, if there be a man
Subtill in curses, that exceedes the rest,
His worst wish on thee. Thou hast broke my hart.

Gob. How Sir? Have I preserv'd you from a childe,
From all the arrowes, malice or ambition
Could shoot at you, and have I this for pay?
Arb. Tis true thou didst preserve me, and in that
Wert crueller then hardned murderers
Of infants and their mothers; thou didst save me
Onely till thou hadst studdied out a way
How to destroy me cunningly thy selfe:
This was a curious way of torturing.
Gob. What doe you meane?
Arb. Thou knowst the evils thou hast done to me,
Dost thou remember all those witching letters
Thou sentst unto me to *Armenia*,
Fild with the praise of my beloved Sister,
Where thou extolst her beautie; what had I
To doe with that, what could her beautie be
To me, and thou didst write how well shee lov'd me,
Doest thou remember this: so that I doated
Something before I saw her.
Gob. This is true.
Arb. Is it, and I when I was returnd thou knowst
Thou didst pursue it, till thou woundst mee into
Such a strange, and unbeleev'd affection,
As good men cannot thinke on.
Gob. This I grant, I thinke I was the cause.
Arb. Wert thou? Nay more, I thinke thou meantst it.
Gob. Sir I hate a lie.
As I love God and honestie, I did:
It was my meaning.
Arb. Be thine owne sad Judge,
A further condemnation will not need:
Prepare thy selfe to die.
Gob. Why Sir to die?
Arb. Why wouldst thou live, was ever yet offendor
So impudent, that had a thought of mercy
After confession of a crime like this?
Get out I cannot, where thou hurlst me in,
But I can take revenge, that's all the sweetnesse
Left for me.
Gob. Now is the time, heare me but speake.
Arb. No, yet I will be farre more mercifull
Then thou wert to me; thou didst steale into me,
And never gavest me warning: so much time
As I give thee now, had prevented thee
For ever. Notwithstanding all thy sinnes,
If thou hast hope, that there is yet a prayer
To save thee, turne, and speake it to your selfe.
Gob. Sir, you shall know your sinnes before you doe um
If you kill me.
Arb. I will not stay then.
Gob. Know you kill your Father. *Arb.* How?
Gob. You kill your Father.
Arb. My Father? though I know it for a lie

Made out of feare to save thy stained life:
The verie reverence of the word comes crosse me,
And ties mine arme downe.

Gob. I will tell you that shall heighten you againe, I am thy Father, I charge thee heare me.

Arb. If it should be so,
As tis most false, and that I should be found
A bastard issue, the dispised fruite
Of lawlesse lust, I should no more admire
All my wilde passions: but another truth
Shall be wrung from thee: If I could come by
The spirit of paine, it should be powr'd on thee,
Till thou allowest thy selfe more full of lies
Then he that teaches thee. *Enter Arane*

Arane. Turne thee about,
I come to speake to thee thou wicked man,
Heare me thou Tyrant.

Arb. I will turne to thee,
Heare me thou Strumpet: I have blotted out
The name of mother, as thou hast thy shame.

Ara. My shame, thou hast lesse shame then anything:
Why dost thou keepe my daughter in a prison?
Why dost thou call her Sister, and doe this?

Arb. Cease thou strange impudence, and answere quickly,
If thou contemn'st me, this will aske an answere,
And have it.

Ara. Helpe me gentle *Gobrius.*

Arb. Guilt dare not helpe guilt, though they grow together
In doing ill, yet at the punishment
They sever, and each flies the noyse of other,
Thinke not of helpe, answere.

Ara. I will, to what?

Arb. To such a thing as if it be a truth,
Thinke what a creature thou hast made thy selfe,
That didst not shame to doe, what I must blush
Onely to aske thee: tell me who I am,
Whose sonne I am, without all circumstance;
Be thou as hastie, as my Sword will be
If thou refusest.

Ara. Why you are his sonne.

Arb. His sonne?
Sweare, sweare, thou worse then woman damn'd.

Ara. By all thats good you are.

Arb. Then art thou all that ever was knowne bad. Now is
The cause of all my strange misfortunes come to light:
What reverence expects thou from a childe
To bring forth which thou hast offended Heaven,
Thy husband and the Land: Adulterous witch
I know now why thou wouldst have poyson'd me,
I was thy lust which thou wouldst have forgot:
Thou wicked mother of my sinnes, and me,
Shew me the way to the inheritance
I have by thee: which is a spacious world

Of impious acts, that I may soone possesse it:
Plagues rott thee, as thou liv'st, and such diseases
As use to pay lust, recompence thy deed.

Gob. You doe not know why you curse thus.

Arb. Too well:
You are a paire of Vipers, and behold
The Serpent you have got; there is no beast
But if he knew, it has a pedigree
As brave as mine, for they have more discents,
And I am every way as beastly got,
As farre without the compasse of a law,
As they.

Ara. You spend your rage, and words in vaine,
And raile upon a guesse: heare us a little.

Arb. No I will never heare, but talke away
My breath, and die.

Gob. Why but you are no Bastard.

Arb. Howe's that?

Ara. Nor childe of mine.

Arb. Still you goe on in wonders to me.

Gob. Pray be more patient, I may bring comfort to you.

Arb. I will kneele,
And heare with the obedience of a childe;
Good Father speake, I doe acknowledge you,
So you bring comfort.

Gob. First know our last King your supposed Father
Was olde and feeble when he marryed her,
And almost all the Land as shee past hope
Of issue from him.

Arb. Therefore shee tooke leave
To play the whoore, because the King was old:
Is this the comfort?

Ara. What will you find out
To give me satisfaction, when you find
How you have injur'd me: let fire consume mee,
If ever I were whore.

Gob. Forbeare these starts,
Or I will leave you wedded to despaire,
As you are now: if you can find a temper,
My breath shall be a pleasant westerne wind,
That cooles, and blastes not.

Arb. Bring it out good Father,
Ile lie, and listen here as reverentlie
As to an Angell: If I breathe too loude,
Tell me; for I would be as still as night.

Gob. Our King I say was old, and this our Queene
Desired to bring an heire; but yet her husband
Shee thought was past it, and to be dishonest
I thinke shee would not; if shee would have beene,
The truth is, shee was watcht so narrowlie,
And had so slender opportunitie,
Shee hardly could have beene: But yet her cunning
Found out this way; shee fain'd her selfe with child,

And postes were sent in haste throughout the Land,
And God was humbly thankt in every Church,
That so had blest the Queen, and prayers were made
For her safe going, and deliverie:
Shee fain'd now to grow bigger, and perceiv'd
This hope of issue made her feard, and brought
A farre more large respect from everie man.
And saw her power increase, and was resolv'd,
Since shee believ'd shee could not have't indeede;
At least shee would be thought to have a child.

Arb. Doe I not heare it well: nay, I will make
No noise at all; but pray you to the point,
Quicke as you can.

Gob. Now when the time was full,
Shee should be brought abed; I had a sonne
Borne, which was you: This the Queene hearing of,
Mov'd me to let her have you, and such reasons
Shee shewed me, as shee knew would tie
My secresie: shee sware you should be King;
And to be short, I did deliver you
Unto her, and pretended you were dead;
And in mine owne house kept a Funerall,
And had an emptie coffin put in earth:
That night the Queene fain'd hastilie to labour,
And by a paire of women of her owne,
Which shee had charm'd, shee made the world believe
Shee was deliver'd of you: you grew up
As the Kings sonne, till you were six yeere olde;
Then did the King die, and did leave to me
Protection of the Realme; and contrarie
To his owne expectation, left this Queene
Truly with Childe indeed of the faire Princesse
Panthea: Then shee could have torne her heire,
And did alone to me yet durst not speake
In publike; for shee knew shee should be found
A Traytor, and her talke would have beene thought
Madnesse or any thing rather then truth:
This was the onely cause why shee did seeke
To poyson you, and I to keepe you safe:
And this the reason why I sought to kindle
Some sparke of love in you to faire *Panthea*,
That shee might get part of her right agen.

Arb. And have you made an end now, is this all?
If not, I will be still till I am aged,
Till all my heires are silver.

Gob. This is all.

Arb. And is it true say you Maddam?

Ara. Yes, God knowes it is most true.

Arb. *Panthea* then is not my Sister. *Gob.* No.

Arb. But can you prove this?

[*Gob.*] If you will give consent: else who dare goe about it.

Arb. Give consent?
Why I will have them all that know it rackt

To get this from um: All that waites without
Come in, what ere you be come in, and be
Partakers of my Joy: O you are welcome. *Ent. Mar: Bessus, and others.*
Mardonius the best newes, nay, draw no neerer
They all shall heare it: I am found no King.
Mar. Is that so good newes?
Arb. Yes, the happiest newes that ere was heard.
Mar. Indeed twere well for you,
If you might be a little lesse obey'd.
Arb. On, call the Queene.
Mar. Why she is there.
Arb. The Queene *Mardonius, Panthea* is the Queene,
And I am plaine *Arbaces*, goe some one,
She is in *Gobrius* house; since I saw you
There are a thousand things delivered to me
You little dreame of.
Mar. So it should seeme: My Lord,
What furi's this.
Gob. Beleeve me tis no fury,
All that he sayes is truth.
Mar. Tis verie strange.
Arb. Why doe you keepe your hats off Gentlemen,
Is it to me? in good faith it must not be:
I cannot now command you, but I pray you
For the respect you bare me, when you tooke
Me for your King, each man clap on his hat at my desire.
Mar. We will: but you are not found
So meane a man, but that you may be cover'd
As well as we, may you not? *Arb.* O not here,
You may, but not I, for here is my Father in presence.
Mar. Where?
Arb. Why there: O the whole storie
Would be a wildernesse to loose thy selfe
For ever; O pardon me deare Father,
For all the idle, and unreverent words
That I have spoke in idle moodes to you:
I am *Arbaces*, we all fellow subjects,
Nor is the Queene *Panthea* now my Sister.

Bes. Why if you remember fellow subject *Arbaces*, I tolde you once she was not your sister, I say she look't nothing like you.

Arb. I thinke you did good Captaine *Bessus*.

Bes. Here will arise another question now amongst the Swordmen, whether I be to call him to account for beating me, now he's prov'd no King. *Enter Ligones.*

Ma. Sir, heres *Ligones*
The Agent for the Armenian King.
Arb. Where is he, I know your businesse good *Ligones*.
Lig. We must have our King againe, and will.
Arb. I knew that was your businesse, you shall have
You King againe, and have him so againe
As never King was had. Goe one of you
And bid *Bacurius* bring *Tigranes* hither,
And bring the Ladie with him, that *Panthea*

The Queene *Panthea* sent me word this morning
Was brave *Tigranes* mistresse.
Lig. Tis *Spaconia.* *Arb.* I, I, *Spaconia.*
Lig. She is my daughter.
Arb. Shee is so, I could now tell any thing
I never heard; your King shall goe so home
As never man went.
Ma. Shall he goe on's head?
Arb. He shall have Chariots easier than ayre
That I will have invented; and nere thinke
He shall pay any ransome; and thy selfe
That art the Messenger shall ride before him
On a Horse cut out of an entire Diamond,
That shall be made to goe with golden wheeles,
I know not how yet.
Lig. Why I shall be made
For ever, they belied this King with us
And sayd he was unkind.
Arb. And then thy daughter,
She shall have some strange thinke, wele have the Kingdome
Sold utterly, and put into a toy.
Which she shall weare about her carelesly
Some where or other.
See the vertuous Queene. *Enter Pan.*
Behold the humblest subject that you have
Kneele here before you. *Pan.* Why kneele you
To me that am your vassall?
Arb. Grant me one request.
Pan. Alas, what can I grant you?
What I can I will.
Arb. That you will please to marry me,
If I can prove it lawfull.
Pan. Is that all?
More willingly, then I would draw this ayre.
Arb. Ile kisse this hand in earnest.
Mar. Sir, *Tigranes* is comming though he made it strange
To see the Princesse any more.
Arb. The Queene, *Enter Tig. and Spa.*
Thou meanest: O my Tigranes pardon me,
Tread on my necke I freely offer it,
And if thou beest so given; take revenge,
For I have injur'd thee.
Tig. No, I forgive,
And rejoice more that you have found repentance,
Then I my libertie.
Arb. Maist thou be happie
In thy faire choice; for thou art temperate:
You owe no ransome to the state, know that;
I have a thousand joyes to tell you of,
Which yet I dare not utter, till I pay
My thankes to Heaven for um: will you goe
With me, and helpe me; pray you doe. *Tig.* I will.
Arb. Take then your faire one with you and your Queene

Of goodnesse, and of us; O give me leave
To take your arme in mine: Come every one
That takes delight in goodnesse, helpe to sing
Loude thankes for me, that I am prov'd no King.

FINIS.

The following verse variations have also been noted between the Act printed above from A and the quartos B, C, D and G.

p. 434, ll. 46 and 47. B, C, D, G] two lines, *him*, *rope*.

p. 436, ll. 19 and 20. B—D] two lines, *better*, *Grandsire*.

p. 437, ll. 16—18. B, C, D, G] six lines, *Whore*, *satisfied*, *Dancer*, *Musitians*, *thee*, *whore*.

p. 438, ll. 40 and 41. B, C, D, G] four lines, *laming*, *fall*, *Sword-men*, *Stock-fish*.

p. 442, ll. 22 and 23. B, C, D, G] two lines, *in-*, *affection*.

p. 443, ll. 24 and 25. B, C, D, G] three lines, *impudence*, *me*, *answere*. ll. 44 and 45. Three lines, *all*, *cause*, *light*.

p. 446, ll. 17 and 18. B, C, D, G] one line, *this*. ll. 19 and 20. B, C, D, G] one line, *truth*. l. 26. Two lines, *hat*, *desire*.

p. 447, ll. 16 and 17. B, C, D, G] two lines, *ever*, *us*. ll. 23 and 24. B, C, D, G] one line, *Queene*. ll. 29 and 30. B, C, D, G] one line, *will*.

THE SCORNFUL LADY.

(A) The | Scornful | Ladie. | A Comedie. | As it was Acted (with great applause) by | the children of Her Majesties | Revels in the Blacke | Fryers. Written by | Fra. Beaumont and Jo. Fletcher, Gent. | London | Printed for Myles Partrich, and are to be sold | at his Shop at the George neere S[t] Dunstans | Church in Fleet-streete. 1616.

(B) The | Scorneful | Ladie. | A Comedie. | As it was now lately Acted (with | great applause) by the Kings | Majesties servants, at the | Blacke Fryers. | Written by | Fra. Beaumont, and Jo. Fletcher, | Gentlemen. | London, | Printed for M. P. and are to be sold by | Thomas Jones, at the blacke Raven, in | the Strand. 1625.

(C) The | Scornefull | Ladie. | A Comedie. | As it was now lately Acted (with great | applause) by the Kings Majesties Servants, | at the Blacke-Fryers. | Written | By Fran: Beaumont, and Jo: Fletcher, | Gentlemen. | The third Edition. | London. | Printed by B. A. and T. F. for T. Jones, and are to be sold at his | Shop in St. Dunstans Church-yard in Fleet-street. | 1630.

(D) The | Scornfull | Ladie. | A Comedy. | As it was now lately Acted (with great | applause) by the Kings Majesties Servants, | at the Blacke-Fryers. | Written by Francis Beaymont, and John Fletcher, Gentlemen. | The fourth Edition. | London, | Printed by A. M. 1635.

(E) The | Scornfull | Lady. | A Comedy. | As it was now lately Acted (with great | applause) by the Kings Majesties Servants, | at the Blacke-Fryers. | Written by Francis Beaumont, and John Fletcher. Gentlemen. | The fift Edition. | London, | Printed by M. P. for Robert Wilson, and are to be sold at | his shop in Holborne at Grayes-Inne Gate. | 1639.

(F) The | Scornfull | Lady. | A Comedy. | As it was Acted (with great applause) by | the late Kings Majesties Servants, | at the Black-Fryers. | Written by Francis Beaumont. and John Fletcher. Gentlemen. | The sixt Edition, Corrected and | amended. | London: | Printed for Humphrey Moseley, and are to be sold at his Shop | at the Princes Armes in St. Pauls Church-yard. 1651.

(The British Museum copy lacks the printer's device on the title-page, possessed by other copies seen; it varies also slightly in spelling etc.)

(G) The | Scornful | Lady: | A | Comedy. | As it is now Acted at the | Theater Royal, | by | His Majesties Servants. | Written by Francis Beaumont and John Fletcher Gent. | The Seventh Edition. | London: | Printed by A. Maxwell and R. Roberts, for D. N. and T. C. and are | to be sold by Simon Neale, at the Three Pidgeons in | Bedford-street in Covent-Garden, 1677.

p. 231, l. 5. A *omits* list of Persons Represented in the Play. B—E print the list on the back of the title-page, under the heading 'The Actors are these.' In F and G the same list is printed on a separate page following the title-page. G] The Names of the Actors. l. 8. B and C] the eldest. D—G] the elder.

p. 232, l. 1. A] a Userer. l. 4. A] Savill make the boate stay. B *prints* '*Savil.* Make the boat stay,' as if the rest of the speech were spoken by Savil. C—G for '*Savil*' print '*Yo. Lo.*,' thus giving the words to Young Loveless. l. 9. E and G] at home marry. l. 10. A—E and G] your countrey. F] your own country. A and B] then to travell for diseases, and returne following the Court in a nightcap, and die without issue. l. 15. Here and throughout the scene for 'Younglove' D—G] Abigall. l. 16. A—C] Mistres. D] Mistrisse. E—G] Mistris. l. 22. A and B] for me. l. 33. E—G *omit*] Exit.

p. 233, l. 2. G] acted Loves. l. 3. A, B and E—G] murtherers. l. 6. A and B] that shall be. l. 12. A—G] woman. l. 25. A—G *omit*] and. l. 31. F] out there. l. 35. D—G for *Younglove*] Abigall.

p. 234, l. 5. F] time of place. l. 16. E—G *omit*] Yes. l. 19. E—G] that can. l. 27. F] deadfull. l. 37. G] and put. l. 39. A and B] with you for laughter.

p. 235, l. 10. A and B] and so you satisfied. l. 17. B] doeth. l. 28. A] Hipochrists. E and F] Hipocrasse. G] Hippocrass. l. 34. A and B] his yeere. l. 31. G] said she.

p. 236, l. 9. B] doeth. D and E] with you. l. 17. G *omits one*] that. l. 19. G] I'le live.

p. 237, l. 1. A and B] with three guards. l. 4. D] wesse. E—G] wisse. l. 10. D—G] Abigall. l. 14. E—G] happily. l. 21. A—E] may call. l. 25. A—G] as on others. A—G *omit*] that. l. 27. A—G] A my credit. l. 30. A and B] beginnings. l. 31. G] maid. l. 32. E and G] bed. l. 33. D—G] doe you not. l. 35. D—G] Abigall.

p. 238, l. 2. A and B] rid hard. l. 25. A] other woemen the housholds of. B—G] of the households. G] of as good. l. 28. F and G] tho not so coy. D—G] Abigall. l. 36. A—G] God.

p. 239, l. 7. G] Call'd. l. 17. A] your names. l. 32. A] the weomen. l. 33. A and B] an needlesse. E—G *omit*] a. F] her comes. G *and sometimes* F] here comes.

p. 240, l. 4. E—G *omit*] of. F and G] I do inculcate Divine Homilies. l. 13. G] man neglect. l. 16. A and B] I pray ye. A—G] and whilst. l. 19. B] your Lay. l. 20. C—F] ingenuous. l. 23. A] I shall beate. l. 25. A—E] forget one, who. F and G] forget then who. l. 34. A and B] how Hoppes goe.

p. 241, l. 6. A—G] to keep. l. 14. F and G] like a Gentlemen. l. 15. F *omits*] me. l. 23. D—G] Yet, that. l. 25. A—E *omit*] of. F and G] Ile here no more, this is. l. 30. A—E and G] comes. l. 39. A] Gent.

p. 242, l. 6. A—G *omit*] etc. l. 7. B—G] help all. l. 22. A and B] warre, that cries. l. 27. G] has knockt. l. 32. D—G *omit*] even. A—G] a conscience. l. 34. A—E *omit*] he.

p. 243, l. 6. E—G] pound. l. 11. A and B] We will have nobody talke wisely neither. F] Will you not. l. 17. A—C] ath Coram. l. 25. F and G *omit*] that. l. 27. F and G] sir, to expound it. l. 28. 2nd Folio *misprints*] iuterpretation. l. 37. A and B *omit*] Sir. l. 40. F *omits*] keep.

p. 244, l. 1. F and G *add after* part] Savil. l. 6. D—G *add*] Finis Actus Primus. F and G *add*] *Omnes*. O brave Loveless! (F = Lovelace) Exeunt omnes. l. 12. F and G *omit*] Lady. l. 13. F and G] that complaint. l. 28. F and G] it loveth. l. 34. A] premised.

p. 245, l. 11. D—G] reprov'd him. l. 22. F and G] hath made. l. 23. A and B *misprint*] Maria. l. 25. F and G] with a. l. 27. A and B] He's fast. l. 39. F and G *omit*] Sir.

p. 246, l. 4. A, B and G] Gentlewoman. l. 23. G *omits*] indeed. l. 26. F and G] smile hath. l. 28. A—E and G] cropping off. l. 34. E and G] meditations. l. 36. F and G] and experience the. E—G] collection. l. 39. F and G] thus to.

p. 248, ll. 3 and 4. G] and fornication. l. 24. A and G] set.

p. 249, l. 10. A—C, E—G] appeares. l. 11. A] drown. l. 12. G] Sir Aeneas. l. 34. A and B] Gentlewoman.

p. 250, l. 15. A—G] a Gods name.

p. 251, l. 11. A and B *add*] Drinke to my friend Captaine. l. 14. A, B, F and G *add at end*] Sir. l. 15. A—G] cursie. F] a tittle. l. 16. G] would strive, Sir. F] I will strive, Sir. l. 22. Second Folio *misprints*] Youn. l. 24. A] to feede more fishes. l. 30. F and G] pray you let. l. 34. A] a ful rouse. ll. 36 and 37. D and F] I bear. l. 39. A—G] a your knees.

p. 252, l. 12. A] finde. l. 32. F and G *for* Capt. (character) *read* Sav. *and add* 'Let's in and drink and give' etc.

p. 253, l. 5. F and G] be you your. l. 27. D—F] love chamber. G] dares. l. 34. A—C] will stoop. l. 35. A] feede ill. l. 36. A—G] which for I was his wife and gave way to. l. 39. F] in patience of.

p. 254, l. 1. D and E] gossip too. l. 3. E and F] from whence. l. 9. F *misprints*] crown'd at. l. 21. E—G] have the money. l. 23. F and G] provided my wise. l. 26. F] Here's here. ll. 30 and 31. F and G] for thine. l. 32. F *omits*] well.

p. 255, l. 1. A] the faith. l. 11. D—G] mony fit for. l. 13. A—D, F and G] afore. l. 14. G *omits*] all. ll. 18 and 19. D—G] turne up. l. 20. G] Ship. l. 22. G] poor man. l. 26. D, F and G] against the. l. 28. A—G] thy staffe of office there, thy pen and Ink-horne. Noble boy. l. 29. A] sed. ll. 30 and 31. A—G] thy seat. l. 34. F and G] men immortal. l. 37. A] that shall. l. 40. A] What meane they Captaine.

p. 256, l. 8. F and G] pounds. l. 9. F and G] by this hand. l. 13. F and G] There is six Angels in earnest. l. 17. A] all in. l. 25. F and G *omit*] so be it. l. 35. A and B] at charge. l. 40. A—G *add*] Finis Actus Secundi.

p. 257, l. 2. A *omits*] and drops her glove. l. 3. A—C] tels. l. 8. A, B and D—G] Lenvoy. l. 16. F and G] No, Sir.

p. 258, l. 10. D, E and G] come here to speak with. l. 18. F and G] I say I. l. 26. A *misprints*] ralkt. F and G] with the. l. 29. F and G] Troth guess. l. 33. F] Gentlewomen. l. 36. A and B] But one, I am. C] or Woman.

p. 259, l. 1. A] shall not you. l. 16. A—C and E—G] no such. l. 19. A—C and E—G] tender Sir, whose gentle bloud. l. 29. A *omits*] be. l. 31. A and G] as he. l. 34. A *omits*] They draw. l. 36. F and G *omit*] Jesus.

p. 260, l. 4. A and B *omit*] Why. l. 11. F] but none so. l. 26. A] wilde. B, C and E—G] vild. l. 31. F and G] sword. l. 33. E and G] a hazard.

p. 261, l. 1. A and B] which is prone inough. C—G] are prone. l. 5. A] anger lost. l. 10. F and G] least share in. l. 25. D, F and G] are you. l. 33. A and B] self from such temptations. G] self from temptations. l. 34. A—D, F and G] Pray leape. G] the matter. C] whether would. l. 38. A—C, E and G] should.

p. 262, l. 6. F and G *omit*] a. l. 11. A—C] see. l. 12. E] Of any. l. 20. F and G] his ruin. l. 27. C *omits*] him. E—G] with these. l. 37. E—G] leave them to others. l. 40. C] works a mine.

p. 263, l. 13. A] certaine. l. 18. E—G] spoken. l. 19. F] ask you. l. 20. E—G] forward. l. 32. G] hard-hearted. l. 35. F and G] me to do.

p. 264, l. 4. E—G] could redeem. l. 10. D, F and G] This. l. 24. A] you have so. l. 27. E and G] By this light.

p. 265, l. 10. F] by your troth. l. 11. A] could. l. 15. C] cold meats. l. 23. F and G] we would. l. 27. F and G] that thou art here. l. 29. F and G] use thee. l. 33. A and B] offending. l. 34. F and G] Thou art nothing...for love's sake.

p. 266, l. 3. G *omits*] I hope. l. 13. F and G] thy face. l. 14. A—G *omit*] for. ll. 21 and 22. F and G] companion. l. 25. A] amable. l. 38. G *adds at end*] I hope.

p. 267, l. 4. A, B and D—F] Don Diego, Ile. l. 11. A, C and E] saies. l. 15. E—G] you may. l. 20. E] wine here. F and G *add before* All] Mr Morecraft. l. 21. A—G] Sir. *Savill?* l. 31. G] and yet they. l. 33. F *omits*] pray. l. 36. A—C and E—G] God a gold. 2nd Folio *misprints*] expouud.

p. 268, l. 3. A] not you. l. 7. A and B] is much is much. l. 18. G] in tenements of. l. 22. F and G] I shall not dare to. l. 23. A] By blithe. l. 33. A and B] of satten. l. 37. A—G] necessary. D—G] and consuming.

p. 269, l. 10. 2nd Folio *misprints*] nor. l. 16. A—G] a' my knowledge. l. 20. F and G] the. F] Morall. l. 27. B and D—G] worst on's. l. 31. A] your complement. l. 34. F and G] paid back again.

p. 270, l. 4. F and G] we have liv'd. ll. 4 and 5. F and G] be the hour that. l. 14. A *misprints*] *Yo. Lo.* l. 15. F and G] A thirsty. l. 17. F *omits*] Sir. l. 20. A] raile. l. 24. D—G] to'th.

p. 271, l. 1. A] hee's your. l. 4. A—G] fall. l. 19. A—G] who you left me too. l. 20. F *omits*] for. l. 23. F and G] be leaping in. l. 24. E—G] nights. l. 25. F *omits*] my. l. 27. E] thirtie. l. 34. B] you fellow. l. 37. A—G] Cresses sir to coole. l. 39. A—C] fornications.

p. 272, l. 3. E—G] get no. l. 4. A—G *add*] Finis Actus tertii. l. 6. A—G] solus. l. 8. A] thee to? to what scurvy Fortune. l. 9. E] of Noblemen. l. 15. B and E—G] profit. 2nd Folio *misprints*] Eccle. l. 16. F] eats out youth. l. 22. 2nd Folio *misprints*] abolishth, is. l. 25. D and E] in his. l. 33. A] neglectingly. l. 34. A] broke.

p. 273, l. 9. F and G] abused like me. A—F] Dalida. l. 11. F and G] you may dilate. l. 27. F and G] could not expound. l. 28. A] and then at prayers once (out of the stinking stir you put me in). l. 29. A] mine owne royall [F and G *also add* royal] issue. l. 34. D and E] for you. l. 35. B] and thus. l. 36. A, F and G] contrition, as a Father saith. l. 39. A—G] Comfets. l. 40. A, F and G] then a long chapter with a pedigree.

p. 274, l. 3. A] lovely. l. 4. F and G] when due time. l. 8. F and G] but have. l. 14. A—E] cunny. l. 17. A *omits*] in. F and G] the hanging. l. 19. A, F and G] more with the great Booke of Martyrs. l. 23. F and G *add after* beloved] Abigail. l. 31. E—G] chop up.

p. 275, l. 3. A and B] wise Sir. l. 7. A, B, F and G] make. l. 14. F and G] thank Heaven. l. 19. E—G *omit*] Lord. l. 22. A and B] some sow. l. 23. F and G] brought forth. l. 26. F and G] will not. l. 29. E] a cleere. E—G] would take. l. 39. A] and yet would.

p. 276, l. 3. A—F] errant. l. 5. A—F] pray be. l. 9. A] the gods (B=God) knowes. C] God the knowes. F and G] Heaven knows. l. 15. 2nd Folio *misprints*] Lo. l. 18. A *omits*] so. l. 19. A—C *omit*] for. l. 38. E—G] that has.

p. 277, l. 1. A and B] turne in to. l. 4. A *omits*] pray. l. 13. G] have you. l. 14. G] light, as spirited. l. 21. G] sheeps. l. 22. G] with two. l. 23. F and G *add at end*] I can. l. 33. F and G] your use of. l. 37. A, B, D, F and G] now then.

p. 278, l. 7. A—G] Rosasolis. l. 16. G] in presuming thus. l. 19. E—G] to any end. l. 23. D, E and G] heap affliction. B—D, F and G] on me. l. 28. F and G *add*] ha. l. 33. F and G *for* a *read*] ha'. l. 37. E—G *omit*] Sir.

p. 279, l. 1. G] no so. l. 2. A] know. l. 6. F *omits*] that. ll. 6—8. D and E *omit*] at you...not laugh *and runs on the remainder of* Lady's *speech as part of* Mar.'s. F and G *omit*] Sir...not laugh. l. 7. A—C *omit one*] 'ha.' l. 15. A and B] for it then. l. 20. E—G] And you may. l. 28. G] crack. l. 36. A—C] fit ath. l. 38. B] will you cure.

p. 280, l. 5. A and C] Let him alone, 'is crackt. l. 6. D—G] he's a beastly. A and B] to loose. l. 7. A—G] is a. ll. 9 and 10. G] foh (soh F) she stinks. ll. 19 and 20. F and G] ye have...hate ye. l. 23. A and B] in intercession. D—G] make intercession. l. 25. A] not all. l. 26. F and G] and will. l. 32. A and B] safer dote. l. 33. F] disease.

p. 281, l. 8. A—C] I hope 'is not. l. 16. A] There is. l. 28. A] Carrire. D—G] carriage. l. 29. A—C, F and G] now I. l. 30. A—G] a horse back. l. 31. A—C and E—G] to looke to.

p. 282, l. 3. A—C] 'is fleet. l. 10. 2nd Folio *misprints*] sweed. l. 11. F] not your. A—E] Reasens. F and G] your rotten Reasons. l. 13. F and G] civil and feed. l. 16. A—G] pounds. l. 18. A, F and G] defend.

p. 283, l. 2. F and G] Ordinaries do eat. l. 3. F and G] to a play. l. 6. E] Bootmaker. F and G] to a bear-baiting. l. 13. A, C—G] aire. l. 15. A] as little. l. 18. E] if they may. ll. 22 and 23. F and G] ask me. l. 23. A and B] a modesty. l. 24. A—F] Wardrope. l. 28. E—G] to dogs. l. 36 E] cheate. A—G] *add*] Finis Actus Quarti.

p. 284, l. 27. F and G] the Gentleman. l. 31. A and B] house Sir.

p. 285, l. 5. B] for your. l. 10. A—D] be lest. E—G] be left. l. 15. E] never-worme. l. 25. F and G] the elder hath. l. 31. 2nd Folio *misprints*] Gentlewomau.

p. 286, l. 7. G] goodly. l. 8. A and D] beliefe. l. 10. E—G] you cas'd. l. 29. A—G] in thy. l. 30. G *omits*] I. l. 31. F] years.

p. 287, l. 1. F and G] vilely. l. 3. A and D—G] shall want uryne to finde the cause by: and she. B and C] shall want uryne finde the cause be. l. 14. A and B] I stoppe.

p. 288, l. 7. E *omits*] did. F and G] he does. l. 25. A and B *omit*] be. l. 34. F and G] till death.

p. 289, l. 1. 2nd Folio *misprints*] berroth'd. E and G *add at beginning*] Ah. l. 5. A and B] mind is. l. 6. G] womens. l. 22. F] not any. l. 26. F and G *omit*] Godlike. l. 27. A and B] passions. l. 28. F and G] is her law. l. 39. D—G] and colour.

p. 290, l. 7. 2nd Folio *misprints*] yon. l. 7. F and G] you, though unknown. l. 18. F and G] Heaven to comfort. l. 34. A and B] Milde still as. l. 37. B] ends. l. 40. F and G] never find.

p. 291, l. 7. A and B] I will. l. 12. G] spoken. l. 25. A—F] judicially. l. 27. G] off her. A—C] sound. G] her Love. F] lovers. l. 33. A, B and E—G] a bed. l. 37. D] at a third. F and G *add after* Balls] admirably.

APPENDIX

p. 292, l. 2. A, F and G] forgot. ll. 4 and 5. F and G *omit*] I'll not... you joy. l. 9. G] there was. l. 10. A, B, F and G] meant. G *omits*] you. l. 19. G] rather then. l. 20. A, B and D—F] forsooke. l. 34. A, E and G] I had rather.

p. 293, l. 4. D—G *add after* so] a most ungodly thing. ll. 5 and 6. D—G *omit*] Since a...ungodly thing. l. 30. D and F *omit*] and Young. l. 32. A and B] all uncivill, all such beasts as these. C] are uncivill, all such beasts. D and E] wee are uncivill, as such beasts as these. F and G] all uncivil. Would, etc.

p. 294, l. 7. G] are you. l. 11. A—C] learning new sir. E—G *omit*] Sir. l. 14. A] rouge. l. 16. A] capassions. l. 17. 2nd Folio *misprints*] Goaler. l. 25. F and G] indeed I do.

p. 295, l. 8. 2nd Folio *misprints*] A I. l. 27. F and G] Heaven quite. l. 31. F and G] thou help. l. 34. F and G *omit*] the Cleve. l. 36. F] all this.

p. 296, l. 30. F, *some copies*] hankt it. l. 34. G] O Heaven.

p. 297, l. 1. F and G] with this. l. 12. F and G] who I. l. 17. B, F and G] hold out. l. 22. A] witnes to. ll. 26 and 27. F and G] this Welford from.

p. 298, l. 5. 2nd Folio *misprints*] turn. l. 8. A, B, D, F and G] tyr'd. l. 12. A] sore Ladies. D—G *omit*] four. l. 19. F and G] I think I. l. 23. A] I see by her. l. 38. A and E] make.

p. 299, l. 2. E—G] he is. l. 10. A and B] A will. C] I will. l. 13. F and G] make you well. l. 15. G] unconverted. l. 20. F and G] tell you. l. 26. B] yon. l. 34. F and G] Who's.

p. 300, l. 8. F and G] must wear. l. 9. G *omits*] Of. l. 19. A and B] pound. l. 22. E and F *omit*] a. l. 29. G] you wall grare. l. 30. F and G] once again. l. 33. F and G] your Worship. l. 38. G] Why now.

p. 301, l. 3. F and G] As fast as. l. 11. C] helps. l. 17. A and B *omit*] the. l. 24. F and G] and lead. l. 25. A—G *add*] Finis.

[During the passing of these sheets through the press, a copy of the quarto named G (1677, 'The Seventh Edition') has been found in England by the writer of this note. Its existence has been ignored by every previous editor of Beaumont and Fletcher, and, apparently, by English bibliographers, the folio of 1679 being presumed to be 'Ed. 7.' The knowledge that a copy existed in America led to a fruitless search for it in English libraries, until accident, a few months ago, brought one to light in time to enable a collation of its text to be included in the above notes. It will be seen that many of the readings are of considerable interest.

A. R. W.]

THE CUSTOM OF THE COUNTRY.

A=The First Folio.

p. 302, l. 2. A *omits* Lists of Persons Represented in the Play and of principal Actors. l. 49. Second Folio *misprints*] Arnolda.

p. 303, l. 5. A] And that. l. 17. A] a conscience. l. 21. A] Customes. l. 24. A] In the world.

p. 304, l. 25. A] it can. l. 36. A] I A dainty wench. l. 37. A *omits*] I.

p. 305, l. 3. Second Folio *misprints*] yon. l. 11. A] wilde minde. l. 24. A] a heritage.

p. 306, l. 14. A] De'e doubt tis day now. l. 15. A] pulses.

p. 307, l. 32. A] This rogue that breaks.

p. 308, l. 7. A] speake.

p. 311, l. 31. A] alarums.

p. 312, l. 14. A] this marring. l. 15. A] sheckles. ll. 26—28. A adds in the margin] *Boy ready for the songs.*

p. 313, l. 13. A] But such a ransome. ll. 28 and 29. A *adds* marginal stage-direction] *Bowle of wine ready.* l. 31. A] And blushing and unloose.

p. 314, l. 39. A] alarums. ll. 7 and 9. Second Folio] Arn.

p. 316, l. 2. A] Pompean. l. 19. A] Ile ha' your life. l. 20. A prints this line as part of Charino's speech.

p. 317, l. 8. A *omits*] A. l. 23. A *omits*] o're.

p. 319, l. 8. A] Lisborne.

p. 321, l. 21. A] renders. l. 35. A] Lisborne.

p. 322, l. 14. A] aboord. l. 15. A] Yet my disguise. l. 30. A] the contempt.

p. 325, l. 10. A] And he in Lisbon. ll. 22—26. This speech is printed in A as a continuation of Arnoldo's.

p. 326, ll. 18 and 19. A *adds* in the margin] Tapers ready. l. 20. A] so, like a Turke. l. 26. Second Folio *misprints*] Of what. l. 34. Second Folio *misprints*] embace.

p. 327, ll. 2—10. A gives all these lines to Rutilio.

p. 328, ll. 5 and 6. A *adds* in margin] Lights ready. l. 33. A *omits*] Fight. l. 35. A *omits*] Falls. l. 38. Second Folio *misprints*] Governous.

p. 329, l. 4. A *omits*] 1.

p. 331, l. 30. A prints marginal direction] Hold a purse ready.

p. 333, l. 14. In A the words 'my state would rather ask a curse' are printed by mistake between ll. 16 and 17. l. 23. A] sight. l. 30. A] her Chamber.

p. 334, l. 17. A] but to a fortune. l. 21. A] bucket. l. 39. A prints the marginal direction (Musicke) at the end of the following line.

APPENDIX

p. 335, l. 1. A *omits*] 1. l. 19. A] strike indeed.

p. 336, l. 1. A] attend her.

p. 341, ll. 14—16. A by mistake gives these lines as a continuation of Sulpicia's speech. l. 33. A] beaten off.

p. 342, l. 23. A] blow that part.

p. 344, l. 12. A] affection.

p. 345, l. 33. A] give that.

p. 346, l. 4. A] may cease.

p. 350, l. 18. A] a larum.

p. 352, l. 5. A] had. l. 13. Second Folio *misprints*] Portual.

p. 353, l. 29. A *omits*] will.

p. 354, l. 25. Second Folio] comanded.

p. 358, l. 31. A] angers.

p. 359, l. 13. Second Folio] you. l. 25 and 26. A transposes these lines. l. 26. A *omits*] not.

p. 361, l. 10. A] hopes. Lords againe. l. 38. A *omits*] and.

p. 365, l. 27. A] it will not hold. l. 33. A] lost me an. l. 34. Second Folio *misprints*] strengthing. l. 39. A] a dores.

p. 367, l. 4. A] adventure. l. 20. Second Folio *misprints*] unwhosom.

p. 368, l. 38. Second Folio *misprints*] To may you.

p. 369, l. 27. A *omits*] do. l. 28. A] maugre.

p. 371, l. 9. A] sorrowes. l. 27. A *omits*] and.

p. 372, l. 18. A] visitance.

p. 373, l. 3. A] but to read.

p. 375, l. 11. A] Gives.

p. 376, l. 2. A] banding.

p. 379, l. 1. A] a foote. l. 9. A] stick. l. 23. A] welcome home Gentlemen.

p. 380, l. 36. A] eye.

p. 381, l. 19. Second Folio] If.

p. 383, l. 13. A] Doore in.

p. 384, l. 25. Second Folio *misprints*] rrue.

p. 387, l. 13. A *adds*] For my Soune Clarke.

END OF VOL. I.

CAMBRIDGE: PRINTED BY JOHN CLAY, M.A. AT THE UNIVERSITY PRESS.

LaVergne, TN USA
13 October 2010
200669LV00003B/112/P